MUQADDAMA-E-SIRAJUL ABSAR

VOLUME TWO

BY ALLAMA SYED YAQOOB BAZMI(Rh)
S/O HZT. SYED MUSTAFA TASHRIFULLAHI(Rh)

TRANSLATED BY

SYED SHARIEF KHUNDMIRI
S/O HZT. SYED QASIM KHUNDMIRI(Rh)
American Edition

Order this book online at www.trafford.com
or email orders@trafford.com

Most Trafford titles are also available at major online book retailers.

Printed in the United States of America.

ISBN: 978-1-4907-0825-6 (sc)
ISBN: 978-1-4907-0824-9 (e)

Trafford rev. 11/04/2013

www.trafford.com

North America & international
toll-free: 1 888 232 4444 (USA & Canada)
fax: 812 355 4082

List of Contents
VOLUME TWO

The end of Muqaddama-e-sirajulabsar

End of the book in two volumes

Index and of Muqaddamāt e individual [?]

and at the beginning volume [?]

PART 111
Imamana's (As) Companians and their Characters
Chapter One
Bandagi Miyan Syed Mahmood (Rz)

Alim Billah Miyan Abdul Malik Sujawandi (Rh) had argued in " Sirajul Absar" that

Characters of the companions of Imamana(As) were comparatively equal to that of the companions of the Holy Prophet (Slm). Thus on that basis he argues when these prominent personalities had recognised Imamana (As) as the Promised Mahdi, then why should any doubt arise? In this connection, to further substantiate it, he had described the sublime characters of his contemporaries who were the descendants of the companions of Imamana (As). (vide "Sirajul Absar" p.174)

Author of Hadia in order to refute that argument what had been written in 'Sirajul Absar" he had written chapter 3 to 7 including chapters 2 and 8 and tried to create doubts about characters of those companions of Imamana (As) and through these unwanted vulgar writings he had indirectly behaved impudently by attacking even the personality of Imamana (As).

However, it is a fact that the companions of any Prophet are not innocent. They may be having some importance and others may be ordinary ones. And if anyone commits mistakes, how his mistakes affect the Prophet?

Author of "Asnai Ashria" had written that:

"Ahl-e-Sunnat believe in Prophets' innocence, but do not agree the same to his companions."

نزد اهـل سنـت عـصمت خاصهٔ انبیاء دست صحابه را معصوم نمی دانند

Abdullah Ibn Abi Sarha was a hypocrite for a long time; reported by author of "Madarijul Nabuwwat".

"Akrama Ibn Abbas narrated that Abdullah Ibn Abi Sarha was the writer of Revelations for the Holy Prophet (Slm); but he was misled by Satan and under the influence of Satan, started to tell that Mohammed (Slm) does not know what he was dictating; therefore I wrote whatever I thought better. Thus he became hypocrite and became one of the infidels."

عـكرمه از ابن عباس روایت می كند كه بود عبدالله بن ابی سرح كه می نوشت برائی آنحضرت صلی الله علیه وسلم وحیٔ پـس گـمـراه گردانید اوراشیطان وگفت مـحـمـد نـمی داند كه چه می گوید من هر چه خواستم می نوشتم پس مرتد شد ملحق گشت بكفار الیٰ آخرهٔ

Whether his hypocrisy would in any way effect the characters of the Holy Prophet (Slm)?

There are so many such episodes stated in the traditions. But by presenting them we do not want to disgrace the companions of the Holy Prophet (Slm). But our intention is just to blame the decliner and his followers. Because he had maliciously on the basis of some unauthentic and unfounded narrations had presented impudently such instances just to attack on the personality of Imamana (As) indirectly.

Through the following, we are going to repudiate those inauthentic narrations, maliciously presented by the biased decliner.

Dog of Miran Syed Mahmood's dairah:

The decliner had written in chapter 3 of Hadia that Miran Syed Mahmood (Rz) had reared a dog which is against Shariat. Thus he had written as below:

"One day a dog by name Lala was passing in front of the house of Bibi Malkan (Rz). Bibi hit it with a piece of brick. Miran Syed Mahmood(Rz) uttered: Had it been a dog, your hitting was correct, but it was not a dog, therefore your hitting it, was not correct. With that remark, Bibi Malkan (Rz) inquired: Was it like Bhai Kaloo? Miran Syed Mahmood (Rz) told: yes, it was the brother of Bhai Kaloo. (P. 195)

It comes to the notice that the dog was not a home grown dog , but it was living in the daira, which was like a colony. On just seeing the dog passing in front of her house, Bibi Malkan (Rz) hit it with a piece of brick. It means to say that Mahdavi do not rear dogs. When its very passing in front of the house was not permissible, then how could one guess that dogs were reared by Mahdavis in their houses? Miran Syed Mahmood's assertion on hitting the dog: "if it was a dog, your hitting was correct? But it was not a dog. Many issues emerge at this point:

1. The dog should not be kept in house. If a dog enters the house it must be ejected from the house.

2: In fact that dog was not a dog, but it was a Jinn who changed itself to a dog. And traditions prove that Jinns change themselves into the shape of a dog or snake.

3: This particular Jinn which changed itself to a dog, was like the dog living in the dairah of Imamana (As), to which Miran Syed Mahmood (Rz) stated that it was Bhai Kaloo's brother; which informs that the dog which was living in the dairah of Imamana (As) was a Jinn (and not a dog).

Miyan Yousuf Circumambulates a Room:

The decliner had reported in chapter 3 that;" During the period of Miran Syed Mahmood (Rz) brother Miyan Yousuf came to him (there was another Miyan Vali Yousuf (Rh) who gathered "Naqliat-e-Imamana"(As), and asked permission for performing Hajj. He was, instead, directed to circumambulate the room of Miyan Shah Dilawer (Rz) with a remark that if this did not turn into a Hajj, then he could go to Hajj. He did go (to the room of Shah Dilawer (Rz) and might have done what was asked to him and came back and told that he had the vision of Allah. (P. 196)

There are certain conditions for performing Hajj and also for the offering prayers. Unless those conditions are fulfilled neither prayer gets completed nor the Hajj. Therefore the circumambulation of the room of Shah Dilawer (Rz) was a slang expression and not a real one. Actually it means to say that" go to Shah Dilawer (Rz) and serve him first and then go to Hajj". It is a fact that the most important tenet of Hajj is performance of circumambulance seven times around the Kabatullah, hence the word Cicumuimbulance was used. This sort of saying is in vogue by using those words what were really told by Miyan Yousuf, and thus it served his purpose.

"Madarijul Nabuwwat" informs that:

"After that, Abu Baker (Rz) came and whatever was with him he brought. The Prophet (Slm) inquired: "had you hoarded anything for the family"? Abu Baker (Rz) told he had hoarded Allah and His Rasool (Slm)."

بعد از آن ابوبکر آمد هرچه تمام آور دبه وے نیز فرمود برائے عیال چه ذخیره کرده گفت اذخرت الله و رسوله

Now we have to ask the decliner whether the words of Abu Baker "hoarded Allah and His Rasool" were really meant, as if "Allah and His Rasool (Slm)"are commodities for hoarding? Abu Baker (Rz) used the same words what the Holy Prophet(Slm) had used "what have you hoarded". In the same manner Miran Syed Mahmood (Rz) too used the word "circumambulate", because Miyan Yousuf asked permission to perform Hajj. Therefore Miyan Yousuf was directed to circumambulate the room of Shah Dilawer (Rz), it means actually to serve Shah Dilawer (Rz) and nothing else. Thus it has also to be ascertained whether Miyan Yousuf had funds for the journey or not? Had he shown the provision, then he would not have been directed to go to Shah Dilawer (Rz).

Thus, he was not at all stopped for going to Hajj, instead he was told to serve Shah Dilawer (Rz) first and " then go to Hajj".

There is a tradition in which it is stated that a man came to the Holy Prophet (Slm) and asked his permission for going to jihad. But the Prophet (Slm) asked him to serve his mother:

"Narrated by Ahmed Nisaai (Rz) who said to Behaqi that one person by name Muaviyia Bin Jahamta came to the Holy Prophet (Slm) and informed that he intends to go for Jihad, and requested Holy Prophet's permission for going to Jihad. The holy Prophet (Slm) inquired whether his mother was alive? He said Yes. Then Holy Prophet (Slm) directed him to serve his mother since, under the feet of the mother, there lies the Paradise."

رواه احمد النسائی والبیهقی فی شعب الایمان عن معاویةبن جاهمةان جاهمةرضی الله عنه جاء الی النبی صلی الله علیه وسلم فقال یا رسول اردت ان اغزو وقد استشیرک فقالو هل لک من ام قال نعم فقال فالزمها فان الجنة تحت رجلیها

The Holy Prophet (Slm) directed him to serve his mother, but did not give permission for Jihad. Thus, should anybody object that the Holy Prophet (Slm) did not permit him to go for Jihad?

Thus in the same manner Miran Syed Mahmood (Rz) did not permit him for Hajj but asked Miyan Yousuf to serve Shah Dilawer (Rz) instead.

Saintly Line:

The decliner had blamed that Miran Syed Mahmood's elder son Miyan Syed Abdul Hai (Roshan Munawer Rz.) did not have his saintly line with his father. It was not correct, as mentioned by the author of "Shawahedul Vilayet": that he had heard from Syed Raji Mohammed (Rz) son of Miyan Syed Sadullah (Rz) that Miyan Abdul Hai Roshan Munawer (Rz) was trained by his father Miran Syed Mahmood (Rz).

"Elder son Miran Syed Abdul Hai (Rz) had the Saintly Line with Bandagi Miran Syed Mahmood (his father)."

پسر کلاں میاں سید عبدالحی علیه الرضوان تربیت بدم خجسته بندگی میران سید محمود رضی الله عنه بودند

Thus it is a confirmed fact that Miran Syed Abdul Hai (Rz) had the Saintly Line of his Father Miran Syed Mahmood (Rz), and it was famous even before 1052 H.

CHAPTER TWO
Bandagi Miyan Syed Khundmir (Rz)

The decliner had pointed out some objections in his book's chapter third, argument 17 about Bandagi Miyan Syed Khundmir's "Bu'azul Aayaat pamphlet" that:

"Every Prophet has one specimen from his Ummah".

(۱) لکل نبی نظیر فی امته

It is an inauthentic version which had been mentioned maliciously by the decliner.

What Bandagi Miyan (Rz) had written it is correct according to the following tradition:

"There is no Prophet who does not have his example".

مامن نبی الاله نظیر

Another tradition supports it::

"Prophets were sent by Allah to every region of the world Like your Nabi , Mohammed; like Adam, Adam; like Noah, Noah; like Ibrahim, Ibrahim; like Isa, Isa."

فی کل ارض نبی کنبیکم وآدم کآدم ونوح کنوح وابراهیم کابراهیم و عیسیٰ کعیسیٰ

This tradition too speaks about example of each Nabi.

Author of "Zubdatul Haqaeq" had written that :

"No Nabi was there who does not have his example."

مامن نبی الاوله نظیر فی امته

Thus what "Bu'aazul Aayaat" had presented, it is correct, according to the traditions of the Holy Prophet (Slm). Such stupid remark by the decliner shows his lack of knowledge of the traditions who is in the habit of making malicious remarks. Unfortunately he does not know that his such utterane goes against the Holy Prophet (Slm) also. Now remains his doubt whether there would be any example of the Holy Prophet or not? It shall be discussed while discussing about Imamana (As).

B. The decliner had taken a narration from "Maktoob-e-Multani":

انی لاعرف اقواماً هم بمنزلتی الی آخره.

"Indeed I know those people who would be of my rank."

The same objection he had labeled what he had already stated about the first narration.

What Author of "Zubdatul Haqayeq" has narrated, the same had been written in"Maktoob-e-Multani": Thus the wordings are:

مگره که این حدیث دیگر نشنیده که گفت انــی لاعــرف اقواماهم بمـنزلتی عندالله ماهم انبیاء ولا شهداء یغبطهم الانبیاء والشهداء بمکانهم عندالله هم المتحابون بروح الله

"But you did not hear that tradition in which the Holy Prophet (Slm) had said:

"Verily I know those Ummahs who would have my ranks before Allah, like mine. They are neither Nabi nor martyrs, still they would envy for those ranks which Allah had granted to them, They love each other with the Grace of Allah."

Author of "Bahrul Muaani" had also narrated these words " Hum Ba Manzaliti":

(۱) باز این فرمود انی لاعرف رجالا من امتی فی لیلة المعراج منزلتهم بمنزلتی عندالله تعالیٰ

"Verily, I recognized them in Mairaj who were from my Ummah; whose ranks are like mine before Allah"

Accordingly, the following tradition of "Sihah" proves the previous ones:

عن عمر قال قال رسول الله صلی الله علیه وآله وسلم ان من عباد الله لا ناساماهم بانبیاء ولا شهداء بطهم الانبیاء والشهداء یوم القیامة بمکانهم من الله قالوا ایا رسول الله تخبرنا من هم قال هم قوم تحابو بروح الله الی آخره

"Narrated by Omer (Rz) who heard the Holy Prophet (Slm) saying that "among the people, there are certain people who are neither Prophets, nor martyrs, to whom even Prophets and martyrs would envy for their ranks on the Day of Judgment. Companions requested the Holy Prophet (Slm) to inform about them who are they? Replied "They are those who love each other by the Grace of Allah."

Whether those people about whom tradition speaks, are not they equal to those about whom the words"Hum Ba Manzilati" had been used? The decliner had no knowledge of the language of the traditions. His objection is that, Mahdavis believe equality of the ranks of the companions of Mahdi (As) with the companions of the Holy Prophet (Slm). Before it, we have proved and stated that "to have the ranks or to officiate or to be immersed in the entity of a Nabi", does not mean that someone becomes a Prophet or equal to that Prophet. We have referred to a tradition which was narrated by Abu Dawood Tayalsi (Rz) that:

"It seems certain that every one of the Ummah may become Prophet."

كادت هذه الامة ان تكون انبياء كلها

Does it mean that every one of the Ummah would actually become a Nabi or a Prophet?

Some traditions suggest that whoever had loved the Holy Prophet (Slm), he would be in the paradise along with the Holy Prophet (Slm).

These are the wordings of the tradition:

"Whoever had loved me (the Holy Prophet (Slm), he would be in the Paradise along with me."

من احبنى كان معى فى الجنة

With reference to this tradition, author of "Madarijul Nabuwwat" said that:

"It may not be hidden that to be along with the Holy Prophet (Slm) should not be presumed that he would become equal to the prophet, even though in some traditions it was said that they would be holding my rank."

پوشیده نماند کـه مـراد بـه معیت مساوات در درجه نـخواهد بود اگرچه در بعضی احادیث کان فی درجتی نیزواقع است

Author of "Madrijul Nabuwwat" further states that :

"To be with me" does not mean to become equal to me; although other traditions in which it was said by the Holy Prophet(Slm) that: " They shall hold my rank."

It also had been said by the Holy Prophet (Slm):

"Whoever befriended with Hasan (rz) and Husain (Rz) and their father Ali (Rz), then he would be with me on the day of Judgment, having my rank."

مـن احب هذین یعنی الحسن و الحسین و اباهما کان معی فی درجتی یوم القیامة

When "to be with me in my rank" does not make any one equal to the Holy Prophet (Slm), then how could the words of the tradition : "to have my rank " shall make any one equal to the Holy Prophet (Slm)?

Apart from this, the Holy Prophet (Slm) desired Abu Baker (Rz) that:

"Oh Lord, on the Day of Judgment, keep Abu Baker (Rz) with me in the rank (as of mine)"

اللّهم اجعل ابابکر معی نی درجتی یوم القیامة

In those traditions the word "Fi Jannati" (My rank) had been used. If that does not make equal to the Holy Prophet (Slm), then how the words" Ba Manzaliti" makes one equal to the Holy Prophet (Slm)?

Yet another objection was raised by the him from "Maktoob-e-Multani" which is:

"(Holy Prophet (Slm) said) Ah! I have desired to meet my brothers who would come after me and whose dignity would be like of the Prophets (As)."

واشوقا الى لقاء اخوانى يكونون من بعدى شانهم كشان الانبياء

Same narration had been written by author of "Bahrul Muani":

"Ah!. I have the desire to meet my brothers who would come after me and they are like Prophets and martyrs recognized by Allah and they are like me."

واشوقا الى لقاء اخوانى يكونون من بعدى وهم كالانبياء وهم عندالله بمنزلةالشهداء وبمنزلتى

Ainul Quzzat Hamdani had narrated in "Zubdatul Haqaeq" that:

"Again said (Holy Prophet (Slm)) Ah! I desire to meet my brothers who would come after me. Their splendour would be like that of the Prophet (As)."

ثم قال واشوقا الى لقاء اخوانى يكونون من بعد شانهم كشان الانبياء

If copying of these traditions is by Bandagi Miyan (Rz) becomes rude and objectionable, then all saints and mystics who had also copied these traditions or those who had accepted them, all shall be labeled as rude and unholy also? according to the decliner!

These narrations are correct to their meanings, since "Muslim" had reported about Abu Huraira (Rz) what he heard from the Holy Prophet (Slm) that:

"I yearn to see my brothers"

وددت انا قدر اينا اخواننا

These wordings do not make someone equal to the Holy Prophet (Slm), but they say that his dignity shall match the splendour of the Prophets (As).

Just by saying "Rasool's brothers" could the said "Brothers" become equal to the Prophets?. It only says that their ranks resemble to the ranks of the Prophet. Previous to this we had already referred about the tradition which informs about those dignitaries who were neither Nabi nor Martyrs, but even Prophets and martyrs would envy for them.

If it is not objectionable that the Prophets (As) would be becoming envious of the people of the Ummah, then why any objection be raised if it is said that "Brothers of the Holy Prophet (Slm) would enjoy ranks of the Prophets (As)?

When Prophets (As) are envying to the status of certain people of the Ummah is not objectionable, then how just by equalizing the dignity of the Prophet (As) to the dignity of the brothers of the Holy Prophet (Slm) becomes objectionable?

Author of "Maktoob-e-Multani" had referred to "Alwa'ul Makhtoom" and presented some of its couplets:

"It points out that the Holy Prophet (Slm) had narrated regarding the commissioning of the Khaatimul Aouliah."

اشـارت بـرایـں دارد کـه از رسـول الله خبر آمده است
به تعین ختم الاولیاء

It may be pointed out that "Alwa'ul Makhtoom" was not written by any Mahadavi which informs about commissioning the last of the saints.

Apart from this the decliner had copied at page 307 of Hadia what Sheik-e-Akbar (Rz) had said that this tradition was found by him in a Persian city in the year 594 H. Thus it is confirmed that the tradition of "Khatmul Aouliah"was accepted by all mystics. Thus Imam Mahdi (As) became known as the "Khatimul Aouliah" about whom the Holy Prophet (Slm) had said that he (Mahdi (As)) would be the "Khatim-e-Vilayet"; as mentioned in "Uqudud Durer":

"Allah shall complete the religion through Mahdi (As), as He had started from me."

یختم الله به الدین کما فتحه بنا

Miyan Abdul Malik Sujawandi (Rz) - had answered to the 12th question put by Miyan Sheik Mubarak (Rh) Nagori in "Minhajut Taqweem" that:

"And those words which have come in the traditions referring to Mahdi (As) as Imam, Khaliphatullah and "Khaatim-e-Deen" as designated by the Holy Prophet (Slm) that Allah shall complete the Deen (Religion) through Mahdi (As) as He had started from us. Thus, there is a similarity in Deen and Vilayet(Mysticism). The Word "Khaatim-e-Vilayet" is confirmed from this tradition."

والـذی وقع فی الاحادیث من الفاظ الامام والخلیفه و
خـاتـم الـدیـن کـمـا ذکرنا قبل وهو قوله علیه السلام
یـخـتـم الـله به الدین کما فتحه بناوبین الدین والولایة
مناسبة فلعل المقتبس اخذلفظ خاتم الولایة

The intention of Bandagi Miyan (Rz) in referring this tradition was to emphasize that without Imam Mahdi (As) the Deen would not come to its completion as mentioned in the tradition.

2. Taiyyun Means Fixed Income:

Author of "Insaf Nama" had stated in chapter nine that:

"Whoever gets some pension, he requests Hazrat Bandagi Miyan (Rz) to permit him to rerceive the pension. He thus used to issue permit(after verification)."

کسے راجائے وظیفه بودے وپیش بندگی میاں سید خوند
میرؓ اذن طـلبیـد (ع) کـه آنجا برویم اگر رضائے خوند
کار باشد بیاریم رضا دادند

Author of Hadia had objected to it by telling that when Imamana (As) had declared any fixed income is a curse, then how could Bandagi Miyan (Rz) permit it? This problem had been discussed in previous chapters. However it may be said that it was permitted only when it was ascertained that fixed income if legitimized by Shariah then only Bandagi Miyan (Rz) had permitted.

3. Recitation of Qur'an and Zikrullah:

Narrated in "Insaf Nama" that:

"Narrated that Malik Bakhan (Rz) inquired Bandagi Miyan (Rz) in Khanbail that someone reads Qur'an every time. Is there any benefit by such reading? Bandagi Miyan (Rz) answered if his reading is to understand and to ponder over what Allah had ordained, it is good, still there remains a curtain in between Allah and the reader; but the remembrance of Allah cuts down that curtain too."

نقل است که در کها نبیل پیش بندگی میاں سید خوند میرؒ ملک بخن پر سید که فلاح کس قرآن بسیارمی خواند چیزے از خواندن فائده می شود بعده بندگی میاں فرمودند که قرآن را رایتلونه حق تلاوته میخواند هم پردهٔ نورمیان بنده و خدا می شود و ازیادخدا پردهٔ نور هم دریده می شود۔

On this the decliner had misunderstood that "remembrance of Allah is better than recitation of Qur'an" thus objected and presented three traditions in support of his objection.

A."Narrated by the Holy Prophet (Slm) that Allah has remarked: "if Qur'an stops any person from my remembrance and from his asking from me, what I give to anyone, I shall give more to that man". Venerability and supremacy of Kalamullah are like what supremacy of Allah is over his creation. Reported by "Tirmizi", Dari and Behaqi in Mishkat and Shobul Iman."

(۱) قال رسول الله صلی الله علیه وسلم یقول الرب تبارک وتعالیٰ من شغله القرآن عن ذکری ومسئلتی اعطیته افضل ما اعطیٰ السائلین وفضل کلام الله علی سائر الکلام کفضل الله علیه خلقه (رواہ الترمذی والدارمی والبیهقی فی شعب الایمان کذفی المشکوٰة)

The decliner although had written the tradition as mentioned in "Mishkat", but he had forgotten that according to "Tirmizi" this tradition is indigent and poor.

Another point on which the decliner became jubilant when it was said that the recitation is supreme to remembrance, but he ignored the fact that it was used in a literary sense and not in the conventional sense. However this traditional recitation of the Qur'an does not make superior to remembrance:

b."Recitation of the Qur'an is superior in prayers to other than in prayers. And its recitation other than in prayers is better than praising Allah or telling the beads also better than offering fast while fast is a shield from Hellfire."

(ب) قرأة القرآن فى الصلوٰة افضل من قرأة القرآن فى غير الصلوٰة و قرأة القرآن فى غير الصلوٰة افضل من التسبيح و التكبير والتسبيح افضل من الصدقة والصدقة افضل من الصوم و الصوم جنة من النار .

By presenting this tradition the decliner could not prove recitation is supreme to rememberance since praising Allah is to say "Subhanallah", or telling beads means "Allahu Akbar". But the significance of remembrance is established by repeating "La Ilaha Illallahu" the best among all recitations.

C. Narrated by Ahmed Hunbal (Rz) that he had witnessed Allah in the dream and asked which worship is superior? The answer came: Recitation of Qur'an, second time asked : with meanings . Answered yes, with meanings or without meanings. This narration tells that recitation is a better worship; however it does not prove that it is better than all worships. But there are traditions which prove Remembrance of Allah is the best worship among all:

"Abi Darda narrates that the Holy Prophet (Slm) stated: "should I not tell you which is the best worship? And what is the best offering to the king by you ? Which is greater than silver and gold and even better than fighting against your enemy; then told " It is Zikrullah". Reported by Malik, Ahmed and tirmizi, Ibn Maja."

(ا) عن ابى درداء قال قال رسول الله صلى الله عليه وسلم الانبئكم بخير اعمالكم ازكٰها عند مليككم وارفعها فى درجاتكم من انفاق الذهب والورق و خير لكم من ان تلقو اعدوكم فتضربوا اعناقهم ويضربوا اعناقكم قالوا بلىٰ قال ذكر الله رواه مالك و احمد و ترمذى ابن ماجه الان مالكا وقفه على ابى درداء

This tradition emphasizes on "Zikrullah'. Although Recitation also is a good worship but Zikrullah is better than recitation. Muaz Bin Jabal (Rz) stated what the Holy Prophet (Slm) told about "Zikrullah":

"Narrated that from all the worships, "Zikrullah" is the best worship which saves from the hellfire. Reported by Tirmizi, Malik and Ibn Maja."

قال ما عمل العبد عملا انجى له من عذاب الله من ذكر الله رواه مالك والترمذى و ابن ماجه

"Zikrullah" is the best worship as had been narrated by the following tradition:

"Narrated by Abdullah Bin Busar (Rz) that an Airabi came to the Holy Prophet (Slm) and asked who is the best of Creation? Holy Prophet answered: "Glad tidings to the one who got lengthy life and whose practice was virtuous." Again inquired which practice is better? Answered: "You pass from this world with zikrullah with your moist tongue". Narrated by Ahmed Hunbal (Rz) and Tirmizi."

عن عبدالله بن بسر قال جاء اعرابی الی رسول الله صلی الله علیه وسلم فقالوا ای الناس خیر قال طوبی لمن طال عمره احسن عمله قال یارسول الله ای الاعمال افضل قال ان تفارق الدنیا و لسانک رطب من ذکر الله(رواه احمد والترمذی)

Narrated by Jaber that:

"Holy Prophet (Slm) said that "La Ilaha Illallahu" is the best remembrance and the best Blessing is "Al Hamdo Lillah" reported in "Tirmizi" and "Ibn Maja."

قال قال رسول الله صلی الله علیه وسلم افضل الذکر لا الـه الـله افضل الدعاء الحمد الله رواه الترمذی و ابن ماجه

Allah Himself ordains that:

"My remembrance is the best worship"

ولذکر الله اکبر (العنکبوت ع۵)

"Zikrullah" is greater than prayer. It is stated by Imam Jassas (Rz) who had commented on this verse which is mentioned in "Madarik' that:

"Narrated Salman that Zikrullah is greater than every worship."

قال سلمان ذکر الله اکبر من کل شئی

Bandagi Miyan (Rz) had stated about Zikrullah which is "La Ilaha Illallahu" and this is the conventional Zikr about which Sheik Abdul Haq had said that:

"Among all worships, Zikrullah is supreme. Although there are so many items of remembrance, but 'La Ilaha Illallahu' is one of the tenets of Islam which is known as Kalma-e-Towheed" and without this tenet Iman is not complete. Its perpetual remembrance opens so many Divine secrets of Allah, therefore you must be busy with it by remembering continuously. It cleanses your inner self, cleanse your heart, and it opens the secrets which are in your heart but hidden in the chest."

فاضل ترین ذکر لاله اله الله است اگرچه اذکار بسیار است هر چه بدان یاد خدا حاصل شود از اقوال و افعال ذکر است لیکن این کلمۀ تو حید است و ایمان بے آن صحیح نه داشتغال و مداومت این کلمه راخواص عجیب و اسرار غریب است ورتطهیر باطن و تصفیه قلب و ظهور سری که مودع است درون

The Qur'an is a Light. When it is recited the curtain of light comes in between Allah and the Reader of Qur'an. And when the Zaakir indulges in Zikrullah, then that curtain is turned off and Zakir witnesses the vision of Allah, because Zikr is very effective as has been said by Sheik Abdul Haq:

'Zikr is very effective and opens the Divine secrets, while Qur'an's recitation is slow in its effectiveness."	ظهـوراثـر در ذكـر اسـرع و اظهر است وحصول آں در قرآن بطی است

As the Holy Prophet (Slm) had said that:

"There is no curtain for "La Ilaha Illallah", therefore it reaches directly to Allah."	لا الـه الا الـلـه ليـس لهاحجاب دون الله حتى تخلص عليه

Bandagi Miyan (Rz) also had commented on this tradition. Thus the remembrance of Allah is superior to the recitation of the Holy Qur'an. Therefore to tell it rudeness is a denial what had been said by the Holy Prophet (Slm) in his traditions.

Whatever had been said was in connection with that tradition which the decliner had presented . But as a matter of fact it is not stated in "Insaf Nama" that Zikr is superior to recitation of Qur'an. Instead it presents Zikrullah as the basic ingredient for the Vision of Allah, thus Whoever stops Zikrullah for the purpose of recitation of the Holy Qur'an he would never get the vision of Allah. Because Zikrullah is an equivocal order of Allah which if neglected, one cannot have the vision of Allah.

4.I Company of Allah Possible While Playing:

Author of Hadia had presented an inauthentic narrative and blamed Bandagi Miyan (Rz). But the fact is that such narrative is not available in "Tazkeratul Saleheen" which was written by Hzt. Syed Mahmood's descendants. It is narrated that Khatemul Murshad being still a child, was playing near the door of the Khanbail Dairah. Miyan Doulat Shah brought Hzt. Saidanji by holding his hand to Bandagi Miyan (Rz) and stated that (the boy) was playing alone. I had brought him so that none should kidnap him. Bandagi Miyan (rz) took (the boy) in his lap and asked "tell me truth who was with you when you were playing"?. Hzt. Saidanji (rz) answered that he "was not alone, Allah was playing with me". After hearing, Bandagi Miyan (Rz) reprimanded Doulat Shah "not to disturb the boy, since Allah also was playing with him". From these two issues emerge:

1. To correct Miyan Doulat shah's statement.

2. To pacify Saidanji who became sad for being stopped from playing.

Although Bandagi Miyan (Rz) had repeated the words of Saidanji (Rz), but actually he had confirmed his opinion that Allah's company is always available. This way of dialogue is proved from the following tradition:

"Then Abu Baker (Rz) came and brought whatever he was having. The holy Prophet (Slm) inquired whether he had hoarded something for the family? Answered Abu Baker (Rz) that "I had hoarded Allah and His Rasool (Slm)."

بعد از آن ابوبکر آمده هر چه داشت تمام آورده بوے نیز فرمود براۓ عیال چه ذخیره کردهٔ گفت اذّ خرت الله و رسوله

Here hoarding of Allah means to have complete trust in Allah. The decliner cannot deduce from this that Allah can be hoarded. Thus, in the same way, Bandagi Miyan (Rz) also repeated8u what Saidanji (Rz) had told. Thus he actually confirmed his conviction that Allah's company is always available for everyone whether someone is playing or sleeping. In support of Bandagi Miyan's statement this verse is submitted:

"And He (Allah) is with you, wherever you are."

وهو معکم این ماکنتم (حدید ع)

In its support a tradition is submitted:

"Be engaged in play and sports, as well, because I feel it loathsome if you feel harshness in the religion."

الهوا و العبوافانی اکره ان یری فی دینکم غلظة

This play or sport what had been referred in the tradition is not contemptible nor it was used to brand it as mean.

It may be pointed out that in sports or playing there is some wisdom in it. Author of "Tuhfai-e-Asnai-e-Ashria" had reported that the Holy Prophet (Slm) took Bibi Ayesha (Rz) to witness the play of the Negroes. It may be a game, but actually it teaches wisdom. The narration is this:

"The fact is that the Negroes used to play with swords and arrows to get acquainted how to fight with the infidels and also to prepare ammunition for use in the Jihad and this was actually meant for training purposes. Naturally they are games, but actually they give understanding and wisdom how to drive horses and how to shoot arrows. In fact the Holy Prophet (Slm) used to visit such games and sometimes he had taken part in them and told that in such games angels too take part."

دیگر آنکه لهو و لعب حبشه بسپروو نیزه هابود که براۓ مهارت حرب کفار وبه طریق اعداد آلات الجهاد دمشق این هنر میکر دند پس به صورت لعب و بازی بود و به معنی سراسر حکمت و رنگ دانیدن اسپان و تیر اندازی و بلا شبه آنحضرت دراین قسم حاضر شده اند بلکه در بعضی اوقات شریک هم شده و فرموده که ملائکه نیز دراین قسم بازی ها حاضری شوند

"Bukhari" and "Muslim" also have references to such games which were being played in the Masjidun Nabavi:

والحبشه بلعبون بالحراب فى المسجد

"And the Negroes used to play with small arrows in the Masjid (un Nabvi)."

Shah Abdul Aziz had mentioned that the Holy Prophet (Slm) helped Bibi Ayesha (Rz) in playing with dolls.

مدعا از تجويز لعب براۓ زنان خرد سال باين بنات تمرين ايشان هست براۓ امور خانه دارى و آموختن و دوختن وقطع كردن آراستن فرش و زيب و زينت وادن مجلس چنانچه اطفال ذكورراللعب باسپ چوبين شمشير چوبين و تير و كمان و نيزه كه ازين جنس باشد نيز بنا بر حكمت با تجويز كرده اند

"To arrange playing with dolls for minor girls actually it was to teach them household works, stitching , cutting clothes, arranging floors and cleaning them and to train them for arranging parties and horse riding for boys, arrow throwing, sword play, using ammunition etc. these were for training purposes and wisdom."

Thus arranging doll playing for minor girls to get training in household affairs and for boys training for horse riding, sword playing through wooden horses and wooden swords was meant for training and understanding those arts were based on the tradition and should not be blamed as being abominable and mean, if told, it is just to blame the Holy Prophet (Slm).

Apart from this Psychologists have accepted the fact that games help in the development of kids' physical and mental development, then how could it be disgraced when such games are morally permitted. Further they help in the development of wisdom. Then if Allah's presence by partaking in such games how could they be blamed.? Particularly when according to the tradition Allah becomes hand and a leg for His servants. And also that the Holy Prophet (Slm) had permitted games which are permissible morally in order to describe that religion does not make life miserable but allows playing games often. Now we have to look into that verse which the decliner had presented:

وما خلقنا السموات والارض ومابينهما لعبين (الدخان ع ٣)

"We have created heaven and earth and whatever is in them not for useless sport purposes."

From this it comes to light that Allah does not play games. We have also discussed that games are good for children for their body and mental development. When the Holy Prophet (Slm) had helped Bibi Ayesha (Rz) in her doll playing, and if Bandagi Miyan (Rz) had permitted his minor son to play; how could that be objected.? "Madarijul Nabuwwat" states that:

"The Holy Prophet (Slm) competed in running along with Bibi Ayesha (Rz), but Ayesha (Rz) became successful. When they again ran second time, the Holy Prophet (Slm) surpassed, it was a period when Ayesha (Rz) became fatty and chubby, On that Holy Prophet (Slm) said I had equaled her."

آنحضرت با عائشه مسابقت کرد یعنی ملا عبت کردند بایکدیگر بدویدند پس درگذشت عائشه از آنحضرت پیش وقتے دیگر بازدویدیس در گذشت آنحضرت از عائشه این وقتے بود که گوشت گرفته بود عائشه و تندار شده بود و گفت آنحضرت که این پیشی من از تو در بدل آن پیشی تو بو دازمن (جلد اول ٤٤)

5. Imamana (As) not Recognized properly:

Author of Hadia had presented the following narrative against Bandagi Miyan (Rz) in chapter 7 of his book:

"At this place Bandagi Miyan's narrative is submitted in which he said that "as Imamana (As) came, so he went away", none recognized him properly as should have been recognized and in this connection he presented this verse of the Qur'an: "People did not respect Allah, as He should have been respected."

درایں جانقل بندگی میاں سید خوند میر صدیق مهدیؐ جلوه گرمی نمایند که فرمودند ' مهدی موعود چنانچه آمده بود همچنان رفت' هیچ کس حق شناختن اور نه شناختن ودرایں آیت کتاب خواندندماقدر والله حق قدره (انعام ع ١١)

The fact is that Bandagi Miyan (Rz) was expressing inability of the people to recognize Imamana (As) properly, as should have been recognized, which shows the dignity of Imamana (As) who was not recognized properly. How can any person deduce about the opinion of Bandagi Miyan (Rz) that he had made Imamana (As) a deity? In this regard, we submit what Allah has said:

"(They) recognize the Holy Prophet (Slm) as they recognize their sons".

یعرفونه کما یعرفون ابناء هم (البقره . ع١٧)

While discussing about the children of the infidels, if the Holy Prophet's name was mentioned, does not it mean a praise for the Prophet (Slm)? If not, why should there be any objection on Bandagi Miyan's statement about Allah that "He was not recognized as should have been recognized", in the same manner Imamana (As) was not recognized properly. If the parable is objected then the following verse also becomes objectionable:

"Those who are offering their allegiance on your hand, actually they are offering their allegiance to Allah. Allah's hand is on their hands."

ان الذین یبایعونک انما یبایعون الله یدا لله فوق ایدیهم (الفتح ع١)

Does this verse make the Holy Prophet (Slm) a deity? If not how the narration of Bandagi Miyan (Rz) makes Imamana (As) a deity?

6. Annihilating Into Entity of Allah:

Author of Hadia had presented the following narration against Bandagi Miyan (Rz) in chapter 7:

" One day Bandagi Miyan (Rz) asserted that we were just mortal men, but in the company of Imamana (As) we were able to recognize Allah properly. Further he said that unless a man becomes Allah he cannot recognize Allah. "

Here to become Allah means, man's heart, tongue, eyesight, audition, hands, legs all should become Allah. That is to say one should annihilate himself unto the entity of Allah then only he would be able to recognize Allah. Allah ordains that:

"And you did not throw, but Allah had thrown".

وما رميت اذرميت ولكنّ الله رمىٰ (الانفال ع ٢)

In this verse, it is a fact that on the Command of Allah, the Holy Prophet (Slm) did throw the pebbles upon the infidels. But this act of throwing, Allah emphatically states that "It was not thrown by you, but it was thrown by Us!" We have to ask whether this verse becomes objectionable to the decliner? If not, then how annihilation into the entity of Allah, becomes objectionable?

7. Secrets Not To Be Reported:

Author of Hadia had objected on Bandagi Miyan (Rz) on his assertion that:

'"Whatever we have heard from Imamana (As), if we say openly to the commoners, they would stone us to death. It means that "those mystic secrets told by Imamana (As) if narrated openly before the commoners who could not understand their intricacies properly, they may stone us." How this would become a point of objection when Abu Huraira (Rz) had said a like statement:

"I had received two vessels from the Holy Prophet (Slm). One I had disclosed. If I disclose the other I shall get my neck cut."

قال حفظت من رسول الله صلى الله عليه وسلم وعائلين فاما احد هما فبثثته واما الآخرلو بثثه لقطع هـذا البـلعوم (صحيح بخارى كتاب العلم باب حفظ العلم)

From this tradition it is clear that there are some Divine Secrets, if disclosed as Abu Huraira (Rz) was fearing to tell, how can anybody say that this tradition refers atheism? Then how the words "we would be stoned to death" stated by Bandagi Miyan (Rz) becomes objectionable?

Here stoning to death does not indicate mercy but acute disgust. This way of discussion had been used in traditions :

" I like persons who do not abandon joining the group (for prayers) otherwise I shall burn them till death.."

Here "burning to kill" has been just an abomination, and not actually burning them to death. Because in another tradition the Holy Prophet (Slm) had forbidden burning any one till death.

8. Desire for Martyrdom if Confronted by Enemy:

Author of "Tazkeratul Saleheen" had reported in chapter one that:

"Bandagi Miyan (Rz) asserted that if someone informed him the enemy's army had advanced from the village Kadi (towards Khanbail-his Dairah), he would fill his mouth with sugar candy."

فرمودند هر که پیش این بنده خبر آرد که لشکر درموضع کری پیشتر آمد دهن اور ابانبات مصری پرکنم ۔

Author of Hadia had objected in chapter One page 30 that Bandagi Miyan's desire is against the verse "Do not desire to meet the enemy." It means to say that do not desire to get slaughtered by the enemy. The author had referred a small portion of the tradition only, but complete tradition is as below:

"Abdullah Ibn Abi Oufi (Rz) narrated that the Holy Prophet (Slm) on some occasion was waiting for the enemy who may come before sunset. Still, he told the people not to wish to meet the enemy in a battle. He advised, instead, to implore Allah for their safety. However, once you confront the enemy, be patient and believe that paradise is under the shadow of the sword. Then prayed "Oh Lord, Revealer of the Book, and Driver of the clouds and Defeater of the groups of infidels, defeat them and bestow upon us victory."

عن عبدالله بن ابی او فی ان رسول الله صلی الله علیه وسلم فی بعض ایامه التی لقی فیه العدو انتظر حتی مالت الشمس ثمه قام فی الناس فقال یا ایها الناس لا تتمنو القاء العدو واسالوالله العافیة و اذا لقیتم فاصبرو اواعلموان الجنة تحت ظلال السیوف ثم قال اللهم منزل الکتاب و مجری السحاب و هازم الا حزاب اهز مهم و انصرنا علیهم

It is evident that Holy Prophet's assertion was before confronting the enemy. It has four issues:

1. The holy Prophet (Slm) waited till the sun set.

2. Asked not to desire to confront the enemy and implore safety from Allah.

3. When the enemy is before you, have patience, since paradise is under the shadow of the sword.

4. The holy Prophet (Slm) prayed for victory over the enemy by defeating the enemy.

Holy Prophet's assertion was not to desire confronting the enemy is clarified by the succeeding para in which he implored Allah for providing safety. It means sword fighting becomes fatal when confronting the enemy.

Apart from this Prophet's persuasion to the companions to have patience while imploring Allah for granting victory by defeating the enemy shows the situation was grim and very serious.

Here by telling that paradise is under the shadow of the sword denotes the excellence of confronting the enemy.

Fuzala Bin Ubaid narrates in Tirmizi that:

"I heard Omer Ibnul Khattab (Rz) saying that he heard the Prophet (Slm) who had categorized martyrs into four groups:

A. "Man of faith who confronted the enemy and affirms the Omnipotence of Allah, is such a person to whom people honor him with respect."	قـال سـمـعـت عمر بن الخطاب يقول سمعت رسول الـلـه صـلـى الله عليه وسلم يقول الشهداء اربعة رجل مـومـن جيـداالايـمان لقى العدو وفصدق الله فذلك الذى يرفع الناس اليه اعينهم يو القيامة الى آخره

For the cause of Allah, confronting the enemy is a worship. Neither this worship is objectionable nor its desire, because the Holy Prophet's assertion was not to desire confrontation with the enemy. It denotes the seriousness and hardship of the battle which may take place after the confrontation. And surely it is not an easy job or a mere sport. This way of assertion is in vogue. Nisai had narrated that Abu Huraira (Rz) had heard the Prophet (Slm) telling:

"Do not make my grave Eidgah but invoke Allah's Blessing on me , because it (Darood) reaches me from where you are invoking."	لا تـجعـلـو اقبـرى عيد اوصلو اعلى صلوتكم تبلغنى حيث كنتم

Here the advice is given to Muslims not to make Prophet's grave an Eidgah. It means the Holy Prophet (Slm) advises Muslims not to take troubles every now and then to visit his grave and make it an Eidgah, since the salutation reaches him from anywhere a person invokes Allah's Blessings to the Prophet (Slm). It is just to save you from hardship of visiting the grave. However, it is simply an advice, and Muslims are free to visit the grave any time they like. However it does not contradict the advice given in the tradition. In the same sense Holy Prophet (Slm) had advised not to desire for confronting the enemy because it is not an easy job for which the Holy Prophet had advised to implore Allah's Blessings for safety. How can it be said it is prohibiting the confrontation of the enemy?

This discussion was in reference to the tradition, but the fact is that Bandagi Miyan's desire of confrontation is not proved from any source. This is evident from Shah Burhan's narration that:

"When news regarding enemy's arrival at the village Khariayal was heard by Amir Syed Jalal (Rz) and Amir Syed Husain (Rz), they rushed to inform the fact to Bandagi Miyan (Rz), he became happy. He made both sons to sit on his lap and filled their mouth with sugar asserted "Alhamdu Lillah what Imamana (As) had prophesied those symptoms are visible."

چوں این خبر آمد لشکر جهان به موضع کها ریال بزبان امیر سید جلال و امیر سید حسین شنیدند بسیر خرم و خوش حال شده برخاستند وهاون دسته بدسته مبارک خود گر فتند بنات باریک کرده میده ساخته هر دو فرزندان را برزانوئے مبارک خود نشانده دهن هر دو جگر گوشگان خود راپر از بنات کردند فرمودند که الحمد الله انچه فرمودهٔ مهدی موعود بود علامات آن ظاهر شد آثار آن باهر گشت (دفتر اول رکن هفتم باب دهم)

Last words point out that Bandagi Miyan (Rz) was waiting for the accomplishment of the prophecy of Imamana (As) that "after twenty years from his demise the battle would take place, and Bandagi Miyan (Rz) would become successful on the first day, while the next day he would be martyred". He was waiting to become a martyr in the cause of Allah, and to prove the authenticity of Imamana's prophecy on which Imamana's Mahdiat was substantiated. Surely it was not to confront the enemy, but a desire which was expressed by Abu Huraira (Rz):

"Narrated Abu Huraira (Rz) that the Holy Prophet (Slm) had informed about the battle which would be fought in India. In which I shall invest all of my wealth and even my life. If I was martyred I would become leader of the martyrs and if come back alive I am that Abu Huraira (Rz) to whom Hellfire was forbidden."

عن ابی هریره قال وعدنا رسول الله غزوة الهند فان ادرکتها انفق فیهما نفسی و مالی فان اقتل کنت من افضل الشهداء وان ارجع فانا ابو هریرة المحرر

This zeal informs Abu Huraira's desire to get martyrdom into the battle of Hind which was prophesied by the Holy Prophet (Slm). It was only a desire of Hazrat Abu Huraira (rz), but here it is a fact that Bandagi Miyan (Rz) had the zeal to become martyred since Imamana (As) had prophesied and that was a Hujjat-e-Mahdi", a condition that if it happened, Immana(As) emphatically assserted that take me as the true Mahdi, otherwise an imposter. It proved Imamana's Mahdiat. Imamana (As) with utmost certainty had prophesied: "**If that battle did not take place between Bandgi Miyan (Rz) and the government's army, then take me as an Impostor; and if that happened as prophesied by me, believe me that I was the Real Promised Mahdi** (As)". Such a big challenging prophecy to happen after twenty years from his demise, was going to be accomplished, then why should not Bandagi Miyan (Rz) become happy at that news of coming of the army? The battle started on the 12th. Shawwal 930 H. And as per the prophecy he became victorious. Confrontation on 14th. Shawwal 930 H., was the day of his martyrdom along with his elder son Syed Jalal (Rz) and sixty companions. It was Bandagi Miyan's firm believe in his Mentor Imamana (As) that whatever he had prophesied about him should happen and had happened word by word. Thus in such circumstances desiring for becoming martyr could not be objected.

(Note: Thus Imamana's Prophecy that at three places,1. Bandgi Miyan's Body was buried at Sudrassan,2. his bones of the head and face were buried at Patan, and 3. the skull filled with straw were buried in Chapneer along with other four martyrs, Hzt Syed Jalaluddin,Son,Malik Hammad, Malikji Mehri, and Malik Bakhan(Rz) . These three shrines are the undisputed facts which are enough to substatiate Imamana's Mahdiat, since Imamana(As) himself prophesied that if these facts would not occur, "Take me as an Imposter, otherwise, believe me as the "True Promised Mahdi". It was such a challenge that (Naoozo Billh) had it not happened, Imamana's claim of Mahdiat would have become questionable. These three Shrines are the undeniable and a concrete Proof of his Mahdiat.Among these three, Chapaneer's Shrine is in a good condition. While other two were in a delapidated condition.

In order to refurbish Patan's Shrine, this translator took personal interest and provided required funds for construction. Hzt. Ghazi Baba, Hzt. the Late Dawood Baba, Inayetullh Miyan, Salamullh T.Syed, Mutavalli, Azmatullah Syed, Photographer, and Syed Sultan Naseer of Hyderabad,all joined to supervise the construction, for that they got plans prepred. First of all, the 500 year old masjid was demolished and reconstructed on the old basement, along with a broad room, were constructed, two Living Rooms of 30' X 20.', two bath rooms, one for gents another for ladies, a kitchen and a common abluton palce with water tank were consdtructed. Some 30 graves were on ground level, all were reconstructed by fixing their epitophs with their names engraved on marble, and an all round boundary wall with a strong iron gate. As the Mujawer is a Hindu, his quarter was constructed outdside the boundary and his own Latrine. Water arrngements were maid from the neighboring Bore Well. The original Shrine was carefully refurbished .Now it is available for scores of Zaereen to stay and offer their humble prayers. Patan is 36 miles from Palanpur.

*The third Shrine is of Sudrasan which is abetting to a river, which destroys every effort to maintain it in a good condition. Hence, the Mutvalli, Janab Salmullah T. Syed and others have aproached concerned authorities to help in constructing the Shrine. Government had sanctioned Rs.35 lakhs, last year, just to divert the flow of the river, away from the Shrine. The plan and the estimate was prepared by the late Talib Khundmiri, Architect, which comes to about Rs.25 lakh, apart from governments's Funds. It is said that after the end of the Rainy Season, Insha Allah, Govt.work may start. Now it is our responsdibility to collect required funds for constructing afresh the Shrine.Sudrasan is just 12 miles from Patan, where in, on the second day battle martyrdom occurred. Therefore this third Shrine's construction afresh is compulsory, which is one the three shrines of Hzt.Bandagi Miyan (RZ)as prophesied by Imamana(AS) a living proof of Imamana's Mahdiat. We must come forward to collect funds for constructing the third shrine, to declare and inform to the decliners that notice the last prphecy of Imamana(As) **who challenged that "If after 20 years from his demise, if the battle did not take place between Bandagi Miyan(Rz) and the Government forces, and on the second day Bandagi Miyan along with his 60 companions are not martyred, and Bndagi Miyan's body, bones of the head and face and the skull filled with straw were not burierd at three different*** *places, Imamana(As) made it his Hujjat that he my be taken as Imposter, and if that happened word by word, then believe me, with your heart and mind, that I am the real Promised Mahdi(As), as prophesied by the Holy Prophet (Slm).*

I appeal the generosity of the readers to provide funds to safeguard the shrine, for the sole purpose mentioned above and kindly contact the Mutavalli, Janab Salmullh T.Syed at his phone No<011 91 2742-246382>for providing the funds to the right person and to know the facts about the shrine........Khundmiri).

Bandagi Miyan (Rz) Before Meeting Imamana (As)

Author of Hadia had become so mean and jealous by reporting absurd and unauthentic narratives and had tried to create false objections against Bandagi Miyan (Rz) that before meeting with Imamana (As), he was engaged in the nightingale, lamb and cattle fighting in his chapter 3, argument 9. These bogus and baseless accusations are not available in any book of Mahdavis.

"Moulood" is the oldest biography written by Miyan Abdul Rahman (Rz) who has minutely reported about the very first visit of Bandagi Miyan (Rz) to Imamana (As) as under:

"Malik Bakhan (Rz), alias Malik Barkhurdar, informed Bandagi Miyan (Rz) that a pious and a supreme personality, about whom he was curious to meet, had arrived here. Hearing this news, Bandagi Miyan (Rz) became very happy and got himself ready to meet Imamana (As) and at the very sight of Imamana (As), Bandagi Miyan became senseless ."

ملك بـخـن عرف ملك برخوردار ميان سيد خوند ميرؒ راگفتنـد كه چنانچه شمامى خواستيده همچنين ذات باركات آمده است چنانچه شمامى خواستيدهمچنين ذات باركـات آمده است شنيده بسيار منشوط روان شـدنـد و بـه مـلازمـت عـالـى درجت مشرف گشتند چونكه نظر بر حضرت ميران عليه السلام افتاد ے هوش شدند (مولود ميان عبدالرحمن ٨٤)

It denotes that he was busy not in the cattle fighting, but very enthusiastic to see such a pious personality who could satisfy his ambition to witness the vision of Allah.

Miyan Mansur Khan a disciple of Bandagi Miyan Syed Mahmood (Rz) had described this meeting in the following words:

"Miyan Syed Khundmir (Rz) was an elite among the nobles (of Ghadiwal). When he visited Imamana (AS) for the first time, on account of Imamana's splendour, he became unconscious at the very first sight of Imamana (As). He was taken away into a corner by Imamana (AS) and informed him that "it was not our ritual", at this, he came out to his senses and informed that "he did not see Imamana (As) but to Allah who was manifested in him."

میاں سید خوند میرؓ از امرا زادگان بودند چوبه ملازمت میراں آمده مشرف گشته بشرف آمدهٔ مشرف گشته بشرف دیدار مشرف شدند چنان بے هوش شدند که در هوش خود نماندند برداشته در گوشه بردند چون به هوش آمدند گفتند من میران راند بدیم بلکه خدائے خود را دیدم ۳۳ـ۳٤

Here no cattle fighting had been reported, but actually he had the zeal to meet such a Godliman who could satisfy him regarding the secrets of the Divinity which could lead him to have the vision of Allah. Thus, can anyone imagine a person who is immersed in the desire to see Allah could he take interest in filthy affairs as stated by the decliner who is a mean, vicious and malicious and a biased manipulator.

Author of "Matleul Vilayet" had reported Bandagi Miyan's first visit to Imamana as under:

"Bandagi Malik Bakhan (Rz) informed Bandagi Miyan (Rz) about the arrival of a dignified, pious and auspicious personality about whom Bandagi Miyan (Rz) was serious and desirous to meet. Thus on hearing, Bandgi Miyan (Rz), a true seeker, longing for the vision of Allah for long, went on Friday to meet Imamana (As) and when he had Imaman's very first sight he became unconscious and fell down".

بـه سیـد الشهـداء میـان سیـد خونـد میـرؓ خبـر کـردند مرشدیکه شما طالب آن هستید چه آن صفت ها که هر جـامی جستید چنیـن ذات فـائض البرکـات جـامع الـصفات تجلی ذات آمده است ، پس آن عاشق عارف طـالب صـادق مستثنیٰ به ثنائے بے نهایت حامل خاص حمـل ولایـت بعـد نمـاز جمعه متوجه ملازمت آنحضـرت گشـت، هـر گـاه نظرش بر آں ذات عالی صفـات افضل الدرجات افتاد فی الحال به تجلی جلال مست و بے هوش شده افتاد

Here too there is no news about his being busy with filthy affairs but had a longing to have the vision of Allah and thus he met with Imamana (As) for the first time on Friday. Author of "Shawahedul Vilayet" had narrated:

"After having a meeting with Imamana (As), Malik Bakhan (Rz), who was residing near the house of Bandagi Miyan (Rz) went to Bandagi Miyan (Rz) and informed that a dignified Godliman, a real mystic, has come to Pattan, and he is the one to whom you were searching."

ملك مذکور از حضرت امام البروا البحور رخصت شده بخانه آمدند که خانهٔ ایشان و خانهٔ بندگی میان در قـلعـه کهنه عنقریب بود بندگی میان رامبارك باد داده خبـر کـردند که چنانچه شمامیخواستید پیرکامل آمده است(باب پانز دهم)

Here also there is no information about cattle playing. These are the oldest sources of information about Bandagi Miyan (Rz) in which nothing is recorded about his cattle playing etc.. If any other book written later by any anonymous author which does not get sanctity, if the author of Hadia referred that unauthentic book and had raised objections, those bogus objections are null and void. Apart from this it is a fact that Bandagi Miyan's life was clean from all sorts of innovations and bid'ats and he was living in a very secluded and mystic life from the very beginning. When he met Imamanas (As) he had given a Glad Tiding to Bandagi Miyan, saying:

"Imamana (As) said brother Khundmir (Rz) had brought the lamp, along with oil and wicks, just remained to be lit, which is lit through the flame of the "Vilayet-e-Mustafavi."

فرمودند برادرم سید خوند میر چراغاں وروغن وفتیله مستعد کرده آور دند مگر روشن کردن مانده بود بچراغ ولایت روشن چراغدان و روغن وفتیله مستعد کرده آوردند برادرم سید خوند میر چراغاں و روغن و فتیله مستعد کرده آوردند مگر روشن کردن مانده بود بچراغ ولایت روشن کرده شد(شواهد الولایت باب ۲٦)

"Tazkeratul Saleheen" says that:

"Imamana (As) said that Miyan Khundmir (Rz) had brought with him the lamp, oil and wick, yet to be lit, which was lit from the flame of "Vilayet-e-Mustafvi"; thus he became "Noorun Ala Noor."

فرمودند که روغن و فتیله و چراغدان همه استعداد چراغ به میان سید خوند میر موجود بو دیگر کار افروختن باقی مانده بو دآں هم از چراغ ولایت افروخته شدپس نور علی نور گشت (باب اول)

Had the life of Bandagi Miyan (Rz) was served in absurdity, how could he become "Noorun Ala Noor" on the very first meeting with Imamana (As)?

As regards Bandagi Miyan's characters it is stated:

"It is said that all nobles of Baadiwal had their best opinion about the characters of Bandagi Miyan (Rz), even the uncle of his mother, Mubarzul Mulk, was so fascinated with the character of Bandagi Miyan (Rz), that he used to say if Bandagi Miyan (Rz) proclaims his Mahdiath (at that period the environment was very thick about the advent of Mahdi) we shall surely offer our allegiance to him."

به نقل تواتر رسیده است که همه امرایان باڑی وال معتقد خاص حمیده خصال بندگی میان بوده اندتا به حد سے که سرحلقه ایشان که عموے مادر شان ملك مبارزالملك محب و معتقده و عاشق بندگی میان بوده اند که کرات ومرات می فرمودند که اگر میان دعویٰ بینه آخر الزمان کنند ما تصدیق می کنهم (دفتر اول)

It is narrated from so many sources that even before meeting with Imamana (As), Bandagi Miyan (Rz) had been always busy in meditation in seclusion. He never bowed his head before any worldly priest or person. He declared it was against the Shariah to offer allegiance to the grave of a so called Murshid who died long back. He felt loathsome to offer allegiance to the worldly mashaequeen.

9. Bandagi Miyan's Childhood:

"Hadia-e-Haqaeq" reports about the answers given by Bandagi Miyan (Rz) to those who tried to get his father's Mansub transferred in his name:

"Even in his childhood he used to say that he had witnessed the vision of Allah. We are engaged in the service of the Almighty, therefore we do not want to become servant of any worldly man nor we offer salutations to others".

آں حبیب ذو الـجـلال در آں خـورد سـالـی جـواب بـاصـواب میـدادی کہ معبود خود را دیدہ ایم، نوکری و چاکری و بندگی ھمان معبود خالق خودی کنیم چاکر و نوکر مخلوق نمی شویم و مخلوق را سر فرو کردہ سلام نمی کنیم ـ(دفتر اول رکن اول باب اول)

Just think over Bandagi Miyan's sublime thoughts, then guess how can such a person would indulge in absurdities of cattle playing etc.? Thus author's objections on the characters of Bandagi Miyan (Rz) on the basis of unauthentic and baseless versions, are utterly unfounded and malicious.

10. Firework on a Wedding Ceremony:

Author of Hadia had objected on a baseless narration that on the wedding ceremony of Miyan Syed Hameed, son of Imamana (As), Bandagi Miyan (Rz) arranged for the firework which the decliner states that it was against Shariat.

It is a fact that at the wedding ceremony of another son of Imamana (As) he had arranged a grand gala function just to propagate the name of Imamana (As). "Dafter-e- Shah Burhan" Narrates:

"It is narrated that Bandagi Miyan (Rz) had arranged a princely wedding function for Miyan Syed Ibrahim, son of Imamana (As) in which he had invited all companions of Imamana (As). On that night, while on the city rounds according to the traditions, "The Nikah was announced on the trumpets of the Duff". He provided all sorts of musical instruments just to enhance the name of Allah and Mahdi (As). The bridegroom sat on a horse and he himself, along with other companions, was treading slowly in front of the horse. The descendants were holding sweets and betels on the trays, he directed them whoever comes and asked about whose wedding is that to "tell that it was the wedding of the beloved son of our Imamana (As)".

بنقل تواتر رسیده است که بندگی میان استعداد کا رخیر جگر گوشۂ صاحب زمانه به مقابله شاهانه کرده اند و دروقت کہ خائی شان جمیع مهاجرین خلیفۃ الرحمن علیهم الرضوان را طلبید ه اند وهمه مصدقان را حاضر گردانید اند و در شب شهر گشت به مقتضائ حدیث نبوی صلی الله علیه وسلم که اعلنو النکاح بضروب الدفوف اچه از انواع سورنی و نقاره و دف می باشد برائ الله و به جهت آشکارا کردن کلمۃ الله حاضر فرمودند و حکم چراغ هائ بسیار نموه داند وامیر سید ابراهیم رضی الله عنه را براسپ سوار کرده اندو خود با جمیع مهاجران علیهم الرضوان حزب الرحمن در پیش اسپ شهزادهٔ خود پیاده می رفتند و بدست اکثر تابعان خود طبق هائ شیرینی و برگ تنبول پر کرده داده اند ومیفرمودند که هر که به می تماشامی آیدومی پرسد که این شهر گشت کیست این شیرینی و برگ تنبول به هیدو وبگوئید که این شهر گشت پسر حضرت امیر سید محمد مهدی علیه السلام است

Here also arrangement of a grand gala function had been mentioned, but nowhere the words "Firework" had occurred. Then how anybody can imagine that yet with another son of Imamana(As), Miyan Hameed's wedding ceremony, arrangement of Firework had been made by Bandagi Miyan (Rz)?

Very important words of this narration were that:

'Tell them it is the City Round of the wedding of the son of Hazrat Mahdi-e-Maoud".

بگوئید که این شهر گشت پسر حضرت سید محمد مهدیّ است

It was just to propagate the name of Mahdi (As) and for that arrangement of lightning was done which was necessary at a period when there were no street lights available. However, In order to announce the matrimony there are so many narrations:

"At the ceremony of matrimony to blow Duff and announcing loudly is just to differentiate between Matrimony and Adultery."

(۱) الفصل مابین الحلال و الحرام ضرب الدف والصوت فی النکاح

In "Ashatul Lam'aat" it is reported about the sound at the time of Niklah that:

"Sound means to announce and propagate among the people about the matrimony ceremony by blowing Duff. It means that a faithful had married and not indulged in adultery. It is not a secret and unless the sound of Duff is not heard or smoke is not spread, announcement of matrimony is not complete."

مراد به آواز ذکر و تشهیر است میان مرم

(۲) اعلنو ا هذا النکاح و اضربو اعلیه بالغربال

(۳) کمل دینه النکاح ولا السفاح ولا نکاح السر حتی یسمع دف اویری دخان

These narratives show that announcement of Matrimony is done (1) either by blowing Duff or (2) by burning fire by spreading smoke. These are two carriers of news of matrimony. Hence no filthy objection is tenable. Thus firework at matrimony cannot be branded as a play or a thing of sport. Particularly when the intent has been just to propagate the name of Imamana (AS).

We have never read anything which proves that the city round of a bridegroom along with the firework had been branded as a filthy display. In this connection, the Holy Prophet (Slm) himself had sanctified such things as a source of enhancement of religious purpose. Before the fall of Makkah, the Holy Prophet (Slm) had ordered to burn fire before the all tents, four miles ahead of Makkah, to show pomp and glory of his arrival. This is mentioned in "Madarijul Nabuwwat":

"Thus Holy Prophet ordered to his companions to burn fire before every tent."

پس فرمود آنحضرت اصحاب خود راکه هر کس برده خیمه خود آتش افروخت (جلد دوم ۲۸۵)

When burning fire becomes a source of announcements (of the arrival of a grand lashker), then why firework of a matrimony becomes a filthy act?

It all boils down to say that the biased decliner is trying to blame Bandagi Miyan (Rz) on an unauthentic and baseless narrative, just to blame about his characters. If some person brands firework at matrimony is a filthy act, then how Duff blowing becomes appreciative custom at the matrimony?

Thus objection was on a baseless narrative, therefore nobody could point out finger towards the characters of Bandagi Miyan (Rz). Even if we accept that the firework was arranged, then it was arranged just to make famous the name of Imamana (As). Therefore it cannot be said a disgraceful act. For example go through the narration of by Bibi Ayesha (Rz):

"Narrated by Ayesha (Rz) that when the Negroes were playing with swords and arrows on the Eid Day, the Holy Prophet (Slm) was covering me under his cloak."

قالت بردایه و انا انظرالی الحبشة یلعبون بالدرق و الحراب یوم العید

This narration speaks about the Holy Prophet (Slm) who himself took part along with Bibi Ayesha (Rz) in witnessing the games of the Negroes who were showing their art of warfare. When the Holy Prophet (Slm) did not designate these games as absurd which were being performed in the Masjidun Nabavi, then why Bandagi Miyan's actions are objected?

Shah Abdul Aziz narrates:

"Another thing is that the play of the Negroes was with swords and arrows. They were practicing to gain mastery over the art of warfare against the infidels to prepare for Jihad with all sorts of ammunition. As a matter of fact it was a game being played openly, but actually it had a wisdom in gaining perfection in horse riding and arrow shooting. In such plays the Holy Prophet (Slm) had taken part in them and sometimes he himself practiced and used to say the angels attend these games too."

ديگر آنكه لهو و لعب حبشه به سپر و نيز ها بود كه برائى ممارست حرب كفار و بطريق اعداد آلات الجهاد مشق اين هنرى كردند پس به صورت لعب و بازى بوده به معلى سراسر حكمت ورنگ ، دانيدن اسپان و تيرا نداى بلاشبه آنحضرت در اين قسم حاضر شده اند بلكه در بعضى اوقات شريك هم شده و فرموده' كه ملائكه نيز در اين قسم بازى ها حاضرى شوند-

When such games are not absurd and they were being played in the Masjid and were branded for enhancing wisdom, then how they become absurd for Bandagi Miyan?. Furthermore arrow throwing and horse riding also are the acts of play and sport, since they are supposed to help in training for Jihad; that is why the Holy Prophet (Slm) himself had taken part in them personally and where according to the Holy Prophet (Slm) angels too took part in them; then Bandagi Miyan's arrangement for lightning at the City Rounds after the wedding ceremony if arranged, how could it be disgraced, when the intent was just to propagate the name of Imamana (As)? This firework, based on an inauthentic narrative, even though it is doubtful, however had it been actually arranged, in view of the above said traditions, cannot be branded as an act of disgrace?

Blame for Tampering (with the text):

Author of Hadia had blamed Bandagi Miyan (Rz) that he had tampered with the text of "Futuhat-e-Makkiah" as mentioned in his chapter 3 argument 8. It is an accepted fact that while copying any book some differences of versions occur on account of misunderstanding by the copier and thus it cannot be branded as tampering the very text of the book. The fact is that Bandagi Miyan (Rz) had written his "Maktoob-e-Multani" in 928 H. addressing to the scholars of Multan which became very famous. He had discussed, at the beginning, about the reasons for the commissioning of the Prophets by Allah Jalley Subhanahu and had arguably emphsised about the wisdom inherited in it. Thus the same wisdom is witnessed in commissioning of Imamana (As) by Allah mainly to spread monotheism and the Divine Message of Allah. Then he had mentioned those traditions in which Imamana (As) and his companions have been referred. In order to clarify his purpose, he had presented excerpts from "Makkiah" which refer to Imamana (As) and his companions. And at the end of the letter he had quoted those verses which pertain to Imamana (As) and his companions. Excerpts from "Makkiah" have presented in support of the claim of Mahdiath of Imamana (As); particularly in view of the fact that at a time when the air was thick with the news of the Advent of Mahdi in India and particularly since the Indians had great faith in Sheik Akbar (Rz) who had supported Imamana's Mahdiat. It may be noted that after mentioning traditions and narrations the excerpts of "Futoohat-e-Makkiah" had been presented. However, Bandagi Miyan (Rz) had a firm faith in the signs regarding Imam Mahdi (As) as mentioned in the traditions as well as in the "Futoohat" and through these excerpts he proved that those signs were applicable to Imamana (As) in entirety. Thus how could it be blamed that Bandagi Miyan (Rz) had tampered the text of the "Futoohat"?

Old volume of "Futoohat" Found in Fouqania:

According to Shirani the old volume of "Futoohat" was found in Fouqania which had been signed by the Author, Sheik Akbar (Rz) himself. But it might have been tampered in due course of time as the Bible and Torah had been tampered. The details are presented hereunder:

"All traditions and narrations which had been mentioned in them about Imam Mahdi (As) and those signs and symbols mentioned are proved on the person of Imam Syed Mohammed Mahdi Alaihis Slaam since they perfectly fit on him. Then those issues were presented pertaining to Sharia supported by the Ummah's consensus. It is said that Sheik Abu Taher who had brought that volume from Makkah had compared the the signatures of Sheik Akbar (Rz) available with the signature on that copy which was found in Fouqanai. He (Shirani) says that In order to make it a concised one, "I had deleted those items which I haven't seen in the volume given to me by Sheik Abu Taher."	جميع ما عارض من كلامه ظاهر الشريعة وما عليه الجمهور فهو مدسوس عليه كما اخبرنى بذلك سيدى الشيخ ابو طاهر المغربى نزيل مكة الشريفة ثم اخرج لى نسخة الفتوحات التى قابلها على نسخة الشيخ التى بخطه فى مدينة قونيه فام ارفيها شيئا كنت توقفت فيه وحذفته حين اختصرت الفتوحات

Further Shirani states that:

"Sheik Mohiuddin Arabi (Rz) had written in chapter 366 that: It may be known that Imam Mahdi's advent is necessary, since the Earth is filled with oppression and cruelty and thus after appearing he (Imam Mahdi (As) would establish justice and tranquility. It is eminent to happen at any time soon, if even one day is left for the Dooms Day, his appearance is must and Allah shall enlarge that day, so that Imam Mahdi (As) would establish his caliphate. He would be from the progeny of the Holy Prophet (Slm), a descendant of Bibi Fatima (Rz); whose grandfather was Imam Hussain Ibn Ali Ibn Abu Talib (Rz). *(Upto that point it is correct, but what he wrote afterwards crerates ambiguity of tampering by the Sheites)*. Because he further states that "Imam's father would be Hasanal Askari bin Imam Ali Naqi, bin Imam Mohammed Taqi bin Imam Ali Raza, bin Imam Moosa Kazim (Rz) , bin Imam Jafer-e-Sadeq (Rz), bin Imam Mohammed Baqer (Rz), bin Imam Zainul Abedeen (Rz), Bin Imam Hussain (Rz) bin Hazrat Ali Ibn Abu Talib (Rz)."

وعبارت الشيخ محى الدين فى الباب السادس الستين و ثلثمايه من الفتوحات واعلمو انه لابد من خروج المهدى عليه السلام لكن لايخرج حتى تمتلى الارض جوراوظلمات فيملو ها قسطاوعدلا ولولم يكن من الدنيا الا يوم واحد لطول الله تعالى ذلك اليوم حتى يلى ذلك الخليفه وهومن عترة رسول الله صلى الله عليه وسلم من ولد فاطمه رضى الله عنها جده الحسين بن على بن ابى طالب والده حسن العسكرى ابن الامام على النقى بالنون بن محمد التقى بالتا وابن الامام على الرضا بن الامام موسى الكاظم ابن الامام جعفر الصادق ابن الامام محمد الباقر ابن الامام زين العابدين على ابن الامام الحسين ابن الامام على ابن على ابى طالب

From this writing Sheik Akbar (Rz) was of the opinion that Mohammed bin Hasanal Askari should be the Mahdi-e-Maoud. If these words had not been available in that volume under question, then there was no reason that Shirani had mentioned in it. Since that sentence was available in the volume in which Sheik Akbar's signature was found, and the same volume was copied by Sheik Abu Taher. Thus it is a fact that the said sentence was available in that volume in which Sheik Akbar's signature was found. It is out of question that Sheik Akbar (Rz) belonged to Asnai-e-Ashri. Thus it is a fact that the volume was already tampered in favor of Mohammed Bin Al Askari, because Sheite people have faith that Mohammed Bin Al Askari should become the Promised Mahdi. In this connection author of "Izalatul Ghain " had written that:

Author of "Izalatul Ghain" thus mentioned that:

"Author of "Futoohat" had never mentioned that Mahdi-e-Mauood (As) should be the son of Hasan the second. This was the belief of Imamiah sect that Mahdi would be the Eleventh Imam."

صاحب فتوحات زینهار نه گفت که مهدی موعود فرزند امام حسن ثانی است که امام یاز دهم به طور امامیه باشد

If the above mentioned narration was not found In his book, then Shirani would never have mentioned in his book. It proves that the particular narration was available in Sheik Abu Taher's copy and that copy had the signature of Sheik Akbar (Rz). It cannot be presumed that Sheik Akbar (Rz) was a Shia, belonging to the Asnai Ashria, hence it is confirmed that the copy in which Sheik Akbar (Rz) had signed was a tampered one. Therefore except Asnai Ashria none had accepted Mohammed Hasanal Askari as Imam Mahdi.

Apart from this, Shirani had written "Al Kibriatal Ahmer" which is a concised version of "Futoohat". Chapter 366 of the "Futoohat" presents the signs of Imam Mahdi (As) based on the traditions mentioned in "Sihah" and other sources. However, "Al Kibriatul Ahmar" lacks in the signs for Imam Mahdi (As). Probably Shirani might have thought that Sheik Akbar (Rz) was not sure about them, hence deleted.

Thus Sheik Akbar's "Futoohat" had been certainly tampered. In such a situation we cannot prove which volume was authentic and the other was a tampered one. But what Bandagi Miyan (Rz), had written was the true copy of what was written in the original one; therefore no blame should be inflicted as such on Bandagi Miyan (Rz) for tampering.

Not only 'Futoohat' had been tampered, but Imam Ghazali's "Kitabul Ahyah" too had been tampered which was recorded by Shirani:

"In this manner, several issues had been included in "Kitabul Ahyah " under the name of Imam Ghazali (Rz). Qaazi Ayaz found out a copy which was later on was tampered, thus he asserted to burn it.

وکذالک دسوا علی الامام الغزالی عدة مسائل فی کتاب الاحیاء وظفر القاضی عیاض بنسخة من تلک النسخ فامر باحر اقها

Futoohat-e-Makkiah" was the first book in which the signs of Imam Mahdi (As) had been written based on both strong and weak traditions and they had become well known among the Ummah. That is why Bandagi Miyan (Rz) had presented some excerpts of "Futoohat" in his "Maktoob-e-Multani" which he thought necessary to be furnished.

As against Bandagi Miyan's narrations, the author of Hadia had asserted to have copied also from the "Futoohat", that Imam Mahdi (As) would appear in Damascus and at a place, named Ghotha, who would kill Sufiani under a tree. As regards "Sufiani" It may be pointed out that the name Sufiani is not available in "Sihah". Then how could we believe that this particular name of Sufiani, which is not found even in Sihah, how Shaik Akber(Rz) wuld refer?. Particularly when we have proved that gthis "Sufiani" was a creation by Shaites only. To negate the issue of Sufiani, we present an authentic statement of the calibre like Ibn Hazam (Rz) who had empahatically contradicted the very concept of Sufiani by saying that "son of Hasan Askari and emergence of sufiani is the accepted sign of Asanai-e-Ashria only and none else". Thus, on reading the words of the Futoohat that both, son of Hasan Askari and Sufiani, would emerge at one time, author of "Reehanatul Adab" had written about Sheik Akbar (Rz) that:

"Whatever had been written by Sheik Akbar (Rz) about the signs of Imam Mahdi (As), were copied from the books of Asnai Ashria".

عـلامـات ظهـور آن ولـى عصـر.........موافق كتاب
علمائ اماميه نگارش داده

The author of "Reehanatul Adab" was a Shia. (Being a Shia) he accepts the tampered version of the "Futoohat" in which Sheik Akbar (Rz) is said to have written about the different signs of Imam Mahdi (As). (But since the text of "Makkiah" had been tampered) therefore what was written was based on the beliefs and from the books of Asnai Ashria only. And on that score, author of Hadia maintains that whatever had been written about the signs of Imam Mahdi (As), are correct since those signs are mentioned in the tampered book of Sheik Akbar (Rz). Thus the author blindly accepts the narration which was copied by Shirani in which the name of Mohammed bin al Askari was written as Imam Mahdi (from the tampered copy of the "Futoohat"). Thus we it is an accepted fact that one of the copies of the "Futoohat" was certainly a corrupted copy in which different and baseless signs of Mahdi (As) had been incorporated based on the Shiete sources. However, the author of Hadia accepts those false signs mentioned in the corrupted copy of the Futoohat and blames Bandagi Miyan (Rz) for tampering which is nothing but malicious and unfounded allegation. However we refute his objections as malicious based on prejudice and bias only.

A. Bandagi Miyan (Rz) had written in his "Maktoob-e-Multani" with reference to "Futoohat" about the characters of Mahdi (As):

"Characters shall be like that of the Holy Prophet (Slm)." (as predicted by the Prophet (Slm) himself.)".

يشبه مع رسول الله فى الخلق بضم الخاء

As against Bandagi Miyan's version, Author of Hadia had written in chapter 3, the tampered version No.2 of the "Futoohat" that:

"Face shall be like that of the Holy Prophet (Slm), but Characters shall be not like him, because none could have such characters like that of the Holy Prophet (Slm)."

يشبـه رسـول الله فى الخلق بفتح الخاء وينزل عنه فى الـخـلـق لانـه لايـكـون احد مثل رسول الله صلى الله عليه وسلم فى اخلاقه

This narration of "Futoohat" does not match the traditions. the Holy Prophet (Slm) had said "Khul qohu Khulqi."/ characters shall be like mine. These are the words of the Holy Prophet (Slm) regarding the characters of Imam Mahdi (As). Apart from this, Sheik Akbar (Rz) had maintained that Mahdi (As) shall be called "Rahmatullil Alameen" par with the Holy Prophet (Slm). The following is from "Futoohat":

"Thus Mahdi (As) is Allah's Blessings comparing to the Holy Prophet (Slm). Allah had stated that We had made you "Rahmatullil Alameen. Mahdi would follow your footsteps and would not Err." Thus it is certain that he is a Blessing of Allah."

فالـمـهـدى رحـمة الله كما كان النبى صلى الله عليه وسـلـم رحـمة قـال تـعـالىٰ وما ارسلناک الا رحمته للعالمين والمهدى يقفو اثره ولايخطى فلابدان يكون رحمة .

The person who believes Imam Mahdi (As) to be the "Rahmatullil Alameen" as the Holy Prophet (Slm), how can he say that the characters of Imam Mahdi (As) would be different from the characters of the Holy Prophet (Slm)? as blamed by the biased decliner.

The author himself had accepted in chapter 8 that the characters of Mahdi (As) would be equal to that of the Holy Prophet (Slm). It is strange that he had preferred to present narration from the corrupted copy of the "Futoohat" which contradict the real version and which is certainly against the traditions too. Sherani died in 973 H. and before him, Sheik Abu Taher died in 955 H. While the "Maktoob" was written in 928 H. It proves that Bandagi Miyan (Rz) had referred the oldest possible volume of "Futoohat" which was available to him as an original one.

However, if there was a difference in two volumes, it cannot be said that Bandagi Miyan (Rz).had tampered.

B. Bandagi Miyan (rz) had stated regarding signs of Mahdi (As) with reference to "Futoohat":

"One person would come to Mahdi (As) in the evening. He would have been a miser, illiterate and coward, when he visited Imam Mahdi (As), still he would become generous, well educated and a brave man in the following morning after meeting with Immana(As)."

يـاتيـه الـرجـل يمسى جاهلا بخيلا جبانا فيصبح اعلم الناس اكرم الناس اشجع الناس

Author of Hadia had objected on this narration by telling, Bandagi Miyan (Rz) had added "Yatiul Rejla" because had it not been added it would not apply to Imamana (As). The author thinks that these words have been added by Bandaghi Miyan (Rz). But, as a matter of fact, these words had been mentioned in other copies of the "Futoohat" also with a little difference as mentioned by Shirani who had referred "Futoohat"and had narrated the following:

" If a person might have been an illiterate and a miser, at the evening when he came (to see Mahdi (As), but he shall become brave and generous in the following morning, (after meeting Mahdi (As)."

يـمسى جاهلا بخيلا جبانا فيصبح اعلم الناس اشجع الناس

These words are available in "Futoohat" which was published in Egypt in the year 1293 H. Thus it is proved that Bandagi Miyan (Rz) did not add "AL Rijl". Thus in both volumes it is narrated that "a man would come to Mahdi and within a little time he would become perfect in Islam and become faithful". Therefore the words "Yatiul Rijl " are suitably mentioned. While Shirani had mentioned the words "Yamsi" and Bandagi Miyan (Rz) used the words "Yatiul". This difference is due to the different copies referred by both personalities. However since it is a little difference should be ignored.

Apart from it, in one of the copies of "Futoohat", the words "Yarfaul Mazaheb" had been used, while Shirani's copy lacks those words.

The wordings of "Futoohat" prove that whoever joins the company of Mahdi (As), his bad qualities would change into virtuous qualities. For example, if he was a coward, he would become brave; if he was an illiterate, he would become well educated; and if he was a liar, he would become a truthful man. Therefore the words "yatiul Rijl", used by Bandagi Miyan (Rz) are more appropriate than" Yamsiul Rijl" as mentioned by Shirani. However, it is certain that a man would visit Imamana (As) and in a very short period he would become a perfect Muslim on account of Imamana's beneficence.

Author of Hadia maintains that according to Shirani's copy the text is as below:

"When Allah commissioned Mahdi (As) in the night:

"When Allah commissioned Mahdi (As), whoever was an illiterate, miser and weak, in the evening, he would become literate, generous and strong in the following morning (After meeting with Mahdi (As)".

يـمسى الـرجـل جاهلا وجبانا وبخيلا فيصبح عالما شجاعا كريما

What Shirani had written it contains the word "Yamsi ur Rijl" as under:

"That person might have been illiterate, weak and miser, but in the following morning he would turn to be literate and generous and strong. (After meeting with Mahdi (As)"

The same version is available in the copy which was published in Egypt in the year 1293 H.

Bazranji had also copied the same narration from page 366 of the "Futoohat" in "Al Ishaa fi Ashrathus Sa'a", as below:

"In the period of Mahdi (As) one person might have been an illiterate, weak and miser in the evening, but he would turn to be most strong, literate and generous in the following morning."

يـمسـى الـرجـل فـى زمانه جاهلا بخيلا جبانا فيصبح اعلم الناس اكرم الناس اشجع الناس

In this version the period mentioned refers to the period of Mahdi. This also supports what Bandagi Miyan (Rz) had written the words "miser and illiterate" have nothing to do with Imamana (As), but these qualities belong to the one who comes to Imamana (As) for his beneficence.

Apart from this Allah had made the Holy Prophet (Slm) to tell the infidels as mentioned below:

"I had spent a whole lifetime among you (did you hear anything uttered by me like this before), then do not you understand (the difference)?" (10:15)

فقد لبثت فيكم عمرا من قبله اف لا تعقلون (سوره يونس ع ٣)

Through this verse the life of the Holy Prophet (Slm), before his Prophethood, had been presented as a proof of his Nabuwwat. Imam Mahdi (As) who would tread on the footprints of the Holy Prophet (Slm), how he would not have such (exemplary) qualities, even before his proclamation of Mahdiat?

Shame on the author and his coterie who had maliciously admitted that Imam Mahdi (As) would carry contemptible character before his Mahdiat, although they know very well, that the Holy Prophet (Slm) had asserted that Imam Mahdi (As) would carry Holy Prophet's Characters by saying "Khulqahu Khulqhi" that means to say Imam Mahdi's character shall be what the Holy Prophet (Slm) had and Imam Mahdi's characters would resemble to Holy Prophet's characters.

Thus it is certain that what exemplary characters the Holy Prophet (Slm) had before his Nabuwwat, the same exemplary characters Imam Mahdi (As) would have carried from the beginning, of course, before his Mahdiat.

"Bukhari" had reported what Jabeer Bin Mut'am (Rz) had narrated to have heard the Holy Prophet (Slm) telling:

"You never found me a miser, a liar, nor a weak person".

لاتجدونى بخيلا ولا كذوبا لاجبانا

It tells that the Holy Prophet (Slm) did not carry such filthy characters before his Nabuwwat. As regards Imam Mahdi (As) it had been stated that Imam Mahdi's character shall be like that of the Holy Prophet's. That is to say Imam Mahdi (As) also would not have any filthy character before his Mahdiat.

As the words "Mohammed Bin al-Askari" had been added in the version of "Futoohat", it is possible that the enemies of the Ahl-e-Bait might have deleted the word "AL Rujl" from the version of "Futoohat" so that the illiterate persons like the author who is ignorant about the art of traditions, may wrongly form an opinion about Imam Mahdi (As) to possess such filthy characters before his Mahdiat.

The tradition as reported by "Ibn Maja" tells:

"Mahdi (As) is from the Ahl-e-Bait,   المهدى من اهل البيت يصلحه الله فى ليلة
Allah would infuse in him an exemplary
capacity in a single night."

Here the word "Lail (night)" denotes to a little period and not to a single night and the "reform" means to infuse capacity of Mahdiat. It is possible only when Allah educates Imam Mahdi (As) directly without any medium. This tradition refers towards granting of the position of Mahdiat.

It is nowhere mentioned in that narration that Imam Mahdi (As), before his Mahdiat, would carry such filthy characters like, miser, liar or weak. Whereas the version of "Futoohat" tells that whoever joins the company of Imam Mahdi (As), the new comer's filthy characters would convert into good habits. Had he been a week, he would convert to a strong person. If he was an illiterate, he would become a literate one. If he was a liar, he would become a truthful worthy person.

As a matter of fact the novice only had tampered on account of which differences have erupted in so many copies of the "Futoohat". If any version had been copied from a volume which was tampered, then how could the copier be blamed? And the remark is inflicted upon him as if he had tampered?. Particularly when the decliner's objection is against the traditions.

Thus it is certain that some volumes of "Futoohat" had been tampered and if any person refers any narration from that tampered volume, how that man would be designated as a tamperer?

Examples of Tampering:

The very decliner had tampered. Examples of his tampering are submitted hereunder:
Bandagi Miyan (Rz) had copied two couplets from "Futoohat" of Sheik Akber (Rz):

"Ala Un Khatimul Aouliah Shaheed" "Wa Ain Imamul Aalamain Faqeed"
"Hu As Syedal Mahdi Min Al-e-Ahmed" "Hua Sarimul Hindi Hainey Yabeed"

A. Author of Hadia had blamed for tampering the meanings, but as a matter of fact Bandagi Miyan (Rz) did never change the meanings.

1. The Author's contention that "Khatmul Aouliah"means Jesus Christ (As) is utterly wrong. In this connection we submit Nawab Siddiq Hussain Khan's clarification about that couplet:

2. "Khatmul Aouliah means Mahdi   مراد به ختم الاولياء مهدى است
(As)".

3. Barzanji also maintains: "Khatmul   مراد به ختم الاولياء المهدى
Aouliah" means Mahdi (As)."

B. The version regarding "Khatimul Vilayet" starts with these words:

"Al Khatam, Khatman, Yakhtamullahi Bihil Vilayet-e-Mutlaqa WA Khatm-e-Yakhtamullah bihil Vilayet-e-Mohammadia." author maintains that the version is a part of "Maktoob-e-Multani", whereas it is not the part of "Maktoob". "Khatime Sulaimani" maintains about this "Maktoob" that:

Regarding Makateeb, Bandagi Miyan (Rz) had stated about "general Vilayet and particular Vilayet"

> In the name of Allah……
> There are two Khatims…..

It is clear that Bandagi Miyan (Rz) had written a letter, but it is not necessary that the version of the letter should be according to the "Futoohat".

Khatim-e-Vilayet, Qur'an & Traditions:

The word "Khatim-e-Vilayet"had not come either in the Qur'an or in the traditions. This is a term used by mystics. Therefore Bandagi Malik Sujawandi (Rh) had described it as under:

"Thus, brother, you cannot trace the word "Khatim-e-Vilayet" in the Qur'an or traditions; because it is well known to scholars that this title had been attached to Mahdi (As) by the mystics. There exists not even a week tradition in this regard, leave aside the strong one; thus it is not referred in the holy Qur'an. This is only created by the mystics to differentiate Mahdi (As) from other mystics.

"However other titles which had been used for Mahdi (As), they are Imam, Khalifa and "Khaatim-e-Deen", about which we have already stated above. As asserted by the Holy Prophet (Slm) that : "the Deen would complete by Mahdi (As)"or to say " on Mahdi (As)", as it was started by the Holy Prophet (Slm)."

فـاعـلـم ايهــا الاخ ان طـلب بيـان لفظ خـاتم الولاية بـالـقرآن والاحاديث الصحيحةغير صحيح اذلايخفى عـلى الـعـالـم ان اطـلاق هـذا الـلفظ على المهدى من مـصـطـلحات الصوفية ليس عليه حديث ضعيف فضلا عـن الـصـحـيـح والـكتاب وهل عليه دليل سوئ اقوال الـصـوفية والـذى وقع فى الاحاديث من الالفاظ الامام الخليفة وخاتم الدين كماذكرنا قبل وهو قوله يختم الله به الدين كما فتحه بنا (منهاج) التقويم ١٣١ و٣٢

In the same manner the words" Khatimul Aouliah" also had not come in any of the traditions, however in "Sihah" the words "Khalifatullah Mahdi (As)" had been written. Thus this term was certainly used by the mystics to differentiate Imam Mahdi(As) from other Mystics.

Author of Hadia had deliberately omitted some words from the tradition in order to describe it in a wrong sense. The Author had maintained that after Hzt. Ali (Rz), nobody could be declared as "Siddiq-e-Akbar (Rz)". For that purpose he had copied the tradition of "Ibn Maja" as under:

"I am Abdullah (Rz), brother of the Holy Prophet (Slm) and Siddiq-e-Akbar (Rz). None would declare except a liar."

انا عبدالله و اخو رسول الله صلى الله عليه وسلم وانا الصديق الاكبر لايقولها بعدى الا كذاب .

But the actual tradition adds the words " I had offered prayers seven years ago earlier to the people." The author had tampered it in the tradition by omitting the said words. As a matter of fact without those words which were omitted by the author, correct meanings of the tradition cannot be understood.

Hzt. Ali (Rz) had presented the argument that he had offered prayers seven years earlier than the people. Among the people Hzt. Abu Baker (Rz) also is included. It means to say that Hzt. Ali (Rz) had performed prayers seven years earlier than to Hzt. Abu Baker (Rz). On that basis Hzt. Ali (Rz) shall rightly become the "Siddiq-e-Akbar (Rz)". According to the author from the companion of the Prophet (Slm) no one could be called "Siddiq-e-Akbar (Rz) except Hzt. Abu Baker (Rz)?. Is it the belief of the decliner?

The Author's contention that "Siddiq-e-Akbar (Rz)" cannot be applied to Bandagi Miyan (Rz) and as a proof, he had submitted an incomplete tradition of "Ibn Maja" so that the commoners may understand that after Abu Baker (Rz) none could be called "Siddiqu-e-Akbar (Rz). His contention is absurd and unacceptable since this tradition cannot apply to the companions of Mahdi (As) or of the Prophet Eisa (As).

But in that tradition nowhere it is mentioned that the ranks what the predecessors (Companions of the Holy Prophet (Slm) got, could not be claimed by the descendants means

(Companions of Imam Mahdi). Particularly when the Holy Prophet (Slm) had prophesied that " They would love more intensely with me who would come after me." This had already been discussed under the chapter" Ranks of Companions".

Since there was a "Siddiq-e-Akbar (Rz)" among the companions of the Holy Prophet (Slm), thus there should also be any Siddiq-e-Akbar among the companions of Mahdi (As) and of Jesus Christ (As).

Further, Bandagi Miyan (Rz) did not claim himself to be the "Siddiq-e-Akbar (Rz), but this title was given to Bandagi Miyan (Rz) by Imamana (As) as "Siddiq-e-Vilayet". Because he was the first to declare Imamana (As) as the promised Mahdi (As) when Imamana (As) proclaimed his Mahdiat for the third time in 905 H. at Badhli as prophesied by the Holy Prophet (Slm). And at that time Imamana (As) granted him the title as a Glad Tiding to Bandagi Miyan (Rz).

"You are Siddiq-e-Vilayet".   شما صدیق ولایت هستید

"Aqeeda-e-Shariefa" and Author's Objections:

Bandagi Miyan (Rz) had written "Aqeedai-e-Shariefa" and at the very beginning he stated that:

قال امام المهدى صلى الله عليه وسلم علمت من الله
بـلا واسـطة جـديـد اليـوم قل انى عبدالله تابع محمد
رسـول الـلــه مـحـمـد مهدى آخر الزمان وارث نبى
الـرحـمـان عـالم علم الكتاب والايمان مبين الحقيقة
والشريعة والارضوان.

"Narrated by Imamana (As) that I get Revelations directly from Allah and that I am a servant of Allah, follower of Mohammed Rasoolullah (Slm), named as Mohammed Mahdi, Akhiruz Zaman, successor to the Holy Prophet (Slm), knower of Allah, the knowledge of the Qur'an and the Faith, narrator of the Shariah and carries Allah's Blessings."

الـمـقـصـود بنده سيد خوند ميرؒ عرف چهجواى احكام
اززبـان سيـد مـحـمـد مهدى عليه السلام شنيده است
واوفـرمـوده اسـت هـر حـكـمـے كـه بيان كنم از خدا و
بامرخدا بيان كنم الىٰ آخره

"Thus I, Syed Khundmir (Rz) son of Syed Moosa, alias Chajjo, had heard these words from the mouth of Imamana (As) as asserted by Imamana (As): "whatever he heard from Allah the same he announces before all.""

This Arabic version was written by Bandagi Miyan (Rz) in the beginning of "Aqeedai-e-Shariefa", then he wrote in Persian language. Author of Hadia in chapter 8, argument No, 7 had maintained that whatever was written, was as if narrated by Imamana (As). He thus writes in chapter-8 argument-7, that he regarded all to have been said by Imamana (As) and states that " Now hear about the narration of the Qur'an by Mahdi (As), the controversial (according to his belief),....... As a matter of fact Bandagi Miyan (Rz) had particularly written "Stated by Mahdi (As)", that means " it was stated by Imamana (As)". The Arabic version had three portions: First states "Narrated Imamana Mahdi Salle Alahi Walahi Sallam" this version was written by Bandagi Miyan (Rz). Second starts from, "Alamtu Min Allah" and ends at "Mohammed Rasololullah (Slm)" This version pertains to Imamana (As). Third portion starts from" Mohammed Mahdi (As)" and ends at : Ar Rizwan." This pertains to Imamana's ranks written by Bandagi Miyan (Rz).

Imamana's statement that "Allah ordains me" which Imamana (As) had described that Command, need not necessarily to be what had Allah spoken. We have many traditions in which the Holy Prophet (Slm) has stated that "Allah has commanded me." The following is an example of such narration of the Holy Prophet (Slm):

وان ربى قال يا محمد انى اذا قضيت امر فانه لايرد

"And verily Allah stated that "oh Mohammed when we issue orders for anything it is not reversible."

Whether such traditions shall be categorized as the verses of the Holy Qur'an?

Thus the second portion contains what Imamana (As) had stated while first and third portions pertain to Bandagi Miyan's version..

Thus the author had objected about Imamana's contention and the version of Bandagi Miyan

(Rz). There are four objections in technical terms based on grammar on both the versions of Imamana (As) and of Bandagi Miyan (Rz) which demonstrate that the decliner himself has no knowledge of Arabic language of the Qur'an and of the traditions.

(This lengthy discussion about the grammar and technical terms had been omitted from translation for the brevity purpose) . (Urdu Pages 649 to 652 not translated).

12. Blaming for Lack of Understanding:

Author of Hadia had objected that what Bandagi Miyan (Rz) had copied from "Futoohat" was to show the excellence of the companions of Imam Mahdi (As) and particularly about Bandagi Miyan (rz) does not fit on them. The excerpts from "Futoohat" are being scrutinized below:

"They would follow the footsteps of the companions of the Holy Prophet (Slm). And they proved right what they had promised to Allah. Although they would be Ajmi and none would be an Arab, still they speak Arabic and understand Qur'an as well. There is one who would be a protector, He would never disobey orders of Allah, he would maintain a distinct position among the companions because of his trustworthiness."

وهم على اقدام الرجال من الصحابة صد قواما عاهدو الله عليه وهم من الاعاجم مافيهم عربى لكن لايتكلمون الا بالعربية لهم حافظ ليس من جنسهم ماعصى الله قط هو اخص الوزرا وافضل الامناء

The fact is that they would follow the footsteps of the companions of the Holy Prophet (Slm). Mullah Abdul Qader Badayuni had proved in his "Najatur Rasheed" about the descendants of the Imamana (As) by stating: "if their particulars are written, it would become another "Tazkeratul Aouliah". By stating he had proved their ranks and importance among the Ummah.

Their most significant attribute is that they would all be Ajami (Non Arabs), none would be an Arab. It is a fact that the companions of Imamana were non Arabs, because they were born in places other than Arabian lands, therefore they were called Ajmi. However prominent Arabs too had accepted Imamana (As) as the promised Mahdi (As). Imamana's Muhajirs were from Baghdad also, Miyan Abdul Rahman's "Moulood", the oldssdest written biography of Imamana (As) confirms that:

"One day Miyan Abdullah Baghdadi (Rh) requested (Imamana (As))."

روزے میان عبدالله بغدادى عرض کردند الیٰ آخره

It may be pointed out that "Futoohat" had described the ranks of the companions of Mahdi (As). It was not necessary that their language too was to be mentioned. Just speaking Arabic, was not a distinguishing feature for the companions, since any man of mean nature also can speak Arabic.

The fact is that it refers to "Al Arabia'; it means one who refers Qur'an in his speech which is a matter for prominence. Now remains whether by mentioning "Al Arabia" can we deduce Qur'an from it or not? Author of "Nahaiyah" had referred about Hzt. Omer (Rz):

لاتنقشو افى خواتمكم العربيه

"Do not engrave Arabic in your fingers."

With reference to this it also had been said that:

كان ابن عمريكره ان ينقش فى الخاتم القرآن

"Ibn Omer (Rz) disdained engraving Qur'an on the finger Rings."

Now we can understand the words "La Yatakal lemoona Illa Bil Arabia"; it means to speak with reference to Qur'an only. Further, "Takal Lum Bil Qur'an" can be well described by Darmi's narration which he had reported from Abu Huraira (Rz):

قال قال رسول الله صلى الله عليه وسلم ان الله قرأطه ويسن قبل ان يخلق السموت والارض بالف عام فلما سمعت الملائكة القرآن قالت طوبى لا مة ينزل عليها و طوبى لاجواف تحمل هذا و طوبى لالسنة تتكلم بهذا

"Narrated by Abu Huraira (Rz) who heard the Holy Prophet (Slm) telling that one thousand years before the creation of Earth and skies Allah had recited the Sooras of Taha and Yaseen and when heard by the angels they exclaimed good news for them to whom these Sooras were revealed, and also blessings for them whose bosoms are able to hold them and also Blessing to those languages which speak with it (Holy Qur'an.)"

The last words "Takallum Ba haza" of the tradition means "Takallum Bil Qur'an" that means they speak by referring to the Qur'an. Since the recitation of the Qur'an may be construed as "Takallum Bil Qur'an". Therefore after reading the Holy Qur'an giving description also is called "Takallum Bil Qur'an" This vouchsafe by both "Bukhari and "Muslim":

ويتكلمون بالسنتنا

"And speak in our language, that is in Arabic".

"Ashaatul Lam'aat" states that:

تكلم مى كنند بقرآن و حديث و مواعظ و حكم

"(They) Speak by referring to the Qur'an and traditions with wisdom in their sermons."

Here also "Takallum Bil Qur'an" means to deliver lectures with reference to the Qur'an and Traditions is meant.

From this what "Futoohat" had referred becomes clear that the companions of Mahdi would speak Arabic while referring to the Qur'an and the traditions. This refers to their "Narration of

Qur'an" which was the speciality of the Dairah. The narration had become known as commentary of the Holy Qur'an in real sense. In order to form an opinion about the narration of the Qur'an by the descendants of Imamana, what Mullah Abdul Qader Badayuni had written is enough which had been already stated before. For example Badayuni had written about Sheik Burhan (Rh) of Kalpi is furnished here:

"(Sheik Burhan Kalpi (Rh) used to follow the system of breath reckoning (Pass-e-Anfas) of Mahdavia. Although he didn't learn the Arabic, but was well versed in Arabic to narrate commentary of the Qur'an in Arabic eloquently. He had the inspiration to read the minds of others."

اوقـات بيـاس انفاس بطريق مهدويه ميگذرانيد و باآنکه عـلـوم عـربيه هيچ نخواند بود تفسير قرآن بوجه بليغ مى گفت و صاحب کشف قلوب بود

From this it is clear that Sheik Burhan (Rh) of Kalpi although did not have command in Arabic, still his commentary of the Qur'an was so impressive and eloquent that any person could understand it . Could it not be ascertained as "Takallum Bil Quran? From this you may imagine how best had been the narration of Qur'an by the companions of the Imamana (As).

Fourth point was of a "Hafiz" not of a Qur'an, but a protector. This refers to "Nasir-e-Deen." As mentioned in "Shawahedul Vilayet":

"Narrated Imamana (As): Bhai Syed Khundmir (Rz): You are "Sultanun Naseer (Rz)", protector of the Vilayet-e-Mustafa (Slm)"

برادرم سيـد خـونـد ميرّ ذات شماسلطانا نصير ااست ناصر ولايت مصطفى هستيد

In the "Naqliat-e-Syed Alam" it had been described that Imamana (As) had given the title of "Protector of Religion" to Bandagi Miyan (Rz). And Allah had stated that:

"Provide protection to Allah and His Rasool (Slm)."

وينصرون الله ورسوله(الحشرع)

Author of "Madarik" had commented for the above verse that:

"That is, to protect Allah for Deen (Religion) and provide help and assistance to Allah's Rasool (Slm)."

اى ينصرون دين الله و يعينون رسوله

The fifth point is that he would not belong to the progeny of the companions. This also fits to Bandagi Miyan (Rz). The fact is that except Bandagi Miran Syed Mahmood (Rz), and Bandagi Miyan (Rz) other three companions of Imamana (As) were not from the progeny of Bani Fatima (Rz). Thus Bandagi Miyan (Rz) belonged to the progeny of Bani Fatima (Rz) Therefore this also fits on Bandagi Miyan (Rz). The details of Bandagi Miyan's martyrdom had been described in detail.

Sixth point is that he would be prominent among the companions (ministers). This also fits on Bandagi Miyan (Rz) because according to the tradition of "Artat", Bandagi Miyan's martyrdom took place just after twenty years from the date of demise of Imamana (As) as prophesied.

Seventh point is that : "He would be prominent as trustworthy among the companions. This refers to the fact that he would be "Haamil-e-Bar-e-Amanat". This title of Bandagi Miyan (Rz) was well known even before 930 H.

Eigth point is that Bandagi Miyan (Rz) would not go against orders of Imamana (As). But Author of Hadia had maintained that Bandagi Miyan (Rz) had gone against Imamana (As). For that he had presented two issues. One: Cattle fighting's accusation and Two: Firework (at wedding of Imamana's son). These malicious accusations had already been refuted based on the dictates of the Qur'an and the traditions.

13.Accusation of Following non believers:

Author of Hadia had accused that Bandagi Miyan (Rz) had followed the non Mahdavis for prayers. And for that he had presented a narrative from "Insaf Nama":

بندگی میان سید خوند میر فرمودند که در مسجد جامع و در نماز عید مستعد شده باجامه نیك پوشیده باسلاح و جمعیت برویم تامخالفان خشم خورند و سوخته شوند و بگویند که ایشان این چنین بسیار هستنده واز مومنان تبر سند (باب هشتم)

"Bandagi Miyan (Rz) ordained his followers. while going to Jamai-e-Masjid for Eid, go by wearing gorgeous clothing in congregation so that the non Mahdavis become jealous and by seeing so many Mahdavis, they would become afraid."

Of course it proves that they had gone to Jamai-e-Masjid, but did they really offer prayers behind the non believers is not proved. In the same way for Eid Prayer also they had gone. But in "Naqliat-e-Miyan Abdul Rasheed" (Original) the words "Non Mahdavi Congregation had come:

نیز فرمودند که روز عید و جمعه درمجلس مخالفان باستعداد سلاح و جامهٔ نو پوشیده بازینت باید رفت تامخالفان سوخته شوند (باب پنجم)

"And ordered to go for Eid and Friday prayers keeping ammunition in the non Mahdavi congregation so that they become envious and afraid."

Although it is proved that they had gone to the Jamai-e-Masjid, but how can you prove that they actually had offered prayers behind a non believer? Certain examples are submitted:

A."Haashia Sharief" states that:

نقل است بندگی میان سید خوند میرؒ در لباس درویشی به موضع پٹن آمدند روز جمعه و نزدیك منبر نشستند ا زحجت مهدیت، علماء میان خود گفتند سید خوند میرؒ آمده است چون خطبه شد همه گریختند آری پیش حق باطل نماند

"Bandagi Miyan came in a saintly robe on Friday near the Podium and sat down. Scholars said that Syed Khundmir (Rz) had come. When the sermon was over all fled away. Before virtue evil flees."

Here it is proved that he had gone to the Masjid and sat down near the podium for the purpose of deliberation of a lecture, but how can it be proved that he had offered prayer behind the leadership of non believers?

Shah Burhan (Rh) had reported that:

"It is narrated that under the pressure of the scholars, the king did not meet the companions of Imamana (As) and then the companions had gone to their places. At that time Bandagi Miyan (rz) went to Peeran Pattan on Friday and met with Mulla Shamir who was sitting after completion of Friday prayer for teaching."

نقل است که چون بادشاه گجرات را علمائے لصوص الدین وفقهائے قطاع الطریق المبین مانع شدند و بااصحاب حضرت مهدی ملاقات کردن ندادند و یاران خلیفة الرحمن بجاهائے خود انتقال کردند بندگی میان در پیران پٹن روز جمعه یا ملاشهمیر که استاد علمائے گجرات بود ملاقات کردند آورده اند که ملائے مذکور بعد از فراغ نماز جمعه بامجمع انبوه بجهت درس نشسته بود (رکن پنجم باب سوم)

Here also it is proved that he went to Masjid on Friday, but offering prayer is not proved.

Author of "Insaf Nama" reports that:

"We have never seen that Bandagi Miyan (Rz) Syed Mahmood (Rz), Bandagi Miyan Nemat (Rz), Miyan Dilawer (Rz), and many migrants used to attend sermons or for learning purposes, nor they were going to the Non Mahdavi Masjid for keeping friendships with them."

بندگی میران سید محمود میاں سید خوند میر و میاں نعمت و میاں دلاور بلکه اکثر مهاجرین مهدی راند یدیم که برائے وعظ شنیدن در مسجد و برائے خواند ن علم پیش مخالفان رفته بودند علم خواند ن و وعظ شنیدن نشان دوستی است بایشان (باب چهارم)

But as a matter of fact Bandagi Miyan (Rz) never had attended any sermon in non Mahdavi Masjid nor he had advised his followers to go for hearing sermons or for learning purposes. He had replied to Mullah Moinuddin in this way:

"None from our Dairah would come to you for obtaining knowledge or for learning purposes, whether you make truce or not. We would never surrender before the falsifiers of truth."

پیش شما احدے هم از دائره ما برائے خواندن علم نخواهد آمد صلح کنید یا نه کنید پس تکذیب کنندگان حق را اطاعت نباید کرد (باب چهارم)

In these circumstances, was it possible that offering prayers behind the non Mahdavis be tolerated?

"Hashia Sharief" reports that:

"Bandagi Miyan (Rz) asserted that a true Mahdavi shall not befriend with any non believer, if he did not do like that then how can we believe that he had accepted Imamana (As)?"

بندگی میاں سید خوند میر فرمودند همارا کوئی منکر کون دیکھے پیچھے تین جاگا تیڑا ہودے اگر اتنا بھی کرنہ دکھلایا تو اس نے مہدی کی تصدیق کیا کیا۔

14. Tradition Regarding "Hostility for the sake of Allah":

The above version is the correct description of the tradition of the Holy Prophet (Slm) who said that this pleases Allah the most:

"Narrated by Abu Zarr (Rz) that the Holy Prophet came to them and asked : "do you know which actions please to Allah the most"? One companion said prayer and Zakat, another told Jihad. The holy Prophet (Slm) said that "verily it is to befriend Allah and to be hostile for the sake of Allah."

عـن ابـی از قـال خـرج عـليـنا رسـول الله صلی الله عليه وآلـه وسـلـم قـال اتـدرون ای الاعمال احب الی الله تـعالیٰ قال قائل الصلوٰة والزکوٰة قال قائل الجهاد قال النبی صلی الله عليه و آله وسلم ان احب الاعمال الی الله تعالیٰ الحب فی الله والبغض فی الله .

Narrated by Ahmed Bin Hunbal (Rz) and Abu Dawood (Rz).

When Bandage Miyan (Rz) asked Mahdavis to become hostile with any non Mahdavi, then is it possible that he permits for offering prayers behind the non Believers? Thus wherever it is said that Bandagi Miyan (Rz) or any Mahdavi had gone to a non Mahdavi Masjid, it was not for offering prayer behind the non believers but for other purposes or for offering prayers together themselves.

15.For Hajj Provision Necessary:

"Narrated that Bandagi Miyan (Rz) went for Hajj along with all persons of the Dairah. The command came to ask others to go back. Bandagi Miyan (Rz) asked them to discontinue. He took only three persons along with him. On reaching Kabatullah, they had some provision for sale. Companions informed Bandagi Miyan(Rz) that "we would try to sell somewhere else to get the highest price". Bandagi Miyan (Rz) told them that we had come for Hajj and not for business."

نـقـل است بندگی میاں سید خوند میر بادائره همه روان شـدنـد بـرائے حج فرمان آمد اے سید خوند میرؒ مرد ماں کـه بـرابر تواند ایشاں را باز بگر داں بندگی میاں بازبگر دانـیـدند سه مرد ماں راہ همراہ خود گرفته رفتند چونکه بـه کـعبته الله رسیدند برائے خرچه چیزے کالائے بود به بـهـائـے ایـنـجـا مـیـفـرد ختند بـرادراں عـرض کـردند ایـنـجـا بسیار گـراں اسـت و قیـمت زیـادہ مـی آید میاں فـرمودند بـرائے الله به حج آمدم نہ بـرائے سوداگری آمدم

This narration proves that when Bandagi Miyan (Rz) came for Hajj, he had some provision for sale. The opponents maintain that while going for Hajj, provision for sale should not be kept. But Allah ordains that:

"Pilgrimage to Kabatullah is a duty. Men owe to Allah. Those who can afford the journey (3:97)"

وللـه عـلی الـنـاس حـج البيت من استطاع اليه سبيلا (آل عمران رکوع ۱۰)

Author of "Madarik" had reported that the Holy Prophet (Slm) advised to have provision and means of traveling. And there is also a tradition:

" Ibn Omer (Rz) narrated that a person came to the Holy Prophet (Slm) and asked what was necessary for the Hajj?

"The holy Prophet (Slm) told provision and means of traveling. Reported "Tirmizi" and "Ibn Maja."

عن ابن عمر رضى الله عنهما قال جاء رجل الى النبى صلى الله عليه وسلم فقال يا رسول الله مايوجب الحج قال الزادو الراحلة رواه الترمذى وابن ماجه .

Bandagi Miyan (rz) when went to Hajj, kept some provision which is permitted by Qur'an and tradition. To tell against it means, the opponent is unaware of Qur'anic dictation and the advice of the Prophet (Slm),

16. Delay After Azan For Prayer:

"Whenever Bandagi Miyan (Rz) used to have dinner, he used to tell the Muazzin to delay the Call for prayer." (Hashia Shrief)

نقل است میان سید خودند میر طعام خوردن نشستی پیش از آن موذن راخبر کنانیدے که قلیلی تاخیر کنید

The opponent says that this practice is against Sharia. It may be pointed out that Bandagi Miyan (Rz) was the leader of the dairah. Whatever was received as Lillah, he used to distribute equally among all. Sometimes it happened that many were hungry for want of provision. Still whatever was received was being distributed. And sometimes someone would be busy in eating. In such circumstances he used to ask the Muazzin to delay for calling for prayers just to accommodate companions to finish their dinner. This delay was permitted only for the convenience of the companions.

Tradition says to wait for those who are busy in eating or drinking. Jaber had reported in "Tirmizi" that:

"Between Azan and standing in prayer allow some time so that anyone who is eating or drinking or had gone for nature's call, they should complete their job and join."

اجعل بین اذانک و اقامتک قدر مایفرغ الآ کل من اکله والشارب من شربه والمعتصر اذا دخل لقضاء حاجته

It is narrated in "Insaf Nama " that:

"Miyan Syed Khundmir (Rz), since he already sat for dinner, he advised the Muzzan to delay so that he could finish his dinner."

میان سید خوند میرؓ طعام خوردن نشست بودند پیش موذن خبر کنانید ندکه قلیلی تاخیر کنید (باب ۱۱)

For the purpose of congregational prayers, Iqamat(proclaming Takbeer, before Prayer) may be delayed. In such circumstances to facilitate Ahl-e-Dairah, Call for prayer may be delayed for a short period. It should not be objected.

17.Bandagi Miyan Became Muslim When He met Imamana (As):

It is narrated in "Hashia Sharief" that:

"Narrated by Bandagi Miyan (Rz) that he became Muslim after meeting Imamana (As)."

نقل است میان سید خوند میر فرمودند پس از حضرت میران ما مسلمان شدیم

The opponent had objected to this statement, although in another place it had been said that:

"Now we have become Muslim under the guidance of Imamana (As). In the presence of the sun, stars are dimmed and when the sun sets, stars become brightened".

میاں خوندمیر فرمودند......اکنوں بصدقہٴ مہدی علیہ السلام مسلمان شدیم لینے بہ مقابلہ ٬ آفتابہ ستارگان محو شدندے و پس آں زماں روشن شدندے

This is clear that Imamana's presence was like that of the sun. Just as in the presence of the sun stars become dim; and when the sun sets down stars glitter, like that after the demise of Imamana (As) the companions became visible and they showed their piety and abilities and people benefited from their teachings.

18. Bandagi Miyan's Affirmation of Imamana (As).

Imamana (As) had proclaimed himself to be the promised Mahdi(As) at Badhli, for the third time in 905 H. (As prophesied by the Holy Prophet (Slm) upon which Bandagi Miyan (Rz) was the first to attest and affirm Imamana's Mahdiat by proclaiming loudly "Amanna Saddaqna."

"I accept and affirm". Hence he was declared as Siddiqu-e-Vilayet (Rz) by Imamana (As) himself."

At the time of "Emphasized Proclamation" by Imamana (As) at Badhli, Bandagi Miyan's affirmation had significance because from that day onwards the non believers of Imamana (As) were designated as infidels. Therefore Bandagi Miyan (Rz) was named "Siddiqu-e-Vilayet (Rz)" by Imamana (As) himself.

19. Threatening orders of Allah.

An opponent had objected that if a servant accepts a threatening order of his boss, how could it become proficient? In this way the opponent also is objecting on Imamana (As) that Imamana (As) had accepted a threatening dictation from Allah. According to "Matleul Vilayet" Imamana (As) stated in Hindustani language that "Allah ordains me to proclaim your Mahdiat otherwise I shall enroll you along with unjust persons". That way of command by Allah to Imamana (As), the opponents took it as a threatening order from Allah to Imamana (As). It seems the opponent does not know how Allah had ordained the Holy Prophet (Slm).

"Thus declare it openly which you had been ordered and avoid the infidels."

فاصدع بما تؤ مروا واعرض عن المشرکین (سورۃ الحجر ع۲)

This verse is a clear threatening order from Allah to the Holy Prophet (As) who was preaching in secrecy for three years. Thus the opponent's objection is not only on Imamana (As), but even on the Holy Prophet (Slm).

20. Bandagi Miyan's Head Prostrated:

It had already been proved that Bandagi Miyan (Rz) was martyred as reported in the traditions of "Artat" and "Nisaai". But the author of Hadia had based his malicious objection on the basis of a very late book which even Mahdavis do not like to read or keep it in their homes. "Tazkeratus Saleheen" is the oldest source which narrates:

"In the city (Pattan) everywhere call for Zuhar prayer was given. At that time five heads (being beheaded by the enemy after their martyrdom), came out of the basket, one head (of Bandagi Miyan (Rz) took the position of leader and the other four followed behind him , facing towards Kabah and offered Zuhar prayer jointly by keeping their foreheads on the ground."

بانگ نماز ظهر جابجا در شهر خوانده شد بنا بر آن هر پنج سرهاز سبد برزمین فرودآمده مقابل قبله صف کشیده سربندگی میان پیش همه سر هاشده نماز ظهر باجماعت بر پیشانی ها ساجد گشته ادا کردند (باب اول)

"Even older than "Tazkera", "Hashia Sharief" states :"The cut heads of Bandagi Miyan (Rz) and other four of his companions were kept in a basket and they (army) brought them to Pattan and kept it on the ground. At Zuhar time all the cut heads came out of the basket. Bandagi Miyan's head led the prayer while other four heads followed and completed the Zuhar prayer."

سر بندگی میان سید خوند میر و سربرادران در سید داشته به شهر پٹن بردند آنجا وقت بانگ نماز شد سر ها از سید بیرون شدند سر بندگی میان پیش شده و سرهائی برادران پس شده ساجد شدند

The objection is that how the cut heads could prostrate? This objection shows his lack of knowledge and tells upon the decliner his illiteracy and foolishness. Let this decliner be known that the cut-head of Imam Husain (Rz) too had spoken. Shah Abdul Aziz had narrated what Ibn Asaker had told:

"Thus Allah provided speaking power to the cut-head of Imam Husain (Rz) in an eloquent language and the head said "My murder and holding of my head is stranger than that of the cave men."(*Explanation required*)

فانطق الله الراس بلسان ذرب فقال اعجب من اصحاب الکهف قتلی و حملی

In the same manner the cut head of Prophet Yahiya (As) also had spoken addressing the king:

"After all the crooked king had killed Yahiya (As) and cut the head from his body, then the cut head addressed the king and said that "it was irreligious and illegal to marry your wife's daughter." (Qasasul Ambiah p. 365 Lahore.)

When the heads of Imam Husain (Rz) and Prophet Yahiya (As) could speak and there had been no objection, here a silly objection is raised for the cut head of Bandagi Miyan (Rz) who led the Zuhar prayer, which is a clear miracle; how could anybody dare to object. His objection is based on malice and prejudice.

21.Shah Khundmir (Rz) - and the verse "La Talqoo Be Aideekum"

Opponent had raised an objection on this verse, but he had failed to present the complete verse which is as below:

"And spend in the name of Allah and do not put yourself into peril and do good to others. Verily Allah befriends those persons who do good things."

وانفقوا فی سبیل الله ولا تلقوا بایدیکم الی التهلکة واحسنوا ان الله یحب المحسنین (البقره ۲۴۶)

This verse directs to spend for a good cause in the name of Allah and those who avoid, they put themselves in peril. Author of "Madarik" had stated that:

"It means spending for the purpose of Allah and whoever stops the spending, he is putting himself to destruction."

والمعنی النهی عن ترک الانفاق فی سبیل الله لانه سبب الهلاک

Thus whoever does not spend for the cause of Allah he renders himself to grave danger. This verse abhors misery. Author of "Muheb-e-Aliah" writes:

"And do not push yourself towards grave danger, misery surely puts you in jeopardy."

ومیفگنید خود راه بدست های خود بورطۀ هلاکت یعنی بخل مکنید که مودی به هلاک است

Further stated that:

"The miser is far from Allah, far from paradise and near to the hellfire."

البخیل بعید من الله بعید من الجنة قریب الی النار

The same is repeated by "Tirmizi" as narrated by Abu Huraira (Rz). Thus both from the Qur'an and traditions it is proved that whoever does not spend for the cause of Allah, he puts himself to misery and peril.

The opponent's objection is unfounded since as per "Matan Sharief" Bandagi Miyan (Rz) had distributed what was available in his house in the cause of Allah and only reserved one blanket for himself:

"Bandagi Miyan distributed everything of his household and kept a blanket for himself; as Hazrat Abu Baker (Rz) had brought whatever he had, except a blanket and distributed to the needy ones."

بندگی میان سید خوند میرؒ گلیم پوشیده انچه در خانه بود همه دادند چنانچه ابوبکر صدیق گلیم پوشیده بود همچنین صدیق مهدی کردند (باب پانزدهم)

****

CHAPTER THREE
Bandagi Miyan Shah Nemat(Rz)

1.Author of "Insaf Nama" in chapter 8 reports:

Legacy of Muhajir Belongs to Muhajirs only:
"It is stated that Miyan Ali (Rh) of Dolqa died in the Daira of Shah Nemat (Rz) at Nagore. He left 50 Ferozi coins as a legacy. Shah Nemat (RZ) distributed equally among the residents of the Daira, instead of sending any share from the legacy to the heirs of Miyan Ali (Rh) by telling that the legacy of a muhajir is the property of the residents of the daira."

نقل است که میان علی دهولخیه (دولقیه) در شهر ناگور در دائره بندگی میان نعمتؓ نقل شد و پنجاه فیروزی ترکه گزاشته میان نعمت سویت کرده تمام دائره را دادندو پسر و دختر میان علی در دهولخه بودند ایشان را انفرستادند که حق از آن فقیران دائره ه ست

Author of Hadia raised an objection that the legacy of the migrants was not given to the descendants of the deceased. This allegation is absurd since Shah Nemat (Rz) did it according to the dictates of the Qur'an: Allah ordains that:

"And those people who had accepted Faith but did not migrate, thus you (non migrants) do not have any connection to their legacy, until they migrate."

والذین آمنو ولم یهاجرو ا مالکم من ولایتهم من شی ءٍ حتیٰ یهاجرو ا(الانفال ع ۱۰)

A. Mohammed Ibn Hajeer Tabri (Rh) comments on this verse that:

"Tradition was disclosed by Mohammed Bin Abdul Ali (Rz) who heard it from Mohammed Bin Soor (Rz) who heard from Qatadah (Rz) that you have no share to the legacy of your relatives, if they left after migration, therefore, until you too migrate; because Migrants are successors to each other. On the basis of migration, the Holy Prophet (Slm) established brotherhood. Thus on the basis of migration Muslims are successors to each other. Those who, although accepted Islam, but did not migrate, they cannot demand share in the legacy who had migrated and died after migration."

حدثنا محمدابن عبدالاعلی قال ثنا محمد بن ثور عن معمر عن قتاده مالکم من ولا یتهم من شی حتی یهاجروا قال کان المسلمون یتوارثون بالهجرة وآخی النبی صلی الله علیه وسلم بینهم فکانو ایتوارثون بالاسلام والهجرة وکان الرجل یسلم ولا یهاجر لایرث اخاه

B. Author of "Kasshaf" had written under this verse that:

"Migrants and Helpers are successors to each other because of migration and heirs of such helpers, forfeit their share in the legacy of the deceased after his migration."

وکان المهاجرون والانصار یتوارثون بالهجرة والنصرة دون ذوی القرابات

Imam Fakhruddin Razi (Rz) had commented that:

"Thus told Wahid what Ibn Abbas (Rz) had told that all commentators had agreed that ownership of a legacy is based on migration and assistance as decreed by Allah and not to the kinship. Any heir who accepted Islam, but did not migrate or help had no share in the legacy of his relative who died as a migrant.."

فقال الواحدى عن ابن عباس والمفسرين كلهم ان المراد هو الولاية فى الميراث وقالو اجعل الله تعالىٰ سبب الارث الهجرة والنصرـة دون القرابة وكان القريب الذى آمن ولم يهاجر لم يرث من اجل انه لم يهاجر ولم ينصر

D. Author of "Mualamul Tanzeel" had referred to Ibn Abbas (Rz) that:

"Ibn Abbas (Rz) had told about the legacy that Muslims are successors to each other on the basis of migration. Thus muhajirs and ansars are successors to each other, and not their kins, if the kins did not migrate along with their relatives. Thus even if one accepts Islam, but did not migrate, hence the heir cannot claim share in the legacy of his relative who died during and after migration."

وقال ابن عباس فى الميراث وكانو ايتوارثون بالهجرة فكان المهاجرون والانصار يتوارثون دون ذوى الارحام وكان من آمن ولـم يهاجر لايرث من قريبه المهاجر

Thus from the above verse and the narratives, it is proved that once migration had been completed, then there remains no relationship between the migrant and his heirs who had not migrated although they were legally successors to the deceased.

According to "Insaf Nama" Miyan Ali's son and daughter were in Dholqa, but Miyan Ali (Rh) had migrated from Dholqa to Nagore and died in the dairah. Therefore the legacy of Miyan Ali (Rh) was distributed among the migrants residing in the dairah. Hence Shah Nemat's decision was correct according to the Qur'an and traditions. The illitrate decliner had no knowledge of the dictates of Allah and the traditions, hence his objection is null and void. However there still remain two issues which require consideration.

First: Migration which had been discussed as one of the obligations. Here we present what Imam Fakhr-e-Razi had commented about that Verse:

"Said Hasan (Rz) that migration had not been snapped forever. Now remains what the Holy Prophet (Slm) had asserted that after victory (of Makkah) there is no migration. This migration is particularized because that migration is meant after the victory of Makkah. Second point relates to the order:

"Malikum Min Vilayetahum":

قال الحسن الهجرة غير منقطعة ابد اواما قوله عليه السلام لاهجرة بعد الفتح فاطراد الهجرة المخصوصة فانها انقطعت بالفتح

It may be known that the Dictates of Allah Revealed in the Holy Qur'an are Eternal having no limitation of time and place. For example order for jihad, wherever arises in such situations Jihad is an obligation. The same is the situation for Migration. If the situation becomes dangerous (for fulfillment of the dictates of Islam) migration becomes an obligation. We have already discussed about no verse of the Holy Qur'an had been abrogated.

Thus the author of Hadia maintains that the said verse had been abrogated, which is wrong and against the dictates of Allah. Because the Verse which is said to have been abrogated, is the description of the previous verse. We quote here both the verses:

"Those who had accepted Islam and did not migrate, they owe no share in the legacy unless they migrate.." (8:72-Part)

والذين آمنو ولم يهاجروا امالكم من ولا يتهم من شئٍ حتى يهاجروا

"Those who accepted Islam and after wards migrated and fought for the Faith in your company, they are one among you. But kindred by blood have prior rights, against each other as mentioned in the book of Allah" (8:75)

والذين آمنو امن بعد وهاجرو واوجاهدو امعكم فاولئك منكم واولو الارحام بعضهم اولىٰ ببعض فى كتاب الله (الانفال ع١٠)

From the first verse who even after accepting Islam did not migrate, they had forfeited their share in the legacy of their relatives who died after migration and from the second verse who had accepted Islam and migrated they have right in the legacy of the migrants. Both these verses give importance to migration and whoever abandoned migration, his right to share in the legacy is forbidden.

First verse could only be abrogated when the second verse ordains that even if not migrated, share in the legacy would not be forfeited. Thus what Shah Nemat (Rz) had done was perfectly under the commands of the Qur'an and traditions.

Another objection was that Miyan Ali (Rh) had hoarded 50 Ferozi coins which was against Tawakkul (Trust in Allah). The decliner must know that while going to Hajj provision has been permitted to be kept, therefore at the time of migration too it is necessary to have some cash to meet eventualities. Therefore it should not be objected.

Hazrat Jafer-e-Tayyar (Rz) and other companions who had migrated to Habsha under the orders of the Holy Prophet (Slm), can anybody say that they had no trust in Allah; and whether they did not keep amount during the journey? Read what "Tabri" states:

"Those who migrated in the beginning, they very secretly left Makkah. They were 11 men and 4 women and they reached Shaiba (a valley). Some of them had horses and others were peddling. Luckily they find two boats which were traveling for trade and these migrants were accommodated in the boats and they were charged just half a Dinar up to Habsha. They migrated from Makkah in fifth year in the month of Rajjab."

خرج الـذيـن هـاجـروا الهجرة الاولىٰ متسللين سـرا وكـانـوا احد عشر رجلا واربع نسوة حتىٰ انتهوا الى الشعيبة منهم الراكب والماشى ووفق اللـه للـمـسـلـمـين ساعة جاوا ااسفينتين للتجار حمـلـوهـم فيهـا الى ارض الحبشة بنصف دينار وكـان مـخـر جهـم فى رجب فى السنة الخامسة من حين بنى رسول الله صلعم .

This is a proof that the companions had amount with them when they migrated and they reached Habsha by paying the boat fare. Thus if Miyan Ali (Rh) did keep 50 coins as provision for journey what objection could be raised?

It is narrated that Shah Nemat (Rz) told one day that I am the servant of Allah. And sometimes I become Allah. Sometimes being His servant, witness His vision. Sometimes Allah declares "you are from Me and I am from you". But on the day of judgment my position shall be:

"On the Doomsday the pan of the scale would be kept. While others would go towards paradise, I shall proceed to meet my friend Allah".

روز قيامت شود پله به ميزان نهند
خلق به جنت رودمن بروم سوئ دوست

This tells that Shah Nemat (Rz) had merged and annihilated himself into the entity of Allah. It does not mean that Shah Nemat (Rz) had taken himself as Allah, otherwise he would have told the words "Allah says that you are from Me (Allah)". And he also had told that he is a meager servant of Allah..

The words" From Me you are": This is also correct, because we have been created, then only we can guess about our Creator. If there is no creation then who would know who is the Creator?. Allah is the "Rabbul Alameen". However when we say " I am from you (Allah) or Allah is from us". These are the exclamation of fraternity and love. Omer Bin Haseen (Rh) states that:

"Verily, the Holy Prophet (Slm) told that Ali (Rz) is from me and I am from Ali and he is a friend of all Faithful."

ان النبى صـلـى الله عليه و آله وسلم قال ان عليا منى
وانامنه وهو ولى كل مومن رواه الترمذى

Sheik Abdul Haq had commented on this tradition that:

"It is narrated that the Holy Prophet (Slm) told that Ali (Rz) is from me and I am from Ali (rz). This is a metaphorical expression of complete unity of thought and fraternity."

روایت کرده است که آنحضرت گفت که علی ازمن است ومن از علی کنایت است ازکمال اتحاد و اتصال و اخلاق ویگانگی

The same words also had been said by the Holy Prophet (Slm) for Hazrat Abu Baker (Rz):

"I am from Abu Baker (Rz) and Abu Baker (Rz) is from me."

ابوبکر منی وانامنه

These metaphors are indications of affection, sincerity and fraternity and never to utter that Hazrat Ali (Rz) or Hazrat Abu Baker (Rz) were(Naoozu Billah) Prophets like Our Holy Prophet (Slm). In the same sense if the author of Hadia states what Shah Nemat (Rz) had stated " I am from You (Allah) and You are from Me (Allah"), it only tells that Shah Nemat (Rz) had annihilated unto the entity of Allah when Allah himself states that "when my servant comes towards Me, I become his hands, legs, wisdom, audition, eyesight etc.". What sort of objection could be raised, if raised it is just malicious on account of ignorance.

Declaration of Truth is Prohibited:

"It is narrated that a Godliman of the early period told Shah Nemat (Rz) that in our period if we say about our Faith, it is as if we are declaring of selling beef mutton in the area of infidels. This act would invite the infidels to kill us, Thus our position is like that."

نقل است از بندگی میان نعمت که یکی از بزرگان پیشین گفته بود که درزمانه ماحکایت دین کردن آنچنان شده است که کسی گوشت گائو برچارپائی نهاده برسر کرده در کفرستان بآواز بلند گوید که گوشت گائو بگیر یدپس خلق اور ایکشندیا نه یعنی بکشند و سنگسار کنند این زمانه حکایت مهدی یاران وی همچنان شده است ـ

It only denotes that declaration of truth has become unbearable to the listeners.

Shah Nemat (Rz) and Deposits:

"Tazkeruts sadequeen" states that when Shah Khundmir (Rz) and Shah Nemat (Rz) had come from Kaha (Sindh) to Gujrat on orders of Imamana (As), Sultan Mahmood Begdha's sisters Raje Soon and Raje Murari both had handed over to Shah Nemat (Rz) some Futooh (Lillah) to be given to Imamana (As). Shah Nemat (Rz), while returning from Gujrat, reached Radhanpur where Bandagi Miran Syed Mahmood (Rz) (son of Imamana (As) demanded from Shah Nemat (Rz) to hand over those Futoohs (deposits), on which Shah Nemat (Rz) told him that he would not breach the trust. Then some persons came and told Shah Nemat (Rz) that they want to visit Imamana (As), and asked him for help. Shah Nemat (Rz) helped them by paying for their journey to Farah. On reaching Farah Bandagi Miran Syed Mahmood (Rz) complained against Shah Nemat (Rz) before Imamana (As), on which Imamana (Rz) disliked his way of treatment for his son, Miran Syed Mahmood (Rz).

Author of Hadia had narrated this episode with some alterations which is being investigated hereunder:

1. Shah Nemat's denial by saying he would not breach the trust. It tells that whatever was deposited with him in the name of Imamana (Rz) he took it as a trust and wanted to present to Imamana (As) only. This cannot be objected because he did not like to breach the trust of the persons who had deposited with him to be given to Imamana (As).

2. Miran Syed Mahmood (Rz) felt much and did not come out from his room.

It cannot be said that Shah Nemat (Rz) loved wealth. He was such a Godliman who did not accept even the villages of Sanchoori and Bairamgaon which were being awarded to him as Jagir by Sultan Mahmood Begdha; but he preferred to proceed to visit Imamana (As), and to hand over what was entrusted to him by the sisters of the king. Thus he did not like to breach the trust.

Author of Hadia had dishonestly remarked against Miran Syed Mahmood (Rz) that when Bandagi Miyan (Rz) presented the deposits, then only Bandagi Miran Syed Mahmood (Rz) came out of the room. It is utterly wrong. It was a time for Maghrib prayer when Miran Syed Mahmood (Rz) heard Azan for the prayer, then he came out and after prayers only Bandagi Miyan (Rz) handed over some amount to Miran Syed Mahmood (Rz).

According to "Tazkeratus Saleheen":

"After hearing the Call for Maghrib Prayer, Miran Syed Mahmood (Rz) came out of the room and offered prayers and after wards Bandagi Miyan (Rz) handed over whatever he had brought on behalf of Imamana (As), some 15 horses, and amount whatever was with him."

بندگی میاں سید محمود این سخن شنیده زود بیرون آمده ملاقاتی شده نماز عصر و مغرب ادا کردند بعده بندگی میاں انچه بنام حضرت میراں پانزده خود داشته همه آن را پیش میراں سید محمود نموده

This episode also is recorded in the "Moulood" of Miyan Abdul Rahman (Rz) which is the oldest biography of Imamana (As) which says that:

"After completion of the evening prayer, Bandagi Miyan (Rz) placed before Miran Syed Mahmood (Rz) whatever he had with him to be given to Imamana (As)".

پس ازادائی نماز شام ٔ امتعه مذکور که بودپیش میراں بداشتنند

It is reported in" Tazkeratus Saleheen" that:

"On that Miran Syed Mahmood (Rz) became very happy (on Bandagi Miyan's behavior) and brought whatever was with him and handed over to Bandagi Miyan (Rz) and told that this is all yours; keep all with you and spend according to the need during our journey."

بعد میراں سید محمود بسیار خوش حال شده چیزے مبلغ که باقی مانده بود آورده همه یك جاکر ده به بندگی میاں سپرده فرمودند که اے میاں سید خوند میر این همه از آن شما است بقدر ضرورت خرج کنید۔

On that Imamana (As) told to Shah Nemat (Rz) that: "Did you forget what is said in Gujrat? That son is the heir of his father"? And there should be no objection when the son uses his father's property.

At the time of demise, Imamana (As) read out the tradition:

"We are from the category of the Commissioned ones, hence we are neither inherited by any one , nor we inherit any one.".

At that point Bandagi Miyan Syed Mahmood, Sani-e-Mahdi (Rz), distributed Imaman's sword and belongings among the companions and he himself did not take anything from the legacy of Imamana (As). This action was according to the tradition of the Holy Prophet (Slm) which states that:

"Narrated by Abu Baker (Rz) that the Holy Prophet (Slm) had emphasized that "we do not leave any legacy, whatever we have left, it is charity only."

عـن ابـى بـكر رضى الله عنه قال قال رسول الله صلى الـله عليه وسلم لا نـرث ولا نـورث مـاتركناه صدقة (متفق عليه)

What Imamana (As) had said to Shah Nemat (Rz) was correct, because in view of the circumstances the property belonging to Imamana (As) should have been given to Bandagi Miyan Syed Mahmood (Rz) since Imamana (As) was alive at that time, and the amount was required by Miran Syed Mahmood for meeting expenses for his journey to Farah.

The fourth point is that Instead of handing over to Bandagi Syed Mahmood, Shah Nemat (Rz) spent that amount on those persons who were desirous of going to Farah to meet Imamana (AS). This action should not be said as Shah Nemat's dishonesty.

Further, there should arise no doubt that Shah Nemat (Rz) preferred to help those persons who were desirous to visit Imamana (As) and avoided to hand it over to Bandagi Miran Syed Mahmood (Rz). Somehow he had decided to hand over the remaining deposits to Imamana (As) alone. Further he thought that it was out of the question that a well to do person like Bandagi Miran Syed Mahmood (rz) should be facing any hardship. Thus Shah Nemat (Rz) thought that some how Bandagi Miran Syed Mahmood (Rz) would arrange for his journey. However Bandagi Miyan had handed over whatever he had with him to Bandagi Miran Syed Mahmood (Rz).

From "Shawahedul Vilayet " it comes to knowledge that even Shah Nemat (Rz) also was feeling shortage of provision therefore he thought that whatever is left that should be handed over to Imamana (As). That is why he avoided to hand over to Bandgai Miran Syed Mahmood (Rz).

From "Tazkeratus Saleheen", it is reported that Bandgi Miran Syed Mahmood (Rz) also had a little provision. However, Shah Nemat (Rz) preferred to provide to those who were really in hardship to continue their journey to Farha, that is why he provided them and did not give to Bandagi Miran Syed Mahmood (Rz).

Thus it could be said that Shah Nemat (Rz) acted against the will of the sisters of sultan Mahmood Begda who handed over amounts to Shah Nemat (Rz) to be given to Imamana (As), and he instead gave to those who did not have provision for the journey to Fararh. However it was given Lillah to those who were in need.

The fifth point is that Shah Nemat's departure at Imamana's remarks, should not be objected. For example, once the Holy Prophet (Slm) was delivering a sermon in the Masjid-e-Nabavi, the audience heard the bells of a caravan, and left the Holy Prophet (Slm) and avoided to listen the sermon in order to get grocery.

"Ubaid Bin Hameed had narrated that when the Holy Prophet (Slm) was delivering a sermon of Jum'aa the same time a Makkah's caravan reached near the masjid-e-Nabavi, people rushed towards it leaving the Prophet (Slm) except some companions including Abu Baker (Rz) and Omer (Rz), then at that time this verse was revealed. Thus the Holy Prophet (Slm) exclaimed, "I Swear on Allah in whose hands is my life that even all of you had left me and went away then there would be a flood of fire would have enveloped to you."

اخرج عبد بن حميد عن الحسن قال بينا النبى صلى الله عليه وسلم يخطب يوم الجمعةاذ قدمت عير المدينة فانفضوا الهاوتر كوا النبى صلى الله عليه وسلم فلم يبق معه الارهط منهم ابوبكر و عمر فنزلت هذه الآية فقال رسول الله صلى الله عليه وسلم والذى نفسى بيده لوتتا بعتم حتى لايبقى معى احد منكم لسال بكم الوادى نارا

Was that action of the companions wrong? It is a fact that the situation was very bad at Madinah. There was an acute shortage of foodstuff, naturally companions rushed leaving the Prophet (Slm) just to get grocery. It was but natural. In the same situation Shah Nemat (Rz) left Imamana (As) and went away. Therefore his action should not be objected.

The author of Hadia had taken a wrong view of this action of Shah Nemat (rz) and alleged that Imamana (As) had scolded him and his group as transgressors. The author had misunderstood what was written in "Tazkeratus Saleheen":

"Tazkeratul Saleheen" states that:

"However Imamana (As) demanded the amount from Shah Nemat (Rz) who told that the amount was spent on those who arrived here to meet you. Then Imamana (As) told that those who were not present who told that they were the seekers of Allah?

الغرض بعده حضرت ميران فتوح خودرا نزديك ميان شاه نعمتؒ طلب فرمودند شاه مذكور جواب دادند كه ايں طالبان خدا كه آمده اند درميان ايشان خرچ شد حضرت ميرانؑ فرمودند كه غائبانگاں را طالبان خدا كه كردـ

From this three issues come out:

One: Imamana's demand for the Futooh. Second: Shah Nemat's answer that he had spent for persons who were desirous to meet Imamana (As). Third: Imamana's utterance that who had so far did not come, how they could be said that they were the seekers of Allah? Somehow Imamana (As) was not happy with the action of Shah Nemat (Rz). It is a fact that at Thatta Imamana (As) himself had asked Shah Nemat (Rz) to go back to Gujrat and bring those who want to come to see him. Then how could it be deduced that Imamana (As) had forgotten his own orders? Because Imamana (As) told to bring those who are really seekers of Allah,. This had been narrated in "Moulood" also:

"Go and bring those who are desirous to come".

بروید آیندگان را بیارید

جاؤ اور آنے والوں کو لاؤ

Then how could it be said that Imamana (As) had forgotten about his own wish?

"Shah Nemat (Rz) had brought such persons who were desirous to get Blessings from Imamana(As)".

میان نعمتؒ کسانیکه برحمت حق لائق بودند آورند

On that basis only that group which came along with Shah Nemat (Rz) is called "Rahmatullahi Group". About whom Shah Burhan (Rh) wrote:

"It is narrated that when Shah Nemat (Rz) decided to go to Imamana (AS) at Farah, then some one hundred persons who had accepted Imamana (As) as the Promised Mahdi (As) and who had relinquished the worldly affairs and had a desire to meet Imamana (AS), but they lacked funds to reach Farah,then only Shah Nemat (Rz) provided provision for their journey and brought them to Farah. Therefore this group was known as "Rahmatullahi Group".

آورده اند چون بندگی میان نعمتؒ از احمد آباد به جانب حضرت امام علیه السلام متوجه گشتند چند صد کسان از مصدقان امام آخر الزمان دنیا ترک داده برائے صحبت خلیفۃ الرحمن همراه بندگی میان شار الیه می شدند که ایشان رادر اصطلاح گرده حضرت مهدیؐ رحمتہ اللھی می گفتند (دفتر اول رکن دوم باب پنجم)

Bandagi Shah Burhan (Rh) further states that:

"Shah Nemat (Rz) came before Imamana (As) and submitted the accounts to Imamana (As) and informed the expenses he borne for journey who were desirous of meeting Imamana (As)."

ادا کردن امانت بندگی میان نعمتؒ درپیش حضرت خاتم الولایت حساب دادن انچہ خرج رحمتہ اللھی کہ ترک دنیا کرده آمده بودند مشهور است (دفتر اول رکن دوم باب پنجم)

Thus the author of Hadia's allegation about that group that they were hypocrites is ridiculous, Imamana (As) himself came to Shah Nemat (Rz) and consoled him.

Seventh: According to "Tazkeratus Saleheen" it is stated that when Shah Nemat (Rz) left Imamana (As), that group also left Imamana (As), but other books lack that information. Imamana's coming to console Shah Nemat (Rz) should not be objected.

It is reported that when once Hzt Ali (Rz) was displeased with Bibi Fatima (Rz), slept in the Masjid-e Nabavi., The Holy Prophet (Slm) came to him and cleaned him from the dirt and addressed him "Stand up Abu Turab".

"Narrated by Suhail bin Sa'ad who said that Hazrat Ali (Rz) came to Bibi Fatima (rz). Then he went to the Masjid and slept. When the Holy Prophet (Slm) came to Fatima's house he did not see Ali (Rz). The holy Prophet (Slm) asked where was Ibn Um? (That is Ali (Rz) (This is the way in Arabic language not to mention Ali (Rz) as her husband.) Fatima (Rz) informed that something unpleasant happened among them, and he went out. The Holy Prophet (Slm) asked someone to search him out where was he? Someone came and informed that he was sleeping in the Masjid. Thus the Holy Prophet (Slm) went to him who was sleeping on his one side. On account of which his body was filled with dirt. Then the Holy Prophet (Slm) addressed him "wake up Abu Turab" From that day Ali's patronymic name became "Abu Turab."

بخاری ومسلم از سهل بن سعد ساعدی آورده که گفت درآمد علیؓ بر فاطمه رضی الله عنها پستر بیرون فت و خسپید درمسجد چوں حضرت رسول الله صلی الله علیه وسلم ودربیت فاطمه آمد علیؓ راند ید پر سید کجا است ابن عم تو یعنی علی و این به عادت زبان عرب است که گویند ونخواسته که زوج وماننده آن گوید، فاطمةؓ گفت میان من وی یزے واقعه شده پس غضب کرو بیرون رفته و قیلوله نزد من نه کرد پس آنحضرت کسی را فرمود که یہ آن بیند کجاست پس آن کس آمد و گفت یا رسول الله هست درمسجد خواب می کندپس آنحضرت علیه السلام درمسجد بر سروے آمد ودید که بر پهلوئی خفته و رواش از پهلو افتاده و بدن شریفش خاك آلوده گشت پس آنحضرت صلی الله علیه وسلم فرمود قم اباتراب از آن روز کنیت سے ابوتراب آمد

Just as Holy Prophet (Slm) went to Hazrat Ali (Rz) and consoled him, in the same manner Imamana (AS) went to Shah Nemat (Rz) and consoled him. How could this action be objected? Particularly when Imamana (As) said to Shah Nemat (Rz), whether you like me or not, I like you.

"Bandagi Shah Nemat (Rz) became sad (after hearing from Imamana (As) about the deposits) and went towards a Masjid in a Jungle. Imamana (As) himself went to that Masjid and searched him out and told him "Whether you like me or not, I like you."

بندگی میاں نعمت بدان واسطه دلگیر گشته مسجدے که در صحرا بود رفتند حضرتؑ رفته دست میاں نعمتؓ گرفته آور دند درآں محل این سخن فرمودند توں مجھ موڑ نلوڑ ہوں تو تجھ لوڑ بنار۔

According to "Shawahedul Vilayet" it is certain that Shah Nemat (Rz) had paid the balance of amount to Imamana (As) by explaining the expenses he borne on those persons who accompanied him. When accounts were clarified, then there arise no allegation on Shah Nemat (Rz) as the author of Hadia had raised.

Son of Imamana got martyrdom in lieu of Shah Nemat (Rz):

Author of Hadia had written about Shah Naimat (Rz) in chapter 2 that "Shah Nemat (Rz) was relieved from his captors only on offering a peerzada (Syed Ali (Rz), son of Imamana (As)

who was buried alive in a wall of a fort in lieu of Shah Nemat (Rz) as his ransom."

Here Peerzadah refers to Bandagi Miyan Syed Ali (Rz), son of Imamana (As). It is utterly false what had been mentioned by the author of Hadia. The fact is that Shah Nemat (Rz) did not offer Miyan Syed Ali (Rz) as his ransom, but actually Miyan Syed Ali (Rz) got Shah Nemat (Rz) released from the opponents as mentioned by the author of "Tazkeratus Saleheen":

"Narrated that opponents of Imamana (As) got hold of Shah Nemat (Rz) and were driven away in an ox cart. Suddenly Miyan Syed Ali (Rz), aged 15, went to them and asked them as to why they were taking away Shah Nemat (Rz)? They told to present him before the king. Miyan Ali (Rz) asked for what reason? They said "In the name of Mahdi (As). Miran Syed Ali (Rz) told them that if the son of Mahdi (As) presents himself on behalf of Shah Nemat (Rz), then shall you let Shah Nemat (Rz) go? They accepted his offer. Miyan Syed Ali (Rz) informed them that he was the son of Mahdi (As) and asked them to leave Shah Nemat (Rz) and instead take him into custody."

نقل است روزے بندگی میاں شاہ نعمتؓ رامنکر ان مہدی در گردن نشاندہ می بردند ناگاہ میاں سید علیؓ در اثنائے راہ ملاقاتی شدہ فرمود کہ ایشاں راکجامی برید منکراں گفتند بحضور بادشاہ ' میاں فرمودند برائے چہ کار باز گفتندبرائے نام مہدی فرمودند اگر فرزند مہدی بدست آید ایشاں را خواہید گزاشت گفتندآرے ' میاں سید علی فرمودند کہ من فرزند ذات مہدی ہستم مرا برید ایشاں رابگزارید (باب دوم)

"Khatim-e-Sulaimani" also reports this episode as below:

"Bandagi Miyan Syed Ali (Rz), son of Mahdi-e-Mouood (As), got Shah Nemat (Rz) released and in lieu of Shah Nemat (Rz) he himself got imprisoned."

بندگی میاں سید علی بن مہدی موعود شاہ نعمتؓ اخلاص کنانیدہ خود درجس شدند (گلشن ہشتم چمن اول)

Thus the author of Hadia's contention that Shah Nemat (Rz) made Bandagi Miyan Syed Ali (Rz) his ransom and got released, is against facts, maliciously framed to disgrace Shah Nemat.

Now remains another blame on Shah Nemat that he confronted the army is nothing but a distortion of facts. Facts are narrated by "Khatim-e-Sulaimani"that:

"Narrated that Nizam Shah, becoming afraid of the Mughal Army left Doulatabad and came to Logadh Fort which was said to be a safe place. He brought his family and left them for safety under the supervision of an eunuch who was a very wicked man and a deadly enemy of Mahdavis. While so, Shah Nemat (Rz) and his disciples were absorbed in Zikrullah in the Masjid, suddenly an army passed in front of the Masjid with a disturbing noise of "Be away, Be away" which sound did not disturb the Godlimen who were absorbed in Zikrullah. Noticing their inaction the army started slaughtering all 18 Godlimen including Shah Nemat (Rz) and went away."

نقـل اسـت کـه از بـلـدهٔ دولـت آباد نظام شاه بادشاه از خـوف افـواج مـغل هـراسان شده حرایم اسمت قلعه لوه گـڈه کـه جـائـی مـحـفوظ و متمکن و مکان محروس و مـامـن اسـت روانـه کـرده بـود کـه در قلعه چند روز بـگـذراننـدو حـواله کار حفظ و ضبط بیگمات خواجه سـرا خـوار هـر دوسـرا بود و تخم عناد و حسد مهدویان درارض دل خبـث مـنـزل کا شته بود قضاء را گذر فوج قبائل شاه بردائره حضرت نعمت اللهی واقع شده گویند آنحضرت بـعـد عـصر یا بعد مغرب باگروه فقیران بر صـفـوف در بـحـر مـشـاهـده و مشکافه غرق بودند ناظر مـذکـور سـواری رسید اهتمام دور شوید دور شوید آغز کـرد شـاه وفـقیران درامـر جـوعـه خبـری نـداشتندبر نخاستندناظر خبـث منظر حکم قتل کرو ودر اندک زمانی شاه رضی الله عنه با هیجده کسان فقراء شهیدشدند(گلشن هشتم چمن اول)

Shah Nemat's life Prior to Meet Imamana (As):

Author of Hadia had critically condemned the characters of Shah Nemat (Rz) by saying that before meeting Imamana (As) he was engaged in burglary and murderous activities.

The fact is that Shah Nemat (Rz) had confessed his sins before Imamana (As) as reported by Miyan Abdul Rahman (Rh) in his "Moulood":

"Shah Nemat (rz) relinquished the worldly life and confessed his all sins and told that he had been a guilty man in the past and asked in what manner his guilty and sins would be redeemed?"

همان ساعت تارک دنیا و طالب مولیٰ شده تائب گشتند جـریـمـه' خـود رامـن وعـن فرانمودند که ازمن ثقیل تر گنهگار دیگر کس نبا شد چنین گناهان راچگونه عفو نوانم کرو

"On that Imamana (As) consoled him and said Allah is the Redeemer. Whatever sins occurred against Allah's dictates ask forgiveness from Allah and whatever sins were rendered against public go and get pardon from them individually."

فـرمـودند که خدائی تعالیٰ غفور الرحیم است گناه اوباو بخشائید وگناه خلق پیش خلق به بخشائید

On hearing from Imamana (AS, Shah Nemat (Rz) went to each and every one whom he had hurt them in any way and obtained complete pardon from them. When they witnessed his humility they pardoned him. Miyan Abdul Rahman (Rh) had reported in his "Moulood" that:

"Shah Nemat (Rz) had gone to everyone whom he had somehow or other hurt in any way and asked them to take revenge. Witnessing his humility and sincerity in offering himself, all pardoned him and withdrawn their claims against him".

به خانه هائے هر ایك دعویٰ داران خود رفتند و گفتند که قصاص خود بگیر یدچوں درمیان ایشان حالت دیگر دید نداز دعوئ هائے خود در گذشتند

In such circumstances when the hurt ones had pardoned him, no body can pointout against his characters when he had relinquished his worldly life and became a pious, Godliman and the remorseful person from his past life to which Allah also might have pardoned and absolved him from his past sins.

****

CHAPTER FOUR
Bandagi Shah Nizam(Rz)

Author of Hadia on page 199 had blamed Shah Nizam (Rz) on the basis of an inauthentic narration that he had got written a man's fate as "approved" while he was already designated as reprobate in Allah's old books. This is such an unacceptable narration that no Mahdavi could believe, because it is not found in any of the Mahdavi literature that any of the companions of Imamana (As) or even Shah Nizam (Rz) had dared to do such manipulation in the Books of Allah.

"Hashia-e-Sharief" reports about the manner in which companions of Mahdi used to provide religious instruction:

"Narrated the way in which companions of Imamana (As) used to train their disciple is that: A man brought his son to Bandagi Shah Nizam (Rz) and asked him to provide him religious instructions. Shah Nizam (Rz) delayed for it. He tried much and after some time brought his son again and requested. Then Shah Nizam (Rz) looked into the Divine Tablet and when he found everything was good, then only he provided religious teaching."

نقل است تلقین کردن مهاجران ایں چنیں بود که یکی مرد بندگی میان شاه نظامؓ راعرض کرو فرزند مرا تلقین کنید میاں تاخیر کردند بعده کوشش بسیار کرد بعده میاں نظر در لوح محفوظ کردند ابتداء و انتهائ او معلوم کردند که خیریت است انگه تلقین کردند ـ

From the above narrative it is evident that whenever any person came to any of the companions of Imamana (As) for Bia'at and teachings they used to become satisfied about some one's character first. by inspiration, and if they found that everything was OK for him then only, after much persuasion, they used to admit anyone as a disciple.

As regards Shah Nizam's way of teaching the above narration does not mention anything unusual about Shah Nizam (Rz) that he had made to change the verdict of Allah about certain person. Thus the blame is unfounded and unbelievable about Shah Nizam (Rz).

Shah Nizam's Adventure of Koh-e-Qaff:

Author of Hadia had again blamed Shah Nizam (Rz) on the basis of a cooked up version regarding, as if Shah Nizam (rz) had stated that "Sikander Zul Qarnain" had sexually intercoursed with a fruit of a tree; and further blamed that Shah Nizam (Rz) had claimed to have witnessed the ruins of Shaddad's paradise. The old record thus states about him that:

"During the course of the journey, Shah Nizam (Rz) had stated that he had visited Koh-e-Qaff and saw a tree whose fruits are just like the moon.

"At this place Godliman traveled and he brought that moon shaped fruit and put it into the left over water and whoever drank it he got the inspiration. He said that he had visited two times."	وقتے کـه بندگی میاں شاہ نظام در سفر بودند بکو ہ قاف رسیدند آنجادرختان اند آن را پھل همچو ماه اند آنجا بندگان بندگان خداسیری می کنند آن پھل رامی آرند ورپس خورده اند کے می ریزند هر کسے را کہ می دهند آں راکشف مـی شود بندگی میاں شاه نظام فرمودند بنده دوباره رفته بودم بعد ازاں نه رفتم (حاشیہ شریف ۱۷۳)

The same narration is also recorded in "Naqliat-e-Miyan Syed Alam:

"Shah Nizam (Rz) stated that he had seen such a tree in Koh-e-Qaff whose fruits are like the moon. Godlimen used to travel there and bring that fruit and put it into water. If the left over water was given to any person he got the inspiration. Bandagi Shah Nizam (Rz) said that he had visited Koh-e-Qaff two times."	میـاں نـظـام فـرمـودند کہ در کوه قا فدرختان آں میوه بـمثل ماه می شود بندگان خدا آنجا سیری کنندآں ثمر مـی آرنـد و بـخـور نـد ذره پـس خورده هر کس رابد هنداومکشوف می شود بندگی میاں فرمودند دوبار آنجارفته بود (نقلیان میاں سید عالم ۲۹)

The vulgar blame against Shah Nizam (Rz) by the author is malicious, unfounded and shows the vulgarity of his own in presenting ill-founded episode by the author himself.

Koh-e-Qaff is also known as Qafqaaz which is a land in between the Black Sea and Bahr-e-Khizr. It is out of question that Shah Nizam (Rz) might have traveled up to that place. It is a confirmed fact as mentioned in "Tazkeratus Saleheen".

"(Shah Nizam (Rz) had traveled to Syria, Rome (Turkey) and Iraq and also passed from cities of India."

درملك روم و شام و عراق گشته و از ديار هندوستان هم گزشته (باب يازدهم)

These narrations had no reference about the shameful intercourse by Sikander Zul Qarnain with a tree nor about the so called Paradise of Shaddad. But it just refers only about his journey to Koh-e-Qaff and sighting fruits resembling to the moon which were tasty. Thus the author's allegation based on an inauthentic narration is simply based on bias and prejudice about our Faith. Hence unacceptable.

Ranks of Imamana's Companions:

Author of Hadia had recorded a narration on page 235 that Miyan Abdul Rahman (Rh) was referring to a tradition from Abu Zarr Ghiffari (Rz) saying: "when he reached at a certain point while reading, the Holy Prophet (Slm) told, "this is about my brothers who have my ranks". On hearing Shah Nizam (Rz) said that such ranks do ever belong to the companions of Imamana (As) as well?. The biased author had translated the words" Ikhwanihum Ba Manzilati" (My brothers they are of my ranks). The Author does not know the way the commentators treat the Holy Prophet (Slm). They never make companions equal to the Holy Prophet (Slm). From this no one can deduce any sort of similarity or equality with the Holy Prophet (Slm).

"Whoever had an affection with me, he is in my rank".

من احبنى كان فى درجتى

Does this tradition make equal to the Holy Prophet? the one who loves the Holy Prophet (Slm)?

Author of "Madarijul Nabuwwat" had commented on this tradition that:

"Narrated by Anas (Rz) that the Holy Prophet (Slm) told "whoever shows affection to me he would accompany me in the paradise". It does not mean that he becomes equal to his ranks. Although in some traditions the words "Kana Fi Darjati" (on my ranks) also have been said."

درحديث انس رضى اللـه عنـه آمده كـه فـرموده آنحضرت من اجنبى كان منى فى الجنة ـ پوشيده نماند كـه مرادبه معيت مساوات در درجه نخواهد بود اگرچه در بعضى احاديث كان فى درجتى نيز واقع شده است

When "Kana Min Darjati" (would be in my rank) does not prove equality then "how can "Ba Mazilati" Could make any one equal?

These narratives only point out that whoever had intense affection with the Holy Prophet (Slm) he would be with the Holy Prophet (Slm) on the Day of Judgment. Further informed by the Prophet (Slm) that:

"Among my Ummah those would have intense affection with me who would come after me."

من اشد امتی لی حباناس یکون بعدی

Thus there is a difference of affection. Simple affection and intense affection. Therefore those who had intense affection should be having higher ranks than those who had simple affection.

Author of "Zubdatul Haqaeq" had maintained that:

"If the status and position of the Holy Prophet (Slm) would become known, then only you may think the status of that group." (Which Group?)

اگر منزلت و مقام مصطفی توان دانستن وداشتن انگه ممکن بود که منزلت این طائفه دریابی۔

Author of "Shawahedul Vilayet" had commented about "Hum Ba manzilati":

"First of all you have to recognize the sublime status of the Holy Prophet (Slm), to understand his position."

اول مقام ومنزلت رسول الله صلی الله علیه وسلم باید شناخت تامقام و منزلت ایشان علیهم الرضوان معلوم شود

Above narrations agree on one point regarding the Holy Prophet (Slm), but how can you deduce that the group would be more prominent than the Holy Prophet (Slm)?:

Thus, just by telling "Kana Fi Darjati" does not equalize the Holy Prophet (Slm) with that group.

Divine Secrets Not Be Disclosed:

The decliner has recorded his objection on page 235 that Shah Nizam (Rz) said whatever he had heard from Imamana (As), if he disclosed it, he would be stoned to death. This is the same as told by Abu Huraira (Rz) that if he disclosed what the Holy Prophet (Slm) had told, he would be stoned to death.

Allah's inquiry from his Servant:

The biased decliner had blamed on his book's page 235 that Shah Nizam (Rz) maintained that Allah in order to grant blessings to anyone inquires Shah Nizam's opinion: "If you agree I shall grant someone mercy otherwise not". Thus Shah Nizam (Rz) affirmed: "what I recommended Allah then only grants". The Word "Recommendation" had not been used, instead it was told that" "By imploring request for consideration."

From the above two issues emerge: one : Whenever Allah grants mercy to anyone, it becomes known to Shah Nizam (Rz) and Two: When Shah Nizam (Rz) invokes Blessings for anyone, Allah grants it.

Allah's Command: "Salamun Ala Ibrahim" had been commented in "Baizavi":

"Thus, Gabriel came to Ibrahim (As) once and asked whether he had any desire? Hzt. Ibrahim (As) informed: Yes, I do have a requirement, but not from you". Then Gabriel asked him "to invoke from your Allah". Ibrahim (As) told: "I do not want to request, because my Allah knows my position."

فقال له جبريل هل لك حاجة فقال اما اليك لا فقال فسل ربك فقال حسبى عن سوالى علمه بحالى.

From this, can we infer that before granting anything Allah wanted Ibrahim (AS) to request? Gabriel's coming to Hzt. Ibrahim (As) was just to inquire his requirement ? In the same manner Allah wanted to know what Shah Nizam's desire had been for a certain person?

Yet there is another tradition which informs that Allah wanted to know from the Holy Prophet (Slm) whether he wanted to live as a Prophet and servant, or as a king and a Prophet? Narrated by Bibi Ayesha (Rz) that:

"Thus the Angel told that Allah had sent His Blessings to you and is asking whether you like to live as a Prophet and a Servant or as a king and a Prophet? "

فقال ان ربك يقراء عليك السلام ويقول ان شئت نبيا عبد اوان شئت نبيا ملكا ....فقلت نبيا عبدا .

Is it not clear from this that Allah had asked the Holy Prophet (Slm) to tell his desire which position he would like: as a king and Prophet or as servant and Prophet? Nisaai comments thus:

Narrated by Abi Talha (Rz) that one day he saw the Holy Prophet (Slm) was in a jubilant and pleasant mood. And informed that Gabriel had come to him and conveyed:

"Allah's message that do you agree if any one of my follower implores Darood on me once, then Allah would send darood ten times for me.?"

عن ابى طلحة ان رسول الله صلى الله عليه وسلم جاء ذات يوم و البشر فى وجهه فقال انه جاء نى جبرئيل فقال جبرئيل ان ربك يقول اما ير ضيك ان لايصلى عليك احد من امتك الا صليت عليه عشرا .

Do not the words "Ama Yarzika" denote that Allah is asking his servant's consent?

Thus the decliner, it seems that he, had no knowledge of the traditions in this respect.

Bandagi Malik Ilahdad's Rank:

Chapter one of "Tazkeratus Saleheen" reports:

"Then Shah Nizam (Rz) permitted Malik Ilahdad (Rz) to go and then he put his hand on the back of Malik Ilahdad (Rz) and said "whatever I had bestowed to you now, had not given to anyone before. And would never give to anyone in future also."

بعده بندگى شاه نظام بندگى ملك را رخصت داده بوقت وداع دست خود بر پشت ملك نهاده فرمودند که الهداد الهداد انچه داد وانچه داد پیش کسى رانه داده است نه پس کسى را خواهد داد ۔

Shah Nizam (Rz) had said about Malik Ilahdad (Rz), that among all the companions of Shah Nizam (Rz) what Bandagi Ilahdad (Rz) got no one was given. This shows the greatness and significance of Bandagi Ilahdad (Rz).

What Shah Nizam (Rz) had disclosed the position of Bandagi Ilahdad (Rz) the same can be ascertained from Mullah Abdul Qader Badayuni had written in "Najatur Rasheed" about him:

"Faani Fillah, Baqi Billah Sheik Burhanuddin (Rh) of Kalpi stayed for three days with Bandagi Malik Ilahdad (Rz) in the village Bari and attained nearness to Allah (from the teachings of Malik Ilahdad (Rz)."

الشیخ الفانی والباقی به برهان الدین مشهور ساکن کالپی سه روزه در صحبت شیخ الهداد وساکن قصبئه باری رسید واز مقربان درگاه کبر یاگشته۔

The kind of blessings Shah Nizam (Rz) gave to Bandagi Ilahdad (Rz) became known through Mullah Abdul Quader that Burhanuddin (Rh) of Kalpi obtained the secrets of Mysticism, from just a three days company of Bandagi Ilahdad (Rz) and became "Fani Fillah -Baqi Billah" in a short period. It shows greatness of Bandagi Ilahdad (Rz) and Shah Nizam(Rz).

****

CHAPTER FIVE
Bandagi Shah Dilawer (Rz)

Description of "Yalid yawalid":

Author of Hadia had reported a narrative against Shah Dilawer on page 237 . The same is written in "Tazkeratus Saleheen":

"Narrated that one day Miyan Yousuf (Rh) was listening the commentary of Soora-e-Ikhlas (from Shah Dilawer (Rz) and when he came at "Lum Yalid Walam Youlud" at this Miyan Shah Dilawer (Rz) left the word "Lum" and read only "Yalid wa youlad", on which Malik Yousuf (Rh) commented how could you leave the word "Lum" since they are definitive commandments of Allah without any interpretation. At this Miyan Abdul Malik (Rh) asked Miyan Yousuf (Rh) to keep quiet since Miyanji is describing the dignity of Vilayet."

نقل است روزے دربیان سورۂ اخلاص میاں یوسف سامع بودند چوں به لفظ لم یلد ولم یولد رسیدند بندگی میاں شاہ دلاور یلد ویولد بترک لم خواندند میاں یوسف باثبات لم خواندند باز شاہ مذکوربترك لم خواندند میاں یوسف عرض نمودند که این محکمات بے تاویل است میاں عبدالملك گفتند میاں یوسف خاموش باشید میانجی شرف ولایت بیان می کنند (باب هفتم)

Shah Dilawer's contention was that although Allah had no siblings, yet his beneficence is available (through His Emissaries). Here the beneficence or bounty of Allah had been described as a simile in the shape of man. Such resemblance is not new and there should arise no objection. What Bandagi Shah Dilawer (Rz) had commented on the "Soora-e-Ikhlas" is that His Benevolence is described as His sibling which is flowing through generations to generations. Thus, it is a simile and nothing else which is not a new thing therefore should not be objected..

"Bukhari" and "Muslim had reported about Abu Huraira (RZ) that:

"Prophets are step brothers with different mothers."

الانبیاء اخوۃ من علات و امهاتم شتی

Author of "Madarijul Nabuwwat" states that:

"Narrated by (Prophet) Isa (As) that Prophets (As) are step brothers, their father is one and mothers are different."

عیسیٰ می گوید که انبیاء همه برادران علاقی اند که پدر ایشان یکی است ومادر ایشان متعدد

The commentators had deduced from this that the reference to mothers means different Shariaths of the Prophets. Therefore when the Prophets (As) had become step brothers and their Shariah is their mother, then their father should become the Beneficence of Allah alone and who else?

Therefore Holy Prophet (Slm) although is the Last of the Prophets (As), yet Allah's Beneficence has not been exterminated because as per Holy Qur'an there shall be an interpreter of the Holy Qur'an, and he is Imam Mahdi (AS). What Miyan Abdul Malik Sujawandi (Rh) had referred to the dignity of Vilyet, it refers to the same personality of Imam Mahdi (As) who is the Khalifatullah. The Word "Yelid" means as stated above since the Prophets (As) are step brothers and get Allah's Beneficence directly, so also Imam Mahdi (As) as His Khalifatullah should get Beneficence directly from Allah. Thus not only Imam Mahdi (As) will get the beneficence directly from Allah, but by virtue of his coming from the progeny of the Holy Prophet (Slm) he would get this bounty by hereditary also. Thus by deleting the word "Lum" the continuity of the flow of the Bounty of Allah is perpetuated till the Day of Judgment. (*Wallahu Alam Bis Sawab.)* Thus this is confirmed by Qur'an also:

"Thus bestow me from You one son who would be my heir and also of Yaqoob"

فهب لى من لدنک ولیا یرثنی ویرث من آل یعقوب (سوره مریم ع ۱)

Thus by the words "Yalid and Walud" minus "Lum" Beneficence of Allah is continued till the Day of Judgment. This is the commentary of kalamullah and not a distortion of Qur'an.

(Note:it was previously reported that the holy Prophet(Slm) recited the words before his demise: "Neither we are heir of any one. nor any one is heir of ours".The plural is used for all of the prophets. As against this, according to the above verse,the Prophet is requesting Allah for bestowing his heir not only to him but also to Prophet Yaqoob(As).And according to the commentary of "Soora-e-Ikhlas" whole scenario changes and man becomes the heir of Allah, by deleting the word "LUM" before the words "Yalid and Walid"(Naoozu Billah). Reaquires clarification minutely). Khundmiri.

Punishment with Fire and Coldness:

From a cooked up narrative, Author of Hadia had objected on Shah Dilawer (Rz) that Shah Dilawer (Rz) was agreeable to say that whoever is an Aatashi (made of Fire) would be punished with utter coldness.

According to the narrations of the predecessors neither Aatashi is mentioned nor punishment with "Za Muhareer" (Utter coldness) has been indicated.

It is narrated in "Hashia-e-Sharief" That:
"Narrated by Miayn Abdul Karim: One day a thought came to Shah Dilawer (Rz) that what would be the situation of those who worshiped a lot? Allah's order came to Angels to bring them in the shackles before our Servant (Shah Dilawer (Rz) who thought about them). When they were brought, a voice came:

نقل است از میان عبدالکریم که میان دلاورؒ یك روز در خاطر آوردند که .... خلقت عظیم بودند و بسیار ریاضت ها کشیده‌اند حال اوشان چون باشد ملائکان را فرمان خدائی تعالیٰ شد که بنده ماآنهار ایاد کرده است پیش آن به برید ملائکان .... باغلال وسلاسل بسته به پیش میان شاه دلاورؒ آور دندهاتف شد که نگران شوید میان دیدند که خلقت

"Look at them carefully". A large creation was before him. Shah Dilawer (Rz) asked what is your position? They said they did not regard Allah, whatever we did it was for the worldly things only and others worshiped us which pleased us. Thus we are in permanent punishment . Then the angels took them away towards the Hell."

عظیم استاده شده اند میان پر سیدند حال شما چون است اوشان گفتند درمیان ما مقصود خدانه بود، همه ریاضت از روئے دنیا کردیم همه مردان مارا پرستش کردند مارا خوش آمد از آن سبب این عذاب ابدی روزی شد باز ملائکان بدوزخ بردند ۔

Here neither punishment of fire is mentioned nor of utter cold/Za Muhreer.

Miyan Syed Alam also has narrated about it, but he did not mention of any punishment either of fire or of utter cold water. The author however had presented to substantiate his wrong contention through a verse:

"Ordered: Enter the hell with other Ummahs who had already passed before you pertaining to Jinn and Men."

قال ادخلو فی امم قد دخلت من قبلکم من الجن والانس فی النار (اعراف ع۴)

It is clear from the Qur'an that Za Muhreer has to be recognized by Kalamullah. Allah had praised paradise in these words:

"Neither fire will be seen in it nor utter cold."

لا یرون فیها شمسا ولا زمهریرا (الدهر غ)

Author of "Nihaya" had written about Za Muhreer" that:

"Za Muhreer means intense cold, it is that punishment which Allah had prepared for the infidels."

الزمهریر شدة البرو و هو الذی اعده الله عذابا للکفار فی الدار الآخرة

Infidels include both Jinns and Men. But how could it be said that those Jinn who are infidels would not be punished by Za Muhreer/ intense cold. There are Traditions in which the category of infidels pertaining to punishment of Za Muhreer also available in the hell .

"Bukhari" states that:

"The Holy Prophet (Slm) advised: "when there is intense warm, prayer of Zuhar may be delayed, till the intensity of warm is reduced and offer prayer when you feel somewhat cool (in the atmosphere)". Another narration of "Bukahri" reported by Abi Sayeed is that "Instead of prayer the word "Zuhar" had come. The intensity of warmness is due to the Hellfire , and thus Fire complained before the Almighty that some of my portions have been eaten away by my other portions. Then Allah permitted the fire to have two Breaths. From one Breath intense warmness is produced and from the other intense cold is produced.. "Bukahri" and "Muslim" confirmed that the intense warmness comes from the Hellfire and the intense coldness comes from Za Muhreer."

قـال قـال رسـول الـلـه صـلى الله عليه وسلم اذا اشتد الـحـرفـا بـردوا بـالصلوٰة وفى روایة للبخارى عن ابى سـعـید بـالظهر فان شدة الحرمن فیح جهنم واشتكت الـنـار الىٰ ربها فقال التراب اكل بعضا فاذن لها بـنـفسیـن اشد ما تجدون من الحرواشد ماتجدون من الـزمهریر متفـق عـلیـه فى روایة للبخارى فاشد ماتجدون من الحرفمن سمو مها و اشد ما تجدون من البرد فمن زمهریرها

Za Muhreer had been mentioned in the tradition as Breath of the hell Fire. Therefore where there is Fire there is Za Muhreer also. Abdul Haq had commented on this tradition that:

"Where the word Fire had come in the tradition it may be taken to Hell , which contains Zamuhreer also."

مـراد بـنـار كـه در حـدیـث واقع شده محل اوست كه دوزخ است اور دوزخ طبقه ، زمهریر هم هست

Thus the author's contention is wrong that the Jinn are punished by Hell Fire and not by ZaMuhreer.. Because Hell contains both Fire and Zamuhreer. Jinn and Men get punishment of the hell. Thus it is proved that both Jinn and men get the punishment of both intense fire and intense coldness.

Thus the cooked up narrative presented by the author of Hadia is nowhere written in our Mahdavia literature

Thus Allah decides on the Day of Judgment among the following:

"There should be no doubt that Muslims, Jews, Sabiens, Nasara and Majoos and those who are polytheists, Allah shall decide His judgment about them individually."

ان الـذیـن آمنـو والـذیـن هادو والصائبین والنصارى والـمـجـوس والـذیـن اشركو ان الله یفصل بینهم یوم القیامة (الحج ع٢)

It is clear from this except Muslims, other including Jews, Christians and Sabianes and others shall come under the category of infidels.

Shah Dilawer (Rz) and Abdul Malik Sujawandi (Rh)

Author of Hadia had narrated at the end of the chapter 3, that Miyan Abdul Malik Sujawandi(Rh) had been the disciple of Bandagi Shah Dilawer(Rz) who wrote "Sirajul Absar" which contains some defects. Hadia states that: " I do tell that the contention of Shah Dilawer(Rz) was wrong, because this book(Sirajul Absar) has many flaws of scholastic philosophy and apologetics. Even though he had asserted about flaws in the book, but he could not list out the flaws of scholastic philosophy or apologetics or dialectics. One who is not proficient in the art of dialectics he should not raise such silly objections which could not be interpreted to the best of the satisfaction of other party.

The author of Hadia had read, scrutinized and gone through the book word by word of "Sirajul Absar" and also by a group of competent scholars of that period who at least read it for four years and that group of scholars could find out just three flaws in it according to them. Those flaws as pointed out by them are:

1. Chapter 3, Argument 4, 5 and 15: objection has been raised on the traditions presented in "Sirajul Absar", stating that they do not fit to the personality of Imamana(As). About those traditions we have elaborately discussed and proved that these traditions correctly apply to Imamana(As).

2. Under Argument five, they have demanded to rectify the narration mentioned in "Tanbihul Tahurruz" Answer to this shall be given in Part four, Chapter Three.

3. Third objection is regarding the end of the chapter 3. This is regarding criticism of Miyan Abdul Malik Sujawandi(Rh) who had criticized on the language used in the "Risala-e-Rudd" of Shaik Ali Muttaqui. The decliner had slept over nine criticism and just pointed out on a single review that to on a fragment of that review. And that too does not stand to our criticism. This will be answered in our Part four, Chapter two. Now we leave the matter to the eminent scholars to decide whether those objections have any bearing on the Scholastic philosophy, or dialectic principles. Shah Dilawer's greatness can be ascertained from the caliber like that of Miyan Abdul Malik Sujawandi(Rh) who sat respectfully before him and became his disciple by offering allegiance on the hands of Shah Dilawer(Rz) and through him he accepted Imamana(As) as the true and the Promised Mahdi(As). As regards "Sirajul Absar" it was completed after many years from the demise of Shah Dilawer(Rz) which will be discussed in part Four, chapter one.

The author should have written his answer for "Sirajul Absar" on an academic style, since it was not in his capacity, thrrefore he had chosen an absurd way of objecting by tracing narrations from the books of biography and narratives and had un-characteristically based his objections on unauthentic narratives which are not found in any of the old sources of Mahdavia literature.

Dignity of Shah Dilawer's Servant:

Author of Hadia had submitted a narrative on page 211 which states that Shah Dilawer (Rz) had praised about his servant Miyan Yousuf (Rh) before Bibi Khund Buwa (Rh) describing that the Holy Prophet (Slm) and Imamana (As) are sitting on a wooden cot and Miyan Yousuf (Rh) was standing near them and the grandfather of Bibi Khund Buwa (Rh), Mahboob Alam (Rz) also was there. Unfortunately the details are nowhere recorded in the old sources of Mahdavia literature, except in "Hashia Sharief" that:

"Bandagi Shah Dilawer (Rz) had married into the family of Shah Alam (Rz). His wife used to always praise by saying "Shah Alam (Rz) said". On her such utterances Shah Dilawer (Rz) taunted by saying that in this Dairah there are many Shah Alams, about which Shah Alam you are speaking?

نقـل اسـت در اهـل شـاه بندگی شاه دلاورؒ نکاح کرده بودند هر بار گفتندے شاه عالم میاں فرمودند ۔ بی بی چندیں شاه عالم در دائره ما افتاده اند شما چند شاه عالم گوئید (۱۳٤)

Here neither there are Holy Prophet (Slm), nor Imamana (As), who had been said to have been sitting on the cot, and not even Mahboob Alam (Rz) was standing before them. It was just told that like Shah Alam (Rz), the grandson of Mahboob Alam (Rz), there are so many Shah Alams are in the dairah. There should be no objection when Malik Sujawandi (Rh) like eminent scholar was living in that dairah,. Author of "Tazkeratul Saleheen" refers that:

"One day Bibi Munawer (Rh) inquired about Miyan Yousuf as to where he had gone, since she did not see him for a long time. Shah Dilawer (Rz) was not happy on such utterances of Bibi Munawer (Rh) and told her to take Miyan Yousuf's name with respect, because he receives Allah's Blessings every day. Bibi told that Miyanji I am also the granddaughter of Shah Alam (Rz). Shah Dilawer (Rz) asked where Shah Alam and where Miyan Yousuf ? Then Bibi asked whether Miyan Yousuf is greater than Qutub Alam (Rz)? He told that like Qutub there are many Qutubs in his dairah".

روزے بی بی منور گفتند که میانجی یوسف کجا رفته است کـه اورانمی بینم بعدهٗ شاه دلاورؒ ناخوش شده فـرمـودنـد کـه هشیار باشید نام میاں یوسف با ادب و تـعظیـم بـگـوئیـد روز ایشـان را اسـلام خدامـی آید گفتندکه میانجی ماهم نبسه شاه عالم هستیم فرمودند شـاه عـالـم کجا ومیاں یوسف کجا باز ٬بی بی عرض کردند که چه ایشان از قطب عالم بزرگ اند فرمودند که چندیں قطب در دائره ما افتاده اند (باب هفتم)

Here Also nowhere mentioned that Holy Prophet (Slm) and Imamana (As) were sitting on a wooden cot and no where Mahboob Alam's name was mentioned. From both books it comes to light that Shah Dilawer (Rz) had told that like Shah Alam (Rz) there are many Shah Alams are in his dairah. The dignity is bestowed by Allah and anyone can reach to the dignity of Shah Alam (Rz) or Mahboob Alam (Rz).

Both "Hashia Sharief" and "Tazkeratus Saleheen" say that like Qutub Alam (Rz) there were many Qutubs in the dairah.

One tradition states that:

"It is near that the whole of the Ummah would become Prophets."

كادت هذه الامة ان تكون انبياء كلها

When the Ummah could get the status of Prophets then what is strange that a person of the Ummah becomes Shah Alam (Rz) or Qutub Alam (Rz) or even greater than them.

Zaeda was the maid servant of Hzt. Omer Bin Khattab (Rz). The Holy Prophet (Slm) gave her a glad tiding:

"Allah had granted one of my Ummah's woman the position of Maryam."

خدائى تعالىٰ زنى را از امت من بدرجه مريم رسانيد

If the maid slave of Hzt. Omer (Rz) gets the rank of Bibi Mariyam (Rz) and when it is not objectionable, then if Shah Dilawer's servant gets higher rank than Mahboob-e-Alam (Rz) why should he be criticized?

(Note: Such criticism and comaprison should be avoided to safe-guard harmony among the present generation of the followers of Immana(As).   Khundmiri)

SHAH DILAWER'S GLAD TIDINGS FOR A DROWNED MAN:

The Author has submitted a narrative that :

A. A man from the Dairah of Miyan Abdul Fatah (Rz) had gone to collect cucumber, but drowned in a river and died.

B. Miyan Abdul Fatah (Rz) declared that the death was carrion/Haram Mouth.

C. Shah Dilawer (Rz) states that he was given the place of Ba Yazid (Rz), but he was not accepting even that position.

The Author had blamed that the man after witnessing cucumber of a creeper jumped in the river and died. The Narration is about an episodeof a flood in the river, to witness the people of the Dairah were gathered and were alarmed by witnessing the gravity and devastation caused by the flood and cautioned others not to grab anything which may be flowing in the gushing waters: it states that:

After a long period there was a flood in the river Haikri and brothers of the diarah were standing to witness it. It happened that when some cucumbers were flowing near one brother, he just wanted to catch it, but slipped into the river while the creeper surrounded him and he could not come out and died. The Author had objected his action for picking up the flowing cucumber. Although if a thing is dropped, and someone picks it up, it does not tantamount as illegal, since there were none to claim it. There is such narration reported in "Kanzal Ammaal":

"Narrated by Sa'ad that he was going along with the Holy Prophet (Slm) who saw a piece of cloth in which two palm dates were found. One date he took and the other he gave to Sa'ad."

عن سعد قال كنت امشى مع رسول الله صلعم فوجد مقرومة فيها تمرتان فاخذتمرة واعطانى تمرة .

This tells that the Holy Prophet (Slm) picked up a thing from the ground for himself. If that was not proper he would not have picked it up. Like that Abu Dawood reports that:

"Narrated by Abu Sayeed Al Hazri that Ali Ibn Abi Taleb (Rz) found a Dinar and brought it to Bibi Fatima (Rz) and asked the Holy Prophet (Slm) as to whether was it correct to pick up the Dinar?. The holy Prophet (Slm) said that it was a gift from Allah. Thus the Dinar was utilized by them all. Just after that a woman came searching the Dinar. The Holy Prophet asked Ali (Rz) to hand it over to that woman."

عن ابى سعيد الخدرى ان على بن ابى طالب رضى الله عنه وجد دينار فاتى به فاطمه فسال عنه رسول الله صلى الله عليه وسلم فقال رسول الله صلى الله عليه وسلم هذا رزق الله فاكل منه رسول الله صلى الله عليه وسلم واكل على و فاطمه فلما كان بعد ذلك اتت امرأة تنشد الدينار فقال رسول الله صلى الله عليه وسلم يا على اد الدينار

As the Holy Prophet (Slm) told that the dinar was a gift of Allah, in the same sense the cucumber flowing in the water might have been taken as the gift from Allah. If the biased decliner thinks that picking up the cucumber was not legal, what should be his opinion about the dinar and the palm dates? Thus his objection is not valid since he had no knowledge of traditions. Fatawa Alamgiri states that:

"Thus if apple and guava were found flowing in a river, picking and eating them there should be no fear for entertaining them."

وكذلك التفاح والكمثرى اذوجد فى نهر جارلا باس باخذه والا نتفاع به وان كثر (الجز ، الثانى طبع مصر ٢٥٧)

Thus cucumber also comes under this category which was flowing in the water.

****

On the death of that man, Miyan Abdul Fatah (Rz) maintains that his death was declared to have become carrion/Haram Mouth. Miyan Abdul Fatah (Rz) thought that the man purposely dived into the river to pick up the cucumber and died, hence it was unlawful. But as a matter of fact he just wanted to pick it up and for that purpose put his hand, but his leg slipped and drowned in the water and died. The objection had been raised on Shah Dilawer's verdict that he was presented the place of Ba Yazid (Rz), but he was not accepting that position. Why should there be any objection to his not acceptance? The words" Not accepting" indicate that he was expecting still higher reward. At a time when the Holy Prophet (Slm) gave glad tidings that the whole of Ummah would become Prophets, then if a person of the Ummah expects higher place than granted to Ba Yazid (Rz)because he was categorized as a martyr.

This person was from the descendants of Imamana (As). Mullah Abdul Qader had stated about the followers of the successors that:

اگر مجملے از آن ہادر قید کتابت آرند تذکرۃ اولیاء دیگر بایدنوشت

"If we write about them (successors) even in brief then there would be another Tazkeratul Aouliah."

Whether Ba Yazid (Rz) was a mystic? Whether descendants' rank is not greater than the successors? The drowned man's claim that he is from the Imamana's Ummah, therefore he stressed that "I am not content with Ba Yazid's place". Thus he was claiming the rank of the descendants. When according to "Najatur Rashid" if the ranks of the successors are greater than the rank of the descendants, then his rank should be greater than Ba Yazid (Rz).

It is not clear why the author had presented these verses of Qur'an with reference to this tradition: Thus Allah states that:

(ا) انی لا اضیع عمل عامل منکم من ذکرو انثیٰ

"Certainly, I shall not waste (good) action of any man or woman."

When Allah does not waste any person's action, then should that man keep silence? Or why should not he invoke Allah's Blessings for a greater rank?

The Author had presented another verse:

من جاء بالحسنۃ فلہ خیر منھا

"Whoever does good work, he would be granted a better reward."

When Allah does not waste any person's action and He grants better rewards for good deeds, then should one not invoke Allah's Blessings?. If it is said that our actions are enough for our salvation, then what is the purpose of any recommendation?

The drowned man asserts that he belongs to Imamana's Ummah (As), therefore he did not accept even the rank of Ba Yazid (Rz). He claimed higher rank since he belonged to Imamana's group.

(Note:The Sayings of he Holy Prophet(Slm) and of Imamana(As) that Allah will never ask whose son or dughter you are, but shall enquire about the sincerity in your day to day religious dealings, for the purpose of awarding judgment. In view of the above sayings, the drowned man's assertion to get higher position than Ba Yazid, may not get notice by Allah,because he belongs to the Mahdavi Giroh. Then why waste time on this meaningless issue?)

703

703

Description of the Rank of Apostles:

Author of Hadia had recorded two narrations regarding Shah Dilawer (Rz) on page 235 that (1) he had granted the position of the Apostles to his descendants and even greater. (2) Another, granting position of "Hum Ba Manzaliti" to his descendants or even greater than that.

It is clear that the Position of a Nabi and the Rank of a Nabi are just used as a nominal terms. With reference to "Zubdatul Haqaeq" we have already presented this narrative:

اگر منزلت و مقام مصطفی توان دانستن و داشتن انگه ممکن بود که منزلت این طائفه دریابی (تمهید اصل ثالث)

"If anyone can understand the position and rank of the Holy Prophet (Slm), then he could understand the rank of that group".

It is not our purpose to designate equal rank according to one's status and dignity. But to inform someone who possesses, by nature, the attributes of a particular Nabi. This term is known as "Sair-e-Nabi" when someone is immersed in a particular Nabi's entity.

Author of Hadia had translated "equal" for "Ba Manzaliti" which is wrong. It denotes status or position.

Apart from this the Holy Prophet (Slm) had blessed for Abu Bakr (Rz):

اللهم اجعل ابابكر معی فی درجتی یوم القیامة

"Oh my Lord, grant my status to Abu Bakr (Rz) on the Day of Judgment".

From this can it be inferred that the Holy Prophet (Slm) and Abu Bakr (Rz) held the equal status and position?

Now remains the doubt that what is the greater position with reference to "Ba Manziliti"? The answer was given by the Holy Prophet (Slm):

من احبنی کان فی درجتی

"Whoever had an affection with me , he would be in my rank."

These are the degrees of absolute affection. Thus it is clear that whoever had intense affection with the Holy Prophet (Slm), his degree of affection would be greater. The Holy Prophet (Slm) said that "those who had intense affection with me they would come after me".

من اشد امتی لی حبانا س یکونون بعدی

"In my Ummah those who had intense affection with me they would come after me." (That means: not yet born)

Thus who had intense affection shall get greater rank than those who had nominal affection.

There are certain persons to whom prophets (As) would envy, thus their position would be even greater.

According to a tradition:

یغبطهم الانبیاء والشهداء یوم القیامة بمکانتهم من الله

"On the Day of Judgment, prophets and martyrs would envy for the position of those who held before Allah."

Thus it is clear that their position is greater than the apostles.

The meaning of the terms "Status" "Rank" and "Sair" (being immersed) is described as a simile in the traditions:

It is stated in "Tuhfa-e-Asnai Ashria" that:

"In the traditions of Ahl-e-Sunnat, Abu Bakr (Rz) has comparison to Prophet Ibrahim (As) and Jesus Christ (As), while Prophets Noah (As) and Mosses (As) are compared to Omer (Rz), and Abu Zarr (Rz) compared to Jesus Christ (As)."

در احادیث صحیحہٴ اهل سنت تشبیہ ابوبکرؓ با ابراهیمؑ وعیسیؑ وتشبیہ عمرؓ بنوحؑ وّ موسیؑ وتشبیہ ابوذرؓ بعیسیؑ مروی شد۔

This term is known as "Status of a Nabi or Position of a Nabi".

Divine Secrets not to be Disclosed:

Author of "Insaf Nama" narrates that:

"It is narrated by Miyan Raji Mohammed bin Mina (Rh) that Bandagi Shah Dilawer (Rz) had told many a time that whatever he had heard from Imamana (As) if disclosed he would be stoned to death".

نقل است ازمیان راجی محمد بن مینا کہ از زبان بندگی میان دلاور چند کرات شنیدیم کہ فرمودند انچہ از حضرت میران شنیدیم اگر پیش بعضی مهاجران بگوئیم ایشان مرا سنگسار کنند (باب ۷)

How could this narrative becomes objectionable when the same narration was stated by Abu Huraira (Rz) in this connection, although already been stated many a time, still is repeated again:

"Abu Huraira (Rz) had said that "he had received two vessels from the Holy Prophet (Slm), one he had disclosed and the other, if I disclose, my neck would be cut."

قال حفظت من رسول اللہ صلی اللہ علیہ وسلم دعائین فاما احد هما فبثتہ و اما الآخر لوبثتہ لقطع هذا البلعوم

The theme is common in both narratives, with a difference that one tells "he would be stoned to death" and the other told "his neck would be cut". However they represent stern action as a sharia punishment. However, both reprimand not to disclose divine secrets openly.

Shah Dilwer (Rz) Stood on a Grave:

Author of Hadia had blamed Shah Dilawer (Rz) that he had ruined a grave. Although in Mahdavia literature such information of ruining a grave is nowhere available. However it is mentioned in "Hashia Sharief" that:

"One day Shah Dilawer (Rz) went to a forest. There was a grave on the road. The command came to him that he should stand on that grave so that it would become a source for salvation of that man, buried in the grave. He did as per orders of Allah and salvation was granted."

نقل است بندگی میان شاه دلاورؓ یک روز در صحرا رفتند آنجا یک قبر بود درمیان را فرمان خدا شد تو اینجا آمده برای قبر سوار شو، خاک کفش تو برا او افتد اور از عذاب نجات دهم میان اور اهمچنین کردند خدائی تعالیٰ اور از عذاب خلاص کرد (۲۱۲)

(Will he be free from questioning on the day of Judgment? Khundmiri)

The same is narrated in "Naqliat-e-Syed Aalam":

"Shah Dilawer (Rz) happened to go in a forest where there was a grave on the road. Command of Allah came to him to tread over the grave for its salvation. Shah Dilawer (Rz) stood over the grave and Allah granted salvation."

نـقـل است که بندگی میاں دلاور یك روز به صحرا می
رفتـنـد در آنـجا یك قبر دیدند حکم از خدائی تعالیٰ شد
بـرایـس سـوار شـو گـرد کـفش توبرایں افتداز عذاب من
نجات یابد۔

(Note: It is just an exaggeration on the part of Shah Dilawer (RZ) since granting of salvation is dependent on one's good deeds and not at all by a godliman's treading the grave of a person, when Imamana (As) had categorically told to Miyan Barkhurdar (Rz) that "if even you wore my skin, and did not act what I taught to you in my sermons between Asr and Maghrib prayers, my Allah will take my skin from you and give it to me and punish you". In such conditions, just by treading the grave of a person by Shah Dilawer (Rz), the man got salvation is nothing but ridiculous. Hence such exaggeration should not be emphasized any more and must be disregarded and scrapped from our literature to avoid undue criticism and misinterpretation by others.   Khundmiri)

In these two narratives Shah Dilawer's standing on the grave had been mentioned, but he had ruined the grave was not at all mentioned. By standing on the grave means standing near the grave for invocation of Blessings from Allah.

Allah asked the Holy Prophet (Slm):

""Do not stand on the grave."

ولا تقم علی قبرہ (التوبة ع ۱۱)

Author of "Madarijul Nabuwwat" had explained the action of the Holy Prophet (Slm):

"Along with companions he used to stand on the grave and invoke salvation."

باصحابہ بالائے قبر اوایسادی واوراد عاکردے

How could it be inferred that the Holy Prophet (Slm) used to stand on the graves of Muslims?. It only describes going nearer to the grave for invocation of Blessings.

******

CHAPTER SIXTH
Bandagi Miyan Ilahdad Hameed (Rz)

Bandagi Miyan Ilahdad(Rz) and ranks of Imamana(As):

Author of "Matleul Vilayet" had reported that:

"Reported by Miyan Ilahdad Hameed (Rz) that he had written a pathetic Elegy in praise of Imamana (As) after ten days from Imamana's demise which contains praise of Imamana (As) which determines the day, date, month and year of Imamana's demise and read at the grave in the presence of all companions".

نقل است از میان الهداد حمید بعرس دهم روز از مرثیه دل سوزو جگر دوز در الم و ماتم و پشیمانی مشتمل تعریف خاتم الاولایت مع تاریخ وسال وماه روزه و ساعت ساخته و پرواخته در مجمع جمیع صحابه پیش قبر منور آنحضرت خواندند ۔

Author of Hadia raised objection on some couplets which says that::

"On command by Allah he would recommend on the Day of Judgment.

بادابروز حشر شفاعت گر از احد

The biased decliner had complained that Mahdavis, (Naoozoo Billah) prefer Imamana (As) over the Holy Prophet (Slm). This is against Mahdavia Faith and thus utterly false. Further the couplet also does not indicate such faith. From the other couplet author's allegation is again nullified:

"The world had been darkened on the demise of Imamana (As), just as it had become darkened when the Holy Prophet (Slm) had passed away."

دهر آنچنان است تیره که بعد رسول حق

Had Bandagi Ilahdad (Rz) preferred Imamana (As) over the Holy Prophet (Slm)? Then should such couplets not have been written?. Abdullah Bin Omroo states that:

"He heard the Holy Prophet (Slm) saying that sky did not cover nor the Earth holds anybody except Abu Zarr (Rz) the most trustworthy."

قال سمعت رسول الله صلی الله علیه آله وسلم یقول ما اظلت الخضراء و ما اقلت الغبراء باصدق من ابی ذر.

On the basis of this tradition can it be deduced that Abu Zarr (Rz) surpassed in truth worthiness even upon all prophets (As) and even on the Holy Prophet (Slm)? It is just an exaggeration as maintained by "Ashatul Lam'aat".

"Tirmizi" reported what Hzt. Anas had said:

"Stated that the Holy Prophet (Slm) had a bird roasted for eating. Before eating alone, he implored Allah to send such a person who was most loved by You (Allah) to share that bird. Hzt Ali (Rz) came and shared the bird along with the Holy Prophet (Slm)."

قال کان عندالنبی صلی الله علیه آله وسلم طیر فقال اللههم آتنی یا حب خلقک الیک یا کل معی هذا الطیر فجاء ه علی فاکل معه .

On this tradition Abdul Haq Dehalvi had commented that::

"This tradition confirms that Hzt. Ali (Rz) was the most loved one among the Ummah by Allah."

ایس حدیث دلالت دارد بر آنکه علی مرتضیٰ رضی الله عنه رحب خلق خدا بودنزد خدا

From this tradition it comes to light that Hzt. Ali (Rz) was the most loved one by Allah, but the Holy Prophet (Slm) is exempted. Like that the couplet of Miyan Hameed exempts the Holy Prophet (Slm).

"It may be pointed out that Miyan Ilahdad (Rz) had written a dot less Dewan" under the title"Kalaam-e-Ilahdad" in 911 H. In one of the couplets he believed "Imamana (As) to be equal to both Prophet Adam (As) and the Holy Prophet (Slm)" the couplet which is in Persian mentions his belief in Imamana (As).

اعلام داد همسر احمد ره صلاح آگاه کرد همدم آدم ره ملام

Bandagi Malik Ilahdad's Dairah:

Malik Abdul Malik Sujawandi (Rh) on page 174 of "Sirajul Absar" had mentioned about his contemporaries who were the successors of the companions of Imamana (As), particularly about their piety and abstinence. By presenting their attributes he had advised to guess the greatness of the companions.

Author of Hadia had tried to malign even Miyan Abdul Malik Sujawandi (Rh) for his deliberations about the companions and their successors. Detailed answer for this is already given in Part 4, chapter two.

He had also described about the dairah of Bandagi Malik Ilahdad Hameed (Rz) in a sarcastic manner and written on page 32 of Hadia that when someone on the death bed asked another brother the reason of his weakness; the dying man showed towards the bread. Author of Hadia had copied this episode from "Tazkeratus Saleheen" which is also recorded in "Hashia-e-Sharief" and "Naqliat-e-Miyan Syed Alam". that:

"The dairah of Malik Ilahdad (Rz) was in Baakhar. Many Godlimen died on account of hunger. One brother asked another about his condition. He pointed with his hand towards the bread and he too died in that condition."

دائره بندگی میان ملک الهداد در موضع باکهر بود بسیار فقیران جهت فقر متوفی شدند یکی برادر دائره را کسی پرسید اوراز اشارت دست نمودند چیزے نان ، اوشان به همین حال رحلت شدید

This narrative tells that someone asked about the condition of the Dairah, he showed towards the bread. It means that on account of "lack of food provision" people were dying on account of becoming hungery. It does not mean that the man who was himself at the death bed, was asking for the bread to eat, even if the bread is supplied can one imagine that he could eat it, while gasping the last of his breaths ?

At the time of gasping the last breath, by pointing out bread it may be deduced that the dying man was explaining his severe condition was the result of non availability of foodstuff. Thus, there is no reason to raise false allegations against the condition of a Dairah.

Even if a dying man demands bread; what is wrong in it; because the companions of the Holy Prophet (Slm) too had expressed about their hunger as mentioned in "Sihah":

"Narrated that one night the Holy Prophet (Slm) came out from his house and luckily met with Abu Bakr (Rz) and Omer (Rz). The holy Prophet (Slm) inquired "what made you both to come out during the night? They told "hunger". The Holy Prophet answered that "the same thing also brought him out."

قال خرج رسول الله صلى الله عليه وسلم ذات يوم اوليلة فاذاهو بابى بكر و عمر فقال مااخرجكمامن بيوتكماهذه الساعة قالا الجوع قال وانا والذى نفسى بيد لا خرجنى الذى اخرجكما الىٰ آخره

Thus it comes to light that the Holy Prophet (Slm) and his companions when confronted with acute shortage of food stuff they too had expressed their need. It is but a human requirement.

If anyone from the dairah of Miyan Ilahdad Hameed (Rz) had pointed out on account of lack of food many had died or he might have expressed condition on account of his hunger, there should arise no ugly objection like that raised by the Author of Hadia. In view of the above tradition, since it is a human requirement, Author's objection stands absurd and futile.

Revelation of Khaatimul Murshid (Rz):

Miyan Syed Mahmood (Rz) (Khatimul Murshid) got the caliphate from Bandagi Syed Shahabul Haq (Rz) his elder brother:

"(Bandagi Syed Shahabuddin Shahabul Haq (Rz) called Miyan Syed Mahmood (Rz) (his younger brother) at his death bed and handed over him the Caliphate and advised."

بندگى ميان سيد محمود رانزديك خود طلبيد ه وصيت رحلت و عطائى خلافت فرموده

Author of "Tazkeratus Saleheen" narrates that:

"(Someone asked): After your demise (of Miyan Syed Shahabuddin) (Rz) who would hold the Caliphate? He answered "Syed Mahmood (Rz)."

بعد از خوند کار خلاف بر کیست فرمودند که برسیدنجى (باب اول)

Author of "Insaf Nama" had narrated a dream of Bandagi Miyan Syed Mahmood (Rz) in which he saw that the Dooms Day had been established and Allah's command came for accounting etc:

"First the Holy Prophet (Slm) was commanded. Then the Holy Prophet (Slm) directed Imamana (As) who, in turn directed Bandagi Miyan Syed Khundmir (Rz) to account for the inhabitants of the whole world. Upon that Bandagi Miyan (Rz) conducted an accounting of all inhabitants of the world and there was a Divine Vision which is inexpressible."

اول فرمان رسول الله رامی شود بعد از آن رسول الله سوائے میران می فرمائیند و میران ؑ، بندگی میان سید خوند میر رامی فرماید که شما حساب عالم بگیرید بعده حساب تمام عالم بندگی میان سیدخوند میر ؓ می کنند و ظهور حق چنان شده است که در بیان نیاید (باب ۱۷)

Author of Hadia had objected on the details of the dream at page 207 of Hadia. As a matter of fact in such cases the importance is given on intent and not on minor things as reported by the Holy Prophet (Slm):

"I did see my Allah in my dream who was personified as a young man whose beard was thick, wearing the shoes made of gold and drops of gold water were seen on his face."

رایت ربی فی المنام فی صورة شاب موفر فی الخضر علیه نعلان من ذهب و علیٰ وجهه فراش من ذهب

It depicts the grandeur of the Almighty. The details are irrelevant. As Sheik Abdul Haq had stated that:

"The intent is that to describe the grandeur and magnificence of the Almighty, the details are irrelevant."

خلاصہٴ معنی وزبدہ آں بیان عظمت الهی وکبریائی اوست و معنی مفردات کلام در اینجا ملحوظ نیست

The intent of the dream is that Bandagi Miyan (Rz) had a clean chit, therefore he was entrusted the accounting of all the inhabitant of the world except the Khaatemain (As). A tradition also points out that:

"Thus enters (Bandagi Shah Khundmir (Rz) in the paradise without his account being checked".

فیدخلون الجنة بغیر حساب

Shah Dilawer (Rz) vouchsafe this Saying of Imamana (As) about Bandagi Miyan (Rz) as reported in "Naqliat-e-Syed Aalam":

"Narrated Shah Dilawer (Rz) that he had seen on the door of the paradise: 1.Creed of the Holy Prophet (Slm) 2. Acceptance of Mahdi (As) and 3. Affection to Bandagi Miyan (Rz)."

میاں دلاورؓ فرمودند که کلمۂ محمد و تصدیق مهدی و محبت میاں سید خوند میرؓ بردر بهشت نوشته دیدم (۱۰۹)

It means to say that whoever had affection to Bandagi Miyan (rz) he would enter the paradise. Author of "Insaf Nama" had written in chapter 17 that:

"It may be known that Miyan Syed Mahdmood (rz) witnessed a dream in Khanbail that he reached the Divine Throne of Allah and witnessed some companions of Imamana (As) were dancing with spreaded hair and clapping, also saw Bhai Muhajir there."

نیز معلوم باد که در کها نبیل میاں سید محمود معامله دیدند که ازیں عالم عروج کردند تاعرش وکرسی آنجا چه بینند که پیش حضرت حق تعالیٰ بعضے اصحاب مهدی موی هائے خود را واکرده رقص می کنند و دستك هامیز نند و در آں حال میاں بهائی مهاجرؓ رادیدم۔

Author of Hadia had objected on this dream too at page 207. If we verify the contents of the dream it comes to light that the companions of Imamana (As) are close to the Almighty because of their exalted position; that is why they were near the Almighty, for that position, they were jubilant and dancing. It is but natural. In "Madarijul Nabuwwat" it is reported that:

"On receiving favors from the Holy Prophet (Slm) Jafer (Rz) became very jubilant and started dancing on one leg around the Holy Prophet (Slm). When asked why you are dancing? He told that "In Abi Sina (Habsha) the same sort of dance was being performed around the king, when King Najashi, grants some favors to any man, thus the man dances on one leg around Najashi". When the Holy Prophet (Slm) addressed Zaid (Rz) as brother and titled him as Moula, he started dancing around the Holy Prophet (Slm) on his one leg."

پس جعفر باین عنایت که درباب وے واقع شد بسیار خوش حال گشت و در روایتی آمد کـه بـرخـاست گرد رسول خدا صلی الله علیه وسلم بیك پائی بگشت، حضرت پر سید از دے که این چیست جواب داد کـه درحبشه دیده ام که باباد شاهان خود چنیـن مـی کنند و نجاشی نیز چون کسی رااز خود خوشنـود ساختی آن کس بر کاستی و گرد اوبیك پائے بگشتی و نیز آور ده اند که چون بـازید گفت انت اخونا ومولانا، زید حجل کرد یعنی رقص کرد از فرح و سرور

In the same manner Hazrat Ali (Rz) too had danced. Reported author of "Keemia-e-Sa'adat" that:

"When the Holy Prophet (Slm) declared Ali (Rz)" to be from me and I am from you". Then Ali (Rz) danced and dashed legs while dancing."

رسول الله صلی الله علیه وسلم با علی رضی الله عنه گفت که توازمنی و من از تو علی از شادی این رقص کرد وچند بار پائے برزمین زد

Thus the dream of Hzt. Saidanji (Khaatemul Murshid (Rz) points out (1) the companions of Immana's nearness to Allah 2. On the position of being near to Allah, they became jubilant and 3. Their hair was spreaded. It means that they were following Shariat-e-Mustafavi (Slm).

Author's foolish objection on such dream is based on jealousy and bias. He did not know that the remark goes against the Holy Prophet (Slm) too.

Author of Hadia had written at the end of chapter one about the demise of Miyan Syed Mahmood (Rz) Ibn Hazrat Bandagi Miyan Syed Khundmir (Rz) that: One night this pious man was sitting on the prayer mat after Tahajjud prayer that the soul of Yazid entered into a dog. Miyan drove it away, but the dog inflicted wound on his hand which resulted in death after 43 days on the 15th of Muharram."

"Tazkeratus Saleheen" reported this episode:

"Bandagi Miyan Saidanji (Rz) was sitting on a prayer mat after Tahajjud on 3rd. of Zil Hajja in Jalore, that the soul of Yazeed entered in a dog or pig and came into the room and this Satan Yazid inflicted wound by a spear on the hand of Hzt.Saidanji (Rz), on that he yelled: Be off evil spirit, Be off evil spirit twice."

آخر الامردر موضع جالور درماه ذی الحجه بتاریخ سـوم بـعد ادائے نماز تهجد بندگی میان سید نجی بـرجـائے نماز نشسته بودند نا گاه روح یزید لعنت مزیـد بصـورت سگ یا خوك در حجره آمد میان بـدست مبارك خود اورابر اندندیزید ید لعین ابلیس قریـن دردست بندگی میان برچهی بزدور آن حال فرمود پهٹ پلید پهٹ پلید (باب اول)

It is clear that a dog or pig cannot use spears to inflict wounds. It must be his enemy who inflicted wound. The detail of the wound had been given in "Tazkeratus Saleheen" that:

"On hearing the words "Be of Paleed" two times, Bandagi Syed Noor Mohammed (Rz) (his son) came out from his room. He saw that the light was off, he lit a lamp and saw that the wound was visible from one end to the other end of his palm and was profusely bleeding which drenched the prayer mat."

ناگاه آواز..... بندگی میان سید نور محمدؓ پهٹ پلید شنیده و شتاب آمدند و یدند که چراغ گل شده است زود چراغ روشن کرده دیدند که زخم سه رویه دردست میان ازیں جانب به آن جانب گشت و تمام مصلیٰ در خون تر شده است (تذکرۃ الصالحین باب اول)

Thus the author's contention that on account of dog's biting he died after 43 days is utterly wrong malicious and is nothing but a white lie.

This episode had been narrated in Miyan Abdul Rahman's "Daftar" also that:

"At Sirohi along with people of the diarah Saidanji (Rz) stayed. He was meditating in a room on a dark night that suddenly he heard the walking sound of a man or an animal (God knows better) He moved his hand and raised his right hand's palm and he got a wound which crossed from one side to another and was bleeding profusely. As his stunning voice went outside, brothers who were also meditating, rushed to him with a lit up lamp and saw that his hand was bleeding profusely. They searched for the culprit, but none were there. They administered bandage on the wound."

در سیر وهی بادائره کلهم اجمعین اقامت فرموده بودندو درشبی از شب هائے تاریک در خلوت خانه خود باحق مشغول بودند که ناگاه بے آگاه اثر پائے جنبده خواه آدمی خواه غیر وے الله اعلم در آنجا ظاهر شد و آنحضرت دست مبارک هیبت کرده جنبانده اند که چوں دراز کرده انددرمیان کف دست راست برابر یک عباسی زخم کرده رسید هر دورخ و خون بسیار جاری شدو آنحضرت که هیبت کرده بودند آواز مبارک بیرون خلوت رسیده بود و برادرها که برائے نوبت نشسته بودند وغیر ایشانهمه در آنجا رسیدند و چراغ آوردند و تحفص کردند اثر هیچ کس نیافته اندوزخم دست مبارک در حال بسته اند (دفتر دوم رکن دواز دهم باب دهم)

Author's objection was about the "soul of Yazeed entered in a dog". Such old sayings are in usage since who inflicted wounds could not be determined. However such foolish objections by the author of Hadia is just on account of his enmity with Mahdavis.

Thus whatever blames, doubts and objections had been raised by the jealous author had been completely answered and refuted against Imamana (As) and his companions with befitting arguments.

****

PART FOUR
CHAPTER ONE
Sources Of The Opponents

1."AL Risalathul Rudd":

Sheik Ali Muttaqi, a pupil of Ibn Hajrul Hitimi, had written "Al Risalatul Rudd" against Mahdavis on the basis of a Decree (Fatwa) issued by his teacher against Mahdavia Faith. The details are as below:

"You had questioned about a group who had faith in a person who died forty years ago and that he is Mahdi-e-Maood (As)" because his advent had been at the last period with a firm opinion that whoever denied his Mahdiat he was an infidel".

وسئلت عن طائفة يعتقدون فى رجل مات من منذاربعين سنة انه المهدى الموعود بظهوره آخرالزمان و ان من انكر كونه المهدى المذكور فقد كفر

From this it came to light that the decree was issued in the year 950 H. (910+40= 950). The opening paragraph of The "Rudd" written by Sheik Ali states that:

"But a group of people in India had the faith that he was the Mahdi-e-Maood (As) who died about fifty years ago."

ثم طائفة فى البلاد الهند يعتقدون فى شخص مات و له نحو خمسين سنة انه هوالمهدى الموعود .

This tells that the "Risalatur Rudd" was written in 960 H after ten years from the date of the Fatwah.

Imamana (AS) and the Traditions regarding Mahdi (As):

"Now remains first reason to repudiate those traditions which have reached in a continuity which shall be discussed now".

اما الاول فلخالفته لصريح الاحاديث التى كادت نتواتر بخلافه كما ستملى عليك

Sheik Ali's version in the Rudd is just like that:

"Certain real traditions are against him".

والاحاديث الصرائح تخالفه

Here both the teacher and his pupil agree on this point.

Denial of Mahdiat:

Ibn Hajr had repudiated Imamana's Mahdiat in these words:

"The referred man who had died is not the Mahdi (As)".

هذا الميت ليس المهدى (سراج الابصار معه مقدمه طبع اول ٢١٦)

Sheik Ali too states that:

"Thus it became known that the Late Syed was not the Mahdi (As)".

فعلم ان السيد الميت ليس بمهدى

Although Ibn Hajr kept secret the progeny of Imamana (As), but Sheik Ali had accepted it.

Ibn Hajr's Denial of Mahdiat:

Ibn Hajr Makki had designated Mahdavis as infidels, because we Mahdavis believe in Imamana Syed Mohammad Juanpuri as Mehdi-e-Maood (As), consequently we do not believe in any other Mahdi which the opponents say that he would arrive in future and to Ibn Hajr Makki the future Mahdi would be the real Mahdi for him: and not our Imamana (As): these are his words:

"These people deny that Mahdi who would appear in the last period. This certifies by a tradition which narrated by Abi Bakerul Askaf who heard the Holy Prophet (Slm) saying that whoever denies the Anti Christ (Dajjal) he is an infidel and who denies Mahdi (As), he too becomes an infidel. Thus these people certainly deny that Mahdi (supposed to appear when Dajjal appears) hence it is feared that they would become infidels."

وهؤلاء منكرون للمهدى الموعود به آخر الزمان وقد ورد فى حديث عند ابى بكر الاسكا فى انه صلى الله عليه وسلم قال من كذب بالدجال فقدكفرو من كذب بالمهدى فقد كفرو وهئولاء مكذبون به صريحا فيخشى عليهم الكفر

Sheik Ali Muttaqi has the same opinion that we Mahdavis, who deny their so called Mahdi to come in the future (maybe when Dajjal appears), would become infidels in his opinion. The Sheik had written thus:

"Thus on account of the denial of appearance of a (their so called) Mahdi in the future, whom the signs would apply, may render them (We Mahdavis) to infidelity; because they have already accepted and believe Imamana Syed Mohammad Juanpuri as the true Mahdi (As)."

فعلى هذا يلزم كفرهم لاعتقادهم مهدوية هذا الشخص المستلزم انكار مهدوية المهدى الذى سيوجد فيه هذه العلامات (سراج الابصار معه مقدمه)

Decree for Killing Mahdavis:

Ibn Hajr Makki had issued a decree against Mahdavis:

"Obviously Ghazali (Rh) had decreed against such a sect by saying: " killing of one man of that sect equals to the killing ashof 100 infidels."

وقد قال الغزالى رحمة الله تعالىٰ فى هئو لاء الفرقة ان قتل الواحد منهم افضل من قتل مائة كافر

Sheik Ali too issued a like decree (against Mahdavis):

"To wage jihad against the innovators (we Mahdavis) is superior to waging jihad against infidels".

والجهاد معه المبتدعة افضل من الجهاد مع الكفار (سراج الابصار مع مقدمه طبع اول)

Daira-e-Mahdavia:

Ibn Hajr Makki, however, had accepted the piety and abstinence of Mahdavis and declared "these qualities have become a strong reason for the propagation of their faith" **Consequently:**

"But these people pretend to be pious and reformers for the public, still believe in unchaste faith. The public becomes cheated on account of their appearance and become obsessed of their chastity and accept whatever they say; although it is an innovation and concealed infidelity (according to him)."

واما هئولاء فيظهـرون للنـاس بـزى الفقـراء والصالحيـن معـه الطـوائهم عـلى العقائد الفاسدة ....فيغتـرون بظـواهـرهـم ويعتقدون بـسببها فيهـم الـخير فيـقبلـون مـايسـمعون منهم من البـدع والكفر الخفى و نحو هما

Sheik Ali too toes in his teacher's footsteps: "After witnessing their actions in performing prayers, fasting and separation from the public, people accept this heretic innovator's sect. A commoner does not understand their apparent actions and is easily deceived and becomes their prey."

والـعـوام يعتقدون لهذه الطائفة المبتدعة لانهم يرون اعمـالهم الظاهرة من الصلوة والصوم والانزواء من الـخـلق ....والعامى لايعرف هذه المسئلة و يغتر بظاهر عملهم فيقع فى شبكتهم (سراج الابصار مع مقدمه ٢ ٣،٥٣)

Sheik Ali too is bound to accept Mahdavis' piety and abstinence as his teacher confirmed. He is just copying what his teacher utters and sometimes his words resemble his teacher's.

Ibn Hajr's assertion that Mahdavis show themselves to be pious and reformers (*Is it not a fact?*), does it not prove that these qualities of Mahdavis became known in the Arabian lands too? And Sheik Ali's assertion that the public become prey to them creates two issues for discussion:

1. Mahdavis' abstinence and piety survived even the adverse propaganda of the opponents. 2.The propagation of Mahdavis was very impressive. Further Sheik's assertion that only the commoners used to become impressed by the propagation of Mahdavis is utterly wrong. This issue was discussed in our previous chapters in detail under the topic: "Propagation of the Faith". Ironically one of the relatives of the Sheik had accepted Mahdiat who was a pious man of mystic qualities and was living in Makkah.

Sheik Abdul Haq Dahalvi had written about his teacher Sheik Abdul Wahab Muttaqi (D.1001 H) who said to have met with that Mahdavi relative of the Sheik:

" Narrated by Shah Abdul Wahab that a relative of Sheik Ali who had accepted Mahdavia Faith, came to Makkah. When Sheik Ali heard about his arrival, Sheik wanted to celebrate his arrival and for that he handed over some money to Abdul Wahab by asking him to say to his relative that this feast is just because he is a blood relative and not for his religious connection.

"And asked to tell that his arrival was good for some reason that if you still had any doubt you can clear from me. Come into our company to eradicate if you have any misconception, get it verified and be penitent. Abdul Wahab states that he went to that gentleman, who came out from his house lamenting and weeping. We said to him whatever the Sheik had told. He heard it and kept quiet (*Since keeping silence was better than answering to an ill-fated decliner*)."

می فرمودند یك بارے از قرابتان ایشان ، كه در مذهب مهدویه درآمده به مكه آمد ایشان چوں خبر آمدن اور اشنید نـد خـواستند كه اور اضیافتے كنندیك ابراهیمی بـدست فقیر دادند و گفتند كه این رایش آن شخص ببریدو بـدهیـد و بـگویـد كه این رابرهیم ضیافت پیش شما فرستاده ایم و بگویید كه این ضیافت بجهت قرابت بـطنی نه نسبت دینی و بگویید كه آمدن شمادر این دیار خوب شده است اگر شبه داشته باشید در اینجار فع آ

بكنیدویه صحبت مادر آئید و تحقیق این مسئله كه شمارا در آنـجـا اشتباه شده است رفع بكنیده تائب شوید میفرفرمودند نـزد آن مـرد رفتیم ازخلوت برآمد گریه كنان و آه زنان مبلغ رابه وے رسانیـد یـم وایـس حـرف كه شیخ فرموده بودند نیز گفتیم خاموش ماند۔

Abdul Wahab after coming back had spoken to the Sheik about that man's weeping and lamenting posture. The Sheik remarked:

"This sort of lamenting and weeping impresses and indeed he must be having fervor and zeal but his weeping is not impressive to me. Good Faith is essential."

ایں گریه و حـالـت خـود امـرے مرغوب و مطلوب است ایشان را مگر دردے و ذوقے می باشد فرمودند عجائب گریه سردے ناموثر بود كه اصلا نشان ذوق و بـوے صدق نـداشت گریـه را اعتبار سے نیست اعتقاد خوب می باید

From the above it is clear that:

1. A relative of Sheik Ali had converted to Mahdiat, and the Sheik had tried to reverse his conversion, but failed.

2. This point had reached to such a certainty that the life of Mahdavis of that period was so impressive and captivating that even a rigid opponent would become impressed which is evident from the Abdul Wahab's assertion that the Sheik had repudiated just on the basis of prejudice and bias.

3. The further assertion of Abdul Wahab is that the lamenting and weeping were such qualities that impresses others and this quality was not found in the company of the Sheik.

4. Sheik's assertion" if doubt had arisen, come and get it repudiated". This points out that Sheik's relative was a well versed scholar of that time.

From the particulars of the relative of the Sheik, as spoken by Sheik Abdul Wahab, anybody can guess how captivating and impressive should be the life in Mahdavi Dairahs and certainly was not available in any place either in Arab lands or non Arab lands.

Advent of Mahdi (As) and the Traditions:

Ibn Hajr (Died 971) was the first to spread a wrong theory that all signs described in the traditions mentioned in "Sihah" and other than "Sihah" should apply to Imam Mehdi (As). Thus he did not distinguish between the signs of Mahdi (As) as narrated in "Sihah" and narrated in other than "Sihah". On the other hand Muhaddiseen did never try to mix up signs reported in the traditions of "Sihah" and other than "Sihah" and never directed to apply all the signs irrespective of being mentioned either in the "Sihah" or other than "Sihah".

Thus it was not possible for the opponents to distinguish and determine the signs as advised by the Muhaddisseen. Hence they put a condition that whatever signs had been prescribed in the "Sihah" or "Non Sihah" books they should apply to the personality of the Promised Mehdi (As). Ibn Hajr Makki had selected a less number of signs from the "Sihah" and many signs from "other than Sihah" and wrote that:

"These traditions negate the contention of these people who have been referred in the questionnaire."

فهذه الجملة من الاحاديث تكذب اولئك المذكور ين فى السوال

Sheik Ali Muttaqi too had maintained the same logic:

"Thus determination of Mahdi (As) was subject to fulfillment of all signs which had been mentioned in those traditions."

فالحاصل ان المهدى لايتحقق الا وان يوجد فيه جميع ماور دفى شانه من الاحاديث

Whatever Sheik Ali Muattaqi had written about the signs of Mahdi (As), it is based on the Fatwa of Ibn Hajr with a difference that while Ibn Hajr Makki had written in detail, the Sheik had simplified it by telling emergence of Sufiani was made an essential sign of the advent of Mahdi (As). But Ibn Hajr had suggested more details, a part of which is presented below:

"Thus Mahdi (As) shall slaughter Sufiani under a tree whose branches would be hanging down towards Tabriah Sea."

فيذبح السفيانى تحت الشجرة التى اغصانها الى بحيرة طبرية . (الفتاى الحديثيه)

As a matter of fact the word "Sufiani" is not at all mentioned in any of the books of "Sihah", leave aside mentioning of a tree under which their so called Mahdi would slaughter the so called Sufiani near the Sea of Tabriah.

The fact is that the source of the "Risaltur Rudd" is the Fatwa of Ibn Hajr Makki. Thus "Sirajul Absar" is not only the answer of the "Rudd", but also the answer for the fatwa of Ibn Hajr Makki.

Note:"Sirajul Absar" was written under consultation of Bandagi Miyan Syed Shahabuddin Shabul Haq (Rz) as mentioned by Syed Fazlullah in "Hashi-e-Ziaul Quloob":

"When Sheik Ali's Risala was received, Bandagi Miyan Abdul Malik Suijawandi (Rh) brought it to Bandagi Miyan Syed Shahabuddin (Rz) who after reading, advised Miyan Abdul Malik (Rh) to write a befitting rebuttal as the answer to the Risala."

Bandagi Shahabul Haq (Rz) passed away in 972 H., thus "Sirajul Absar" was written before that year. Author of "Sirajul Absar" had referred to the murder of Sultan Mahmood

Shah of Gujrat. This happened in 961 H. Thus it was written either from this year or after 961 H. The author had also referred about the murder of Abu Abdullah al Mahdi of `````````` `Maghrib, which occurred in 964 H. Thus it is certain that "Sirajul Absar" was written between 964 and 972 H, during the period of Bandagi Shahabul Haq (Rz). Miyan Abdul Malik (Rh) had great respect for Bandagi Shahabul Haq (Rz) which had been mentioned by Bandagi Shah Burhan (Rh) that:

" Bandagi Miyan Abdul Malik (Rh) had stated that only two personalities had recognized him: one: his Murshid Bandagi Shah Dilawer (rz) and second: Bandagi Miyan Syed Shahabuddin (Rz). Thus "Sirajul Absar" was written after the demise of Bandagi Shah Dilawer (died in 944 H). Thus after twenty years (964 H) on the advice of Bandagi Miyan Syed Shahabuddin (Rz) "Sirajul Absar" was written. This ends the wrong belief that it was written under the advice of Shah Dilawer (Rz). (Author Hzt. Bazmi (Rh)

"Risalatur Rudd and Hostile Scholars:

"Sirajul Absar" is the answer of that "Risala" which had been mentioned by the hostile scholars. Details are as mentioned below:

1. Abdul Haq Muhaddis-e-Dehalvi with reference to his teacher Shah Abdul Wahahab Muttaqi (D.1001 H.) had written about Sheik Ali Muttaqi:

"After this event of writing of the rebuttal against Mahdavi Faith, just to defame this Sect, pamphlets were written."	بعـد از وقوع ایں واقعہ رسائل درد مہدویہ وافساد ایں فرقہ ضالہ نوشتند

1. This points out to "Risala Burhan" and "Risal-e-Rudd". Since these pamphlets were written against the Mahdavia Faith, which became famous both in Arabia and Ajam. Therefore without writing their names just reference had been given.

2. He (D.1052 H.) also had written about this event without giving his own opinion. Thus it tantamount to his admission (of the fact that these pamphlets were written to defame the Mahdavia Sect.)

3."**Shuhab-e-Muharraqa. Asad Makki** (D.1162 H) a literate in Arabic, who had studied Traditions under the guidance of Arabian Scholars as stated by Mir Ghulam Ali Azad Bilgirami and Tajuddin, had written in support of Sheik Ali Mutaqi's "Risalatur Rudd" and against some arguments of "Sirajul Absar" wrote a pamphlet under the title "Shuhab-e-Muharraqa" who had recognized that the "Risalatur Rudd" was written by Sheik Ali Muttaqi that:

"Sheik Ali Muttaqi had written a Risala under the name "Ar Rudd" against those people who have declared that Imam Mahdi (As) had come and gone."

Asad Makki eventhough he being a literate in Arabic and a resident of Makkah could not answer to any of the criticism made in"Sirajul Absar"against Sheik Ali's utterances in his"Ar-Rudd".

4. **Hadia-e-Mahdavia".** Author of "Hadia-e-Mahdavia" (published in 1287 H.) along with a group of scholars had accepted "Risalatur Rudd" being written by Sheik Ali Muttaqi, and they treat this pamphlet to be of high standard that even Miyan Abdul Malik Sujawandi (Rh) could

not understand it. He writes that Aalim Billah Sujawandi (Rh) had mistaken to understand the construction of syntax on some passages. On the other hand, Miyan Abdul Malik (Rh) had criticized on the language of the "Rudd" and pointed out eleven mistakes, but the protesters could not clear those mistakes, that means to say that they had accepted those mistakes, except on one point they had criticized.

5. Author of **"Nuzhatul Khawathir"** has written about Sheik Ali Muttaqi that he had written pamphlets against proclamations of "Syed Mohammed Juanpuri as Mahdi-e-Mauood" (As).

6. Abul Kalam Azad had written in his **Tazkera (published in 1335)** regarding Sheik Ali who had written "Risala Rudd" against the "exaggeration and innovations of Mahdavis", but "As regards the Syed (As) he refers him as a man of intense divinity" and wrote that: "somehow we cannot say that "he too was an innovator". Wallahu Aalam Bis Sawab".

Thus Sheik Ali Muttaqi's pupil, from Sheik Abdul Wahab to Moulana Abul Kalam Azad, all have confirmed that "Risala-e-Rudd" was written by Sheik Ali Muttaqi.

Apart from "Risalatur Rudd", Sheik Ali had written **"Kanzul Ammal" and "Al Burhan Fi Alaamat-e-Mahdi-e-Akhiruz Zaman".** While Sheik Ali maintains that "Denial of Mahdi does not make the denier infidel", but in his other book "Al Burhan" he had admitted that the denier becomes an infidel. From the following statement of Miyan Abdul Malik (Rh) it comes to light that Sheik Ali had the company of Mahdavis:

"Sheik's heart had been sealed by Allah. He had become deaf and blind. On account of which he did not benefit himself from the company of Mahdavis."

طبع الله على قلب الشيخ فاصمه واعمى بصيرة قد صحبهم مرة ولم يظهر له شئى مما منحوا.

Miyan Abdul Malik (Rh) had written about Sheik Ali's hatred against Mahdavis:

"As an enemy of Mahdavis, Sheik had exaggerated about Mahdavis and he came back from Makkah to Gujrat, and just for the enmity he tolerated many hardships with a hope that he would put out the flame of Allah, but his dirty plans were dissolved like salt in the water. Thus he was unsuccessful in his aim. Then he went again to Makkah. Then after a long time again came to Gujrat and poisoned the ears of the king of Gujrat and instigated him to issue orders for killing Mahdavi brothers which resulted in the martyrdom of nine brothers. And within four months he himself paid the price of this massacre."[258]

بالغ الشيخ فى عداوة اصحابنا حتى جاء من مكة الى كجرات بنفسه و اتعبها فى انكار هم مريد الاطفاء نور الله بفيه ويابى الله الا ان يتم نوره فانما ع كيده كماينماع الملح فى الماء فلم يحصل مقصوده ثم ذهب الى مكة ثانيات بعد مدة مديدة كتب الى سلطان كجرات ليقتل اخواننا فامتش امره فقتل احد عشر رجلا من اخواننا صابرين فاخذ الله ثارا اخواننا فى مدة اربعة اشهر الى آخره(سراج الابصار معه مقدمه طبع اول ٢٣٤)

Yet at another place he writes:

"I had seen a pamphlet which came from Makkah which is also attributed to Sheik Ali Muttaqi."

رایت رسالة جاء ت من مكة المشرفة المنسوبةالى الشيخ المشتهر بعلى المتقى (سراج الابصار)

"Hadia-e-Mahdavia":

The second source of the opponents was "Hadia-e-Mahdavia". It is better to discuss about the writer first and then about his book as well.

The name of the writer of this book is Mohammed Zaman Khan, known as Abu Rija. He was born in Shahjehanpur in the year 1242. He has written his travelogue under the title "Dastan-e-Jehan.":

"Started first journey from my birthplace, Shahjehanpur at the age of twenty years for the purpose of learning. Came to Kanpur in 1262 in the service of Moulana Shah Salamatullah. Then after three years went to Farukhabad, Barili, Rampur, Koel, Akbarabad, Dholpur, Gawaliar, Jhansi, Dataetri, Sagar, Bhopal, Hoshangabad, Amrawati and via Nanded arrived Hyderabad and settled down there finally."

سفر اول كه از مولد شاهجهان پور در عمر بست سالگى براى طلب علم بخدمت مولانا شاه سلامت الله صاحب مرحوم بطرف كانپور ۱۲۶۲ء واقع شدواز آنجا بعد سه سال فرخ آباد و دهولپور وگواليار و جهانسى ' و دتيا ويٹريو ساگر و بهوپال وهوسنگ آباد و امراوتى وناندیڑ گذركنان به حيدرآباد رسيدم و توطن ورزيدم ۔

Nawab Nasirud Dowlah was the king of Hyderabad, where Zaman Khan came to Hyderabad for the study of Traditions under the guidance of Moulvi Karamat Ali Dehalvi. He got an audience of Nawab Nasirud Dowlah through Ghulam Mohiuddin Khan and Hakim Mohiuddin Ahmed Yar Khan and was able to get a grant of Mansab of Sixty Rupees monthly. According to the author of "Hayat-e-Masih", Nawab Afzalud Dowlah, Heir Apparent, became his pupil for learning Persian and Gulistan. During Nasirud Dowlah's period he was appointed as the principal of Darul Uloom, which post he relinquished after four years.

The reason for his resignation from Darul Uloom had been stated to be the differences between Nawab Mukhtarul Mulk, known as "Sir Salar Jung Bhadur", and Zaman Khan. It is stated that while Zaman Khan was the principal of Darul Uloom, Mukhtarul Mulk, a Shia, wanted to get prepared a separate curriculum for Shiate students of the Darul Uloom which Abu Rija did not obey. Finally Mukhtarul Mulk had withdrawn his proposal only because both Nawab Afzalud Dowlah and Nawab Shamsul Umarah sided with Zaman Khan who were against writing a separate curriculum for the Shia community.

On account of his defeat, Mukhtarul Mulk took revenge by appointing Moulvi Nasrullah Khan and Deputy Nazeer Ahmed as the tutors of Nawab Mahboob Ali Khan, Heir Apparent. But here again Mukhatrul Mulk was defeated on account of Nawab Rafiuddin Khan, Shamsul Umra-e-Sani who did not like new appointments of Nasrullah Khan and Deputy Nazeer Ahmad, instead Zaman Khan was appointed as the tutor of Mahboob Ali Khan against a monthly salary of Rupees one thousand. This generated intense enmity between Mukhtarul Mulk and Zaman Khan, consequently Zaman Khan resigned as principal of Darul Uloom, and established his own

"Mahboobia School" and started imparting education to the students of the New School.

Zaman Khan went on traveling to the Islamic countries in the year 1283 and returned after eleven months and 21 days. After returning from the journey he happened to meet Hazrat Aalam Miyan Saheb, a staunch Mahdavi Preacher of that time in Hyderabad. Zaman Khan wanted to study Mahdiat, therefore requested Aalam Miyan Saheb to provide some books on Mahdiat, thus Aalam Miyan Saheb provided some books along with a pamphlet "Shubhatul Fatawi" also was given to him which was printed in Bangalore in the year 1283 H.

Before meeting Zamana Khan, Hazrat Aalam Miyan sahib had met with eminent persons like Moulvi Abdul Haleem Lukhnavi, Moulana Niyaz Mohammed Badakhshani, Moulvi Mohiuddin Khan Dehalvi, Moulvi Hyder Ali and others. But these scholars avoided discussing about Mahdiat with Aalam Miyan Saheb, because the arguments presented in "Sirajul Absar" have weight against the arguments of "Risalatur Rudd" of Sheik Ali.

It seems, on getting his required books, including "Sirajul Absar", "Kanzul Ammal" and "Shubhatul Fatawi" instead of discussing the issues with Aalim Miyasn Saheb, Zaman Khan decided to study the books minutely, for that reason he convinced Mukhtarul Mulk and got issued orders of exile of Aalim Miyan Saheb. The covert plan of Mukhtarul Mulk, was to make Zaman Khan busy in writing against Mahdavis with an ulterior motive of creating enmity between Sunnis and Mahdavis. Thus Mukhtarul Mulk again befriended Zaman Khan in this respect cunningly. But actually in this way he was taking revenge from Zaman Khan since he did not obey his orders to write a separate curriculum for the Sheite students who were studying in Darul Uloom.

On orders of the exile, Aalam Miyan left Hyderabad and reached Pindyal. But after some days he returned to Hyderabad and submitted a petition against Mukhtarul Mulk to the Madarul Muham, stating that he had, without any legal problem, issued orders for his exile. When this petition was sent for remarks to Muktarul Mulk, who, in turn, asked Miyan Syed Aalam to give a written understanding that he would never meet with Zaman Khan. On that advice, Aalam Miyan wrote that letter and handed over to Mukhtarul Mulk, on which he issued orders for canceling orders of Aalam Miyan's Exile.

Soon after obtaining the letter from Aalam Miyan sahib, Zaman Khan's Hadia-e-Mahdavia was published and a copy was sent to Aalam Miyan Saheb. Thus it opened a Pandora's box. Had Mukhtarul Mulk not helped Zaman Khan in publishing "Hadia-e-Mahdavia" there would have been no reason for the tussle between Mahdavis and Sunnis. This was a clear game of Mukhtarul Mulk who wanted to take revenge against Zamaan Khan by disrupting the cordial relationship between the two communities. As a matter of fact Mukhtarul Mulk was taking revenge from Zaman Khan and played this dirty game. Thus enmity grown between Mahdvis and Zaman Khan which resulted in Zaman Khan's murder at the hands of Hzt. Abji Miyan Saheb Shaheed (Rh) of Musheerabad.

(NOTE: Hzt.Abji Miyan Shaheed(Rh):

It seems necessary to give details about Hzt. Syed Mohammed Abji Miyan Saheb Shaheed

(Rh) of Musheerabad who took the strong step to kill Zaman Khan, the writer of "Hadia-e-Mahdavia" which is against Imamana (As) and Mahdavis:

Hazrat Abji Miyan Shaheed (Rh) comes from a dignified noble family of saadath known as Mujtahid-e-Giroh of Musheerabad. Seventh in succession to Hazrat Bandagi Miyan Shah Qasim Rh. He was born on 8th Safarul Muzzaffer 1274 H. His father Hzt. Syed Noor Mohammed alias Namkeen Baday Miyan (Rh) died in 1276 H. (Just after two years of his birth), who was a Mansabdaar under Mukhtarul Mulk Sir Salar Jung Bahadur. Hzt. Abji Miyan was 6 feet tall, with broad shoulder and handsome with clear white complexion.

After his Bismillah he was taught and groomed under the guidance of his elders. He had the zeal to learn Arabic and Persian languages in which our Faith is written. Therefore he was sent to Syed Shah Mohammed Hussain Qadri, alias Sheereen Sukhan, in 1285, at the age of eleven. He was the pupil among the noble personalities like Ameerul Hind Walah Jah, Nawab Mohammed Ghous Khan and Nawab Aziz Jung of Hyderabad.

He learned to the extent he could understand the difference between the faiths of Ahl-e-Sunnat and Mahdiat. He had cultivated the taste of poetry and started writing some poems too. He had the zeal to learn the art of soldiery and became perfect in dagger and sword wielding under the guidance of Munawer Khan, Ghazi, of Chanchalguda battle 1238 H. and became perfect in dagger wielding.

Suddenly at that time the atmosphere of Hyderabad became very thick with the un-wanted publication of "Hadia-e-Mahdavia" in 1287 H., a derogatory book written by Abu Rija Zaman Khan, the teacher of Mahboob Ali Khan Sixth Nizam of Hyderabad.

The book was purposely got written, published and distributed under instigation by Mukhtarul Mulk, a Shia noble of Hyderabad against our Faith and against Imamana (As), just to disrupt the cordial relationship between Sunnis and Mahdavis of Hyderabad.

Hzt. Abji Miyan could not digest it after reading this distorted and highly biased book, against our Faith and ultimately came to conclusion to finish that Abu Rija, who dared to write against Imamana (As) in a very filthy language. Thus, Hzt. Abji Miyan, a perfect and staunch Mahdavi, a young man of just seventeen years, decided to avenge the honor of Mahdavis by killing Abu Rija.

In order to avenge, Hzt Abji Miyan, very prudently and schematically, joined the Mahboobia School run by Abu Rija Zaman Khan near Shah Ali Banda in 1292 H. just to educate himself with the environment available in the school. The school was running in full swing where about a hundred students, including himself, were engaged in studying under Abu Rija Zaman Khan.

He then wrote to several Religious Scholars and authorities and asked their Fatwahs against a person who blatantly and blasphemously wrote against the traditions of the Holy Prophet (Slm) regarding the advent of Imam Mahdi (As) and got some Fatwahs against that Zaman Khan and made up his mind to finish the mischief monger once for all so that it become a warning against those who inadvertently, one way or the other, try to disrupt the peace of mind in the Mahdavia Community.

Thus with a firm intention of mind and thought , Abji Miyan (Rh), with a sublime humility and very ceremoniously visited his mentor's shrine of Hzt. Shah Qasim (Rh) in the dead dark night of 6th Zil Hajja 1292/ 3rd. January 1886 and demanded ultimate decision for his venture in the cause of his faith and to offer his head in propagation of the cause and name of Imamana Mahdi-e-Maood Alaihis Salaam .

He became satisfied and went to his Murshid in the morning and presented his Qur'an to him as a gift, distributed some sweets among the children and came to his mother and asked her benevolence and blessings for his decisive action what he was going to take that day. He was clad himself with a best clothing with an onion colored turban on the head, by folding a 14 inch long dagger in a Roomal on his shoulders, started his final journey after offering Asr prayer, went towards Shah Ali Banda his final destination. He reached the Masjid (presently bearing No.20-6-321) near Zaman Khan's School and offered his Maghrib prayer.

Abu Rija Zaman Khan used to visit Nawab Mahboob Ali Khan every evening at Purani Haveli, to teach him and then come to the Masjid for Isha prayer and after reading some verses from the Qur'an used to go to his house for the dinner. That night he was reading the verse of Soora-e-Aaraf (7) Verse No. 103:

"Summa Ba'asna Mim Ba'dihim Moosa, be aayatina ila Firauna wa Malayehi Fa zalamoo biha Fanzur Kaifa Kana Aaqibatul Mufsideen". (7:103). Its translation:

After (those messengers,) we sent Moses with our signs to Pharaoh and his people, but they transgressed. Note the consequences for the wicked. (submission.org)

When Zaman Khan was busy in reading the Qur'an, Hzt. Abji Miyan entered the Masjid of Zaman Khan and pierced the dagger first at his shah rug (Jugglery vein), then on his head and the third on his left side of chest. Thus Zaman Khan was finished and his blood stains dropped on that verse 103 of Soora-e-Aaraf. These blood stains were seen and certified both by Sunni and Mahdavi scholars to have been dropped on that line.

A big hue and cry started that Zaman Khan was murdered. Zaman Khan's younger brother, Masihus Zaman Khan came rushing at the spot along with 62 students of Zaman Khan. Hzt. Abji Miyan threw his dagger in front of the gathering and informed them that "I had accomplished my mission, do you what you want to do and presented himself boldly to them".

Rustum Ali Khan Kotwal and Mirza Vali Baig of Police department came and took away Hzt. Abji Miyan with them, first brought to the Rikab Gunj Police Station, then transferred to Khana Bagh of Salar Jung known as Bara Dari, where the Salar Jung Museum stands now.

After burial of Zaman Khan at his Masjid on 9th.Safar 1292 H. a public gathering at Charminar started going towards Chanchalguda with the words "Revenge, Revenge". Nawab Mukhtarul Mulk pacified the crowd and tried to stop but failed. The crowd crossed Gulzar House and reached Purani Haveli and Masjid-e-Shah Lagan. In order to stop the crowd, the Government ordered to close the Dabeerpura Door. Again Mukhtarul Mulk pacified the crowd not to take Law and Order in their hands since Government is investigating the Reason and Cause of this murder. But the crowd passed with deaf ear and tried to open the Dabeerpura door. Meanwhile Mahdavis of Chanchalguda came out of their houses and gathered near the Takia of Shah Ibadullah for defense.

When the news of gathering of Mahdavis reached to Mukhtarul Mulk, he conveyed the message to Mahdavis that the Government had taken measures to curb the onslaught of Sunni crowd, therefore be satisfied and do not initiate any confrontation. On the other hand he ordered the Sikh Regiment to shoot on sight if anyone crosses the Dabeerpura Door. Two unfortunate youngsters crying "Deen Deen" crossed the door and were shot down by the Sikh Regiment. Seeing the bodies of these men, the crowd ran away from the sight. Those two were buried near the corner of Purani Havili where now wooden utensils are being sold.

Mukhtarul Mulk took another drastic action by dismissing Mahdavi Policemen and Mahdavi Jamedars of the Police Department and army, just to please the crowd. Then he issued orders on the 5th. Muharram 1293 to Mahdavi Jagirdars and officers and generally to Mahdavis to exile beyond the limits of the dominion. With this drastic order Mahdavis had to migrate to the adjacent states, for the second time, particularly to Kurnool and Mysore.

Then he appointed Moulvi Akbar Ali Khan (Sabahat Jung) and Abul Fazal Syed Mahmood, Naazim-e-Nazm-e- Jamiat for investigating the issue with remaining Mahdavis who had yet to exile. After completion of the investigation they prepared a report by bursting and twisting the facts submitted to Government on First of Saferul Muzaffer 1293 H.

When Hzt. Abji Miyan, a young man of 17 years, was asked to say who had instigated him to take such drastic step. He frankly told that it was his own decision, because Zaman Khan had written a very derogatory book against our faith and particularly against our Imamana Alaihis Salaam. The book instigated me when read, then only I decided to kill this man whose absurdity, foolishness and derogatory remarks against our faith provoked and instigated me to teach him a lesson and also it is a warning to others who are trying to defame and vilify our faith and Imamana (As). Had I been instigated by someone else I would not have surrendered myself so easily but I would have run away to take shelter of those who had instigated me. This blunt and fair reply dumbfounded the investigators and they could not harass others in this personal case except they questioned Aalam Miyan Saheb for his writing that "this book-Hadia- would take the life of the writer some day", and for that he was decreed for permanent exile and sent behind the bars at Jagtial Court.

The report went to Darul Quzza and a panel of seven Mufties was appointed to declare their judgment in the shape of a fatwa under the chairmanship of Mufti Mir Vilayet Ali, Shaher Panah. They issued a fatwa to murder Hzt. Abji Miyan in Revenge (Khisas).

Thus under the decree of Fatwah, Hzt. Abji Miyan was brought to a spot in between Muslim Jung Bridge and Purana Pul, and placed him face down under a Gorakh Amli tree abetting Moosa Nadi on the afternoon of the 14th. Safarul Muzaffer 1293 and as per orders the Jallad cut his head. After this tyrannical action they buried the body of the Martyr near the tree which is no more now.

But Mahdavis started their agitation to get the body of the martyr which took three days and finally Mukhtarul Mulk agreed to hand over the body to just four Mahdavis with instructions to dig the grave and take out the body during night time and take it where they want to take without making any hue and cry.

Accordingly on 17th. Safaerul Muzaffer 1293, Hussain Khan Jamadar and three Mahdavis dug out the grave and brought the body from the grave and placed it on a Cot. They were amazed to see the face of the martyr which was as fresh as if martyred the same day and a fragrance spread all around the atmosphere. They started towards Musheerabad :

"Main Akela hi chala tha Janib-e-Manzil Magar ---- Log sath hothey gaye aur karavan Banta gaya.

"I started my journey alone towards my destination--- But people joined me and a big caravan emerged."

By the time they reached thousands gathered through the way and reached Musheerabad Hazeera. A grave was dug at the northern portion of Hzt Shah Qasim's Masoleum and was buried. A white Washed big grave still visible from far and near and draws attention of every Mahdavi visitor that it was Hzt. Abji Miyan who died for the cause of Mahdiat more than 142 years ago and whose Martyrdom drove Mahdavis on a Second Exile (First was after the Chanchal Guda Battle in 1238 H.)

The family of the martyr came to Channapatna. One lady among them was my grandmother, Chandkhan Saheba Bibi (Rh), niece of the martyr, daughter of martyr's elder brother Hzt. Syed Qasim alias Shah Saheb Miyan (Rh). She was married to my grandfather Hzt. Syed Roshan Munawer (Rh). My father carried the name of Martyr's brother, Hzt. Syed Qasim, father of my grandmother.

Once she came to Hyderabad in 1938, at her age 85, had visited Musheerabad Hazeerah and profusely wept at the grave of the martyr and then moved to the third grave of her father on the left side then, moved southward to the grave of her grandfather, and finally offered flowers to all the graves of her relatives which are in three lines on the left side of the Martyr. And declared that her seven generations are absolved from the Hellfire on account of the martyrdom of her uncle Hzt Abji Miyan Shaheed. (Wallahu Alam Bis Sawab)

After a long time the migrated Mahdavis returned to their homes and four localities became known as Mahdavi localities: They are Musheerabad, Kachi Guda, Begum Bazar and Chanchalguda. Yet another martyr, Bahadur Yar Jung rests in Musheerabad, who was a political victim and was martyred in the night of the 4th. Rajjabul Murajjab 1364 H/ 1944 in a covert plan hatched in the house of his thick friend Hashim Yar Jung, where he was poisoned and died spontaneously, was forced to be buried without Post Martem or Investigation under the Dictatorial orders of Mir Osman Ali Khan, last king of Hyderabad, who too died in 1967 and was buried in Judi Masjid, Sher Gate, King Koti. --- Translator.)

Here Mukhtarul Mulk's diplomacy played weell. He was playing a double trick. At one time he was helping Zaman Khan to write the book against Mahdavis to create tussle between Sunnis and Mahdavis and on the other hand he was trying to entangle Zaman Khan in various difficulties because he did not obey his orders for writing a separate Curriculum for Sheites. Thus Zaman Khan was entrapped, which he did not realize. He informed through a letter to Mukhtarul Mulk that he had completed the book under the name and title "Hadia-e-Mahdavia" in 1285, which was published in 1287 at Kanpur.

Those books which were received from Aalam Miyan Saheb were returned to Nawab Junaid Khan Jamadar for handing over to Hafiz Miyan, brother of Alam Miyan Saheb, who was out of Hyderabad on orders of his Exile. It was a period in which Mukhtarul Mulk was all in all in Hyderabad. He could have averted this tussle between the two communities, instead he, in order to take revenge, instigated Zaman Khan to write against Mahdavis. After all he was a Shia, he just wanted to entangle Zaman Khan in a "River of no return"situation that created hardship to Zaman Khan's presence in Hyderabad. Thus he took revenge of his defeat regarding Shiete Curriculum and Zaman Khan was no more.

After five years of the book's publication, Zaman Khan was murdered in 1292. And Aalam Miyan sahib was blamed for this murder, because some time back it is said that Aalam Miyan Saheb had prophesied in a pamphlet that "as a revenge for writing against Imamana (As) and Mahdavis, Zaman Khan would be killed", which came true. On this remark, Aalam Miyan was called for to testify his writing. He wrote his statement in a pamphlet as below:

"Although I have no knowledge about this murder by a young Mahdavi, I was called by Nawab Salar Jung to testify before some scholars at the Darul Qazat. They thought that this Faqeer had instigated that boy (Abji Miyan Saheb aged 17 years). When I wanted to go to meet them, my people opposed to my appearance before the Darul Qazat. But I convinced my people if I would not go they would catch me for non appearance and the entire blame would go on me. On which my people left me. I was questioned about the murder by the scholars in the Darul Qazat, Aalam Miyan Saheb answered:

" When they questioned me "I asked them to point out who was the Complainant"?. They told that they were all the complainants. Then they referred to that pamphlet in which Aalam Miyan Saheb had opined "under the dictates of Sharia that one day Zaman Khan would be murdered". And asked why he had written that? I answered by just mentioning Holy Prophet's Sharia. And it was a miracle that it came true and proved our Imamana (As) as the Promised Mahdi (As). With that, they issued orders for my confinement, coupled with permanent Exile from the city and I was sent to Jagtial Fort."

The bold and fearless answer given by Aalam Miyan Saheb proved illegality of the decree issued by the Durul Qazat against Aalam Miyan Saheb. However after serving a confinement he was released in Rajjab 1309 and wrote all these episodes in "Mai'yar-e-Sidq wo Kizb" and died in 1311 H.

It is my firtm desire to give a befitting reply to Zaman Khan's book "Hadia-e-Mahdavia" through Muqaddama-e-Sirajul Absar".(Declared Allama Bsazmi (Rh).

3. Tanbihul Ghafeleen":

One more source for the opponents was Mullah Qari's "Tanbihul Ghafeleen" which furnishes some cooked up vulgarities about the characteristics of Mahdavis which is so vulgar that could not be presented in this book. But Editor of Nigar had taken some sexual taste out of this vulgarity and to depict his enmity against Mahdavis, he had recorded those cooked up material to malign mahdavis.

But the fact is that who was the real writer of "Tanbihul Ghafeleen" is not clear. Just one person, Najmul Ghani, author of "Mazahebul Islam" had referred it in his book. According to him Mulla Ali Qari was the writer of this controversial book who had recorded a cooked up episode of an opponent of Mahdavis. This is a concocted and nothing but malicious and unfounded blame against Mahdavis. However Mulla Ali Qari's and Najmul Ghani's contemporaries who were not Mahdavis had still praised piety and abstinence of Mahdavis.

Mulla Ali Qari had written about "Idrees-e-Roomi" and "Mahdi-e-Maghribi" which is the translation of Sheik Ali Muttaqi's "Risalatur Rudd".

1. **"Mahdi Maghribi"** Mulla Ali Qari had written under the chapter Mahdi in the year 965 H. that a noble Syed had proclaimed his Mahdiat in the region of Western India. His reputation still spread in the West to the extent of four Manzil which was under his control. (Mazaheb-e-Islam) is a translation of Rudd.

2. **Idrees-e-Roomi:** Mulla Ali Qari had written in his Pamphlet in the year 965 under the chapter Mahdi that a person who is called Idrees had proclaimed his Mahdiat in the period of Sultan Ba Yazid. He had 80 disciples. One day he called his disciples that he had inspiration that he is the promised Mahdi. Therefore you concentrate on this inspiration and let me know about your inspiration. His disciples came after a long period to him and precariously told that what he had told was correct. Thus it was brought to the notice of the Sultan who was a pious man and told them to adopt it. After some days the Sultan concentrated and found that it was not an inspiration from Allah, but it was from Satan. This narrative also is a translation of Rudd (Vide "Sirajul Absar").

With a difference that Najmul Ghani wrote Idrees in place of Owais.

According to the author of "Mazaheb-e-Islam" if "Tanbihul Ghafeleen" is written by Mulla Ali Qari, then the answer for this narrative is that it was a creation of an opponent who wrote nothing but fabricated facts against Mahdavis. It is a fact that his contemporaries who were not Mahdavis, still they had accepted piety and abstinence of mahdavis and reject that book as a false propagandas against Mahdavis.

Even Sheik Ali had written in his "Kanzul Ammal" that he had been in the company of Mahdavis and then he wrote "Risala-e-Al Burhan" and through this he had even recognized the piety and abstinence of Mahdavis. Mullah Abdul Qader Badayuni, a contemporary of Sheik Ali Muttaqi, had written about Mahdavis that:

جمعی را ازین سلسله ملازمت کرده ام و اخلاق رضیه و
اوصاف مرضیه ایشان رادر فقرو فنا به مرتبهٔ عالی دیده و
بیان قرآن و اشارات آن و دقایق حقائق و لطائف معارف
بے کسب علوم رسمی چنان شنیده ام که اگر خواهند
مجملے از آنها در قید کتاب آرند تذکرة الاولیائے
دیگر باید نوشت۔

"I lived with many persons of Mahdavia Sect. Their pleasant manners and their captivating attributes regarding their Trust in God and forbearance in hunger and poverty were heart touching. Although they were not well versed in formal education, yet their commentary of Qur'an and interpretation of Divine secrets I have heard so many times from them that if I start compiling a book, then it would become another "Tazkeratul Aouliah."

This writing certifies that Mahdavis of his period were Godlimen and mystics among whom he lived.

On further investigations, it comes to light that Mullah Ali Qari does not belong to India, still he had referred to a cooked up vulgar episode and did not mention from where he got that news about Mahdavis. It is later on known that he was born in Herat (Afghanistan) and went to Makkah and became the pupil of Ibn Hajr Makki and started writing, Just to malign Mahdavis, under instructions by his teacher, invented a vulgar episode to curb propagation of our Faith in Khurasan.

Mulla Ali Qari werote sa false snd unfounded narrative just to malign Mahdavis. In this connection a narrative is presented from Tabri with reference to Abi Bakrah and Mugheera Bin Shoba:

كانا بالبصرة وكانا متجاورين بينهما طريق وكان فى
مشربتين متقابلتين لهما فى داريهما فى كل واحدة
منهما كوة مقابلة الاخرى فاجتمع الى ابى بكرة
نفر يتحدثون فى مشربته فهبت ريح ففتحت باب الكوة
فقام ابوبكرة ليصفقه فبصر بالمغيرة وقد فتحت الريح
باب كوة مشربته وهو بين رجلى امرأة فقال للنفر قوموافا
نظروا وافقا موافنظروا وائم قال اشهد واقالوا و ومن

"Hzt. Abi Bakrah and Mugheerah bin Shoba were in Basrah and were neighbors. They had a single route who were living in front of each other having a single window for both. Some persons came to Abi Bakrah and were busy in talking. Suddenly the door of the window was opened by air. He saw Mugheerah was in between the legs of a woman. Abi Bakrah told persons to see and be a witness. Persons inquired who was that woman. She was Umm-e-Jameel, daughter of Uqum. She was from the Bani Aamir tribe who used to come to Mugheerah every now and then. Also she used to visit nobles. Some woman had that fashion. When she left, Mugheera wanted to lead the prayer, persons stopped him from leading. Then this narrative was brought to the notice of Omer Bin Al Khattab (Rz)".

هذه قال ام جميل ابنة الا فقم و كانت ام جميل احدى
بنى عامر بن صعصعة و كانت غاشية للمغيرة و تغشى
الامراء والاشراف و كان بعض النساء يفعلن ذلك
فى زمانها فقالوا انما راين اعجازا و لا ندرى ماالوجه
ثم انهم صمموا حين قامت فلما خرج المغيرة الى
الصلاة حال ابوبكرة بينه وبين الصلاة وقال لا تصل
بنا فكتبوا الى عمر بذلك

This episode had been narrated by Sheik Ali Muttaaqi in his "Kanzul Ammal". If this episode does not malign Islam, then how Mulla Ali Qari's episode could malign Mahdavis. If such vulgar episode was written in Mahdavi Books how much hue and cry would have been raised against Mahdavis?

Wedding Rituals of Lukhnow:

It is strange that the Editor of Nigar, Niyaz Fatehpuri had presented a vulgar episode of Mulla Ali Qari by stating that Mahdavis used to keep a hole in their huts to view others anytime just to malign Mahdavis. Mirza Mohammed Hasan Qateel Lukhnavi (died 1222 H.) had written "Haft Tamasha-e-Qateel" in Persian. The Sixth Entertainment under the title "Sixth entertainment is one of the rituals of Muslims of India". He had written about the wedding rituals that:

"The night when the bride and the bridegroom are together........., women used to stand behind a curtain and by tearing the curtain used to view what was happening among both:"

شبى كه داماد عروس رابه كنار گرفته به كشتى اولين
پردازد نيز زنان عقب پرده استاده شوند و چادر پرده را
شگافته حال هر دو رابه غور بينند

When such vulgar rituals do not malign Islam, since Islam never tolerated such vulgarity like that. Thus how Mulla Ali Qari's episode would affect Mahdavis.

Whether Lukhnow's episode is accepted by Muslims or not, but it was enjoyed by the Fatehpuris and the Lukhnowis!!!

There are still many opponents, among them like, Rahman Ali author of "Tazkeratul Ulema", Najmul Ghani Rampuri, author of "Mazaheb-e-Islam"; Rafique Dilaweri, author of "A'emmai-e-Tilbees" who had written just by referring "Hadia-e-Mahdavia" or Niyaz Fathepuris' writings in "Nigar"of February 1935. But they have failed to scrutinize this vulgar episode written by Mulla Ali Qari or as written in "Mazaheb-e-Islam" which has nothing to do with Mahdavia literature nor they had corrected or inquired from any Mahdavi.

4."Nuzhatul Khawathir:"

Syed Abdul Hai, director of Nadwatul Ulema, Lukhnow had written this book in Arabic in which he had written about tenth Century's scholars and while writing about Imamana (As) and Mahdavia Faith, he had mostly referred to "Hadia-e Mahdavia" as if there were no books available about us. Had he read about those historians of India who had painstakingly written about Mahdavis and Imamana (As); like "Tabkhat-e-Akbari, Najatur Rasheed, Mu'asir-e-Rahimi, Tuhfatul Kiram, Juanpur Nama and Tazkeratul Waasileen" which were available in every library or with any scholar of repute. It means to say that they had written without scrutinizing the facts from other sources, as had been mentioned above, it only shows his prejudice against Mahdavis, but he is such a peculiar writer who does not take pains to refer and research before blaming on any person or any Sect.

Margoleouth had written even from England about Mahdavis with reference to "Muntakhabat-e-Tawareekh"; it is strange that the author of "Nuzhatul Khawathir", an Indian, had written from Lukhnow and never referred "Najathur Rashed" or any other book on Mahdavis.

In order to write about Mahdavis by referring only "Hadia-e-Mahdvia" is just like referring the book "Hidayetul Muslimeen" written by a Christian Priest Imaduddin who wrote about Islam; or by referring to Dr. Tusdal's Book "Sources of the Qur'an" who started to write on facts about the Qur'an.

Just see the research ability of the Author of "Nuzhatul Khawathir" that he had written father's name of Imamana (As) as being "Yousuful Juanpuri" How amazing!!! That this new name was neither available in Mahdavi or non Mahdavi literature. We have to ask him to show his source of information.

Other Sources:

A. Even after the publication of "Hadia-e-Mahdavia" many Non-Mahdavi writers have written about Mahdavis and Imamana based on real facts to a great extent. Among them is one Khaja Ibadullah Akhter Amratsiri, who had written a chapter on" Syed Mohammed Juanpuri (AS)" in his book "Mashaahir-e-Islam." Another being Moulana Abul Kalam Azad who had written "Tazkerah" in which he had subscribed his worthwhile research work on Imamana (As) and about Imamana's second generation disciples in a plausible and admirable manner and his peculiar style. Third is Saheb-e-Mithialvi who through his "Paisa" Newspaper of Lahore, on 30th May 1940 and 6th. June 1940 wrote about "Hazrat Syed Mohammed Juanpuri (As)" in a very appreciable and convincing manner. We appreciate these writers who had painstakingly studied and referred sources and jotted down their impressions about our Faith and Imamana (As)

As against these publications, important books and Newspaper of Lahore, some writers had deliberately written impudently against the descendants of Imamana (As). For example: Nazeerul Haq author of "kitabul Islam" who had mentioned some signs about Imam Mahdi (As) and maintained about a rare and unimaginable sign which, he says, should be found on a person who claimed to be Mahdi. According to his ill-found knowledge that Sign seems to be very peculiar and he deliberately states that: "Mahdi's tongue should have stammering defect, on account of which, whenever he felt difficulty in speaking, then he would strike his knees with his hands." When he was asked to provide the source of such peculiar sign, he failed to provide the source and faded away.

There is no tradition which presented this absurd sign of Stammering and striking hands on the knees. However, this ridiculous sign had nothing to do with such a condition for Mahdiat, because Characters are the best signs of Mahdiath, since in the case of the holy Prophet (Slm), his venerable Characters alone became the proof for his Nabuwwat. Apart from the characters, as far as other signs are concerned according to the traditions in Sihah and other famous books of the Traditions, they were fully applied and found on the person of Imamana (As).

1. The Holy Prophet's prophecy that Mahdi (As) shall be from my progeny is the most cocrete proof of Imamana's Mahdiat. Since it had been proved many a time that Imamana (As) was from the genealogy of Imam Moosa Kazim (Rz) coming from the line of Ahl-e-Bait (Rz).

2. His father's name was Abdullah, and mother's name was Aamina as prophesied by the holy Prophet (Slm), this fact became true from the writings of Juanpur Nama, by a non Mahdavi writer and also by other prominent non Mahdavi writers.

3. He would be from the genealogy of Imam Hasan (Rz). It was already proved from Juanpur Nama that mother of Imamana (As) belonged to Imam Hasan's genealogy. Thus from the mother's side he belonged to Imam Hasan's genealogy. Apart from this, he comes directly from Imam Moosa Kazim (Rz) who is the descendant of Imam Baqer (Rz) and Imam Baqer's mother Fatima (Rz) was the daughter of Imam Hasan (Rz). As per Jami who reported in "Shawahedul Nabuwwat" that: His patronymic name was Jafer and his epithet was Baqer (Rz)....... his mother was Fatima (Rz), daughter of Imam Hasan Ibn Ali (Rz).

4. Imamana (As) having broad forehead and straight nose. That had been proved from the writings of both Mahdavi and non Mahdavi literature.

5. Would fill up with peace and tranquility in the world. Wherever his followers were residing there was a permanent peace and order. Now to say that the entire world would be in peace and tranquility, such tranquility was not possible even during the period of " Rahmatul Lil Alameen" then how could it be possible for Imamana (As) to fill the whole world with peace and tranquility when he did not acquire a worldly empire as the Holy Prophet (Slm) acquired?

6. To emerge as Mahdi (As) in his fortieth year was also proved through Imamana's record of migration which he undertook under the Commands of Allah at his age 40 and invited public openly towards following the Holy Qur'an and the Shariat-e-Mustafavi (Slm) and himself correctly was toeing the footsteps of the Holy Prophet (Slm).

Author of "Kitabul Islam" had stated that Mahdi (As) would conquer Qustuntunia, whereas no tradition was presented from any authentic books of Traditions about it. Further details shall be provided in chapter four.

5. Erroneous Assumptions of Author of Shiraz-e-Hind, Juanpur:

In 1963 a book under the title "Tareekh-e-Shiraz-e-Hind" was published in which under the chapter "Hazrat Maqdoom Syed Mohammed Juanpuri (As)" particulars of Imamana (As) had been written. The inaccuracies mentioned in it are being refuted hereunder:

A. Author of "Shiraz-e-Hind" had written the word "Maqdoom" along with the name of Imamana (As). But no book mentions "Maqdoom" along with Imamana's name so far either

Mahdavia or Non Mahdavia literature. As against this, Khairudduin Mohammed Allahbadi, author of "Juanpur Nama" had used the words "Khaja" and "Miranjeo" which were in usage in Juanpur for Imamana (AS).

B. Author of "Tareekh-e-Juanpur" had maintained that Imamana (As) had taken the oath of allegiance on the hands of Sheik Daniyal at page 653. Whereas there is no evidence regarding such an allegiance. However our books certify that in his childhood Imamana (As) was under the care of Sheik Daniyal (Rh) for his elementary education. And at a later stage Sheik Daniyal (Rh) himself had taken oath of allegiance on the hands of Imamana (As) as mentioned in "Moulood" of Miyan Abdul Rahman (Rh). Opponents claim that Imamana (As) was the disciple of Sheik Daniyal (Rh). It is an allegation which is just like that the Holy Prophet (Slm) even before his proclamation of Nabuwwat, had obtained religious teachings from a Jew priest from Syria named Buheera, when he visited Syria on behalf of Bibi Khudaija (Rz) to sell her merchandise.

C. The same author at page 677 maintained that Imamana (As) had just proclaimed himself to be Mahdi (As) and not as the Promised Mahdi (As). "Aqeedai-e-Shariefa" was the authentic and approved book by all the companions of Imamana (As) which was written within ten years from the demise of Imamana (As) which maintains that:

"And those who based their argument on the tradition that Mahdi (As) would fill the entire Earth with peace and tranquility against its tyranny and oppression and all the inhabitants of the world would accept him. Thus he answered that all faithful had accepted him (as the Promised Mahdi (As) and obeyed him."

وآں کسانی کہ این حدیث راپیش حجت آوردند کہ یملاء الارض قسطا وعد لاکماملئت جوراو ظلما یعنی ھمہ عالم مھدی راایمان آرند و اطاعت کنند جواب فرمودند کہ ھمہ مومنان ایمان آوردند واطاعت کردند (عقیدہ شریفہ)

The tradition "Yamlaul Arz" refers to Mahdi (As) alone. The opponents' presentation of this tradition and Imamana's clarification in this regard proves that he had proclaimed as the "Promised Mahdi (As)" and never as a simple "Mahdi". And this is a fact that the Indian Historians had also accepted that Imamana (As) had proclaimed himself to be the "Promised Mahdi (As)".

D. The said author at page 687 while referring to Shah Valiullah's name, he had written that if Imamana's proclamation is accepted, it would be a matter of astonishment. But the author did not mention the name of the book in which Shah Valiullah ever had said such a baseless remark in any of his writings. However, Shah Abdul Aziz, son of Shah Valiullah, had written about Imamana's proclamation in these befitting words:

"Mir Syed Mohammed Juanpuri (As) had proclaimed his Mahdiat with full force in India."

میر سید محمو جونپوری در ھندوستان بیانگ بلند ادعائ مھدیت نمود

The words "Full force" determine no ambiguity in Imamana's proclamation, then why should there be any sort of astonishment as mentioned above said to have been told by his father.

E. The said author had stated on page 687 that Imamana (As) at the time of his demise had declined to be the Mahdi. And in this regard, he has submitted what Mulla Abdul Qader had narrated about a Mughal of Sar-e-Hind who said that when Imamana (As) at his last moments had declined his Mahdiat by telling even that he was not the Mahdi.

It may be pointed out that the year of birth of Badayuni was 947 H., 37 years after the demise of Imamana (As) and he had gone to Sar-e-Hind in 980 H. at his age 33. At the time of Imamana's death there were 313 companions. None of those 313 companions had ever told about such denial, then how could an opponent's lone statement could become a denial of Mahdiat by Imamana (As)? Particularly when the antecedents of that Mughal were not known as to who was he and what was his age and for what purpose he had visited Farrah from Sar-e-Hind? In the absence of these fundamental questions, this statement should be taken simply as fabricated, malicious and merely a white lie. In this connection A. S. Ansari had reported with reference to a book of Ishtiaq Hussain: which reports about that Mughal in these words:

"He, however, survived the ordeal and lived to a ripe old age of 94 years. He died thirty eight years later in 993 H. (Thus, when Imamana (As) passed away he was just 11 years old (he died at his age 94 in 993. It means he was born in 899 H. Hence he was of 11 years in 910 H when Imamana (As) passed away. Thus on what Sharai basis a minor's statement, if at all he had utterred, could become authentic? In these doubtful circumstances the Mughal's fabricated and false statement is just nothing but a white lie. And it is also doubtful that a caliber like Mullah Abdul Qader would have reported this unreliable narrative, seems against his wisdom to rely on such fabricated lone statement. Since that bare statement could not be verified from any reliable source?

(And it is a fact that Badayuni who lived with so many Godlimen of Mahdavia Community for so many years and praised their charming manners and loving attributes, how could he report such a false and fabricated thing about Imamana (As) to whom he had praised in his books as the most trustworthy Mystic of that age!!! It is just unimaginable that he had written such a derogatorty remark against Imamana(As)or it may be that his book might have been fabricated by the enemies of our Faith.)

6. Wrong Statement of Anwarul Bari:

Sayeed Ahmed Bijnoori had written "Muqddama-e-Anwarul Bari" in two volumes. One pertains 240 pages which describes about those traditionalists who were the predecessors of "Bukhari". It also discusses about Fiqha-e-Hanafia and interpretation as stated by Imam Abu Hanifa (Rh). The Second contains 300 pages which describe the traditionalists from "Bukhari" to his period. On page 66 of the second volume a description of Sheik Ali Muttaqi Burhanpuri has been given, and on page 169 he has written about Mohammed Bin Taher Gujrati, and had copied the description what Taher Gujrati had stated. On page 171 Sheik Abdullah Khan Niyazi's description had been recorded. With reference to Miyan Abdullah Khan Niyazi, who was a staunch Mahdavi, he had intentionally tried to provide a wrong statement about Miyan Niyazi and Mahdavia Faith. The following are his wrong statements which are baseless hence rejected in limini:

A. On page 166 of the second volume, Imamana's father's name had been written as "Yousuf

Juanpuri" which is wrong as per authentic record of "Juanpur Nama" and other books.

B. On page 172, with reference to "Nuzhatul Khawathir" objections had been raised on the fundamental beliefs of Mahdavia Faith. It is a fact that, on page 325 while he had referred what "Nuzhatul Khawathir" had recorded about Mahdavia Faith with reference to Hadia-e-Mahdavia, but he avoided to give reference of "History of Palanpur", although both books were before him. How deceptive Bijnoori is, while he had referred an opponent's statement from Hadia, he had avoided to write the statement of Mahdavis from "Tareekh-e-Palanpur" in which it is clearly mentioned that "Any statement of Mahdi Juanpuri (As) if found against Qur'an and traditions should be taken as untrue as against Imamana's declaration that "My religion is Qur'an and I follow the Holy Prophet (Slm)."

C. He had sarcastically taunted Moulana Abul Klam Azad by telling: "An Scholar of the present period had written much in favor of Mahdi Juanpuri (As) (2nd. Volume p.171)" And further wrote that: "if some scholars had accepted him as Mahdi (As), should not be taken as authentic; because many scholars of Egypt and eminent Traditionalists like Sheik Ali Muttaqi, an arch rival of Imamana (As) had written rebuttal." How could these be overlooked? Bijnoori should know that the Holy Prophet (Slm) had propagated Islam in Makkah for thirteen years , while a few only had understood Qur'an and accepted it, but many among eminent scholars of that period did not accept Qur'an as the Word of Allah". We have to ask Bijnoori whether he is not overlooking those eminent scholars who did not accept the Qur'an as the word of God?

It is a fact that the standard of education was far greater of the companions of Imamana (As) than that of the opponents. For example "Sirajul Absar" of Miyan Abdul Malik Sujawandi (RH) is far better in its standard than the " Al-Rudd" of Sheik Ali Muttaqi who resided in Makkah for most of his life."

D. Bijnoori had objected on Moulana Abul Kalam Azad at page 171 of his second volume. As regards truthfulness he had presented about Abdullah Khan Niyazi and others, and stated wrongly that those persons have denied the faith at the end. Here Bijnoori had written in the plural form "Hazraat", then he must prove who were the others who were said to have denied the Faith?

"On orders of Saleem Shah, Miyan Sheik Niyazi was being whipped in Biayana, and until he was in his senses these words were on his tongue "Oh Allah keep me steadfast and grant me victory over these infidels." And on account of continuous whipping he became senseless and never denied the faith. As against this basic fact, he had conceded by telling the fact that even after getting traditions from scholars of Arabia and Egypt, Sheik Niyazi came to Gujrat and Deccan and then preferred to accept Mahdavia Faith finally. This is a proof that the standard of Islamic teachings were being imparted in Mahdavia dairahs was so higher and impressive that it was no where available, leave aside Saudi Arabia or Egypt, that is why Miyan Niyazi had accepted Mahdavia Faith after searching truth which was not found even in Arabia and Egypt. This fact Bijnoori himself had admitted.

7. Islamic Studies: Karachi:

Central Islamic Research Bureau, Karachi, issues a Journal in every three months under the title" Islamic Studies". A. S. Ansari had published his Essay under the caption "Sayeed Mohammed Juanpuri (As) and His Movement;" in which he had discussed about Islam,

Imamana Alaihis Salaam and about Mahdavia Faith, but his remarks are full with absurdities, still he thinks it was his research work; for example:

1. On page 42 of the Journal he writes that Taftazani did not even indirectly mention about Mahdi (As). The writer even does not know that Taftazani had written "Sharh-e-Maqasid" in which he states that wherever the word "Leadership/Guidance is used it refers to the advent of Imam Mahdi (As)."

2. Another blame he had lodged on page 42 that the doctrine of Mahdiat is the creation of the Shias. But he had ignored the traditions mentioned in "Tirmizi", "Abu Dawood" and "Ibn Maja". And these are the authentic books of traditions of the Ahl-e-Sunnat. In view of these authentic sources, he had stated that the doctrine of Mahdiat is the creation of Shias tantamount to his lack of knowledge of the fundamentals of Islam. While negating the doctrine of Mahdiat he utters that the murderer of Anti Christ /Dajjal has been accepted by Ahl-e-Sunnat as the Revivalist.

3. On page 42, the so called research scholar states that the date of birth of Imamana (As) had not been found in any of the Mahdavia literature. What sort of bogus research he had conducted. Had he gone through the oldest biography of Imamana (As) "Moulood" of Miyan Abdul Rahman (Rh)? Which states that:

"At the appointed time, on Monday, just after the date of migration of the Holy Prophet of eight hundred and forty seven years the auspicious birth had taken place in the city of Juanpur."

بعد از مدت معین درایں عالم فی یوم الاثنین بعد از حضرت رسالت پناه که هشت صدو چهل و هفت انصرام گشتند در بلده جونپور ....
........تولد مطهر اظهار یافت

From this it is ascertained that Imamana (As) was born on Monday in the year 847 Hijri.

4. Author's standard of research is so outdated that he bases his argument on a person who was born in 957 H. and does not accept the man who was born in 908 H in respect of Imamana's particulars. Miyan Abdul Rahman (h) has written at the beginning in "Moulood" that:

"Mother of Imamana (As) was a chaste lady, pious, devotee, virtuous, immaculate, well behaved, pleasant mannered, selfless worshipper of Allah, ever fasting, enjoining virtue and abhorring evil, well educated, whose glorious name was Bibi Aamina (Rz)"

والدهٔ حضرت میران علیه السلام عفیفه عابده صالحه زاکیه زاهده مخلصه رابعه ساجده صائمه حنیفه کریمه علیمه عظیمه اسمها شریفه بی بی آمنه امام شب خیز و صائم النهار و قائم اللیل بودند (٦)

Thus Imamana's mother's name has been confirmed to be Bibi Aamina (Rz) (as had been prophesied by the Holy Prophet (Slm) that Mahdi's mother's name would be Amina (Rz). In the same manner, name of Imamana's father was Syed Abdullah (Rh), also prophesied by the Holy Prophet (Slm) that Mahdi's father's name would be Abdullah. As mentioned in "Moulood":

"Thus Sheik (Sheik Daniyal (Rh) discovered from a reliable source that Allah had bestowed a son to Miran Syed Abdullah (Rh)."

پس شخص مذکوره در تفحص افتاد، از بعضی مردم خبر یافتند که

Sources favoring Imamana (As)

1. Tuhfatul Kiram and Imamana (As):"

How shameless is he who although had referred the name of the father of Imamana (As) was Syed Khan with reference to "Tuhfatul Kiram", but did not mention what "Tuhfatul Kiram" said about Syed Khan which was a title. These are the words of "Tuhfatul Kiram":

"Syedul Aouliah Syed Mohammed (As), known as Miran Mahdi Ibn Miran Syed Abdullah, known as Syed Khan was directly connected to Imam Moosa Kazim (Rz)."	سيـد الاوليـاء سيد محمد المقلب به ميران مهدى بن مير عبـدالـلـه الـمـعـروف به "سيد خان"كه نسبتش به امام موسىٰ كاظم می پيوند"

2. History of Eliot refers Descenting to Holy Prophet (Slm):

History of an English writer, Elliot, proves that Saadaths had been awarded the title of Khan. This has been mentioned by Elliot with reference to "Tareekh-e-Dawoodi" which is mentioned with reference to Sultan Sikander Lodhi:

"When this (news of the arrival of Sultan Sikander Lodhi) reached to Sultan Hussain Sharkhi, he sent one of his chief nobles Miran Sayyid Khan, as an ambassador to Sultan Sikander who addressed to Miran Sayyid Khan "You are children of the Prophet (on whom be the mercy of God) why do you not teach him (Sultan Husain Sharqi) to be reasonable, since, he will afterwards may have cause to repent?" History of India (By N. M. Elliot) Vol. 1V. When historically it is proved that Syed Khan was the title (and Sikander Lodhi addressed him "You are sons of the Holy Prophet (Slm)" what more proof this unscrupulous and so called research scholar requires to accept that Syed Khan was the title of Imamana's father, and whose actual name was Abdullah?

Another wrong version reported by him that, on account of differences, the people of Farah denied burial of Imamana (As) at Farrah. Whereas according to "Moulood" it is clearly written that:

"Thus residents of Farrah and of Rich (village) held a different view: Farrah people told that our fort is large, hence we bury here. On which people of Rich told that Imamana died at their land therefore they had the right to bury in Rich. On this quarrel, Miran Syed Mahmood (Rz), son of Imamana (As), sent Bandagi Miyan Nizam (Rz) to inform them that it was their right to decide where to bury, therefore both should not fight each other."	درميـان اهـل فـراه ورچ اخـتـلاف برخواست اهـل فـراه گفتند قلعه ، ما كلان است به فراه است بـه فـراه بـريـم و اهل رچ گفتند كه بر زمين ماواصل حق شدند همين جابداريم بعد ه ميـران سيـد مـحـمـود بـنـدگی ميان نظام را فـرسـتـاده گوياندند نبايد كه منازعت كنيد ، ايـن نعمت ماست هر جاكه قابل ماآيد آنجا خواهيم سپرد

From the above version it is clear that both people of Farrah and Rich were trying to bury Imamana (As) at their land (to give credence to their land to be the burial place of Mahdi-e-Akhiruzzaman.) Then how this so called scholar says that people of Farrah denied burial of Imamana (As) at Farrah. Does he understand Persian well? It is on account of jealousy and enmity such filthy unfounded remarks have been written by a so called research scholar!!!

Age of Imamana (As):

On account of fictitious narratives, the author had titled them as one of the narratives of Miyan Abdul Rasheed (Rz) and stated under narrative no. 292 that "Imamana (As) did not know his own age". The original Narratives of Miyan Abdul Rasheed (Rz) had been published which has eight chapters and pertains 64 pages. The unscrupulous author is called upon to show from where he got that Narrative No.292?

The fact is mentioned in "Shawahedul Vilayet" also that: Miyan Yousuf Suheet of Peeran Pattan had noted the date of the advent of Mahdi (As) from a Godliman who was lost in Divine Meditation. When he inquired the age of Imamana (As), it was stated that:

"Miyan Yousuf Suheet inquired the age of Imamana (As) who directed him to inquire from Miyan Abu Baker (Rz), the son-in-law of Imamana (As), who told the age of Imamana (As). To which Miyan Yousuf compared with the date what he wrote from that Godliman and found to be correct."	به حضور معلی عرض کردند که میرانجی عمر خدام چه قدر است آنحضرت فرمود که میان ابوبکر رابه پر سید داماد آنحضرت بودند اوشان عمر مقدار امام الابرار گفتند چونکه برقعه مقابله کنند که هیچ تفاوت نیست ۔

Migration: Prophet's Tradition:

The author had objected on the migration of Imamana (As) from Juanpur. It means to say that he does not know the traditions of the Prophets. "Madarijul Nabuwwat" it states that:

"Thus the Holy Prophet (Slm) keenly inspected the situation and made the decision to migrate, since it was the tradition of the Prophets."	پس آنحضرت از مشاهده، این حال قصد هجرت کرد که سنت انبیاء است سلام الله علیهم اجمعین ۔

Further he states that migration upsets the equilibrium of the society. It seems he is blind even after studying Islamic history and fails to accept as an obligation when it becomes necessary for Muslims to keep their Faith at a time when they cannot follow the tenets of Sharia peacefully, they have to migrate.

Dairah of Sani-e-Mahdi (Rz):

The author has objected in his Essay about the Daiarah of Miran Syed Mahmood (Rz) by telling that legal issues used to be decreed as the Tribal Jirgas of Pakistan deliberate today. From this objection we come to conclude that he is an illiterate who failed to understand the basics of the Society's problems. In this regard author of "At Touzeeh" had reported about Hazrat Omer Ibn Mugheera (Rz):

A. "Narrated that Hazrat Omer (Rz) had whipped a woman for a certain sin she committed. On account of this whipping she aborted. Hzt. Omer (Rz) consulted with the companions who said it was not his fault, since his motive was to punish. But when consulted with Hzt. Ali (Rz), he told that he has taken a false step."	روی ان عمر رضی الله عنه ضرب امراة لجنایة فاسقطت الجنین فشاورة الصحابة رضی الله عنهم فقالوا لاغرم علیک فانک مؤدب وما اردت الا الخیر و علی رضی الله عنه ساکت فلما ساله قال اری علیک الغرة

Now we have to ask the research scholars that whether Hazt. Omer's consultation with companions was an act of toeing the line of Sharia or it was like the procedure of the tribal Jirga of Pakistan?

B. When the case of Mugheera bin Shoba came before Hzt. Omer (Rz), on the basis of differences of a witness he was acquitted. Shah Abdul Aziz had commented on this decree which was based as per Sharia. Here Hzt. Omer (rz) was a judge. We have to ask the scholar what was the legal position of the companions who had gathered there. Had they had the authority to certify or deny the Decree, as had been accepted by Shah Abdul Aziz. It seems the author feels this action was also like that of the Jirga of Pakistan.?

Life in the Mahdavi Dairahs:

The author designates the way of living in a Mahdavi dairah as the joint family system of Hindus. As a matter of fact the system of dairah was based on Qur'anic dictates and traditions. Chapter seven of "Uqudud Durar" states about Mahdavis that:

"Allah shall gather such a group here who would weep like clouds and they would have love in their hearts."

فيجمع اللـه له قوم‌افرغ‌اكفرغ السحاب يولف بين قلوبهم

This is a fact that the companions of the Holy Prophet (Slm) had complete love and affection with each other. And the same trend had been adopted in Mahdavi Dairahs. Imam Ahmed Hunbal (Rz) had written in his "Musnad" that "Mahdi (As) shall distribute equally among people." (And it is a fact that the doctrine of Sawiath, Equal distribution was the system adopted first by Mahdavis as per the dictates of Imamana (As) about which system Imam Abu Hunbal (Rz) had mentioned in his "Musnad" .

Brotherhood Among Migrants and Ansars:

Brotherhood was established by the Holy Prophet (Slm) among the Migrants and the Ansars which had been narrated in "Bukhari" that:

"Ansar Rabi (Rz) had two wives. He told to his brother Muhajir: You look both of them, whichever you select I shall inflict divorce to her and when she completes her probationary period you could marry her".

"Narrated by Ismail Bin Abdullah , having heard from Ibrahim bin Sa'ad that he heard from his father who heard from his grandfather that when the Migrants arrived in Madinah, the Holy Prophet (Slm) established brotherhood among the migrants and the people of Madinah; Abdul Rahman bin Auf (Rz) was the migrant, Asad Bin Rabi (Rz) became his brother. Sa'ad Abdul Rahman told that he was rich among the Ansars. He told to his Muhajir brother that "Whatever I had

حدثنا اسماعيل بن عبدالله قال عدثنى ابراهيم بن سعد عن ابيه عن جده قال لما قدموا المدينه اخى رسول اللـه صلى الله عليه وسلم بين عبدالرحمن و سعد ابن ربيع قال لعبدالرحمن انى اكثر الانصار مالا

with me, I make two portions, one I keep and the other I give it to you. Another Asad Bin Rabi (Rz), Ansar told his Muhajir brother that I have two wives. I told him : You look both of them, whichever you select I shall inflict divorce to her and when she completes her probationary period you could marry her. Hearing this Abdul Rahman told it was not necessary. Allah may bestow upon you His Mercy in your family and wealth."

فـاقسـم مـالی نصفین ولی امراتان فانظرا عجبهما الیک فسـمهـا لی اطلقها فاذا انقضت عدتها فتنر وجها قال بارک الله لک فی اهلک ومالک

A. S. Ansari should point out the depth of fraternity shown above in the Narration which depicts the way of life? If he knew that the same system of life was in vogue in the Dairahs, what would have been his opinion?

12.Opponents of Nabuwwat and Mahdiat:

Author had sarcastically taunted foolishly that Imamana (As) had told that the persons who live in his dairah, they are not only faithfuls, but they might be infidels and even hypocrites, but he failed to mention Imamana's assertion that "Allah would not cause death of any infidel or the hypocrite in his Dairah". Under these circumstances author's taunt is baseless since it was made clear by Imamana (AS) that "No infidel or hypocrite would die in the dairah". It means that even if any one was an infidel or hypocrite he would convert as a perfect Mahdavi and die as a Mahdavi only, because whoever used to enter dairah they used to leave every belongings and come clean having no worldly relations, then the question of living of any infidel or a hypocrite in the Dairah does not arise, as objected by the author of Hadia.

13.Bandagi Meeran Hameed and grape:

The Author had objected at pages 60 and 61 that a companion of Imamana (As) gave a grape to the minor son of Imamana. Imamana (As) took away that grape from minor's mouth and told that it was the property of the Fuqara. Imamana (As) did not favor his minor son and at this act of Imamana (As), the author taunted. However no where such episode of taking out grape from the mouth of the minor son had been narrated. The same is stated in "Hashi-e-Shariefa" that:

"On getting grapes in the dairah of Imamana (As), Bandagi Syed Salamullah (Rz) gave a bunch of grapes to Miran Hameed (RZ), minor son of Imamana (As). Imamana (As) objected by telling:"this is the property of the Fuqaras". Companions told that they forgive their right in favour of the minor. Then Imamana (As) asked them to get it forbidden by all companions."

نقل است حضرت میـران علیه السلام را خـدائی تـعـالیٰ انگور رسانید بود ، میاں سید سـلام الله ایك خوشه بدست میاں سید حمید دادند ، میـران علیه السلام فرمودند که حق فقیران چرادادی ، برادران گفتنند میرانجیو معـاف کنیم حضرت میران علیه السلام فرمودند که پیشن همه فقیران معاف کنید ۔

Such episode happened also in Nabuwwat, as narrated in "Bukhari and Muslim" that:

"Narrated by Abi Huraira (Rz) that Hasan Ibn Ali (Rz) took a palm date and kept in the mouth. The Holy Prophet (Slm) asked Hasan (Rz) to take it out from his mouth. Then he asked Hasan (Rz): "Did he not know that we do not eat anything from charity"?

عـن ابـى هريرة رضى الله عنه قال اخذ حسن بن على تمرة مـن تـمـرـة الصدقة فجعلها فى فيه فقال له النبى صـلى الـلـه عـليـه وسلم كخ كخ يطر حها ثم قال اما شعرت ان لانا كل الصدقة

It means that charity is forbidden to the "Saadaat, who come from the Ahl-e-Bait (Rz)."

Now we have to ask what remarks he would pass on the Holy Prophet's action?

14. Treatment of a Slave and a Kaneez:

The Author had confronted on a narrative regarding Imamana (As) who informed that the very existence of a slave or a kaneez in a house, deprives the Blessings. It is reported in "Hashia-e-Sharief" that:

"One day, in the house of Miyan Syed Salamullah (rz), a kaneez was being beaten. Miyan Shah Nemat (Rz) prevented the beating. There was a loud discussion between Syed Salamullah (Rz) and Shah Nemat (Rz); then the matter gone to Imamana (As). Imamana (As) told that a house which keeps slave or kaneez is deprived from Faith. "

يك روزه در خانه ' ميان سيد سلام اللّٰه شورشد كنيز ك را مى زدند ' ميان شـاه نـعمتّ منع كردند ، ميـان سيـدسـلام اللّٰه و ميان نعمتّ راگفتگو شد ' آن قصه را پيـش حضرت ميران عـرض كردند ' حضرت ميراں فـرمـودنـد درخانه كسى كه كنيزك يا غلام باشد اور ايمان شدن محال است ـ

On beating a slave or kaneez, the atonement is, to free him or her.

"Narrated by Ibn Omer (Rz) that he heard the Holy Prophet (Slm) telling whoever beats or slaps on the face of his slave without any wrong doing, the atonement is to let him free. Narrated in "Muslim."

عـن ابـن عـمـر قال سمعت رسول الله صلى الله عـليـه وسلم يقول من ضرب غلامـاله حدا لم ياته او لطمه فكفار ته ان يعتقه رواه مسلم

"Narrated Ibn Masood (Rz) that he was beating his slave. I heard a voice telling that "Allah is more Omnipotent than you over him". I turned and saw the Holy Prophet (Slm) who was behind me. Then and there I set the slave free . The holy Prophet (Slm) admonished him by telling that had you not freed him you would have been burnt by Hellfire. Narrated by "Muslim".

عـن ابـن مسعـود الانصارى قال كنت اضرب غلامـالى فسـمعت مـن خلفى صوتا اعلم ابا مسـعـود الله اقدر عليـك منك عليه فالتفت يـا رسـول الـلـه صـلى الله عليه وسلم فقلت يا رسـول اللـه هو حر لـوجه الله فقال امالو لم تـفـعـل لـلفحتك النار اولمسك النار رواه مسلم.

Thus when the matter came before Imamana (As), he informed whoever keeps slave in his house, Iman is forbidden from that house. The Holy Prophet's command that if you beat without any reason, you have to release him free, otherwise Hellfire is your punishment.

Another tradition tells that a Muslim should not hurt either by hand or by tongue another Muslim. It may be pointed out that Islam treats slaves and kaneez as members of the house. Tradition says:

"Narrated by Abu Zarr (Rz) that the Holy Prophet (slm) told that your slaves are your brothers. Although Allah had made them under your command. Therefore provide them what you eat and clothe them what you clothe yourself. Both "Bukhari" and "Muslim" confirmed it."

عـن ابـى ذر قـال قـال رسول الله صلى الله عليه وسلم اخـوانكم جعـلهـم الله تحت ايديكم فمن جعل الله اخـاه تحت يديه فليطعمه مما ياكل وليلبسه ممايلبس متفق عليه

Thus the slaves are not treated as slaves, but like brothers and as per another tradition Holy Prophet (Slm) ordains to treat slaves as sons:

"Thus favor them as your sons and provide meals what you eat."

فاكر موهم ككر امة اولادكم واطعموهم مما تاكلون

Thus under these traditions what Imamana (As) said is correct, because if a slave or kaneez is not treated as a brother and sister or as son and daughter and instead was being ill-treated or beaten without their fault, surely that man should not be called a momin. Thus whatever was told by Imamana (As) was just according to the commands of the Holy Prophet (Slm).

14. Author had blamed Imamana (As) on page 52 that Imamana (As) had told a person who had two clothes and did not provide to the one who did not have any clothing, then he becomes hypocrite:

"Narrated by Imamana (As) that whoever keeps two clothes and one brother is naked, then he must hand over one, otherwise he would become a hypocrite."

حـضـرت ميران عليه السلام فرمودند كه كسى دوجامه دار ديكى بـرادر بـرهـنـه بـاشد اور ابدهد وگرنه منافق است

Here the word hypocrite has been used and not infidel as the author blames. In a tradition the one who speaks lies had been designated as an hypocrite.

15."**The hypocrite**" has three signs:

1. Whenever speaks, he speaks lies; 2. If promised, would not keep it up; 3. Breaches the trust."

٢٨٤. آية الـمنـافق ثلث............اذا حدث كذب و اذا وعد اخلف واذاوتمن خان

Commentary about this tradition had been given in "Ashatul Lam'aat" that:

"It is not necessary that a person of these qualities need not be a hypocrite, but it tells that hypocrites may carry these qualities as well."

صـاحب اين خصال به حقيقت منافق نيست بلكه مراد آن است كه اين صفات لايق منافقان است

Seyouti had narrated with reference to Abdullah Masood that:

"That man could not be called a momin who eats to his satisfaction and does not provide to his neighbour who is looking after him that he would provide something to eat."

ليس المومن الذى يشبع وجاره جائع الى جنبه

Here's the one who does not provide meals to his hungry neighbor had been designated as not a momin. In the same manner whoever does not provide clothing to a naked neighbor is called a hypocrite. Both carry the same meaning.

16.Zikrullah vs. Satan:

Imamana (AS) did not condemn Satan, instead he stressed for zikrullah. The narrative is this:

"Someone asked Imamana (As) how would you rate condemning a Satan? Imamana (As) answered: "Allah and the angels are condemning him, if you too condemn, he is pleased because you had been diverted from Allah's Zikr and have wasted your time in condemning him."

حضرت میران راکسی پر سید شیطان را لعنت کردن چنو است ‘ میران فرمودند اور اخدا وفرشتگان لعنت کنند از لعنت کردن شما اوخوش می شود ویا د خدا فراموش کناند ـ

What Imamana's intention in this regard is that the time you serve in condemning Satan , it is better that the same time be served in Allah's Zikr, which is an obligation:

"Oh Faithful be busy in abundance with Zikrullah." (33:41)

یا ایها الذین آمنو االذکر واالله ذکر اُکثیرا (احزاب ٣ع)

17.Preferable not to Ask:

The Author had pointed out on page 54 that Imamana (As) had forbidden from asking because it tells upon one's self respect. As a matter of fact the word "Self respect" was not used:

"Whatever you want, ask from Allah, do not ask from others, ask only from Allah."

هر چه خواهی از خدا خواه پیش مردم سوال مکن ‘اگر سوال کنی پیش خدائ تعالیٰ بکن (حاشیه شریف ٦٤)

The Imamana's assertion is just according to the Holy Prophet's dictates:

"Narrated Soban who heard the Holy Prophet telling: "Is there anyone who assure me that he would not ask anything from other people? So as I could assure him that I become Guarantor for him in the paradise". Soban told he assured the Prophet (Slm). Thus Soban did never ask anything, afterwards from any person. Narrated by "Abu Dawood" and "Nisaai."

عن ثوبان قال قال رسول الله صلى الله علیه وسلم من یکفل لی ان لایسال الناس شیئا فاتکفل له بالجنة فقال ثوبان ان فکان لایسئال احد اشیئا رواه ابو داود والنسائى

Thus Imamana's assertion was in toeing the footsteps of the Holy Prophet (Slm). Thus, the author is not only blaming Imamana (As), but actually blaming the Holy Prophet (Slm) as well!

18.Description of Divine Love:

Author had objected at page 54 that Imamana (As) had asserted about Qur'an that it is a Divine Book of Love Message, which is mentioned in "Hashia-e-Sharief" that:

"It is narrated that Imamana (As) asserted "Qur'an is an "Ishque Nama" "Divine Message of love of Allah."

نقل است حضرت میراں فرمودند قرآن عشق نامه است

Here "Nama" means book and thus Qur'an is a book which educates how to love Allah, not a worldly love but a divine love, pure love with Allah. Since "Allah befriends one who loves Allah profusely", as stated in a verse, hereunder:

"Thus Allah shall arrive with that Sect who loves Allah, Allah too loves him."
(5:57 beginning part)

فسوف یاتی الله بقوم یحبهم ویحبونه (المائده ۷ ع)

Whoever loves Allah, his life is the evidence of this verse:

"Tell them with certainty that my prayer, and my entire worship, my life and death are for Allah alone who is the Creator of these worlds."

قل ان صلاتی و نسکی و محیای ومماتی لله رب العالمین .

Does this verse not show the correct sense of love with Allah? For that reason alone Qur'an had been asserted as "Divine Love Message (of Allah). Allah thus asserts:

"Those who are faithful have an intense love with Me."

والذین آمنو اشد حبا لله (البقره ۲۱ ع)

Thus to tell Qur'an " message of love to Allah" is nothing but describing the intent of the Qur'an.

19.Perfect vs. imperfect:

The Author had objected at page 54 that Imamana (As) had informed that they should not fear from the Hellfire and quoted the following narrative:

"Who desires Allah, he is a "man", the one who desires, world he is a "woman", and the one who desires Hereafter, he is an "Eunuch". Here, Hereafter means Doomsday, in which there is either paradise or hell. If it is paradise then heavenly nymphs are for him. Comparatively it is said that the man who desires Allah is a man and who desires heavenly nymphs is an eunuch. The word fear from Hell is nowhere used. Then the objection has no value. "Insaf Nama", in chapter 5 says:

"Narrated Imamana (As) that "Oh Infidels: world is for you, Oh imperfect faithful, Hereafter is for you and Allah is for me and for him who follows me."

الدنیا لکم ایها الکافرون و العقبی لکم یا یها المومنون الناقصون والمولی لی و لمن اتبعنی (۳۱)

It is clear from this narrative that whoever desires Allah, he is a perfect faithful and who desires Heavenly nymphs, he is an imperfect faithful. However "Kanzul Ammal" states that:

"World is forbidden for those who desire Hereafter and Hereafter is forbidden for the worldly men; and world and Hereafter are forbidden for the Faithful."

الدنیا حرام علی اهل الآخرة والآخرة حرام علی اهل الدنیا والدنیا والآخرة حرام علی اهل الله

Whether there shall be the same objection since here also advice is being given not to fear from the Hellfire.?

20.Governor of Jalore's Acceptance:

Author negates that the Governor of Jalore had accepted Mahdiat, because Osman Khan had died when Imamana (As) arrived in Jalore according to "History of Palanpur". Whereas "Khaatim-e-Sulaimani" reports that:

"Imamana (As) stayed in Jalore for four and half month. And Malik Jabdal, Lohani Pathan, Governor of Jalore, accepted Imamana's Mahdiat along with his subjects."

در بـلـدۀ جـالـور چهار نیم ماه اقامت شده و ملك جبدل پـٹهـان لـوهانی حاکم آنجا معه قبائل به تصدیق مشرف شده(گلشن چهارم دوم)

Just on account of the difference in names the fact could not be negated. Hence it is proved that the Governor of Jalore had converted as Mahdavi along with his subjects. His descendants who are the Nawabs of Palanpur are still Mahdavis and, Insha Allah, shall remain Mahdavi.

21. Mahdavis of Farrah:

The Author had objected by telling at pp 52,53 that on account of Farrah's Qazi's opposition, none from Farrah converted to Mahdavia Faith. It may be pointed out that Imamana (As) lived there for two years and five months. During this period many had converted. Particularly Sheikul Islam Harvey had sent four scholars to discuss with Imamana (As). Those four scholars after complete satisfaction converted and resided with Imamana (As) at Farrah till Imamana's demise. They wrote to Shiekul Islam that "Imamana (as) was one of the signs of Allah and no one could defeat Imamana (As) in discussion since his mystic knowledge is more superior than ours". And they suggested to come over to Farrah and accept the faith. Mullah Abdul Qader Badayuni had written regarding Farah in "Najatur Rasheed" (page 177) which is enough as a reply to these filthy objections of a so called research scholar. As regards opposition, the entire Makkans were against the Holy Prophet for thirteen years and on account of which Holy Prophet (Slm) had to migrate to Madinah. Was his Mission failed? Like that even after opposition of a Qazi, hundreds converted at Farah and Imamana's Shrine has become a sacred place still now.

22.Imamana's jihad:

The Author had opposed regarding Imamana's fighting and killing Rai Dalpat, saying that it is fictitious, since no such battle took place. But if the battle had not been recorded in history the fact could not be suppressed. There were certain Ghazwat of the Holy Prophet (Slm) which are not recorded by the Jews and the Christians, then shall the author dispute about them? However he had accepted the battle of Khanbel and Sudrasan.

"Bukahri" had written"Tareekh-e-Kabeer" which lacks information about some eminent Hanafi godlimen; on account of his prejudice and anger. Hence for non inclusion in his "Tareekh", would those eminent personalities be denied of their existence? Was the author unaware of an eminent historian Farishta's writing that "Sultan Hussein Sharqi had fought against Rai of Oraisa (Rai Dalpat) with his three hundred thousand army and 400 elephants". Can he deny the facts on account of his enmity and jealousy with the venerable Mahdavia Faith?

What sort of research the author had conducted?

Farishta wrote:

"(Sultan Husain Sharqi) had amassed three hundred thousand army and 400 elephants for battle against Rai of Orisa"

نخست س ۳ لك سوار و هزار و چهار صد زنجیر فیل جمع نموده متوجه ولایت اوریسه گردید

"Matleul Vilayet" reported that:

"Sultan was so impressed with the divine personality of Imamana (As) that he never waged a war without Imamana (As)."

چنان معتقد این درگاه بود که به هیچ مهمی بغیر آنحضرت نه رفتی

As "Tareekh-e-Farishta" reported about the battle of Orisa which took place in 871, at that year Imaman's age was 24 years. This occurred before the period of his Trance. Sultan's waging war against Oraisa has been historically proved, then how could it be asserted that the Sultan did not fight with Rai Dalpat whose dominion was in Oraisa? Author of "Maqdoom Zaadagan-e-Fatehpur" had written about battle of Oraisa. At that period Lukhnow was a part of kingdom of Sharqia. The English Gazetteer of Lukhnow had referred about a victory of the fort of Kakor Gadh. Apart from this old historical record, the memoirs of the Kakori dynasties state that:

""Sultan Husain Sharqi under Islamic pressure of a sense of honor in order to crush the Susuns dynasty, dispatched a strong army which captured the fort of Rae-Bareili, the Raja Sathan fled to Kakor Gadh and obtained refuge. The Sharqi army was following him, but suddenly the revolt spread in Bengal, therefore Sultan Sharqi left the mission of capturing Raja, went towards Bengal and crushed the revolt in Bengal. However the legends mentioned about Rai Dalpat's defeat by Sharqi are perfectly true. Thus Imamana had waged a war aginst Rai Dalpat is a proven fact which cannot be denied. And it is alo a fact that Raja's nephew was brought by Sultan Husain Sharqi as a captive, who was given to Imamana(As) as his personl servant, later on he converted and was named Shah Dilawer, and became the fifth Caliph of Imamana(As).Who can deny these facts?

23. Defence is not Revolt:

'Bandagi Miyan's mission was nothing but to spread the Mahdavia Faith. He did not attempt to capyure and controle any territory to establish his authority, then how can any person declare battle of Khanbel or Sudrasan was a revolt? Allah's command is that:

"Wage a war for Allah's cause against the offenders"ﺝ

وقاتلو افی سبیل الله الذین یقاتلو نکم

Here command for waging a war is for self defense. Mahdavis confronted the offenders to save their life and honor. The same zeal is embedded in Chanchalguda battle also. (P293).

24. Non Muslims in the army:

Author further objects on pp. 45,46 that the battle which was fought between Sultan Husain and Rai Dalpat can not be said to be a Jihad. He had described the reason that the army had non Muslims also, hence it cannot be called a complete Muslim army. If it is taken as a fact then how would you categorize the battles fought by the Holy Prophet (Slm) and Hzt. Omer (Rz) since in those armies non Muslims also were included? Before the victory of Makkah, Abbas Ibn Abdul Mutallib (Rz) had reported:

"At that time Banu Ka'ab Bin Omroo reached with five hundred cavalry and his army's flag bearer was Bashir Bin Abu Sufian and Abu Sufian personally verified the army which was friendly to the Holy Prophet (Slm)."	انگاه بنو کعب بن عمر که میان ایشان پانصد سوار نامی بودند رسیدند وعلم این فوج بشر بن سفیان داشت ابو سفیان تحقیق این فرقه نمود عباس گفت که ایشان خلفائ محمد اند

From this it is clear that before reaching Makkah, the Holy Prophet's army had included those who were not Muslims, but who was a mutual agreement that both would not fight each other.

At the time of Ghazvai-e-Hunain:

"When the Holy Prophet (Slm) heard that the enemy wanted to fight, then Holy Prophet (Slm) assembled an army on Monday of Shawwal, containing ten thousand from Madinah and two thousand from Makkah along with Talaqas and Halafahs, non Muslims, still they agreed not to fight each other and to whom general amnesty had been granted, they were more than 80 who were infidels of Makkah including Sufwan Ibn Ummyya."	چون آنحضرت صلی الله علیه وسلم شنید که این جماعه قصد محاربه دارند بیرون آمد از مکه روز شنبه شوال در دوازه ده هزار مسلمانان از اهل مدینه و دو هزار از مکه از طلقاء و حلفا ....وهشتاوکس دراین میان از مشرکان هم بودند مثل صفوان ابن امیه وغیره
"While sufwan was considering to become Muslim or not, still he was with Muslims for the Hunain and Taef Ghazwas."	صفوان هنوز در اختیار اسلام مترد د و متوقف بود باوجود شرک در غزوه' حنین و طائف در رکاب همایون بود

During the period of Hzt. Omer (Rz), even infidels were recruited for the Army. Shibli Numani writes that when Hzt. Omer (rz) expanded his army, he did not discriminate between any nation or country; nor even religion or infidelity; nor for any particular country, he had put no bar on caste and creed. As far as volunteer regiment is concerned, thousands of Majoosis were recruited who were getting same salaries as that of Muslims. Even in administration there were Majoosis also. The Author's assertion that in view of the inclusion of non Muslims in the army of Sultan Husain, that battle could not be categorized as Jihad, is indirectly an objection on the Holy Prophet (Slm) and Hzt. Omer (Rz).

25. Sheik Ahmed Sar-e-Hind:

It is ridiculous to say that religion of Sar-e-Hindi was based on "Unity of Divine manifestation". " Meaning of "Shahood"had been described by "Ghiasul Lughat" that:

"Shahood means to have the witness of
Allah's vision according to the Seekers.
One who considers the creations and his
own whims and fancies contemplate into
the Divinity, where all of the creations
become one and a single entity which
melts down into an ultimate unity, thus
at that stage what ever remains is
nothing but reality."

شهـود در اصطلاح سـالـکان رویت حق است کـه از
مـراتب کثرات مـوهـومات صدری عبورنموده به مقام
تـوحیـد عیانی رسیده در صور جمیع موجودات مشاهدۀ
حق نماید وغیریت دور شده هر چه بیند حق بیند

Thus it is a stage in which all creations of Allah's splendour are witnessed and everything becomes manifested into the Ultimate Entity. And the same had been described by Sheik Ahmed himself as transcending to the Ultimate Unity, the all powerful Unity of natural forces are visible as the manifested Unity of the Omnipotent. For that an example is presented:

Sar-e-Hindi himself had used the words " Omnipotence of Allah" a "Mystic experience" a "Divine manifestation" He described it that "all is one" to witness "One' and nothing but one."

"When the sun rises, stars, although they
also exist in the sky, but unable to be
seen on account of the brightness of the
sun, thus every one knows that stars are
existing but invisible."

وقتی کـه آفتـاب رادیـد البتـه ستـاره هـارانخواهد دیدو
شهـود ادجـز آفتاب نخواهد بود و درای زمان کـه ستاره
هـارانمـی بینـد میداند کـه ستاره ها معدوم نیستند بلکه
میداند کـه هستند اما مستور اند ـ

If everything is manifested as the Divine Unity and if it is what Islam teaches, then they must explain how those 360 idols which were kept by the infidels in and around the House of Allah were regarded by the Holy Prophet (Slm) as idols? After all they were emblems of infidelity and Shirk. The author had maintained that the movement of Sar-e-Hindi had eclipsed the Mahdavi Movement; then by preaching this theory of "Divine Manifestation" are you not eclipsing Islam?

26.Sar-e-Hindi vs. Muslim:?

The author had objected to Imamana's teachings that they are lacking in moderation. Whereas they are totally based on the Qur'an and the traditions; while the Sar-e-Hindi movement had been presented as a "Creative Movement" from the Islamic concept. One aspect of this creative movement is conditional to Islam. Therefore Sheik Sar-e-Hindi had written a letter to Sharfuddin Yahiya Muniri about the stipulation of Islam that:

"Until one mates with mother, he is not
a Muslim." (Naoozu Billah)

تـابـه مـادر جفت نه شود مسلمـان نـه شود (ارشـاد
السالکین)

If such Islamic condition had been written in Mahdavia books, what would have been the author's impression about us, we do not know. Such sort of Islamization is the domain of the research scholar alone. If he accepts Sheik's movement then it is certain that he is practically following the above practice. Tuff on him.

27. Author vs. Mahdavis:

Author on page 27 maliciously accused by alleging deception by Mahdavis and for that he submitted as a proof that: In Ahmed Nagar some Mahdavi scholars had asserted before Aurangzeb that we accept Oneness of Allah, Nabuwwat of the Holy Prophet, Four Caliphs of Raashida and four Schools of Thought. We cannot say what was wrong with it? As far as four Schools of Thought are concerned we adopt that one which is mostly based on Qur'an and traditions. Then only we accept (which is Aaliat, most preferable). And that is our Fiqha. From his objection we are constrained to deduce that he denies all these basic fundamentals. If such declaration of faith is called subterfuge (hiding), then what will be his opinion on offering prayers in hiding at Dar-e-Irqam? Or what is his opinion on propagating Islam in hiding for three years ?

28. Mysticism and Shariat-e-Mustafavi:

The author had ascertained that Imamana's way of teaching was based on the teachings of the Bughdadi Mystics. But it is a fact that Imamana (As) had torn down the curtain of secrecy which enveloped for centuries by the anti Arabinism. The following vouchsafe this:

"One priest and a follower were going to Makkah. The priest spread his prayer mat on the water and started treading over it and asked his disciple to stand over it.

"He instructed his follower that "When I say Allah", you say "Peer". But the follower uttered Allah and was drowned. Because he did not tell what the peer asked him to tell "Peer". When the follower told "Peer" he came out from the water over the prayer mat. When this episode was narrated to Imamana (As). Imamana (As) told: It was not fair, why should he not let be drowned? By saying Allah, if drowned he becomes a martyr."

يك پير و مريد به مكه مى رفتند ـ پير مصلىٰ به آب گسترانيد ه سوار شد مريد را گفت غرق شد باز پير گفت پير بگو ، بارب گفت " برآمد اين نقل برادران پيش حضرت ميران عرض كردند ، حضرت ميران عليه السلام فرمودند خوب نكرو ، چراغرق شدن نداد ، بنام خدائى تعالىٰ غرق شدے شهيد شدے(حاشيه شريف) (١٦٥)

The dialogue between the peer and the disciple was based on the Mystic way of discussion , but what Imamana told was just based on Shariat-e-Mustafavi (Slm).

29.Consistancy of Qur'an:

The author had used the word, "Hearsay" on the very first page regarding Mahdavia Faith which shows his prejudice, since he does not know about our faith which is based on the Qur'an and traditions. We believe that Quran's consistency in revelations is perfect. But unfortunately his religion is against this consistency and the verses of the Holy Qur'an which are the emblem of Brightness, he abrogates five hundred verses of the Qur'an as was done in the Bible and Torah (by the Jews and Christians). Is it not his faith based on hearsay?

30. A. S. Ansari vs. facts:

"Tazkera-e-Indian Scholars" was published by the Pakistan Historical Society. Actually it is a translation of the "Tazkera of Rahman Ali" who had written in Persian. The same was published a second time by Nowal Kishor Printing Press in 1914. Rahman Ali had written about

Imamana (As) with references from "Hadia-e-Mahdavia" of Zaman Khan from pp 197 to 201; and on page 149, he had written about Sheik Alaai Mahdavi of Biyana. About Zaman Khan he has written on pages 189,190. He has referred the second Edition of "Hadia-e-Mahdavia" which was published in 1292. Whatever wrong Rahman Ali had written about Imamana (As), Mahdavia Faith and history of Mahdism; had been refuted in the previous pages by us emphatically, but from the following we are going to refer the ridiculous writings of A. S. Ansari which is against the historical facts. It is regarding the murder of Zaman Khan that:

"Even after search the whereabouts of the murderer became not known." هر چند تجسس نمودند سراغ قاتل نه رسید

It is wrong to say that murderer Hzt. Abji Miyan's whereabouts became not known. It is a fact that after killing Zaman Khan, Hzt. Abji Miyan did not run away from the scene, but stood boldly when Zaman Khan's brother and 62 students surrounded him and he threw the Dagger before them by saying: "I had accomplished my Mission. Do what you want to do". The then Police Commissioner arrested him and took to the Rikab Gunj police Station. He was under custody till his martyrdom on the 14th. Saffer of 1293 H. The author seems ignorant of the historical facts, that on the basis of a Fatwah of Qisas, Hzt. Abji Miyan was martyred on 14th Saferul Muzaffer 1293 H. and he was buried in Musheerabad Graveyard.

A. S. Ansari had followed what "Tazkera" had jotted down that "the murderer made good his escape." Which is wrong as this statement is utterly against the facts. **These so called research scholars are advised if they are trying to write about Mahdavis or about Mahdavia Faith it would be better for them to go through "Muqaddama-e-Sirajul Absar", chapter by chapter, (and other authentic writings of Mahdavis to ascertain about our facts.).**

31.A. S. Ansari recognizes Imamana (As):

After all, A.S. Ansari had somehow conceded and accepted Imamana (As) that:

"All non Mahdavi sources are unanimous in saying that the characters and teachings of Syed Mohammed (As) were above reproach. His honesty of purpose, integrity with his Mission, selflessness, contempt for worldly gains, resignation to the Will of Allah and above all his own examples inspired the Muslims of those days with a new zeal and fervor and many forsaking the comforts of a settled life, dedicated themselves to the service of religion and to the fellow travelers on the path of deliverance". (pp 58,59)

Even after writing such facts about Imamana (As) and still not accepting him as the deliverer, then what would be his opinion about the tradition of Hirql,as reported in "Bukhari" about the signs referred by Hirql regarding the Holy Prophet (Slm) and about his proclamation of Nabuwwat?

32. Accusation of Editor of Tajalli:

Aamir Osmani, Editor of Tajalli, of Dev Bund had resorted to abusive language about Imamana (As) and Mahdavia Faith in his Issues on November 1963, January 1965 and April 1965 whose replies were given in December 1963, February 1965 and May 1965, simultaniously in the "Supplement of Muqaddama-e-Sirajul Absar" under the captions: First Scene, Second Scene and Third Scene, individually and separately for his three issues. Now their gist along with some additions being narrated hereunder:

33.Religion of the Editor:

Mohammed Ismail Dahlavi in his pamphlet "Ek Rozi" had written that:

"Not uttering lies" is one of the qualities of Allah Jalle Subhanahoo. We praise this quality of Allah as against Dumb man and stones which do not speak lies as well."	عـدم کـذب را از کـمالات حضرت حق سبحانه، می شــما رند داور اجل شانه، بآں مدح می کنند بر خلاف اخرص و جماد

It means to say that Allah's "non utterance of lies" is not a reason for his prominence, because a dumb man or stones too are unable to speak a lie. Thus in view of the decliner, Allah, dumb man and stones come under one category. Further the Editor of "Ek Rozi" had written that:

"Although a man having perfection in telling lies, but on account of expediency in order to avoid any doubt may not speak lies".	صـفت کمال همیں است که شخصی قدرت برتکلم بـه کـلام کـاذب داردوبنـا بر رعایت مصلحت و مقـتضـائی حکـمـت به تنزه از شوب کذب تکلم به کلام کاذب نه نماید۔

From these unscrupulous statements, according to them, it comes to light that "Allah also can tell lies", and according to the editor of "Ek Rozi" it becomes an attribute of Allah. (Naozoo Billah)

On the basis of this unholy utterance, author of "Mazaheb-e-Islam" has also sided with "Ek Rozi" Editor and asserts that "it is possible that Allah too can speak lies." (page 662)

(The two pages pertain to this sort of writing has no bearing to our Faith or about Imamana (As), therefore omitted from the translation- PP 758 to 761)

34.Decliner's Religion Defames holy Prophet (Slm):

Mohammed Ismail Dahlavi had written in "Taqviyatul Iman" that:

"Every creation whether he is small or big, he is not more than a cobbler before Allah's grandeur,"

Although "Darmi" and "Tirmizi" had reported what Ibn Abbas (Rz) had said about the Holy Prophet (Slm) who asserted:

"I am the friend of Allah."	انی حبیب الله

Being "a Beloved of Allah" he had reached at the highest level, that Allah informs the Holy Prophet (Slm) that:

"And We have raised high your esteem for you in which you are now. (Alam Nashrah)	ورفعنا لک ذکرک

The personality of the Prophet (Slm) is such that he is most beloved Prophet (slm) of Allah whose esteem Allah had raised among his followers, then how can he become a "cobbler" as determined by Qasim Dahelvi? How loathsome is the editor and his mentor who degrade even the Holy Prophet (Slm)?.

Yet another defamation had been uttered by Aamir Osmani against the Holy Prophet (Slm) that : If by chance during the prayer the notion of the Holy Prophet (Slm) occurs, then it is even inferior to the notion of a bull or of an ass. And his teacher Mohammed Ismail had written on "Straight Path" that:" Oh Muslims think over such filth and unchaste sentences that" to get the idea of the Holy Prophet (Slm) during the prayer is so absurd that you are thinking about intercourse with a prostitute"! (What sort of vulgar and mean scoundrel is he?)

Author of "Ateebul Biyan" had commented on it that "No momin can utter such filth and nonsensical remarks from his mouth about the Holy Prophet (Slm) on account of which our hearts and body start shivering. This Ass utters that" if during prayers the notion of the Holy Prophet (Slm) comes, then it is as if the notion of an ass or a bull had come to you" !!. How this scoundrel could think that when we are reciting Tasshahud we are expressing the name of the Holy Prophet (Slm) with utmost dignity, and without that Tasshahud our prayer is not complete. If that scoundrel, who is certainly a faithless disbeliever and a hypocrite should forthwith stop his prayers to ALLAH, and instead we have every reason to believe that this scoundrel had become an infidel. Shame and tuff on him and his followers.

The editor thinks about the Holy Prophet (Slm) as if he is his elder brother, thus in view of this, this scoundrel Mohammed Ismail who had written in "Taqwiatul-e-Iman" that men are all brothers, any Saintliman is his elder brother, then you have to respect him accordingly.

Author of "Madarik" had commented that:

"Mujahed expressed his opinion that every Nabi is the father of his Ummah., thus Momineen are brothers to each other, because the Holy Prophet (Slm) is their father."

قـال مـجـاهد كل نبى ابو امته ولذلك صار المومنون اخوة لان النبى صلى الله عليه وسلم ابو هم فى الدين

Allah Ta'alla states that:

"The wives of the Holy Prophet are the mothers of the Momineen." (33:6 Beginning part)

ازواجه امهاتهم (الاحزاب ع ا)

According to this dictate of Allah when Ummehatul Momineen are mothers of Monineen then the Holy Prophet (Slm) becomes father of the Muslameen. And surely not an elder brother as these scoundrels Ismail, Aamir and editor of Ek-Rozi had proclaimed about the Holy Prophet (Slm). Shame on them!

35.Mahdi's Traditions vs. Aamir Osmani:

Editor of Tajalli had branded the traditions of Imam Mahdi as doubtful. If these traditions are doubtful, then how other traditions regarding Mairaj, splitting of Moon etc. could become reliable? And on which ground the Editor confirms their reliability? Particularly when Revelations descended on the Holy Prophet (Slm) through Gabriel, who is said to have come in the shape of a dog sometimes.!!!.

For his knowledge, Editor's leader Hafiz Ibn Taimia had certified those traditions in these words:

"Traditions of Imam Mahdi (As) are recognized. Narrated by Imam Ahmed (Rh), Abu Dawood (Rh) and Tirmizi (Rh)."

احادیث المھدیؑ معروفۃ رواھا الامام احمد وابو
داود وترمذی الی آخرہ

The advent of Mahdi (As) was accepted by Ibn Tamima (Rh) and the traditions regarding Mahdi (As) were proved by Ibn Tamima (Rh) and he had also proved their reliability as well:

"Thus those traditions which are the proof of the advent of Mahdi (As) are correct. Narrated by Abu Dawood, Tirmizi and others".

فالجواب ان الاحادیث صحیح بھا علی خروج
المھدی احادیث صحیحۃ رواھا ابو دائود والترمذی
واحمد وغیرھم

The Editor in the Issue of April 1965 of Tajalli had published an essay of Hakim Abdul Rasheed Gangohi in which objection has been raised on Moudodi that he does not accept the traditions of Mahdi (As). Hakim Gangohi had written about Hafiz Hajr Makki and Sheik Ahmed Sar-e-Hindi that they had designated those traditions as unreliable. But when Ibn Taimia (Rh) had accepted them as reliable, if Moudodi or Ibn Khaldun deny, their denial is weightless in the presence of Imam Abu Tamima's acceptance. But as a matter of fact Moudodi also had accepted them as reliable but he had wrongly elucidated the position of Mahdi (As). To him: "The doctrine of the Advent of Mahdi (As) were recognized by many, but what I had understood that whoever would emerge he would be of a new type of a "leader!!!."

The Holy Prophet (Slm) had prophesied about Mahdi (As) that he would be the Khalifatullah and through him the Deen /Religion would be completed. Look up the religiosity of Moudodi who brands Mahdi (As) as a new type of a "leader" as against the prophecy of the Holy Prophet (Slm) that "MAHDI is the Khalifatullah."

However, Hzt. Abu Bakr (Rz) although presented himself to be the deputy of the Holy Prophet (Slm) but abstained to name himself as "Khalifatullah" as reported by Ibn Abi Sheeba that Abu Bakr (rz) was the leader of his people and deputy of the Holy Prophet (Slm), but he was not the "Khalifatullah", how the so called new type of a "leader" of Moudodi could become Khalifatullah. We have already discussed this issue in detail in "Traditions of Mahdi (As) and Ibn Khaldun".

36.Divine Revelations:

Editor of Tajalli had objected on the "Divine Revelations" of a sacred noise which sounded at the time of the birth of Imamana (As). With this objection, he is actually objecting what author of "Muwaheb-e-Ludunia" had reported about a voice was heard by Bibi Aamina (Rz), when the Holy Prophet (Slm) was born and she heard also about the newborn that "he is having Adam's characters, mystic knowledge of Shees (As), bravery of Noah (As) and fraternity of Ibrahim (As), so dip him into the sea of the Prophets (As)."

He had actually objected this narrative in order to refute any such voice regarding Mahdi (As). Both revelations are correct. Since he cannot accept one and deny the other; he has to deny both. But his such denial has no value since those revelations had been accepted by one and all and the entire Ummah.

37.Imamana vs. Editor:

Editor's belief is represented by his mentor Mohammed Qasim Nanotvi's assertion as written in "Mubahisai-e-Shahjehanpur."

"The Nabuwwat and venerability of Prophets Moosa (As) and Isa (As) are recognized and whoever denies them is an infidel, so also we are not sure about Sri Krishan and Sri Rama Chander."

On one hand, such is his perfect belief and as regards Imamana (As), he says: name him Mystic, or Qutub, but not as an Appointee of Allah. Editor of Tajalli's contention is like that of those Christians who declared the Holy Prophet (Slm) as a reformer, but not as the Holy Prophet (Slm), because they say that in him those signs are not visible for example: he would have emerged from Faaran which is in Syria and not in Makkah.

In order to refute such silly objections, Scholars of Islam have presented Characters of the Prophet (Slm) as the proof of his Nabuwwat instead of prophesied signs and in the same manner, Imamana's characters are being presented as a proof for his Mahdiat. In order to negate Imamana (As) as an appointee by Allah, he sometimes tells that he proclaimed when he was in a trance and absorbed in Divinity, further he says that Imamana's proclamation was a mistake of authoritative interpretation.

This abusive language is just like that abusive language of the Atheists who used against the Holy Prophet (Slm) as written by Abdul Haleem Ahrari:

"Some say that he was suffering from epilepsy and during this disease whatever feelings he got he would take them that these are the revelations from Allah."

Thus the author in order to console his own mind and heart he indulges in a different sort of accusations. But he must understand that these foolish accusations had been refuted long back. For details please see Part one, chapter Three of this "Muqaddama".

It would be better if he goes through what his mentor's father, Shah Abdul Aziz had said about Imamana (As).

"Mir Syed Mohammed Mahdi (As)   "میر سید محمد جونپوری در هندوستان بیانگ بلند

had proclaimed his Mahdiat with full   ادعائی مهدیت نمود

force."

"The words "With Full Force" denotes that the proclamation was not in the "state of being absorbed in Divinity" but that he was firm on his proclamation till his last breath. However the author had accepted to name him a Mystic and a Qutub knowing that the Mystic does not speak lies. Thus Imamana (As) had never repudiated his own claim to be the "Promised Mahdi (As)" and this proves his Mahdiat.

However the editor had tried to negate Imamana's Mahdiat by presenting a single narrative which is like the one which the Jews or Christians present a single prophecy from either Torah or Bible and declared that the Huzoor Prophet (Slm) was not the one who was commissioned by Allah.

Our firm belief is that the argument through which Holy Prophet (Slm) had been commissioned by Allah as the last Prophet (Slm), the same argument fits to prove the commissioning of Imamana (As) as the Promised Mahdi (As). In our previous discussion we have refuted all such silly objections. Now we go to prove some other issues hereunder:

38. Editor and Signs of Imam Mahdi (As):

Neglecting all other signs, the editor is sticking up to a single sign, it is just like the Jews and Christians too are still thinking about a single sign for the Holy Prophet (Slm) that he would appear from Faraan (Syria) and not from Makkah. And thus they are denying his apostleship. In the same manner the Editor wrongly is sticking to a single sign and rejects Imamana's Mahdiat.

Our belief is that on what basis the apostleship of the Holy Prophet (Slm) had been accepted and confirmed the same criterian should be adopted to confirm the Mahdiat of Imamana Syed Mohammed Juanpuri (As) which had been already discussed in previous chapters. But now we discuss about some signs about which the Editor speaks:

A. Change of Throne and Crown :

This condition was not referred in any of the narratives. Thus when there was no such condition of changing the throne or the crown, his silly objection is just nothing but a malicious accusation on the Holy Prophet.

B. Starting of an Earthquake:

Historically it was proved that there was an earthquake in between 905 and 907 in Juanpur.

Now remains that part of the narrative that the earth would be filled with peace and tranquility which is being investigated. Allah states that:

"Do not spread rebellion on the Earth once it had been reformed. (7:85 Part)"

ولا تفسدو افى الارض بعد اصلاحها (اعراف ع ١١)

Author of "Muaheb-e-Alaih" had commented that:

"After reforming the earth, Allah , commissioned the Prophets and revealed the scriptures."

بعد از صلاح آن زمين به بعث انبياء وانزال كتب (جلداول)

Here Earth means residents of the Earth and by reforming means to infuse faith in the inhabitants of the Earth. Thus to fill the Earth with peace and tranquility means to educate the inhabitants of the Earth regarding the religion and faith. Now remains to see, how many persons would be benefited from the teachings of the religion; this had been described by the Holy Prophet (Slm):

"Narrated by "Muslim" through Uns that he heard Holy Prophet was telling:

"It is a fact that out of the prophets there had been one Prophet to whom none accepted him except one person."

ان من الانبياء نبيا ماصدقه من امته رجل واحد (اشعته اللمعات)

From this tradition it comes to light that even if one person accepts any Prophet, as per Qur'an, reformation of the Earth should be considered as complete. This refutes the contention of the Editor of Tajalli that unless a huge number of persons of the Earth accept the dignity of proclamation, he could not be accepted as a commissioned personality of the Almighty Allah. In view of the above presented tradition, imposing any such condition is not only to falsify Qur'an and traditions, but such nonsensical assertions make the teller an infidel. It also contradicts the claim of the editor that whoever is the commissioned dignitary he would overturn the throne and crown. It had been ordained for the Holy Prophet (Slm) that:

"When he stood, he shook the Earth; and when he started, he trembled the nations."

وقف وقاس العرض نظر فرجت الامم (اصحاح آيت ٤٠٣)

Now the editor is put to question that had anything of such stated things happened during the life of the Holy Prophet, either in Makkah or Madinah? And if it did not happen then could he dare to de-recognize the Holy Prophet (Slm) as an Apostle of Allah? To tell that after the Holy Prophet (Slm) whoever is commissioned by Allah, he would shake the earth or cause the earth trembling is nothing but misleading. Bible of Yuhanna had prophesied about the Holy Prophet (Slm) that:

"Leader of this World is coming."

رئيس هذا العالم ياتى

Whether the editor would dare to negate the Prophethood of the Holy Prophet (Slm), because the Holy Prophet (Slm) did not establish his authority over the whole Earth as prophesied in the Bible?

It was also narrated in the Book "Habqooq" that:

"Whole world would be filled up with his glory."

والارض امتلاء ت من تسبيحه

The fact is that at the time of the demise of the Holy Prophet many tribes had become hypocrite, except people of Makkah, Madinah and Owais people who were from Bakhran. Still he was accepted as the commissioned one and was affirmed by all. In such situation had the editor courage to negate the Holy Prophet's Prophethood? Or dare to say, since the whole of the Earth did not fill up with his glorification, the holy Prophet (Slm) should not be recognized as the Apostle of Allah? Or that all the inhabitants did not convert as Muslims? Therefore can the editor dare to say that the Holy Prophet (naozoo Billah) did not fit to the prophecy of the Torah or Bible?

Under the said tradition it is reported for Imam Mahdi (As) also that after his advent the Earth would fill with peace and tranquility.

According to the Book of Habqooq the Holy Prophet (Slm), did he fill up the world with peace and tranquility? Then how can anybody demand Imam Mahdi (As) that he would do what the Holy Prophet (Slm) could not do, since he was a perfect follower, by toeing the footprints of the holy Prophet (Slm)?

Sarcastically the editor of Tajalli had attacked indecently that Imam Mahdi (As) did nothing in this regard. For that we had taunted at him that such indecency he got from his Mentor only who had given the opinion that if a person get the idea of the Holy Prophet (Slm) during the prayer it would be like he is thinking about a bull or an ass. (Naozoo Billah)

Having read our befitting replies to his unethical ideas, he mended his behavior, still his indecency did not go, because of his mentor. It is his fate!

Allah ordains the Prophet (Slm):

"If you give judgment, then administer them based on justice." (5:45)

وان حكمت فاحكم بينهم بالقسط (مائده ع ٦)

Here Allah is asking the Prophet (Slm) to issue orders based on justice. Even otherwise neither the whole of the world became Muslim nor the Holy Prophet (Slm) was the administrator of the whole world. It is a fact that the Holy Prophet (Slm) propagated Islam for 23 years, but one hundred twenty four thousand only became Muslims. Among these Muslims there were hypocrites also and also those who were weak in their faith and the Holy Prophet (Slm) used to assist them monetarily; and those who after obtaining shares in the booty from the battle of Hunain only became Muslims. And at the time of the demise of the Prophet (Slm) except people of Makkah, Madinah and Najran, all tribes had become hypocrites, although their language, their culture, their nationality was one and they belonged to the same country. Just read what the author of "Muaheb Alaih" had written:

"Just after the demise of the Holy Prophet all tribes became hypocrite, except Muslims of Makkah, Madinah and people of Abul Qais belong to Najran."	بعد از وفات حضرت رسالت پناه تمام عرب مرتد شدند الا اهل مکه و مدینه وعبدالقیس از نجران (جلد اول ۱۳۸)

Now the editor is put to test to verify the ratio of the Muslims under the domination of the Holy Prophet (Slm) at the time of his demise and the population of the whole of the world!

(It should not be taken that as if we are (Naoozoo Billah) comparing between the holy Prophet (Slm) and Imamana (As), but we are just presenting facts, which cannot be denied.)

The specialty of Imamana's migration for propagation of Mahdavia Faith was very much captivating and impressive that the public from all walks of life, left the family, property, wealth and position, came to the diarah for peace of mind and heart. They travelled from India to Sindh and then to Khurasan by enduring ordeal, turmoil and hardships of the journey just to have the company of Imamana (As). These facts are narrated by the Non Mahdavi scholars and historians.

Another peculiarity was that the public consisting of different peoples of different caste, creed, color, language and culture, joined together to listen and accept Imamana's sermons. The country was alien, still none became hypocrite at the time of the demise of Imamana (As). What more proof is required to show the gravity of Imamana's impressive teachings. Whether this is not the miracle of the Huzoor Prophet (Slm) that his prophesied Khalifatullah dominated a large section of the peoples of three different regions?

Imamana (As) undertook journeys of thousands of miles. Wherever he went people welcomed him and offered their allegiance on his hands and got beneficence. Just go through the writings of Mullah Abdul Qader Badayuni's "Najatur Rasheed" about the people of Farrah who embraced Mahdavi Faith on his hand that: "During the period of Mir Zunnoon, governor of Qandhar, Mir Syed Mohammed Juanpuri's arrival from Hijaz via Gujrat, raised a hue and cry in Qandhar and a multitude of people accompanied him". This is an historically recorded proof which is verifiable.

According to the Holy Qur'an when a single person's acceptance of a commissioned personality, brings reform into that piece of land, then why should not it become a proof of Imamana's Mahdiat on account of numberless people accepted him as the Khalifatullah?

Jubair Bin Mu'tim narrated what the Holy Prophet (Slm) said about himself:

"I am that eradicator of infidelity that
Allah eliminates it completely".

انا الماحى الذى يمحو الله بى الكفر

During the period of the Holy Prophet (Slm) infidelity could not be eliminated from all parts of the world. Still he was the eradicator of infidelity as declared by Allah. Allah addresses the Holy Prophet (Slm):

"That thing which was revealed to you is
a truth from your Allah, but many
persons do not believe it." (8:1)

والذى انزل اليك من ربك الحق ولكن اكثر الناس لايومنون (الرعد ع ا)

Qur'an certifies that many persons did not embrace Islam, then how is it possible that during the period of the commissioned personality like Imamana (As) who arrived later on, people still embraced Mahdiat in multiples? For that reason only Allah again ordains that:

"Thus very few embrace (Islam)."

فقليلا مايومنون

This confirms that Muslims are in minority only. As against this clear indication, the Editor maintains that during the period of the commissioned personality a vast number of people should have embraced Islam? By for such foolish utterances, isn't he going against Qur'an?

The Qur'an declares the Holy Prophet (Slm) as"Rahmatul Lil Alamin", does the editor thinks that only the people of Makkah, Madinah and Najran are supposed to be the whole world?

Tumult and tyranny are embedded into the human nature. To eradicate them completely, it is out of question to eradicate from all parts of the world. When during the period of the Holy Prophet (Slm) it was not practically possible, then how can the editor imagine that during the period of Imamana (As) it would become possible? It has been just a fool's imagination indeed!

Whether during the period of the holy prophet (Slm) the punishment of stoning to death was not operative? Whether the punishment of cutting of hands was not inflicted? Whether in view of the weakness of persons instead of whipping 100 flagging, 100 soft branches were not used? Whether the holy prophet (Slm) did not ask Hz. Ali (Rz) to whip even his own slave girl ? According to the traditions and Qur'an if even a single person of a place embraced Islam it was thought that the whole people of that place had embraced Islam, comparatively here, as regards Imam Mahdi (As), countless people accepted Mahdiat during the period of Imamana (As). Author of "Isbath-e-Mahdi (As)" while referring about those who accepted prophet Noah (As), state that during the short period of five years of his Mahdiat by Imamana (As) not only thousands, but hundreds of thousands of people embraced Mahdism.

When during the period of the Holy Prophet (Slm) the tyranny could not be eradicated even from Makkah and Madinah, leave aside from the whole of the world, then to put a condition on Imamana Mahdia-e-Maoud (As) that "He had not eradicated it from the entire world" is just like living in a Fool's paradise.

Author of "Isbaathul Mahdi (As)" had written about Imamana (As) that:

"Within a short spell of time of five
years, not thousands, but hundreds of
thousands had embraced Mahdiat."

بلكه چندلكهه مومنان ايمان آور دند

Mahdi's Birth after Holy Prophet:

Editor of Tajalli utters in Tajalli of November 1964 that after the Holy Prophet no other person would be commissioned by Allah. Such foolish utterances are nothing but to negate and falsify the very Qur'an and traditions of the Holy Prophet (Slm). Allah addresses Adam (As) and Eve (As):

"Allah Ordained to get down both of you. There would be enemies among you. Thus if you receive any guidance from Me and whoever follows guidance he would never be misled, nor become wretched."	قال اهبطا منها جميعاً بعضكم لبعض عدو فاما ياتينكم منى هدى فمن اتبع هداىٰ فلايضل ولايشقىٰ (طهٰ ٤٧)

This verse does not stipulate a particular time or place. Nor it mentions that after the Holy Prophet (Slm) there would never come any guidance. Just read the verse "Summah Inna Alaina Biyanahu". This verse asserts that "Still its (Qur'an's) Biyaan (Interpretation) rests with Allah". Thus as it was possible that the guidance had come before the Holy Prophet (Slm), so also guidance should continue to be provided even after the demise of the Holy Prophet (Slm). The said verse has also informed that whoever brings the guidance, his denial makes one wretched and misled. And further that if whoever does not accept the Commissioned one, he becomes an infidel. Thus Allah ordains further that:

"Whoever does not accept what Allah had revealed, he becomes an infidel."	ومن لم يحكم بما انزل الله فاولئك هم الكافرون

Thus whatever is revealed in the Qur'an, its description is provided by the traditions. For example Qur'an asks for offering prayers, but it does not mean that all the 24 hours you have to perform the prayers.

(However, according to the above verse, Imamana (As) had particularly and emphatically advised his followers to remember Allah in all circumstances as Allah Himself had ordained to remember him standing, sitting and even when lying on the bed. Further he advised his son and his followers to be with Allah always wherever they go.)

Thus, the Holy Prophet (Slm) had prescribed how to offer prayers and when to offer. In the same way he had prophesied that after him someone, by the name Mahdi (As), carrying my name, Mohammed (Slm), would come as a guide. Thus, if someone denies the Holy Prophet (Slm), he would become an infidel, hence denial of the "Promised One" also makes one infidel. Thus if denial of Mahdi (As) does not render anyone as infidel, then the denial of any one from Adam (As) to the Holy Prophet (Slm) who were commissioned by Allah would not make any one infidel?.

The editor of Tajalli in April 1965 states that he is not ready to read any book which is written in proof of Imam Mahdi (As) being a promised one. But how wretched is he who reads "Shahjehanpuri" written by his mentor Mohammed Qasim Nanotavi in which he had tried to designate Sri Ramchander and Sri Krishan as Commissioned ones like the Holy Prophet (Slm) Shame, Shame!!!

40.Denial of the Commissioned One?

According to the editor it is a stupid cruelty if a person is designated as an infidel, if he denies the Commissioned personality who emerges after the demise of the Holy Prophet (Slm). How stupid is the editor who even accuses Allah the Almighty by telling (Naoozoo Billah) that He is not free from the defect of false telling". When he made the Holy Prophet (Slm) his "Elder Brother" is it not his stupid cruelty? Then why should he determine stupid cruelty for designating a person as infidel because he denies to accept a Khalifatullah? This stupid man is trying to issue a verdict on the basis of majority and minority; while the Holy Qur'an warns that:

"And uttered that the Satan would (comparatively) attract a sizeable portion of persons."

وقال لاتخذن من عبادك نصيباً مفروضا

Author of "Madarik" states what Satan had uttered before Allah: "Out of every 1000, only one will be yours, and 999 will be mine":

"In every 1000, nine ninety nine shall be mine (Satan's) and one to You (Allah)."

لى من كل الف تسعمائة و تسعة و تسعون و واحد لله

From it becomes clear that 999 are the followers of Satan, and only one out of 1000 worships Allah, then how is it possible that during the period of Imamana (As), the whole of the world would be filled with justice? Previously we had presented a tradition which says that even if one person is benefited by a Khalifatullah, the purpose of Allah completes in all respects.

Qur'an too certifies that the minority always enjoins Faith and the editor should know that Muslims are always lesser in number than the infidels in the world always.

(Out of 193 countries of the whole world, just 58 countries are Muslim countries. The world population is more than 7 billion, Muslims are hardly 1.75 billion; that is to say, hardly one fourth, means a minority only.)

It may be pointed out that the Christians believe in Allah, believe in all Prophets including Jesus Christ (As), they believe the Dooms Day, paradise and Hell as well, and also have the faith that "Faar Qaleet" would appear in the future. But they just deny our Holy Prophet (Slm) by saying he was not "Faar Qaleet": according to their arguments. And just for that reason only they all are branded as infidels. However, Islam permits Muslims to marry a Christian woman, taking into consideration that the siblings are legitimate. Still it is a fact that married women, even though her children are Muslims, she remains as an Infidel, because she does not believe the Holy Prophet (Slm) as an Apostle of Allah. Does the editor claim this attitude against her as a stupid cruelty (on the part of Muslims)?

Thus, just because the Christian married wife of a Muslim and mother of her Muslim children, does not accept our Holy Prophet (Slm) as the last Prophet (Slm), she is an infidel for both her husband and children and for all Muslims, then if the Khalifatullah is denied even after the Holy Prophet (Slm) and even Qur'an had declared him to be the Commissioned one by Allah, as Khalifatullah (As), should not he or she be branded as infidels? And on what grounds it becomes a stupid cruelty for the editor?

The person who does not believe Khalifatullah (As) is branded as an infidel not just because he does not believe him to be commissioned by Allah, but because he is denying the prophecies of the Holy Prophet (Slm) and of the Holy Qur'an. And to us whoever denies the prophecies he is an infidel and if that telling is branded as stupid cruelty, then the verse "Al Kaferoon" would not have been revealed (by Allah) in the Holy Qur'an, which is revealed to our Holy Prophet (Slm) who is an emblem of the "Best of His Creations". If the editor thinks that branding Infidel is a great abuse then what does he think about the teachings of Islam, while permitting to marry a Christian woman and bestow authority of rearing the children and then abuse her by branding her an infidel? Does the editor think still it is our sublime and secular Islamic culture? As had been said that if Infidelity is a great abuse, as per his absurd thinking, then Qur'an would have not used this word frequently, nor the slaughtered animals by the Christians be permitted as lawfully slaughtered according to the tenets of Islam and never any Christian woman would have been permitted to be married, still those Scripture holders are called Infidels as per this verse:

"If at all you would like to decree
among them, then do it with justice."

قل يآهل الكتاب لم تكفرون بآيات الله .

This verse allows the Holy Prophet (Slm) to do justice, but still neither the whole world became under Holy Prophet's control, nor the whole of the world became Muslim. However Allah had legitimized for Muslims the slaughtered meat by any Christian, and Muslims are permitted to marry Christian women according to the following verse:

"Today legitimized for you the chaste
things and permitted you to eat the meat
of the slaughtered animals by the
scripture holders and that is legitimized
for you and the virtuous and chaste
Muslim women and those women who
had been bestowed with heavenly
Scriptures" (5:6 Part)

اليوم احل لكم الطيبات وطعام الذين اوتو االكتاب
حل لكم وطعامكم حل لهم والمحصنات من
المومنات والمحصنات من الذين اوتو الكتاب من
قبلكم (المائده ع ١)

Whether the editor thinks that these are the Islamic teachings that while the children are brought and bred by a Scripture holder and in the result they can abuse their own mother, hurting her by branding her as an infidel?

It may be pointed out that the words" Prayer and fasting", Prayer and Payment of Zakaat" and the word infidelity had been used frequently in the Qur'an even at the advent of Islam in particular sense which had been accepted as approved by the Qur'an and the traditions.

The editor tells that "to tell infidelity" is an abuse. Then we have to ask him, if branding infidelity is an abuse, then why the word Infidelity had been used in Qur'an in so many verses and at so many times?

The editor states in Tajalli of April 1965 that even telling infidel to a person who denies Imamana (As) creates engrossment in his (fickled) mind. Then we ask the editor does his mind get engrossed in reading or hearing the above said verse, which legitimizes eating of the meat of the animal if slaughtered by 'an infidel Scripture holder? And a Muslim is legally permitted to marry an infidel Scripture holder?

41.Beliefs of the Editor of Tajalli:

Commissioning by Allah of a Khalifatullah after the demise of the Holy Prophet (Slm), in view of the Verse " "Khaatimun Nabbiin" is not objectionable to the editor, since his mentor, Mohammed Qasim Nanotavi, had written in his pamphlet "Taqvitul Eiman" that even after the period of the Holy Prophet (Slm) any Nabi would be born (Naoozoo Billah) - Is he not an Ahmedi? Since he admits that even after the Holy Prophet any Nabi may emerge as the Ahmadis call Ghulam Ahmed as a Nabi (Naoozubillah). If it is his belief, then why should he become angry if the Holy Prophet himself declared Khalifatullah about Imam Mahdi.

42.Fabricated Letter of the Editor:

We have already written to the editor previously that before scribing any remark against Mahdiat, he must twice think before writing, so that same sort of objection should not be inflicted on the Holy Prophet (Slm) or any Khalifatullah (As) and that any prophecy mentioned in the Qur'an and the tradition is affected so as to avoid being accounted for in the presence of Allah on the Doomsday. Therefore, this time he himself did not raise any objection but in the June 1965 issue of Tajalli he had printed a fabricated letter of a so called hypocrite stating that Imamana (AS) does not belong to Saadaat progeny and the names of the parents are not as mentioned in the tradition,

The so called hypocrite, named "Nematullah" of Pakistan, does not live in Chanchalguda. It may be pointed out that Muslims of northern India, as against Southern India, every now and then renounce by repenting Islam and convert to Christianity very often. Should such hypocrites' action prove that Islam is a false religion? We just question directly to the Editor that if any hypocrite converts to Christianity and write to Aamir Osmani, should he publish that letter in its original form? Priest Imaduddin had converted to Christianity and had written a book under the title "Hidayetul Muslameen-Guide to Muslims", will Aamir Osmani inform the new generation of Muslims to read that blasphemous book by publishing it and also printing some excerpts from that unholy book?

This hypocrite's letter states that the traditions regarding Mahdi (As) are not applicable to Imamana (As). As a matter of fact traditions mentioned in "Sihah" confirm and apply to the personality of Imamana (As) completely, as the prophecies mentioned in Torah and Bible apply perfectly on the personality of Huzoor (Slm) except the mountain Faaran, they say it locates in Syria, and we Muslims take it being located in Makkah. It is a fact that the Holy Prophet (Slm) used to go for meditation at Jabal-e-Noor's Cave named "HIRA". About this topic refer part one, Chapter three.

43.Name and Title of Imamana's Father:

On page 12 of Tajalli of June 1969, he had written with reference to "Matleul Vilayet" that: "In Juanpur Syed Khan used to live; while in "Matleul Vilayet" the name "Syed Khan" not at all written. Thus it is a white lie. Lastly he wrote shamelessly that he became a Muslim after invoking Kalema. This sort of lie only could be uttered either by a Neo Muslim or a non Muslim, readers may decide about whether Aamir Osmani is a Neo Muslim or a converted Non Muslim? Since:

1. On Page 7 of "Matleul Vilayet" Imamana's genealogy had been clearly written which is Syed Abdullah son of Syed Osman.

2. The mother's name was written as Agha Malik by the hypocrite, while the mother's name

has been written in "Matleul Vilayet" as "Bibi Amina", further at page 8 it is written that:

"Mother of Imamana being Bibi Amina, Syeda, Saleha, Abida and night Worshipper."

والـده آنـحـضـرت بـی بی آمنه نیز سیدی صالحه عابده شب خیز بودند "

3. He objected the genealogy by saying that there was no child by the name "Nematullah" in the lineage of Imam Moosa Kazim (Rz). This is not the objection which was raised for the first time. This objection is the same what Abu Rija Shahjehanpuri had raised. Here it is enough to write that in a book "Kanzul Ansab" published in Bombay, at page 61, out of eight sons of Ismail Bin Syed Moosa Kazim, one son's name has been written just as "Nemat" It confirms Imamana's genealogy as written in books like 1. "Hadeeq-e-Haqaeque", 2. "Mairajul Vilayet", 3. "Khaatim-e-Sulaimani" and 4. "Mazahebul Islam."

In some Mahdavi Books instead of writing "Nematullah bin Ismail bin Syed Moosa Kazim" has been written as "Nematullah bin Moosa Kazim". Such writing represents like that of the Holy Prophet who told about himself as "Ana Ibn Abdullah bin Abdul Mutallib" but was mistakenly written as "Ana Ibn Abdul Mutallib."

4. An objection is raised with reference to "Insaf Nama" that Imamana asserted : Whether Allah is not powerful to make Syed Khan's son the MAHDI (As)? This too is not a new objection which was also raised by Abu Rija Shahjehanpuri. Imamana (As) did say those words just by repeating the opponents' words. However Father's name was Syed Abdullah and the title was "Syed Khan" as per the recorded and accepted facts by both Mahdvi and non Mahdvai scholars and historians. Imamana's genealogy had been written in part one and chapter one of this book.

According to the belief of the editor of Tajalli, Allah is omnipotent to speak even lies; does Allah not have that power to designate "Syed Khan's" son as "Mahdi (As)"?

5. The quality of the decliner's research may be seen that even when the word "Syed" is written as "Syed Khan", he does not use the word "Syed" which denotes to "coming from Sadat family". But he had used the word "khan" and preferred to name him as a "Pathan" on account of the word "Khan"; that is how he had purposely ignored the word "Syed".

Author of "Rouzatul Ahbab" had written that in the genealogy of the Holy Prophet (Slm) in between Adnan and Ismail (As), there had been fourteen generational gaps, while others say forty six generational gaps. Thus while there is a gap of forty six generations in the genealogy of the Holy Prophet (Slm), and still it becomes a confirmed fact that the Holy Prophet (Slm) was the descendant of Prophet Ismail (As) son of Prophet Ibrahim (Rz). On the other hand while in the case of Imamana (As) there is only one, purposely created gap; then why should the genealogy of Imamana (As) becomes doubtful to these unscrupulous and the so called research scholars?

While we have the oldest source about the biography of Imamana (AS) written by Miyan Abdul Rahman, born in 908 H., just two years before the demise of Imamana (910 H.) under the title "Moulood", but, on the other hand, unfortunately, we do not have any old source of biography of the Holy Prophet. The "Moulood" states the correct name "Miran Syed Abdullah" as the father of the Imamana (As) and mother's name as Bibi Aamina. If that old Source does not get sanctity of these so called scholars, then how could those books of Traditions which were compiled after two hundred years from the demise of the Holy Prophet be accepted as authentic and genuine? In order to support the contents of "Moulood" we present "Juanpur Nama" written by Khairuddin Mohammed Allahbadi in which Imamana's father's name Syed Abdullah and mother's name as Bibi Aamina were clearly mentioned:

"His ((Syed Mohammed) father Syed Abdullah got the title of "Syed Khan" from the kingdom and his mother Aamina Kahtoon was the sister of Qiwamul Mulk and she was also known as "Agha Malik". Both father and mother come from the genealogy of Sadat of Bani Fatima (Rz)."

پدرش خواجه عبدالله از جانب سلطنت سید خان خطاب داشت مادرش آمنه خاتون که خواهر قوام الملك باشد به آغا ملك مخاطب بود ، هر دو پدر و مادر از اجلّه سادات نبی فاطمه بودند (جونپور نامه باب پنجم)

Thus it is confirmed that Imamana's father's name was Syed Abdullah, who was granted the title "Syed Khan" by the Sultan of Sharqi Dynasty. And mother's name was Bibi Aamina and was known as "Agha Malik" since the word "Agha" is a Turkey word used for ladies, by prefixing the name of the ladies in Persian style.

After "Matleul Vilayet", was written, "Shawahedul Vilayet"was written, in which "Agha Malik" was not written for the mother of Imamana (As) upon this Abu Rija (Zaman Khan) had objected for not writing. But his objection is silly because in the oldest biography the names of the parents are correctly written in "Moulood" the same names are written in "Shawahedul Vilayet". In this regard we have presented "Juanpur Nama" which is based on the history of Juanpur and the legends available in Juanpur, about which either Zaman Khan or the editor of Tajalli seems to be unaware, since they both failed to research the facts and tried to write on hearsay gossips.

Thus the names of the parents of Imamana (As) are confirmed from the old sources of Imamana's biography and also about his genealogy coming from Sadaat of Bani Fatima (Rz) which also is a recognized fact by an accredited Writer of "Tuhfatul Kiram" which was written in Sindh (Pakistan). Thus both, "Juanpur Nama" and "Tuhfatul Kiram" are unanimous about the father's name of Imamana (As). That means to say that Imamana (As) belongs to the genealogy of Bani Fatima (Rz), that is a concrete proof, nobody could deny the historical facts.

44. Holy Prophet's Inherant Name:

If there is more than one name of the Holy Prophet (Slm), we have to select that name which had been prophesied. In the case of the Holy Prophet (Slm), Prophet Jesus Christ (As) had prophesied:

"And I am conveying the good news that a Prophet who would come after me , his name will be Ahmed." (61:6)

ومبشرا برسول یاتی من بعدی اسمه احمد (الصف ع ۱)

But our Holy Prophet's name is "Mohammed" designated by his grand Father Abdul Mutallib:

محمدرسول الله

"Allah informs in the Holy Qur'an that
He has revealed Soora-e-Mohammed
since he is the Messenger of Allah". (67)

On such difference of names, has the editor courage to question the Holy Prophet (Slm), as to why he claimed himself as a Prophet, since his name is Mohammed and not Ahmed as prophesied by Jesus Christ? Shall he object on the name "Mohammed (Slm)"? because Jesus Christ (Slm) had proclaimed the name Ahmed (Slm) who was to come after him? Thus according to the prophecy of prophet Jesus (As), name Ahmed bears much weight than the name"Mohammed (Slm) given by his grandfather. In these circumstances, we have to ask the Editor his opinion? Will he agree to the name "Mohammad (Slm)" or he would deny, by saying that the holy prophet's name should be Ahmed (Slm) as per the prophecy, therefore is he doubtful of the prophethood of the holy Prophet (Slm)? The Editor must know that the Holy Prophet (Slm) was known and was called as "MOHAMMED (Slm)" for at least forty years and only after he became Messenger of Allah, his name "Ahmed" became known through the Revelations. Thus with such difference of names the personality of either the Prophet(Slm) or Mahdiat does not change.

Thus it is proved by the holy Qur'an that the name of the holy Prophet (Slm) was Ahmed (Slm), as well as Mohammed (Slm), according to the holy Qur'an. Now we ask the decliner, how can he deny these facts about the difference of the name's of the holy prophet (Slm)? As regards, in the case of Imamana (As), there is no difference in the name of his father. His Father's name was recognized as "Syed Abdullah (Rz)", who was awarded the title as "Syed Khan" by the Sharqi Government. That's also a recognized fact, which cannot be denied.

So also, Imamana's mother's name was Bibi Aamina (Rz), but she was known as "Agha Malik (Rz)". According to the tradition Bibi Aamina (Rz) is correct therefore it fits on to Imamana (As). Thus the traditions certify that Hz. Abdullah (Rz) and Bibi Aamina (Rz) are the parents of Imamana (As).

45. Prophet (Slm) known as "Ibn Abi Kabsha:

"Infidels used to call the Holy Prophet
(Slm) by the name "Ibn Abi Kabsha".

مشرکین آنحضرت را صلی الله علیه وسلم ابن ابی کبشه خواند

The tradition of Ibn Masood also refer this name:

"Told infidels: it is certain that Ibn Abi
Kabsha had mesmerized you".

گفتند کفار به تحقیق سحر کرد شمارا بن ابی کبشه

Bukhari" presents a lengthy tradition which is regarding questions and answers between Hirql and Abu Sufian, as under:

"Thus I told my companions that Bani
Asfara the second (Hirql) is afraid of Ibn
Abi Kabsha, thus he (the Holy Prophet)
had gained his purpose."

فقلت لاصحابی حین خرجنا لقد امرا مرا بن ابی کبشه انه لیخافه ملک نبی الاصفر

From this it is clear that the Holy Prophet (Slm) was also being called as Ibn Abi Kabsha, that is to say his father's name also was Kabsha. Does it mean that his father's name was not Abdullah? But Kabsha? In the same way if the title was "Syed Khan" then does it mean that

Imamana's father's name was not Abdullah? When being Kabsha's son the Prophethood could not and should not be questioned, then how could Imamana's Mahdiat be questioned simply for the reason of the title of his father being "Syed Khan"?

Apart from this, When even after the prophecy regarding the next Prophet's name, being "Ahmed (Slm)" as Jesus Christ (As) himself reported as against his given name "Mohammed (Slm)" did it repudiate the Prophethood of the Holy Prophet (Slm)? In the same sense if as objected that Imamana's parents' name were not according to the traditions, then why should Imamana's Mahdiat be questioned?

46.Tareekh-e-Dawoodi confirms "Syed Khan" comes from Ahl-e-Bait (Rz):

The so called hypocrite doubts that "Syed Khan" is not from the genealogy of the Saadaat which shows his lack of knowledge of history. "Tareekh-e-Dawoodi" was written during the period of Jehangir in the year 1012 to 1027 whose author is Abdullah who had written about Sultan Sikander Lodhi that:

"Sultan Husain Sharqi, after hearing (Sultan Sikander Lodhi's arrival), sent Mir Syed Khan, one of his eminent nobles as ambassador to Sultan Sikander Lodhi. The Sultan addressed Miran Syed Khan: **"you are the son (descendent) of the Holy Prophet (Slm); why do not you teach him** (to Sultan Husain Sharqi) to behave properly, otherwise he would have to repent (afterwards)."

سلطان حسین شرقی بعد از اطلاع بهم رساند میر سید خان (را) که از مرایان کلان سلطان حسین بوده به ایلچی گری فرستاده ....

This is clear that even the kings (of Delhi) knew about Syed Khan that he was the descendent of the Holy Prophet (Slm), still if the editor is doubtful, then it may be said that he lacks in the knowledge of History, therefore he is advised again to object if he is thorough in the subject matter, otherwise he would be termed as a muff and dumb.

Objections raised by a so called hypocrite who said that he became Muslim only after invoking the Kalema-e-Tauheed". That is why he had become a hypocrite because he did not read the complete Kalema which includes "Mohammadur Rasoolillah" Thus to him, it seems that "Mohammedur Rasoolullah" is not the part of the First Tenet of Islam.

47.Imamana's Patronymic Name:

The names of parents of Imamana (As) are correct according to the traditions, his patronymic name also had been mentioned in the tradition. Author of "Jannatul Vilyet" states that:

"After some time the Sheik (Sheik Daniyal Rz) asked Syed Abdullah (Rz) _ about the new born as to how he was doing. He (Syed Abdullah (Rz) replied: Good. Then Sheik (Rz) asked whether any patronymic name had been suggested? He replied that his grandfather's patronymic name was Abul Qasim, therefore sometimes we call Abul Qasim also to him (Imamana (As)"

بعد از چند مدت يك روز شيخ الاسلام سيد عبدالله را پرسيدند كه سيد محمد خوش حال است گفتند آرى، شيخ باز پرسيدند كه نام كنيت دى چيزى هست يانه گفتند جد ما ابوالقاسم بود بناء،بر آن گاهى ابوالقاسم مى گوئيم (٧)

The same is reported in "Shawahedul Vilayet":

"After a lapse of a period (Sheik Daniyal Rz) inquired: whether any patronymic name was suggested? (Hzt. Syed Abdullah (Rz): replied, our grandfather's name was Syed Qasim (Rz), hence we call him "Abul Qasim" sometimes."

بعد از مدتى پرسيدند كه آن پسر را به چه كنيت مى ناميد، جواب دادند كه نام جد ما سيد قاسم بود بناء بر ان گاه گاه ابوالقاسم مى خوانيم (باب چهارم)

There is no reason not to name Mohammed and the patronymic name Abul Qasim, both to Imamana (As) together, since it was the name and the patronymic name of the Holy Prophet (Slm) because Imam Maalik (Rh) had permitted:

"To name Mohammed (Slm) and patronymic name Abul Qasim (As) is permissible as per Imam Maalik (Rh)."

جمع ميان كنيت و اسم روا است وين قول را با مام مالك نسبت مى كنند وايشان مى گويند كه احاديث منع منسوخ اند

Author of Ashatul Lam'aat" also had written the same:

"To name Mohammed (Slm) and patronymic name Abul Qasim (As) is allowed by Imam Maalik (Rh) with a clarification that those traditions which had forbidden this usage, now became obliterated."

جمع نيز درست است وين قول را با مالك نسبت مى كنند و ايشان مى گويند كه احاديث منع منسوخ اند ٣ ـ

Thus Syed Abdullah (Rz) named his son "Syed Mohammmed (As)" and also called him "Abul Qasim"; which is permitted according to the Imam Maalik (Rz). Hence no objection should be raised.

Particularly because the Holy Prophet (Slm) himself had informed that the Mahdi's name would be Mohammed (As) and his patronymic name was Abul Qasim (As).

Author of "Uqdud Durer" had written that:

"Narrated Abdullah Bin Omer (Rz) who heard the Holy Prophet (Slm) saying that from my descendents one person would emerge in the last period whose name would be of mine and whose patronymic name also would be that of mine. He would fill the Earth with peace and justice against its tyranny."

قال قال رسول الله صلی الله علیه وآله سلم یخرج فی آخـر الزمان رجل من ولدی اسمه اسمی وکنیة کنیتی یملاء الارض عد لاکما ملئت جورا ۳ا،

Although Zaman Khan did not object on this issue, but objection was raised on "Shawahedul Vilayet's reference to this issue and objected that since there was no other son by name Qasim, hence on grandfather's name patronymic name was suggested as Abul Qasim to the only son. Thus his objection has no value because just to give the patronymic name of Abul Qasim, it is not necessary that there should be any son; as mentioned in " Safarus Sadat" that:

"Patronymic name is given with reference to an elder son of a family to a newborn one. And if there had been no offspring, then as a good omen it is kept."

کنیـت گاهی باضافه ولد می باشد خصوصاً باکبر اولاد گـاهے بے آن کـه اور اولدے باشد اضافه بوے کنند تفاولاً ـ ۱ ـ ؎

Abu Dawood's tradition also refers that even during the lifetime of the Holy Prophet (Slm) a kid's patronymic name was given as "Abul Qasim."

48. 2nd.Fabricated Letter of the Editor of Tajalli:

Now we try to answer to another fabricated letter of the editor under the title: " Mahdait ki jhalkian" (Glimpses of Mahdiat): printed by Aamir Osmani in Tajalli of September and October 1965:

His fabricated letter also could not prove the validity of his "religious view" that Allah also can speak lies.(Naoozoo Billah)

49.Mahdi as Allah's Khalifa:

The prominence of Bai'at/ oath of allegiance, to become a disciple of the Holy Prophet (Slm) had been mentioned by Allah in this manner:

"Those people who are offering oath of allegiance (on your hand) in fact they are offering (on our hand) to Allah" (68:6)

ان الذین یبایعونک انما یبایعون الله (الفتح ع ا)

The Holy Prophet (Slm) had instructed to offer allegiance to Imam Mahdi (As):

"Thus offer allegiance to him (Mahdi (As) even if you had to crawl over the snows, since Mahdi (As) is the Khalifatullah."

فبایعوه ولو حبوا علیٰ الثلج فانه خلیفة الله المهدی

(Note: "To crawl over the snows" for offering allegiance to Mahdi, who is Khalifatullah, points out Imamana's advent shall be on to the East of Baghdad, to a place which is beyond snow clad Mountains of Hindu Kush, therefore after crawling the Hindu

Kush only, one could reach India upto Karara, now Juanpur, which is itself a prophecy of the Holy Prophet (Slm) who pointed out Imamana's Birth Place." It may be pointed out that in one of the traditions, the place where Imam Mahdi would born was given as Karara. According to the historical facts, Juanpur was founded after dismantalling the Kararabeir temple of Karara. Still the name of Karara is available near the fort of Juanpur. Khundmiri)

It may be pointed out that the Leaders of Traditions have accepted these traditions regarding Imam Mahdi (As) as mentioned in "Sihah" and the Commentators like Ibn Tamima etc. had also authenticated those traditions.

Apart from this the Traditionalists have also accepted the continuity of these traditions as

(Muthawatir). (vide Part 1, chapter 7) Allah had ordained the Holy Prophet that:

"Tell; verily, my Lord had guided me." قل انی هدانی ربی (الانعام ع ٢٠)
(6:161)

When Allah had guided the Holy Prophet (Slm), then the Holy Prophet's personality too may be known as Mahdi (As), therefore the name "Al Mahdi" is one of the names of the Holy Prophet (Slm) as well.

Ahmed Ibn Hunbal (Rz) had referred the name "Khalifatullahil Mahdi (As)" as had been reported by Soban. It means to say that since Mahdi is Khalifatullah (As), every Prophet (As) is also the Khalifatullah (As). As per commentary of the Verse "Inni Jaaelun Filarzi Kahalifa":

"I am going to create (depute my) Khalifa on the earth." "Madarik" states that:

"Since Adam (As) was the Khailfa of Allah on His Earth, therefore all Prophets (As) (also are Allah's Khalifas)." لآن آدم کان خليفة الله فی ارضه و کذلک کل نبی

Author of "Ruhul Mu'ani" states that:

"The meaning of Adam (As) being His First Khalifa on the Earth, thus Allah made all Prophets His Khalifa on the Earth." ومعنی کونه خليفةالله انه تعالیٰ فی ارضه و کذلک کل نبی استخلفهم ٣

Thus the Holy Prophet (Slm) also had been bestowed with the Khilafat as Prophet Adam (As) (had been bestowed). Therefore "Mu'ahebul Aliah" had written that:

"Being "Allah's Khalifa was also an approved fact for the Holy Prophet (Slm) also." خلافت حق مر آنحضرتؐ را ثابت بوده

The importance of allegiance to Imam Mahdi (As) is evident in view of the fact that the Holy Prophet (Slm) had asserted that Mahdi Khalifatullah (As) is also the Repellor from extinction of the Ummah as himself. Reported Razzeen that:

"How could the Ummah be extinct, in whose beginning I am there, Mahdi (As) is in between and Christ (As) is at the end."

كيف تهـلك امة انـا اولهـا والـمهـدى وسطهـا والمسيح آخرها

Author of "Mirqaat" had termed the linkage mentioned in the tradition as a "Golden Chain". (vide Part 2, chapter 3)

Thus it is clear that Imam Mahdi (As) is Khalifatullah as the Holy Prophet (Slm) and Christ (As)are, and all the three are the Repellors from extinction of the Ummah. It is a proof that Khalifatullah is Innocent as the Prophet (Slm). Hence "Bukhari" narrates:

"Narrated Abu Sayeed that the Holy Prophet (Slm) said that Allah did not send any Prophet and did not make any one His Khalifa, but that there are two personalities internally; one orders for virtue and instigates to enjoin it, while the other orders for evil which instigates to commit it. But innocent is the one who is saved by Allah from (evils and to commit sin). Reported by Bukhari."

عن ابى سعيد قال قال رسول الله صلى الله عليه وسلم مابعث الله من نبى ولا استخلف من خليفة الا كانت لـه بـطـانتـان بـطـانة تـامـره بالمعروف و تحضه عليه و بطانه تامره بالشرو تحضه عليه والمعصوم من عصمه الله رواه البخارى ۵ﮬ

From this tradition it comes to light that every Khalifa is innocent as the Prophet (Slm) is also innocent. This tradition further informs that khilaphat is meant for Allah's khilafat and not the worldly Khilafat.

50. Ranks of Mahdi (As):

Since the Prophets, including our Holy Prophet (Slm), are guided by Allah, Mahdi, as Khalifatullah, is also the guided personality by Allah. Still there are other attributes for Imamana (As) which are discussed hereunder:

Reported by "Uqdud Durer" that the Holy Prophet (Slm) told:

"His name would be as of mine; and his characters shall be like mine."

اسمه اسمى وخلقه خلقى (الباب ثانى)

Characters here are reported in an abstract sense. Therefore it covers all issues. Thus Imamana's characters should be as that of the Holy Prophet's. For further details read Chapter "Characters of Imamana (As)."

"Narrated Holy Prophet (Slm) that Mahdi (As) is from us. Allah would complete the Deen/religion on him in the manner it started from me."

ب . قال رسول الـلـه صـلى الله عليه وسلم الـمهـدى مـنـا يختم الله به الدين كم فتحه بنا (عقد الدر الباب السابع)

This proves that Mahdi (As) would bring the Deen to its completion by openly teaching the third pillar of Deen, AHSAAN, as taught by Gabreil (As), which is known as "Hadees-e-Jebrail"; thus he completes the purpose of the Faith, religion, Deen, term it as you may think fit to its entirety. Hence Imam Mahdi (As) is also called "Khaatim-e-Deen-e-Ilahi."

"Narrated Ibn Siereen when asked: Was Mahdi (As) better than Abu Bakr (Rz) and Omer (Rz)? Replied: Mahdi (As) is better than both, rather he is equal to the Holy Prophet (Slm)."

ج. عـن مـحـمـد ابـن سـيـرين قال قيل لـه الـمـهـدى خير ام ابـوبـكر و عمر قال هو خير منهما و يعدل بالنبى ١ ﺐ

Abu Abdullah Nayeem Bin Hammad (Rz) had deduced, in his Book "Kitabul Fittan," about this tradition, and author of "Uqdud Durer" had commented on it that Mahdi (As) was superior to both Abu Bakr (Rz) and Omer (Rz) and is equal to the Holy Prophet (Slm). Because both Holy Prophet (Slm) and Mahdi (AS) are Khalifatullah, while Abu Bakr (Rz) was not the Khalifatullah, since this fact Abu Bakr (Rz) himself confirmed it as narrated by Ibn Abi Sheeba:

"Tradition stated to us by Waqee who heard Naafe-e-Bin Omer and he told to Ibn Abi Malikat that someone addressed Abu Bakr (Rz): "Oh Khalifatullah"! Abu Bakr (Rz) stopped him and said that he was not the Khalifatullah, but just a deputy of Rasoolullah (Slm) and with that I am satisfied being the deputy of the holy Prophet (Slm)."

حـد ثـنا و كيع عن نافع بن عمر عن اب ابى مـلـيـكـة قـال قـال رجل لابى بكر خـلـيـفـة الـلـه قـال لست بخليفة اللـه و لـكـنـى خـلـيـفة رسـول اللـه وانـاراضى بذالك

Based on it, Ibn Siereen deduced that Mahdi (As) was greater than Abu Bakr (Rz) and equal to the Holy Prophet (Slm). Thus Amir Osmani could not object because as per his own version hundreds of thousands of persons are equal to the Holy Prophet (Slm); particularly because his mentor, Ismail Dehalvi had written that:"If desired, He (Allah) would create hundreds of thousands of Prophets, mystics, Jinn's, angels and Gabriel who would be equal to the Holy Prophet (Slm). Apart from it, another mentor of the editor, Mohammed Qasim Nanothavi had written in "Discussions of Shahjehanpuri" that even Sri Ramcahander and Sri Krishan could become Khalifatullah and therefore, they are also equal to the Holy Prophet (Slm). Therefore he could not object to Ibn Siereen who had equaled Mahdi (As) to the Holy Prophet (Slm) for the reason that both are Khalifatullah.

It informs that even before Adam (As) and Eve (As) were shifted to the Earth, Allah had ordained that whenever you receive my Guidance, you are bound to obey it, if you do not obey, you would become wretched and misled from the right path.

51.Mahdi (As) and Apostles (As):

Allah Ordains whoever brings guidance, he would be questioned:

"Thus We shall question to those to whom they were sent and also We shall question to those Apostles who were sent. (7:6)

فـلـنـسـئـلـن الـذين ارسـل اليهـم ولـنسئلن المرسلين (الاعراف ع ا)

In this verse "Almursaleen" had been used which is in the plural form of "Murassal" which had a different meaning as per Ajamis. However Allah States:

"Do you really believe that (Prophet) Saleh (As) had been sent by Allah?." (7:75)

اتـعـلـمون ان صالحاً مرسل من ربه (الاعراف ع ٠١)

It means to say that all Messengers are sent by Allah. Thus whomever Allah sent, He sent for Guidance to the people. Therefore they are called "Mursaleen". As per above verse if we say that it was meant for a single Messenger, then whether other Apostles would not be put into question?

Then how could it be said that Mahdi (AS) is not Innocent and the one who denies his

Mahdiat, why should he be not termed as an infidel? Otherwise it tantamount to the denial of Qur'an and traditions. When the disciples of Ahmed Raza Khan Barailvi do not offer prayer behind the disciples of Mohammed Qasim Nanothavi (founder of Darul Uloom, Devband), on account of difference of beliefs, becomes infedil, then a person who does not accept Mahdi (As) as one among the Commissioned one then, behind such a denier how a Mahdvi could offer prayer, like the followers of Ahmed Raza Khan?

52.Qasim Nanothvi and Ranks of Holy Prophet:

Aamir Osmani does not believe in the doctrine of "khaatim-e-Nabuwwat". His mentor is Qasim Nanothavi about whom, the author of "Hussamul Harmain" had stated that:

"A book under the title "Tahzeerunnass" was written by Qasim Nanothavi. According to him, in the presence of the holy Prophet (Slm) if some person declares himself as Nabi, this Nabi would cause no effect on the position of the Holy Prophet (Slm) since he is the Last Messenger of Allah. Further to this, even after the Prophet's demise if there emerges a new Nabi, then also, the Holy Prophet's position as the Seal of the Prophets remains intact. Generally, the public gives importance to the Holy Prophet (Slm), because he was the last of the Apostles, but those who are persons of misunderstanding do not give any importance for the Prophet (Slm) as being the last of the Prophets (Slm)." *(They are known as Ahmadis, designated as Infidels/Kafir).*

القاسميه المنسوبة الىٰ قاسم النانوتى صاحب تحذير الناس وهو القائل فيه "ولو فرض فى زمنه صلى الله عليه وسلم بل لو حدث بعده صلى الله عليه وسلم نبى جديد لم يخل ذلك بخاتمية وانما تخييل العوام انه صلى الله عليه وسلم خاتم النبين بمعنى آخر النبين معه انه لا فضل فيه عند اهل الفهم آخر

According to Qasim Nanothavi, two issues arise: 1. Even if any Nabi emerges after the demise of the Holy Prophet (Slm), it does not affect the position of the Holy Prophet (Slm) as he was the Seal of the Apostles. 2. Holy Prophet's position as the last of the Apostle has no importance to him. Because he admits that even a new Nabi does not cause any effect on the person of the Holy Prophet (Slm), then how could he say that Imam Mahdi's inclusion among the Commissioned ones, would in any way affect the position of the Holy Prophet (Slm) as the last of the Apostles? Particularly when the Holy Prophet (Slm) already had given glad tidings to Imam Mahdi (As), as the Kahlifatullah, protector of the Ummah from destruction and Khaatim-e-Deen-e-Mohammedi (Slm).

53. Status of Mahdiat and Nabuwwat:

Now remains the point for discussion that what is the ground to claim the status as Imam Mahdi (As)? We may say the same status what Nabuwwat acclaims, the same laudable traits of character should grant the status for Imam Mahdi (As) and his claim for Mahdiat as well.

When Allah declared that "I shall descend similar to the one which I had descended prior to this". With reference to this it is stated that when the Writer of the Revelations wrote the words: "Laqad Khalaqnal Insana Min Salalatin" and when he reached at "Summa In Shanahu Khalaqa......"then suddenly the following words uttered by the writer "Fatabarakallahu Ahsanal Khaleqeen". A. Author of "Mualam-e-Tanzeel" had stated that"

"When this verse was revealed: "certainly we created man from the extract of soil (food)"; Holy Prophet (Slm) asked the "Writer of Revelations" to write down in the Qur'an.Listening this Abdullah became very much fascinated about the Creation of man, then the writer suddenly exclaimed"Fatabarakallahu Ahsanul Khaleqeen." At this point, the prophet (slm) asked him "to continue to write down the same words what he had just spoken, since those words also have been revealed to me by Allah". On that Abdullah became suspicious about the Holy Prophet (Slm), "by wrongly surmising whether the Prophet (Slm) was trustworthy? Because the holy Prophet (Slm) is asking me to incorporate those words what had I uttered, were the words of Allah who also revealed to him and to me simultaneously." Thus he became hypocrite and joined with the infidels."

فلمـا نـزلـت لـقد خلق الانسان من سلالة من طين
املاهـا رسـول الله فعجب عبدالله من تفصيل خلق
الانسـان فـقـال فتبـاركـ الله احسن الخالقين فقال
الـنبى اكتبها فهكذا نزلت فشكـ عبدالله وقال لئن
كـان مـحـمـد صادقا لقد اوحى الّى كما اوحى اليه
فارتد عن الاسلام ولحق بالمشركين الىٰ آخره

B. It is also reported in Tafseer-e-Kasshaf: "Certainly we created man with the extract of the Soil (Food), this was appreciated by Abdullah (the writer of Revelation), then he exclaimed : Thus how much grandeur he had, which surpassed all creations: Then the Holy Prophet asked him to write down what Abdullah had expressed. It is because the same was also revealed to the Holy Prophet (Slm). Abdullah became doubtful as to how could those words sa by me become the part of the Revelation? The same to have been revealed by Allah to the Prophet (Slm)? If he is a liar, then how could it be a revelation that those words which were said by me could be the words of Allah. Hence he became hypocrite and converted back as an infidel."

فلـما نزلت ولقد خلق الانسان من سلالة من طين الىٰ آخر الآية عجب عبدالله من تفصيل خلـق الانسـان فقـال "فتبارک الله احسن الخـالقـين" فقـال عليـه السلام اکتبها فکذلک نـزلت فشک عبدالله وقال لئن کـان محمد صادقا لقد اوحی الیّ کما اوحی اليـه ولئـن کـان کـاذبـالـقد قلت کما قال فارتدعن الاسلام ٢؏

C. Author of "Tafseer-e-Madarik states that:

"Abdullah Bin Sa'ad Ibn Abi Sirha was the writer of the Revelations. The Holy Prophet asked him to write "Wa Laqad Khalakhal Insana Khalaqan". Thus suddenly Abdullah uttered the words" Tabarakallahu Ahsanul Khalequeen". On that Holy Prophet asked him to write what he had just spoken as a revelation.

"Since this is a revelation also to me. (Said the Holy Prophet Slm). Abdullah became perturbed and thought whether the Prophet is trustworthy? He thought if these words were revealed to the Prophet, then those words, as if, were also revealed to me. Then he joined the infidels of Makkah. (Presuming himself to be also a Nabi)."

هـو عبـداللـه بن سعد بن ابی سرح کاتب الوحی وقد أمـلـی النبی عليه السلام عليه ولقد خلق الانسان الی خـلـق آخـر فـجری علـی لسانه فتبارک الله احسن الخـالـقـين فقـال عليه السلام اکتبها فکذلک نزلت فشک وقال ان کان محمد صادقا فقد اوحی الیٰ کما اوحی اليه وان کان کـاذبـاً فقد قلت کما قال ولحق بمکة

D."Tafseer-e-Madarik" speaks about:

"It is stated that Abdullah bin Saad bin Abi Sarah used to write the revelation as dictated by the holy Prophet (Slm) but before the holy Prophet (Slm) said he wrote two verses from himself, on that the holy Prophet (Slm) accepted his words and told "your words are correct, because the verse is revealed to me also like that". Then Abdullah said if Mohammad is a Nabi and revelation comes to him in the same manner, I also receive the revelation thus he became hypocrite.

E. "Asbabul Nuzool" states these words:

"Thus Abdullah praised what had been told by the Prophet (Slm) about the creation of Man. On that Abdullah exclaimed "Fatabarakallhu Ahsanal Khaleqeen" in praise of Allah. On that the Holy Prophet (Slm) told that the "same words had been revealed to me also."

قيل ان عبدالله بن سعد بى ابى سرح كان يكتب للنبى عليه السلام فنطق بذلك قبل املائه فقال له رسول الله صلى الله عليه وسلم اكتب هكذانزلت فقال عبدالله ان كان محمد نبيا يوحى اليه فانا نبى يوحى الّى فارتد

فعجب عبدالله من تفصيل خلق الانسان فقال تبارك الله احسن الخالقين فقال النبى صلى الله عليه وآله وسلم هكذا انزلت على

Thus it is a fact that those words were told by Abdullah first, then those words revealed by Gabriel (As) on to the Holy Prophet (Slm). On this author of "Tareekh-e-Habeeb Ilah" had commented that: From the experience in writings, it came to light that sometimes what the teacher wants to describe, the pupils get the reflection of even before he explains. Such was the situation with Abdullah who exclaimed even before the Holy Prophet (Slm) explained to him. Abdullah took it otherwise being instigated by Satan and he became infidel."

We have firm believe and have opinion on the assertions and as already confirmed by the Holy Prophet (Slm) that those words were certainly revealed by Gabriel (As) to the Holy Prophet (Slm) and we accept the Holy Prophet's assertion since he is known as the trustworthy person even before he was commissioned as an Apostle. This fact had been recorded in "Madarijul Nabuwwat:

"The Qureysh used to call the Holy Prophet (Slm) as Trustworthy, even before he was proclaimed as the Prophet himself"

آنحضرت را تمام قريش پيش از ظهور نبوت محمد امين مى خواندند ٤ ٮ

Even before he was proclaimed as an Apostle of Allah, therefore, none could blame the Holy Prophet (Slm) to have ever lied; as mentioned in "Bukhari" and "Muslim":

"Hiraql inquired to Abu Sufyan whether you at any time had blamed him for lying even before he was chosen by Allah? Abu Sufian told: Never. Thus I became convinced that he could not tell lies."

وسـالتک هـل کـنتـم تتهـمو نه بالکذب قبل ان يقول ماقال فزعمت ان لی فعرفت انه لم يكن ليدع الكذب علی الناس ثم يذهب فيكذب علی الله .

It is reported about the Holy Prophet (Slm) during his stay in Makkah for 13 years that:

"His stay in Makkah (after becoming the Apostle) for thirteen years, but some say for ten or fifteen years."

مدت اقامـت آنحضرت صلی الله علیه وسلم در مکه سنیزده سـال بود چهـانکه مشهور و مختار است و برواتی ده و پانزده نیز آمده ۱ـ

During this lengthy period very few eminent scholars accepted the Holy Qur'an as the word of Allah. But they were impressed by the Prophet's appreciable character. Thus his laudable character became the best proof for his Nabuwwat. So also it is an affirmed fact that the Holy Qur'an was revealed to the Holy Prophet (Slm) by Arch angel Gabriel (As). Still his appreciable character is the touchstone for his Nabuwwat.

Mohammed Qasim Nanothavi had attributed three features as the standard for Nabuwwat:

1. Love of Allah 2. Appreciable characters 3. Intelligence . Thus he wrote:

Intelligent people should judge intelligence, appreciable character and practice of a Nabi, then they decide who is Nabi and who is not.

Thus the standard through which we have to judge for a Nabi, the same standard should be applied to judge for Imam Mahdi (As). Now remain signs, some may fit and some may not fit. Still appreciable character is enough as the proof (which will never change).

Now we have to determine whether Hzt. Syed Mohammed Juanpuri (As) alone is the promised Mahdi (As), about whom the Holy Prophet had prophesied? The answer is that:

The Holy Prophet (Slm) was known as the most trustworthy person and that this quality of truthfulness was accepted by all even before his Prophethood, thus what he asserted about Imam Mahdi (As) should be accepted as true in all respects. Holy Prophet asserted about Imam Mahdi (As) that "He will never tell lie, nor he will err, and will follow me." Imamana (As) also is known for his exemplary characters, since the holy prophet (Slm) had predicted that "Mahdi (As) shall have my character - Khuluqahu Khulqi". Apart from these predictions, Imamana (As) was acclaimed by the scholars of Juanpur as "Asadul Ulemah" and "Syedul Aoulia" even before he proclaimed himself to be the "Promised Mahdi (As)". His characters were like that of the Holy Prophet (Slm). Such a venerable personality left his house, his city, his country for the cause and in the name of Allah without having provision, having complete trust on Allah for his sustenance and started his Mission with a firm belief in Allah who is the lone Sustainer. He traveled thousands of miles from Juanpur via so many places to Makkah, back to India then went to Sindh and finally to Farrah, Afghanistan, borne many hardships and turmoil of the journey just for the cause of Allah, to spread the message of the Holy Prophet (Slm) about Islam in its original shape and proclaimed his Mahdiat four times at different places and did never repudiate as other false claimants had done. Thus, when appreciable character is the best criterion as the proof of Nabuwwat of the Holy Prophet (Slm), in the same manner, Imamana's appreciable character is the best touchstone for his Mahdiat. Now remains applicability of the signs: As the prophecies regarding the Holy Prophet mentioned in the Scriptures, some of them, correctly apply to him and some do not apply, in the same manner all the narratives mentioned in "Sihah" regarding Mahdi (As), apply completely to the personality of Imamana (As). However, Aamir Osmani had accepted Mahdi (As) as a Mystic and a Qutub and helped us to close our discussion now. His words are: Accept Imamana (As) as "a Venerable personality, a Vali, even a Qutub, a Saintliman, all attributes are thus acceptable to him (but not Mahdi-e-Mouood). (Tajjalli Monthly, January 1965, P.63)

Even Aamir Osmani accepted Imamana (As) as a Mystic who must be an innocent, now he turned back and says that Mahdi (As) could not be an innocent one and for this he submits that Imamana (As) had studied under the patronage of Shaikh Daniyal (Rz) who was not an innocent one, because any innocent should not get education from a person who is not an innocent one. But all biographies of Imamana (As) confirm that Shaikh Daniyal (Rz) himself had benefitted by the teachings of Imamana (As). The first issue is that, even before his Mahdiat, Allah had provided him such an exemplary capability to understand education which became the cause of his being awarded the title of "Asadul Ulema" by the learned people of Juanpur at his tender age of twelve. Of course, preliminary studies in learning the Arabic Language and basic knowledge, Imamana (As) were under the guidance of Shaik Daniyal (Rz) when he was of the age of four years and afterwards. Of course he became qualified in Arabic and Persian languages under the supervision of Hazt. Shaik Daniyal (Rh). On account of which at the age of 12, he was recognized by the scholars of Juanpur that Imamana (As) was the "Asadul Ulemah" and further at his age 21 years he was awarded the title of "Syedul Aoulia" These titles he earned not because he went to the school of Shaikh Daniyal (Rz) in his early childhood, but because Allah had provided him necessary teachings to become "Asadul Ulemah and Syedul Aoulia."

It may be pointed out that in his childhood the Holy Prophet (Slm) learned the idioms and usage of the Arabic language when he was under the care of his childhood nurse, Bibi Haleema (Rz), through whom he could challenge the eminent Arabic scholars of his period, particularly Ibnul Zubairi who was an eminent poet of that time. As mentioned in "Madrijul Nabuwwat".

"When the verse was revealed: "Verily, you oh Infidels and those idols to whom you worship in place of Allah, shall be thrown into the Hellfire" On that Zubairi told that from this verse it seems that Jesus Christ too would be thrown in that fire, because Christians worship him. Then he said what if our idols are thrown in that fire. At that assertion of Zubairi, the Holy Prophet (Slm) told: "Alas you are so ignorant of our language that the word "Maa" is used for those who lack in the capacity to understand as mentioned in the grammar."

چون نازل شد آیئہ کریمہ "انکم وما تعبدون من دون اللہ حصب جھنم" ایں ابن زبعری گفت ازیں آیت معلوم می شود کہ عیسیٰ پرستیدن اور انصاری او نیز درجھنم باشد چون او درجھنم باشد گو معبود ان ما نیز باشند آنحضرت فرمود "ویلک ما اجھلک بلسان قومک اشارت کردبآنکہ کلمۂ مابرائے غیر عقلا است ـ چنانچہ درکتب نحو مقرر شدہ است (مدارج النبوۃ جلد دوم ۳۰۳)

In "Ashatul Lamm'aat" it is reported that: "When Ibn Zubairi, who was an infidel uttered, the Holy Prophet (Slm) retarded "Alas you are too ignorant of our language."

آوردہ اند کہ ابن زبعرا کہ یکے از مشرکان بود ایں بحث کرد آنحضرت صلی اللہ علیہ وسلم اور اگفت وائے برتوچہ خوش خوش جاہل بودۂ تو بزبان قوم خود (اشعتہ اللمعات جلد اول ۱۴۵)

The verse of Kalamullah tells that both infidels and their idols would be thrown into the Hellfire. On that Ibn Zuibairi told that the Christians worship Isa (As), then Isa (As) too would be put into that fire. The Holy Prophet (Slm) retarded by telling as per grammar the word "Maa" does not apply to Isa (As). Years before the Revelations started to descend onto the Holy Prophet (Slm), the Holy Prophet (Slm) was well proficient in Arabic, because he was a Qureyshi and was brought and bred among the Qureysh, who were Non Innocent, thus he himself said that:

"My early period was served with my foster mother Halima Saadia (Rz) of Bani Sa'ad bin Bakr who were very proficient in the Arabic language."

ناشی شدم من در بنی سعد بن بکر کہ قوم مرضعہءوی صلی اللہ علیہ وسلم حلیمہء سعدیہ اند و ایشان افصح عرب بودند (مدراج النبوۃ جلد اول ۱۰)

Thus he learned the use of the language by the non-innocent people, and when it is not objectionable, then if Imamana too learned Arabic and Persian and got juist the elementary education from non-innocent peoples, why should that issue be raised at all?

54. Qur'an's Consistancy Proved:

At the time of the Holy Prophet (Slm) there was nothing like exclusive sentences, or distinct, terminated, omitted, in the text of the Holy Qur'an and Qur'an was considered to be consistent in all respects, but as time passed on, the Commentators invented a new way of studying the Qur'an in which a new vocabulary was introduced like "repetition of verses, extra alphabets and abandoned verses" etc., through this, Qur'an for them became mostly inconsistent. In Juanpur before the birth of Imamana (As), Qazi Shahabuddin Doulatabadi wrote a Commentary in four volumes under the title "Bahr-e-Mouwwaj" in which verses have been rearranged and from the beginning to the end it had been pointed out that, in the very text of the Holy Qur'an, the "exclusive sentences, parenthetical sentences, distinctive features, even terminated and abandoned verses" etc. are existing which made the holy Qur'an completely an inconsistent one. (God Forbid).

As otherwise the Holy Prophet (Slm) by using the colloquial language and its usage proved Qur'an's lingual eloquence. In the same way Imamana (As) with his proficiency in Arabic had virtually negated any sort of "abrogation, exclusive sentences" etc. and proved Qur'an's consistency as it was during the period of the Holy Prophet (Slm). Details of which you may read in Part 2, chapter 6.

55. Early Worship of holy Prophet (Slm):

The life of the Holy Prophet (Slm) before he became the Apostle of Allah has been mentioned in "Madarijul Nabuwwat":

"(He) Followed Ibrahim's Shariat and Shariats of other Prophets if he found them comprehensible, (to his understanding) had adopted."

عـمـل مـی کرد به شریعت ابراهیم علیه السلام یا هر چه ثـابـت مـی شـد نـزد وی یـعـنـی از شرائع انبیـاء و یـا بـه استحسان عقل (جلد دوم ۳۰)

Before his Prophethood, he used to go for Hajj and had performed Umrah as mentioned in "Madarijul Nabuwwat"

"He had firm belief in the Oneness of Allah. Hated Idol worship. Used to perform Hajj and Umrah and never drank liquor."

پیش از بعثت ‘ توحید مـی کرد از خدا ‘ دشمن مـی داشت اوشـان و عبـادت آن راوحـج وعـمـره مـی کرده هر گز شراب نه خورده (جلد اول ۹۳)

After becoming Prophet (Slm) Gabriel (As) used to teach him as mentioned in "Madarijul Nabuwwat":

"Instructed him how to perform ablution and prayers."

جبـرئیـل گفت که وضو کردن و نماز گز اردن همچنین است (جلد دوم ۳۱)

56. First Revelation and Varqa Bin Noufil:

After becoming Prophet, Gabriel (As) had taught him about ablution and how to offer prayers. Now Aamir Osmani has to explain why the holy Prophet (Slm) had become afraid of Gabriel (As) of getting the first Revelation and informed Bibi Khadija (Rz) his experience?

And he said that he is afraid of his life. Bibi Khadija (Rz) consoled him by telling that "on account of your sublime character, Allah would never let you down" and then she took him to her cousin Varqa Bin Noufil who had converted to Christianity and was translating the Bible into Arabic. He asked him to tell what he had witnessed? He informed him what he had witnessed and heard. Then Verqil told:

"This is the same Angel which was sent by Allah to Moses (As)."

هذا النا موس الذی انزل الله علیٰ موسیٰ ا

This fact has been mentioned in "Bukhari and Muslim" accordingly as narrated by Bibi Ayesha (Rz). It confirms that after receiving the first Revelation he got consoled by a non-innocent lady and he came to know from other non innocent man about the Angel sent by Allah to Prophet Moses (As). When these instances are not against his Nabuwwat, then why should there be any hue and cry if Imamana (As) got an Arabic teaching from a non innocent teacher and how this teaching alone could negate his institution of Mahdiat.

57. Recitation of Bible and Torah appreciated:

After becoming Prophet, the Holy Prophet (Slm) had heard the recitation of the Torah and Bible as reported by the author of "Mu'alm-e-Tanzeel" that:

"Narrated Abdullah bin al Hazrami that he had two slaves by names Yasar and Jabar who used to recite Bible And Torah. Whenever Holy Prophet (Slm) passed their way he used to stop and listen to their recitation."

"قال عبدا لله بن مسلم الحضرمى كان لغا عبدان من اهـل عيـن التمريقال لاحد هما يسآر يكنى ابافكيهة و يقـال الآخـر جبرو كان يصنعان السيوف بمكة وكانا يقرآن التورية فيقف ويستمع."١ﻫ

Tafseer-e-Kasshaf" states that:

Narrated that there were two slaves, Yasar and Jabar who used to manufacture swords while reciting from Torah and Bible. Whenever Holy Prophet (Slm) used to pass their house, he used to stop and listen to their recitation."

وقيـل عبـدان جبـرو يسـآر كـانا يصنعان لسيوف بمكة و يـقرآن التورات والانجيل فكان رسول الله صلى الله عليه وسلم اذا مرو قف عليهما يسمع مايقران ٢

Mu'alam-e-Tanzeel had also written that:

"Whenever he got hurt by the infidels, he used to sit with those slaves and get satisfaction through their recitation."

وكان النبى اذا اذا ه الكفار يقعد اليهم و يستريح بكلا مهم.٣ﻫ

Even after the Revelations started to come to the Prophet (Slm), the Prophet (Slm) used to go to the slaves just to listen the Bible and Torah and get satisfaction. When this is not objectionable, then Imamana's obtaining a preliminary education at the age of 4 years to 12 years, why should it become a point of objection? It is also stated that those slaves used to come to the Prophet (Slm) at night and get teachings of the Holy Qur'an from the Prophet (Slm). In the same manner those teachers who taught Imamana (As) Arabic and taught Qur'an how to recite in his childhood, were also benefited with the Divine teachings of Imamana (As) later on he was declared "Asadul Ulema' at his tender age of just 12 years.

58. Prophet appointed a Jew to arbitrate:

As per the Jewish tradition, Jews were of the opinion that an adulterer/fornicator should be punished by whipping only and not by stoning to death. On that important issue the Holy Prophet (Slm) appointed Ibn Sariyah a Jew, the most learned scholars of Torah, as an arbitrator. It is reported in "Mualam-e-Tanzeel" that:

"Thus Gabriel (AS) instructed the Prophet (Slm) to appoint Sariyah as an arbitrator in between both of you, by informing the attributes and qualities of Sariyah, who was a Jew. Then the Prophet (Slm) asked the Jews whether they knew a youth with fair color and single eyed man whose name is Sariyah. Jews replied: yes. The Holy Prophet (Slm) asked: is there anyone who knew Torah which was revealed to Prophet Moses (As), better than him? They said: Sariyah alone was perfect in Torah. Thus the Holy Prophet asked them to call him and he was called. When he came, the Prophet (Slm) asked him: Was he Ibn Sariyah? He replied positively. Then the Prophet (Slm) asked him whether he was the most learned among the Jews? He replied people think like that. Then the Prophet (Slm) inquired the Jews whether you agree to make him an arbitrator between you and me? Jews replied yes."

The same is reported in"Muaheb-e-Alaih":

"The Prophet (Slm) inquired about a youth, a simple man, with fair color having a single eye, whose name was Ibn Sariyah. They replied: Yes. Then the Prophet (Slm) further said he is the most learned man of Torah among you; therefore on the basis of the Torah, it is better if he becomes the arbitrator between us both. Jews told that whatever he decreed we shall comply. Prophet (Slm) asked them to call him. When he came, Prophet (Slm) asked him whether he was Ibn Sariyah? He replied yes. The Prophet (Slm) asked him to become an Arbitrator; because you are the best known learned Jew. Ibn Sariyah agreed to be the Arbitrator."

فقـال لـه جبـرئيـل اجعـل بينـک و بينهم ابن صـور يا وصـفه لـه فقال رسول الله هل تعرفون شابا امر دابيض اعـور يسـکـن فدک يقال له ابن صور يا قالو انعم قال فاى رجـل هـو فيـکـم قـالوا هو اعلم يهودى بقى على وجه الارض بما انزل الله تعالىٰ علىٰ موسىٰ فى التوريۃ قـالّ فـارسلو االيه ففعلوافاتا هم فقال له النبى انت ابن صـوريـا قـال نـعم قال و انت اعلم اليهود قال کذلک يزعمون قال اتجعلونه بينى و بينکم قالو انعم ۲

حضرتؐ فرموده درميان مردم شما در فدک جوانى است سادہ اوسفيد پوست يک چشم که اور يا ابن صور يا گويند گفتنـد آرى دانـاتـر هـمـه اهل زمين است بـه توريت حضرتؐ فـرمود که درميان ماوشما در حکم توريت او حکم باشد گفتند آرے به حکم اوراضى باشيم حضرت بـه حضـور او امـر فـرمود وبـعد از چند روز اوراحاضر کـردنـد حضـرت رسـالت پناه گفت ميان من و اينها تو حکـم بـاش کـه دانا تر يهودى، ابن صور يا قبول کروــ

Thus even after being designated as the Apostle of Allah, the Prophet (Slm) suggested to appoint a Jew as an arbitrator, who was a non innocent man, because he was adhering to the dictates of Allah:

"Thus, you better ask those people who read books (Torah and Bible) revealed to them earlier than you."

فسئل الذين يقرئون الكتاب قبلك (يونس ع ۱)

In view of these traditions, if Imamana (As) before he was commissioned as the promised Mahdi (As), had obtained preliminary education, how can he be questioned, particularly when he had defeated his adversaries through his dialectic discussions?

59.Rasool and Mahdi to be Unlettered Men:

No where it was written that Mahdi (As) would be an unlettered man, like the Prophet (Slm). But some traditions report that the Holy Prophet (Slm) started learning, writing and reading before he died. (In 8 Hijri Treaty of Hudaibia was written. At that time he was still an unlettered man. Thus did he get some education and became learned? Is verifiable?.

According to "Madarik" it is said that:

"Narrated Sha'abi and Mujahed that the Holy Prophet (Slm) did not die without learning and writing."

عن مجاهد والشعبى مامات النبى صلى الله عليه وسلم حتى كتب و قراء

Author of "Ashatul Lamaat" tells that:

"The Holy Prophet never died without learning and writing."

نرفت آنحضرتؐ از عالم مگر آن كه خواند ونوشت
ـ ۱

Author of "Muaheb-e-Alaih" had commented: "Ma kuntu tathloo" that:

Prophet Moses (As) answered:

"Ibn Abi Sheeba had written in his book with reference to Aoun Bin Abdullah that without learning and writing the Holy Prophet (Slm) did not pass away and that he wrote and read, and this is not against the version of Qur'an that he was an unlettered man, because at the time of starting of the Revelations, he was actually an un-lettered man."

ابن ابى شيبه در مصنف خود از طريق عون بن عبدالله نقل مى كند كه مامات رسول الله حتىٰ كتب وقراوايں صورت مثانى قرآن نيست زيراكه در آيت نفى كتابت راوتلاوت را مقرر ساخته به زبان قبل از نزول قرآن

60.Occupation Before Prophethood:

Before being designated as the Apostle of Allah, he was busy in shepherding goats and sheep. Then he became a businessman and undertook journeys to Syria for about 25 times. When these occupation did not hinder in getting the Prophethood, then how Imamana (As) who was very busy in learning the Qur'an and the traditions, 28 years before he was designated as the promised Mahdi (As), could not claim his Mahdiat on the commands of Allah?

(Note: God Forbid, the above discussion should not be taken as a comparison between the Holy Prophet (Slm) and Imamana (as). Imamana (As) was the perfect Follower, and the Tabay Taam of the holy Prophet (Slm) who declared his religion was based on Qur'an and Following Mohammed Mustafa (Slm). These are the historical facts about the attributes of these venerable personalities which have been discussed for the sake of academic knowledge of the readers to get acquainted with these facts, and to repudiate the allegations by the Editor of Tajalli and nothing more.)

61.Description of of Expediency:

Aamir Osmani does not understand what is expediency and what is avoidance of any given order. Some examples:

1. What order Allah had given to Prophet Moses (As) is mentioned in the Qur'an:

"Your Sustainer called Moses (As) and ordered him to go to these tyrant people, Pharaoh and his men; and to see whether they are afraid of US?"	وازنادیٰ ربک موسیٰ ان ایت القوم الظالمین قوم فرعون الایتقون (الشعراء ع ۲)

Prophet Moses (As) answered:

"Moses (As) replied: My Lord, I am afraid that they may falsify me. I feel pressure on my chest and my tongue does not speak properly. Therefore instruct Haroon (As) too."	قال رب انی اخاف ان بکذبو نی و یضیق صدری ولا ینطلق لسانی فارسل الیٰ ہٰرون (الشعراء ع ۳)

These verses are clear that when Allah ordained Prophet Moses (As) to go to Pharaoh, Moses (As) requested Allah to direct Haroon (As) (to accompany him when Moses (As) attends the court of Pharaoh). This is not disobedience but a request to Allah in view of the situation.

62.Tradition of Mairaj:

Reported by Muslim that: When Allah fixed 50 obligatory prayers on the Ummah under these orders:

"Thus Allah fixed 50 prayers as an obligation during day and night (to be performed by Muslims)."	ففرض علی خمسین صلوٰۃ فی کل یوم ولیلۃ .

Prophet Moses (As) advised the Holy Prophet (Slm) that your Ummah may not be able to bear it, therefore he advised him to beg and represent to Allah to reduce the number of prayers. Thus Holy Prophet (Slm) went to Allah and requested thus:

"Spoken the Holy Prophet (Slm): Thus I approached to My Lord many times and requested to reduce this burden on my Ummah."	قال فرجعت الی ربی وقلت یارب خفف علی امتی

Thus in this way the Prophet (slm) repeated his request and got fifty prayers reduced to five, in this regard "Ashatul Lam'aat" had written that:

"From this tradition it comes to light that with an installment of five, he approached nine times (to Allah for reducing the burden.)"

ازیں حدیث معلوم شده پنج پنج نماز کم کردپس مراجعت نه بارشد

Thus got fifty prayers reduced to five. This is not disobedience but expediency.

63. Secret Propagation By the Prophet (Slm):

Allah ordained through Gabriel (SA) to propagate jinn and men, as reported by " Madarijul Nabuwwat":

"When Gabriel (As) came to the Prophet (Slm) with a revelation of glad tidings, who informed that I am Gabriel (As) and Allah had sent me to you to tell that you are the Apostle of Allah (Slm) for your Ummah, therefore invite Jinn and men towards:

چوں آمد اور افرشته بومی گفت مژده باد ترائی محمد که من جبرئیلم و خدا مرابه تو فرستاده است و تورسول خدائی بریں امت ، برجن و انس دعوت کن به قول لاله الا الله ۲ ؎

"La Ilaha Illallah".

Even after clear orders, the Prophet (Slm) propagated secretly as narrated in "Madarijul Nabuwwat" that:

"Thus the Holy Prophet (Slm) continued invitation for Religion in secrecy." (for a period of three years)"

پس آنحضرت خفیه دعوت می کرد ؎

"Mu'aheb Alaih "reported that:

"The Holy Prophet (Slm), even after being commissioned, invited people secretly towards religion, thus in this way three years passed."

حضرت رسالت پناه بعد از بعثت مردم رابه خفیه دعوت می فرمود تا ۳ سال به گذشت ٤ ؎

Then this verse was revealed, reprimanding to him:

"Whatever ordained (to you), propagate openly, and ignore the infidels."

فاصدع بما توء مرو اعرض عن المشرکین (الحجر ٦ع)

In "Madarijul Nabuwwat" it is mentioned that orders came to announce without fear that "idol worshipers are doomed to Hell". Thus the Holy Prophet (Slm) announced openly only after strict orders of Allah came to the Prophet (Slm) (as a firm command).

"Holy Prophet (Slm) objected idol worship by the Qureysh and reprimanded them that idols as well as their worshipers are doomed to the Hell."

آنحضرت معترض شد آلهیه ، ایشاں راوحکم کرد که بتاں و عبادت کنندگان در نار خواهند بو د ۱ ؎

Even after clear orders, avoidance by the Holy Prophet (Slm) not to propagate openly for three years, it should not be termed as disobedience, but an expediency. And after three years infidels were informed about the punishment. Imamana (As) did propagate for 18 years, not as the Promised Mahdi (As). Then he was also reprimanded to propagate openly. Thus the question of disobedience does not arise on either of them.

64. Proclamation of Mahdiat:

Aamir Osmani objects to Imamana (As) that he avoided to proclaim for twenty years. This objection is malicious and prejudiced, since Imamana announced (As) his Mahdiat in 887 H. In Juanpur for the first time and then final declaration was made at Badhli, (Gujrat) in 905 H., thus it comes with 18 years and not 20 years as wrongly stated by the editor of Tajalli. During this period also he had proclaimed at many places as reported in "Hashia-e-Sharief" which is older than "Matleul Vilayet":

"Reported that Allah ordained Imamana (As) that you are the "Promised Mahdi (As) about which he reported to his family. Bibi Alahdadi and Miran Syed Mahmood (Rz) accepted him as the "Promised Mahdi (As)", when came out from the house, Miyan Dilawer (Rz) too accepted.

حضرت میران علیه السلام را فرمان شد تو مهدی موعود هستی اول درخانه دست بیعت میران سید محمود کردند، بیرون آمدند میان دلاور دست بیعت کردند حضرت میران علیه السلام به کعبته الله رفته بودند بالائی منبر نشسته دعوت کردند من اتبعنی فهو مومن آنجا میان نظام دست بیعت کردند، در بڑلی فرمان عتاب رسید میان سید خوند میر دست بیعت کردند۔ الیٰ آخره

When he went to Kabatullah, he sat on the podium and announced whoever accepts me (As the "Promised Mahdi" (As) he is Faithful. Miyan Shah Nizam (Rz) and others who were present there accepted his Mahdiat. At Badhli Imamana (AS) was reprimanded by Allah (to declare openly), Bandagi Miyan Syed Khundmir (Rz) and many more who were present there accepted and became Mahdavi."

At different places Imamana (As) had declared his claim for Mahdiat which had been reported in detail in "Shawahedul Vilayet" of Shah Burhan (Rh):

"When Imaman's age was 40, Allah's command came in 887 H, when he came out from his trance, then only Imamana (As) had proclaimed his Mahdiat and this was the first proclamation in Juanpur. Then he lived for 23 years. The second time he might have proclaimed at Bidar in 900 H. on account of which, the people of Bidar started asking, whether he was Mahdi? And third time in Makkah in between Hajr-e-Aswad and Muquam-e-Ibrahim in 901 H. He lived nine years after that proclamation. Fourth time at Ahmadabad in Taj Khan Salar's Masjid in 903 H. Then he lived seven years. Fifth and the last time at Badhli, near Peeran Pattan in 905 H. He lived five years afterwards."(As prophesied by the Holy Prophet(Slm), that Mhdi will live for nine or seven or five years, just came true).

چون عمر آن ذات پیغمبر صفات به چهل رسیده بود که سنه' هشت صد هشتا دوهفت سال بود به فرمان رب العزت دعوئ مهدیت اظهار فرموده اندوای دعوئ اول در جونپور بوده است که بعد ازیں دعوئ بست و سه سال حیات بود دوم بار دعوئ مهدیت درمیان حجر الاسود و المقام اظهار کرده اند که سنه' نهصدویك سال بود بعد ازیں دعوئ نه سال حیات شده شده سوم بار دعوئ مهدیت باجمله اخلاق نبوت بامر کردگار در مسجد تاج خان سالار در شهر احمد آباد کرده اند

Imamana (As) passed away in 910 H. Apart from this in some non Mahdavi literature it has been reported in "Ma'danul Jawaher" that at Bidar in 900 H. Imamana had proclaimed his Mahdiat also. Like that total five times he proclaimed his Mahdiat with full force.

65. Emphasised Assertion and non-Emphasised:

Aamir Osmani must know about Mahdavia Faith, then object. He does not know what is Emphasized and Non Emphasized Assertions? Imamana (As) asserted for 23 years. During this lengthy period, the Emphasized Assertion was for 5 years and the Non Emphasized one was for 18 years. As mentioned in "Shawahedul Vilayet":

"Imamana (As) declared that for 18 years it was a "Non- Emphasized Order" that "you are the Promised Mahdi", hence assert and proclaim", I just digested that order. Then lastly in 905 H. orders became "Emphasized One" in which I was reprimanded to declare that you are the Promised Mahdi."

بنده راهژده سال امر غیر موکدبود که تومهدی موعود هستی دعوئ بکن اظهار کن بنده هضم کردیم' پنج سال است که امر موکد شده است و عتاب می شود که اے سید محمد تو مهدی موعود هستی اظهار بکن (باب

(۲۸)

Non-Emphasized assertion is that in which Imamana (As) did not declare: " whoever does not accept him as the promised Mahdi, he did not designate his decliner as infidel"; and the Emphasized Assertion is that "when he declared that anyone who denies me as the "Promised Mahdi" (As), he would be accounted for before Allah, on the Day of Judgment."

The Holy Prophet (Slm) had asserted his Nabuwwat secretly for three years and only from fourth year when the Verse "A'raza Minal Mushrekeen" was revealed then only he openly proclaimed and reprimanded infidels about the punishment of the Hell. The question of disobedience does not arise for the delay on the Prophet (Slm) nor on Imamana (As). Editor of Tajalli must know.

Now we have to verify those narrations which Aamir Osmani had presented:

"Hum Ba Manzaliti"explained:

A. In the real narrative the words " Ikhwani Hum Ba Manzilati" have been written which was wrongly translated by the author of Hadia, instead, he has translated :"Brothers they are of my rank" Ba Manzaliti means to be equal in rank. Then what should be the meanings of "Fe Darjati":

من اشد امتی لی حبا نا س یکونون بعدی.٣

"In my Ummah there would be those who would love me with utmost intensity and they are in my rank.?"

Thus it is clear that whoever would love with utmost intensity with the holy Prophet (slm) his rank must be higher than others.

B. Another narrative presented by Aamir Osmani: "Hum Ikhwani Ba Manzalati " along with "Muqam-e-Mursaleen" has been referred.

"Muqam-e-Nabi" and" Manzalat-e-Nabi" are terms about which Author of "Zubdatul Huqaeqe" states that."

اگر منزلت و مقام مصطفیٰ توان دانستن وداشتن رنگ ممکن بود که منزلت این طائفه دریابی (تمهید اصل ثالث)

"If you can grasp the dignity and position of the Prophet (Slm) and ability to absorb it, then you will be able to know the dignity of that group."

Dignity and position are not equal, but to absorb the qualities of a Nabi, means, "Sair-e-Nabi" "immersed in Nabi," and as per tradition "to be on the heart of Nabi, then what should be the position of those people about whom it is stated that even Prophets (As) would envy on their position which they have before Allah.

یغبطهم الانبیاء والشهداء یوم القیامة بمکانهم من الله

"Even Prophets and martyrs would be envious of them for their position which Allah had granted to them."

This position is greater than the position of the Mursaleen. (vide Part 3, chapter 5)

68.Qur'anic Dictates:

This must be known that if there is any order in the Qur'an then that order must be carried out without any reservation. In the same manner if there is any order for not to do anything, then that also should not be done. But the Devbandi editor of Tajalli and Shahjehanpuri author of "Hadia-e-Mahdavia, have made sixteen kinds of such Qur'anic dictates as not obligatory. That is why they neglect other Qur'anic orders like "Relinquishing Worldly affairs, Migration etc." are supposed by them not obligatory since, if they observe them as obligations, they are unable to perform them. About these obligations please read Part One, chapter 8. However a brief note is submitted below to consider whether these are obligatory or not?:

A. Relinquishment:

Allah had determined punishment of the Hell for those who are busy and engaged in worldly life always. To them Allah ordains:

"Whoever desires worldly life and glory of life we grant him in this world only and there is no dearth of them. Those are such that in the hereafter they deserve nothing but Hell." (11:16,17)

من كان يريد الحيوٰةالدنيا و زينتها نوف اليهم اعمالهم فيهـا وهـم فيها لا يبخسون اولئك الذين ليس لهم فى الآخرة الاالنار (هود ع ٢)

For that reason only the Holy Prophet (Slm) has directed:

"Leave the world to those who desire for it."

اتركو الدنيا لا هلها)

Aamir Osmani had described it as a monasticism. Aamir does not know how Monasticism had been described in the tradition:

"Islam forbids monasticism since it means relinquishing matrimony".

لارهبانية فى الاسلام و مراد به رهبانيت ترك نكاح است

On the other hand Mahdavia Faith inculcates asceticism and abstinence and does not relinquish matrimony (vide Part 1, Chapter 8)

B. Desire for Divine Vision of Allah:

Allah ordains that:

"I Did not create the Jinn and Men, but to worship (Me)." (51:57)

فمـن كـان يـرجـو لـقـاء ربـه فليعمل عملا صالحا ولا يشرك بعبادة رب احدا (الكهف ع ١٢)

وما خلقت الجن و الانس الا ليعبدون (ذاريات ع ٣)

"Thus whoever is desirous of witnessing our vision, he must do righteous deeds and never add anything while worshiping Allah. (18:111)

Man is created for worshiping Allah:

And how to perform worship Allah, the holy Prophet (Slm) had described it:

"Worship Allah as if you are witnessing Allah".

ان تعبدو الله كانك تراه (اشعته اللمعات)

Thus the creation of man is just for witnessing the vision of Allah. Therefore witnessing the vision of Allah is an obligation?

Aamir Osmani had maliciously accused that in Mahdavia Faith if a worshiper does not witness Allah and still offers prayer, he is an infidel.

"Aqeedai-e-Shariefa" which was confirmed by all companions of Imamana states that:

"Thus instructed (Imamana (As) to every man and woman to have at least the DESIRE of witnessing the vision of Allah, thus it is an obligation."

نیز حکم کرده است که برهریکی مردوزن طلب دیدار خدا فرض است

The meaning of "To have a staunch desire of witnessing the vision of Allah" Aamir Osmani had wrongly taken as "If a worshiper does not witness Allah and offers prayer, he is an infidel" Is not Aamir Osmani's prejudice and ignorance? (Part 1, chapter 8)

C. Migration:

For those who avoid Migration, Allah reprimands:

"(Angels) say: was the land of Allah not expansive? Then why they should not have left the country and go elsewhere. For them who deny their abode is Hell". (4:98)

قالوا الم تکن ارض الله واسعة فتها جروا فیها فاولئک مأواهم جهنم (النساء ، ع ۱۳)

This verse informs the punishment for the avoidance of Migration is Hell, when the situation becomes serious to maintain Faith. It clarifies that Migration is an obligation, provided there are reasons for Migration. Just migration from Darul kufr to Darus Salaam is not Migration, but migration from Darul Kufr to Darul Aman also is called Migration. (vide Part 1`, Chapter 8)

D. Ushr:

Allah Ordains:

"Oh Faithful, spend (give charity) from your chaste income (which you derive with your skill) and whatever we have given you from the land." (2:268)

یا ایها الذین آمنو انفقو امن طیبات ما کسبتم و مما اخرجنا لکم من الارض (البقرة ع ۳۷)

From this verse it is ordained that whatever income a man earns through his skill, and whatever is produced by land, we are ordained to spend towards charity from those incomes. How much to spend has been described in a tradition. Thus "Kanzul Ammal" narrates Hzt. Ali (Rz) had said that a person came to the Holy Prophet (Slm) and told that he earned 100 Uquias and out of them he gave in charity ten Uqias. Another person told that he had 100 dinars and he had given 10 dinars as a charity, the third man said he had 10 dinars and he had given one dinar. The Holy Prophet (Slm) said to them that:

"You all have done a good job. All of you are equal in reward, for the reason that you had all given ten percent of your income."

کلکم قد احسن انتم فی الاجر سواء تصدق کل رجل منکم بعشر ماله

To give Ushr is an appreciable and excellent thing as per Holy Prophet (Slm). But to state payment of Ushr is against Sharia is nothing but to contradict the Holy Prophet. It may be said that Ushr is not Zakat nor even substitute for the Zakat as per the tradition:

"It is certain that over and above zakat you still owe from your property (as charity)."	ان فى المال حق سوى الزكوٰة

As per tradition: whatever land produces give Ushr ten percent of the land produce. Thus so also whatever income a man gets from his services he is also obliged to give Ushr.

E. Lailatul Qadr:

Soorai-e-Qadr (Soora 97,) determines the prominence of Lailatul Qadr. If worshiping in this night is not considered as an obligation then the prominence of this night has no meaning. Prayer means to offer at least two Rak'ats as a thanksgiving worship to Allah. And it is a fact that the Holy Prophet (Slm) offered two Rak'ats at the first time when he worshiped Allah.

70. Difference of Opinion:

Aamir Osmani contends that Relinquishment, Desire to witness Vision of Allah, Migration etc are against Sharia. His objection is based on his ignorance, since such objection is against the dictates of the Holy Qur'an and the traditions. If the jurists have any objection, then there are so many sectarian differences among these jurists as well. On these differences "Safarus Sadaat" states that:

"As regards fundamental principles, there are 125 problems for which Ahmed Ibn Hunble (Rz) and Abu Hanifa (Rz) have agreed, while Imam Shaafai (Rz) disagreed for some."	یکصد وبست وپنج مسئله از اصول مسائل نوشته اندکه احمد با ابو حنیفه موافق است در آن و باشافعی مخالف –

71.Examples of These Differences:

A. Imam Shaafai (Rh) permits the follower (Muqatadi) to recite "Al Hamd", during the congregational prayers, but Imam Abu Hanifa (Rh) does not permit. The details are as under:

"One youth from the Ansars was following the Holy Prophet (Slm) in offering the prayer. Whatever the Holy Prophet was reciting he was copying. On that occasion this verse (73:20 Part) was revealed."	جوان انصاری در عقب رسول الله صلی الله علیه وسلم نماز می گزار دو هر چه آنحضرت قرأت می فرمود اونیزمی خواند آیت آمد.

From the above, two issues emerge from the recitation of Qur'an.

1. To listen with concentration;

2. To hear quietly;

Author of "Madarik" had commented on this verse that:

"This entails that during the prayer when the Qur'an is being recited, just listening and keeping quiet is an obligation."	ظاهره وجوب الاستماع والانصات وقت قرأة القرأن فى الصلاة و غیرها .

Further "Madarik" comments that:

"Consensus of the Jurists is that the follower has to listen only."

وجمهور الصحابة رضى الله عنهم على انه فى استماع المئوتم

Tradition of Abu Huraira (Rz) states that:

"The Holy Prophet (Slm) directed that everyone should follow the Imam. Thus when he utters Takbeer, you too say it and when he recites, then you keep quiet. Narrated by Abu Dawood, Ibn Maja and Nisayi."

قال قال رسول الله صلى الله عليه وسلم انما جعل الامام ليوتم به فاذاكبر فكبر واواذا قراء فانصتو ارواه ابو ائودو النسائى و ابن ماجه

Thus it is confirmed that during the prayer the follower should listen and keep quiet.

As against this there is a tradition which also says that:

"Whoever did not recite the Opening chapter (Al Hamd) his prayer is not complete."

لا صلوة لمن لم يقراء بفاتحة الكتاب

1. First is Allah 's command:

"Thus recite Qur'an that much which could be recited with ease." (73:20 part)

فاقروا ما تيسّر من القرآن (المزمل ع٣)

"That much which could be recited" mentions to recite small sooras like " Ikhlas" or "Al Asr", Al Hamd etc.

Thus advised by the Holy Prophet (Slm):

2."Thus when you wish to offer a prayer: first complete ablution, face towards Qibla, say Takbeer, then recite which you can recite easily from Qur'an."

فقال اذاقمت الى الصلوة فاسبغ الوضوء ثم استقبل القبلة فكبرثم اقرأ ما تيسّر معك من القرآن .

This tradition also has been narrated by Abu Huraira (Rz) and confirmed by "Bukhari" and "Muslim" as well. Thus recitation of "Soora-e-Al Hamd" had not been particularized in it also.

3. From the above referred tradition of "La Salaat", the follower who hears the recitation, is exempted, because from another tradition of "Sihah"which directs to keep quiet when the Imam is reciting, it has also been validated by the Qur'an, which is clear from Allah's assertion that:

"And the angels praise Allah's greatness and invoke the Blessings of Allah for the inhabitants of the Earth."

From this verse the infidels are exempt, because Allah had ordained even to the holy Prophet (Slm) not to invoke Allah's blessings even for his infidel relatives as under:

"Neither the Prophet (Slm) nor the momins should invoke Blessings from Allah, even for their infidel relatives."

From the words of the verse "Mun Fil Arz", the infidels are exempt, in this manner, the tradition of "La Salaat" exempts as advised by the holy prophet (Slm):

"When the imam

recites, you have to keep quiet."

4. The traditions "La Salaat" and "Mun Kana Lahu Imam" have no difference, since if one listens to the recitation of the imam with concentration, it amounts that the follower himself has recited. Thus Allah ordained that:

"And when they hear what had been revealed to the holy Prophet (Slm) you would see tears are coming from their eyes."

From this verse it is clear that whoever hears the recitation, he may be weeping by listening those verses.

5. Still Abu Huraira (Rz) maintained:

"To recite Al Hamd by heart."   اقراء بها فی نفسک

6. The words "Iza Qural Qur'an" assert a common Command. They do not ask you not to hear during the prayers, but listen away from the prayers.

7. The Holy Prophet (Slm) emphasized on hearing the recitation quietly, since listening with concentration itself, becomes reciting personally. "Sifrus Sadaat" tells:

"The Holy Prophet (Slm) preferred to hear the recitation. "Bukhari", "Tirmizi", "Muslim" and "Abu Dawood" all books of Traditions, confirmed the holy Prophet (Slm) asked Abdullah Bin Masood (Rz) to "let me listen recitation of Qur'an by you". On that, When Ibn Masood (Rz) questioned: "How can he recite when the Qur'an was revealed on you!", Then the Prophet (Slm) informed: "I prefer to listen recitation of the holy Qur'an from others."

آنحضرت صلی الله علیه وسلم درست داشتی که قرآن
را از دیگرے بشنود چنانچه بخاری ومسلم وترمذی و
ابوداؤد آورده اند که عبدالله ابن مسعود رافرمود قرآن
بخوان برمن او گفت یار سول الله آیامن خوانم و حال
آنکه فرستاده شده است بر توفرمود درست میدارم من
که بشنوم قرآن رااز غیر خود (٣٤٣)

Thus during "Jahri" prayers, just listening by the followers is appreciated.

8. When we are following the Imam in prayers, we have to just listen the Imam what he is reciting and keep quiet. Thus in Jahri Namaz (where Imam recites loudly) follower's recitation is against the dictates of Allah that" when the Qur'an is recited, just hear and be quiet".

Under this verse hearing is first, and keeping quiet is secondary. Therefore in "Sirri Prayers" (where Imam does not recite loudly), here the question of hearing does not arise, then the question of "not to recite" does also not arise. Therefore you must recite slowly.

Note: If it is said that Imamana (As) has asserted that "without Surah Fatiha the prayer of the follower does not become complete". It's answer is that such statement is not recorded in Mahdavia Literature. Even if it is accepted that the verse 'when the Quran is recited' then its connection is with the "Sirri" prayer only, and not with the "Jahri" one. When the followers of Imam Shaafai (Rh) were permitted to read Surah-e-Fatiha in Jahri Namaz (even against the verse of the Quran), on the basis of Imam Shaafai, if mahdavis read Sura-e-Fateha in every Rakaat, whether Jahri or Sirri, then why the faith of Mahdavis, becomes against the Shariah?.

B. As against other Imams, Shaafai (Rh) and Ahmed Hunbal (Rh) assert that Sperm is chaste. Thus in "Asatul Lamaat" it is stated that:

"Both Shaafai (Rh) and Ahmed Hunbal (Rh) regard Sperm to be chaste. Their argument is that because Sperm is a thing which creates man, then how can we brand it as un-chaste? Dar Qatni and Tabrani had narrated that when the Holy Prophet (Slm) was asked about the sperm, the Holy Prophet (Slm) stated that "it is just like mucus or salvia. Therefore it may be cleaned by just scratching it by a rough article".

نزد شافعی و مشهور از مذهب احمد منی طاهر است، و دلیل ایشان آن است که منی اصل ماده پیدائش دوستان خداست پس چگو نه گویم که نجس است ودار قطنی و طبرانی از ابن عباسؓ روایت آورده اند که گفت پرسیده شد پیغمبر خدا صلی الله علیه وسلم از منی که می رسد جامه راپس فرمود که آن به مثابۀ آب بینی است و آب حلق اسست کفایت می کند کریمال آن را بخرقه یا به خشتی ۔

Generally all Muslims take Sperm as an un-chaste thing, except Shaafai (Rh) and Ahmed Hunbal (Rh) who assert that sperm is chaste, hence, when it is not regarded as against Sharia, then how the "Migration and the prayer of Lailatul Qader" which Mahdavis accept them as an obligation, become against Sharia?

As a matter of fact our Faith is based on the Qur'an and the traditions of the Holy Prophet.

Founder of Devband's belief : Allah is their Khanazad (Naoozoo Billah).

Now Aamir Osmani has to inform the basics of his belief regarding Allah as "Khanazad/ Devoted person" which had been asserted by his mentor Qasim Nanootvi in his pamphlet "Hujjatul Islam" which states that "Allah is He whose existence is like a devoted person (Khanazad)". Now we are asking the readers to decide themselves about the status of the religious belief of Aamir Osmani, the so called Editor of Tajalli, why he should not be termed as an infidel along with his mentor and his coterie.?

72. Wrong Description of Traditions- by Devbandis:

Tayyab Qasmi of Devband contends that every inhabitant of the world would accept the religion (of Islam) is nothing but wrong and against the verdict of Allah in the holy Qur'an and traditions. The explanation is given hereunder:

A. Allah ordains Jesus Christ (As):

" And those who are your followers shall be dominant over those who have denied you; and became infidel"

وجاعل الذین اتبعوک فوق الذین کفروا الیٰ یوم القیامۃ (آل عمران ع ۳)

Here it is ordained by Allah that Jews who denied Jesus Christ (As) as the Apostle of Allah, shall be dominated by the Christians till the Day of Judgment.

B. Allah further ordains:

"Thus we spread between them enmity and prejudice to each other till the Day of Judgment." (5:15) 424

فاغرينا بينهم العداوة والبغضاء الى يوم القيامة (المائده ع۳)

The word "Between them" means either the Christian sects or in between Jews and Christians. It is certain that till the Day of Judgment they shall remain infidels. It is a proven fact as per Qur'an.

C. Allah further informs:

"And we instill between them enmity and hostility till the Day of Judgment." (5:65)

والقينا بينهم العداوة والبغضاء الى يوم القيامة (المائده ع۹)

Here "Between them" means sects of Jews like Qareeza and Nazeera.

Thus this verse contends that till the Day of Judgment there shall be infidels everywhere.

D. Allah also informs that:

"Had Allah desired, you all would have become one Ummah, but He had made it a test for you."

لو شاء الله لجعلكم امة واحدة ولكن ليبلوكم فى ما اتكم (المائده ع۳)

H. This is a proof that all inhabitants of the world would never become one Ummah and this is the Will of Allah. If every inhabitant embraces Islam as his or her religious faith, then the question of "Testing" would not have arisen. Further it is described that:

"Had Allah Willed all inhabitants would become one Ummah, but they would always be fighting among each other, except one whom Allah shows His mercy." (11:119)

(۵) لوشآء ربك لجعل الناس امة واحدة ولا يزالون مختلفين الا من رحم ربك ولذلك خلقهم (هود ع ۱۰)

This is a proof that there would be always a tussle between Faithful and the infidels in every period and in every region of the world. Thus Tayyab Qasim's contention that every inhabitant would become Muslim, is nothing but a mere contradiction of Holy Quran's dictates. And just imagine what would be the fate of a man who contradicts the Words of Allah ? The Holy Prophet (Slm) informs:

"One group of people from my Ummah shall always be on the right path, upholding the true Faith. None of their opponents would inflict any harm to them till Order of Allah Dominates in the shape of the day of Judgment.:"

لا يزال طائفة من امتى على الحق ظاهرين لايضرهم من خالفهم حتى ياتى امر الله (اشعته اللمعات)

"Narrated by Nuwas Bin Sam'aan in Muslim that the Holy Prophet (Slm) told":

"Thus the fragrance of the air shall cause the death of every Muslim and every Faithful, leaving the wretched ones who would intercourse on land like donkeys, thus the Day of Judgment would come on them."

فتقبض روح كل مومن و كل مسلم و تبقى شرار الناس يتهار جون فيها تهارج الحمر فعليهم تقوم الساعة (اشعته اللمعات)

In this way till the Day of Judgment there shall remain both faithful and the infidels on the Earth. Thus Tayyab Qasimi's contention is null and void for all practical purposes because infidels will remain on the Earth as stated by the Qur'an and by the Holy Prophet (Slm). No one could dare to contradict these statements.

Now we have to investigate that tradition on which Tayyab Qasimi had based his wrong contention.

The tradition says:

"Narrated Meqdad that he heard the Holy Prophet (Slm) telling that no house of mud would remain on the Earth nor there would be any tent made up of camel's skin, but Allah would infuse the tenets of Islam and Allah would honor them and they would become obedient. Meqdad told that it may happen."

عن المقداد انه سمع رسول الله صلى الله عليه وسلم يقول لا يبقى على ظهر الارض بيت مدر ولا وبرالا ادخله كلمة الاسلام بعز عزيزو ذل ذليل اما يعزهم الله فيجعلهم من اهلها او يذلهم فيه نيون لها قلت فيكون الدين كله لله (رواه احمد)

The first thing is that this tradition does not have reference about Imam Mahdi (As), nor any Muhaddis had kept it under the chapter "Babul Mahdi"

Secondly, Author of Mishkat had kept it in "Kitabul Iman". This is a proof that this tradition had nothing to do with Imam Mahdi (As) or about the period of Imam Mahdi (As).

Thirdly, Author of "Mishkat" had written about it under "Zahrul Arz" that:

"It is specifically known as the Arabian island or near to it."

اى وجهها من جزيرة العرب و ماقرب منها

Thus just Arabian island or any surrounding land is wrong to mean the whole of the world.

Fourthly, the word "Al Arz" referred to in the said tradition does not mean the whole of the world. It refers about a tent made up of the skin of a camel. It just points out the custom of the Arabs who used to live in those tents. Thus it only mentions that the whole of the Arabian peninsula would convert to Islam. And it is an historical fact.

Fifthly, Whatever that traditionally contains, it has nothing to do with "Akhiruz Zaman" (As). Otherwise we have to accept that there would be no building made up of stone, or cement or iron. And even if such a building would be available in Islam, shall have no place in it. Because it is stated in that tradition that Islam would have entered into the houses of mud or tents made up of the skin of a camel. Thus the tradition does not mention about the concrete buildings. However even if we accept that "Al Arz" means the whole of the world then it also is highly impossible that all the inhabitants of the world would convert to Islam.

Sixthly, whether the living place is made up of mud or of the tent which is made up from the camel skin, even if a single person among them converted to Islam then it tantamount to say that Islam had entered into it. Thus from this it cannot be claimed that whole inhabitants of the world would have embraced Islam.

It may be pointed out that in that tradition there are two ways to enter Islam, one with honor and another with disgrace. As regards honor, Islam had entered in the mud house and camel's skin tents. Thus the prophecy became true.

As regards disgrace, it means that those who do not accept Islam still they would accept domination of Islam and live in those houses of mud and camel skin made tents by paying "jazia"/ Capitation tax. Thus this prophecy also was fulfilled.

Thus it seems that Tayyab Qasimi had only read a portion of the tradition which mentions about mud houses or tents made from camel skins. And he did not care to look the other portion of the tradition which refers about those who were living along with Muslims by paying Capitation Tax for their safety. Thus as had been said earlier this tradition had no reference to Imam Mahdi (As) or about the period of Mahdi (As). Further this tradition does not speak that whole of the world would convert to Islam...

Apart from this Allah had addressed Prophet Ibrahim (As) That:

"Then put one, one, piece on each mountain." ثم اجعل على كل جبل منهن جزءً

Here "Kul Jabal" does not mean all mountains of the world. Thus from "Al Arz" how could you mean whole of the world? Now remain those words that inform the Deen shall be of Allah alone. But these words are not told by the Holy Prophet (Slm), but were told by the narrator, it tantamount to say that Islam shall be flourishing everywhere. Thus "Madarik" states that:

"This speaks about the domination of Islam through signs and by arguments." هو اظهاره بالحج والآيات

It is clear that real domination is about the signs and arguments not about the mere numbers. Thus the last sentence of the tradition does not speak about all people of the world would embrace Islam. Therefore this sort of statement by Tayyab Qasimi is nothing but to blame the Holy Prophet (Slm) or to negate the verses of the Qur'an which is un-wanted and also unthinkable.

☆☆☆

Chapter Two.

Criticism on "Sirajul Absar" and its Verification:

1.Allegation of Omission:

Miyan Aalim Billah (Rh), author of "Sirajul Absar" had sometimes written a portion of the tradition according to the subject matter of the article. Author of Hadia had criticized that it contains "omission, distortion and plagiarism". It is also a fact that it had been the practice of Imam Bukahri (Rh) to categorize a tradition according to the subject matter and place them under different chapters. Thus on such categorization by Imam Bukhari (Rh) could it be termed as omission, distortion or even plagiarism on the part of Imam Bukhri (Rh)?

Miyan Aalim Billah (Rh), while discussing the argument regarding characters he had submitted various narratives, including the following narrative also:

"Hazrat Ali (Rz) asked the holy Prophet (Slm) whether Mahdi (As) is from our family or from others? The holy Prophet (Slm) replied that "Mahdi (As) is from our genealogy and Allah shall complete the Deen through Mahdi (As) as Allah has started the Deen from us".	(۱) ومنها ما قال علی رضی الله عنه قال قلت یا رسول الله امنا المهدی ام من غیرنا قال رسول الله بل منا یختم الله به الدین (سراج الابصار ۳۰۶)

A. The criticism of this tradition is said to be that author of "Sirajul Absar" had copied half portion of the tradition and the other half he had omitted. The complete tradition as narrated by Nayeem Bin Hammad and Abu Nayeem is as under:

"Hazrat Ali (Rz) narrated that I asked the holy Prophet (Slm) as to whether "Mahdi (As) is from our descendants or from others"? The Prophet (Slm) replied that "Mahdi (As) would be from our descendants. The Almighty Allah would conclude the Deen through Mahdi (As), as He had started it through us and through us only it would be saved from the evil, as we have protected it from infidelity and through us only their hearts shall be changed from the enmity as were changed from infidelity and through us only they shall become brothers as it practically happened during my lifetime".	عن علی قال قلت یا رسول الله امنا آل محمد المهدی ام من غیرنا فقال لا بل منا یتخم الله به الدین کما فتح بنا بنا ینقذون من الفتنة کما انقذو من الشرک و بنا یولف الله بین قلوبهم بعد عداوة الفتنة کما الف بین قلوبهم بعد عداوة الشرک وبنا یصبحون بعد عداوة الفتنة اخوانا کما اصبحو ابعد عداوة الشرک اخونافی دینهم.

After writing it, Miyan Aalim Billah had mentioned at the end that he had copied these traditions from "Uqudud Durer." Whatever he had presented in it, is from the Chapter one of "Uqudud Durer", whose title is "Mahdi (As) is from the genealogy and the progeny of the Holy Prophet (Slm)."

The criticizer had presented the tradition of the "Uqudud Durer" mentioned in chapter 7, whose title is"Seventh Chapter regards Mahdi's nobility and sublimity of his status."

"Uqudud Durer's old volume published in Damascus in 1092 H. is available in the Central Library, Hyderabad, in which it may be noted that what Miyan Aalim Billah (Rh) had copied the same portion is available in the first chapter of "Uqdud Durer" (which may be verified from the copy available in the Central Library, Hyderabad.) in order to verify what Aalim Billah (Rh) had copied, whether he had omitted any portion from it or not? Thus it may be said that the volumes of "Uqudud Durer" available in India and Arabian countries in which the same portion is available what had been presented by Miyan Aalim Billah (Rh). Apart from this, a pamphlet written by Ibn Yousuf Al Muqaddasi al Hunbali under the title "Fawaidul Fikr Fe Imam Mahdi-e-Muntazir", printed in 1186 H., whose First Chapter is about " Facts about Advent of Mahdi (As)", it also presents the same portion what had been copied by Miyan Aalim Billah (Rh).

Author of "Uqdud Durer" too had written in his chapter 7, with reference to what Hafiz Abu Baker Behiqi also had written about that portion only:

Thus the objection that the author of "Sirajul Absar" had copied half of the tradition and did not write the other half is baseless. Actually the objection should be made against the author of "Uqdud Durer" for such half way writing; but as a matter of fact he also could not be blamed because he had written as required under the subject matter of the article; since Imam Bukhari (Rh) had mentioned one tradition in different chapters. Apart from this Miyan Aalim Billah (Rh) had written this tradition while discussing Qur'an and Imam Mahdi (As).

"Hazrat Ali Ibn Abu Talib (Rz) reported that he asked the holy prophet (Slm) about Mahdi (As), the holy Prophet (Slm) replied that "Mahdi (As) is from Bani Fatima (Rz) and Allah shall complete the Deen (-e-Islam) through Mahdi (As) as he has started from us". This has been inferred by Hafiz Abu Bakr Baihiqi.

٤٣٦. عـن عـلى ابـن ابى طالب رضى الله عنه قال قال رسول الله صلى الله عليه وسلم المهدى منا يختم الـلـه بـه الـدين كـمـا فتحه بنا اخرجه الحافظ ابوبكر بيهقى.

"Hazrat Ali (Rz) reported that when he asked the holy Prophet (Slm) about Mahdi (As) the holy Prophet (Slm) replied that "Mahdi (As) is from us. And Allah shall complete the Deen of Islam through Mahdi (As) as he had started Islam from us."

٤٣٧. فـمـنـهـا عـليه السلام عن على رضى الله عنه قـال قلـت يا رسول الله امنا المهدى ام من غيرنا فقال رسـول الـله صلعم بل منا يختم الله به الدين كما فتحه بنا الىٰ آخر الحديث (سراج الابصار معه مقدمه طبع اول ١٠٠).

All the volumes of "Sirajul Absar" are in agreement with "Ila Akhirul Hadees." This shows that he knew the full text of the tradition, but he had copied a portion only what was required under the subject matter. As regards the remaining portion of the tradition is concerned about the fact that when all the inhabitants of the world did not get freedom from polytheism during the period of the Holy Prophet (Slm), then how could it be possible that during the period of Imam Mahdi (As) the whole of the world would get freedom from wicked tribulations? As regards to live in an atmosphere of fraternity, the same was available in the Mahdavi dairahs only, where poor and peer, illiterate and soldier and the head of the army, after relinquishing the world and property, used to live like brothers. Still the critic admits that those who would be freed from the polytheism, the same people would be free from wickedness.

This peculiarity and dependence is not correct, because it entails that Imam Mahdi's birth should be among the companions of the Holy Prophet (Slm) which is against the prediction of the holy Prophet (Slm).

B. Miyan Aalim Billah (Rh) had presented another tradition whose last portion ends with these words:

وهذا معنى يملاء الارض قسطا وعدلا .

"And these are the meanings that Allah shall fill the earth with justice through Mahdi (As).

"Criticizer objects that in this tradition also, he had omitted a portion of Abu Nayeem's tradition which is as below:

الدنيا عدلا كما ملئت جوراً"

"Imam Mahdi (As) would fill the world with peace and tranquility against the tyranny."

As regards the tradition of "Yamla ul Arz", Miyan Aalim Billah (Rh) had accepted it and in the beginning he had elaborately discussed this issue; but to object that he had omitted it at the end is not justifiable. The second point is that in connection with "Kama Qumta Bihi Fi Awwaliz Zaman" had written just in two lines that:

"Wa Haza Mu'ani-e-Yamla wal Arz Qistoun wa Adla" by writing these words he had described the tradition of "Yamlaul Arz", but still to say that he had omitted the words "Yamla ud Duniya" for the sake of interpretation is wrong.

The fact is that the aforesaid passage had been mentioned in some volumes of "Sirajul Absar" and in some it is omitted. We have two volumes of "Ziaul Quloob". This passage is written in the text of those volumes; which we too have included in our "Muqaddama" at page 212.

C. Miyan Aalim Billah (Rh) had written with reference to "Qulooba Ghalfa" that:

فا نظر ايها المنصف الى قوله عليه السلام وقلوبا غلفا وهو عطف تفسير لقوله حصون الضلالة فعلم ان المهدى يفتح القلوب بفيضه فيملاء ها بعد له وهذا معنى يملاء الا رض فسطا وعده لا كما ملئت جورا كما ذكر الا ماماحمد بن حنبل فى سنده و يملاء الله قلوبهم امة محمد غنا و يسعهم عدله.

"A man of understanding must realize the meanings of the statements made by the Holy Prophet (Slm) 1. Veiled hearts 2. Fortresses of wickedness. These two are interlinked to each other. It means to say that Imam Mahdi (As) would raise the veils upon the hearts of the people of the Ummah and through his beneficence and good influence, fill the Earth with justice and tranquility against its rampant tyranny. That is what Imam Ahmed (Rh) had mentioned in his "Musnad"that Allah will fill the hearts of Muslims with riches, duly infusing in them the attribute of justice.

It is objected that the commentary of Imam Ahmed (Rh) was subverted, which is utterly false.

It may be clarified that Miyan Aalim Billah (Rh) had inserted passages of traditions in his "Sirajul Absar" according to the subject matter. For example some are presented hereunder:

1. While discussing the tradition of "Yamla ul Arz, a passage regarding Dajjal has been discussed by saying" Fa A'sa yamina wa A'sa Shimala ya Ibadallahi Fa as bitu."

2. While discussing about Mahdavi Sect, a passage from the tradition reported by Niwas bin Samaan has been inserted.

3. While discussing interpretation of permissible (Amer Bil Ma'aroof) and commentary of forbidden (Nahi Unil Munkir), where the rank of Imamana (As) had been pointed out, this passage had been inserted from another tradition.

In these circumstances to tell that author of "Sirajul Absar" had omitted a portion of Imam Hunble's writings which negates Imamana's Mahdiat is utterly wrong. If that passage which the criticizer had referred to have been omitted because Imamana's Mahdiat was negated.

Miyan Aalim Billah (Rh) had described the words "Qulooba Ghulfa" (as told by the Holy Prophet (Slm) and in support of his description, he had inserted that portion of the narrative of Imam Ahmed (Rz) which is directly related to the statement under discussion and had omitted to insert that portion which had no direct link to the subject matter. Imam Ahmed's narrative is submitted hereunder:

In this tradition there are eight issues:

1. Imam Mahdi (As) to be from the progeny of the Holy Prophet (Slm). (2) Appearance of differences and earthquakes (3) Filling up of the Earth with Justice (4) acceptance of Imamana (As) by the inhabitants of the skies and of the Earth. (5) Equal Distribution of Futooh (Any monetary help is received, Lillah, in the Dirah used to be distributed equally) of property equally and Ummah's hearts becoming rich (6) Announcement of the Call. (7) Demanding property by a man, his demand was rejected and was not accepted. (8) Imam Mahdi (As) would be living for five, seven, or nine years.

It is now clear that as regards the description of "Yaftahu Qulooban Gulfa, Yam laul Quloob-a-Ummath-e-Mohammadi (Slm)" was the befitting passage to be inserted. Therefore the other passage, as per the criticizer's opinion was derogatory to Imamana (As), therefore was not referred is absolutely incorrect and wrong.

1. Imamana's coming from the progeny of the Holy Prophet has been accepted and narrated by Shaikh Ali Muttaqi. Even though he had not accepted Imamana (As) as the Promised Mahdi (As), but he had accepted that Imamana (As) was the descendant of Bibi Fatima (Rz). Sheik Ali also confirmed that Imamana's name was Mohammed (Slm) and he belonged to the Ahl-e- Bait (Rz).

Shaikh Ali's father was born in Jaunpur which is confirmed by Mir Ghulm Ali Azad. Mua'sirul Kiram states that he belongs to Juanpur and was born in Burhanpur.

A. Therefore his acceptance of Imamana's genealogy was based on his family knowledge which is also supported by "Juanpur Nama" and "Mua'sirul Kiram" that he comes from the descendants of Imam Moosa Kazim (Rz).

B. (a) This tradition refers to the emergence of differences. It is correct since there were so many sects in the Ummah. There had been differences relating even to the concept of Mahdiat, which is also true; because Imamana's birth took place when the difference of opinion about the "advent of the Promised Mahdi (As)" had already surfaced about Imamana (As) which had been stated as" Differences regarding the fact about Mahdi (As)" erupted in the Ummah as narrated by Baihaqi.

(b) As regards the earthquakes, it is also a fact that during the life and after the demise of Imamana (As) there had been earthquakes also in many cities of the then world.

(c) Author of "Juanpur Nama" had stated about the Sultans of Sharqi that Sultan Sikander Lodhi had attacked Juanpur in 905 H. and in view of Sultan Husain Sharqi's wrong postures, Sikander Lodhi ordered demolition of the palaces and mausoleums of the Sharqi Dynasty. Thus in this connection "Juanpur Nama" states that:

"Thus in the year 905, Sikander Lodhi ventured towards Juanpur and in view of the bad temperament and intolerable postures of Sultan Husain Sharqi, Sultan Sikander Lodhi ordered demolition of the palaces and mausoleums of the Sharqi Dynasty."

"پس در سال نهصد و پنج به صوب جونپور مراجعت کرددر پاداش حرکات سلطان حسین فرمان دادتا اماکن و مقابر سلاطین شرقیه از پادر آرند ـ"

And further wrote that:

"Royal palaces which were equal to kaiwan were trampled by the horses and within two years their names were obliterated. Further to this there was a great earthquake which demolished thousands of buildings."

وقصر هائی ملوکانه که بایوان کیوان پهلو می زد اکنول پامال سم ستوران شد و درعرصهٔ دوسال نامی ونشانی از آن نمـاند .... طرفه تر آنکه درآن عرصه زلزله عظیـم پدید آمد، عمارات ابالی شهر از هزار ها متجاوز زبر زمین ریخت ـ

2. Earthquakes in India and Elsewhere:

These facts confirm that during the life of Imamana (As) there had been earthquakes in between 905 and 907 H. "Emphasized Declaration" was made by Imamana (As) in 905 H. at Badhli.

Author of "Shazrathul Zahab" had written that in the year 908, the city of Eden experienced heavy earthquakes occurred for days and nights continuously.

The year of Imamana's demise witnessed many earthquakes outside India as reported by Abdul Qaderul Idroos that in the year 910 H the city named Zubaid had a great earthquake and one another city named Zeela'h had experienced a heavy earthquake which destroyed hundreds of houses and people ran towards the banks of the river. Even after the demise in the year 911 H India witnessed a very heavy earthquake, reported by Farishta in which many cities were devastated. He has given the date of the earthquake as being 3rd. Safer, the Sunday of 911 H. This fact had also been supported by "Tareekh-e-Dawoodi" that:

"Such a devastating earthquake was never occurred in India from the period of Prophet Adam (As) for the period of Sultan Sikander Lodhi and nobody remembered such an earthquake occurred previous to this."

از زمان آدم تا زمان سکندر لودی زلزله ، درهندیه وقع نیا مده وهیچ کس یاد نه دارد۔

2. Thus it is historically proven fact that during the time and after the demise of Imamana (As), there had been many devastating earthquakes in various parts of the world, particularly in India. Thus this was the true sign of the "Advent of the Promised Mahdi (As)". The world also had witnessed similar earthquakes before the birth of the Holy Prophet (Slm) and it was a proven fact that the parapet turrets of the palace of Kisra fallen to earth. This does not mean that Mahdi (As) could stop such earthquakes as the author of Hadia contends.

3. To say that whole of the world would be filled up with justice and tranquility is not supported by either Qur'an or any traditions. Miyan Aalim Billah (Rh) had discussed this issue in detail with reference to the tradition of "Yamlaul Arz". However, it is mentioned that the hearts of the Ummah would get rich. This does not mean the whole of the earth, because there are other followers of different religions also.

Novavi had reported a tradition:

"I am that destroyer through which infidelity would be annihilated." About this tradition he writes that:

"In another tradition the meanings of "Mahi" have been mentioned that "Mahi" is the one through whom the voices of those who follow him would be eradicated. Verily, annihilation of infidelity is meant by that."

وجاء فى حديث آخر تفسير الماحى بانه الذى محيت به سيئات من اتبعه فيكون المراد بمحو الكفر هذا.

In the same sense, those who would follow Imamana (As) would spread justice to the extent they could.

4. Acceptance of Imamana (As) by the inhabitants of skies and of the Earth:

If the inhabitants of the skies accept him, then it is not necessary that all inhabitants of the earth also should accept? Imam Ahmed Hunbal (Rh) had narrated a tradition of Abu Huraira (Rz) that:

"Narrated that the Holy Prophet (Slm) told that "when Allah loves any person, He ordains Gabriel (As) to love that person, and to cultivate friendship with him. Then Gabriel (As) informs inhabitants of the skies that your Sustainer had befriended with that person, therefore you too befriend him. Thus the people of skies befriend him, then he becomes famous on the Earth."

قال قال رسول الله صلى الله عليه وسلم ان الله اذا احبَّ عبداً فلانا فاحبه عبدا قال لجبريل انى احب فلانا فاحبه قال فيقول جبريل لاهل السماء ان ربكم يحب فلانا فاحبوه قال فيحبه اهل السماء قال ويو ضع له القبول فى الارض .

All Prophets and the mystics are loved and befriended by the inhabitants of the skies, but all the inhabitants of the Earth did never favour any Prophet or the mystics except a few. Thus Imamana (As) was acclaimed as the best of the mystics, hence as per the tradition, Imamana (As) was the most favoured one of the inhabitants of the skies. Allah had addressed the Holy Prophet (Slm) in these words:

"Virtue and vice are not equal. You may avoid vices by doing virtuous ways and you will see that some person who had ill-will against you, surely will become friendlier to you." (41:34)

ولا تستوى الـحسنة ولا السيئة ادفع بالتى هى احسن فـاذا الـذى بينك وبينه عداوة كانه ولى حميم . (حٰم السجده ۵ع)

Even otherwise all the enemies had not become friends of the Holy Prophet (Slm).

5. Distribution of property among the members of the Dairah was unique among Mahdavis since equal distribution is known as "Al Sawwiyah". This feature had been reported by Mullah Abdul Qader Badayuni with reference to Shaikh Alaai (Rh) by stating that whatever was received in the dairah as Lillah, Shaikh Alaai (Rh) used to distribute among the members of the dairah equally then and there.

Author of "Juanpur Nama" had also written in chapter 5, with reference to "Khaja Syed Mohammed (As)" that whatever was received, Lillah, in the dairah that was never hoarded for the next day, but used to be equally distributed among the members of the dairah.

In this connection Miyan Vali Yousuf (Rh) had written that:

"It is narrated that the brothers of the dairah used to say to Miyan Shah Nemat (Rz) to follow the system what Imamana (As) was doing. Imamana (As) used to give three sawiyeths to Bibi Malkan (Rz) (Imamana's wife). So also why did you not follow by giving to your wife three Sawiyeths? Shah Nemat (Rz) answered that all the brothers of the dairah had agreed because many visitors used to come to Imamana's house. On that all the brothers unanimously agreed and also asked Shah Nemat (Rz) to follow the system of Imamana (As). On that Shah Nemat (Rz) told that Imamana (As) was our Mentor, and I am his disciple to whom Imamana (As) had given one only and which is sufficient to me."

نقـل است كه ميان نعمت رابر ادران دائره مى گفتند پس روى ميراں چرانمى كنيد، ميراں بى بى مـلـكـان راسه سويت ميداند، شما درخانه چرانـمى دهيد ميان نعمت رحمة اللہ فرمودند همه ياران مهـدى اتـفـاق كـرده دهانيد نـد از جهت آنكه مهـمـان بسيـارى آمـدنـد بـرادران ميان نعمت راگفتنـد، هـم راضى هستيم پـس روى ميراں بكنيـد، ميـان فـرمودند ميراں مرشد بودند و مـاطالب هستيم، ميراں بنده رايك سويت داده بودند و همين ايك پسنده است

This tells us that extra Sawyeth was allowed only on the occasion of the continuity of the visitors coming to the dairah. It provides two issues. 1. That whoever comes to the dairah, he would receive his share equally. 2. Even after facilitating visitors, if Bibi Malkan (Rz) was also given only one Sawiyeth, it would be an injustice to her; therefore extra Sawiyeths were allowed to her. It may be noted that Imamana (As) never increased her Sawiyeth with his own will, but all brothers agreed that Bibi Malkan (Rz) should be allowed to get more, hence she was given more. Thus there should be no criticism on this point as to why Bibi Malkan (Rz) was given three Sawiyths?.

Author of Hadia had purposely neglected to inform the fact of visitors' arrival and their felicitation by Bibi Malkan (Rz). Still there is one inauthentic narrative that Imamana's son Syed Mahmood (Rz) and his family got ten Sawiyeths, has no record available in our sources.

"Narrated that Bibi Kad Bano (Rz) (wife of Miran Syed Mahmood, Sani-e-Mahdi (Rz) asked Miyan Shah Dilawer (Rz) to request Miran Syed Mahmood (Rz) for extra sawiyeths to meet enhanced expenses on account of felicitation of the visitors to her house. When Shah Dilawer (Rz) requested for extra sawiyeths to Bibi Kad Bano (Rz), Miran Syed Mahmood's eyes became tearful and told Shah Dilawer (Rz) that she was not telling on her own self, but was made to tell. Imamana (As) had given me ten sawiyeths, that is sufficient for me."

نقل است که بی بی کد بانو میاں دلاور فرمودند که میران سید محمود را بگوئید که چند سویت ما را زیادت بدهید از جهت مهمانی که خرج بسیار می شود' میان دلاور عرض کردند میران سید محمود چشم ها پر آب کردند وفرمود که شما از کود نمی گوئید گویاینده کسی میگوئید' بی بی کد بانو پیش این بنده نصیب دنیاوی طلبید ند بگوئید که حضرت میران این بنده راده سویت داده بودند' همان بس' بعد از چند فرزند تولد شدن میاں سید محمود زیارت نه گرفتند(باب نهم)۔

It is now clear that Bibi Kad Bano (Rz) wanted extra sawiyeths only because she had to facilitate the visitors coming to her house frequently. But Miran Syed Mahmood (Rz) did not give extra sawiyeths to Bibi Kad Bano (Rz) by saying that ten sawiyeths are sufficient for her, her children, her servants and the visitors.

But there is no such record that Imamana (As) had given ten sawiyeths to his son, instead Shah Burhan's second Dafter, had mentioned that:

"It is narrated that Imamana (As) had given equal sawiyeth to his son as well along with other brothers of the dairah and never distinguished."

نقل است که حضرت امام علیه السلام آل خود را برابر برادران دائره یك یك سویت داده اند هیچ فرق نه کرده اند۔

Thus there had been no distinction in distribution of sawiyeth. Of course in view of the visitors, extra sawiyeths were allowed to be given just to felicitate the visitors. As regards Bibi Malkan (Rz) the reason for extra sawiyeth given was on the basis of consensus by brothers of the dairah, the extra sawiyeth was allowed to felicitate the visitors. On such matters, Imamana (As) should not be criticized because it was allowed on the basis of necessity, just to meet extra expenses of the visitors coming to Imamana's house and that too was allowed by the consensus of the brothers of the dairah. A like occasion had been noticed that the Holy Prophet (Slm) had released his son-in-law, husband (who at that time was an infidel) of Bibi Zainab (Rz), without obtaining any ransom on the consensus of his companions:

"Manzar Bin Omer had narrated that Manzar Bin Sa'ad, who was the slave of Bani Asad bin Abdul Uzza, had narrated what Bibi Ayesha (Rz) had said that Abul A'as Bin Rabi (husband of Bibi Zainab (Rz), daughter of the Holy Prophet (Slm), who had not accepted Islam yet) was the one who came to Badr along with other infidels and was arrested by Abdullah Bin Jubair Bin Abdullah. When the inhabitants of Makkah sent ransom for the release of their prisoners, brother of Abul A'as, Omru Bin Rabi also brought ransom in the shape of a necklace, belonging to Bibi Zainab (Rz) who was in Makkah, which was given to her at her wedding by Khadija Binte Khuweled (Rz). When the Holy Prophet (Slm) saw it and recognized it to be belonging to his daughter, Zainab (Rz), he felt touchy and blessed her and asked his companions if they agree the necklace would be returned to the owner Zainab (Rz) and Abul A'as would be released without taking any ransom? To which the companions agreed and released Abul A'as, husband of Bibi Zainab (Rz), Abul A'as was asked to send Bibi Zainab (Rz) to Madinah, on which Abul A'as did comply by sending Bibi Zainab (Rz) to the Holy Prophet (Slm)."

اخرجنـا محمد بن عمر حدثنى المنذر بن سعد مولى لبنى اسد بن عبدالعزى بن عيسىٰ بن معمر عن عباد بن عبدالله بن زبير عن عائشه ان ابالعاص بن الربيع كان فى من شهد بدر امع المشركين فاسره عبدالله بن جبير بن النعمان الانصارى فلما بعث اهل مكة فى فداء اسارهم قدم فى فداء ابى العاص أخوه عمروبن الربيع وبعثت معه زينب بنت رسول الله وهى يو مئذ بمكة بقلادة لها كانت لخديجة بنت خويلد من جزع ظفارو ظفار جبل من اليمن وكانت خديجة بنت خويلد من جزع ظفار و ظفار جبل من اليمن وكانت خديجة بنت خويلد أدخلتها بتلك القلادة على ابى العاص بن الربيع حين بنى بها فبعثت بها فى فداء زوجها ابى العاص فلما رأى رسول الله صلعم القلادة عرفها ورقها لها وذكر خديجة و ترحم عليها وقال ان رايتم ان تطلقو الها اسير هاوتردو االيها متاعها فعلتم قالوا نعم يارسول الله فاطلقو اباالعاص بن الربيع وردواعلى زينب قلادتها واخذ النبى صلعم على ابى العاص ان يخلى سبيلها اليه فوعده ذلك ففعل .

Abu Dawood (Rz) and Ahmed Ibn Hunbal (Rh) also had reported that:

"When Holy Prophet (Slm) saw that necklace, he became very touchy and said if you agree to let the prisoner be freed for Zainab (Rz) and return the necklace to Zainab (Rz) which she had given as a ransom of her husband. Companions agreed (and Abul Aas was freed and the necklace was returned to Bibi Zainab (Rz)."

فلمار أها رسولُ الله رق لهارقة شديدة فقال ان رايتم ان تطلقو الها اسير ها وتردوا عليها الذى لها قالو انعم

From this, it comes to light that the Holy Prophet (Slm) had released his son-in-law without obtaining any ransom on the consensus of his companions. Likewise, the companions of Imamana (As) had allowed Imamana (As) to give Bibi Malkan (Rz) extra sawiyeths just to meet expenses for the visitors who come to Imamana's house. Imamana (As) agreed only on the advice of his companions. Thus in view of the necessity, such actions are permissible and justifiable which should not unnecessarily be questioned or criticized. It may be pointed out that ordinarily he had never distinguished between his members of family and the brothers of the dairah.

6. Now remains the fact of becoming hearts of the Ummah filled with riches. Here the intension regarding the Ummah means those who accepted Imamana (As) as the promised Mahdi (As) their hearts were filled with the riches, but not whole of the Ummah of the Holy Prophet (Slm). It does not mean that on account of equal distribution of the sawiyeth their hearts were filled with riches. A tradition of Abdullah Ibn Abbas (Rz) says that:

"The Holy Prophet (Slm) stated that if you give a person's wealth of two valleys worth, he would ask for another valley's worth. Man's belly could be filled with dirt alone and nothing else."

قال لو كان لابن آدم واديان من مال لابتغى واديا ثالثا ولا يملأ جوف ابن آدم الا التراب.

Apart from this, obedience based on property cannot be said to be real and for the cause of Allah ? Author of "Kasshaf" had presented the following":

"Verily, We have sent you, oh Prophet (Slm), as a dervish(poor Man), because whoever becomes follower to you, his obedience should be for the cause of Allah alone and not for worldly greediness."

فانما بعثناك فقيرا ليكون طاعة من يطيعك خالصة لوجه الله من غير طمع دنيوى ٣

Abdul Haq Muhaddise Dahalvi had thus stated that:

"When there would be no greediness for any property in the hearts of the people, then they would abstain and they would have no charm for any wealth or property and they would be absorbed in offering prayers to Allah."

مردم را چون رغبت درمال نه ماند از آن اعراض نمايند ودربذل مال فضيلتى ومجتبى نماند' پس نماند ذوق و محبت جز درنماز

Azizi had told that greediness for wealth hinders worship of Allah and Abdul Haq said that with the love of worship to Allah, love of wealth vanishes away. The same sense is visualized, as narrated in "Shawahedul Vilayet":

"Narrated (Imamana (Rz) that whoever is desirous of wealth, he could not reach to Allah and who desires Allah, he abstains from wealth."

فرمودند هوكه طالب مال باشد بخداى تعالىٰ نرسد دهر كه طالب خداى تعالىٰ باشد مال نخواهد (باب ٢٣ ـ)

It means to say that whoever desires Allah, he gets his heart filled with the riches. But it does not mean that all the Ummah would be filled with the riches. Apart from this the hearts of Ummat-e-Mohammadia (Slm) should be filled with the richness with reference to the traditions, but this is not the case with every person of the Ummat. One example is reported by Hzt. Abu Huraira (RZ):

"The holy Prophet (Slm) asserted that the day of Judgement would not establish unless my Ummath followed the rituals of the Ummath of the previous generations completely. The companions inquired 'are you pointing out about Persia and Rome', then the holy Prophet (Slm) said that who will be other than those persons." 456/1	قال رسول اللّه صلى الله عليه وسلم لا تقوم الساعة حتىٰ تاخذ امتى ماخذ القرون قيلها شبرا بشبر و ذراعا بـذراع قالو يا رسول الله كفار فارس و الروم قال ومن الناس الا اولئك .

It does not prove from the word 'Ummath' the prophet's Ummah is exempted, and that every infidel of Persia and Rome were performing such rituals; because another tradition proves that one group from the Ummath-e-Mohammadi (Slm) would be busy in fighting for the cause of Allah.

Muslims had referred a tradition narrated by Jaber:

"Narrated Jaber that he heard the Holy Prophet (Slm) telling that from my Ummah, a group of people would be always busy in fighting for the cause of Allah till the day of Judgment and it would be always dominating others."	قال قال رسول الله صلى الله عليه وسلم لا تزال طائفة من امتى يقاتلون على الحق ظاهرين الىٰ يوم القيامه .

From this also becomes clear that Ummah means not all of the Ummah, but a certain group of people from the Ummah. Therefore the hearts of those only who accept Imamana (As) would be filled with the riches. Now we have to see how the Holy Prophet (Slm) had described about that group who would be fighting for the cause of Allah?

"Narrated by Abu Huraira (Rz) who heard the Holy Prophet (Slm) speaking about Ghina- (the riches/ opulence)- that it is not because of excessive property or wealth, but the real opulence is that of the baser self or passion."	(ا) عـن ابـى هريره قال قال رسول الله صلى الله عليه آلـه وسـلـم لـيـس الـغنى عن كثرة العرض ولكن الغنى غنى النفس

This tradition had been reported by both "Muslim and Bukhari" real opulence is the indifference of the baser self. The Holy Prophet (Slm) also had said that:

"Whatever Allah had destined for you, be satisfied with that so that you become most contented."	ارض بـمـا قسم اللّه لك تـكن اغنى الناس . (اشعة اللمعات جلد رابع)

Allah had addressed the Holy Prophet (Slm) and ordained that:

" And Allah found you poor and made you rich." (93:8)

ووجدک عائلا فاغنی

Although Allah had made the Holy Prophet (Slm) a contented person, still, there came such times on him that he did not eat continuously for three days. "Madarijul Nabuwwat" thus states:

"Narrated Ayesha (Rz) that for three days continuously the Holy Prophet (Slm) could not eat wheat bread or anything and in this condition he passed away from this world."

از عائشه آمد است که گفت سیر نشد رسول الله صلی الله علیه وآله وسلم سه روز پیاپی از نان گندم تا گذشت ازین عالم ۔

Diarah Mahdavia had this sort of contentment what the Holy Prophet (Slm) had experienced.

7. Announcement of the Call.

In chapter 9 of "Insaf Nama" it has been mentioned that a Call was used to be loudly given for the distribution of the sawiyeth in the dairah particularly for those whoever was desperate, that he should come forward and receive his share:

In chapter 23 of "Shawahedul Vilayet":

"Soon after Imamana's assertion, Miyan Salamullah (Rz) announced to all men and women who are in need for Sawwiyeth, may come forward and get it. On that Call all uttered jointly that "we do not need anything other than Allah".

چنانچه اززبان مبارک آنحضرت صادر گزشته بود بجمیع مردان وزنان گفتند که حضرت میراں فرمودند هر کرا مال درکار باشد بروید بگیر ید همه کسان مردان وزنان بیک بار گفتند که مارا بجز از ذات باری تعالیٰ هیچ درکار نیست

It is stated that an angel used to announce over the head of Imamana (As) that he is Mahdi (As):

"Abdullah Bin Omer (Rz) narrated that whenever Mahdi (As) would come out, a patch of cloud would hover over his head. From it an announcer would announce that he is Mahdi (As), Khalifatullah, if you hear it then you have to obey him."

(ا)عن عبدالله بن عمر رضی الله عنهما یخرج المهدی علی راسه غمامة فیها منادینادی هذا المهدی خلیفة الله فاتبعو ه.

Abu Nayeem had said with reference to this tradition that:

"Narrated by Abdullah Bin Omer (Rz) that there would be an angel over the Mahdi's head who would announce that he is Mahdi (As), hence you have to follow him."

(ب) عن عبدالله بن عمر رضی الله عنهما یخرج المهدی وعلی راسه ملک ینادی ان هذا المهدی فاتبعو ه.

Three issues emerge from these two narrations:

1. Presence of an angel.

But it is not mentioned whether any person would see that angel? However it is seen from a particular point, who would be able to witness it, he may become senseless, since when the Holy Prophet (Slm) witnessed the Angel, he became senseless as reported in "Madarijul Nabuwwat":

"No person had witnessed Gabriel (As) in the shape of an angel, except the Holy Prophet (Slm). And he had witnessed two times in its real face, the Holy Prophet (Slm) became senseless; and when he came out his senses he saw Gabriel (As) sitting beside him."

وهیچ کس جبرئیل را در صورت ملکی ندیده غیر ا ز حضرت مصطفی واوراد و نوبت دیده در نوبت اول که اورا بر صورت اصلی خود بدید بیهوش شد، چون به هوش آمد جبرئیل را یافت نزدیك خود نشسته الیٰ آخره۔

Even the Holy Prophet (Slm) became senseless after seeing Gabriel (As), then how ordinary people could dare to see the angel? Hazrat Hamza (Rz) too became senseless when he witnessed the angel, as did the Holy Prophet (Slm).

"Holy Prophet (Slm) narrated that Hamza (Rz) witnessed Gabriel (AS) at Makkah and became senseless and fell down."

نمود آنحضرت صلی الله علیه آله وسلم بحمزه جبرئیل را در کعبه پس بیهوش افتاد حمزه ۔

It means to say that if any angel would be hovering over Imamana (As), it is not necessary that every person would witness it and if seen by anyone he would not bear to witness it.

2. To hear the Call: the tradition does not specify whether every person would hear the call? One who had been enabled by Allah only could hear it.

3. The purpose of the Call is that he is Mahdi (As), Khalifatullah, to whom everyone should obey.

However, whether there would appear an angel or not, or any person hears the call or not, purpose of these traditions is to inform that Mahdi (As) is Khalifatullah to whom every person should obey.

The call of an Angel has been described as under:

"Narrated Abu Durda (Rz) that the Holy Prophet (Slm) informed that the sun would not rise until two angels come on both sides of the sun to announce to the creation, except men and Jinn by saying:"come towards Allah for subsistence, but it is better to be thrift which would not hinder from worshiping Allah."

عن ابی الدرداء قال قال رسول الله صلی الله علیه وسلم ما طلعت الشمس الا بجنبتیها ملکان ینادیان یسمعان الخلائق غیر الثقلین یا ایها الناس هلموا الی ربکم ما قل و کفی خیر مما کثرو الهی۔

From certain narratives it had been asserted that a piece of cloud always had been seen as hovering over the head of Imamana (As):

"It is also said that over the head of the Holy Prophet (Slm) also a piece of cloud used to hover as stated by "Madarijul Nabuwwat"

معجزۀ هشتادو چهارم آن که برسرمبارك میران همیشه ابر سایه کردے (افضل معجزات المهدی)

"Thus called the Holy Prophet (Slm) (to witness) that a piece of cloud hovering over his head."

پس آنحضرت رانیز طلبید ند وآن ابر پاره همراه آنحضرت و برسر مبارك وے سایه کرده نیز آمده ۔

It has also been reported that angels had been hovering over the Holy Prophet:

"Khadija (Rz) was sitting along with some ladies at the upper storey of her house, she saw that two birds were flying over the Holy Prophet (Slm). "Rouzatul Ahbab" reports that Khadija (Rz) did see two angels, in the shape of birds, which were hovering over the head of Holy Prophet (Slm)."

خدیجه در بالا خانه باجمعی از زنان نشسته بودید که دو مرغ برسرش سایه کرده ودر روضته الاحباب همچنین گفته و در مواهب گفته که خدیجه دید که دو فرشته برسرآن سرور سایه کرده اند وخود ظاهر است که فرشته ها بودند متمثل به صورت مرغان والا چه جائے سایه کردن مرغان است

It is also proved that angels would Call that he is Mahdi (As), the Khailifatullah:

"Miracle 15 is that an angel always use to give a Call that he is Mahdi-e-Mauood (As) and Khalifatullah"

معجزۀ هشتاده وپنجم آن که فرشته همیشه ندامیکرد که هذا مهدی موعود هذا خلیفة الله(افضل المعجزات المهدی)

It is also a fact that wherever Imamana used to pass by, plants and stones used to call that he is Mahdi (As). Whoever had that divine proficiency could hear that call. Author of "Shawahedul Vilayat" in chapter 32 had written about Miracle 20 that:

"Wherever he went plants and stones used to announce that He is Mahdi (As). Whoever had that beneficence might have heard that Call."

هر طرف که روان شدے تمام حجر و شجر منادی می کردے که هذا مهدی هذا مهدی وآن راکه گوش دل حاصل بودے شنیدے

7. Now remains about a person who got his share and then returned it. It is just an example. The real thing is contentment of heart. According to the tradition a man who gets wealth, he may become a greedy man. Thus he would say I am the greediest man in the Ummah. There seems nothing peculiar that his reference had been made in a tradition.

Muhaddis-e-Dehlavi had referred about the prophecy of the Holy Prophet (Slm) in his Book "Ashiah":

"Thus reported that in the Haram goats and wolf would live together."

وهمچنین ذکر کرده حرم راکه گرگ و بزیک جابچرند
٢ـ

8. Imamana (As) had proclaimed himself to be the Promised Mahdi (As), first time at Makkah in the year 901 H. He lived until 910 H. Thus he lived for nine years after his first proclamation. And when it is proved that he lived for nine years, then other years like 7 or 5 could be proved easily.

Thus what Aalim Billah (Rh) had reported the portion of the tradition of Imam Ahmed (Rh) was appropriate to the subject matter. For the description of "Yaftahoo Qulooba Ghulpha" he had presented "Yamla Allahu Quloob Ummathi Mohammad (Slm)."

Author of "Uqdud Durer"also had reported that portion of the tradition which ends on"Sakinul Arz". This also is appropriate according to the subject matter. How could any objection be raised regarding theft or distortion?

3. Literal Meaning of RAAS:

A.Miyan Aalim Billah (Rh) had mentioned a tradition in which the words "Innal laha Yab'asu Ala Raas-e-Kul Mayathe Santha" had been quoted. The objection had been raised on it by saying that"Raas-e-Suddi"denotes to the end of the century. But Imamana (As) proclaimed his Mahdiat in 905 H, then how was it possible that he belonged to the tenth century?

It may be clarified that in Arabic the word "RAAS" denotes to both the beginning and the end of a century. Here beginning of the century should be taken. Now remains to see in what meaning the word "RAAS" was used in the tradition of Abu Dawood (Rh)?

As against the author of Hadia, the commentators of Traditions had given the meanings of Raas as Starting or beginning. Miyan Aalim Billah (Rh) did not mention whether he had used the word for the Beginning or for the End., but he had copied the words as " Fil Mayathi Aashira" which means"Tenth Century". Author of "Koukab-e-Muneer" had stated that:

ولذا قال شيخنا المراد من راس كل ماية مايورخ بهافى مدة الماية

"Therefore our Shaikh had said that "Raas-e-kul Maya" means that which is written in history during the period of one hundred years."

Thus the whole century is meant. Therefore the meanings of "Ala Raas-e-Kul Maya" means one century or one hundred years.

B.The traditions presented by the Author of "Sirajul Absar"regarding Imamana (As), there are three such traditions which mention that Mahdi (As) would be "Ghulama Shaba Hadasa" meaning "young lad" had been mentioned, the second one states "Huwa Shaba Murfua Minal Wajhe" and the third one states "Yarjullai him Shab Moufiqya". Author of Hadia had objected on these traditions by saying that these traditions negate Imamana (As) to be the Promised Mahdi (As), because all the three traditions mention that Mahdi (As) would be a " Full bloom young Man." On the other hand Imamana (As) in the beginning of his 58th year proclaimed his Mahdiat and passed away at his age 63. Thus, he states that, the facts are against him.

But as a matter of fact if the meaning of the word "Shaab" is taken as a young man as used in those traditions, then also it fits on to the personality of Imamana (As) in the same manner as it fits with the personality of the Holy Prophet (Slm).

The tradition of "Meraj" which mentioned by Hzt. Qatadah (Rz) in the "Muslim" states that:

"When Moosa (As) was asked which matter makes him weeping? He answered: I weep because a lad would be sent after me and his Ummah was greater than my Ummah and who would enter the paradise."

قيل مايبكيک قال ابکی لان غلاما بعث بعدی يد خل الجنة من امته اکثر ممن يد خلها من امتی ٢.

It is a fact that the Holy Prophet (Slm) was not a lad but a man of 40 years when he was commissioned as the Holy Prophet (Slm). Therefore, for Imamana (As) also the word "Shaab" fits on him at any age. Abdul Haq Muhaddis had commented on this that::

"Sometime the word Lad is taken as a full bloom young man, even after he may be in his middle ages. For that reason the Arabs of Madinah used to call the Holy Prophet (Slm) as a young man and they used to call Hzt. Abu Bakr (Rz) as an old man, although he was younger than the Holy Prophet (As)."

گاهی غلام می گويند ومراد قوی طرب وشاب دارند اگرچه در سن کهولت باشد لهذا اهل مدينه آنحضرت راصلی الله عليه وسلم شاب می گفتند وابوبکر صديق رابا وجود آنکه صغير سن بودا آنحضرت پير می گفتند۔

In another tradition Allah Says:

" I did send Prophets as young men."

مابعث الله نبيا الا شابا.

Author of "Qaboos" describes the meanings of the word :"Kuhal" as an age between 30 and 51. And author of "Muntahiul Arab" described the meanings of "Shaab" to be between 16 and 32 years. That means that after 32 or 34 years the word "Shaab" does not apply to this age because after that age the word "Kuhal" applies. And it is a fact that the Holy Prophet (Slm) was declared as an Apostle of Allah at his age 40. Still he was acclaimed as a young man. Therefore why not Imamana (As) accordingly be known as young msan when his age was 40, Imamana (As) had proclaimed himself as Mahdi (As) and started his journey?

4. Description of Traditions:

At the end, author of "Sirajul Absar" had mentioned some traditions, to which author of Hadia had objected as they do not fit on the personality of Imamana (As). They are as under:

1. Jaber Bin Abdullah narrates that a person came to Jafer bin Abdullah Bin Ali (Rz) and offered 500 Dirham stating that this is his Zakaat. Abu Jafer (Rz) asked him to distribute among your neighbour or poor Muslims. When our Mahdi (As) would emerge who would be from our lineage then he would distribute equally as sawwiyeth and do justice to his people.

Author of Hadia presumed that Mahdi (As) would establish his dominion, which is wrong since to distribute equally it is not necessary that the distributor should be a king.

Author of "Al Uqudul Fareed" had reported that Hzt. Ibn Abbas (Rz) had addressed Mu'awiyah :

"And we swear to Allah: what you give to the world, we give more than that for the hereafter. And what you spend for absurdities, we spend for the cause of Allah. And what you spend for attainment of personal passions, more than that we spend towards virtue and distribute equally and do justice with our followers."

و نـحـن والـلـه اعطی الآخرة منکم للدنیا واعطی فی الـحق منکم فی الباطل واعطی علی التقوی منکم علی الهوئ والقسم بالسویة والعدل فی الرعیة الیٰ آخره

The same practice was in usage in the dairahs. Sawwiyet had become a term which had also been reported in "Tabkhat-Akbari", "Muntakahabatut Tawareekh" and "Juanpur Nama". Under this tradition it had been described that all the inhabitants would practice accordingly and the system of Sawwiyet was promulgated and justice was done to all.

Hzt. Abu Jafer did not receive the amount of Zakaat and returned it back by saying that Mahdi (As) would distribute equally. The person who brought his Zakaat with a firm belief that Hzt Jafer (Rz) would distribute it equally among the poor. But Hzt. Jafer's contention was that it was the privilege of Imam Mahdi (As) to distribute equally, hence he returned it to the person who had brought that amount of zakaat. Thus Holy Prophet's assertion that Mahdi (As) would distribute equally is a fact that Mahdi (As) would distribute equally. It does not mention that a king only could distribute. However Allah ordains to the Holy Prophet (AS):

"Take charity from their wealth." (9:103)

خذمن اموالهم صدقة (توبه ع ۱۳)

This verse was revealed in the Second Century Hijri and from that year the word Charity was being used for Zakaat to be taken from the wealthy people and started being distributed among the poor.

Author of "Madarijul Nabuwwat" States That:

"The more correct is that Zakaat was made obligatory after Migration in the second year Hijri, may be before Ramazan or after Ramazan."

اصح آن است کـه وجـوب زکوة بعد از هجرت است سته ثانیه پیش از وجوب رمضان یا بعد از دیـے

Whether at that time the Holy Prophet (Slm) became a king? Thus in order to distribute Zakaat equally it is not necessary that the distributor should be a king only.

Author of "Sirajul Absar" had reported:

"Including all traditions, one pertains to Tawoos who said that the sign of Mahdi (As) is that he would be harsh with administrators and soft with poor."

منهـا مـا روی عن طاوس قال علامة المهدی ان یکون شـدیـدا اعـلـیٰ العـمـال رحیـما بالمساکین (سراج الابصار مع مقدمه طبع اول ۲۱۴)

Author of Hadia also had presented the same tradition:

"Narrated By Tawoos that when Mahdi (As) comes he would distribute wealth, and he would be harsh on administrators and soft with poor."

عن طاؤس قال اذکان المهدی یبذل المال ویشتد علی العمال ویرحم المساکین .

From the above it comes to light that Mahdi (As) would be harsh on administrators and soft with the poor. However it does not inform that Mahdi (As) would be a king. The word "Ammaal" is used for "Masakeen". However if "Ammaal" means the worker is taken then also it serves our purpose. Here it is only informed that Mahdi (As) would be harsh on workers and soft with the poor, but it did not mention that Mahdi (As) would be a king.

It may be pointed out that the Holy Prophet (Slm) had appointed a few persons for collection of Zakaat, although he was not a king, since he negated kingship for himself. "Madarijul Nabuwwat" states that:

"(Seeing the Prophet (Slm) was approaching towards him) a merchant put down the balance and stood up to kiss the hands of the Holy Prophet (Slm). On that, the Holy Prophet (Slm) pulled his hands and told that "This system is of the non-Arabs who allow others to kiss their hands. I am the son of a woman who used to eat dry meat."

پس آن مرد میزان از دست بنید اخت و برخاست تابوسه زند دست مبارک آنحضرت رٌ راپس آنحضرت دست بکشید فرمودایں کاراعاجم است که باملوک وروساء خود می کنند و من ملک نیستم مردے ام یکے از شما الیٰ آخره ـ

4. It confirms that the Holy Prophet (Slm) never presumed himself to be a king. Still he appointed Receivers to collect zakaat. In the same manner, Mahdi (As) had never taken himself to be as the king, but he was harsh with administrators and soft with the poor. To be harsh on administrators means they should distribute wealth equally with justice. Thus whoever was designated as a distributor, he was known as Aamil or administrator in the dairahs: "Insaf Nama" reports that:

"All Migrants reported that Imamana (As) used to distribute Sawwiyet in his presence. One day Syed Alauddin saw the face of a person who was receiving the Sawwiyet and asked how much you get Sawwiyet? Imamana (As) stopped him from questioning and told him not to see the face of a receiver, keep your eyes lower and do justice. Because when you see a face you may be lenient in distribution."

نقل است از همه مهاجران که حضرت میران سویت به حضور خود می کنانیدند روزے سید علاء الدین مهاجر به طرف روئ سویت گیرند دیدند پر سیدند که شمارا چند سویت هست حضرت میراںٌ منع کردند که میان طرف روئ کسی مبینند ، چشم فروو کرده به پرسید که چند سویت شماراهست چراکه مردم می چوں بروئ کسی مبینند بضرورت رعایت اومی شود(انصاف نامه باب ۹۱)

This sort of harshness was maintained on the distributors because there should be no leniency for any person and justice to be done in all respects.

It is clear that the Holy Prophet (Slm) appointed administrators even though he was not a king. Like that Imamana (As) was harsh on distributors still he was not the king.

Author of "Sirajul Absar" had presented a narrative of Ka'ab-e-Ahbar who said that he had read about Imam Mahdi (As) in the books of the Prophets (As) and that he would never be a tyrant or entertain a flaw. This also had been stated by Abu Abdullah Nayeem Bin Hammad who said that Imam Mahdi (As) himself certified this narrative that his reference has been made in Allah's book and also in the books of Prophets (As). The same narrative is also available in chapter 7 of "Uqdud Durer".

Author of Hadia had commented about this narrative that from the words of Ka'ab-e-Ahbar it comes to light that the name of Mahdi (As) is available in the books of Prophets (As), but it is not mentioned in the Holy Qur'an.

Ka'ab-e-Ahbar had just told that I had seen the reference of Mahdi (As) in the books of the prophets (As), but he did not say that Mahdi's reference is not found in Kalamullah. This narrative proves the prominence of the Holy Prophet (Slm) that a person from Holy Prophet's progeny is the saviour of the Ummah and whose reference is available in the books of the prophets (As). And it is a fact that even a weak narrative about the prominence of the Holy Prophet (Slm) becomes acceptable to all.

Ka'ab-e-Ahbar had also said that he had seen the reference of the Holy Prophet (Slm) in the Torah. Does it mean that he did not see the Bible?

"Reported by Ka'ab-e-Ahbar that he had read in the Torah about Mohammed (Slm) as the apostle of Allah and that he is a prominent Prophet (Slm) also."

عن كعب يحكى عن التوراة قال نجد مكتوبا محمد رسول الله عبدى المختار الىٰ آخره .

According to Behaqi, Anas had reported that a Jewish boy addressed the Holy Prophet as:

"Oh! The Holy Prophet (Slm)! We have read praise about you in our Torah."

يـارسـول اللّـه انـانجـد لك فى التـوراة نعتك وصفتك.

Does it mean that reference of the Holy Prophet (Slm) is mentioned in the Torah and not in the Bible?

In the same sense when the reference of Mahdi (As) is found in the books of the prophets, then does it mean that his reference is not available in the Qur'an?

It is probable that when the reference of the Holy Prophet (Slm) is made in the Torah, then his reference should be available in the Bible too. Like that when the reference of Mahdi (As) is available in the books of Prophets (As), then his reference should be available in the Holy Qur'an as well.

But Imamana (As) had never referred this narrative as a proof of his Mahdiat, but told:

"If anyone wants to know our truth, he must look our precepts and practice whether they tally to the Qur'an and the traditions of the Holy Prophet or not".

اگر كسى خـواهـد كـه صـدق مارا معلوم كند بايد كه از كـلام خـدا واز اتبـاع رسـول اللـه دراحوال و اعمـال مابجويد وفهم كند (عقيده شريفه)

Shaikh Ali Muttaqi had accepted that Mahdi (As) was flawless and never inflicted any cruelty on others. In the preamble of "Al Burhan" Shaikh Ali used the words"Sharieful Azeem" for Imamana (As) and wrote at the end of "Risla-e--Rudd" that "La Yaznu Bi Haza" meaning we cannot distrust him. However the fact of Advent of Mahdi (As) and Kalamullah shall be discussed in chapter 5.

5. Dignity of Honour:

When asked how would Mahdi (As) be recognized? It was told that through the "dignity of honour". Author of Hadia had objected that this sign is not recognized. Then he had presented an episode which said to have been occurring in Sindh that Imamana (As) had grabbed the turban of a Qazi and kept it on his knees at a meeting. Author of "Matleul Vilayet" had reported that when the Qazi informed the order of the ruler to Imamana (As) that he should leave that place, on that Imamana (As) said:

"Country of Sindh belongs to its ruler, Gujrat belongs to its administrator, Khurasan belongs to its king. Thus every piece of land is possessed by one or the other authority. Show me a piece of land which belongs to Allah alone so that the servants of Allah could worship their Lord on that piece of land. Hearing this the Qazi questioned would you grab any person's turban by force?"	مـلك سـند از آن بادشاه سنداست وقطعۀ گجرات از آن حـاكـم گجرات بـوم ملك خراسـان (از آن حـاكـم و ضابطه خراسان هر ملکے را و هر شهر ے رابزعم خود هر کسے حکم ورائت دارد پس اند کے زمین خدا بنما که خـالـص خـدای را باشد که تا آنجا بندگان خدا محض خدائی را عبادت کنند حیران شده گفت آیا دستار کسے بزور خواهید گرفت (مطلع الولایت باب ششم)

Author of Hadia's statement that Imamana (As) grabbed the turban of the Qazi and kept it on his knees is wrong; because in old Mahdavi sources such thing had not been reported. It might have happened that on hearing the words of Imamana "Show me a piece of land which belongs to Allah;" it was possible that the Qazi might have humbly requested Imamana (As) "for my Turban sake please go, otherwise the ruler would punish me by grabbing my turban".

It is not mentioned whether the turban was taken from Qazi's head. Had it been so, then the words would have been reported in "Moulood" in these words: " Dastaar uz sar-e-Qazi kasheeda."

6. Distinguishing: Legitimate and Prohibited:

Another objection was raised by saying that Imamana (As) had offered his prayers behind a non-believer imam. This is a false objection. In support we present the public statement prepared by Shah Dilawer (Rz) in 915 H. Which was accepted and signed by eminent companions of Imamana (As) which states that :

A. "After proclamation of Mahdiat, Imamana (As) never offered prayers behind any non believer."	میران از وقتیکه ظهور مهدیت کرده اند بد نبال هیچ مخالف نماز نگزا رده اند۔

Further, another written document of Miyan Abdul Malik Sujawandi (Rh) who had answered to Shaikh Mubarak's seventh question that:

"None of the companions of Imamana (As) had reported that Imamana (As) had offered his prayers behind a person who happened to be a non believer."	مـانـقل احد من اصحابه علیه السلام انه صلی خلف امام ظهر انکار ه ۔

B. Yet another objection had been raised regarding "La Yahtajo Ila Ahad" saying that it does not apply to Imamana (As). In this connection we have already mentioned the saying of

Abdullah Mohammed Ibn Omer Makki that Sultan Mahmood Begdaha desired many a time to meet Imamana (As), but his courtiers requested not to meet Imamana (As). Now readers have to decide whether Mahmood Begdaha was in need of meeting Imamana (As) or Imamana (As)? Mulla Abdul Qader Badayuni had mentioned in his Book that Sultan Mahmood Begdaha had already met with Imamana (As). It tantamount to say that kings were in need of meeting with Imamana (As) and not Imamana (As). Thus Imamana (As) had no need to meet any king or any person. The fact is that the author had misunderstood the meanings of "Be Hajatunnas-e-Ilahi Wala yahtaj-e-Ila Ahad." The narrative is submitted hereunder:

"And how to recognize Imam Mahdi (As)? Imamana (As) could identify legitimate and prohibited items. And people would need him and he would never need to see any person."	وبای شئی قال معرفة الحلال والحرام وبحاجة الناس اليه ولايحتاج الیٰ احد

It is clear from this that as regards legitimate or prohibited items, Allah would inform Imamana (As). Then he would never require anybody to help him.

In this tradition the responsibility to recognize legitimate and prohibited items rests with Imam Mahdi (As) and it was the domain of the Holy Prophet (Slm) also:

"(Allah informs about the Holy Prophet (Slm): "He legitimizes the pure things and prohibits unchaste things."	یحل لهم الطیبت ویحرم علیهم الخبائث (الاعراف ۵ع)

Since Imam Mahdi's attributes are like that of the Holy Prophet (Slm), therefore he would follow the path of the Holy Prophet (Slm).

The word "Need" had been well described in the following tradition in respect of making the prayer lengthy:

"Verily, among them are old and weak persons and persons who have to attend important work" (therefore do not make prayers lengthy)."	فان فیهم الضعیف والکبیر وذالحاجة

Shaik Tajul Arifeen Abu Wafa used to receive Shaikh Abdul Qader Jeelani with much respect, when he was still young; people asked the reason for such reception, Tajul Arifeen told that a day would come when eminent and ordinary persons would need him most. Thus if ordinary and eminent persons would need him, is it because he was a king?

Now we go to discuss about the narrative recorded in "Insaf Nama":

"Narrated by Miyan Abdul Rasheed (Rz) who heard Imamana (As) telling Miyan Lad Shah Muhajir (Rz) that "if you find that some prayers like Sunnat if not performed (By Imamana (As) due to forgetfulness) then inform him. After some days Miyan Lad Shah (Rz) informed Imamana (As) that the Holy Prophet (Slm), according to the books of Fiqha, had offered Sunnat prayers before and after Farz prayer outside (the Masjid).Hearing it, Imamana (As) told that he would also do the same thing hereafter."

نقل است از میان عبدالرشید که روزے حضرت مهدی علیه السلام میان لائو مهاجر فرمودند که هر چه در صورت نماز سنت باشد وبجا آوری نمی شود بنده را اعلام کنید بعد از چند روز میان لائو فرمود که از کتب فقہ تحقیق شده است که رسول علیه السلام سنت ظهر پیش از فریضه وبعد از فریضه بیرون آمده گزار دند بعده میراں فرمودند که اکنوں بنده هم بیروں خواهم گزارد۔

This narrative is not a confirmed one to have been told by Miyan Abdul Rasheed. We know that Miyan Abdul Rasheed (Rz), father of Miyan Mustafa Gujrati (Rh), who had compiled the Narratives relating to Imamana (As), but in his compilation this narrative is not found.

(Note: It is a fact that Immana (As) used to offer prayers of Sunnat, always in his house and not in the Masjid, as was the practice of the Holy Prophet(Slm). Khundmiri

However the author of Hadia had objected on this narrative by telling that Imamana (As) wanted some person to watch him if he was missing any Sunnat or not. This sort of forgetfulness is but a human nature. The Holy Prophet (Slm) too had asked others to inform if he would forget any Sunnat left unattended. An example is submitted hereunder:

"Abdullah Ibn Masood (Rz) narrated that the Holy Prophet (Slm) had offered five rakats of a Sunnat of Zuhar prayer. Somebody informed that he had offered extra Rakat. The holy Prophet (Slm) after hearing this, offered two prostrations (as Sahu) and told that he was also a human being like you all and might have forgotten as you may also forget. However in future remind me if such thing again happened."

عن عبدالله ابن مسعود ان رسول الله صلی الله علیه وسلم صلی الظهر خمسا فقیل له، ازید فی الصلوٰة فقال وما ذالک قالوا اصلیت خمسا فسجد سجدتین بعد ما سلم وفی روایة قال انما انا بشر مثلکم انسی کما تنسون فاذا نسیت فذکرونی الیٰ آخره

Help me? By asking people to remind for any forgetfulness does not mean that holy Prophet (Slm) was in need of any person to help him to remind his forgetfulness?

In this connection author of "Tuhfai-e-Asna-e-Ashariah" had written that :

"Such forgetfulness is but a human error which occurs by all including Prophets (As) also. As regards matters of propagation such forgetfulness is not permissible. Commentators of Ahl-e-Sunnat had stated that such things happen even by the Prophets (As) for being absorbed in witnessing the Divinity."

سهو در افعال از خواص بشریه است و انبیاء در امور بشریه شریك سائر ناس اند .... سهو در امور تبلیغیه جائز نیست که بجائے امر نهی نماینده و بجائے نهی امر، بعضے محققین اهل سنت نوشته اند که سهو انبیاء از راه کمال استغراق در حضور و مشاهده می باشد۔

Author of "Asshatul Lam'aat" had written about the forgetfulness of the Holy Prophet (Slm) that:

"You must try to understand the situation in which such things happen even by the Holy Prophet (Slm). It is all on account of his being preoccupied and absorption which is out of our imagination and perception."

باید فهمید که وقوع سهود نسیان از آنحضرت از کدام مقام است لابد از مرتبۀ اشتغال و استغراق درمقامی خواهد بود که دست عقول از دامن ادراک آں قاصر است ۔

Insaf Nama's narrative does not mean that those persons who had declared Imamana (As), long back, as "Asadul Ulema", Imamana (As) still needs them to certify that they had accepted him as Mahdi-e-Akhiruz Zaman (As); but it is just to describe the invitation for Mahdiat that how they are reminded regarding orders to do and not to do. The purpose of Imamana (As) is that his every follower should strictly "Enjoin virtue and Abhor evil" as an obligation. And, if by chance if any obligation is left on account of complete absorption, that forgetfulness must be reminded to Imamana (As); in the same manner as the companions of the Holy Prophet (Slm) used to inform him on such occasions. This tantamount to educate them and not to get education from them.

Author of Hadia had wrongly translated the text of the 'Insaf Nama', which is submitted hereunder:

"The Holy Prophet (Slm) used to offer sunnat, before and after the Farz, coming out (of the Masjid)."

رسول الله صلى الله علیه وسلم سنت ظهر پیش از فریضه بعد از فریضه بیرون آمده گزارند ـ(انصاف نامه)

Imamana (As) also used to offer Sunnat prayer in his house, following the practice of the Holy Prophet (As).

"Abdullah Bin Shafeeq (Rz) narrates that when he asked Ayesha (Rz) about Holy Prophet's offering Sunnat, she informed him that the Holy Prophet (Slm) used to offer four Rakats of Sunnat before the Farz in the house and after completing Farz prayers, he used to come in the house, offer two rakats sunnat in the house."

عـن عبـدالـلّه بـن شـفيـق قال سالت عائشة عن صلوٰة رسـول الـلّه صـلـى الله عليه وسلم عن تطوعه فقالت كان يصلى فى بيتى قبل الظهر اربعاً ثم يخرج فيصلى بالناس ثم يدخل فيصلى ركعتين الى آخره.

Now we have to see what was the practice of the Holy Prophet (Slm) regarding Nafils?:

"Narrated in "Nisaai" and "Tirmizi" that when people stood up for offering (Nafil in the Masjid) the Holy Prophet asked them to go to their houses and offer Nafils."

وفى رواية التـرمـذى والـنسائى قام ناس يتنفلون فقال النبى صـلـى الـلّه عليه وسلم عليكم بهذه الصلوٰة فى البيوت

Omer (Rz) states that: In yet another tradition reported by Ibn Omer (Rz):

"Holy Prophet (Slm) instructed to offer some prayers in your houses also and do not make your houses like a graveyard."

قال قال رسـول الـلّه صلى الله عليه وسلم اجعلوافى بيوتكم من صلوٰتكم ولاتتخذوهاقبورا

Here also orders have been given to offer some prayers in houses, particularly Nafil and Sunnt.

"Oh Faithful. Offer your prayers in your houses, because man's prayer in his house is preferable, except Farz prayer."

ايهـا الـنـاس صلوافى بيوتكم فان افضل صلوٰة المرٔ فى بية الا المكتوبة .

Thus four Rakat sunnat, and two Rakat sunnat, before and after the Farz prayer of Zuhar should be offered in houses. Even sunnat of the Maghrib prayer the Holy Prophet (Slm) had offered in his house. The same was the practice of Imamana (As). This does not mean that Imamana (As) was dependant on someone to inform him about his daily prayers. From this narrative it is clear that Imamana's practice was most desirable. But what Miyan Lad Shah (Rz) had pointed out it was not desirable. And the answer given by Imamana (As) was that in certain circumstances non-obligatory prayers sometimes may be offered in the Masjid also.

7. Dismantling evil fortresses:

Author of "Sirajul Absar" had presented a narrative regarding Imamana (As).

"Mahdi (As) would open fortresses of wickedness and curtain covered hearts."

يفتح حصون الضلالة قلوباً غلفا

By describing this, Aalim Billah (Rh) had taken "Qulooba Ghalpha" as congestive exigency. On which the author of Hadia had objected by telling that Aalim Billah (Rh) had applied this tradition on Imamana (As) and for that reason he had explained "Husoonuz Zalalath" as "Qulooba Ghalpha" meaning Mahdi (As) would fill the misled hearts with his beneficence.

In yet another tradition it is said that:

"Mahdi (As) would come from you, and Allah would spread guidance through him and the fire of wickedness would let off".

ومنک الـمـهـدی وبه ینتشر الهدیٰ وبه تطفی نیر ان الضلالة

Here wickedness had been compared to fire and "Husoonaz Zalaltha" had been compared with fortresses of wickedness. Since "Husoon" had been used, therefore the word" To Open" had been used. However, In "Madarijul Nabuwwat" it is said that:

"Narrated Wahab bin Munba that Allah had sent revelation to Prophet Shees (As) by informing that I shall send an unlettered Prophet (Slm) and shall cause to open through him their deafness and blindness and those hearts which are covered by curtains."

از وهب بن مـنبـه آمـده کـه گفت وحی فرستاد خدائ تـعـالیٰ به سوئ شعیا پیغمبر که وحی می فرستم نبی امی راکـه مـی کشـایـم بروی گوش هائ کر راه وچشم هائ کوررو دل هائ پوشیده در پرده را ۔

Since the un-lettered Prophet (Slm) opened the deafness of the ears, and the blindness of the eyes and opened the hearts from their veiled curtains, in the same manner that un-lettered Prophet (Slm) informed about Mahdi (As) who would open those hearts which are covered by curtains and crush the fortresses of wickedness.

8."Establishing Early Islam:

Author of "Sirajul Absar" had presented narrative from "Uqdud Durer":

"On the appearance of Mahdi (AS), which path he would tread? Stated that he would dismantle all the illegal practices as the Holy Prophet (Slm) had done and establish Islam as it was existing at the time of the Holy Prophet (Slm)".

اذا خـرج المهدی بای سیرة یسیرقال یهدم ماقبله کما صنـع رسـول الـلـه صـلـی الـلـه علیه وسلم ویستانف الاسلام جدیدا.

About this, author of Hadia had objected that it does not apply to Imamana (As), because in his period whole of the world did not accept Islam; but his objection is useless because it only states that Imamana (As) would dismantle illegal practices and establish Islam in its original status.

When during the period of the Holy Prophet (Slm) except the Arabian Peninsula, whole world did not embrace Islam, then how the author of Hadia could demand Mahdi (As) to establish Islam in the whole of the world. His objection is nothing but silly and worthless.

The Holy Prophet (Slm) also said that:

"I am a destroyer of infidelity and in my presence Allah annihilates paganism."

انا الماحی الذی یمحو الله بی الکفر

Author of "Madarijun Nabuwwat" had commented on it that:

"If it is meant to annihilate paganism of those who have converted to Islam, then the word "Mahi" (Destroyer) is enough as had been described by Qazi Fayyaz that Mahi is one who destroys evils."

واگر محو کفراز سینهٔ مومنان آنکه گرویده اند بوی ودرربقهٔ اطاعت و انقیادور آمد ند مراد دارند در اطلاق این اسم کافی است وموافق است به این معنی انچه قاضی عیاض تفسیر این را در حدیث نقل کرده که مامی آن که محو کرده شد بوی سیئات کسی که اتباع کرد اورا۔

9. Prayer of Lailatul Qadr.

"Bandagi Syedus Saadath, Waasilul Haq, Bandagi Miyan Syed Khundmir (Rz) had many a time stated that Hazrat Miran Syed Mohammed Mahdi (As), in the Shab-e-Qadr, after offering Farz and Sunnat prayers of Isha; he had offered two Rakats of Dugana and under his leadership all men and women of the dairah had followed him and offered Dugana. Imamana (AS) invoked blessings from Allah that: "Oh Allah made me a meek person, give me death as a meek man and keep me among those who are indigent and meek. With your blessings, with your Grace and Favour , with most kindness among all."

بندگی سیدالسادات منبع الکائنات واصل الحق سید الشهداء بندگی میان سید خوند میرؒ کرات ومرات فرمودند که حضرت میران سید محمد مهدی در شب قدر بعد از ادائ فرض وسنت متصل دوگانه خود امامت کرده گزاردند و تمام برادران دائره اقتداء کردند و بعد از فارغ شدن از نماز دوگانه حضرت میران دعا خواندند وآں دعاء این است۔ اللهم احینی مسکینا وامتنی مسکینا واحشرنی فی زمرة المساکین بفضلک وبکرمک یاارحم الراحمین۔

"Thus it may be known that this Fakheer Wali Yousuf (Rh) had been under the service of Hzt. Bandagi Miyan Syed Khundmir (Rz) who in obedience to Imamana (As) had offered two Rakat Dugana after performing Isha Farz and Sunnat prayers in the night of "Shab-e-Qadr". All brothers of dairah had offered prayers under his leadership and invoked Allah's blessings as Imamana (As) had invoked."

نیز معلوم باد که این بنده فقیر ولی یوسف ده سال درزیر پائ بندگی میانؒ اتباع بندگی میراںؒ کردند در شب قدر بعد از فرض وسنت عشاء متصل خود جماعت کردند برادران نماز دوگانه گزرانیدند و دعا همین نوع شنیدیم بالا نوشتیم

"Thus it is a fact that all brothers and sisters and children of the Dairah offered Dugana under the leadership of Imamana (As). Those who accepted Imamana (As) as the Promised Mahdi (As), alone were getting rid from the innovations.

Author of Hadia had objected for the "Lailathul Qadr", by telling Imamana (As) had invented a sixth Prayer as obligatory and apart from the Zakaat, he had invented Ushr, a new thing.

We have discussed about Ushr in the previous chapter, now we shall discuss about "LAILATUL QADR" which he said as the sixth obligatory prayer !

Allah ordains that "there is no doubt that We had revealed (Qur'an) it in the night of Qadr", means that Allah had revealed Qur'an in the auspicious night of Qadr. From Qur'an itself it comes to light that this auspicious night falls in the month of Ramazan:

"Shahro Ramazanal Lazi Unzila Fihil Qur'an"; in the month of Ramazan We have revealed the Qur'an". Thus Allah had ordained the prominence of the Lailatul Qadr in this manner. Then informed:

"Shab-e-Qdr is better than one thousand months' prayers. On this night the Angels and Ruhul Quds come down to the Earth under the command of Allah and invoke well being (to those who offer prayers) till the break of the dawn."

ليـلة الـقـدر خير من الف شهر تنزل الملائكة والروح فيها باذن ربهم من كل امر سلام هى حتىٰ مطلع الفجر

Mohammed Bin Jareer Tabri (Rz) had narrated about this verse in "Jaamiul Biyan":

"Narrated a tradition by Ibn Hameed who heard from Hukkam Bin Salam that there was a man of the Bani Israel who used to offer prayer the whole night and he used to battle full day against the enemies of Allah. Which continued for one thousand months. Thus Allah revealed this verse: "Lailatul Qadr is better than one thousand months' prayers and offering prayer in that night is better than one thousand month's prayer."

حـدثنـا ابن حميد قال ثنا حكام بن سلم عن المثنى بن الصباح عـن مجاهد قال كان فى اسرائيل رجل يقوم الـليل حتى يصبح ثـم يجاهداللّه بالنهار حتى يمسى ففعل ذلك الف شهر فانزل اللّه هذه الآية ليلة القـدر خيـر مـن الف شهر قيام تـلك الليلة خير من عمل ذلك الرجل

Imam Fakhr-e-Razi had narrated :

"Mujahed informed that a man from Bani Israel who used to offer prayers the whole night and was engaged in Jihad the whole day and like that he did it for one thousand months. On it, the Holy Prophet (Slm) and Muslims became very astonished. Thus Allah ordained that the Lailatul Qadr is better for you, than the prayer of that Israeli's one thousand nights' prayers."

قال مجاهد كان فى بنى اسرائيل رجل يقوم الليل حتى يصبح ثم يجاهد حتىٰ يمسى ففعل ذلك الف شهر فتعجب رسول اللّه صلى اللّه عليه وسلم والمسلمون مـن ذلك فـانزل اللّه هذه الآية اى ليلة القدر لامتك خيـر مـن الف شهر لـذلك الاسـرائيـلـى الذى حمل السلاح الف شهر .

From these narratives, it becomes clear that the prayer during this night is better than the prayers of one thousand months and to wage war against the infidels. In what sense should it be described that this night's prayer is very auspicious and brands it as an obligatory prayer on the Ummah so that no one should avoid this night's prayer.

Now we have to ascertain the date of Ramazan in which this night falls. Hazrat Ibn Abbas had determined it to be on the twenty seventh night of Ramazan. Imam Fakhr-e-Razi had said:

"Narrated Ibn Abbas (Rz) that there are nine words in "Lailatul Qadr" and had been repeated three times in the verse. Thus (9 x 3=27) it is twenty seventh night (of Ramadan)."

عن ابن عباس انه قال ليلة القدر تسعة احرف وهو مذكور ثلاث مرة فتكون السابعة والعشرين .

Abu Dawood narrates Mu'awiyah Ibn Abu Sufuian that:

"Abdullah Bin Mu'az narrated the tradition that his father heard it from Shoba Bin Qatada who heard from Mutraf that he heard Mu'awiyah Ibn Abu Sufian who heard the Holy prophet informed that Lailatul Qadr falls on the 27th. Night of Ramazan."

حدثنا عبدالله بن معاذ ثنا ابى اخبرنا شعبة عن قتادة انه سمع مطرفا عن معاوية بن ابى سفيان عن النبى صلى الله عليه وسلم فى ليلة القدر قال ليلة سبع و عشرين .

Imam Hanafi (Rz) also agrees on this date, author of "Tafseer-e-Husaini" said:

"Ashab-e-Imam Shaafai" adopt 21st and 23rd., while Ahl-e-Hanafi adopt 27th. night."

اصحاب امام شافعى بست ويكم وبست وسوم اختيار كنند وحنفيه شب بست وهفتم را.

As regards Holy Prophet's practice, Abu Zarr (Rz) had narrated that:

"Narrated Abu Zarr (Rz) that they kept Fast along with the Holy Prophet (Slm). He told that in Ramazan there is no night prayer till there remain seven nights, then offered prayers till third of the night remained, then there remain six nights and offered prayers till half of the night was passed. Abu Zarr (Rz) said to the Holy Prophet (Slm) what better would be if you lead us for extra prayer. The Prophet (Slm) told that when any person offers prayer behind the Imam and the Imam's left, even then the whole night would be counted as for worship. When four nights remained, the Prophet did not offer the prayer along with them, and one third of the night remained. When there remain three nights (27th. Night) then the Prophet (Slm) assembled all his Ahl-e-Baith (Rz), women and children and offered prayer en-block till the time of Sahri came. Then in the remaining nights of Ramadan, the Prophet (Slm) did not offer any prayer with them. Reported Tirmizi, Abu Dawood and Nisaai."

قال صمنا مع رسول الله صلى الله عليه وسلم فلم يقم بنا شيئا من الشهر حتى بقى سبع فقام بنا شيئا من الشهر حتى بقى سبع فقام بناحتى ذهب ثلث الليل فلما كانت السادسة لم يقم بنا فلما كانت انحامسة قام بنا حتى ذهب شطر الليل فقلت يا رسول الله لونفاتنا قيام هذه الليلة فقال ان الرجل اذا صلى مع الامام حتى ينصرف حسب له قيام ليلة فلما كانت الرابعة لم يقم بنا حتى بقى ثلث الليل فلما كانت الثالثة جمع اهله ونساء والناس فقام بنا حتى خشينا ان يفوتنا الفلاح قلت وما الفلاح قال السحورثم لم يقم بنا بقية الشهر رواه ابو داود اوالترمذى والنسائى روى ابن ماجه نحوه الا ان الترمذى لم يذكر ثم لم يقم بنا بقية الشهر

Mahdavi books tell us that Imamana (As) had offered Lailatul Qadr Prayer, for the first time, at Kaha of Tattha District (Pakistan) on 27th night of Ramazan. "InteKhab-e-Mawaleed" tells:

"Thus Imamana (As) came out (during the night) and on command from Allah, asked to give Call for the prayer and assembled all men and women and offered two Rakats with loud recitation."

پس حضرت همان زمان از فرمان حق تعالیٰ بیرون آمده بانگ نماز گویا نیده همه مردمان وزنان راجمع کرده خود امام شده دو رکعت نماز "دوگانه لیلة القدر" قرأت بآواز بلند خوانده ادا کردند

There should be no objection as to why only two Rakats have to be offered. It is because

Very First Prayer was of two Rak'ats:

when the Holy Prophet started praying, he offered just two Rakats, as stated in "Madrijul Nabuwwat" :

"First thing which became an obligatory prayer after Faith and Unity of Allah it was two Rakats prayer only."

اول چیزے کـه واجـب شـد از عبـادات بعد از ایمـان وتوحید دو رکعت نماز بود۔

From the above tradition two issues emerge. 1. The Holy Prophet (Slm) offered prayer on the 27th. Night of Ramadan in the congregation, and after it, he did not offer any prayer (as Laiatul Qadr). 2. He assembled his Ahl-e-Bait (Rz) and all men and women and offered prayers.

It is a fact that he did not arrange such congregation for any of the five times prayers. What the Prophet (As) had practiced for that night no where in the Ummah such thing had been seen, except in Mahadvis who even today perform the same practice what the Holy Prophet (Slm) had maintained for this night's prayer from the date when it was informed by Allah that 27th. Night of Ramazan is the Lailatul Qadr and on the command of Allah, Imamana (As) assembled all persons of his dairah at Kaha, Thatta, Pakistan, and offered two Rakats Dugana as an obligatory prayer after performing Isha prayer, and of course before the Vitr prayer. Then how could this prayer be termed as an innovation, when it was performed by the Holy Prophet (Slm) and following his practice, Imamana (As) performed on the commands of Allah, the Almighty.

(Note: Thus Imamana's performance of "Lailatul Qadr" for the first time on a place which is Kaha, now in Pakistan, it comes to my mind that it may be taken as an Inspiration to Imamana (As) that the place would become a Muslim State, sometime in future. And it is a historically proved fact that when the British Government announced Independence to India, they decided the date 15th. August 1947 for official transfer of power to Bharat and Pakistan. Since 14th. August 1947 was the 27th. Ramazan, Qaid-e-Azam demanded the then Viceroy, Lord Mount Batten, to announce Independence of Pakistan one day earlier to the scheduled date of 15th. August. The Viceroy accepted his desire and arrived Karachi (Kaha is just 12 miles from Karachi) on 14th. August 1947 and transferred authority officially at 12.00 midnight (in the auspicious night of Shab-e-Qadr) to Qaid-e-Azam Mohammed Ali Jinnah, as the First Governor General of Pakistan. Thus as per that performance of the Dugana-e-Lailatul Qadr for the first time at Kaha, near Krachi, now Pakistan, by Imamana(As), as a gratitude, became like a foretelling by Imamaman(As) that some time in future this piece of land shall be designasted as an Independant Republic of Pakistan and that offering of prayers was accepted by Allah Jallle Subhanahu in granting the independnt State of Pakistan to the Muslims of those provinces of India where Muslims were living in majority , by carving a new Islamic State among the comity of the nations of the World..) Khundmiri

10. All Prayers Are Gratitude:

It may be pointed out that all prayers are offered as a gratitude to the Almighty for His benevolence.

11. (Note: Pages 848 to 858 of the Urdu Edition deal with grammatical mistakes of Shaik Ali's "Rudd" pointed out by Hzt. Aalim Billah (Rh), hence those pages have not been translated which do not deal with the problems of our beliefs or Mahdiat, but grammatical mistakes of Shaik Ali, hence not translated pertaining to Arabic vocabulary and grammar only.) *********************

☆☆☆

CHAPTER THREE
Demand To Correct The Narratives And Its Answers.

Traditions:

The traditions presented in "Sirajul Absar" have been accepted by the author of Hadia. But for some traditions, he had objected for their translation and had written that whatever narratives were reliable, answer had been given. But his demand to correct them, is baseless; since we have already explained in chapter 2.

Narratives (Riwaiyaat):

Bandagi Miyan Syed Khundmir(Rz) had presented a narrative of "Shubul Ieman" in his Maktoob-e-Multani.

"Regarding Imam Mehdi(As) some differences have surfaced. A group had hesitated to give his opinion and maintained his belief that from the progeny of Bibi Fatima(Rz) a person would appear whenever Allah wished to help assist His religion."

اختلف النـاس فى امر المهدى فتوقف جماعة واحالواالعلم الىٰ عـالمه واعتقدوا انه واحد من اولا د فاطمةؓ بنت رسول الله صلى الله عليه وسلم يخلقه الله متى شاء يبعثه لدينه

Author of Hadia had doubted about the correctness of this narrative, although he had with him the volume of "Shubul Ieman" which may have some defects. Thus he writes that: "Even in this defective volume which is available in this city, this writing is not available. And from the nature of this book it does not seem that at the end also this narrative was recorded. Because it pertains to some traditions. And it is out of his habit to add anything".Author of "Sirajul Absar" too had copied the same narrative with reference to "Shubul Ieman" therefore its correction seems necessary .

Narrative in "Shubul Ieman":

A. Author of Hadia maintains that the author of "Shubul Ieman" after writing the traditions did not add any thing from his own, which contention is wrong. Author of "Mishkot" in his "Kitabul Nikah" had entered three traditions (copied from Shubul Ieman) and after that he had written that:

"These three traditions have been narrated by Behaqi in "Shubul Ieman" and had pointed out that "if the third tradition is taken as correct, then he could not be called a Muslim and none would entertain him and offer him with whatever he had legitimate things."

روى الاحاديث الثلثه البيهقى فى شعب الايمان قال هذا ان صح فلان الظاهران المسلم لايطمعه ولا يسقيه الاما هو حلال عنده !

From this it is clear that if there is any difference in the traditions, then Behaqi tells something he had added from his own and if there is any doubt he is always ready to clears it.

"A volume of "Shuhab-e-Muharraqa" is available in the State Central Library, Hyderabad, along with "Kanzul Ammaal"

Author of "Shuhab-e-Muharriqa"had accepted what Behaqi had referred about Shia's belief about Imam Mohammed bin Al Hasanal Askri:

"They are Shia, particularly who are called Imamaiah and one of their group claims themselves to be "Ahl-e-Kashf" and had hesitated to claim in this connection. Thus Behaqi had pointed out about the hesitation of the Ahl-e-Kashf, as per the Shia belief, to recognize Mohammed Bin Hasanal Askari as Mahdi. Further they are unble to furnish proof of Askari's date of birth and his claim to Mahdiat. According to our belief Imam Mahdi's advent and appearance is based on the reliable traditions of the Holy Prophet(Slm). Particulafrly when no tradition accepts that Mohammed Bin Hasanal Askari would be the promised Mehdi, who would proclaim himself to be the Promised Mahdi in such and such year after emerging from his hideout."

وهو لاءهم الشيعة خصوصاً الامامية منهم وقفهم عليه جماعة من اهل الكشف فاشارا البيهقى الى توقف جماعة من الناس عما اقدم عليه الشيعة بلاد ليل يدل على تعين وقت ولا دته وعلى كونه محمد بن الحسين العسكرى لان المهدى ثبت وجوده وظهوره بالاحاديث النبوية وليس فيها انه ابن الحسن العسكرى وانه يولد عام كذا وكذ

Asad Makki had accepted Behaqi's narration in his letter whose version is as below:

"Now I shall summarize for you what Behaqi had told, so that what Jaluluddin Seuyoti had made it a hodge podge, you should understand. Behaqi had spoken about those people who had difference of opinion regarding Mahdi(As). That is to say, whether the same Mahdi(As), about whom it was prophesied in the traditions of the Holy Prophet(Slm) should be accepted? And whether there is any tradition that Mahdi(As) should be the son of Hasanal Askari and shall be born in such and such year? Although the Shiites had accepted Askari as Mahdi, and have faith in him; but (the fact is that, there is no consensus since) a group hesitated to accept Askari as the promised Mehdi!"

وهـانـا اشـرح لک قول البيهقى مختصر التكون على بـصيـرة من خلط جهول الدين فيقول البيهقى اختلف النـاس فى امر المهدى اى الموعودبه فى خبر رسول اللـه صـلـى الله عليه وسلم هل تقد م على القول بانه مـحـمـد بـن الـحـسـن الـعـسـكـرى الذى ولدعا م كذا وكـذااانـح ويـجـزمبهـفـاقـدم الشيعة عليه وحرمت به وتوقف جماعة عن الا قد ام عليه والجزم به .

Thus, Asad Makki had pointed out about that group which had hesitated to accept Askari as Imam Mahdi. Thus a correct volume of "Shubul Ieman" is available in Southern India, and in Hejaz. Thus the said tradition has been acknowledged, which fact, Asad Makki also had not refused.Thus the Author had wrongly described Behaqi's version that Al Mahdi means the person of Mohammed Bin Hasanal Askari who is supposed to be in the hiding in Samra's Sardaba area, but the fact is that there are differences even in shias about his date of birth. Ahl-e-Sunnata wal Jama'at had hesitated to accept Mohammed Binal Hasan al Askari's Mahdiat and Asad Makki had described the belief of those who had hesitated in these words:

"Those who had hesitated to adopt the belief on the basis of the consensus of the Ahl-e-Sunnata Wal Jama'at among whom there are eminent scholars of the traditions who are trustworthy in matters of beliefs and who have firm belief that Imam Mahdi is he who is from the progeny of Bibi Fatima(Rz) Binte Rasool(Slm) about whom the Holy Prophet had prophesied in his traditions."

واعتـقـدو ما اعتقد جمهوراهل السنة والجماعة الذين منهم جهابذة الحديث المحول عيلهم فى الدين من ان الـمـهـدى الموعودفى اخبار الصحيحة واحد من اولاد فاطمه بنت رسول الله صلى الله عليه وسلم

Asad Makki had used the words of "Ahl-e-Kashf" for those who had hesitated to accept Shia doctrine and he never accepted that Shias and the Imamiah are known as "Ahl-e-Kashf". It is is a fact that the Ahl-e-Sunnat wal Jama'ath had hesitated to accept Mohammed Hasanal Askari as Mahdi because for them Mohammed Bin Askari's Mahdiat is false. And to say that they had hesitated and never announced the truth, it is also wrong. Apart from this the one who has leaning towards Shieath only had hesitated.

"Among Shias, the Imamamiah Sect was of the opinion that Mohammed Binal Hasanal Askari had hidden himself under the apprehension of enemies. But the narration of hiding is false, since as a matter of fact Mohammed binal Hasanl Askari had long back died and was buried in Madinah. Thus Ahl-e-Sunnatwal Janma'at had denied his Mahdiat at any cost".

زعـمـت الامـاميـة مـن الشيـعـة انـه مـحمد بن الحسن العسـكـرى اختـفـى عـن الـناس خوفا من الاعداء ولا استـحالة فيطول عمره كنوح و لقمان والخضر عليهم السلام وانكر ذلك سائر الفرق.

Author of "Kanzal Dalael" had referred Alauddin Samnani's pamphlet "Majalisaat" in which it is asserted about Mohammed Binal Askari that:

"Allah knows it better that Mohammed Binal Hasanal Askari had died and was buried in Madinah, still there should be no doubt about it (that he had died long back)."

دخـدائى مى دانداومروهاست واورا در مدينه رسول دفن كرده اند شبه درايں نيست۔

In this connection Mullah Ali Qari writes :

" He became a saint, and he had hidden himself from the public; then gained highest place among the saints and in this condition he died." 8

صـارمـن الابـدال وغـاب مـن اعين الناس ثم صار قطبا ومات تلك الحال

Taftazani had reported the scholar's faith that"

" Mahdi shall be the Imam who would establish justice and shall come from the lineage of Bibi Fatima(Rz) and Allah shall commission him whenever He would like for the benefit of the Ummah"

فـذهـب العلماء الى انه امام عادل من ولد فاطمة رضى الله عنه يخلقه الله تعالىٰ متى شاء ويبعثه نصرة لدينه

Therefore that narrative of "Shubul Ieman" which is also mentioned in "Sirajul Absar" had been corrected through the version of Asad Makki which has nothing to do with that Mahdi whom Shias accept as Mahdi.

From the "Shub-e-Ieman" which had "Bughvi's consent states that:

"There had been differences among people about Mahdi and one group hesitated, but claimed it's belief that Mahdi is from the progeny of Bibi Fatima(Rz) who would appear at a latter date."

اختـلـف الـناس فى امر المهدى فتوقف جماعة واحالو العـلـم الى عـالـمه واعتقدوا انه احد من اولاد فاطمة عليها السلام يخرج فى آخر الزمان

Hzt. Aalim Billah(Rh) had written at the end of "Sirajul Absar" with reference to "Tanbihul Tuharruz",and with reference to "Nodi" and from the "Sayings of Hazrat Khaja Gaisoo Daraz(IRz)" that Imam Mahdi(As) shall advent in 905 H. Author of Hadia had demanded to correct what ever the autyhor of "Sirsajul Absar" has written about those referred books as to where such words have been written in "Nodi"and "Sayings of Khaja Gaisoo Draz(Rz)" etc.

"Sirajul Absar" was completed in between the years 964 and 972 H. None of the opponants had demanded to correct the narratives. It is a fact that even before the Moghal period, Gujrat was known as the center of Arabic Learning where there were many eminent scholars and the very pupil of the Shaikh, Abdul Wahab Muttaqi, had gone to Gujrat, after the death of the Shaik, then how can any body guess that after returning to Gujrat his pupil had not read the pamphlet written by his teacher, the Shaikh. It is also a fact that "Sirajul Absar" was sent to Makkah as well.

However, the contemporary opponents had accepted those narratives. Previously we have discussed under the chapter "Mahdavia Faith and Aurang Zeb." During Alamgir's stay in Gujrat, he ordered to investigate Mahdavia's faith to Qazi Abu Sayeed. The discussion between Qazi Abu Sayeed and the Mahdavia scholars had already been published as " Alamgiri Discussions" *(and the same is reprinted in this volume for the knowledge of the readers to get guidance from the truthfulness of the discussions between the Qazi and the Mahdavi preachers.)*

Tanbihul Taharruz:

In those discussions reference had been made to"the Sayings of Khaja Gaisoo Daraz(Rz)", but Abu Sayeed Qazi never demanded any correction for those "Sayaings" and when"Shubul Ieman's" narration was presented, Abu Sayeed told tha, the book was not available in his library. Then Miyan Shaik Ibrahim asked him to call from the library of the king and read and if you found that narrative in that book then only take us as correct. From this answer it comes to light that the book was available in the king's library. Then Shaikh Abul Qasim had written that Qazi understood that whatever was being told was correct. Then he kept quite and told tha "It is now the evening had spread, it is not possible to go to the King's library and verify". That means to say that till 1094 H. no person had objected on the writings of "Tanbihul Tahurruz". In the year 1163, Hafiz Mohammed Asad Makki had written the pamphlet "Shuhb-e-Muharriqa" in which he had referred the narratives of "Sirajul Absar" and had written that even after correction of these narratives they became ineffective.

From the statement of Asad Makki it becomes clear that even after correction they are not acceptable to him, as regards demand for the correction he wrote," Allah Knows better" that means to say that these narratives were not wrong. And after a lapse of 125 years from the date of writing of "Shuhab-e-Muharriqa" author of Hadia had demanded for corrections.

It may be pointed out that no volume of "Tanbihul Taharruz" was available. But "Sirajul Absar"had referred about "Tanbihul Taharruz" in which the tradition of the "Revivalist of the Religion" had beenm mentioned. It may be possible that author of "Sirajul Absar" might have written"Tanbihul Taharruz" under his signature, but any one who copied it might have simply wrote"Tahuruuz". Apart from it, Shaik Jalaluddin Siyoti had written a pamphlet under the name: "Tanbih" in which the tradition of the "Revivalist of Deen" had been mentioned. It is possible that author of "Sirajul Absar" might have written "Tanbih", which was later on the calligraphers might have added the words "Tahurruz" or "Tahreez".

Nodi:

Author of "Sirajul Absar" also has referred "Nodi" in connetion with "Tazkerai-e-Huffaz". Nodi is known as a freelance writer. Thus it can be said that as regards Nodi, his "Sharh-e-Muslim" might have been referred by Hzt.Aalim Billah(Rh)also, because he had discussed about Asaama's capital punishment with reference to Nodi. Thus as regards the narrative of the Advent of Imam Mahdi(As), if available in "Sharh-e-Muslim", he would have certainly discussed.

Rasoolullah may not stay in grave beyond 1000 years?

From this it comes to light, as mentioned by Seyuoti in his "Kitabuz Zail" that, Nodi too had argued about a tradition that "the Holy Prophet(Slm) may not stay in his grave before completion of one thousand years". "Kitbul Zail" mentions about this tradition:

" What the people discuss about a tradition as mentioned in "Kitabul Zail?" that the holy Prophet{Slm} after his demise may not stay in his grave for more than one thousand years." About this tradition, Nodi had asserted that it has no validity.

It seems Nodi had invalidated above tradition after simly reading the apparant meanings of that tradition and did not go through its intrinsic meanings which informs that, it is posssible that a Khalifatullah may arrive before the end of the tenth century Hijri, who would be having same traits and characters pertaining to the Holy Prophet(Slm). Thus from the said tradition it is clear that before the end of the tenth Century the common belief about the advent of Mahdi(As) became an acclaimed fact. Nodi died in the yare 676 H. and this tradition became the talk of the town even before his death. What the author of "Sirajul Absar" had written with reference to Nodi may be construed as had been corrected.

There is a possibility that some books may not be available at the time of writing of the "Sirajul Absaer", but you cannot deny their existence. Neither it can be presumed that those books which were referred in "Sirajul Absar" were not under his review. And it also cannot be said that the author of "Sirajul Absar" had written the answer to Shaikh Ali's pamphlet "Al

Rudd", without keeping in mind that in presence of a number of people who were siding the Shaikh might demand corrections to the said tradition. The books which were written by the old writers are not available, still their names and references are available. Thus can any body deny their existence at all? Why go so far, In India itself what Shah Abdul Aziz (D 1239) wrote in his "Tuhfai-e-Asna-e-Ashria" in which reference of "Mahjajus Salekeen" had been given which states that:

Howevr, Seyouti had written "Kitabul Zail", in which he had mentioned that the holy Prophet(Slm) may (not stay in his grave) come back even before one thousand years. Nodi too had discussed about this tradition. "Kitabul Zail" states that:

Thus it cannot be said that the books which were referred by the author of "Sirajul Absar" while writing his "Rebattal", were not actually read by him. The books which are not available now and it cannot be said that those books were not in exisance at that time of writing his "Rebattal". And it is a fact that many books of the predecessors had been read and then only their names were referred.Then can any body deny that they were not written at all?

Example of Mahjjajus Salekeen:

"When Abu Bakr(Rz) found that Bibi Fatima(Rz) was hurt on his actions on distribution of the legacy of the holy Prophet(Slm), for that reason she was not on talking terms with him. Therefore to console her, he came to her house and agreed before her by saying "you are correct daughter of Rasool(Slm), but I knew the procedure the Holy Prophet(Slm) used to distribute after weighing your potentiality and of the others, and had distributed any legacy mainly to poor persons and the travelers". On that Bibi(Rz) asked him to do as the Holy Prophet(Slm) was doing. On that Abu Bakr(Rz) praised Allah and pacified her by saying "I shall follow the holy Prophet(Slm) in such situations." Bibi Fatima(Rz) asked him to swear, Abu Bakr(Rz) sworn as she demanded. Then Fatima(Rz) invoked Allah by telling "Oh Allah you are the witness". Thus she was consoled and thereafter he used to give her share first, and the remaining was distributed among the poor and travelers."

ان ابابکر لـمـارا ى ان فاطمة انقبضت عنه وهجرته ولـم تـكـلم بعد ذلک فى امر فدک كبر ذلک عنده فارا داسترضاء لها فاتا هافقال لها صدقت ياابنة رسول الـلـه صلى الله عليه وسلم فيما ردعيت ولكنى رأيت رسـول الـلـه صـلـى الـلـه عـلـيـه وسلم يقسمها فيعطى الـفـقـراء والـمـسـاكـيـن وابن سبيـل بعد ان يوتى منها قـوتـكـم والـصانعين بها فقالت افعل فيها كما كان ابى رسول الله صلى الله عليه وسلم يفعل فيها فقال ذلک اللہ على ان افعل فيها ما كان يفعل ابوک فقالت والله لتـفـعلن فقال والله لافعلن فقالت اللهم اشهد فرضيت بذلک واخذت العهد عليه وكان ابوبكر يعطيهم منها قـوتهـم ويقسم الباقى فيعطى الفقراء والمساكين وابن السبيل.

In reply to "Tuhfa-e-Asna-e-Asharia" many books have been written but the name of "Mahjjajus Salekeen:" was never mentioned any where. One Syed Mohammed had reported that in no books written by Shias, any reference is made about this book.

The same fate is of the book written by "Nodi" and "Tanbihul Taharruz". Nowadays these books are not available, then how could you say that these books were not available for verification by the author of "Sirajul Absar"? Whose references of those books had been quoted by Hzt.Aalam Billah, properly, more than four hundred years ago? It is a fact that many books have been written in favour of "Tuhfai-e-Asna-e-Ash'aria", but none had corrected the narration of "Muhajjajus Salekeen", rather they had presented the same intent in their books.According to the "Tuhfa"it is a fact that what narration had been mentioned in "Muhjjajus Salekeen",it is not alone, but many other reliable books have also recorded it which we shall present. The same narrative had been written by a very learned person by name Kamaluddin Museem Bahrani in his "Misbahus Salekeen:" However it cannnot be said that Shah Abdul Aziz had referred it in his book without any recourse. He was having his own library and he had access to the libraries of the kings of Delhi, which proves that a caliber like Shah Abdul Aziz had seen those books, but their alternatives might have not be available even to him..

The same is the fate of "Nodi" and "Tanbihul Tharruz". Now a days their availabilty is impossible, but no body can say for certain that the author of "Sirajul Absar" who had written this book more than four hundred years ago, also might have not access to those books. In the Tabri's narrative, if the name of Mahdi(As) is not found in any of its volume, it does not prove that this narrative was not available in that volume to which the author of "Sirajul Absar" had referred to. At that period it cannot be said that "History of Tabri" was not available in Gujrat, It is a fact that when Akbar conquered Gujrat, he took away selected books as a booty.

Author of Hadia objects by saying that "from where the author of "Sirajul Absar" could get original "Tareekh-e-Tabri"? It shows that author of Hadia had no knowledge and access to the Islamic world which has sizeable record of volumes of classical and modern books which could be obtained if someone desires to look into. The original "Tabri" is available in Calcutta and Hyderabad Deccan. For his information we produce to him what was printed in its preamble:

"The Library of the Asiatic Society of Bengal at Calcutta possesses a valuable fragment of the first volume which was lent to us with the greatest liberality". Page 32.

It means to say that the library of the Asiatic Society at Calcutta keeps a valuable portion of "Tareekh-e-Tabri" which was made available by another library with generosity. The Library of Sayeedia at Hyderabad also has a portion of "Tareekh-e-Tabri" in which the portion related up to 21 H. had been mentioned. On the very first page it is written: "Seventh portion from the Tareekh of Shaikh Mohammed Bin Jareer Tabri."

Already it had been said that "Sirajul Absar" was written more than four hundred years ago. We do not know which volume of which year was under author's review. "Tareekh-e-Tabri" was published in Europe, however it should not be considered to be the original volume. Its many portions were collected from various countries which are different from each other which includes that volume which is available in Calcutta. The volume which was printed in Egypt was the copy of the European volume.

Particularly such differences are found in the hand written manuscripts. One volume may have some reference, but another volume lacks it.

Example of "Tareekh-e- Abul Farj":

Moulvi Shibli had reported in his pamphlet "Kutub Khan-e-Iskandaria" that"Tareekh-e-Mukhtasirul Dawal" was written by Abul Farj, for the first time, it came to light by that book that the "Kutab Khana-e-Iskandaria" was burnt down. In this reference Shibli had translated word by word from pages 180 and 181, printed in London in 1263 AD. The last para states that "Umroo Binal Aas" had dumped these books in a washing room of Iskandaria and then started burning them and within six months all books were burnt. How illiterate was he and so foolish and unethical that he burnt the Kutub Khana! is it not deplorable?"

The gist of that pamphelet had been printed in "Al Hilal" by Jarji Zaidan. Then the scholars of Egypt started writing on it. Ali Basha Mubarak had written about "Kutub Khana-e-Iskandaria" in his book "Al Hazattut Toufiquia" by stating that:

The blame of burning of the "Kutub Khana-e-Iskandaria" had been attributed to Umroo Binal Aas. But its reason is not known. The Christian historians and contemporaries of Umroo Binal Aas also did not mention this tragic event and suddenly it came to be known in thirteenth century only. The fact is that even Abul Farj also had not mentioned in his "General History."

ينسب حرقها الى عمر وبن العاص لكن لم يعلم وجه انتساب ذلك اليه فان هذه الحادثة لم يتكلم عليها احد من المورخين فى عصره من النصارى وغيرهم ولم يظهر ذلك الا فى القرن الثالث عشر من الميلاد عن كتاب ينسب الى ابى الفرج بطريق حلب مع انه لم يذكرها فى تاريخه العام.

From this, it comes to notice that even Abul Farj had not mentioned this event in his book. Whereas the volume in which this event had been written by Moulvi Shibli only. Ali Basha Mubarak states that:

"What Ali Basha Mubrak had stated about Abul Farj was not recorded in his history about the pitiable episode of the burning of the "kutub khana". It means to say that the "Tareekh Mutasarul Dawal" which was published in 1890 AD at Bairoot also does not speak about the burning of the "Kutub Khana". But the reality is that we had not read any thing in it about the burning of the "Kutub Khana-e-Iskandria". However Shibli Nu'mani had said that he had read in it."

قوله لم يذكر ها فى تاريخه العام لعله يريد به تاريخ مختصر الدول المطبوع بمطبعة الآباء اليسوعين بيروت سنه ١٨٩٠ فهذا المطبوع حقيقة لم نرفيه ذكر المكتبة الاسكندرية مع ان شبلى افندى النعمانى قد ذكر ان الجملة انما جاءت فى تاريخ مختصر الدول هذا.

Example of "Sunan-e-Nisaai":

Author of "Uqudud Durer" had written traditions of Imam Mahdi(As) with reference to "Sunan-e-Nisaee". An old volume of " Uqudud Durer" is available in the State Central Library (Kutub Khanai-e-Asafia) Hyderabad, published in 1092 H. after being printed at Damascus, and the calligrapher has written his name "Yousuf Bin Yahiyah bin Ali". In that volume some events have been mentioned. A few of those events are reported hereunder:

Umme Salma(Rz) narrated that she heard the holy Prophet(Slm) telling that Mahdi(As) will be from the descendants of Bibi Fatima(Rz). This has been accepted by Imam Abu Dawood(Rz), Sulaiman bin Al-Ashath(Rz), Imam Abdul Rahman(Rz), Hafiz Abu Bakr Baihaqi(Rz) and Imam Abu Umar Waaldani(Rz). 3.

Anas son of Malik(rz) narrated that he heard the Prophet(Slm) saying that my nation (community) shall never be perished since I am in the beginning and Mahdi(As) is in the middle and Masih son of MaryamI(As) is at the end.

Abi Sayeed Alkhudri(Rz) said he heard the holy Prophet(Slm) telling that "Mahdi(As) is from my progeny and he shall establish peace and justice in the world". It has been certified by Imam Abu Dawood(Rz), Sulaiman(Rz) and Imam Abu Abdul Rahman Nisaai(Rz). 5.

عن ام سلمه رضى الله عنها قالت سمعت رسول الله صلى الله عليه وسلم يقول المهدى من عترتى من ولد فاطمة رضى الله عنها اخرجه الامام ابو داؤد سليمان بن الاشعث السجستانى فى سننه والامام عبدالرحمن النسائى سننه والحافظ ابو بكر البيهقى والامام ابو عمر والدانى رضى الله عنهم(الباب الاول)

عن انس بن مالك رضى الله عنه قال سمعت رسول الله صلى الله عليه وسلم يقول لن تهلك امة انا اولها ومهديها (المهدى) اوسطها والمسيح ابن مريم آخرها اخرجه الامام ابو عبدالرحمن النسائى سننه (الباب السابع)

عن ابى سعيد الخدرى رضى الله عنه قال قال رسول الله صلى الله عليه وسلم المهدى منى و ذكر حليته وعدله ثم قال يملك سبع سنين اخرجه الامام ابو داؤد سليمان بن الاشعث السجستانى فى سننه والامام ابو عبدالرحمن النسائى فى سننه (الباب الحادى عشر)

Author of "Uqdud Durer" states that these traditions were available in "Sunan-e-Nisaai", still in the printed volumes these traditions are not mentioned.

In "Sanan-e-Nisaai" those traditions were recorded, but in the printed volumes these references have been omitted by whom, and why, no body knows. There is no doubt that Imam Nisaai(Rz) had written "Sanan-e-Kabeer" first, then a concised book under the name"Mujtameul Mutoon" was written. And those traditions regarding Imam Mahdi(As) were omitted, but who had done such mischief no body knows. If those traditions of Imam Mahdi(As) are not available in that concised book, it cannot be presumed that in the original "Snana-e-Kabeer" also those traditions were not mentioned; and certainly the same might have been under the review of author of "Uqudud Durer."

Jalaluddin Soyuti and "Tareekh-e-Tabri":

Jalaluddin Suyoti had referred a tradition with reference to "Tareekh-e-Tabri", but the same is not available in the printed volume of "Tabri".

Mir Ghulam Ali Azad had mentioned all of the traditions relating to "Arzul Hind" in "Shamamatul Anber" and these traditions he had also written in his "Subhatul Mirjan". "Shamamatul Anber" may be considered the first volume of "Subhatul Mirjan" in which these traditions had been mentioned:

"Tabri had written in his "History" about Prophet Adam's descent from Paradise on the peak of the mountain at Sarandeep on account of his Sin, where he lived for three hundred years, weeping in repentance and on account of his tears from weeping several medicinal herbs were sprouted in India which were being exported to many parts of the world.." 6

قـال الـطبـرى فى تاريخه عند هبوط آدم عليه السلام الى جبـل سـرانـديپ فبـكى على راس ذالک الجبل ثلاث مـائة سـنة لـذلتـه فـنبت من دموعه من جوانب الجبل ادوية تحمل الى جميع الآفاق من الهند

Mir Ghulam Ali Azad after writing the first chapter of "Subhatul Marjan", had written that whatever he had written in"Shamamatul Anber", Seuyoti had described in his "Tafseerud Durral Manshoor". Thus wherever he had written that "Tabri had stated" these are the words of Jalaluddin Suyoti and not of Azad. That means to say that the volume of "Tabri" which was under review by Seuyoti, then only he had recorded the said tradition. Thus in the volume of "Tabri" which was printed in London, from page 119 to 125 all those events have been written which relate to prophet Adam's descent on the peak of the mountain of Sarandeep, but it omits the narration recorded by Seuyoti which informs that from the tears of Prophet Adam(As) many medicinal herbs in India were sprouted.

However it is a fact that the volume of "Tabri" which was referred by Seuyoti had the reference of the Indian medicinal herbs, but the volume which was printed in London lacks that passage. Thus it may be presumed that in the volume of "Tabri" the information about the "Appearance of Imam Mahdi(As)" was available and that was the volume which was under review by the author of "Sirajul Absar". If the printed volume lacks the information of Imam Mahdi(As), no responsibility could be determined on the author of "Sirajul Absar".

"Sayings of Hazrat Gaisoo Draz(Rz)":

Autrhor of "Sirajul Absar" had referred also about the "Sayings of Hazrat Gaiso Daraz(Rz), still he had not referred any particular "Saying". These Sayings are available in "Jawameul Kalam" which were compiled by Syed Mohammed Akber Husiani. Another compilation was prepared by Qazi Alimuddin Bharochi. Author of "Sirajul Absar" had established his daiarah at Ahmadabad and Budhasan (Baroda), Threfore it may be presumed that the compilation of the volume at Bharoch might have been under review of Miyan Aalim Billah(Rh). But we have another compilation known as "Jawamaul Kalam" of Akber Husaini. Mohammed Hamid Siddiqi has written that, from the scrutuiny of the volumes of "Jawameul Kalam" it is seen that all volumes are full with mistakes and at some places events had been added which have no reference to their context. Thus such differences may be seen from the following:

An old volume of "Jawameul Kalam" is available in the Central Library, Hyderabad, which was printed in 1034 H. at page 181 it is mentioned that:

"What Mu'ayiah had done for the Ahl-e-Bait? Hasan(Rz) was murdered; Husain(Rz) was martyred; Ali(Rz) was murdered; Ayesha(Rz) was murdered who was the favourite wife of the holy Prophet(Slm) for whom traditions mention Bibi Ayesha(Rz) had been designsated by the holy Prophet(Slm) as the "Leader of the women of Paradise "It is said that Mu'awiyah paid 30,000 Dirham to a woman for killing Bibi (RZ) . That woman started going to Bibi Ayesha's house frequently and tried to live like a member of the household. That woman dug a well in her house and filled it with limestone and covered the mouth of the well with straws and made false sitting arrangement for Bibi(Rz) near the mouth of the well. She invited Bibi Ayesha(Rz) to her house for a dinner. Bibi(Rz) went and sat where false sitting arrangements were made for her. As she sat, she fell in the well. That woman put water over (the lime) which burnt her completely. Nobody knew where is the grave of Bibi Ayesha(Rz)." (Verfisable?)

معاویه به اهل بیت اوچه کرد' حسن راکشانید حسین راکشانید علی راکشانید' عائشه که محبوب ترین زنان اوبودکه در باب اوست سیدة نساء اهل الجنة فضل عائشة على سائر النساء کفضل الثرید علی سائر الاطعمتہ اوراکشانید قصہ اواین است کہ عورتے راسی ہزار درم داد کہ عائشہ رابنوعے بکش' اودر خانہ عائشہ در آمدکرد چند روزے ملازم شد تایکی ازکسان خانہ شدد رخانہ خویش چاہی کاوانیدو آن راپر بچونہ آب نارسیدہ کرد وخس پوش کرد عائشہ را روزے درخانہ خویش مہمان خواند' عائشہ فقیہہ امت اجابت کرد ہم برچاہ خس پوش بساط فراز کردہ بود و آنجا نشست وفرود رفت واز بالا آن عورت بدبخت آب ریخت تاآنکہ ہم درمیان بمردوگور عائشہ است ہیچ مسافرے زیارت عائشہ نکردہ و گورا اوراندیدہ۔

The said tragic event is recorded in an old volume, eventhough, two traditions regarding Bibi Aeysha(Rz), also have been recorded. But in the printed volume of "Jawameul Kalam", this tragic episode was omitted. Hamid Siddiqi had written about some annexed material which seems to be pointing out to this very episode. If he had any doubt about any version, he must have written the reasons of his doubts in the margin.

Exmple of "Burhanul Mua'asir":

Syed Ali Tabatabai had written "Burhanul Mu'aa'sir"(History of Ahmadnagar) which was publishsd by "Majlis-e-Makhtutat-e-Persia", in Hyderabad. Some portions had been omitted from the book, regarding which Secretary of Association had written that a concised version only was published. About the material which was not printed are said to be not consistent. The question is, if that material was not consistent, then why should the author write that at all? Whether they are consistent or not, they are the portions of the text.

Syed Ali Tabatabai had written questions of Murtuza Nizam Shah, Ruler of Ahmadnager (A mahdavi) and their answers by scholars, but the secretary of the council of Persian Letters had omitted those questions and answers stating that they did not relate to the history since the mentioned material was omitted from the record with a plea that they indicate the mental derailment of the king, therefore omitted by telling that they did not relate to history and with a false accusation that the king was mentally upset. It was a common belief that these questions were related to religion, pertaining to Mahdia beliefs,therefore that portion on account of bias with those beliefs only had been omitted from recording. It was better to keep every word recorded and in the margin he should have mentioned his objections in the margin for their ommission..

"Al Talveeh" and "Bukhari":

Taftazani had written "Al Talveeh" with reference to "Bukhari":

"It had been argued with reference to the holy prophet's statement in which the holy Prophet(Slm) told that after him, many traditions would appear. If you get any tradition with reference to me, then compare it with the holy Qur'an. If it is found that it fits to the holy Qur'an, then accept it, otherwise reject it. Here he says that it had a single source which are particularized with Imam Mahdi(As) and specified as continuous and famous, hence cannot be said to be absolute."

واستدل على ذلك بقوله عليه السلام يكثر لكم الاحاديث من بعد فاذاروى لكم عنى حديث فاعرضوه على كتاب الله فان وافق فاقبلوه وما خالفه فردوه واجيب بانه خبرو احدو قد خص منه البعض اعنى المتواتر و المشهور فلا يكون قطعيا (التلويح على التوضيح الجز الثانى طبع مصر ٩)

Taftazani had declared such traditions coming from a single source. Further he states that:

"It has been accepted as blameworthy by the Muhaddiseen, because one of the narrator is Yazeed bin Rabia and he is unknown. Whatever he presents there is no link between Ash'ass and Suban, thus it was deleted. Yahiya ibn Moin had stated that the tradition was cooked up by Zanadiqa. Still Imam Bukahri(Rz) had included it in his "Sahih Bukahri" eventhough it was deleted on the basis of a single source."

قد طعن فيه المحدثون بان فى رواته يزيد بن ربيعة وهو مجهول وترك فى اسناده واسطة بين الاشعت وثوبان فيكون منقطعا وذكر يحيىٰ بن معين انه حديث وضعته الزنادقة وايراد البخارى اياه فى صحيحه الاينافى الانقطاع اوكون احد رواته غيرمعروف بالرواية (التلويح على التوضيح طبع مصر الجزء الثانى ٩)

It is certain that the said tradition was recorded in "Sahih Bukhari". Taftazani died in 792 H. hence before that year that tradition was recorded, but later on was removed from the current volumes of "Bukhari".

Ibn Khaldun and Karbala Episode:

In the same manner the tragedy of Karbala was omitted from the Muqaddama. In volume 3 of his "Muqaddama" under the caption" Maseerul Husain Ilal Koofa wa Maqutala" on page 21, under that Imam Husain's going to Kofa and was martyred at Karbala was omitted. It ends at page 23 and every thing is blank. Actually he had written six pages about that tragedy, but all pages are blanbk.

"Rouzatul Ahbab" and its Volumes:

Mir Jamaluddin, Muhaddis-e-Shirazi had written "Rouzatul Ahbab" in 788 H. in the city of Herat it conatins three issues:

1. Biographies of the holy Prophet(Slm),2. Ahl-e-Bait and companions of the holy Prophet(Slm). And 3. About Descendants, followers of the successors, eminent commentators., for that there are three chapters. Since the written manuscripts lack the third Section, the printed volumes too lacks this section as well.It seems that during the period of Shah Ismail Safavi (906 when Shia rose to the height, "Rouzatul Ahbab" was tampered to show that author of "Rouzatul Ahbab" was a Shia Scholar. "Reehanatul Adab's" author is a Persian. He had admitted that "Rouzatul Ahbab" was written in three volumes. The third volume is missing pertaining to the Descendants, followers of the successors and prominent Commentators.

Sharh-e-Aqaed:

During the period of Sultan Abdul Hameed "Sharh-e-Aqaed" was published in Qustuntunia. That portion had been omitted in which the discussion about Khilafat had been written. The tradition of "A'e'mathul Qureysh" had been written, to which Moulvi Shibli had certified in his travelogue in these words:

"In my presence "Sharh-e-Aqaed" was being printed in a printing press, But Mu'arif (Director) had striken off that portion of discussion mentioned about Khilaphat. I saw that volume in which the said portion was striken off which made me sad about it. It was a period about 1309 H. Thus it is possible that volume pertaining about the "Sayings of Hazrat Gaiso Daraz(Rz)"might have also been ommitted. Author of "Sirajul Absar" who had written it more than four hundred years, should have read the "Sayings" and the "Traditions about the Appearance of Imam Mahdi(As)", but in those volumes printed afterwards that portion had been omitted. Now a days when any volume comes for printing, it is easy to the printers to omit any "tradition or Sayings" according to their belief, hence on account of prejudice and bias, there is a possibility to omit the traditions of Imam Mahdi(As). Miyan Aalim Billah(Rh) whatever had written is correct according to the purpose of the writing, because other books certify his writings.

Matching narratives:

References of those books supporting Imam Mahdi as mentioned in "Sirajul Absar" are presented hereunder.

1.Ibn Ahdal's Narrative:

There are such books which are not available and there are some books which have differences, but not corrected, in such circumstances we cannot presume that the very contents of the books are wrong. Seyuoti had presented in his pamphlet "Tanbih" the narrative of Ibn Ahdal:

" Mahdi(As) or Eisa(As) would appear in the tenth century when the priod ends at the Arabic number (Alf) "	ويكون المهدى او عيسىٰ ابن مريم فى الماية العاشرة عند تمام الدورو العدد العربى انتهىٰ. (كلام ابن الاهدل)

By telling"Yakuna Mahdi(As) aou Eisa(As)" means either Mahdi(As) or Eisa(As), thus Ibn Ahdal did not have faith in emergence of both Mahdi(As) and Eisa(As) at the same time. He was of the opinion that if Eisa(As) did not appear in the tenth century then Mahdi's appearance was a must.

Imam Ibn Ahdal had told three points: 1. Appearance in the tenth century, which fits to Imamana(As), because Imamana(As) had proclaimecd his Mahdiat in 905 H. and after five years of propagation of Mahdiat, passed away in 910 H. The Tenth Century is calculated from 901. Shaik Ahmad Sar-e-Hindi died in 1034 H. He is known as Mujaddid-e-Alf-e-sani, hence the beginning of a century is taken not the end.

Second point is that Mahdi(As) would appear at the end of the period. Here period means, Lunar period, in whose beginning prophet Adam(As) appeared and the total length of the period has been calculated to be seven thousand years. The source of this seven thousand years is the tradition "Ad Duniya Sabatha Alaf Santha wa ana fi Akhirha Alfa". With reference to this Tradition, and with reference to Rafiuddin Dehalvi's writings, author of Hadia, had written in his chapter 3, Argumnet 5 that:

In order to count a person's age, we count in two ways : if a boy had completed six years, then we say him to be of six years or we may say that he is running in his seventh year of his age. Hazrat Ali(Rz) counted the age of the Earth from the date of appearance of Adam(As) on the Earth as six thousand years upto his time. Thus according to him the world had attained six thousand years. Secondly; he said that the world had entered into its seventh thousand year. Thus according to the traditions at the end of the seventh thousand year appearance of Imam Mehdi(As) was a must.

"When Mahdi(As) appaears at the end of seventh day, when the world completes its seventh thousand years of age.?"	ويتم الظهور بخروج المهدى تتمه سبعة ايام ولهذقالوا عمدة الدنيا سبعة ايام ولهذا قالو امدة الدنيا سبعة الآف سنة

Author of "Ghiasul Lughath" had counted the Lunar time table and had stated that:

"According to the "A'yeen-e-Akbari" upto the year 1242 Hijri, the period from the birth of prophet Adam(As) 7170 years have passed and now lunar period is over and giving way to Zuhal and 170 years have already passed according to Solar years."

مـولف گـویـد کـه چوں از آئین اکبری دریافت می شود کـه تـا امسال کـه سنۀ یك هزار ودو صدد وچهل وهجر یسـت آدم عـلیـه السـلام را هـفت هـزار ویك صـدو هـفتادسـال شمسی گـذشتـه ازیـن معلوم می شود كه بـالـفـعـل دور قـمـر نیست بلكه دور زحل باشد واز آن تاحال یك صدد وهفتاد سال شمسی گذشته ازیـن معلوم می شود که بالفعل دور قمر نیست بلکه دور زحل باشد واز آن تاحال یك صد وهفتاد سال شمسی گذشته اند ـ

That is to say from the starting of the Lunar period to 1242 total age had been 7170 Solar years . According to it the Lunar years come to 7390 years Thus if we count 390 years before 1242 , the year comes to 852. At the end of Lunar period, Imam Mahdi(As) was born in 847 H. Thus it is proved that at the end of the Lunar period Imam Mahdi(As) had appeared. And Imam Mahdi(As) passed away in 910 H. It was the end of one thousand years. In Arabic language there is no word to count beyond one thousand. Therefore they say Alif for one thousand. Imam Al Ahdal(Rz) said that at the end of Arabic number Ailf, Imam Mahdi(As) would appear. Thus Imam Mahdi(As) appeared before the end of one thousand years.

Seyuoti's Pamphelet and the Tradttion:

Seuyoti had mentioned in his pamphlet that the holy Prophet(Slm) would not rest in his grave for more than one thousand years. The purpose of this tradition is well known to the public, still Seyuoti disregarded it.

He says that in Rabiul Awwal of 898 H. a man came to him and presented a paper to him by telling that it was given as a Fatwah by an scholar who had accepted that tradition of the Prophet (Slm) not resting beyond thousand years. Seuyoti says that "since it was given by a scholar, I could not reject it". This writing had three points to ponder:

1 According to a tradition the holy Prophet(Slm) would not rest in his grave beyond one thousand years and this is a well known fact to the public.

2. That fatwah was issued by a prominent scholar who had accepted that tradition to which Seyuoti could not reject.

3. The period of that Fatwah was 898 H. *(Imamana(As) was born on 847 H. and passed away in 910 H., that is, before the end of one thousand year, as stated in the tradition that the Holy Prophet (Slm) would not rest in his grave beyond one thousand years.)*

Mullah Abdul Qader's Narrative:

According to Seyuoti as the scholar had complete belief in that tradition, while according to Mulla Abdul Qader the scholars of Makkah and Madinah also had accepted that tradition. Thus in "Najatur Rasheed" he opined about the Mahdavi Faith that:

"Some people requested the scholars of Harmain and Shariefain to issue a Decree about a tradition in which it was asserted by the holy Prophet(Slm) would not stay in his grave beyond one thousand years. And before the end of that thousand years all important signs have started to appear in which appearance of Imam Mahdi(As) also is a fact. The Muhaddiseen of Harmain Shariefain accepted the facts of the tradition and wrote their decree and when that Decree was received by Shaik Jalaluddin Seyuoti who himself regarded as a Revivalist, did not agree to sign on that Fatwah and when he took that as an exaggeration he wrote a Pamphlet against that Decree under the title "Be kashf fee tajawwuz hazihil ummati anil alf"

بعضی از مردمان چون از علمائے حرمین شریفین استفتاء درست کرده اند د رایں باب کـه حضرت رسالت فرموده که من بیشتر از هزار سال درمرقد منور و مطهر قرار نـمـی گیـرم و پیـش از انقراض هزار سال درمرقد منور ومطهر قرار نمی گیرم و پیش از انقراض هزار سال عـلامـات کبـرئ کـه خروج مهدی موعود وازان جمله است مـی بـایـد که البته ظاهر شود واکثر ے از محدثین آبی امـاکـن شـریـفـه بـرطبـق مستفتی جواب نوشته بر صـحت آن حـدیث امضا فرموده و چون به شیخ جلال الدیـن سیوطی رسیده که خود را امجددمایه عاشره می گـفت اول از روئے مـروت دربـاب امـضائے آں مدافعه نـمـوده بـعـد از مبـالغه بسیار به خلاف آں جماعت در تـضیـعف آں حـدیث رساله نوشته مسمی به کشف فی تجاوز هذه الامة عن الالف

According to the above it is confirmed that the scholars of Harmain were unanimous in accepting that tradition and accordingly the advent of Mahdi(As) was imminent to them before the end of tenth century. But Seyuoti had rejected it against a decision of a group of eminent people.

From the contents of this tradition it is certain that (1). Either the holy Prophet(Slm) would emerge from his grave before the end of thousand years or (2) or Any other person would emerge whose arrival would be like that of the arrival of the holy Prophet(Slm).

Thus from that tradition the period of the appearance of Imam Mahdi(As) is determined. However the contemporary scholars of Seyuoti had come to conclusion that when Mahdi's appearance was a must, then it was possible that Jesus Christ(As) and the Anti Christ also would emerge; thus they had included wrongly these baseless particulars in that Decree. But to Seyuoti it seemed impossible that the thousand year was just coming to an end and how is it possible that all such important events would emerge before the end of 1000 years? It seems that at that time the tradition of Razeen and Mishcot were not before Seyuoti in which it was asserted that "how the Ummah would perish when I am in its inception, Jesus Christ(As) would be at its end and in between Mahdi(As) would be there".

Therefore In "Mishcot" the traditions relating to Imam Mahdi(As), important signs regarding the emergence of Anti Christ and Jesus Christ(AS) were not mentioned although these are important signs before the Doomsday. The scholars took those signs like ignorance, adultery, wine drinking, less number of men comparing to exceeding number of women, would emerge before the Day of Judgment.

Apart from this there is no tradition in which it is stated that along with Imam Mahdi(As) Jesus Christ(As) also would appear at the time of emergence of the Anti Christ.

Thus from that tradition it comes to light that Imam Mahdi's appearance was imminent, still the scholars had unnecessarily and erroneouly included other signs which are related to the Doomsday.

Hazaerul Qud's Narrative:

Hzt. Syed Mohammed Gaisoo Draz(Rz) had written his "Malfoozat" which is available in the State Central Library, Hyderabad (Tasawuf Persian No.409). Although in the list its name is given like "Malfoozat", but actually on the book "Hazaerul Quds" is written whose year of publication is 1068 H. A Seal of Aurang Zeb library had been affixed on it. The particulars of prophets have been written on pages 379 to 386. It is written that Prophet Noah(As) got his salvation on account of the holy Prophet(Slm); in the same way Moosa(As) got manifestation also was caused by Mohammed(Slm). What Jesus Christ's resuscitation is called, was also on account of the holy Prophet(Slm). At page 383 it is written that the holy Prophet(Slm) had given himself the name of Christ and he gives life to the dead and takes life of a living man. After the holy Prophet(Slm) the Ummah would become poverty stricken as under:

"The moon of the holy Prophet(Slm) would have set. And the light of Mohammed(Slm) had disappeared. Islam was poor at the beginning, and after his demise, the same way, again Islam shall become poor. Now the time had come for rising of a new moon. When it would rise, from the date it would rise, every day would become brightened."

هاں قمر محمدؐ غروب کردونور احمدی فرور رفت برآمدن راجا نماند شنیده بد أالاسلام غریبا ھاں اکنوں آں مہ برمی آید تا ایام دولت او طلوع شد ھر روز ھرروز روشن تر بر آمده

This indicates about the appearance of Imam Mahdi(As). After mentioning about the new moon's rising, matters about the appearance of Eisa(As) and blowing of the trumpet of Soor, and finally the Day of Judgment had been mentioned. And at the end, the date of completion of the book was written as 803 H. and it ends by telling that the moon would emerge. Accordingly Imam Mahdi(As) was born just after forty four years in 847 H.

Qiramani's Narration:

"Shaik Owais Bin Ali Qiramani said that Mahdi(As) would appear at the end of nine hundred or at the beginning of nine hundred."

قال الشیخ اویس ابن علی القرمانی ان المهدی سیظهر عن قریب او علی راس التسعمایة البتة

Indian Schoars' Narrative:

The scholars of Akber's period also were of the opinion that in the Tenth Century some one of prominence would appear and that personality should be of Mahdi(As). Thus in order to flatter, the courtiers designated Akber as a man of prominence, and they did mention wrongly the word Mahdi to Akber. Thus Mohammed Husain Azad while discussing about "Jashn-e-Now

Rozi" had written that "Thus the worldly scholars put into the mind of this illiterate ruler(Akber) that in the year one thousand, every thing would change and Akber would become that prominent person." Thus Akber established a nerw religion which they named it "Deen-e-Ilahi."

Sources of Narratives for the Tenth Century:

Those scholars who had particularized the Tenth Century for the advent of Mahdi(As), they based their calculations on some traditions.

A.Abdul Wahab Shirani had referred the faith of Shaikh Taqiuddin (died 702 H.) and had mentioned this tradition: " If my Ummah accepts reforms it will take one day and if there had been any tyranny, it would take half a day."

B.Abu Dawood(Rz) referred this tradition with reference to a like tradition as mentioned below:

"Narrated Sa'ad Ibn Waqqass(Rz) who heard the holy Prophet(Slm) saying that my Ummah would not become powerless before Allah, if it was given even a half day, when Sa'ad asked how much is the half day, holy Prophet(Slm) said five hundred years."

عن سعد بن ابی وقاص عن النبی صلی الله علیه وسلم قال انی لا رجوان لاتعجز امتی عند ربها ان یوخر هم نصف یوم قیل لسعد کم نصف یوم قال خمس مائة سنة

C. Author of "Koukab-e-Munir" had written about this tradition that:

"If my Ummah is on the true path, its life is one yum, one yum means one thousand years. And otherwise it would survive half a day, that is five hundred years."

ان احسنت امتی فبقاء هایوم من ایام الآخرة وذلک الف سنة وان اساءت فنصف یوم

D.Author of "Asshatul Lam'aat" had narrated that:

"The meaning of the above tradition is that my Ummah would get so close to Allah that Allah would keep it alive for five hundred years."

معنی حدیث آن است که ای امت راایں مقدار قدرت و مکنت و قرب مکانت نزد پروردگار تعالیٰ هست که پانصد سال ایشان رانگاه داردوهلاک نه کند

E. The holy pophet(Slm) said:

"How would my Ummah perish, when I am at its beginning, Mahdi(As) would be in the middle and Esa(As) would be in the end."

کیف تهلک امة انا اولهاوالمهدی وسطها والمسیح آخرها ولکن بین ذلک فیج اعوج لیسو امنی ولا انا منهم

Thus from this tradition it becomes clear that Mahdi(As) would emerge as the saviour of the Ummah within one thousand years.

F.Author of "Uqudud Durer" had referred Hzt. Ali(Rz) telling:

"Nayeem Bin Hammad had referred Mohammed Bin Hanafiah who stated that they were sitting with Ali(Rz), when a person asked about Mahdi(AS). Ali(Rz) told it takes a long time and made his fingers to figure out as "nine" and said that he would appear at the end of that period. And people would be guided to fear from Allah. Allah shall arrange such a group of people who would weep like clouds, they would be filled with love of Allah. They would never rejoice if any one joins them nor they would repent if any one goes out from them. Their number would be like the companions of Badr. None would surpass them nor the last one would reach their position and their number would be like Taloot, who would cross the river along with them."

اخرج نعيم بن حماد عن محمد بن الحنفيه قال كنا عند علي فساله رجل عن المهدى فقال هيهات ثم عقد بيده تسعا فقال ذلك يخرج فى آخر الزمان اذا قيل للرجل الله الله الله فقام فجمع الله له قوما فرغا كفرغ السحاب يولف بين قلوبهم لا يستوحشون على احد خرج منهم ولا يفرحون باحد دخل فيهم على عدة اصحاب بدر لم يسبقهم الاولون ولا يد ركهم آخرون وعلى عدة اصحاب طالوت الذين جاوزوا معه النهر

From this, author of Hadia had deduced that by terrifying through fear of Allah they would claim Ba'iat is utterly wrong.

The question was about the period. Hazrat Ali(Rz) made the figure of "nine" by his fingers. As it is already stated that in Arabic there is no word to count more than one thousand which is called "Alf". Here nine means nine hundred years, Imamana(As) passed away in 910 H. In another sense, if nine is counted then also it fits to Imamana(As), since he lived for nine years after first proclamation at Makkah in 901. H.

Now remains another narrative which refers to the signs of the Day of Judgment which would start to appear after two hundred years as reported by author of Hadia which was contradicted by "Safarus Sadaat":

"There is no certainty about two hundred years regarding the emergence of the signs for the Day of Judgment."

در باب ظهور آيات بعد از دويست سال چيزے ثابت نشدنده ـ

How can you prove that Imam Mahdi's appearance would be just after two hundred years from the fall of the Abbasid Caliphzate in Persia?

Those who believe that the twelfth Shia Imam would be Mahdi(As) who was born in 255 or 258 H. they deduce their claim from this tradition.

Other items of this tradition referred by Hzrt.Ali (Rz) fit to Imamana(As):

1.There would be a group of people who would be weeping.

Author of "Sirajul Absar" had mentioned about the followers of the Descendants of

Imamana(As) that they would be absorbed in worship of Allah so much that they would be found always grieving, lamenting and weeping. Before this we have presented the impression of Shaikh Abdul Wahab Muttaqi, the pupil of Shaikh Ali Muttaqi, who told about a close relative of the Shaikh, who had accepted Mahdiat and was living in Makkah and when he met him he found him in a lamenting and weeping position. Further to this, author of "Juanpur Nama" had mentioned about Mahdavis who were weeping and lamenting.

2. To live in harmony and indifference on any one's arrival or departure:

The best example was seen in Mahdavi dairahs where people of different creeds joined in the dairah after leaving their wealth and world, and used to live there with peace and tranquility like brothers together. The same was the position of the companions of the holy prophetI(Slm). The example of indifference on any person's arrival or departure may be noticed that when Ruler of Jalore entered in the gathering of Imamana(As) in which Imamana(As) was delivering his sernmon, no body moved to offer respect even to their Ruler, and even his servants too.

3.The number of Companions of imamana(As) to be like that of the companions of Badr and of Taloot:

It is a fact that the total number of the companions of Badr was 313 and that of Taloot also was 313. Miyan Syed Alam states that:

"At that time Allah's command came to Imamana(As) to obtain allegiance from those who are approved by Us. Then Imamana(As) took their allegiance and they were all 313 in number."	همان وقت فرمان حق تعالیٰ شد که اے سید محمد از ایشان بیعت کن که ایشان مقبول حضرت مااند حضرت میران بیعت کردند در آن سه صد سیز ده مردمان بودند

And also it was a fact that at the time of Imamana's demise there were 313 companions around him.

" Those who were present at the time of demise were all forgiven by Allah and they became Muhajirs of Mahdi(As). It is reported that they were 313 in all"	امام آنانکه بوقت وصال حبیب ذوالجلال حاضر بودند همه بخشیده شندد وهمه ایشان مهاجران نام شده بروادیتی جمله ایشان سه صد وسیزده بودند۔

4. None of the Awwaleen or Akherreen got the position of the Companions of Imamana(As):

We have referred previously what Mulla Abdul Qader Badayuni had written in "Najatur Rasheed" that if he started to write about those Mahdavis of his period it would become another "Tazkera-e-Aouliah". That means to say what venerable position they got. "Kitab-e-Fittan" testifies the above statement:

"Narrated Abu Ayyub in Artat, Who heard Abdul Rahman Bin Jubair bin Jafer who heard the holy Prophet(Slm) was telling that the people of my Ummah would meet surely with Eisa Ibn Mariyam(As), and indeed they would be like you or even better than you."

حـدثنا ابو ايوب عن ارطاة عن عبدالرحمن بن حبيرين نفيـر قـال قـال رسـول الـله صلى الله عليه وسلم ليد ركـن الـمسيـح ابن مـريـم رجال من امتى هم مثلكم وخيرهم مثلكم او خير

Other traditions also confirm that advent of Imam Mahdi(As) would be in the Ninth Century, Hzt. Ali's statement also testifies about Ninth Century. "Najatur Rasheed" also mentions that the scholars of Hejaz were expecting about the appearance of Mahdi(As) in the Tenth Century. Hazrat Gaisoo Draz(Rz) too had stated that appearance of Mahdi(As) would be in the Tenth Century. The same had been mentioned by Imam Ibn Ahdal(Rz) that Imam Mahdi(As) would emerge in the Tenth century. Quiramani's statement testifies that the people of even Rome were guesing Mahdi's emergence at the end of the Ninth Century, And as a matter of fact Imamana(As) was born in Ninth Century(847 H.) and demised in Tenth Century(910 H.). All statements fit on to the personality of Imamana(As).

As at the end of the month of Ramazan as we are all desirous to witness the new moon, the same sort of zeal and enthusism of waiting had been witnessed in most parts of the world about to hear the news of the appearance of Imam Mahdi(As). The same was the enthusiasm when the Holy Prophet's appearance was the talk of many places of the world. And also when he migrated to Madinah from Makkah, the Madnians were eagerly and enthusiastically waiting for his arrival. And aslo when he was commissioned by Allah as the Last Seal of Apostles.The details are given below:

Apostleship of Holy Prophet(Slm):

A.Author of "Asadul Ghaba" writes that Hazrat Abu Bakr Siddiq(Rz) had gone to Yeman before the auspicious event of Apostleship of the holy Prophet(Slm) and he met with a certain Shaikh Azdi, a soothsayer, who informed about coming of the "Akhiruz Zaman"(Slm) and his companions. in the following words :

"From my true knowledge I find that a Nabi would emerge in Haram (Makkah) to whom would assist one young(Hzt.Ali Rz) and another middle aged man(Hzt.Abu Bakr Rz) who would help him in Prophet's thick and thin. Middle aged man would be meek and weak of white colour having a sign of depravity on his stomach and a sign on his left thigh."

اجـد فى الـعلـم الـصـحيح الصادق ان نبيا يبعث فى الـحرم يعاون على امره فتى و كهل فاما الفتى فخواض غمـرات ودفا ع معضلات واما الكهل فابيض نحيف على بطنه شامة وعلى فخذه اليسرى علامة .

Shaik Azdi had written some poem in praise of the Apostle. When Abu Bakr returned to Makkah, by that time the holy Prophet(Slm) had already declared his Apostleship.Abu Bakr(Rz)went to Bibi Khadeja's house and met the holy Prophet(Slm) and offered his allegiance on the hand of the holy Prophet(Slm). Asadul Ghaba writes, Hzt. Abu Bakr(Rz) requested to Prophet(Slm): "I ask to spread your hand that I witness: "there is no god except Allah and you are His Apostle(Slm)".

"The holy Prophet(Slm) informed Hazrat Abu Bakr(rz) that "I am the Rasoolullah(Slm) for you and for all people. Hence accept Allah as One and Alone".Abu Bakr(Rz) asked the Prophet(Slm) "on what basis"? Holy Prophet(Slm) informed about an old man with whom Abu Bakr(Rz) met in Yeman". Abu Bakr asked "with how many old persons I had met in Yeman"? Holy Prophet(Slm) told: "With that old man who read his poem to you in praise of mine". Abu Bakr asked "who informed him(The Prophet(Slm) about that"?: "That Angel who used to go to other prophets(As)."Was the Prophet's answer.

قال يا ابكر انى رسول الله اليك والى الناس كلهم فامن بالله فقلت مادليلك على ذلك قال الشيخ الذى لقيته باليمن قلت و كم من شيخ لقيت باليمن قال الشيخ الذى افادك الابيات قلت و من اخبرك بهذا ياحبيبى قال الملك العظيم الذى ياتى الانبياء قبلى قلت مديدك فانا اشهد ان لا اله الا الله وانك رسول الله .

From this It comes to light that people of Yeman were waiting for the "Akhiruz Zaman(Slm)".

B.Author of "Shawahedul Nabuwwat" had written about Hazrat Abu Bakr(Rz) while referring Abu Masood Ansari, that:

"Abu Bakr(Rz)stated that I reached Dair-e-Bahwara which was the residence of Buhaira Monk. And asked him the interpretation of my dream.He asked me "who was I" ? I told that I belong to Qureysh. He informed me that Allah would conmmission one man from the Qureysh as Nabi and you would be his minister in his life time and afterwards as his Kahlipha. When Mohammed became Rasoolullah(Slm), he will invite towards Islam. I asked Mohammed (Slm) that every Prophet had one sign, what is your sign? "The sign of my Nabuwwat is your dream which you witnessed and Buhaira had interpreted about me". I asked him who told you? He told it was Gabriel(As). Then I did not ask any other sign and proclaimed"I witness that Allah is One and single and no one was His associate and I witness that you are his Messenger(Slm)."

C.Author of "Madarijul Nabuwwat had stated that:

در بعض تجارت بدیر بحوراء که مسکن بحیرا راهب بورسیدم وتعبیر خواب خودراز ویرسیدم گفت توچه کسی گفتم من مردے ام از قریش گفت خدائی تعالیٰ درمیان شما پیغبرے برخواهد انگیخت وتور درایام حیات وے وزیر وے خواهی بود و بعد از وفات وے خلیفه وی پس چوں رسول الله صلی الله علیه وسلم مبعوث شد مرابااسلام خواند گفتم هر پیغمبرے راد لیلی بوده است بر نبوت وی دلیل توچیست گفت دلیل نبوت آن خوابے کے دیدی وآں حبر ا در جواب تو گفت که آن را اعتبار ے نیست و بحیر ا گفت که تعبیر آن چنیں است و چنیں من گفتم ترابایں که خبر کرد گفت جبرئیل گفتم من از تو هیچ دلیل وبرهان نمی طلبم زیارت ازیں اشهد ان الا الہ الا اللہ وحدہ لاشریك لہ واشهد انك عبدہ ورسولہ ۔

" A monk by name Abu Aamer was from the Ous tribe. From both tribes of Ous and Khuzarj he was the most eulogist about the holy Prophet(Slm). He was having close relationship with the Jews of Madinah. He asked them about the holy Prophet(Slm). The Jews used to tell about the characters of the holy Prophet(Slm). They used to tell that Madinah would be his migrated place. Then he went to the Jews of Teemah. They informed the same thing about him. Then he went to Syria and asked the Christians. They also informed about the holy prophet's characters. Abu Aamer used to wear hessian fabrics and used to tell that he was Hanafi, follower of Prophet Abraham(As) and was waiting for the Last of the prophets to emerge."

ابو عامر راهب شخصی بود از اوس هیچ کس از اوس وخزرج و صاف ترازوے مرآنحضرت رانبود والفت و مصاحبت می نمود بایهود مدینه وی پر سید ایشان را ازوے خبر میدادند ایشان اور از صفات رسول رب العالمین صلی الله علیه وآله وسلم ومی گفتند که این دار هجرت اوست پس از آن نزد یهود تیما رفت ایشان نیز خبر داد ند بمثل آں پس از آن به شام رفت وسوال کرد نصاری را ایشان نیز خبر دادند بصفت آنحضرت پس بیرون آمد ابوعامر و ترهب نمود وپلاس پوشیدومی گفت من ملت حنیف و دین ابراهیم دارم و منتظر خروج پیغمبر آخر الزما نم۔

All these soothsayings told that people of Yeman, Madinah, Teemah and Syria were all waiting for the appearance of "Nabi Akhiruz Zaman(Slm)". In the same manner the muslims of the world from India to Hijaz and Egypt were waiting about the advent of Mahdi(As) in the Tenth Century. Just now we have discussed about the apostleship of the holy Prophet(Slm) by the monks and soothsayers who informed about the coming of the "Akhiruz Zaman(Slm)". Thus Ibn Hissham(218 H.) had reported that:

"Scholars of Jews and Christian, Monks and Soothsayers of Arabia used to tell about the apostleship of the holy Prophet(Slm) and they prophesied that the period of appearance had come nearer"

كانت الاحبار من يهود و الرهبان من النصاری والكهان من العرب قد تحدثوا بامرر سول الله صلی الله علیه وسلم قبل مبعثه لما تقارب من زمانه.

When their information about appearance of an "Akhiruz Zaman(Slm)" had been accepted, then why should not the information of eminent scholars of the Ummah and mystics be accepted for the advent of Imamana(As) regarding coming of "Mahdi-e-Maauood(As)"? Thus Author of "Sirajul Absar's writings with reference to "Tanbihul Taharuz" about Imamana's appearance in the Tenth Century for sole purpose of the "Revival of the Religion of Islam" of the original period of the holy Prophet(Slm) was an important issue.

CHAPTER FOUR
Author Of The Risalatur Rudd
And His Belief,
Other Signs Of Imam Mahdi(As)

Denial of Mahdi(As)?:

The argument presented by the Shaikh is full with anguish. At one place he denies and on the other place he subdues. At one place he said that denial of Mahdi(As) is not an infidilety. When Mahadavis tell non believers are infidels, then the Shaikh insists the acceptance of that Mahdi(As) is an obligation who carries all the signs (as mentioned in the traditions). That means to say that if the Shaikh admits a person as Mahdi(As), then only Mahdi's acceptance becomes obligation otherwise not. The problem is that according to the criterion of the Shaikh that particular Mahdi(As) of his belief, had not born so far and he had not proclaimed his Mahdiat also(*and certainly will not born, leave aside prolamation*) . Even before that, any of the so called Mahdi if born, and if some one denies his Mahdiat, according to the shaik that person becomes infidel. Shaikh's contention is nothing but absurd.

As a matter of fact as regards the basics of Mahdiat, whatever the holy Prophet(Slm) had prophesied about Mahdi(As) and those basics are real religion, to whom we Mahdavis have accepted as the fundamental beliefs. It is surprising to note that the Shaikh had obtained a Decree from the Scholars of Makkah in the year 952 H. which includes the Decree of Yahiya Bin Mohammed Hanbali who clearly decreed that the holy Prophet(Slm) had determined the position of that person as an infidel who denies Imam Mahdi(As). That Decree can be verified in the pamphlet "Al Burhan" of the Shaikh. Still the Shaikh insists that no body could declare a person as infidel who denies Imam Mahdi(As). This statement of the Shaikh denotes his anguish. Because at one place he had accepted the denial of Mahdi(As) makes the denier an infidel and at other place he denies what he himself had said. How strange is it not?

Mahdavi Books of Beliefs:

In this regards Shaikh's contention is that no book of beliefs points out about our Mahdi (As). Thus he writes:

"But the books of beliefs do not mention about this Mahdi(As). Although they refer about the grave torture and about the very nature of the pathway (Pul-e-Sarat) had been made whose denial is not an infidilety."

بل لم يذكر فى كتب الاعتقاد يات مسئلة المهدى مع ذكرهم المسائل التى لم يكفر جاحدها كاثبات عذاب القبر وكيفية الصراط وغير ذلك الى آخره (الرد) سراج الابصار

"Sharh-e-Maqasid" speaks about Advent of Mahdi by inserting these words "Amma Khuroojul Mahdi(As) Faman Ibn Abbas Razi Allahu Anhu." It is amazing that the Shaikh himself had referred "Sharh-e- Maqasid" and with reference to that book he had described the conditions of Imamat (leadership). Those conditions what the Shaikh had referred to are available in Chapter 4, and at the end of that chapter the statement about the advent of Mahdi(As) had been made. Which is as under:

"Among all discussions which relate to Imamat (leadership) the discussion pertaining to the advent of Mahdi(As) also are included in them."

مما يلحق بباب الامامة بحث خروج المهدى الى آخره.

How can we assume that the Shaikh had not gone through " Sharh-e-Aqaed" completely. From this we are constrained to infer that the shaikh just to belittle the problem of Mahdiat and to defraud the Ummah had lied shamelessly.

Mahdi(As) and Imamat(Ledership):

Shaikh contends that Mahdiat is bound with Imamat (Leadership). In this regard he had presented three conditions for the inauguration of general Imamat with reference to "Sharh-e-Maqasid" and he stresses about the conditions for Mahdiat. They are:

1. Acceptance (of Imamana(As) by authorities

2. indignation and mastery

3. Appiontment of deputy.

Under these conditions every ruler can become Imam. Not only the ruler, even any sinful and a debauched person also can become Imam. But as far as Nabuwwat is concerned, no such condition was applied, if these conditions are not applicable to Nabuwwat, then how the hell these dubious and unauthentic conditions could apply to Mahdiat? The Shaikh had given the definition of Authorities, by telling to whom people should obey. The tradition of Hirql describes the signs of Nabuwwat according to "Mishkot" venereable persons' acceptance is the proof of Nabuwwat of the holy Prophet(Slm). But it is also mentioned that these persons who accepted the holy Prophet(Slm) were the followers of the prophets. As regards Imamana(As) the people who accepted Imamana(As) are those who were kings, nobles, ministers, scholars, army, military men, captains, commanders and the persons of repute and from every walk of life including authorities and men of ranks, ordinary and eminent people. Against these facts, the Shaikh is lying that the authorities did not accept Imamana(As). This contention is utter false and absurd just to create doubts and defraud the Ummah.

The second condition of indignation and mastery also do not become conditions, because the holy Prophet(Slm) lived in Makkah for at least thirteen years and he never got mastery over the infidels, although he was acclaimed as the NABI. However he had mastery through a r g u m e n t s   a n d   d i a l e c t i c   d i s c u s s i o n s . :

(Note: Ofcourse the holy Prophet(Slm), although he was an unlettered man, still his superb teachings changed the patterns of the life of the peoples to whom he was deputed by the Almighty Allah for their betterment and emancipation. It was not an ordinary job to convert the staunch polytheists of the Arabian soil to become utter monotheists during his life time only. It was the mesmerizing effect of his eloquent oratory that whenever he, with his graceful, exquisitely brilliant and bright eyes, came to the podium with his melodious, lovely, sweet and heart touching voice, recited the verses of the holy Qur'an in a properly worded tone, it seemed as if, not words but flowers were pouring out from his mouth, touching the inner conscience of the listeners, causing tears coming out spontaneously from the eyes of the masses.

In the same manner, Imamana(As) was more than a master over all the scholars of Juanpur that is why just at his tender age 12, he was given the title of "Asadul Ulemah" by the scholars o f   J u a n p u r .   I s   t h e r e   a n y   d o u b t   a b o u t   i t ?

Imamana(As) started his sermons on religious matters. His sermons were filled with simplicity of style and eloquence that whoever heard once became mesmorized. His audience was full with eminent scholars, elites, literates and common men who became astonished to hear such subjects relating to the holy Qur'an which were never heard before. These sermons brought him the title of "Asadul Aouliah" at his age 21 only. It was an historical achievement which had been recognized by eminent scholars of Islmic studies and historians, particulaly of the Sub-Continent and was recorded in gold wateras in the annuls of history of the saints of India. This is what mastery and prominence are known for. Translator.)

Before this, author of "Zafarwala's" narration had been quoted in which it was said that Sultan Mahmood Begdaha wanted to meet Imamana(As), but his courtiers suggested him not to meet Imamana(As), under the apprehension that if the Sultan met, he would become subdued and become Imamana's disciple, leave aside the question of ordinary people. Sultan Beghda was a king who yearned to meet Imamana(As). This is called mastery and prominence. Another example of mastery was presented by the author of "Tuhfatul Kiram" relating to Mulla Sadruddin who happened to have exalted hundreds of his pupils to an eminent position and who, although he denied to meet Imamana(AS) in the beginning for certain reasons, but when Imamana(As) came to Thahtta, it is said that the moment Sudruddin looked at Imamana(As), at the very first sight he surrendered and became subdued. This is called splendour of his complexions.

As regards the third condition of appointing a deputy, had never been a condition for any prophet(As). This is a fact that, had the holy prophet(Slm) nominated his Khalipha, then at the time of his passing away, the question would never had arisen from the Ansar of Madinah that one Khalipha to be from Ansars and another from the Migrants. In this regard Ibn Hissam had written that the Ansars had asserted " Mana Ameer wa Minkum Ameer." Thus when there is no such condition to appoint any deputy even for the holy Prophet(Slm), or by any prophet, *(except Prophet Moosa(As) who requested Allah to make his brother Haroon(As) his deputy)* then why should this condition be suggested to Imam Mahdi (As)? In this connection we have to adhere what Allah had ordained?

"And We made them Imam who guide according to our orders."(21:74)

وجعلنا هم ائمة يهدون بامر نا(الانبياء ع)

In this verse the prophets(As)was designated as Imam and as regards the condition of Imamat, it comes under the dictates of Allah, through which they guide people. For Imam Mahdi(As), the title of Khalifatullah(As) was granted by the holy Prophet(Slm) and which is mentioned in the traditions pertaining to Imam Mahdi(As). Thus under this context, Mahdi(As) also is the Imam, because all the prophets are Imam. Miyan Abdul Malik Sujawandi(Rh) had written about the attributes of Mahdi(As) that:

"Mahdi(As) is a significant Imam who invites people under the direct orders from Allah withot any medium.."

انه امام خاص يدعو الخلق بامر الله

This shows that Imam Mahdi(As) is definitely an Imam as the prophets are Imam. Further it was said by Miyan Abdul Malik Sujawandi(rh) that:

"Mahdi(As) was designated by Allah to invite people towards Allah, as the holy Prophet(Slm) was commanded by Allah."

المهدى يكون مامورا من الله بدعوة الخلق اليه كما
كان رسول الله مامورا بها

That is why Bandagi Miyan Syed Khundmir(Rz) had asserted in "Ba'azul Aayaat" that after the holy Prophet(Slm) Imamat would be awarded to two dignatories: they are: Imam Mahdi(As) and Jesus Christ(As).

" And after the holy prophet(Slm), Imamat is meant for only two persons, Mahdi(As) and Eisa(As). Because Imamat is suitable to that person only who is the saviour of his followers. And his followers get salvation under his Leadership. That is why the holy Prophet(Slm) had said that "how the Ummah would be perished when I am at its beginning, Eisa(As) is in the last and Mahdi(As) is in its middle,who is coming from the Ahl-e-Bait(Rz)."

والامامة لا يـمكن بعد النبى الا لا ثنين وهما المهدى وعيسىٰ لان الامامة لا تصح لمن يكون سبب النجاة لامته وينـجى امته باقتدائه كما قال النبى صلى الله عليه وسلم كيف تهلك امة انافى اولها عيسىٰ فى آخرها والمهدى من اهل بيتى فى وسطها

Miyan abdul Malik Sujawandi(Rh) also had commented on this tradition that after the holy Prophet(Slm) Imamat is meant for the two persons only, Mahdi(As) and Eisa(As):

"From this tradition the holy Prophet(Slm) had granted Imamamt for Mahdi(As) and Eisa(As). Thus categorically the holy Prophet(Slm) designated Mahdi(As) and Eisa(As) as Imam and none else."

فى هـذاالحديث ظهران رسول الله نص الامامة بعده فى حق المهدى وعيسىٰ ومانص رسول الله صلعم فى حق غير هما .

Shah Burhan(Rh) also had asserted that:

"It is clear that the holy Prophet(slm) had designated Mahdi(As) and Eisa(As) for the Imamat of the Ummah and to none else."

ظهـران النبى عـليه السلام نص الامامة بعده فى حق المـهـدى و عيسىٰ عليه السلام ومانص الرسول فى غير هما

Thus from the tradition " Kaifa Tahluka Ummati" proves that after the demise of the holy Prophet(Slm) there would be only two Imams. And Imam is the one who is a saviour of Ummah. Mahdi's Imamat as a Khalifatullah(As) becomes a divine position granted by Allah, therefore the question of appointing of a deputy does not arise at all and such condition has no value. The verse "Jaalnahum Aa'imma" proves that Imam under the command of Allah guides the public, thus Imamana(As) had guided public as an appointee of Allah for 23 years.

Imam Mahdi(As) the Ruler of the Earth ?:

Shaikh contends that" Yamlaul Arz" means whole of the Earth and had submitted this tradition:

"There would be four persons who would be the rulers of the whole world. Among them two would be faithful and two infidels. The faithful are Zulqarnain(As) and Sulaiman(As). Infidels are Nimrud and Bakht-e-Nasr. From my progeny one person would become ruler of the whole world and he would be the fifth, instead of four."

ملوک الارض اربعة مومنان وكافران فالمومنان ذوالقرنين و سليمان وكافران نمرود و بخت نصر و سليملكها خامس من اهل بيتى (الرد)

Asad Makki also had incorporated the same tradition in his "Shuhab-e-Muhrriqa" and writes that a group had adopted this tradition in a different manner. After that, Asad Makki had inserted some five traditions in which the word "Yamlaul Arz" had come. Still he had included one more traditiion of Abu Dawood(Rz) also. After that he had written that: "If we follow this tradition then we may find it with other group of people also". Thus the Shaikh's referred tradition becomes invalid, in view of Asad Makki's traditions. The correct tradition mentioned by Abu Dawood(Rz) have the same meaning as presented by Asad Makki but in a different manner.

Now we would like to discuss their correct meanings of the traditions. The said tradition refers Imam Mahdi(As) to be the person coming from the Ahl-e-Bait(Rz).One doubt arises that, although it is possible that any one of the Ahl-e-Bait may become the owner of a land, but he may not be granted the position of Imam Mahdi(As). Second thing is that what Arabs think about a king, the non Arabs take a different view about a king. Third thing is that in that tradition names of four kings have been mentioned, but none of them had ever ruled the entire world. Thus in this manner the sanctity of the tradition is doubtful particularly when Hijaz and Tahama were not included in their kingdom. Thus this narrative cannot be said to have been told by a true informer.

The Saikh had presented many traditions in "Kanzul Ummal", but none of them had the reference to Imam Mahdi(As) who would be the king of the whole world as Zul Qarnain(As) or Sulaiman(As). Apart from this the tradition of Haakim also mentions four names who would rule whole of the world, but the name of Mahdi(As) had not been mentioned in it also.

"Omer Bin Abdullah narrates that he heard Mu'awiyah telling that there are four kings who would rule the whole world. They are Sulaiman Bin Dawood(As), Zul Qarnain(As) and one from Ahl-e-Halwan and when fourth name of Khizer(As) was mentioned, answer was in negative."

عن عمرو بن عبدالله الوادعى قال سمعت معاوية يقول ملك الارض اربعة سليمان بن داؤد وذوالقرنين و رجل من اهل حلوان ورجل آخر فقيل له الخضر فقال لا .

Thus the Shaikh's tradition has no value in presence of Haakim's narrative. When Shaikh argues with a non existant tradition then why should we not argue with the following real tradition:

" Bibi Aeysha(Rz) narrated that the holy Prophet(Slm) told that if he desired mountains of gold would become mine, and would become my property. An angel came to me whose height of his waste was upto Kabatullah and qauestioned to me "do you want to be a prophet and a servant, or a king and the prophet. I saw Gabriel who was directing me to adopt humility, then I said I want to be a prophet and a servant."

قـالـت قـال رسول الله صلى الله عليه وسلم يا عائشة لوشئت لسارت معى جبال الذهب جاء نى ملك وان حجزتـه تسـاوى الكعبة فقال ان ربك يقرا عليك السـلام ويقـول ان شئت نبيا عبداوان شئت نبيا ملكا فنـظرت الى جبرئيل فاشارا الى ان ضع نفسك وفى روايـت ابـن عباس فالتفت رسول الله صلى الله عليه وسـلم الـى جبرائيل كالمشير له فاشار جبرائيل بيده ان تواضع فقلت نبياء عبدا الى آخره .

Thus Imam Mahdi is the true follower of the holy Prophet(Slm) how could he desire to become the king of the whole world?

Appearnce of Sufiani ?:

Shaikh did not understand correct intent and the meanings of any tradtion. He contends that the most correct and valuable sign of Mahdi is that "one Sufiani would appear, then Mahdi(As) and Eisa(As) also should both come to Palestine together to kill the Dajjal. Shaikh thus writres that :

"This person (Imamana(As) does not have those signs which could be Identified with Mahdi(As), which have been described in the traditions. For example: "Sufiani's appearance in Palestine near Babul Lud along with Jesus Christ to kill Dajjal."

فهذاالشـخص لـم يوجد فيه اكثر العلامات المعتبرة المـخصوصة بـالـمهدى الصحـيحة المصرحة بـالاحاديـث المستفيضة كوجود سفيانى فى زمنه و خروجه مع عيسىٰ عليه السلام لقتل الدجال بباب لد بارض فلسطين وغير ذلك (الرد)

Now we have to investigate about Sufiani, as to whose creation was he? It is correct that these are reliable signs which have been mentioned in the real traditions for Mahdi(As). But in the traditions of "Sihah", no reference of any Sufiani was given, except in Haakim's tradition with reference to Abu Huraira(Rz) who had mentioned the name of Sufiani, but it lacks any reference of Mahdi(As). Instead he mentioned that a person of the Ahl-e-Bait(Rz) would appear.

Sufiani is the brain child of the Shias according to their unreliable sources. For example:

"Omer Bin Qantalah narrates that he heard Abu Abdullah that before the advent of Mahdi(As) five signs would appear:1. Shrill Cry, 2.appearnance of Sufiani, 3. to inflict losses 4.murder of a pious man and 5. of a yamani. Omer Qantala asked Abu Abdullah that, if a person from Ahl-e-Bait appears,before these signs appear, should we join him? Abu Abdullah told No."

قـال سـمـعـت ابـا عبـدالله عليه السلام يقول خمس عـلامـات قـبـل قـيـام الـقـائـم عليـه السلام الصيحة والسـفـيـانـيـوالـجـسـفـة وقـتـل النفس الزكيه واليمانى فـقلت جعلت فداك ان خرج واحد من اهل بيتك قبل هذه العلامات انخرج معه قال لا الى آخره

Mullah Baqer Majlisi described this narrative:

"Abu Jafer narrates that at a time when Sufiani would appear from Syria, and a Yamani from Yemen, and the lunar eclipse would occur at the desert and a person by name Mohammed Bin Nafsi Zakia of the Ahl-e-Bait would be murdered in between Rukun and Muqam and a sound would come from sky telling Allah is with that group, then our Imam Mahdi(As) would appear."

قـال اذا..........خـرج السفيان من الشام واليمانى من الـيـمن وخسف بالبيداء وقتل غلام من آل محمد بين الـركـن والـمـقـام اسمه محمد بن النفس الزكيه وجاء ت صيـحـة مـن السماء بان الحق فيه و فى شيعته فعند ذلك خروج قائمنا الى آخره.

Who is this Sufiani? his description had been stated by Mullah Baqer Majlisi:

"Imam Mahdi's name shall be on the name of the holy Prophet(Slm), and he would appear when a person from Banu Umayya would dominate the Muslims. Sufiani is the same who had been mentioned in the tradition and he is the son of Abu Sufian bin Harab Bin Umayya to whom Imam-e-Fatimi would kill and also kill the Shias of the Umayya and then Jesus Christ(As) would descend from the skies."

وانـه اسـمـه كـاسـم رسـول اللّه وانـه يظهر بعد ان يستولى على كثير من الاسلام ملك من اعقاب بنى اميـه وهـوا لسفيـانـى الـمـوعـود بـه فى الصحيح من ولـدابـى سـفـيان بن حرب بن اميه وان الامام الفاطمى يـقتـلـه و اشـيـاعـه مـن بنى اميه وغير هم وحينئذ ينزل المسيح من السماء الى آخره.

From this tradition the shias are trying to suggest that Imam Mahdi(As) comes from the Shias. Second point is that a person by name Sufiani from the progeny of Abu Sufian would appear and the Imam-e-Fatimi would kill him. Thus his intention is that some one from the progeny of Hazrat Ali(Rz) would appear to kill a person by name Sufiani who is from the progeny of Abu Sufian. (*As if to take revenge of the martyrdom of Imam Husain(Rz).*)

The source of Haakim's narrative comes from an unauthentic tradition stated by the shias. Haakim too is known as a shia, that is why Sufiani's reference has been given by him. There is no such tradition from Ahl-e-Sunnat about Sufiani, and "Sihah Sittah" also lacks such baseless tradition regarding Sufiani. Thus, just for the sake of prejudicial thinking about Imamana(As) the Shaikh preferred and accepted that irreliable tradition and on that basis he attaches an absolutely wrong sign regarding Mahdi(As) by asserting that Mahdi is the one who confronts Sufiani and kills him. Since Haakim's tradition is baseless, Shaikh utterly fails to manipulate his assertion.

Further, author of Hadia also is hand in glove with the Shaik who tells that Sufiani's narratives have continuity, even though Ibn Hazam had confirmed about Sufiani's narratives to be null and void.

Still there are some more narratives in which reference of Imam Mahdi(As) and Sufiani had been mentioned but they have no sanctity with the Muhaddiseen. Therefore to tell that when Imam Mahdi(AS) would emerge, Sufiani also would appear, is nothing but absurd and false.

Ibn Hazam negates Sufiani's Emergence:

Ibn Hazam had denied about emergence of Sufiani at all. His narration is that:

"It is just like Majoos Faras are looking for the appearance of Bahram-e-Humawand, and waiting of Rafzis for the appearance of Imam Mahdi(As) and the Christians who are waiting by seeing the clouds and waiting of Saibeens for other things, like that they are waiting for Sufiani."

كـانتظـار مـجوس الـفرس بهرام همـاوند راكب البقرة وانتظـار الـروافـض لـلـمـهـدى وانتـظار النصارى الذين ينتـظـرون فى الـسـحـاب وانتـظار الصائبين ايضاً لقصة اخرى وانتظار غير هم للسفيانى۔

Author of Hadia had sided the Shaik and had written that the narrative of Sufiani had a continuity; as against Ibn Hazam who denied the very existence of Sufiani dismissing as null and void by saying it is just like waiting for Bahram is meaningless, thus, appearance of Sufiani is totally nullified

Khasaf-e-Lashker:

This is with regard to Abdullah ibn Zubair, narrated in "Muslim":

"Narrated by Abdullah Bin Qabtia who told Haris Bin Rabia that Abdullah Bin Safwan once came to Umm-e-Salma(Rz), the Ummul Momineen, while I was with them. They asked Umm-e-Salma(Rz) about that Lashkar which would be inflicted in Khasaf which happened during the period of Ibn Zubair. Umm-e-Salma(Rz) told that she heard the holy Prophet(Slm) was telling that a person would come and take refuge in Baitullah for which a lashker would be sent by Yazid and when the lashkar reached a forest, it would face intense troubles. I asked about that person who would be in that lashker? Holy Prophet(Slm) told he too would be put to trouble along with them; but on the day of judgment he would be resurrected as per his desire. Abu Jafer told that Baida means that desert which is near the city."

عن عبدالله بن القبطية قال دخل الحارث بن ابى ربيعه وعبدالله بن صفوان وانا معهما على ام سلمه ام المومنين فسالا ها عن الجيش الذى يخسف به وكان ذلک فى ايام ابن زبير فقالت قال رسول الله يعوذ عائذ

بالبيت فيبعث اليه بعث فاذا كانوا ببيد اء من الارض خصف بهم فقلت يا رسول الله فكيف بمن كان كارها قال يخسف به معهم ولكنه يبعث يوم القيامة على نيته قال ابو جعفر هى بيداء المدينة

From this it comes to light that during the period of Abdullah Ibn Zubair such turmoil had happened. Khasaf means to be drowned, to be destroyed. But such thing did not happen. Another meanings are loss or to disgrace. Nehaya had written about Khasaf that:

"Narrated by Ali(Rz) that whoever did not go for Jihad he would be disgraced and he would be at loss. Khasaf means loss and disgrace as an animal is kept in a cage without grass." 47

(وفى حديث على) من ترک الجهاد البسه الله الذلة وسيم الخسف ، الخسف النقصان والهوان واصله ان تحبس الدابة على غير علف ثم استعير فوضع موضع الهوان وسيم كلف والزم

Muslim Bin Aqba's army should have attacked on idols or at the place where idols were kept, instead it attacked Kabatullah, it means avoiding Jihad. The result was witnessed that Muslim himself died of his ailments. After the death of Yazid, when the army returned to Syria being defeated, was involved in troubles and finally was destroyed in the civil war and whoever was alive had to suffer and was disgraced. This was the result of Khasaf.

Muslim Bin Uqba known as Musrif was taking oath of allegiance on behalf of Yazid at Madinah, a man from Qureysh too had taken the oath but not for allegiance but for otherwise; Muslim did not accept his oath, but ordered to kill. At that tragic event his mother swear to Allah that if she was alive, she would kill Muslim Bin Uqba and burn his body. Thus she killed

Musrif and burned his body (as per her oath.)

Shaik Abdul Haq had narrated in his "Jazbul Quloob" that:

"According to Waqdi, that woman was Umme Yazid Bin Abdullah Bin Zu'ma. When Musrif went to Makkah, she went to her tribe and when she heard the news of the death of Musrif, she went to his garve and dug out his body and hanged the body. According to Zehak,

when people saw his body hanging, they started stoning the body, but it was not burnt. But it may be possible that after two three days the body might have been burnt by her as per her oath."

واقـدى ميـگويـدكـه پيش ماچنين يه ثبوت رسيده كه آن زن ام يزيد بن عبدالله زمه بود بعد از توجه مسرف بمكه مـعظمه وى به مسافت دوسه روزه راه از لشكر باقوم خود مـى گشـت چـون خبر مرون مسرف شنيد بيامد واورا از لشكر باقوم خود مى گشت چون خبر مردن مسرف شنيد بيامد اور ازقبر بر آور دوبردار كشيد ضحاك ميگويد كه

كسانـى كـه اور ابـردار كشيـده ديـده بودند بما حكايت كردنـد كـه مـردم همه بردار اور اسنگسار كردند وذكر سـوختن دراى روايت نيامدهٔ احتمال دارد كه سوختن او بـعد از دو سـه روز كـه بـردار كشيده بودند پس آنكس كه سوخت را روايت نكرد ورحالت اول ديده باشد كه هنور ازدار فرودنيا درده بودند ـ

According to "Jazbul Quloob" the body of Musrif was hung by a python from the neck to his toes:

"When the grave of Musrif was dug opened, people saw his body was clung by a python who was sucking from the body's nose; seeing that every person became afraid. That woman asked to bring his body from the feet to which the python was clinging."

چون قبر بكشا د اژ دهـائى ديد كـه بگرو ن مسرف پيچيـدهاست و استخوان بينى اور اگرفته مى مكدمه از معائنـه اى حال ترسيدند ...... گفت اور ازجانب قدم هـائى او بـر آريـد در آن جـانب نيز يدند كه اژدها به همان طريقه پيچيده است

It is reported that the woman made ablution, oferred prayers and invoked Allah's Blessings and asked for help and strength to bring the body from the grave and burn it. She strike the python with a stick which ran away. Then the body was taken out of the grave, hanged it for some time then burnt it. What more disgrace the commander of an army could endure. As regards the disgrace of that Army, "Jazbul Quloob" states that:

"During this period the news of the death of Yazid reached Syria who died from an horrible disease which caused havoc and embrassment to the army which returned being disgraced and finally was ruined and was destroyed."

اثنائى هـميـن حال خبرمرگ يزيدپليد رسيد كه بعلت ذات الجنب رخت حيات بدارلبوار كشيد، پريشانى در اهـل شـال و بنـو اميـه در افتـاد همه خوار و نزار ورسوا برگشتند وروئى هزيمت بفرار نهاوند ـ

Thus both the commanders and the army were destroyed completely.

Regarding "Khasaf-e-Lashkar" in "Sahih" and "Muslim" there is a narrative:

"Holy Prophet(Slm) stated that it is strange that a group of the Ummah would intend to visit Kabatullah, in search of a person of Qureysh who had taken refuge in Baithullah; by the time other people would reach "Baida" they would be put to "Khasaf"/ trouble."

فـقال العجب ان ناسا من امتى يومون البيت برجل من قـريـش قد لجاء بالبيت حتى اذا كانو بالبيد اء خسف بهم (صحيح مسلم كتاب الفتن)

This Khasaf is regarding the people of Ummah. Literally meaning of Khasaf not to thrust under the earth.

"Holy prophet invokated three blessings. 1. Not to thrust my Ummah under the earth. 2. Do not inflict famine and 3. Let them not kill each other. Allah accepted two, but the third was not accepted."

سـر دعـا كـردم من مرامت خود رايكى آنكه كه فرو نه بـردايشـان رادر زيـن' ديـگر آنكه هلاك نه كنند ايشان رابـه قـحـط سوم قتال نه كنند ميان يكديگر پس اجابت كـرده دو دعـائـى اول راو مـنـع كرد ازثـالث (مدارج النبوت جلد اول

From this it is clear that thrusting the Ummah under the earth is out of question. Therefore the meanings of Khasaf as said by Muslim Bin Uqba is correct.

Khasaf and Abdullah Bin Zubair(Rz):

Abu Dawood(Rz) narrates from "Muslim" that it does not refer Mahdi(As) nor about Ahl-e-Bait(Rz). This narrative refers to Abdullah Bin Zubair(Rz) and the episode of Khasaf. The details are hereunder:

1.Differences would arise at the time of demise of the Khalifa.

The difference arose at the death of Muawiyah, because Ummah did not like Yazid to become the Caliph.

2.One person would run away from Madinah to Makkah.

It was Abdullah Bin Zubair(Rz) who disagreed to take allegiance for Yazid and migrated from Madinah to Makkah.

"Ibn Zubair(Rz) was among those persons who did not agree to take the oath of allegiance on the hand of Yazid and migrated towards Makkah"

وكان ممن ابى البيعة يزيد بن معاوية وفرّالى مكه

3.People of Makkah preferred to take allegiance on his hand (On the hand of Abdullah Ibn Zubair(Rz) instead of Yazid.

This is also correct regarding Ibn Zubair(Rz), since people of Makkah, Yeman, Hejaz, Iraq and Khurasan had accepted him and offered allegiance to him. Ibn Zubair(rz) had taken refuge in Kabatullah where allegiance was undertaken on his hand (Ibn Zubair's).

Ibn Zubair(Rz) had taken refuge in Kabatullah, hence it may be presumed that the oath of allegianmce was taken on his hand in Kabatullah as well.

4. Syrian people would wage a war against those who were running from Madinah to Baida, where the army suffered losses and turmoil (khasaf). This was the army of Muslim Bin Oqba about which we had already discussded that at the place of "Baida" the lashkar would face "Khasaf"/turmoil and destruction.

5. Groups from Iraq and Syrian Abdal/mystics would offer allegiance to Zubair(Rz).

This also pertains to Abdullah Ibn Zubair(Rz). Author of "Tahzeeb" had written that:

"Allegiance was offered to Ibn Zubair(Rz), after the death of Yazid bin Muawiyah by the people of Makkah,Hejaz, Iraq, Yemen, Egypt, Syria in the year 64 or 65 H."

بويع له بالخلافة عقيب موت يزيد بن معاوية (٦٣) وقيل سنة (٦٥)وغلب على الحجاز والعراقين واليمن ومصر واكثر الشام

Regarding "Abdaal" author of "Asshathul Lam'at" states about them that:

"Abdaal are a group of mystics with whose beneficence the world is kept safe by Allah. They are seventy in number. Forty in Syria and 30 in other places. If any one of them dies, another person takes his place. This has been mentioned in several traditions."

ابدال قومى اندكه برپا ميدارد خدائى تعالى زمين رابه بركت ايشان دايشان هفتاد تن اند چهل تن در شام دسى در غير آن اگر يكى از ايشان بهمير ددربدل دے ديگرے را از سائرا الناس بجائے دى بنشاننده ذكر ايشان در احاديث آمده

6. One Qureyshi who was maternally related to Ibn Kalab, would attack on the person who would be in Makkah; but he would be overpowered by the Iraqi saints.

Yazid was a Qureyshi and grandson of Mujadal Kalabi from mother side. "Tareekh-e-Khulapha" states that:

"Maisoon was mother of Yazid, daughter of Mujdal Kalabi."

وامه ميسون بنت مجدل الكلبية

Before that it was reported that Muslim Bin Aqba who brought his army to Syria, died all of a sudden and when Yazid also died the Army returned from Makkah and was destroyed in the civil wars.

7.One who went to Makkah from Madinah would be following Shariah completely and maintained his religion intact. This also fits on to Ibn Zubair(Rz).

"He was the son of that companion who belongs to the ten, designated as Jannati"

صحابى بن صحابى ابوه احد العشرة المشهود بالجنة

There are so many famous attributes about him; one of them is mentioned as an example:

"Narrated Omer Dinar that none was better than Ibn Zubair(Rz) in offering prayers. When he was offering prayers, he was being attacked by arrows, but no arrow would touch his body, and he did not care that they were touching his clothes only.."

قال عمرو بن دينار مارايت مصليا احسن صلوة من ابن زبير كان يصلى فى الحجر يصيب طرف والمنجنيق .ثوبه فما يلتفت اليه.

His Khilafat was universally admitted about which Ibn Hajr Asqalani states that:

" His khilafat on the Muslim World was complete, except some villages of Syria, all Muslims accepted him as the Caliph but Mirwan went against him."

وخلافته صحيحة خرج عليه مروان بعد ان بويع له فى الآفاق كلها الا بعض قرى الشام (الجز الخامس)

8. The person on whose hand allegiance was obtained in Makkah, it was said that he would live for seven years or nine years. According to the "Jameut Tawareekh" Ibn Zubair(Rz) ruled for seven years as predicted.

Thus "Khasaf-e-Lashker, the horrible episode, occurred during the time of Abdullah Ibn Zubair(Rz) and this has nothing to do with the advent of Mahdi(As).

Descent of Jesus Christ(As) and Dajjal:

Shaikh's narrative had been mentioned in which according to him another reliable (most un-reliable to mahdavis) sign of Imam Mahdi(As) had been pointed out that Imam Mahdi(As) would appear along with Jesus Christ(As) at the Babul Lud in Palestine and kill Dajjal. Reliable and correct sign is that which had been mentioned in the true traditions as mentioned in the reliable books. But unfortunately this sign was not recorded in any of the tradition that Imam Mahdi(As) would join Jesus Christ(As) in killing of Dajjal at Palistine. But there are certain narratives in "Muslim" which refer to "Jaish-e-Amir" and "Imam". On these words some people have doubted that for the word "Jaish" they took it Mahdi's Lashker and by the Word "Amir" they took it for Imam Mahdi(As). This doubt is baseless. The details are as under:

1."Narrated Abu Huraira(Rz) that he heard the holy Prophet(Slm) was telling that there would be no Doomday until the Romans entered the village of A'amaqe or Yadaeqe. Thus an army would go against them from Madinah. When both armies met in the battle, the Romans would ask Muslims to hand over those Romans whom Muslims had arrested. The Muslims would answer that they would never handover them. Thus battle would start. More than one third of the Roman Army would be massacred by the Muslim army. Thus they(Romans) fled away. The Muslim army followed them and conquered Qustuntunia. The conquerors were engaged by hanging their swords on the Olive plants for distribution of the Booty, then suddenly Satan would loudly declare that Dajjal had entered among their families, which was a false call.

When they were arranging prayer mats for the prayers that Eisa Ibn Mariyam(As) would descend among them and lead the prayer. When the enemy of Allah, the Dajjal, just after seeing the Christ(As), started melting like salt in the water. But Allah's plan was that Jesus Christ(As) should kill Dajjal and after killing Dajjal Christ(As) showed his spear drenched with Dajjal's blood."

Another tradition reported by Jaber Bin Abdullah:

قال قال رسول اللـه صلـى الله عليه وسلم لا تقوم الساعة حتـى تنـزل الروم بالاعماق اويدايق فيخرج اليهـم جيـش مـن المدينة من خيار اهل الارض يومئذ فاذا اتصافو قالت الروم خلوا بيننا وبين الذين سيوامنا نقاتلهم فيقول المسلمون لا والله لانخلى بينكم وبين اخواننـا فيـقاتلو نهم فينهزم ثلث لايتوب الله عليهم ابداو تقتل ثلثهم افضل الشهداء عنداللّه ويفتح الثلث لا يفتنون ابدا فيفتحون قسطنطنيه فبينا هم يقسمون الـغنـائـم قـد عـلـقو اسيو فهم بالزيتون اذ صاح فيهم الشيطان ان المسيح قد خلفكم فى اهليكم فيخرجـون و ذلك بـاطل فاذا جاؤ الشام خرج فبينا هـم يعدون للقتال يسوون الصفوف اذا قيمت الصلوة فينـزل عيسىٰ بن مريم فيؤمهم فاذا راه عدو الله ذاب كمـايـذوب المـلـح فى الماء فلوتركه لا تذاب حتى يهلك ولكن يقتله الله بيده فيريهم دمه فى حربته.

"Narrated by Jaber Bin Abdullah(Rz) that he heard holy Prophet(Slm)telling that one group of my Ummah would be fighting till the Doomsday and would be dominating. Thus Jesus Christ(As) would descend. The Amir of that group would ask Jesus Christ(As) to come over and lead the Prayer, But Jesus Christ(As) would excuse by telling, ofcourse one among you is Amir, and Allah had granted honor to your Ummah." 61

قال قال رسول الله صلى الله عليه وسلم لا تزال طائفة من امتى يقاتلون على الحق ظاهرين الى يوم القيامة قال فينزل عيسى ابن مريم عليه السلام فيقول امير هم تعال صل لنا فيقول لان بعضكم على بعض امراء تكرمة الله هذه الامة

Another tradition reported by Abu Huraira(Rz) in "Muslim":

"Narrated Abu Huraira(Rz) that holy Prophet(Slm) asked him "what would be your position when Ibn Mariyam(As) would descend among you and would become your Imam". Another narration reports Famkum Minkum.(in place of "Imamakum Minkum)"

قال قال رسول الله صلى الله عليه وسلم كيف انتم اذا نزل ابن مريم فيكم واما مكم منكم وفى رواية فامكم منكم

Shaikh Abdul Haq Muhaddis-e-Dehlavi had commented on this tradition that:

"Here Imam means Eisa(As). To be among them means Eisa(As) would order according to our Shariet and as well as according to the Bible. Another narration says "Fa Yumukum be Kitab-e-Rabbukum wa Sunnatha Nabbiukum". It means that he would lead you according to your Allah's Book (Qur'an) and according to your Nabi's Sunnat. Thus Eisa(As) would lead you and he would be in such a position that you may see him as if he is from our Ummat and his orders would be from our Qur'an and holy pophet's Sunnat."

مراديه امام عيسى است ومراد يه بودن اواز شما حكم كردن اوست باحكام شريعت نه به احكام انجيل ودرروايت ديگر آمدهاست فيومكم بكتاب ربكم و سنة نبيكم پس امامت ميكند شمار ابهكتاب پرور دگار ما وسنت پيغمبر شما' پس معنى چنين باشد كه امامت ميكند شمارا عيسى در حال بودن اواز دين شما وملت شما وحاكم به كتاب و سنت شما

Imam Bukhari(Rz) had entered the narrative of "Imamakum Minkum" in Sahih, because it mentions to Jesus Christ(As). Had he taken it as Imam Mahdi(As), according to his practice he would have placed it under chapter of Mahdi(As). According to his practice if threre are two issues in a single tradition, he would enter it in two different chapters according to the nature of the issue.

Author of "Makhzanul Dalael" under discussion regarding "Imamakum Minkum" with reference to "Sihihien" had copied this narration:

"But the cooked up word which has come in the tradition,"Imamakumal Mahdi(As) Minkum": just to prove that Mahdi(As) would lead the prayer as Imam where Jesus christ(As) would follow Mahdi(As). Thus it is clear that it was a unauthentic tradition; hence false. Thus the word Mahdi(As) had not occurred in "Muslim" or "Bukhari" or even in "Mishkot."

امـامـا ذكر والـفـظـامـوضـو عافى هذا الحديث وهو قولهم امامكم المهدى منكم ليثبتوا الامامة للمهدى فى صلوة عيسىٰ فقد ظهر و ضعه و نشر كذبه بمقاملة الصحيحين اعنى البخارى ومسلم فانه لم يذكر فيهما ولا فـى مـنـتـخـبـا تـهـمـا كـالـمـشارق والمصابيح والمشكوٰة هذا الفظ .

Thus it denotes that "Imamakum Minkum" is meant for Jesus Christ(As) only and not to Imam Mahdi(As).

Some people presume that the first tradition in which the word"Jaish" had come, hence may be taken as Mahdi's lashker, and in the second one the word "Amir" has come for Mahdi(As) and in the third one the wortd "Imam" had come. Thus, some presume that these all attributes belong to Imam Mahdi(As). It may have two positions. Either on the basis of their doubt or suspicion or on the basis of similitude..That is to say it is suspected that Mahdi(As) would be the Amir of this Ummah and that person is one who would emerge from the West. Thus such narration creates doubt and suspicion and some scholars have even told that Mahdi(As) would conquer Qustuntunia two times, one time with declaration of Kalemah and the second time through sword in a battle as mentioned in Qartabi:

" Some of our Scholars had said that Abu Huraira's tradition which had been reported earlier proves that Qustuntunia would be conquered through waging war, while the tradition of Ibn Maja contradicts it. As against Abu Huraira's tradition, Qartabi states that possibly Mahdi(As) would conquer Qustuntunia two times, one time by declaring Kalemah and second time by waging war."

قد قال بعض علما ينا ان حديث ابى هريرةُ اول الباب يـدل عـلـى انها تفتح بالقتال و حديث ابن ماجه يدل عـلـى خـلاف ذلك مع حديث ابى هريره والله اعلم قـال الشيـح الـمـولف رحـمـه الـلّه لعل فتح المهدى يكون لها مرتين مرة بالقتال و مرة بالتكبير

Before the above said passage, Qartabi had also inserted the tradition of "Ibn Maja" in which he refers to conquering Qustutunia became a fact on the basis of declaration of Kalemah, in this also Imam Mahdi(As) had not been mentioned.

This must be noted that Qartabi had used the word "probably" which creates doubt for the staunch believers.

This passage indicates the former scholars had clarified by negating the statement, hence they declared it to be uncertain and dubious. Thus their position was correct in view of their trustworthiness. Allah may Bless them. On that basis alone, the first rate scholars have answered that, from these two tradsitions it comes to light that one group of muslims or an army of the people of Madinah would fight in favour of the truth and would overpower the falsehood. As regards holy Prophet's reference to Doomsday it comes to knowledge that when a group is annihilated, then another would fill up the gap till the Doomsday. Thus one of them would conquer Qustuntunia and that person who conquors Qustutunia would offer prayer along with Jesus Christ(As). Here the word "Jaish" should not be taken as the army of Mahdi(As) and where Imam had been used it relates to Imam Mahdi(As) alone. The words Amir and Imam which have been used in those traditions should not be Indentified for Imam Mahdi(As). As the holy Prophet(Slm) said "La Yazala Taefata Min Ummati" the group known for being busy always in fighting would be continuing to live from the period of the holy Prophet(Slm) till the Doomsday; and when that group is destroyed another group would occupy its place, but Imam Mahdi's group is not like that. Mahdi(As) would emerge after the demise of the holy Prophet (Slm) at any time in future. Thus those people would survive and who would live till coming of Ibn Mariyam(AS) and they would be the followers of Imam Mahdi(As). Thus it came to light that the tradition in which the word "Jaish" was used about a group of people who are faithful people and belonging to the prophet Ishaq(As), whose details shall be given in due course of time. That group had nothing to do with Imam Mahdi(As) and the one who would offer prayer along with Jesus Christ(As) might have been absolutely the Amir of his group and not Imam Mahdi(As).

Taftazani had clarified in "Sharh-e-Maqaasid" that:

"There exists no such tradition which confirms that Imam Mahdi(As) and Jesus Christ(SAs) would come together at one time and at one place, except in one tradition which starts with the words"La Yazaalu Taifata Min Ummati" and to say that Christ (As) would follow Imam Mahdi(As) or vice versa, is an unacceptable fact which cannot be relied upon."

ثم لـم يـرد فى حاله اى عيسىٰ مع امام الزمان حديث سـوى مـاروى انـه قـال عـليه السلام لايزال طائفة من امتى يـقاتلون على الحق الحديث فما يقال ان عيسىٰ عـليـه السلام يقتـدى بـالمهدى او بالعكـس شىء لامستندله فلا ينبغى ان يعول عليه .

Thus, from the above, it is clear that descention of Christ(As) would be along with the Amir of that army and surely not with Imam Mahdi(As), because Mahdi(As) had been designated as an Imam and not as an Amir. Thus it is a fact that Imam Mahdi(As) and Christ(As) would never meet together. Still if some people insist that Mahdi(As) and Christ(As) would come together, this statement is just nothing but false, unreliable and unthinkable.

Whatever had been discussed,it is just to negate through the argument that joining of Imam Mahdi(As) and Christ(As) at one time and one place is nothing but false.

Now comparison of the manuscripts is submitted to clear the doubt and such wrong presumption lead them to uncertainty. In this connection Abu Huraira(Rz) contends in "Muslim" that:

"Narrated Abu Huraira(Rz) that the holy Prophet(Slm) asked: "Did you hear about a piece of land whose one side is towards land and the other side is towards the ocean"? Companions replied positively. The holy prophet exclaimed that "Doomsday would not occure until an army of 70,000 of Bani Ishauq(As) arrive in that city and instead using ammunition to fight with the people of that city, they would declare "La Ilaha Illullahu wa Allahu Akber", then that side of the land would perish which is called "SOAR" towards the ocean, and they would utter the same Kalema for the second time then other portion would perish which is towards land. Then they would utter the Kalema for the third time, then a way would appear through which the army would enter the city and get the booty and when they would be busy in distribution of the booty, then suddenly a shrill cry would come telling Dajjal had emerged, they would leave every thing and rush towards Dajjal."

قال قال رسول الله صلى الله عليه وسلم هل سمعتم بمدينة جانب منها فى البرو جانب منها فى البحر قالوا نعم قال لاتقوم الساعة حتى يغزوها سبعون الفامن بنى اسحاق فاذا جاؤها نزلو افلم يقاتلوا بسلاح ولم يرموا بسهم قالوا لااله الا الله والله اكبر فيسقط احد جانبها قال ثور لا اعلمه الا قال الذى فى البحرثم يقولون الثانية لا اله الا الله والله اكبر فيسقط جانبها قال ثور الآخر ثم يقولون الثالثة لا اله الا الله والله اكبر فيفرج لهم فيد خلو نها فيغنمون فبينا هم يقسمون الغنائم اذجاء هم الصريخ فقال ان الدجال قد خرج فيتركون كل شئى ويرجعون .

Thus it may be pointed out that from the first tradition it is said that Romans would arrive in Aamaq. It also refers about an army which would arrive from Madinah under the command of Bani Ishaq(As). It also refers to the victory over Qustuntunia which had been clearly described as a piece of land whose one side reaches to land and the other side reaches to ocean which determines to Qustuntunia by the commentators:

"That city about which holy Prophet(Slm) had informed is Qustuntunia."

وهذه المدينة هى القسطنطنيه

Hazrat Mu'aaz ibn Jabal(rz) narrates that:

"Narrated By Ibn Jabal(Rz) who heard holy Prophet(Slm) telling that a Grand Event of the victory over Qustununia, and then Emerrgence of Dajjal would happen in just seven months.Reported "Tirmizi" and "Abu Dawood."

It is also narrated by Mu'aaz Ibn Jabal(Rz) that:

"Mu'aaz Ibn Jabal(Rz) had heard holy Prophet(Slm) telling that the population of Baitul Muqaddas would perish, it would be a Grand Event, then would follow by the victory over Qustuntunia, and then another Event would appear about the emrgence of Dajjal. It is mentioned in "Abu Dawood" and "Mishkot."

قال قال رسول اللـه صلى الله عليه وسلم الملحمة العظمى وفتح قسطنطنيه و خروج الدجال فى سبعة اشهر رواه الترمذى و ابو داؤد

قال قال رسول الله صلى الله عليه وسلم عمران بيت المقدس خراب يثرب، خراب يثرب خروج الملحمة وخروج الملحمة فتح قسطنطنيه وخروج الدجال رواه ابو داؤد كذافى المشكوٰة

In these two traditions the events of victory over Qustuntunia and emrgence of Dajjal had been narrated, but no where Imam Madi(As) was mentioned. It may also be pointed out that the Prophet(Slm) had mentiond about Qustuntunia which is known to all. Thus it is affirmed that it was Qustuntunia only to which the Bani Ishaq(As) would invade and conquer and the person who would offer prayer along with Jesuus Christ(As) would be one of the Amirs of bani Ishauq(As). This should not be inferred as Amir to Imam Mahdi(As). Since Imam Mahdi(As) is from Ahl-e-Bait, and from the lineage of Bani Ismail(As) and not from Bani Ishaq(As). By chance if Mahdi(As) to be from Bani Ishauq(As), the holy Prophet(Slm) would have never referred as belonging to himself when he clearly said that" Al Mahdi Min Itrati Min Aoulad-e-Fatima(Rz).Umm-e-Salma narrates "If Imam Mahdi(As) had been from Bani Ishaq(As), then how could he have any relationship to the holy Prophet(Slm).

Had, Mahdi who is from Ahl-e-Bait(Rz), been the leader of the Jaish/ army, this must have been described properly about the leader of Jaish, because there are two distinct features for Imam Mahdi(As): One is that Mahdi's genealogy is different, that he is not from Bani Ishauq(As), but he is from Bani Ismail(As); Second is, the manifestation of the eminence of Imam Mahdi(As) is really the manifestation of the eminence of the holy Prophet(Slm). It all boils down to say that with all these particularities, had Imam Mahdi(As) been the leader of Jaish/Lshkar, then his name would never had been kept in secrecy. It is a fact that Imamana's genesalogy is different and does not belong to Bani Ishaq(As), but belongs to Bani Ismail(As). Further Imamana's appearance is like the Holy Prophet's appearance. Thus, Imam Mahdi, with all these attributes, had he been the leader of the Army, his name would not have been kept secret. That tradition regarding Imam Mahdi(As) is a miracle because it is an hidden information and since it is kept secret sometimes it becomes against the miracle which leads the Ummah towards faithlessness and sometimes leads to infidilety even. Because people will opine as per declaration of the holy Prophet(Slm) that Bani Ishauq(As) would conquer Qustuntunia and at other place how could he say that Bani Ismail(As) became conquorers? It would be only possible when the Army is lead by Imam Mahdi(As). This is against the facts, which leads ummah towards faithlessness. But the fact is that Bani Ishauq(As) would conquer Qustuntunia. Thus the question of Imam Mahdi's meetimg with Jesus Christ(As) would never happen. Further the tradition does not refer the descention of Jesus Christ(SAs) and his killing of Dajjal along with Imam Mahdi(As). As far as the city is concerned it has come to light that it is not Madinathun Nabi, but certainly it is Qustuntunia and that person who would offer prayer behind Jesus Christ(As) is the leader from Bani Ishauq(As). Here too reference of Imam Mahdi is lacking. Thus it is a certainty that Mahdi(As) and Eisa(As) would never meet together at any moment of time.

Shaik Najeebuddin Abu Mohammed Waez Dehalvi had written in his book "Madarul Fuzulah" that:

"It creats a doubt that it may be possible that the leader of this group may be Amir Mahdi."

امير هذه الامة يشبه ان يكون المهدى

Further he wrote that:

"Muqaddasi's assertion is not correct regading a doubt he had created by telling that whether Amir denotes to Imam Mahdi(As)? In order to negate this impression there are two traditions and narrations of eminent scholars which certifies that the said Amir is from the Bani Ishauq(As) and Mahdi(As) is from Bani Ismail(As), then why should there be any doubt about their genealogies?

هـذا قـول لا نـفـاذله من وجه فما بال المقدسى اشتبه عـليـه الا مـرحتى قال يشبه ان يكون المهدى فان فى هـذا الـمـعـنى حـديثيـن صـحيـحين واقوال العلمـاء لمشاهير بل الثابت انه امير من بنى اسحاق والمهدى انه من بنى اسماعيل فكيف المشابهة حتى يشتبه

There is a tradition reported in "Muslim" that: had you heard about a city which had land on one side and the other side touches ocean? All replied positively. Then the holy Prophet(Slm) asserted that the Day of Judgment would never come unless an army of 70,000 troops from the Bani Ishauq(As) did not fight against the city's inhabitants.

This narration does not speak about Jesus Christ(As) and the Dajjal. Here madinah stands for Qustuntunia only and not the Madinatul Nabi(Slm).

Another tradition reported in "Muslim" refers Holy Prophet(Slm) telling "the Doomsday would never occur until the Romans enter in A'amaq and at that moment an army from

Madinah, consisting the best people of the world, would fight against Romans.

The common point of both these traditions is that the army of Bani Ishauq(As) would fight against the inhabitants of Qustuntunia, by just exclaiming "Allhu Akber" they would get victory over them. During the period the booty was being distributed, suddenly the satan would announce falsely that Dajjal had arrived. Then that army would leave the booty and rush towards their houses. Muquaddissi further said that there would be seven years between the victory over Qustuntunia and emergence of the Anti Christ/dajjal.

"In this connection Abdullah Bin Bussar states that:

"The holy Prophet(Slm) further asserted that in between the Grand Event and Victory over Qustuntunia six years would lapse and in the seventh year Dajjal would emerge. This is mentioned by "Abu Dawood" as well as by "Mishkot".

ان رسول الله صلى الله عليه وسلم قال بين الملحمة و فتح المدينة ست سنين و يخرج الدجال فى السابعة رواه ابو داؤد وقال هذا اصح كذافى المشكوة

Thus the Romans would start preparations for the battle and they would arrive in the village called Aamaq as reoported in the first tradition. To confront them that army would appear about which it was said that at the very first, they would declare the kalema and the city would be subdued to them and they would arrest the Romans. This fact is supported by the Roman's statement that they requested leader of the muslim army to let them go to our people who were arrested by the muslim army. Thus, after the battle, muslims would conquer Qustuntunia for the second time . At that time Satan would announce a false cry that Dajjal had emerged. Thus they would return to their families and when they start going towards Syria, where Dajjal is said that he would appear. At this time they would prepare for the battle and would arrange prayer mats for the prayer and as they start offering prayer, Jesus Christ(As) would appear and lead the prayer. Some issues emerge at this point, which are being clarified hereunder:

First is that there is no doubt that Banu Ishauq(As) would conquer Qustuntunia by declaring Kalema, as prophesied in the aforesaid tradition. The second is that in the first tradition the holy Prophet(Slm) prophesied that those people would be the best of the people of the Earth of that period. This points out that these people and their leader would not come from the progeny of the holy Prophet(Slm), because the Ahl-e-Bait(Rz) had been declared by Allah as the best people for all periods of the Earth. Thus they were not from the Ahl-e-Bait(Rz), but coming from the Bani Ishauq(As).

Third point is that the Romans requested to let them go to those persons who had captured their brethrens. It tells that there had already been a battle between them on account of which the Romans were arrested by the army of Bani Ishauq(As) only. From this tradition it is also stated that the Amir of the Army would offer prayer under the leadership of jesus Christ(As). And that Amir would fight the Romans and capture Romans as had been mentioned by Allamah Muntakhabuddin in his "Makhzanul Dalael." This book was written four hundred years before.

The author had referred in his book the tradition of"Yamlaul Arz" by writing "Ili Zamanina Haza Qareeb Alf sunntha minal Hijratha."

It is strange that the Shaik had stated the sign of emergence of Dajjal should be taken as one of the sign of emergence of Imam Mahdi(As), although this is a fact that all traditions speak about the appearance of Dajjal only when Bani Ishauq(As) conquered Qustuntunia which he dubiously seems to have forgotton.

Further there is no tradition from "Sihah Sittha" which informs that Imam Mahdi(As) and Jesus Christ(As) would appear at one time and at one place. Thus Shaik's assertion that important sign of Imam Mahdi(As) is that he would emerge during the period of Jesus Christ(As), is just unbelievable and unacceptable.

In the beginning there was no concept regarding emergence of both Jesus Christ(As) and Imam Mahdi(As) at one time and at one place. Therefore when Mukhtar announced Mohammed Bin Hanafia as Imam Mahdi(As), no body objected by telling Jesus Christ(As) would not descend, since his descention was a known fact that he would descend only near the Doomsday. In the year 737 H. the traditions regarding Imam Mahdi(As) were incorporated in "Mishcotul Musabeh", still there had been no reference of Jesus Christ(As) or the Dajjal. But a different chapter was introduced for Jesus Christ(As) and Dajjal. At a time when a decline in understanding the traditions resulted in Muslim Ummah, then only a condition was introduced regarding the emergence of Imam Mahdi(SAs) and Jesus Christ(As) at the same time and place, which is utterly wrong.

From the traditions regarding the Doomsday, ten signs had been mentioned and appearance of Jesus Christ(As) was mentioned but there is nothing about Imam Mahdi(AS). Thus it is certain that Mahdi(As) and Eisa(As) would never meet at any place before the Doonmsday.

Ahmed Hunbal(Rz) And Kitabul Malahem:
Jalaluddin Seyuoti had mentioned that:

Imam Ahmed Hunbal (Rz)had asserted that there are three Essays which are not genuine. They are: Malahem, **Maghazi and Tafseer."**

قال احمد ثلاث كتب ليس لها اصول الملاحم والمغازى والتفسير

Thus in such situation whether narratives regarding victory of Qustuntunia would become baseless? Author of "Mishkot" too had written about Qustuntunia in Malahem.

Imam Mahdi was In the middle:
There are many narratives mentioned in other books, but none could match what Razeen has narrated:

:

How would the Ummah be perished when I am in the beginning, Mahdi is in the middle and Eisa is in the end."

كيف تهلك امة انا اولها والمهدى وسطها والمسيح آخـر ولـكـن بيـن ذلك فـيـج اعـوج ليسو امنـى ولا انـــــــــامـــــنهـــــــم رواه زريـــــن

Author of "Mirqat" had commented on this tradition that this tradition may be called as a "Golden Chain". (holy Prophet(Slm) Imam Mahdi(As) and then Jesus Christ (As)) "Thus this tradition is therefore mentioned in the "Sihah Sitta". In this tradition three periods have been discussed: First period belongs to the holy Prophet(slm); Second period belongs to Imamana(As), and the third one belongs to Jesus Christ(As). Shaikh Abdul Haq, Muhaddias-e-Dehalvi had written just " Baina Zalika" and translated as "During the middle period unscrupulous people would be there. Mulla Ali Qari had written"Risalutul Mahdi" in which he had taken a derogatory view point about Mahdavi Faith. When he found out that Imamana's period and Jesus Christ(As) period are different, then he cunningly changed the very meaning of "Middle" by mixing it to the end. His interpretration of Middle is: "Wa Wasatha Al Mutasil Be Akhiraha", as against these the words used by the holy prophet are "Lakun Baina Zalika". These words are indicative of clear difference of time in between the two periods pertaining to the holy Prophet(Slm) and Imamana(As), and the same difference of time is shown between the two periods of Imamana(As) and Jesus Christ(As). Abdul Haq said that in this middle period those people may be taken as living away from the religion. In the same manner in between the two periods of Imamana(As) and Jesus Christ(As) same sort of people would be living about whom the holy Prophet(Slm) said that they are not from me and I am not from them.

(Notre: And in order to guide these misreants Imama Mahdi(As) was commissioned by Allah to cleanse the Ummah. And that was the right time as mentioned in the tradition that"When Allah desired to cleanse the Ummah,He shall commission Imam Mahdi(As) for that purpose.)

According to the Tradition Imam Mahdi's period lies in the middle and not in the last time as Mullah Ali Qari claims. No tradition recorded in "Sihah" mentioning one and the same period for Imam Mahdi(As) and Jesus Christ(As). If by chance any such tradition comes to light that the period is one and the same for both, then it cannot be relied in view of the aforesaid tradition of the holy Prophet(Slm) which clearly denotes that there are three different periods for each entity.

Holy prophet's assertion that "Lakun Baina Zalika" clearly mentions that there is a long period between Prophet's period and Imam Mahdi's period. So also there is a vast difference in between the periods of Imam Mahdi(As) and Jesus Christ(As). The holy Prophet(Slm) also indicated that during these periods such notorious people would be living certainly away from the true religion and about whom the Prophet(Slm) declared that such people are not from me nor I am from them.

To be away from the straight path, it is necessary that the period should be far away from the commissioned personality as there had been a long duration between the periods of Imam

Mahdi(As) and the holy Prophet(slm). In the same manner there should be much difference in between the periods of Imam Mahdi(As) and Jesus Christ(As) to justify that the religion was not on the straight path.

(Naturally Advent of Mahdi(As) becomes essential for cleansing the Ummah from those people about whom the holy Prophet(Slm) had prophesied that such people are not from me, nor I am from them.)

Thus according to the traditions Imam Mahdi(As) shall be in the middle of the Ummah and not at the end of the Ummah along with Jesus Christ(As).

No narration from "Sihah" points out that the period of Imam Mahdi(As) and Jesus Christ(As) is the same and one.

In this connection we rely on Taftazani who wrote in "Sharh-e-Maqasid" that:

"To assert that Eisa(As) would follow Imam Mahdi(As) or Imam Mahdi(As) would follow Eisa(As), it is such a baseless argument which cannot and should not be relied upon."

فـمـا يقال ان عيسىٰ يقتدى بالمهدى اوبالعكس شئى لامستندله فلاينبغى ان يعول عليه.

Palestine and Appearance of Mahdi(As):

Shaikh Ali Muttaqi is of the opinion that Imam Mahdi(As) would meet Jesuas Christ(As) at Babul Lud in Palestine in order to kill Dajjal and he bases his argument that this is an important sign of Mahdi(As) and pretends that it is one of the accepted signs regarding Mahdi(As). We have discussed in length about this while discussing emergence of sufianai. However true traditions also vouchsafe our argument that no true tradition mentions about joining of Imam Mahdi(As) with Jesus Christ(As). In this connection the Shaikh had mentioned many traditions in support of his baseless contention, thus he failed to submit a clear cut tradition which visualizes that both Imam Mahdi(As) and Christ(As) would come together in Palestine. But as against this Jesus Christ(As) would kill Dajjal at the Babul Lud in Palestine had been mentioned and clearly written in "Muslim" that Jesus Christ(As) would descend in Damascus at the Minar-e-Baiza, then search for Dajjal who would be found at Babul Lud in Palestine.

"Thus Eisa(As) would search for Dajjal till he found him at Babul Lud, in Palestine and kill him."

فيطلبه حتى يدر كه يباب لدفيقتله

It is clear that Jesus Christ(As) only would kill Dajjal and surely not along with Imam Mahdi(As). The shaikh had written "Kanzul Ammal" in 957 H. at that time the legend of Mahdi(As) and Eisa(As) meeting togther was not in the air, therefore he did not mention in it. Then he wrote the "Rudd" in 960 H. at that time this legend he deliberately coined to present his dubious argument and purposely inserted this wrong version in the "Rudd". This shows his indifference about the principle of Commentators. In such a condition when he lacks the knowledge and the principles, he should not have indulged himself in core problems of religious issue. In absence of basic fundmdental facts about the art of traditions, how could he claim himself to be a commentator of the traditions"? His effort is just to malign and disrupt the propagation of Mahdavi Faith; for that purpose he cooked up fictitous arguments to mislead people against Imamana(As) and Mahdavis.

The Shaikh had maintained that Imam Mahdi(As) would appear at Babul Lud and also pushes forward his agenda to give clean chit to the so called wrong and baseless narrative to authentic and very famous also. He must know that true narrative is such which has more than two narrators. When his assertion has no support of truthful narrators, then how can it be said as a famous tradition? This all he is doing in jealousy and hatred and to malign Mahdavi Moverment.

Qur'an and Advent of Mahdi(As):

Shaikh Ali accepts that there are more than three hundred traditions and legends existing regarding advent of Mahdi(As). As a matter of fact when the holy Qur'an speaks about the cutting of hand to the grand journey of Mairaj and beliefs and practices for the Deen/religion, how can we agree by saying that an important issue like that of Mahdiat was not available in it? Author of Hadia also insists that Qur'an lacks any mention of Imam Mahdi Alaihis Salaam.

Under their influence Abul Aala Moududi, author/editor of "Tarjumanul Quer'an" while discussing the verse "Afa Mun kana Ala Baiyanati Min Rabihi" states that Mahdavis erroneously believe that this verse proves Mahdiat.

According to Mahdavi beliefs the holy Qur'an testifies that after the holy Prophet(Slm) an interpretor of Qur'an would come as a final guide to the Ummah. For that purpose we argue from that verse, although Moudodi too accepts it but he acknowledges not one but many such persons (as Mahdi) and he contends that:

"Whoever desires the life of the present and its glitter, to them we shall pay the price; their deeds therein without diminution in respect thereof. They are those for whom there is nothing in the Hereafter, except the Fire. Vain are their designs they frame therein and of no effect are the deeds that they do. Can those who accept a clear sign from their Lord and whom a witness far from Himself doth teach, as did the Book of Moosa before it - a guide and a mercy? They believe therein; but those of the Sects that reject it; the Fire will be their promised place. Be not then in doubtful thereon. For it is the Truth from thy Lord; Yet many among men do not believe."(11:16-18)

من كـان يـريـد الـحيـوة الـدنيـا و زينتها نوف اليهم اعـمـالهـم فيهـا وهـم فيهـا لا يبخسون اولئك الذين ليـس لهـم فى الاخـرـة الاالـنار وحبط ماصنعو ا فيها وبـطـل مـاكـانـو ايـعملون افمن كان علىٰ بينة من ربه ويتـلـوه شاهد منه ومن قبله كتب موسىٰ اماما ورحمة اولئك يومـنون به ومن يكفر به من الاحزاب فالنار مـوعـده فـلاتك فى مـرية منـه انـه الحق من ربك ولكن اكثر الناس لايؤمنون

In this passage of the Qur'an, at the first place information of those persons had been given who are desirous of worldly life. Then information is given about persons who are guided by Allah and this is the difference between these two types of people, therefore both cannot be equal. Allah had commanded the holy Prophet(Slm) to be not in doubt, thus it is certain that the person who is guided is not the holy prophet, but Imam Mahdi. Moudodi accepts it along with some commentators that "Afa Mun Kana" does not mention to the holy Prophet(Slm). Therefore he had translated the above verse in a different manner:

Moudodi had accepted the argument of some commentators who agree with the arguments of Mahdavis that "Afa Mun Kana" does not denote to the holy Prophet(Slm), but to Imam Mahdi(As). Therefore he had translated the verse: "Whether those who have prudence from their Lord and to them one witness had come from Allah, and before that, the book of Moosa had become Imam and mercy, those only would believe him."

Moudodi had translated "Afamun Kana" as "whether those people"; that means "Afamun Kana" does not denote to the holy Prophet(Slm),but to others(Plural).

Saheb-e-Biyyana and Qur'an:

Moudodi was the editor of "Turjumanul Qur'an" for years, but he could not understand the Word "Biyyana", which, when ever it had come in Qur'an it denotes to the personality of Nabi only and not to common people. It is against the purpose of Qur'an. Examples are given hereunder:

He said: Oh My people : See ye if (it be that) I have a clear sign from My Lord and that he Hath sent Mercy unto me from His own presence, but that the Mercy hath been obscured from your sight? Shall We compel you to accept it when ye are averse to it.": (11:28)	(۱) قال يقوم ارايتم ان كنت على بينة من ربى وآتانى رحمة من عنده فعميت عليكم انلزمكموها وانتم لها كرهون (هود ركوع ۳)

In this verse Prophet Noah (As) had addressed his Ummah. Here prophet Noah(As) had been described as a Sign.

" He said:Oh My people do you see? If I have a clear Sign from my Lord and He hath sent Mercy unto me from Himself-Who then can help me against Allah, If I were to disobey Him? What then would you add to my (portion)but perdition." (11:63)	(ب) قال يقوم ارء يتم ان كنتم ان كنت على بينة من ربى واتنى منه رحمة فمن ينصر نى من الله ان عصيته فما تزيد ونني غير تخسير

Through this verse prophet Saleh (As) had addressed his Ummah. Here also prophet Saleh(As) had been granted a Sign.

" He said: Oh My people: See that I have a clear Sign from my Lord and He hath given me Sustennace (pure, and) good as from Himself. I wish not in opposition to you to do that which I forbid you to do." '(11:88/part)

قال يقوم ارء يتم ان كنت على بينة من ربى ورزقنى منه رزقا حسنا وما اريد ان اخالفكم الىٰ ماانهٰكم عنه (ج)

In this vesre prophet Shuyab (As) had addressed his people. In it also Prophet Shuyeb(As) had been denoted as a Sign. Thus wherever "Ala Biyyana Min Rabbi" had come it denotes to the prophets only. "Biyyana" is such a sign which Allah awards to His prophets only as a fulfillment of a condition.

Moudodi also had referred these three verses but he had shown dishonesty in interpretation like this:

In the first verse where "Biyyana" had come, he had translated as "Inherent Prudence" which is available in the person before he is commissioned as the prophet. Like that in the second and third also he had mentioned "Nature and inherent prudence". It is astonishing that he says that this "inherent prudence" is also available in the infidels before they accept faith. Thus in view of his such opinion, Nabi and the infidel are equal. He further writes that: If that which is omitted if opened, then the meaning of the verse would be like this: whether those who have prudence and those who do not have prudence should be equal? As per the verdict of Qur'an they are not equal. Only the first one would believe because he had the inherent prudence awarded by Allah through which they come to conclusion that the Creator of this World is Allah and He is alone having no associates with Him.

Thus for Moudodi the inherent prudence is available to both prophets and the infidels and with the help of that prudence both prophets and the infidels bound to accept faith. Thus, accordingly Moudodi wrongly treats prophet and the infidel as equal.

When it is not necessary to accept a Prophet before he is commissioned, then how that inherent prudence could be accepted which is inherited to any prophet before he is commissioned? Then in these circumstances how could prophets Noah, Saleh and Shuyeb could satisfay their peoples that they had Signs as a fulfillment of a condition?

This was for the previous prophets, now we have to see what order Allah had given to the holy Prophet(Slm)?

" Say: For me I (work) on a clear sign from my Lord. But Ye reject Him." (6:57/part)

قل انى على بينة من ربى وكذبتم به.

In this verse the holy Prophet(Slm) had been mentioned to have the Sign. If the same meaning are taken as Moudodi had taken then how could the holy Prophet(Slm) tell his people that he has the Sign as a fulfillment of the condition. Qur'an witnesses that the "Biyyana" is such a clear proof which Allah awards to His prominent persons if any one denies it, he is undoubtedly beomes an infidel. Examples are given below:

1.We have granted clear Signs to Eisa Ibn Mariyam(As). (Al Baqra)

وآتينا عيسىٰ ابن مريم البينات

2. And Moosa(As) brought before you clear Signs.((Al Baqra)

ولقد جاء كم موسىٰ بالبينات

3.Say that many prophets, before me, had brought many clear Signs.((Aal-e-Imran)

قل قد جاء كم رسل من قبلى بالبينات

4.Many prophets from us were sent to Bani Israel with clear Signs.(Al Maeda)

لقد جاء تهم رسلنا بالبينات

5. No doubt: they brought Signs to them.(Al Aaraf)

لقد جاء تهم رسلهم بالبينات

6.Before that Yousuf(As) had brought to you many Signs.(Al Momin)

لقد جاء كم يوسف من قبل بالبينات

7.We had sent our prophets with clear Signs.(Al Hadid)

لقد ارسلنا رسلنا بالبينات

8.Verily, I had come with clear signs to you from your Allah.(Al Aaraf)

قد جئتكم ببينة من ربكم

From these verses it is clear that Allah grants special signs to his prophets to differentiate between common man and the prophets.

The one Who Conceals Faith:

Now we have to discuss about the fault finder who says that the man who had accepted Moosa(As) as prophet and then he concealed his faith, Allah had made that man also a Sign holder and awarded other signs also to Prophet Moosa(As). This certainly is a temptation. The details are given below:

Pharoah wanted to kill Moosa (As); thus Qur'an says:

"Pharaoh told his people :"Hinder me not in putting Moosa(As) to death; let him call his Lord to save him. What I fear is, lest he should change your religion or cause disturbance in the land." (40:27)

وقال فرعون ذرونى اقتل موسىٰ وليدع ربه انى اخاف ان يبدل دينكم اوان يظهر فى الارض الفساد

When Moosa heard it, he answered:

"Moses Said"I have indeed called upon my Lord and your lord (for protection) against the mischief of every arrogant one who believes not in the Day of reckoning for account." (40:28)

وقال موسىٰ انى عذت بربى و بربكم من كل متكبر لايومن بيوم الحساب

In the court of Pharaoh there was a man who had faith on Moosa (As), but he concealed it. He told to Pharaoh, whether you are going to kill such a person who had brought clear Signs?

Qur'an testifies him thus:

" A believing man from among the people of Pharaoh, who concealed his faith, said: Will you slay a man simply because he says : My Lord is Allah? and who has brought you clear Signs from your Lord? And if he is an imposter, he will be called upon for his imposture, But if he is telling the Truth, then some of that with which he threatens, you will surely befall upon you. Certainly Allah guides not any extravagant imposter." (40:29)

وقال رجل مومن من آل فرعون يكتم ايمانه تقتلون رجلا ان يقول ربى الله وقدجاء كم بالبينٰت من ربكم و ان يک کا ذباً فعليه كذبه و ان يک صادقا يصبكم بعض الذى يعدكم

In this verse the man who had concealed his faith is not he who had Signs, but it denotes to Moosa(As) which also testifies by this tradition which is reported by Ibn Omer in "Bukhari":

"Narrated by Ibn Omer that when we were standing along with the holy Prophet(Slm) at the floor of Kabatullah, that suddenly Uqba Ibn Mugheet (Lanatullahu Alaihi) came and he placed his cloth over the neck of the Prophet(Slm) and tried to strangle him, then came Abu Bakr(Rz) and dragged him off from the Prophet(Slm) and told him whether you are going to kill such a person who declares that my Lord is Allah."

در صحيح البخارى از ابن عمرى آرد كه گفت در اثنائى آنكه ايستاده ايم مابارسول خدا درصحن كعبه ناگاه روى آورد عقبه بن ابى المعيط لعنة الله عليه پس پيچيده جامهٔ خود را در گردن مبارك آنحضرت وكشيد وخفه كرد آن را خفا كردن سخت پس آمد ابوبكر وگرفت ورش آن مدهوش راوبفع كرد اور ااز آنحضرت و گفت اتقتلون رجلا ان يقول ربى الله

That man who had concealed his faith told to Pharaoh that he favoured Moosa(As), in the same manner Abu Bakr(Rz) too had told Uqba in favor of holy Prophet(Slm). It also brings to light that as prophet Moosa(As) is appointed by the Almighty, the holy Prophet(Slm) also is appointed by Allah".

Thus the said verse determines Moosa (As) as having the Signs and not that man who concealed his faith. Further it may be said that the man who had concealed his faith was not telling about himself but telling in favour of Moosa (As) by affirming that Moosa(As) had brought clear signs from his Lord.

A. Author of "Muaheb Aliah" had commented on "Qad Ja'akum Bil Biyyanat":

" As a matter of fact he had brought to you clear miracles and vivid arguments."

وحال آنکه آورده است به شما معجزات روشن استدلالات هویدا۔

It is clear that the man who had concealed his faith is not he who had brought clear signs but it was Moosa(As).

B. Tafseer "Jalaleen" tells that one who brings open miracles is the one who had been designated as Allah's Messenger and not the one who had concealed his faith. Thus it denotes to Moosa(As) alone.

C. Author of "Ruhul Mua'ani" had written with reference to "Qad Jaaum Bil Biyyanat" that:

"To prove his truthfulness, Miracles and convincing arguments are the witness."

الشاهدة على صدقه من المعجزات والاستدلالات الکثیرۃ

D. Fakhar-e-Razi commented on this verse that:

" Miracles point out the prove of Nabuwwat."

اشارۃ الی تقریر النبوۃ باظهار المعجزۃ

Imamana(As) is also on Biyyna as Moosa(As):

Apart from this as per assertion of Imamana (As) it is proved that according to the verse whoever brings signs is the one who is commissioned by Allah and who conceals it is not the faithful.

Author of "Shawahedul Vilayet" in chapter 18 narrates that:

"Narrated that at Badhli some scholars came and put some questions to Imamana(As) that we doubt in your Mahdiat, whether it is true or a lie, how can we accept? Imamana(As) recited one verse from the Qur'an that if he is a liar, his lie is upon him, and if he is true, then surely you will get about which he is warning to you."

نقل است که روزے در قصبه بدلی بعض علماء آمدند و چند سوال کردند باز علماء سوال کردند ما را در مهدیت شما شك می آید که راست است یادروغ ما چگونه قبول کنیم حضرت امام اولوالباب درجواب ایشان این آیت از کتاب ملك الوهاب خواندند وان یك کازبا فعلیه کذبه وان یك صادقا یصبکم بعض الذی یعدکم

Tafseer "Bahr-e-Mouwwaj" states about "Faala Kazzabahu":

"If his assertion of Nabuwwat is false, then its burden would be on him."

اواگر در دعوئ رسالت کاذب بود بروے جزائے کذب او باشد۔

By presenting the said verse, Imamana (As) proved that the criterion on which prophet Moosa(As) and the holy Prophet(Slm) were designated as Apostles of the Almighty, on the same critarion, Imamana (As) also had been appointed as Biyanna. In the manner prophet Moosa (As) and the holy Prophet(Slm) had brought signs and miracles, in the same manner, Imamana(As) also had brought clear signs.

Thus Moudodi and other fault finders are at the same level who think that an infidel who had accepted Islam was on biyyana too?. Moudodi does not know that the commissioned person only is on Biyyanna.

The following are some examples of the previous prophets:

"Tell them that I had been prohibited to worship whom you call other than Allah, and my Lord had sent me his clear Signs and I had been ordained to bow my head before my Allah alone."

قل انى نهيت ان اعبدالذين تدعون من دون الله لما جاء نى البينت من ربى وامرت ان اسلم لرب العلمين

Thus it is a clear proof which clarifies that one who is on Biyyanna from Allah, or who had been granted the attribute of "Biyynna" by Allah to any prophet, or to a Nabi or a dignified person like Imamana(As) who were commissioned for the purpose of "Biyan-e-Qur'an" they are on the Mission of "Biyyanna". In this connection Allah informs that:

"They said to Prophet Hud that he had not brought any Sign"

قالو يهود ما جئتنا ببينة

From this it comes to notice that even the infidels knew that except the one who was commissioned by Allah no one can get the attribute of "Biyyanna".

While Moudodi asserts that an infidel too is equipped with Biyynna is utterly wrong. Now read the verse"Afa Mun Kana Ala Biyyanna Min Rabbihi" According to him,its meaning are: whether they who are not commissioned by Allah can assert that they are on Biyyanna? This is the commentary of Moudodi whose boastfully says that his "Tafseerul Qur'an" is "Bil Qur'an". Moudodi has taken " Afa Mun Kana" as plural, while actual meanings are: whether any one who is not commissioned by Allah, can assert that he is on Byyansa? Thus it has come for a single person who is commissioned by Allah. Moudodi's argument is absurd and against the purpose of Qur'an. Since Moudodi had taken "Afa Mun Kana" as a plural and he asserts that after the demise of the holy Prophet(Slm) a group would emerge claiming to have been granted the attribute of "Biyyanna". Thus from his commentary of this verse Moudodi's understanding about the Qur'an becomes fake and dubious.

Description of the Verse" Afa Mun Kana":

Moudodi claims that from "Afa Mun Kana" you cannot claim that the verse is meant for a particular person, according to him the interpretaion is against the usage of Arabic language. He says that:

The word "Mun" does not particularize any person. First of all, to say "Mun" is for a special person, it is against Arabic usage according to him. It comes for a common noun. Secondly it is clear that it comes for a group because the word "Ulaika" denotes to "Mun " and "Ulaika" is for plural(group of people-Qoum-e-Imamana(As) and not for singular because the verb "U Menoon" also is used for plural.

Moudodi's contention that "Mun" comes only for a common noun is wrong, therefore he thinks that it does not serve any purpose for Mahdavis to claim "Mun" for Imamana(As) alone. But as a matter of fact the Qur'an proves that it is used for a particular person alone.

The verse" Afa Mun Yukhluq Kamun La Yukhliq", means " whether the one who creates is like that who does not create?". Here "Mun Yukhluq" is meant for particular entity and not for common entity. That is, except Allah none could create. Therefore "Mun" is used for a particular entity which is singular and not plural. Probably Moudodi might have been misled by the previous verse "Mun Kana Yureedul Hayatud Dunnia" afer that "Ilaihim A'amalahum is used which points out to a group. As against this in "Afa Mun Kana Rabbahu and Yutluhu" had been used which is meant for single person only.

Thus, according to Moudodi if we accept it to be for a group, then after the demise of the holy Prophet(Slm) there would arise a long list of "Saheb-e-Biyyanna" which is wrong. Correct is that one what we had asserterd that "Afa Mun Kana" particularises for a single person. Thus after the holy Prophet's dfemise there would come a single person who shall be on "Biyyanna".

The holy Prophet(slm) had prophesied that after him Mahdi (As) and Eisa(As) shall save the Ummah from annihilition. If they are not on "Biyyanna" how they could save the Ummah?

Now remains the point that whether the word "Mun", denotes to Imam Mahdi(As) or Jesus Christ(As)?With this verse Allah had informed that there would come a "Saheb-e-Biyyanna". Jesus Christ(As) was born even before the "Revelation of the holy Qur'an", therefore how Jesus Christ(AS) would fit for this verse? On the other hand, Imam Mahdi's appearance is a well established fact that Imam Mahdi(As) would emerge as "Biyyna" afterr the demise of the Holy Prtophet(Slm) and before Jesus Christ(As) descends, thus really Imam Mahdi had actually emerged after the demise of the holy Prophet(Slm), therefore this verse fits on the person of Imam Mahdi(As) alone.

Saheb-e-Biyyanna and his Witness:

In this verse the words ""Yatluhu Shaida Minhu" had come. This denotes that behind the "Saheb-e-Biyynna"(As) one witness would follow him.The word "Yatlu" denotes to follow, thus Jesus Christ(As) would follow the "Saheb-e-Biyyanna", about which Imamana(As) had asserterd that:

"Imamana informed,"verily, Jesus Charist(As) would follow me"

فرمودند که عیسیٰ پس ماخواهد آمد (نقلیات میان سید عالم)

"Khatim-e-Sulaimani" also reports that:

"Imamana(As) asserted that behind him jesus Christ would come."

میراں علیه السلام فرمودند عیسیٰ پس ماخواهد آمد (گلشن پنجم چمن چهارم)

Author of "Risala-e-Muhakkamat" states that:

" The period of Eisa(As) is far off; now we understand that Eisa(As) would become witness for both these Khatemain (Rasool and Mahdi)."

زمانہ مہتر عیسیٰ پیش ای شدہ است اکنوں می پندار برائے گواہی دادن بر دو خاتمین می آیند ـ

From another tradition it is stated that one prophet is the witness to another prophet. Ibn Tamima had commented that Jesus Christ (As) becomes witness for the holy Prophet(Slm):

" He, the Nabi Akhiruz Zaman(As) gives witness for me, as I gave witness to him."

وے گواہی میدھد برائے من چنانکہ گواہی میدھم برائے او ـ

Thus Hzt. Eisa(As) shall be the witness for Imam Mahdi(As) also.

If by the word "following" is taken as consonance as mentioned in "Muaherb Aliah":

"Torah, the Scripture of Moosa(As), on one hand certifies the unlettered holy Prophet(Slm) and on the other hand provides good news of being consonant to the holy Qur'an."

کتاب موسیٰ یعنی توریت چہ اونیز در تصدیق بنی امی و بشارت بوجود وتابع است یعنی موافق است مر قرآن را ـ

It is certain that Jesus Christ (As)would not bring any new Shariat, but as per Qur'an he would testfy the Shariat-e-Mustafavi(Slm). Thus as Jesus Christ(As) is a witness, the Qur'an also becomes a witness. Here witness means Qur'an as Bandagi Miyan(Rz) had maintained that:

"Qur'an follows the Biyyanna." 104

يتبع هذه البينة القرآن

Here "Yatabbehu" means following and not for reading as Moudodi and others have maintained. Third is that "Minhu" denotes not to "Mun" but to "Rubb"/ Allah. Therefore the person who had come with convincing arguments, to him Qur'an witnesses. It means to say that when Qur'an endorses what the Bayyana asserts then who can dare to deny Qur'an being the witness?.

Saheb-e- Biyyanna and Torah:

Allah had referred to the Scripture of Prophet Moosa(As). It points out that Moosa's Scripture also becomes the witness for Imam Mahdi(As). Or it may be said that Torah declares a prophesy for Imam Mahdi(As). This fact also had been mentioned in "Kitbul Ahyar" by telling that the reference of Imam Mahdi(As) had been mentioned in the books of the prophets. Thus Imam Mahdi's description also is available in Torah.

These narratives should not be taken as weak, since Allah gave them strength therefore the question of weakness does not arise. The news of "Farqaleet" in Torah refers to none but Imam Mahdi (As), regarding which Jesus Christ had stated that:

" We(prophets) have brought Revelations, but Farquleet (Imam Mahdi(As) would bring interpretation."105

نحن ناتیکم بالتنزیل وما التاویل فسیانی به الفار قلیط
آخر الزمان (سراج الابصار معہ مقدمہ ۳ ۱۰۴)

" Nahnu Natiakum Tanzeel" points out to those prophets who had been bestowed with the Scriptures. This statement of Jesus Christ(As) is just like that of the holy Pophet(Slm) who said that:

"We are from the category of the prophets, neither we are heir to any one, nor any one is our heir."

نحن معاشر الانبیاء لا نرث ولانورث

Thus the holy prophet brought Qur'an and Farqualeet, that is Imam Mahdi(IAs) who would interpret the Qur'an.

"Olaika Yuminoon Bihi":

Moudodi had commented on it that "Bihi" denotes to Qur'an. As a matter fact it refers to "Saheb-e-Biyyanna" and not to Qur'an. Thus "Bihi" denotes to "Mun"which is a part of "Afa Mun Kana" and that is "Saheb-e-Biyyanna".This is according to the style of Qur'an. An example is this:

"Do they think that they are the kings of this heaven and earth and whatever is in it belongs to them? If that is so then let them bring a rope and climb the sky? But they would be put to fight even by a host of confiderate." (38:10, 11)

ام لهم ملک السمٰوت والارض ومابینهما فلیر تقوافی الاسباب جند ما هنا لک مهزوم من الاحزاب (ص ٰغ)

In this verse Allah informs that an army would be defeated, but it is not known at which place? The word "Hunalika", according to the commentators, denotes to battle field of Badr. Mohammed Bin Jariri had written that It was Badr where the army of the infidels had been defeated.

Imam Fakhr-e-Razi had commented that:

"Said Qatawah that "Hunalika" denotes to Ghazva-e-Badr and Allah had revealed it in Makkah that Allah would defeat the army of the infidels. Thus it is a prophecy and shall be interpreted as Badr. Some say Gazva-e-Qandaq but to me it denotes to Fath-e-Makkah."

قال قتاده هنالک اشارة الیٰ یوم بدر فاخبر الله تعالیٰ بمکة انه سیهزم جند المشرکین

It is a fact that after giving the good tidings by Allah, the infidels were defeated first at Badr thus "Huna Laka" denotes to the battle field of Badr. There should be no reason to ignore Badr and then Qandaq and lastly Fath-e-Makkah, when Allah ordains "Wa Laqad Nasrakum Allah ba

Badr wa Antum Aallah."It is clear from this that Allah had granted victory over the infidels when muslim army was less equipped in the Gazwa-e-Badr.

In the above verse the words"Huna Laka" have come and it was revealed at Makkah before the migration and in Aal-e-Imran the reference of Badr had been given.

The verse"Afa Mun Kana Ala Biyyannathi Min Rabbahu" informs that after the holy Prophet(Slm), the "Saheb-e-Biyyanna" would be commissioned. Thus the word"Olaika" denotes to that "Qoum" for which the holy Prophet(Slm) had prophesied. Allah had addressed the companions of the holy Prophet(Slm):

"Oh the believers, if any one from you turns down, then Allah would come along with such Qoum who will have affection to Allah and Allah will love such qoum."

يـا يها الذين ا منو من يرتد منكم عن دينه فسوف ياتى الله بقوم يحبهم و يحبونه

Mohammed Ibn Jareeri had commented for this verse that:

"This was a warning from Allah for those persons whom Allah knew that after the demise of the holy prophet, some of them would become hypocrite."

وكـان هـذا الـوعيـد مـن الـلّه لـمن سبق فى علمه انه سيرتد بعد وفاة نبيه محمد صلى اللّه عليه وسلم .

It points out that after the demise, some tribes would try to convert and become hypocrite.

Author of "Sirajul Absar" had written about this verse that:

"Hasan Basri asserted that Allah knew this fact that some persons, after the demise of the holy Prophet(Slm), would revert to politheism again, thus Allah informed that at such time Allah would come along with those who loved Allah and Allah also would love them. The same thing is reported in Mua'alima-e-Tanzeel."

قـال الـحسـن الـبـصرى علم الله ان قوما يرجعون عن الاسلام بعد موت النبى عليه السلام فاخبر انه سياتى بقوم يحبهم ويحبونه كذافى معالم التنزيل تحت هذه الآية

The holy Prophet(Slm) had prophesied that after him Mahdi (As) and Eisa(As) would save the Ummah from annihilation. Then if they are not commissioned by Allah and had they not been provided with clear signs and miracles how could they save the Ummah? Now the discussion remains to decide as to who among them are mentioned in the verse "Afa Mun Kana"?

Demise of Holy Prophet(Slm) and occurance of "Mun Yurtid":

Miyan Aalim Billah(Rh) had argued that after the demise of the holy Prophet(slm), there was a revolt occurred in which some tribes revolted against the Prophet(Slm). The same opinion Miyan Abdul Ghafoor Sujawandi(Rh) had given:

"Allah had informed his apostle to warn the audience (present Believers) that if some among them reverted against Islam, let them do that. Allah is indifferent about their Faith. Then Allah shall bring a Qoum in future which will be clean from such hypocrites."

اخبر الله تعالىٰ قل للمومنين الحاضرين من يرتد منكم عـن دينه فليرتد والله غنى عن ايمانه فسوف يـاتى الله بقوم يعنى الله ياتى بقوم فى الاستقبال ليس فيهم شعبة الارتداد

The word "Audience" denotes about those who would turn back from the religion of Islam and became hypocrite and who were present at the time of this revelation. And it happened also that except the inhabitants of Makkah, Madinah and Najran, all tribes of the Arabian Peninsula revolted after the demise of the holy Prophet(Slm).

Peculiarity of "Yati Allhu Be Qoumihi":

The prophesy of bringing such a Qoum which will be clear from such hypocrecies, came true at the demise of Imamana(As) there was no such revolt against Imamana(As) as happened after the demise of the holy Prophet(Slm). It may be pointed out that it was a condition that when the faithful became hypocrite, a new Qoum would emerge at a distant future for which there should not arise any objection. Abu Huraira(Rz) had opined in "Bukhari" that:

"When breach of trust occurs then wait for the Day of Judgment."

اذا ضعيت الامانة فانتظر الساعة

In this verse the news of coming of a "Sahebe-Biyyana" (Difinite Evidence) after the holy Prophet(Slm) had been given. And it is a fact that Jesus Christ(As) was commissioned as a prophet(As) even before the holy Qur'an was revealed. Then how could it be said to have been designated as "Afa Mun Kana"? further it is a fact that Imamana(As) had been commissioned as Imam Mahdi(As) before Jesus Christ would descend from the skies in the remote future. Therefore "Afa Mun Kana" is meant for Imam Mahdi(As) alone.

It also came to be known that after the demise of the holy Prophet(Slm), people were waiting for that "Qoum" about which Allah had foretold. Thus niether Ansar, nor Abu Bakr's "Qoum" or Salman Farsi's qoum" could be considered to be that Qoum, as some commentators had stated; because these people were present when that verse was revealed. The word "Soufa" denotes to distant future only.

Qazi Shahabuddin had commented on this verse in his "Bahr-e-Mowwaj" that:

" That verse points out for that Qoum which would appear in future. Since Abu Bakr(Rz), or Ansars or Salman Farsi(Rz), who were present at that time, therefore they cannot be presumed to belong to that Qoum, about whom Allah had informed. Thus this Qoum is a particular Qoum which is distinguished from the words"Fasowfa Yatiallahu Qoum" which denotes for the Qoum of the future."

لیکن آیه مذکور متضمن وعده آوردن قوم مسطور درزمان مستقبل است روایت درود اددرشان ابوبکر و انصار و سلمان رضی الله عنهم که در وقت دردو آیت حاضر بودند مشکل است مگر آنکه مراد از فسوف یاتی الله یقوم آوردن در استقبال بود ـ

Author of "Gharayebul Qur'an" known as "Tafseer-e-Naishapuri" had opined for that verse about the Qoum which belongs to Imam Mahdi(As). Further it is with certainty asserted by stating the words: "La'alul Murad Yakhroojal Mahdi Huwa Zalika" It is hoped that Mahdi (As) would appear.

It is a fact that wherever heavenly Scriptures prophesied that Allah would come, it means that it refers to coming of a commissioned one only which is clear from "Safarus Tasnih"that:

" Parwerdigar came from Sina, and for them brightened from Sayeer and sparkled from Faaraan."115

جاء الرب من سینا واشرق لهم من سعیرو تلاء لأ من جبل فاران

Allah's Coming from Sina means Moosa's arrival from Mountain of Sina. From the mountain of Sayeer brightened means coming of Jesus Christ(As) from Sayeer mountain and to sparkle from Faaraan means coming of the holy Prophet(Slm) from the mountain of Faaraan.

(Note:*Probably from Jabal-e-Noor, three miles from Kaabatullah, known for "Ghar-e-Hira" where the holy Prophet(Slm) used to visit as a secluded place and where the first revelation was brought by Gabreil to the Holy Prophet(slm)in that auspicious night of 27th. Ramazan. And as regards Imamana(As) the Zikri Mahdavis of Balochistan, maintain that Imamana(As) descended from the "Koh-e-Murad" actually situated two miles from Turbat Town in Balochistan. Wallahu Aaalam bis'sawab.)*

In the same manner through "Fasowfa yatiallhu Beqoumihi" it is asserted that Allah would come along with a Qoum, denote that a commissioned personality would appear. Jesus Christ(As) was born even before the revelation of the holy Qur'an, therefore after the demise of the holy Prophet(Slm), who would come? Surely it is the personality of Imam Mahdi(As) and none else.

"Be qoumihi" denotes to the Qoum of Imam Mahdi (As). This is the same Qoum for which the word "Ulaika" had been used as the words "huna Laka" points out the battle of Badr which was prophesied in Makkah.

Even if the objectioner's contention that "Behi" points out to Qur'an is accepted, then after the holy Prophet(Slm) the coming of a Commissioned personality was eminent; because "Ulaika" points out about the "Saheb-e-Biyyanna " and to his Qoum only. Our description fits to the style of the Kalamullah., One example:

> "Ask them to compile ten verses like ours and let them request any one (to help them to compile), if they are true. Thus if these infidels do not do what you ask; then be sure that this Qur'an was revealed to you from your Lord. And that there is no diety other than Allah (to worship). Thus are you faithful?"

قل فاتو بعشر سور مثله مفتريت وادعوا من استطعتم من دون الله ان كنتم صٰدقين فان لم يستجيبو الكم فاعلمو انما انزل بعلم الله وان لا اله الا هو فهل انتم مسلمون

In this verse, the holy Prophet(Slm) was addressed by the word"Qul". After that "lakum" had been used, Since the word "qul" addresses the holy Prophet(Slm). Some commentators agree that the word"Lakum" points out not only to the holy Prophet(As) but also to his companions.

Imam Fakhruddin Razi(Rz had commented on "Fa Inlum Yestajibu":

> "This addresses not only the holy Prophet(Slm) but also the faithfuls which informs that if the infidels failed to comply (to bring verses like that of Qur'an) then be sure that this Qur'an is revealed from the (Divine) knowledge of your Lord."

هذا خطاب الرسول صلى الله عليه وسلم وللمومنين والمراد ان كفارا ان لم يستجيبو الكم فى الاتيان بالمعارضة فاعلموا انما انزل بعلم الله

In the same manner, through the words "Afa Mun Kana ala Biyyanna", "Saheb-e-Biyyanna" had been mentionecd as "singular absent"; then the word "Ulaika" had been used to point out to that "Saheb-e-Biyyanna" about whom the holy Prophet(Slm) had long back prophesied. Thus in that manner Allah's address is for the "Saheb-e-Biyyanna" and his followers only. It means that "Saheb-e-Biyynna" would accept Qur'an that means to certify it as the previous prophets had certified the holy Prophet's character and advised their Qoum not only to accept the faith but also to help assist the holy Prophet(Slm) in his mission of propagation of Islam. Thus in the same manner "Saheb-e-Biyyanna" will accept the faith and his Qoum also will follow and accept.

If it is said that Imam Mahdi(As) had been commissioned for the Muslim Ummah and that Ummah accepts Qur'an as the word of Allah; then by the words "Ulaika Yuminoona Bihi" is it not that the "Qoum-e-Mahdi" had been particularized by Allah? Because they already have faith in Islam and on the holy Qur'an as the word of Allah, then why again they are asked to accept the Faith? For that we donot have answer, but we invite scholars towards Kalamullah which is our order of distinction. Allah ordains that:

"Oh the people who had accepted the faith, again accept Allah and His Rasool and that book which had been revealed on His Rasool(Slm)."

يـا ايها الذين امنوآ امنو بالله ورسوله و الكتاب الذى نزل على رسوله

Whereever the words" Ya Iyyohal Lazeena Aamino" had been used in the Holy Qur'an, it certainly denotes to muslims only and not to the infidels, nor the Sciripture holders and even not to the hypocrites. The words "Munafeqeen and Munafiqat" had been used for Infidels and the Scriptures holders and they were addressed as infidels who are called Ahl-e-Kitab (Scripture holders).

Thus the verse"Ya Iyyuhul Lazeena Aamino" addresses only to muslims and further by telling "Aamino Billah" emphasizes to be perfect on the faith of Islam. In the same manner "Ulaika Yumenoona Bihi" points out about the Qoum of the "Saheb-e-Biyyanna", who would have complete faith on the consistency of the holy Qur'an, pertaining to the period of the Holy Prophet(Slm). This had been witnessed in the dairahs where Biyan-e-Qur'an was the main source of inviting towards Mahdiat.

CHAPTER FIVE
Ranks Of The "Saheb-e-Biyanna"
(Diffinite Evidence)

Shaikh Ali had asserted in his pamphlet,"Al Rudd", that it is not correct to accept Mahdi(As) as innocent. While the author of Hadia had maliciously accused that Mahdavi believe Mahdi (As) is superior to the holy Prophet(Slm). In order to refute these allegations we shall describe the ranks of Imam Mahdi(As) in this chapter.

The holy Prophet(Slm) is the most distinguished among the prophets to which fact many traditions support. The holy Prophet(Slm) himself had asserted to have been designated as Allah's appointee so also prophets Moosa(As) and Eisa(As) also had informed about the holy Prophet(Slm)who would be commissioned as the last of apostles by Allah, and on whom the sacred institution of the Nabuwwat would come to and end there will come no Nabi or prophet.

In the same manner Imamana(As) also was prophesied by the Holy Prophet(Slm) that Mahdi (As) would be the Kahlifatullah under the commands of Allah as reported in many traditions.

It is our belief that the holy Prophet(Slm) is the last of the apostles, and having the SEAl as the last one, and also declare him as the most distinguished Prophet(Slm) among all prophets, likewise, we also accept the ranks of Imamana(As) as "Mahdi-e-Akhiruzaman(As)". According to Imamana's assertion, whatever ranks are granted by Allah for him, no Mahdavi can deny, in the same manner, whatever ranks are asserted for the holy Prophet(Slm), no muslim dare to deny.

Thus Imamana's commands which are based on "Suunah", become mandatory for us and in order to refute the objection of the opponents we would like to clarify those commands with reference to Qur'an and the traditions.

Significance of Holy Prophet(ISlm) and Imam Mahdi(As):

About Holy Prophet:

Holy Prophet(Slm)is the "Saheb-e-Biyyana"/ Diffinite Evidence/ Roshan Daleel. (call him as you interpret the meaning of "Saheb-e-Biyyanna".) Allah orders him:

"Say" I am a clear evidence/ Diffinite Evidence of Allah"	قل انّی علیٰ بینة من ربی
"Verily, you possess excellent character."	انک لعلیٰ خلق عظیم

Such Glad Tiding was not given to any prophet, but to the Holy Prophet(Slm). Holy Prophet's characters are a complete embodiment of the combined characters of all prophets. Author of " Muaheb-e-Ludnia" states that Bibi Aamina(Rz), prophet's mother, heard a Divine Call at the time of the birth of the Prophet(Slm):

"To him (We inherited unto him) Adam's Politeness; Mystic knowledge of Shees; Bravery of Noah; Ibrahim's Investiture; Ismail's Voice; Ishauq's submissiveness; Eloquence of Saleh; Prudence of Loot; Countenance of Yaqoob; Vehemence of Moosa; Patience of Ayyub; Obedience of Younus; Warring spirit of Yushua; Melodiousness of Dawood; Love of Daniyal; Pompousness of Ilyas; Chastity of Yahiya; Abstinance of Eisa; thus dip him in the river of the amalgamation of the characters of all the prophets."	اعطوه خلق آدم ومعرفة شیث و شجاعة نوح وخلة ابراهیم ولسان اسماعیل و رضا اسحق وفصاحة صالح و حکمة لوط و بشریٰ یعقوب و شدة موسیٰ و صبر ایوب وطاعة یونس و جهاد یوشع وصوت داؤد وحب دانیال ووقار الیاس وعصمة یحییٰ وزهد عیسیٰ واغمسوه فی اخلاق النبین .

The above charming and attractive amalgamation of characters of all prophets were embeded unto his nature. Further to this, his Satan had converted as a muslim; thus he got rid of all vices and evil temptations which shaped him into a sublime personality and embodiment of excellent and attractive attributes, who was pronounced by Allah "Rahmtullil Alameen.

According to the tradition "Kaifa Tahluka", while the holy Prophet(Slm) prophesied

Mahdi(As) and Eisa(As) to be the Saviors of the Ummah, and he proclaimed himself to be the first Savior of the Ummah. Thus par with him, Mahdi(As) and Eisa(As) also are the Diffinite Evidence of Allah as the saviours.

Traditions attest Imam Mahdi's caharacters to be that of the holy prophet(Slm)as the Prophet(Slm) himself pronounced: "khulquhui khulqi". The holy Prophet (Slm) further prophesied in respect of Imam Mahdi(As),that "Yashbahu Fil Khukhi". That means Mahadi's characters and resemblance shall be like that of the holy Prophet(Slm).

Thus Imamana(As) is the Khalifatullah having the sublime attributes of the holy Prophet(Slm) and Imamana's Satan too had become muslim, hence Imamana(As) too was rid of all vices and evil temptations and filthy characters.

Faith of the Holy Prophet(Slm) and of Imamana(As):

Faith of both the holy Prophet(Slm) and Imamana(As) was equal in all respects. Still, author of Hadia remarks that the faith of Imamana(As) was lesser than that of Abu Bakr(Rz).

Traditions prove that foundation of the perfect Faith should be on the basis of attractiveness of characters only. Haakim had said in his "Mustadrik" that:

"Narrated Abu Huraira(Rz) who heard the holy Prophet(Slm) telling that Faith of the Momeneen becomes perfect only of those whose characters are sublime."

عن ابى هـريـره قـال رسول الله صلى الله عليه وآله وسـلـم اكـمـل الـمـومـنـيـن ايـمانا احسنهم خلقاهذا حديث صحيح لم يخرج فى الصحيحين .

Abu Dawood and Dari also narrate that:

"Narrated Abu Huraira(FRz) who heard the holy Prophet(Slm) was telling that Faithful Momineen are those who have best characters among all."

عن ابى هـريـره قال رسول الله صلى الله عليه وسلم وآله وسلم اكمل المومنين ايماناً احسنهم خلقا .

It is clear from the above that perfection of Faith requires sublime attributes. "Shawahedul Vilayet" states:

"Thus Imamana(As) pointed out that his Faith is that of the holy Prophet(Slm)."

پـس آنـحـضـرت فـرمـودنـد كـه ايمان ما ايمان محمد مصطفى صلى الله عليه وسلم (باب بست و سوم)

"Hashi-e-Sharief" states that:

"Narrated Imamana(As) that none could reach the faith of Rasool(Slm) and Mahdi(As)."

فرمودند ايمان نبى و مهدى كسے رار وانيست

This is correct since none could have such sublime attributes of Rasool(Slm) and Mahdi(As) and whose Satan had converted to Islam. Thus author of Hadia's objection becomes null and void for the above reasons.

Mahdi's Resemblence to the Holy Prophet(Slm):

Allah states that:

"Nothing resembles Him,(Allah) and He is all Hearing and Seeing"

ليس كمثله شئى وهوالسميع البصير .

"And none is equal to Him."

لم يكن له كفواً احد (الاخلاص)

It tells that there is nothing in whole of the universe which resembles Allah. However traditions speak about the resemblance of each Prophet(As). Jalauddin Seyuoti had commented on "Allahul Lazi Khalqha Sab'a Samawat":

"Narrated Ibn Abbas(Rz) that there are seven Earths and each Earth had prophets like your prophets; Adam(As) like Adam, Noah(As) like Noah, Ibrahim(As) Like Ibrahim and Eisa(As) like Eisa. Told Behaqi that it is correct"

عـن ابـن عبـاس فى قوله ومن الارض مثلهن قال سبع ارضين فى كل ارض نبى كنبيكم وآدم كآدم و نوح كنـوح وابراهيم كـا بـراهيم وعيسىٰ كعيسىٰ قال البيهقى اسناده صـحيح ولكنه شاذ لا بى الضحى عليه متابعا.

(Note: The discussion of Shahbuddin Asqalani and Farangi Mahili regarding Moulvi Abdul Haq and Moulvi Fazl-e-Haq Khairabadi on pages 930 (After Hzt. Abbas(Rz) tradition, 931, 932 and 933 have been omitted from translation, since that discussion is regarding such prophets said to have existence in other Earths, thus these passages have no bearing to the subject matter about Mahdiat or Imamana(As.) We have only translated that portion which discusses about Equality between the prophets on the basis of the tradition reported by Hzt.Abbas(Rz.)

Thus, there should be the resemblance of the holy Prophet(Slm) too. Yes! Imamana(As) had the resemblance to the Holy Propeht(Slm). In this connection Moulvi Hyder Ali Rampuri had stated that it is not necessary that one who is Khatimul Anbiah, only could resemble the holy Prophet(Slm). To clarify his idea he had given examples as under:

" The purpose is regarding the equality in honour, eventhough there may be a difference in position like: Zaid is an administrator of the country and Omer is the commander of an army, Both enjoy same honour before the king. Thus it can be said that both are equal."

مـراد تسـاوى و بـرابـرى در شـرف وعـزت بـاشد گو وجـوده اسبـاب آن در متسـاوين مختلف باشندچنانكه زيدكه مهتمم ملك است وعمر كه مهتمم عسكراست و نزد و بـادشـاه هر دو شرف و عزت برابر ميدار ندپس مى تـوان گفت كه هر دو نزد بادشاه متساوى اند۔

Thus it is possible to have the resemblance of the holy prophet(Slm), not in all respects, but to some respects at least. And except Imam Mahdi(As) who is a "Saheb-e-Biyyanna", as well as "Khatimul Aouliah" and also "Khatim-e-Deen"as prophedsied by holy Prophdet(Slm), none could resemble the holy Prophet(Slm).Particularly when the Satan of Imamana(As) also had converted to Islam like that of the holy Prophet(Slm) and faith of Imamana(As) is also perfect as that of the holy Prophet(Slm). Thus, in all respects, Imamana(As) resembles perfectly to the Holy Prophet(Slm).

Equavalence in Khatmiat:

What Moulvi Hyder Ali Rampuri had stated, the same is mentioned in"Uqudud Durer's chapter two that:

"Asked Ali Ibn Abi Taleb(Rz): Whether Mahdi(As) is from us? The holy Prophet(Slm) informed that Mahdi(As) is from Ahl-e-Bait(Rz) and Allah would complete the Deen on Mahdi(As) as it started from us in the beginning. This has been stated by a group of traditionalists and had been written by Abul Qasim Tabrani, Abu Nayeem Isfehani, Abdul Rahman Ibn Hatim and Abu Abdullah Nayeem Bin Hammad etc,".

عـن اميـر الـمومنين علي بن ابى طالب رضى الله عنه قـال قـلـت يـا رسول الـلّـه صلى الله عليه وسلم امنا الـمـهـدى اومـن غيرنا فقال رسول الله صلى الله عليه وسـلـم بـل مـنـايختم الله به الدين كما فتحه بناوذكر بـاقـى الـحـديث اخرجه جماعة من الحفاظ فى كتبهم مـنـهـم ابـو الـقـاسـم الـطبـرانى وابـونعيم الاصفهانى وعبـدالـرحمـن ابن حاتم وابو عبدالله نعيم بن حماد وغيرهم

Author of "Uqudud Durer" in Chapter 7 states that:

"Narrated Ali(Rz) that the holy Prophet(Slm) informed that Mahdi(As) is from us who would complete the Deen as I had started in the beginning. Reported Behaqi."

عـن علي بن ابى طالب رضى الله عنه قال قال رسول الـلّـه صـلـى الـلّـه عليه وسلم المهدى منا يختم الله به الدين كما فتحه بنا اخرجه الحافظ ابو بكر البيهقى .

Thus all these traditions vouchsafe that Imamana(As) had the rank of "Khatamiat" by claiming himself to be "Khatimul Aouliah" who would complete the purpose of Deen-e-Islam during his life time. Thus he is also the Khatim-e-Deen-e-Islam.

Innocence of Mahdi(As):

Miyan abdul Malik Sujawandi(Rh) has written about the innocence of Imamana(As) that the tradition prove that Mahdi(As) is innocent. Ibn Maja had narrated in the tradition's chapter of Mahdi(As) that:

" From the Traditions, symptoms and narrations, it comes to mind that Mahdi(As) is innocent."

يـفـهـم مـن الاحـاديث والآ ثاروالا قوال انـه معصوم (منهاج التقويم)

Narration of Soban as reported in "Ibn Maja" the last words of the tradition under the chapter Babul Mahdi(As) are:

"Thus offer your allegiance to him, even if you had to crawl the snows, because Mahdi(AZs) is Khalifatullah."

فبا يعوه ولو حبوا على الثلج فانه خليفة اللّه المهدى

Khalifatullah Mahdi (As) is also innocent like the Holy Prophet(Slm). The following tradition states that :

" Narrated by Abu Sayeed who heard holy Prophet(Slm) telling that "Allah did not send any prophet and did not make His Kahlifa, but created in him two internal friends: One initiates in him the command for enjoying virtue and pushes him towards good deeds only.And the other commands him for doing vice and instigates him to commit sins. But Innocent is one who is saved by Allah from all sins. Reported in "Bukhari".

عن ابى سعيد قال قال رسول الله صلى الله عليه وسلم مابعث الله من نبى ولا استخلف من خليفة الا كانت له بطانتان بطانة تامره بالمعروف و تحضه عليه وبطانة تامره بالشر وتحضه عليه والمعصوم من عصمه الله رواه البخارى .

Thus it is clear that Khailfa (As) also is Innocent as the Prophet(Slm) is innocent. Here Khalifa means Khalifatullah and not the worldly Khalifa. Qur'an also calls "Nabi is a Khalifatullah." In Kalamullah also Khalifatullah had been used for a Nabi. Thus Kahlifatullah also is innocent as the prophet:

"Oh Dawood: verily We made you Khalifa on the Earth."

يد اودانا جعلناك خليفة فى الارض

That is why the holy Prophet(Slm) designated Mahdi(As) as the saviour of Ummah like the prophets; as mentioned by Razeen:

"How would the Ummah be perished when I am in its inception, Mahdi(As) is in between and Jesus Chrsit(As) is in the end of it."

كيف تهلك امة انا اولهاوالمهدى وسطها والمسيح آخرها

Miyan Abduil Malik Sujawandi(Rh) had commented on this tradition that:

"The holy Prophet(Slm) had mentioned the name of Mahdi(As) in between two prophets(As) and made Mahdi(As) the saviour of Ummah as he had referred himself and Jesus Christ(As) as the saviours. Thus on account of these two venerable personalities the ummah became safe. Had Mahdi(As) not an innocent how could he become the saviour like that of the holy prophets? Otherwise he too would have been a common person like other persons of the Ummah."

ذكر النبى عليه السلام بين النبيين وجعله سببا لنجاة الامة عن عذاب الاستيصال كماجعل نفسه وعيسىٰ سبب نجاتها فنفى الهلك بوجود هولاء الثلاثة فلولم يكن معصوما لكان فرد امن افرادهافكيف يكون سببالنجاتها.

"Sanan-e-Ibn Maja" reports in its Chapter of Al Mahdi(As) that:

"Allah shall create in a single night
the perfect ability (in Mahdi(As)."

يصلحه الله فى ليلة

Bandagi Miyan Shah Khundmir(Rz) and Miyan Abdul Malik Sujawandi(Rh) have written
That:

"In one night or in a portion of it, this
episode neither could be written nor it
could be stated due to its length, as a
matter of fact the narrator had reported
what Amirul Momineen, Ali
Karamullahu Wajhu(Rz) had stated."

فى ليلة واحدة اى فى بعضها وهذه القصه لاتدخل
تحت الرقم ولا يذكر لطولها ولقد صدق الراوى عن
امير المومنين على كرم الله وجهه.

This tradition tells that Mahdi(As) will get Beneficence from Allah without any medium.
And whoever gets that Beneficence becomes the Saviour of the ummah, and he is certainly an
Innocent one about whom the holy Prophet(Slm) declared : "Khulqahu Khulqi".Had Mahdi(AS)
not been Innocent as the holy Prophet(Slm) how could he attain the characters and the attributes
of the holy Prophet(Slm)? That is why the holy Prophet(Slm) suggested about Mahdi(As) that:

" Allah shall cause to complete the
Deen through Mahdi(As) as he had
started through me."

يختم الله به الدين كما فتحه بنا

When the Deen/ religion begins with an Innocent one(holy Prophet), how could it be
completed by a non Innocent person? Thus this tradition vouchsafe that Mahdi(As) is innocent.
Miyan Abdul Malik Sujawandi(Rh) tells that:

" Thus we found out that Mahdi(As)
is the true follower of the holy Prophet
(Slm), who did not bring any new Shariat
and that Mahdi(As) is Innocent without
commiting any Sin."

فعرفنا انه متبع لامشرع وانه معصوم من الخطا

That is why the holy Prophet(Slm) said that Mahdi(As) is innocent from sins. "La Yukhti"
never would commit any error (sin). Thus Innocent is the one who is Nabi or one who had been
commissioned by Allah, and also the one whose attributes resemble to the Prophets(As).

Hazrat Bandagi Miyan Syed Khundmir(Rz) had stated that:

"After the holy Prophet(Slm) there
would be no Imam, except two persons
only. One is Mahdi(AS) and the other is
Jesus Christ(As). Because leadership fits
to the one who is the saviour of the
Ummah and by following him his
Ummat gets salvation."

والامامة لا يمكن بعد النبى الا ثنين وهما المهدى
وعيسى لان الامامة لا تصح الا من يكون سبب
النجاة لامته وينجى امة باقتدائه

This creates three issues: one : After the holy Prophet(Slm), Leadership is meant for two
persons only: Mahdi(AS) and Jesus Christ(As), second: The leadership of the holy
Prophet(Slm) and Mahdi(As) who are Innocent.; third : By following Mahdi(As), then only

Mahdi's ummat shall get salvation. Thus it proves that Mahdi (As) has his own Ummat and that one who owns Ummat is surely an Innocent one.

Mahdi(As) is an Authority:

Allah ordains:

"Oh the Faithful who had Faith: Submit ye to Allah, be obedient to the holy Prophet(Slm) and to them who have authority among you."

يَاايها الـذيـن أمنوا اطيعوا الله واطيعوا الرسول وَاولى الامرمنكم.

Author of "Maghzanul Dalael" writes that Mahdi(As) is also the person who has authority:

" Because Mahdi(As) had the authority according to the command of Allah, then pay homage to Allah, His Rasool and Mahdi(As)who had authority among you."

لانـه مـن اولى الامر لقوله تعالى اطيعو الله واطيعوا الرسول و اولى الامر منكم

As holy propohet's obedience is obligatory, in the same sense obedience of Mahdi(As) and Eisa(As) is also an obligation. Thus both Mahdi(As) and Eisa(As) are the Authorities because after the holy Prophet(Slm) they are commissioned and appopinted by Allah as an authority, therefore after the holy Prophet(Slm) the obedience of the above two is an obligation.

Now remains the question about "oolil Amar" which is in plural. Then how could it apply to Mahdi(As) and Eisa(As) only? Because, according to traditioins, even on two it applies; because two are in the least sense constritute plural.

" Narrated by Aqba Bin Aamer that holy Prophet(Slm) ordered me to recite "Mouazzatain" after every prayer. Narrated by Abu Dawood(Rz) and Ahmed(Rz), Nisaaie(Rz) and Behaqi(Rz)."

عـن عقبة بـن عـامـر قـال امرني رسول الله صلى الله عـليـه وسـلـم صـلـعم ان اقرأ بالمعوذات فى دبر كل صـلـوة رواه احمد وابو داؤد والنسائى و البيهقى فى الدعوات الكبير

This tradition referes to two Soorahs: 1."Qul Aaozo Birabbil Falaq" and 2. "Qul Aaoozo Be Rabinnas": Here "Mouzzatain" are plural just for two. Therefore if "Oolil Amr" applies to Khulafa-e-Rashedain", then it would be said that when the Khalifa of the holy Prophet(Slm) is a person of authority, then Khalifatullah must have that authority more than that of the Khalifai-e-Rasool(Slm)

Mahdi(As) is Amrullah:

Bandagi Miyan Syed Khundmir(Rz) asserted that:

"Thus believe that Mahdi(AS) is the perfect follower of the holy Prophet(Slm) in inviting towards Allah who is appointed for such invitation, as the holy Prophet(Slm) was commissioned for that invitation. And if asked what is the meaning of being perfect in following? The answer is that Mahdi(As) would follow completely the holy Prophet(Slm) on the commands of shariat as per the Revelations."

فاعلم ان المهدى يكون تابعاله فى الدعوة الى الله وهو المامور بالدعوة كما كان رسول الله صلى الله عليه وسلم مامورا لان المهدى يكون كاملا فى اتباعه فان قيل ماالمعنى كاملا فى اتباعه اى يتبعه فى احكام الشريعة بالوحى

From this narrative, Mahdi(As) will follow the holy Prophet(As) in Shriath as per revelation from Allah.

Bandagi Miyan Syed Khundmir(Rz) had commented on the tradition of "Kaifa Tahlaka" that:

"The holy Prophet(Slm) informed about this tradition that the Ummah would be saved under the leadership of Mahdi(As) and Eisa(As) by following the holy Prophet(Slm) who would invite towards Allah through the Revelation of Allah."

اخبر النبى صلى الله عليه وسلم فى هذا الحديث ان لاتخرج امته من الهلاك الا بواسطة اقتداء هما واتبا عهما لانهما عليهما السلام يد عوان الى الله بالوحى وبالحجة القاطعة

Author of "Insaf Nama" narrates that: Allah has taken the responsibility of "Biyaan-e-Quran" by telling:

" Thus, verily the interpretation (of Qur'an) is our(Allah's) responsibility, (through the mouth of Mahdi(As), who is the interpreter) under the commands of Allah and the revelation."

نيز فرمودند ثم ان علينا بيانه اى بلسان المهدى مبين القرآن باعلام وحى ربانى(باب١٢)

Miyan Abdul Malik Sujawandi(Rh) also tells that:

" Allah revealed the meanings of the holy Qur'an to Mahdi(As) directly without any medium."

اى اوحى الله الى المهدى معنى القرآن بلا واسطة

Thus from this it is clear that Mahdi (As) shall follow Shariath based on Revelations; and that Mahdi's invitation towards Deen-e-Islam shall be according to the Revelations only.

Now remains to discuss about Revelations to Mahdi(As)? What does it Mean? "Hashia-e-Insaf Nama" describes it:

"It is narrated that a man came to Imamana(As). He had a desire in his mind that if Imamana(As) is the true Mahdi(As) he would offer him watermelon.When Imamana(As)saw him, told him that "Allah had not sent me to offer you watermelon. We are obeying Allah's orders and we only do what is asked us to do and I follow what is being revealed to me."

نقل است یك مرد پیش حضرت میران علیه السلام آمده نیت كرده بود اگرمهدئ موعود حق است مارا خربوزه خوراند چون حضرت دیدند فرمودند مارا خدائے تعالیٰ خربوزه خورانید ن نفرستاده است مابامر الله هستیم هرچه امر می شود می کنیم و می گوئیم چراکه ان اتبع الا مایوحیٰ الّی فرمود

This narration tells that Imamana (As) is doing what had been commanded to do: " I obey only which is revealed to me." Thus Imamana(As) explained about Revelation that it is a Command from Allah. And which had been accepted by the scholars also. Thus "Asshatul Lamat" tells that:

"The word Revelation also comes as Command from Allah."

وبه معنی امر نیز آید

That is why the Prophet(Slm) explained about himself that he is "Abd-e-Mamoorah", Narrated by Ibn Abbas (Rz):

"Ibn Abbas(Rz) narrated that the holy Prophet(Slm)was the one who was appointed just for the Service of Allah."

عن ابن عباس قال کان رسول الله صلی الله علیه وسلم عبدا مامورا

Bandagi Miyan Shah Khundmir(Rz) stated that:

" Mahdi(As) was appointed to invite, in the manner the holy Prophet(Slm) was inviting the people".

هو المامور بالدعوة کما کان رسول الله مامورا.

From the tradition of "Kaifa Tahlaka" it comes to light that Imamana(As) is the saviour of Ummah and this fact must be known that without the command of Allah no one could become the Saviour of the Ummah, if that would have not been the purpose, then the holy Prophet(Slm) would not have told that Mahdi(As) is the Saviour as he and Eisa(As)are the saviours. And it is clear that without any conmmand of Allah, as the Prophet(Slm), none could become saviour of the Ummah. Had that not been the case, then why should the holy Prophet(Slm) included Mahdi's name in between two prophets?

Author of "Madarijul Nabuwwat" had mentioned about Revelations that they are of eight kinds:

1.In the dreams 2.Inspiration on the heart of the holy prophets. 3.Gabriel's appearance in human face. 4. Ringing of bell. 5. Gabriel's coming in his original comlexion. 6.Supernatural Happening like splitting of Moon etc.; 7. Allah's addressing without any medium. 8. Directly speaking without a veil.

Author of "Madarijul Nabuwwat" had mentioned about seventh type like this:

" Speaking by Allah , Jallay Subhanahu, without any medium"

كـلام كـردن حضـرت رب الـعـزت جـل جلالهٔ بے وساطت ملك

It is said that without any medium Allah had spoken with the holy prophet for seven times as mentioned in "Asahtul Lam'at" that:

"Sometimes Allah used to speak with the holy Prophet(Slm) without the medium of Gabriel(As), like Allah spoke to Moosa(As), thus it happened for seven times (in the case of the holy Prophet(Slm)."

گـاهـے كـلام كـرد، بـاوے پـرورد گـار بيواسطهٔ جبرئيل چنانكه به موسیٰ كرد، اى هفت مرتبه شد۔

However, from the books like "Baa'zul Ayaat", "Inasaf Nama", "Sharh-e--Insaf Nama", "Risalai-e-Hashda Ayaat", this fact came to knowledge that Imamana(As) used to get revelations directly. Here the word Revelation stands for Commands of Allah which had been described by Imamana (As). The holy Prophet(Slm) also used to get revelations without any medium from Allah.

1.Author of "Ajooba Aswala" had written that:

" Finally, after some years Imamana(As) announced his Mahdiat and told that I am not telling either from revelation, or dream or inspiration, but I am telling as commanded by Allah personally to me directly."

الـغـرض بعداز چند سال آن ذات مبارك دعوىٔ مهديت كـرده فـرمـود كـه ايـں سـخـن بالهام ورديادو اقعه نمی گويم بلكه بامر حق تعالیٰ می گويم ۔

2.It is mentioned in "Shawahedul Vilayet" that:

"Narrated that Imamana(As) had said that it is not a revelation, or dream or a happening but telling as per the command of Allah."

نـقـل اسـت كه حضرت ميران عليه السلام فرمودند كه ايـں سخن بالهام ورو يادواقعه نمی گويم بامر حق تعالیٰ می گويم ۔

The same narration has been recorded in Shah Burhan's "Dafter" also. Thus Imamana (As) used to get commands directly from Allah, as the holy Prophet(Slm) used to get directly from Allah without the medium of Gabriel(AS).

Author of Hadia had maliciously remaked that Imamana(As) used to get revelations in different languages like, Arabic,Hindi, Gujrati etc. Before this it had been proved that Imamana (AS) had described Revelation as "Command of Allah" and whatever commands Allah gave to Imamana(As), he used to interpret according to the languages of the audiences of different places.

Biagrophies of Imamana (As) prove that Imamana(As) had spoken languages of those places wherever he had gone, like Eastern India, Deccan, Arabian countries, Gujrat, Sindh, Qhandhar, Khurasan Etc. Imamana(As) used those different languages for propagation of his Mission. In this regard "Shawahedul Vilayet" states that:

> "Where ever he went, to which part of the country and city, miraculously he gave sermons on the holy Qur'an in the language of that place.(Was it not a miracle?)

در شهرے کہ رفتی ودرهر ولایت کہ قدم سعادت فرمودی بزبان آن ولایت بیان قرآن کردے۔

Author of Hadia had copied a portion of Imamana's speech mentioning it as Revelation in Hindustani language. " DAWAI-E-MAHDAVIATH KAHLATA HOWAY THO KAHLA, NAHIEN THO ZALIMAN MEIN KA KAROONGA" It points out that whatever Allah had commanded Imamana(As), he had expressed in Hindustani language as a gist only. Author of "Shawahed-e-Vilayet" had not mentioned the words as Revelation, but the sense was explained in Hindustani language :

> "Natrrated that Imamana(As) told in Hindustani language that : ALLAH KA FARMAN HOTHA HAI KE Oh. SYED MOHAMMED DAWAI-E-MAHDIAT KAHLATHA HOWAY THO KAHLA NAHIEN THO ZALIMAN MEIN KA KAROONGA".

نقل است کہ بزبان هندوستانی فرمودند کہ فرمان حق تعالیٰ میشود کہ اے سید محمد دعوئ مهدیت کا کهلاتا هوی تو کهلا نهیں تو ظالمان میں کاکرون گا(بات)

It came to light that whatever Allah ordained Imamana (As), he had spoken the sense of that command in the Hindustani language of that period and place. Author of "Shaweahedul Vilayet" did not tell those words as exact words of the Revelation. But as far as the meanings and the sense are concerned they were spoken clearly. Therefore no filthy remark could be made. For example just see how Allah addressed the holy Prophet(Slm):

> "And do not be of those who deny Allah's signs.Otherwise you would be among the loosers/Khasereen."

ولا تکونن من الذین کذبو بایٰت اللہ فتکون من الخٰسرین .

From the point of view the above said Hindustani passage (of Imamana(AS), it cannot be said to be un-eloquent, because that Hindustani language pertains to five hundred years back. We cannot compare it with the present Urdu language and cannot decide its standard. Because at that period this type of language was colloquel and easily understandable. However Imamana (As) usually used to speak mostly in Persian language only. for example prophet Ibrahim(As) addressed the infidels by expressing his opinion about the idols:

> " Thus it is certain that those idols are my enemy, when Allah alone is my friend."

فانهم عدولّی الارب العالمین

How could the idols become enemy or friend (to Ibrahim (As) , but according to the beliefs of infidels idols are capable for enmity or friendship, therefore to convince the infidels Prophet IbrhimI(As) used their accepted facts that the idols are his enemy. Here does the objectioner feel that prophet Ibrahim(As) had accepted the ability of the idols to become his enemy?

It is said that some Hindi words are included in Kalamullah stated by Mir Ghulam Azad:

" Some Hindi words are part and parcel of the holy Qur'an as well." 161

بعضے الـفـاظ هـندى جزو فرقان عظيم است وجواهر
سلك كلام قديم (سرد آزاد مطبوعه)

Jalaluddin Seyuoti had commented on Allah's assertion about "Tuba" which is a Hindi word for paradise.

When Hindi words are used in Kalamullah and that had not been objected, then if Imamana's deliberations in Hindi language why should it be objected?

Bukhari's chapter "Mun Takkallam-e-bil Farsia"relates to the holy Prophet(Slm) who had spoken in Persian language:

"Narrated by Abu Huraira(Rz) that Hasan bin Ali(Rz) took a date and kept in his mouth. After seeing this the holy prophet reprimanded Hasan in Persian language by telling" Kukh, Kukh, do not you know we do not eat any thing of charity."

عـن ابـى هـريـره رضـى الـلـه عنه ان الحسين بن على
اخـذتمرة من تمر الصدقة فجعلها فى فيه فقال له النبى
صـلـى الله عليه وسلم بالفارسية كخ كخ اما تعرف ان
لا ناكل الصدقة

When the holy Prophet spoke in Persian, which is not contrary to Nabuwwat, then why Imamana's delibrations in the colloquel Hindi language of that period should become objectionable?

It is proved that Gabriel(As) was with Imamana(As). The details are given hereunder:

Narrated in "Tirmizi" that:

"Narrated by Abi Sayeed Al Khadri who heard holy Prophet(Slm) telling that every Prophet had been provided by two ministers from the skies and two from the Earth. My two ministers from the sky are Gabriel(As) and Mechael(As), and two from the Earth, They are Abu Bakr(Rz) and Omer(Rz),"

عـن ابـى سعيد الخدرى قال قال رسول الله مامن نبى
الاولـه وزيران مـن اهل السـمـاء ووزيران من اهل
الارض فـامـا وزيـرى مـن اهل السـمـاء فجبـرئيل
وميكـائيـل وامـا وزير اى من اهل الارض فابوبكر و
عمر

From "Tirmizi" it came to light that every prophet is provided with Gabriel(As) and Mechael(As) and two companions fom the Earth. Through the Tradition"Kaifa Tahlaka" the holy Prophet(Slm) had placed Imamana(As) in between two prophets which brings Imamana(As) one among the commissioned personalities. If that is so, then as had been said by the holy Prophet(Slm) that every prophet had been provided by those referred Angels, then it may be presumed that Imamana(As) also must have Gabriel(AS) and Mechael(As)along with him. "Sirajul Absar" states that:

"Through some traditions it had been proved that Gabriel(ASs) would be in front of Imamana(As) and Mechael(As) would be in the back of him."

المهدی الـذی وقـع فـی حقـه فـی بعض الاحادیث وجبرئیل مقدمته ومیکائیل ساقته

The same narration had been stated by "Uqudud Durer" and had been mentioned in "Shawahedul Vilayet" in chapter 31. Imamana(As) also had certified about this tradition. Bandagi Shah Burhan(Rh) had mentioned what author of "Taswieth-e-Khatimain" had written that:

"Hazrat Miran(As) asserted that Gabriel(As) is here, but I do not claim to have Gabriel(As,) (helping me.) "

حضرت میران فرموده اند.........این جا هم جبرئیل است اما دعوئی جبرئیل نیست ـ

Author of "Sirajul Absar" had stated that:

"Gabriel(As) is on the right side of Imamana(As) and Mechaeil(As) is on the left side."

وعن یمینه جبرئیل وعن شماله میکائیل علیهما السلام

Shaikh Ali Muttaqi had also mentioned in "Risalai-e-Al Burhan" the same narrative.

According to the tradition both Gabriel(As) and Mechaeil(As) used to be along with Imamana(As). Bandagi Shah Burhan(Rh) had mentioned in "Risalai-e-Hall-e- Mushkilat" that:

"In the manner Gabriel and Mechaeil were with the holy Prophet(Slm), but no body saw them; in the same manner both Gabriel and Mechaeil were with Imamana (As), they were not seen by any person.."

چنانچه نزول حضرت جبرئیل ومیکائیل بر رسول بود کسی اوشان راندید همچنان حق سبحانه تعالیٰ در زمانه حضرت مهدی موعود ظاهر گردانید ـ

According to "Tirmizi" every prophet had been provided by two companions. Since Imamana(As) comes from the category of the commissioned ones, Imamana(As) had given Good Tidings about Bandagi Miyan Syed Mahmood(Rz) and Bandage Miyan Syed Khundmir(Rz) to be his two closest companions. Shah Burhan (Rh) stated that:

"Imamana(As) asserted that as Gabriel(As) and Mechaeil(As) are particular among the Angels, brothers Syed Mahmood(Rz) and Syed Khundmir(Rz) are partuicular among my companions."

نیز فرموده است چنانچه درمیان فرشتگان جبرئیل و میکائیل علیها السلام تخصیص هستند همچنان درجمله یاران بنده برادرم سید محمود برادر م سید خوندمیر مخصوص اند ـ

Narrative Regrding Gabriel(As):

The objectioner states that prophet's interinsic strength is Gabriel as Shaik Muhibb-e-illah Allahabadi had mentioned. In that sense, Imamana's assertion that "here is Gabriel(As)": means what intrinsic strength every prophet had with him, the same strength is with Imamana(As) as well, but Imamana(As) did not bring any new Sharaith through Gabreil(As),therefore he did not take any guidance or help.

Imamana(As) had also asserted that he is from the category of the commissioned ones. "Moulood" of Miyan Abdul Rahman(Rh) states in this regard that:

<table>
<tr>
<td>"Narrated by Imamana(As) that we are from the category of the commissioned ones and therefore neither we are inherited nor any body inherits us."</td>
<td dir="rtl">حضرت قرار گرفته فرمودند نحن معاشر الانبیاء لانرث ولانورث</td>
</tr>
</table>

Thus from the above tradition and Imamana's assertion it is proved that Gabriel (As) was always with Imamana(As).

Shariat of Rasool(Slm) and Mahdi(As):

Reported in chapter 12 of "Insaf Nama" that:

<table>
<tr>
<td>"Narrated by Bandagi Miyan Syed Khundmir(Rz) and other companions that Imamana(As) was the perfect follower(Tabay-e-Ta'aam) of the holy Prophet(Slm) in Shariat and "Matboo" in literary sense also."</td>
<td dir="rtl">نقل است از بندگی میان سید خوندمیرواکثر مهاجران شنیدیم که میران تابع محمد رسول الله است در شریعت ومتبوع در معنی ـ</td>
</tr>
</table>

Loyal follower is one who as an appointee of Allah perfectly follows the Shariat-e-Mustafavi(Slm). Thus Bandagi Miyan Syed khundmir(Rz) said that:

<table>
<tr>
<td>"If a question arises: what is meant by loyally following the holy Prophet(Slm), the answer is that Imamana(As) followed the holy Prophet(Slm) on Sharaii Dictates as dirercted by Allah."</td>
<td dir="rtl">فان قیل ماالمعنی کاملا فی اتباعه ای یتبعه فی احکام الشریعة بالوحی.</td>
</tr>
</table>

Imamana(As) loyally followed the Shariat-e-Mustafavi(Slm) since the holy Prophet(Slm) had followed the Shariat-e-Ibrahimi. Allah states that:

<table>
<tr>
<td>"Then We sent you Revelation to follow the Deen/religion of prophet Ibrahim(As) which is clean from evils."</td>
<td dir="rtl">ثم او حینا الیک ان اتبع ملة ابراهیم حنیفا.</td>
</tr>
</table>

Author of "Muaheb-e-Alaih" had stated on this verse that:

" Saheb-e-Tyassir stated that gthe swortd "following" means to follow the path of the mentor. Thus the holy Prophet(Slm) followed prophet Ibrahim(As), not because he was inferior to Ibrahim(As), but because he was born after Prophet Ibrahim(As)."

صـاحب تيسير آورده كه اتبـاع سلوك سبيل متبوع است پـس اتبـاع آنـحضرت مرا ابراهيم رابه سبب آں بود كه بعد ازاد مبعوث شده اند نه بجهت آنكه دوں اوبوده۔

Thus following as an appointee of Allah does not lower the prestige of the follower. Allah had ordained to the holy Prophet(Slm) to follow not only the religion of Prophet Ibrahim(As), but also religions of all prophets:

"These are such persons who had been guided by Allah; thus follow their guidance."

اولٰٓئک الذى هدى الله فبهداهم اقتده

"Allah had directed you towards that religion for which Noah(As) was ordained to follow and to you also. We have sent you Revelations and about which We have ordered to Ibrahim(As), Moosa(As) and Eisa(As) to establish peace and tranquility and not to create discord among them."

شـرع لـكم مـن الـدين ماوصى به نوحاوالذى اوحينا اليک ومـا وصينـا بـه ابـراهيم و موسىٰ و عيسىٰ اں اقيموالدين ولا تتفرقوا فيه

Therefore the holy Prophet(Slm) asserted that:

"All prophets are step-brothers whose mothers (Shriath) are different but their religion is one and the same."

الانبياء اخوة من علات وامهاتم شتى ودينهم واحد۔

Shah Valiullah had commented on it that although religion which was propagated by all prophets was one , but their Shariat/ Divine Law/ Jurisprudence is different. Thus the religion or Deen is one for all , but the way of life to be followed is naturally must be different according to the time, place, region and countries which have different culture and civilizations.

While the holy Prophet(Slm) was directed to follow the religion of prophet Ibrahim (As), Allah had also ordained to prophet Ibrahim(As) to adopt the religion of prophet Noah (As).

Although Prophet Ibrahim(As) was ordered to follow prophet Noah (As), but the holy Prophet(Slm) had stated about prophet Ibrahim (As) to be the Best among the Creations of Allah, thus even though Prophet Ibrahim(As) is the follower of prophet Noah (As), but his rank is superior to prophet Noah (As).To say that the follower could not become equal to his mentor, is a creation of the Non Arab conceptions, because neither in the Holy Qur'an nor in the traditions such conception is existing. Thus if we accept this conception, then by following Noah(As), prophet Ibrahim(As) and by following Ibrahim(As), the holy Prophet(Slm) became inferior respectively. If such criterion is adopted then the holy Prophet(Slm) becomes inferior to even prophet Noah(As).We have to ask the, fault finder what is his opinion about the above said belief?

However the religion brought by the holy Prophet(Slm) was the same what other prophets had brought.The holy Prophet(Slm) had abrogated the Shariats and not the Religion of other prophets. Religion is the same, but the holy Prophet(Slm) had only abrogated the Shariat of those prophets on whom, the Scruiptures were awarded. The same is our belief.

In this respect Miyan Abdul Malik Sujawandi(Rh) had commented that the old Shariats were abrogated. Thus Imamana's following the Sharait of the holy Prophet(Slm) is an accepted fact. If the objectioner contends that on account of the following, Imamana's rank is lesser than the holy Prophet(Slm); then he must accept that on account of the following by the holy Prophet(Slm) to the Shariat-e-Ibrahimi, the rank of the holy prophet(Slm) became lesser to Prophet Ibrahim? It is just Unimaginable!!

Miyan Abdul Malik Sujawandi(Rh) had commented on "Ad'uo Ilalulah...wa Munat Tab'eni" that:

"Thus Allah commanded "Anaa wa Munith tab'aini"(I, and my follower) that I call upon towards Allah's prudence and my follower also would invite towards prudence of Allah. Thus the invitation of both the mentor and the follower are equal in merits and there should be no difference in their Calls. Allah's command is absolute regarding "Manith Tab'aini",without any restrictions or conditions. Therefore the command is for that person who is perfect in the following of the holy Prophet(Slm) and since the word "Mun" points out to Imamana(As), we have to assume that this verse is meant to Imamana(As) only who is the follower of the holy Prophet(Slm) in all respects of the Shriat and religious performances."

فالقرينة فى تخصيص من فى قوله تعالىٰ انا ومن اتبعنى عطفه على المستكن فى ادعوا والمعنى ادعو الى الله علٰى بصيرـة انا ويدعو ايضا من اتبعنى الٰى الله على بصيرـة فهـذا العطف يقتضى ان يكون الدعوة على التابـع والـمتبـوع بمرـتبة واحدة والالزم التفرقة بين الدعـوتيـن والـمناسبة فى عطف الجملة مرعى من محسنـات الـوصـل ..... قـولـه تعاله تعالٰى من اتبعنى مـطـلـق فينصرف الى الفرد الكامل فى الاتباع والفرد الكـامـل فيـه هو المهدى (سراج الابصار معه مقدمه ٨٢و٨٣)

It must be pointed out that the status of the invitation given by the holy Prophet(Slm) and Imamana(As) is the same and merits equally.Thus Miyan Abdul Ghafoor Sujawandi(Rh) had written in "Hashda Aayat" that Mahdi (As) is the perfect follower of the holy Propbhet(Slm). Bandagi Miyan Syed Khundmir(Rz) had pointed out about Imamana(As) in "Maktoob-e-Multani" that "Taba-e-Ta'aam-e-Khatmur Rusl", he is the perfect follower of the holy Prophet(Slm). Thus it is proved that what status the Call of the holy Prophet(Slm)had been given to adopt the Shariath-e-Mustafavi(Slm), the same status has the Call of Imamana(As), particularly because Imamana (As) is Innocent par with the holy Prophet(Slm).

In these circumstances to suggest Reality is against Shraiat, is nothing but to bring some one near infidelity.

It also may be pointed out that to say Reality is not Shariat makes any one near to infidelity. In this connection Ibn Jozi had reported what Imam Ghizali had stated:

Shariat and Reality

Imamana(As) has emphatically asserted that Shariat is verily the Reality. Shah Burhan(Rh) had stated that "Many a time, Imamana(As) had stated that our Shariat is a Reality. If any person says that Reality is not Shariat, then he becomes infidel. That is what Imam Ghizali(Rz) had asserted:

"Imam Abu Hamidul Ghizali((Rz) had written in some books of "Ahyia" asserting that whoever says that Reality is against Shariat or concealed and invisible, then he is near infidelity."	قد بين الامام ابو حامد الغزالى فى بعض كتب الاحيا فقال من قال ان الحقيقة تخالف الشريعة او الباطن يخالف الظاهر فهو الى الكفر اقرب منه الى الايمان،

The following verse suggests that whoever is the perfect follower (like Imamana(As) being the perfect of the holy Prophet(Slm) who had been commissioned by Almighty and had the authority to invite towards prudence of the Almighty. That authority is one of the attributes of the holy Prophet(Slm)also. Therefore Allah ordains that:

"Verily We sent you as witness to express Glad Tidings and to invite towards Allah under our orders." \	انا ارسلناك شاهدا ومبشرا ونذيرا وداعيًا الى الله باذنه

Both Rasool(Slm) and Mahdi(As) Followed same Shariat:

Allah asserts" We have established you on Shariat, to call towards religion, thus adhere to it"	ثم جعلناك على شريعة من الامر فاتبعها

According to this verse the holy Prophet(Slm) is bound to adhere to the Shariat for which he had been commissioned, but as far as Deen is concerned he is the follower of the previous prophets.

Since we cannot deduce that the holy Prophet(Slm) becomes lower in status by following the religion of the previous Prophets; in the same manner, since Imamana(As) is the perfect follower of the holy Prophet(Slm), he also cannot be said to become lower in rank comparing to the holy Prophet(Slm), still, there is no doubt that he is the perfect follower.

Author of Hadia had himself accepted as to what the holy Prophet(Slm) had spoken about Imamana(As):

"Mahdi(As) would follow my foot prints and never commit faults."	يقفو اثرى ولا يخطى

Therefore Imamana(As) had asserted that we are following the Shariat-e-Mustafavi(Slm) and we perfectly adhere to the dictates of the Shariat under the command of Allah. We have already discussed this issue under the caption"Mahdi and Commands of Allah".

Imamana(As) further stated that he had not brought any new Shariat. Thus it is proved that Mahdi(As) was the true follower of the holy Prophet(Slm) and he did not introduce any new Shariat. On that account if the rank of Mahdi(As) is degraded for not bringing a new Shariat, it is just a falsification of the facts based on total ignorance. It, on the other hand, tentamount to behave impudently against both the holy Prophet(Slm) and Imamana(As), particularly when Imamana(As) is following the holy Prophet(Slm) on the commands of Allah; as the holy Prophet(Slm) was following the previous prophets on the commands of Allah.

(Note: Here the fact is that the Holy prophet(Slm) had also did not bring any new religion, but it is the same what had been bestowed by Allah the Almighty to all the prophets, from Prophet Adam(As) to the Last of the prophets(Slm). But the difference between all prophets(As) and the Holy Prophet(Slm) is that he is the Khatimun Nabi who had two faculties:

1. Shariat-e-Mohammedi(Slm) and 2.Vilayet-e-Mustafavi(Slm).

We have never heard about Vilayet-e-Eisawi, or Moosavi, or even Ibrahimi. The faculty of Vilayet is the domain of the Holy Prophet(Slm) only. If he is the Khatimun Nabi, then there should be some one to be named as "Khatim-e-Vilayet-e-Mustafavi(Slm).Thus logically, Imamana(AS) being the perfect follower of the Holy Prophet(Slm), arguably he is the Khatimul Vilayet-e-Mustafavi(Slm), who was designated to complete the Mission of Deen-e-Ibrahimi, or Deen-e-Mustafavi, or even call it Deen-e-Almighty by followiong the Shariat-e-Mustafavi(Slm).

Miyan Abdul Malik Sujawandi(Rh) had answered the seventh Question in his "Minhajut Taqweem" that:

"Mahdi(As) is the follower of Shariat and not the abrogator." 183

المهدى تابع الشريعة لا ناسخها (منهاج التقويم)

On that basis Miyan Abdul Rahman(Rh) had asserted in his "Moulood" that Mahdi(As) is the perfect follower of the holy Prophet(Slm):

"His title "Mahdi-e-Maood" makes him equal, having equal rank comparing to the holy prophet, because he was the perfect follower known as "Taba-e-taam", still he was also commissioned, as others, to invite the humanity towards"Deen-e-Haq T'allah"

خطابش مهدی موعود وهمسر وهم مرتبۀ محمد محمود زیر اچه اوتابع تام است و بعثت اوبر خاص و عام است (۱۳)

It boils down to say that one appointee of Allah if he follows another Appointee of Allah, as per commands of Allah, it does not belittle him as against his Mentor.

Author of "Insaf Nama" had maintained that "Imamana (As) is the follower of Shariat of the holy Prophet(Slm), here the following means that Imamana (As) as an appointee of Allah and as a Khailfatullah perfectly followed the holy Prophet(Slm) as the holy Prophet(Slm) was following the Deen-e-Ibrahimi.

Imamana(As) had addressed Mullah Sadruddin by saying:

" There is no difference between you and me as ragards the following of the Shariat, but as per command of my Lord I am "Mahdi-e-Maood(As)."

درمیان ماهو شما باتباع شریعت هیچ فرقی نیست ......مگر مرا فرمان حق تعالی شودکه تومهدی موعود هستی (شواهد الولایت باب ۲۰)

What Imamana(As) told to Mullah Sadruddin is that: "he and Sadruddin had no difference as regards following the Holy Prophet's Sharait." This is perfectly according to the style of the Qur'an, since Allah addresses the holy Prophet(Slm) that:

" Say: I am likle you a man, but Revelations come to me (from my Lord)."

قل انما انا بشر مثلکم یوحی الّی (الکهف ۲ ا ع)

This verse clearly tells that there is no difference between a man and a prophet since they are human beings, except the prophet(As) receives Revelations from Allah, which makes a difference. What Imamana(ASs) told was also correct to Mulla Sadruddin that he and Imamana(As) were equal in following the Shariath of the holy Prophet(Slm), but as per commands of the Almighty Imamana(AS) is "Mahdi-e-Maood(As)."

As regards the following, "Shawahedul Vilayet" states that:

"Imamana(As) had many a time asserted that I am toeing the holy prophet's footprints and as regards following, Allah causes me to do and I have no choice but to comply as per His orders."

حضرت مهدى كرات ومرات فرمودند كه بنده قدم به قدم رسول الـله هستيم ونيز فرمودند انچه اتباع رسول الـله است حق تـعالیٰ بے اختيار بنده از دست بنده مى كناند (باب ٣١)

However, as regards the "Following", Imamana(As) follows as per the dictates of Allah. He did not bring a new Shariat, as the holy Prophet(Slm) did not bring a new religion. Imamana(As) had followed the Shariat-e-Mustafavi(Slm) as the holy Prophet(Slm) had adopted the Religion of the previous prophets including Deen-e-Hanifi/ Ibrahimi. As prophet Ibrahim(As) adopted the Deen of prophet Noah (As). Abdul Haq Muhaddis-e-Dehlavi had commented on it by saying that:

"Here accepting one's leadership means conformity and consonance. Since those prophets came earlier to the holy Prophet(Slm), therefore acceptance of leadership was implied and in the same way the holy Prophet(Slm) was asked to follow Deen-e-Ibrahimi"

مـرادبـاقتـدا اينـجـامـو افقت است و چوں انبياء پيش از آنـحـضرت بودند اطلاق كرده شد لفظ اقتدا هم چنين است سـخن درامـر كردن آنحضرت ابتاع ملت ابراهيم ـ

Therefore following or accepting leadership of a Disignated person who had been appointed by Allah is called consonance and conformity. Thus unless there is conformity there would be no following. That is why the holy Prophet(Slm) was asked to follow the prophets who came before him. Thus by following the Deen-e-Ibrahimi, the holy Prophet(Slm) does not belittle himself. In the same manner Imamana(As) also had to follow the holy Prophet(Slm) because the holy Prophet(Slm) came before him. But this following does not belittle him as against the holy Prophet(Slm).

Another point is that if the follower is another person appointed by Allah, then his following becomes consonance. In this connection, author of "Muaheb-e-Ludnia" had stated that:

"Book of Moosa(As), that is Torah which not only certifies the Coming of an un-lettered prophet but follows in giving the Glad Tidings, that this following is called conformity and consonance of the Holy Qur'an."

كتـاب مـوسیٰ يعنی توريت چه اونيز در تصديق نبی امی و بشـارت بـوجود اوتابع است يعنی موافق است مقرآن را۔

Thus when we say that a Nabi is following other Nabi, means he is conforming his predecessor. Hence the holy Prophet(Slm) was commanded to follow the Deen of the previous prophets and particularly to the Deen-e-Ibrahimi, it is called the holyProphet(Slm) is confirming that Deen-e-Ibrahimi to be the religion of Allah alone.

.Author of "Asshatul Lam'aat" says with reference to "Wa Hazal Nabi, Wallazeena Aaminoo":

"Here it is pointed out particularly about the personality of the holy Prophet(Slm) who had been directed to follow and confirm the Deen-e-Ibrahimi."

واین پیغمبر اشارت است بذات شریف آنحضرت که مامور است بمتابعت وموافقت ابراهیم دردین۔

Thus it is proved that the following which had been dictated by Allah is nothing but confimity and consonenece. In the same manner Imamana(As) too had followed the holy Prophet(Slm) as per dictates of Allah, hence this following is called conformity and consonenece. Therefore Bandagi Miyan Syed Khundmir(Rz) had written in"Aqeeddai-e-Shariefa" that:

"As a proof for Mahdiat, imamana(As) had asserted his argument from the dictates of Allah, Qur'an, and as confirmed by the holy Prophet(Slm)."

بـرثبـوت مهـدیـت حـجـت از خدا واز کلام خداوبه موافقت رسول بیاورد

Thus wherever the word"Following of the holy prophet" comes it may be considered as"in consonance of or in conformity with", since if one appointee of Allah follows another appointee of Allah, the rank of the follower does no belittle camparing to whom he follows; otherwise as regards following, prophet Ibrahim(As) becomes belittle as against Prophet Noah(As) which is nothing but falsification of the facts.

Thus Imamana(As) as an appointee of Allah follows the Shariat of the holy Prophet(Slm) on orders of Allah, as Allah had ordered the holy prophet(Slm) to follow the Deen of the previous prophets(As), particularly the Deen-e-Hanifi of prophet Ibrahim(As).

Qur'an and Mahdi(As) are Rasoolullah's two Khalifas:

Traditions prove that the holy Prophet(Slm) had ordered to cling to the holy Qur'an and to his progeny. In this regard there are two traditions. "Tirmizi" reports Jaber saying that:

" It is narrated that during Hajj period I had seen the holy Prophet(Slm) riding on his "Qaswa" (camel) addressing people that: "Oh People I am leaving for you such things if you cling to them you would be never on wrong path; they are the Kalamullah and my progeny." 192

قـال رایـت رسـول الله صلی الله علیه وآله وسلم فی حـجة یـوم عرفـه وهـو عـلی نـاقتـه القصواء یخطب فسـمعتـه یـقول یا ایها الناس انی ترکت فیکم ما ان اخذتم به لن تضلوا کتاب الله وعترتی واهل بیتی .

Muslim Bin Zaid Bin Arquam narrates that :

"One day the holy prophet stood up for giving sermon at Qum village which is in between Makkah and Madinah. He started by praising Allah and then asserted that "I am also a human being like you. I assume Allah's Angel may arrive and I must comply his command. Therefore I am leaving two important things for you. First is Kalamullah which contains guidance and teaches saintliness. Keep it firm and cling to it. Then he told about Ahl-e-Bait(Rz) and again reminded to cling the Ahl-e-Bait also."

قال قام رسول الله صلى الله عليه وآله وسلم يوما فينا خطيبا بما يدعى خما بين مكة والمدينة فحمدالله واثنى عليه ووعظ وذكر ثم قال اما بعد الا ايها الناس انما انابشر يوشك ان ياتينى رسول ربى فاجيب وانا تارك فيكم الثقلين اولهما كتاب الله واستمسكوا به فيه الهدى والنور فخذو بكتاب الله فحث على كتاب الله ورغب فيه ثم قال ثم قال واهل بيتى اذكر كم الله فى اهل بيتى اذكر كم الله فى اهل بيتى .

These two traditions are called "Hadees-e-Saqlain".In order to avoid misleading the emphasis is given by the holy Prophet(Slm) to cling not only to the holy Qur'an, but also to the progeny of the holy Prophet(Slm). Further, here Ahl-e-Bait(Rz)" is absolute which refers to a perfect personality coming from the Ahl-e-Bait(Rz) and that is the personality of Imam Mahdi (As). Thus it amounts to say that as Qur'an saves you from misleading, Imam Mahdi(As) also is the authority appointed by Allah to guide properly to the Ummah.

These two traditions absolutely refer to Ahl-e-Bait(Rz), holy Prophet's progeny and other traditions particularly refer to Imam Mahdi(As) that he is from Bani Fatima(Rz) and had the ability to save Ummah from its annihilation and Deen/Religion shall end on him, further he possessed the characters of the holy Prophet(Slm) and he followed the Sharait-e-Mustafavi(Slm) and never committed fault as the holy Prophet(Slm) prophesied.

Therefore as per the directions of the holy prophet it is obligatory to cling to that personality about whom the holy Prophet(Slm) had emphasised. Here the holy Prophet(Slm) had referred Qur'an and his progeny, that means to say that the person from the progeny of the holy Prophet(Slm) would be the right person to interpret Qur'an under commands of Allah.

About this Bandagi Miyan Syed Khundmir had referred the above two traditions in his

"Al Me'yar" and in "Bua'zul Aayat" he had discussed about "Azkuru kumullahi Fi Ahl-e-Baiti":

"And he is Mahdi(As)."   وهوالمهدى

In some other traditions the holy Prophet(Slm) had described Qur'an and Mahdi (AS) as his two Khalifas. The details are hereunder:

A.Imam Bin Hunble(Rz) had reported the narration of Zaid Bin Saabith:

" The holy Prophet asserted that he is leaving two Khalifas. One is Qur'an which is like a rope coming from skies and reaching upto the Earth and second is my progeny Ahl-e-Bait(Rz). It is certain that both of them would never be separated till they reach me at the Kauser."

B.Ibn Jareer had narrated that:

"Narrated by Zaid Bin Saabit who had reported the holy Prophet(Slm) had certified that he had left two Khalifas, Kalamullah and Ahl-e-Bait(Rz), both shall meet the holy Prophet(Slm) at Roud-e-Kausar."(Canal named Kausear)

C .Siyuoti describes that:

"Reported Ahmed and Tabrani that Ibn Saabit referred about holy Prophet's asseretioin that he had left two Khalifas, Kalamullah, is a rope which is drawn from the sky to the Earth and the Ahl-e-BaitI(Rz), both will never set apart and shall meet me at the Kausar.": 197

قال قال رسول الله صلى الله عليه وسلم انى تارك فيكم خليفتين كتاب الله حبل ممدود مابين السماع واومابين السماء الى الارض وعترتى اهل بيتى وانهما لن يتفر قا حتى يرد اعلى الحوض .

عن زيد بن ثابت عن رسول الله صلى الله عليه وسلم انه قال قد تركت فيكم خليفتين كتاب الله واهل بيتى يردان على الحوض جميعاً

اخرج احمد والطبرانى عن زيد بن ثابت قال قال رسول اللّه صلى اللّه عليه وسلم انى تارك فيكم خليفتين كتاب الله حبل ممدود بين السماء والارض وعترتى اهل بيتى لن يتفرقا حتى يرد اعلى الحوض.

The above traditions are called "Hadees-e-Khalifatain" mentioning about two Khalifas, one is Qur'an and the other is Ahl-e-Bait(Rz), the progeny of the holy Prophet(Slm). Thus by telling two Khalifas, one is the Qur'an, and the other one must be a single person from the Ahl-e-Bait(Rz) to be born in future on a firm command of Allah, when He desires to cleanse the Ummah, He brings that personality from the progeny of the holy Prophet(Slm). Had there been many Khalifas, then the holy Prophet(Slm) should have said many Khalifas and not two Khalifas.

Khulafai-e-Rasoolullah(Slm).

Ibn Abi Sheeba reported what Zaid Ibn Saabit had told that:

"Narrated that he heard the prophet telling: really I AM LEAVING TWO KHALIPHAS after me, one is Kalamullah and the other is My progeny, (a person from my) Ahl-e-Baith(Rz) who would arrive at Kausar and meet me."

قـال قـال رسول الله صلى الله عليه وسلم انى تارك فيكـم الـخـليفتين من بعدى كتاب اللّٰه و عترتى اهل بيتى ترد اعلىّ الحوض

As in the Hadees-e-Saqlain, from the Ahl-e-Bait(Rz) means a perfect personality from Ahl-e-Bait(Rz) is meant and that he was the personality of Imam Mahdi(As) alone, in the same manner from the Hadees-e-Khalifatain also the same personality of Imam Mahdi(As) is meant.

Here Mansoor Khan had written about Hadees-e-Saqlain that:

"Know oh my friend the holy Prophet(Slm), with these traditions, had equalled the ranks of the holy Qur'an and Imam Mahdi(As)."

بدان اے عزيز كه رسول عليه السلام دراىں حديث مرتبهٔ قرآن ومهدى برابر نموده است ـ (جنت الولايت ۹۳)

Author of "Risalatul Hujjat" had written about the said Hadees that:

"It is proved for certain that Qur'an and Imam Mahdi(As) are equal."

تحقيق شد كه قرآن و مهدى عليه السلام برابر اند

☆☆☆

Thus it is proved that both Qur'an and Imam Mahdi(As) are the Khalifas of the holy Prophet (Slm).

It may be clarified that the "Wordings of the TASBEEH" which we are accustomed to pronounce after Isha prayer or after other religious gatherings were said to have been witnessed in a dream by Bandagi Miyan Ameen Mohammed Muhajir (Rz). It is just like that the wordings of Azan which were witnessed by Abdullah bin Zaid bin Abdurraba were permitted by Rasoolullah (Slm). Thus, in the same manner, Imamana(As) permitted to recite the Tasbeeh loudly, which was actually heard by Miyan Amin Mohammed (Rz) in his dream. About this Tasbeeh, Shah Burhan (Rh) had reported in "Shawahedul Vilayet" in Chapter 22 whose words are:

"Qur'an and Mahdi (As) are our Imam, We have faith in them and we testtify them."

القرآن والمهدى امامنا آمنا و صدقنا .

It proves that Imamana (As) and the holy Qur'an have been designated by the holy Prophet (Slm) as Imams. This is according to the traditions. Bandagi Miyan Syed Khundmir (Rz) and Miyan Abdul Malik Sujawandi (Rh) had declared Imamana (As) not only Khalifatullah , but Khalifatur Rasool based upon these traditions and as the holy Qur'an is the Khalifa of the holy Prophet (Slm), Imamana (As) too is the Khalifa of the holy Prophet (Slm). That means to say as we have to cling to the Qur'an as directed by the holy Prophet (Slm), same way we have to cling to Imamana (As) as an obligation.

Mahdi (As) and Imamat:

Kalamullah states that:

"Asserted Allah (to Ibrahim (As) that verily I am going to make you Imam of the nations, then Ibrahim (As) pleaded: also make Imam from my progeny ."

قال انى جاعلك للناس اماما قال ومن ذريتى (البقرة ١٥ع)

Author of "Madarik" had stated with reference to "Wa Min Zurriati" that:

"Make Imam from my progeny who would be followed (by the people)".

اجعل من ذريتى اماما يقتدى به

"Risalai-e-Hashda Aayat" narrates with reference to that verse that:

"Make me Imam and also from my progeny one Imam."

اجعلنى اما ما ومن ذريتى اماما (٣)

From the above verse it is proved that prophet Ibrahim (As) requested Allah to make one Imam from his progeny. This was his prayer:

"Our Lord! Send amongst them an apostle of their own, who shall recite Thy Versess to them and instruct them in the Scripture and sanctify them." (2: 129)

ربنـا وابـعـث فيهـم رسـولاً مـنهم يتلوا عليهم ايتک ويعلمهم الكتاب والحكمة ويزكيهم (البقرة ع ١٥)

This prayer was granted and an apostle was commissioned; Thus Allah says that :

"It is He Who Hath sent amongst the unlettered an apostle from among themselves, to recite to them His verses, to sanctify them and to instruct them the Book (Quran) and teach wisdom." (62:2)

هو الذى بعث فى الاميين رسـولاً منهم يتلوا عليهم ايته ويزكيهم ويعلمهم الكتاب والحكمة (الجمعة ع ١)

Further Allah again confirms His above assertion that:

"He sent among them an apostle from among themselves reciting unto them the Verses of Allah, sanctifying them and instructing them in scripture and teach wisdom." (3:164/Part)

اذبـعـث فيهـم رسـولاً مـن انـفـسهم يتلوا عليهم آياته ويزكيهم ويعلمهم الكتاب والحكمة (آل عمران ع ١٧)

Thus Prophet Ibrahim (As) had pleaded two requests. One for an apostle (holy Prophet (Slm) and the other for an Imam (Imam Mahdi (As). The attributes of the apostle had been described as being reciting the verses (of Quran), instructing scripture, and sanctifying them". And the attributes of the "Ummieain" also had been described. It points out with certainty that prophet Ibrahim (As) had pleaded for commissioning of an another Imam also. Thus Seyuoti had commented on this verse that:

"Narrated By Ibn Sa'ad (in "Tabaqat") has said and Ibn Asaker that Prophet (Slm) has said I am the result of the prayer of my father Ibrahim (As), who pleaded when he was making the basement for Kabatullah and prayed: "oh our Lord send one apostle from among themselves."

اخرج ابن سعد فى طبقاته وابن عساكر من جويبر عن الضحاک ان النبى صلى الله عليه وسلم قال انا دعوة ابى ابـراهيـم قـال وهـو يـرفـع القواعد من البيت ربنا وابعث فيهم رسولاً منهم الىٰ آخره

Thus the holy Prophet (Slm) himself attested that he is the result of the prayer of Prophet Ibrahim (As) who pleaded"Ba'asa Fihim Rasoolan".

Another prayer "Min Zurriati Imama" does not belong to the holy Prophet (Slm). Therefore author of "Muheb-e-Aliaha" had stated about the other Verse that:

"And also send an Imam from my sons and grandsons."

واز فـرزندان ونبير گان من نيز اماماں پيداکن (جلد اول ١٥)

From the above writing, as per "Muaheb-e-Aliaha" the verse "Min Zurriati Imama" does not pertain to the holy Prophet (Slm). But it pertains to *(one of the Venerable personality from the Progeny of the Ahl-e-Bait (Rz), as prophesied by the Holy Prophet, being the Khalifuttullah)* Imam Mahdi (As).

Author of "Sirajul Absar" writes that:

"Ka'ab-e-Ahbar narrated that I had read about Imam Mahdi (As) in the scriptures of all prophets. The orders issued by Imam Mahdi (As) shall have no flaws nor would they be unjust. Narrated by Imam Abu Abdullah Nayeem bin Hammad (Rz)."

روى عـن كـعب الاحبـار انـه قال انى لاجد المهدى مكتـوبا فى اسفار الانبياء ما فى حكمه ظلم ولا عيب اخرجـه الامـام ابوعبدالـلّـه نعيم بن حماد (سراج الابصار معه مقدمه ٢١٠و ٢١١)

Prophet Ibrahim (As) had prayed for another Imam from his progeny. Prophet Moosa (As) also prayed for an Imam from the progeny of the holy Prophet (Slm). Thus Imam Mahdi (As) had emerged about whom all Scriptures inform. Imamana (As) also had asserted that the verse "Min Zurriati" refers to him alone; about which Miyan Abdul Malik Sujawandi (Rh)had written that:

"Prophet Ibrahim (As) prayed to Allah "designate me Imam and also designate Imam from my progeny" and that Imam is Mahdi (As). It was narrated by Qazi Alauddin Alam Danishmand of Deccan about Imamana (As)."

قـال اجعـلـنى اماما ومن ذريتى اماما والامام من ذرية ابراهيمُ هوالـمهـدى نقله قاضى علاء الدين العالم النحرير الدكنى عن المهدى

Thus Imam Mahdi (As) is the Imam as prophet Ibrahim (As) was the Imam and his Imamat was not separate from Khilafat-e-Ilahi.

Miyan Abdul Ghafoor Sujawandi (Rh) had written with reference to "Min Zurriati: that :

"Narrated Imamana (As) that Allah ordains me that prophet Ibrahim (As) prayed for the Imam of muslims, and that Imam is your self and none else."

روى عـن الـمهـدى الـمـوعود عليه السلام انه قال ان الـلـه تعالى امرلى ان الامام المسلم الذى دعا ابراهيم من ذريته هو ذاتك فقط لاغير .

Author of "Anwarul Oyun" writes that:

"It is narrated by Haz. Mahdi (As) that "Almighty Allah instructs me that the prayer, that was supplicated by Haz. Ibrahim (As) for an Imam from his progeny, is no one but yourself only."

روى عـن الـمهـدى عليه السلام انه قال ان الله امرلى ان الامـام الـمسلـم الـذى دعا ابراهيم من ذريته هوذ اتك فقط لا غيرك

Thus it is proved that Imamana (As) is the Imam as was prophet Ibrahim (As). Thus Ibrahim's Nabuwwat, Imamat and Risalath would never separate from Khilafat-e-Ilahi. Therefore Imamana's Imamat is like that of Prophet Ibrahim (As), hence it is a proof that Mahdi should have his own Ummat. For that Bandagi Miyan (Rz) says that:

"And Imamat is meant for the two only after the holy Prophet (Slm). They are Mahdi (As) and Eisa (As). Imamat fits to the person who becomes saviour of his Ummat and on account of his following the Ummat shall get salvation."

والامـامة لا يـمكن بعد النبى الا الاثنين وهما المهدى
وعيسـى لان الامـامة لا تـصـح الا لمن يكون سبب
النجاة لامته وينجى امته باقتدائه (بعض الآيات ٢)

This proves that Imamana (As) is the Imam in the sense as the holy Prophet (Slm), Eisa Nabiullah (As) and Ibrahim Khaleelullah (As) are Imams. Second point is that Imam Mahdi (As) has his own Ummat who would be liberated through following him.

Mahdi's Precepts and Practice:

Imam Mahdi(As) is a Diffinite Evidence and a Khalifatullah whose precepts and practice become obligatory. "Sirajul Absar" thus describes that Imam's words are final: For example, if he says straw a king and a stone a diamond we have to accept it as an obligation. Author of "Insaf Nama" writes that:

"Thus it was the consensus held at one night in which, Bandagi Miyan Syed Khundmir (Rz), Miyan Shah Naimat (Rz), Miyan Shah Dilawer (Rz) , Miyan Shah Nizam (Rz) and many companions were present. They were discussing about Imamana's Sayings. Bandagi Miyan (Rz) pointed out towards a stone and said that if Imamana (As) told it was a diamond, then what will you all say? Then Miyan Salamullah (Rz) took a straw from the floor and said it is a straw, but If Imamana (As) told it a king, then what would you say? Shah Nizam declared that the stone was a diamond and the starw was the king (if really said by Imamana (As)."

نيـز اجمـاع كهانبيل اين است ، شبى بودر در آں شب
بعـد از عشـاء ميان سيد خوند ميرؓ ميان نعمتؓ وميان
دلاورؓ ميـان نظامؓ واكثر مهـاجران حاضر بودند چيزـ
حـديـث گفـت و گـودر فـضـل بـود، بندگى ميان سيد
خـونـدميرؓ فرمودند كه اين سنگ است كه سيد محمد
مهـدى ايـں راه گوهر فرمودند شما چه ميفرمائيد، بعده
ميـان سيد سلام الله يك خاشاك از صف جماعت خانه
گـرفتـند وفرمودند كه ايں گياه است و سيد محمد ايں
راشـاه فـرمودند شماچه ميفرمائيد بعده ميان نظام فرمود
كه آں سنگ گوهر است وايں گياه شاه است۔

From this Consensus it comes to light that if Imamana (As) said a stone, diamond; and a straw, a king; then we have to accept it without asking for any evidence. But as a matter of fact Imamana (As) would never say a stone, diamond nor a straw a king. When the people of the Arabian desert became muslims, then the holy Prophet (Slm) declared some of them to be like Isa (As) and to some like Ibrahim (As). Thus exigency of Faith requires to accept it without any evidence.

So also what Imamana (As) had declared about his companions, must be accepted without any reservation. But the point to be considered is that on what conditions that was said.

Bandagi Shah Dilawer was the nephew of Rai Dalpat. But on account of the beneficence of Imamana Shah Dilawer became such a pious mystic under whose guidance scholars like Miyan Abdul Malik Sujawandi offered their allegiance to him. Although he was like a straw before he met Imamana (As), but under the guidance of Imamana (As) became a pious mystic, he was previously like a stone, but later he became a diamond.

"Yu minoona Bilghaib" is the attribute of a pious person who has faith in the unseen. It is as if we are saying a straw a king. When there is any mental reservation for acceptance, but if we accept it if asked by our Mentor/guide/leader, without any reservation is a proof of our Faith. But condition is that it must have authority of the Saheb-e-Biyyana. As a matter of fact there is no such precedence that Imamana (As) had ever said any thing which contradicted facts.

According to Bandagi Miyan Syed Khundmir (trz) Imamana's precept and practice have to be accepted without reservation since he is the final authority as the Khalifatuulah. prophets (As) are innocent and pious since they are the Messengers deputed by Allah and we cannot demand any further proof from them and they are not dependent to any argument. Therefore Imam Mahdi (As) also is commissioned by Allah, hence no further proof is required. Thus Ibn Omer (Rz) said that :

"He heard the holy Prophet (Slm) saying that "Hajr-e-Aswad" is a stone and Muqam-e-Ibrahim also is a stone on which Prophet Ibrahim's impressions of his feet are engraved. They are two Rubies among the Rubies of Paradise, but Allah had obliterated their brilliance. Had Allah not obliterated their brilliance their brilliance would have brightened the whole world."

قال سمعت رسول الله صلى الله عليه وسلم يقول ان الركن والمقام ياقوتتان من ياقوت الجنة طمس الله نورهما ولولم يطمس نورهما لا ضاء مابين المشرق والمغرب.

It proves that the Hajr-e-Aswad is a Rubi came from paradise whose brilliance had been obliterated by Allah. For this tradition Abdul Haq, Muhaddis-e-Dehalvi, had commented that:

"There is so much of wisdom (hikmat) in obliterating its brilliance, so that people believe in the unseen and it is only a test of their faith."

گویا حکمت ورطمس نور آن است تا ایمان به غیب باشد امتحان ایمان دراین صورت است ۔

Thus if there is any legend that Imamana (As) had said a stone, diamond; it amounts to test our Faith. However such exaggeration was never spoken by Imamana (As). Imamana's companions presented such things as an example only that if Imamana (AS) had told by chance a stone, a diamond, we have to accept it without asking any question. But this example is pricking the eyes of the decliner, since example is not the reality and thus not objectionable. By presenting example it is being asserted that whatever Imamana (As) had said we have to accept it because Imamana (As) is the Khalifatullah as well as a definite evidence of Allah. It is just like to accept the "Hajr-e-Aswad" a ruby from paradise, which is a test of our Faith.

Sayings of Imamana (As) and Interpretations:

Author of Hadia had stated in chapter one, that interpretation of the Qur'an is not the domain of Imam Mahdi (As). But it is a fact that the responsibility of interpretation of kalamullah by Imamana(As) in view of the Verse" Summa Inna Alaina Biyanahu". That is to say Allah has informed through that Verse that it was His responsibility andf gthat responsdibiolity ewas bestowed by Allh to to Imamana(As). However, as for as Muhkkamat/commands, are concerned they are clear in their meanings. Hence there is no necessity for their interpretation. And as regards Mutashabihat or similies, we have to accept them as it is as a part of our faith. It is stated in Kalamullah that:

"We have Faith in Mutashabehat which are from our Lord."

آمنا به کل من عند ربنا

The word "Kul" includes Muhkkamat also.

The holy Prophet (Slm) asserted that :

"Practice on Muhkamat and have faith in Mutashabehat."

اعملو ابالمحکم و آمنو بالمتشابه

It tells that we must not unnecessarily question about the Mutashabihat.

Author of "Mualam-e-Tanzeel" under this verse states that:

l. "Narrated by Sufian Soori wal Ouzavi wal Lais bin Sayeed Sufian Ibn Uyaina and Abdullah Bin Mubarak etc, of Ahl-e-Sunnat to have faith on those verses regarding Mutashbehat without any reservation and any question."

مروی ان سفیان الثوری والاوزاعی واللیث بن سعید و سفیان بن عیینه و عبدالله بن المبارک وغیر هم من علماء السنة فی هذه الآیات التی جاء ت فی الصفات المتشابهات آمنو بها کما جاء ت بلا کیف

It proves that to have complete faith on Mutashbehat is the religion of Ahl-e-Sunnat (and ours too).

With reference to the above verse, author of "Mualam-e-Tanzeel" had further narrated that:

"The rationlists had interpreted the word "Istawa" as overwhelming, but according to Ahl-e-Sunnat "Istawa Alal Arsh" is an attribute of Allah, hence people are duty bound to have faith in it and leave it to Allah alone as He has the real knowledge."

اولت المعتزلة الاستواء بالاستیلاء فاما اهل السنة یقولون الاستواء علی العرش صفة الله تعالی بلاکیف یجب علی الرجال الایمان به ویکل العلم فیه الی الله عز وجل.

The same is the opinion of Imam Abu Hanifa (Rz), and Imam Malik (Rz). Author of "Tafseer-e-Madarik" had asserted about"Summastawa Alal Arsh" (Thus Allah established himself on the Arsh):

"Saadaq, Hasan, Imam Abu Hanifa and Imam Malik had asserted that they knew about "Istawa" whose condition is little known to which you have to accept it as the Faith; its denial is an infidelity and questioning about it becomes hearsay (innovation)."

والمنقول عن الصادق والحسن وابی حنیفہ وما لک رضی اللہ عنھم ان الاستواء معلوم والتکییف فیہ مجھول والایمان بہ واجب والجھودلہ کفر والسوال عنہ بدعۃ.

Mahdavia faith also accepts it. Imamana (As) too asserted:

"Imamana (As) asked to read the verse "Yadullahi Fouqa Aidihim" whose meaning Imamana (As) told that "Allah's hands are on their hands" while the commentators told that "Possession by hands of Omnipotenet. Imamana (As) questioned about their understanding? Allah asserted that there is nothing in the worlds which is like Allah. Allah hears and sees. Allah has hands, but not like the hands, eyes and ears of a man."

نقل است حضرت میران علیہ السلام این آیت رابخواندید اللہ فوق ایدیھم معنی بدی وجہ فرمودند دست خدائے تعالیٰ بردست ایشان مفسران این چنین گفتند قبضۂ دستِ قدرت، میران فرمودند ایشان راچہ فھم شدہ است خدائے تعالیٰ فرمودہ است لیس کمثلہ شئی وھوالسمیع البصیر خدائے رادست ھست فاما بہ مثل کسی نیست۔

The above said Alla's handa, eyes, ears are Muteshabihaa, t We need not interpret Muteshabehat , but accept them without reservation. We have to follow the Arabic usage in understanding them, as author of "Asshatul Lam'aat" had said that:

"The Usage of Arabic is that when we have to praise about generosity of some one, we say " he is open handed", although he may not be having his hands or his hand might have been cut or by birth he may not be having hands at all. Or when we have to praise for his administration, then we say that he sat on his throne, eventhough when he did not sit on it. Or there may be no place to sit at all. Thus while describing Muteshabehat we may not give unwanted meanings for any simili."

روش کلام عرب این است کہ چوں یکی راخواھند وصف کنندبجو دوکرم گویند دست وے فراخ وکشادہ است باآنکہ تواند اور ادست نبود و دست ھائے وے بریدہ شدہ باشد یا از اول خلقت بے دست آفریدہ یاکسے رابہ سلطنت وملک رانی وصف کنندہ گویند فلاں برتخت نشست اگرچہ اورتختی نبود ونشستی نہ دایں مسلکے سدید است درفھم متشابھات قرآن و حدیث کہ بے آنکہ تاویل کنندہ بگویند مراد بدست این و تخت این۔

Therefore it is better not to interpret any Muteshabehath at all and if interpretation is necessary then we have to see what is the usage in Arabic about that. As regards Imamana's narrations they are in Persian language, hence we have to interpret according to the Persian usage. As regards Mahdavi traditions we adopt what Qur'an and traditions allow us to interpret. Miyan Abdul Malik Sujawandi (RH) states that:

"Our religion regarding Muteshabehat is to follow the practice of our predecessors and to accept it as our faith, and should not unnecessarily indulge in unwanted interpretations about it."

مـذهبنـا فى الـمتشـابـه مـذهب السلف نومن به ولا نشتغل بكيفيته

Shah Burhan (Rh) had narrated about this faith in his "Hadiqatul Haqaeq":

"Thus we know about"Istawa" and we should not indulge about its particularity. We must have Faith in it and we should not question about; because questioning about it is an innovation (Bed'at)."

فـالا ستـوى مـعـلوم والكيفية غير معقول والايمان به واجب والسوال عنه بدعة

Predecessors of Mahdavia faith did not indulge in interpretation for Kalamullah. As regards Traditions, if the holy Prophet (Slm) has given some orders we have to adhere to them without objection. If that tradition gives any information, then as the Faith is concerned we have to accept it according to its meanings. For example Ibn Abbas (Rz) narrates that:

"Hajr-e-Aswad was descended from Paradise and it was more white than milk, but the sins of men had made it black, Reported in "Tirmizi."

نـزل الحجر الاسود من الجنة وهواشد بياضامن اللبن فسودته خطايا بنى آدم رواه احمد والترمذى.

Faithful is the one who accepts what had been said by the Prophet (Slm) or Imam Mahdi (As) that Hajr-e-Aswad was descended from paradise; it was more white than milk, but became black on account of the sins of men. Author of "Asshatul Lam'aat" had commented on this tradition that:

"If one has complete faith, he would accept it without any reservation."

اگر كامل الايمان است قبول مى كنند آں راے تردد وے تاويل ـ

And that is the straight path what "Asshatul Lam'aat" had stated.

"This all hesitation and anxiety for the interpretation is on account of internal darkness and cunningness, therefore it is better to accept it as it is without reservations."

هـمـه تردد و شك و تاويل از ظلمت باطنى و حيلۀ نفس است راهِ راست آن است كه بظاهر آں ايمان آرند ـ

The sublime character of Haz Imam Mahdi (As) is just like the character of Haz Rasoolullah (SAW). He is the saviour of Ummah and Sahab-e-Bayyana. So his sayings also cannot be questioned. That is why the predecessors did not interpret any of the 'Naqliat-e-Mahdi'. Having such God Given Beneficience, Imamana's devotees never contradicted his dictates. For example, as mentioned in 'Insaf-nama', if Imamana (As) took a pebble and named it a diamond and so also if he took piece of grass and named it a king, his devotees accepted as was asserted by Imamana (As) without giving any interpretation against his dictates. He had such a God Given auhority that none could defy his dictates and none had the capacity to interpret his dictates.

"Almost 46 year have passed that I, Vali Yousuf, had compiled the Naqliyat-e-Imamana (As) after hearing from Miran Syed Mahmood (Rz) and other companions of Mahdi (As) and never got any interpretetion against any of the Sayings of Imamana (As).

چهل دش سال شده است که بنده ولی یوسف نقل هائے مهدی که از میران سید محمودؓ وازیاران مهدی شنیدیم وازایشان تاویلی و تحویلی۔ نه شنیدیم ۔

Hazrat Bandagi Miyan (Rz) stated if any one tried to interpret that:

"If a person tries to reinterpret any command of Imamana (As), I loose my patience."

وقتی که کسی سخن مهدی را تاویلی و تحویلی می کند حلم بنده نمی ماند (انصاف نامہ باب چهارم)

Thus to reinterpret is nothing but to show internal darkness and cunningness. Therefore reinterpretation is not permissible by any one.

Correctness of the traditions:

Imamana (As) had asserted that:

"There are many diferences in traditions and it is difficult to correct them. The tradition which corresponds to the Book of Allah and the statement of this servant (Imamana As) should be taken as true and correct."

در احادیث اختلاف بسیار است وصحیح شدن آن مشکل هر حدیثی که موافق کتاب الله و حال این بنده باشد آن صحیح است (عقیده شریفہ)

From this we get two issues: Any tradition should correspond to kalamullah then only we accept it as genuine and no objection is raised. Another point is that it must tally to the statement of Imamana (As)and to that of the Holy Prophet(Slm)

Imamana asserted firmly that:

"If any person wants to verify our truthworthiness then he had to examine our precepts and practice from Kalamullah and our following of the Sahariat-e-Mustafavi (Slm)."

اگر کسی خواهد که صدق مارا معلوم کند بایدکه از کلام خدا واز اتباع رسول اللہ در احوال واعمال ما بجویده وفهم کند (عقیده شریفہ)

Imamana's precepts and practice were according to Kalamullah and the traditions. No tradition can be contrary to the statement and practice of Huzoor Mahdi (As). If it is contrary it means it is not correct. Allah commands that:

"... for indeed he (Gabriel) has brought it (this Quran) down to your heart by Allah's permission, confirming the scriptures that came before."

فانہ نزلہ علی قلبک باذن اللہ مصدقا لمابین یدیہ

Our firm belief is that Qur'an tells the truth. and nothing but truth.

Imam Bukhari (Rz) maintained his own principle to check the correctness of the traditions and if anyone did not fit to his principles he rejected those traditions. Other Muhaddiseen also accepted the same critarion. Imamana's characters were the touchstone for correctness of the traditions; then why any objection should arise, particularly when Imamana (As) is "Saheb-e-Biyyana".

Apart from this, the decliner himself had accepted that sublime characters become the standard for the traditions. That is why we have discussed about Imamana's characters in the beginning chapters to narrate sublimity of his characters which had been accepted by one and all. Therefore decliner's objection has no value.

Imamana's supernatural Events:

Supernatural events of the prophets are called Miracles as reported by author of "Madarijul Nabuwwat":

"Any supernatural event that happend by prophets is called a Miracle."

انچہ ازمدعی رسالت واقع شود آں رامعجزہ گویند۔

Predecessors of Mahdavia had used the word Miracle for any supernatural event of Imamana (As)also. Author of "Risalai-e-Isbat-e-Mahdi" has referred the book "Risala-e-Miracles" of Imamana (As) which contains more than a hundred Miracles and states that:

"If any one wants to know the attributes of Imamana (As), our Mentor,then he must go through the book of "Miracles of Mahdi" (As) in which more than one hundred Miracles are recorded,(by a non Mahdavi Writer) like that of the prophets, so that he would become satisfied of Imamana's truthfulness."

اگر خواہی کہ از احوال حضرت مہدی کہ متبوع ایشاں است معلوم کنی از کتاب معجزات المہدی کہ در اورزیادہ از صد معجزات است چوں معجزہ انبیاء علیہم السلام از کتاب معلوم کسنی ترا یقین حاصل آید بہ صدق او۔

Bandagi Shah Burhan (Rh) had recorded more than forty Miracles of Imamana (As) in his "Shawahedul Vilayet" chapter 32. Miracle 40 petrtains to the martyrdom of Bandagi Miyan Syed Khundmir (Rz) and wrote that:

"Just with one such Miracle is sufficient to prove his all miracles, as well as the proof of his Mahdiat itself.

دریس یك معجزہ چندیں معجزہ ہابر ثبوت مہدیت آنحضرت صادر شد۔

Imamana's rank and attributes are: 1.Getting Allah's Commands; 2. innocence (Ismat), 3. Propagating Khilafat-e-Ilahi, 4. According to the Holy Prophet (Slm), he is the Saviour of the Ummah, 5. Carrying magnificent characters like that of the Holy Prophet (Slm); 6.Having Gabreil's unique company; 7. Clear Evidence, 8.His Satan became muslim too, 9. Deen's Completion on him, 10.Imamat.

Inview of these attributes Bandagi Shah Burhan (Rh) did not differentiate between the ranks of the holy Prophet (Slm) and of Imamana (As). Therefore he wrote about them that:

"Both are internally and externally one and the same and there is no difference of ranks between them."

يك درجـه ويك مـرتبـه درآشكار ونهاں هستند درميان ايشاں فرق مراتب نيست ـ

As there is no difference in their ranks their equality (Taswiyat) is proved.

Innoncence is the virtue of the prophets as stated by Shah Abdul Aziz:

"To be innocent is the attribute of the prophets, according to the Sunat wal Jama'at."

ومعصوميت نزد ايشاں خاصۀ انبياء است ـ

Thus Imamana (As) asserted that Allah is superior to Mahdi. A particular companion of Imamana (As) declared Imamana (As) being equal to the holy Prophet (Slm) and it was a consensus of all.

Mastery and excellence:

No body could deny the excellence of the holy Prophet (Slm) which is recorded by the author of Hadia in chapter Eight, but how can we shut our eyes from such traditions as relating to the excellence of other prophets, about whom Abu Huraira (Rz) stated that he heard what the holy Prophet (Slm) was telling same which are recorded in "Bukhari and Muslim":

"Do not give me preference over Moosa (As). When people will become unconscious on the Day of Judgment and I too be among them, I shall be the first to to regain consciousness and I would see that Moosa (As) is clinching one side of the Arsh. I do not know whether he also became unconscious along with others and then regained consciousness even before me or he was among those whom Allah had exempted from becoming unconscious?"

لاتـخيـر ونـى عـلـى مـوسـى فـان الناس يصعقون يوم القيٰمة فـاصعق معهم فاكون اول من يفيق فاذا موسىٰ باطش بجانب العرش فلا ادرى كان فيمن صعق فافاق قبلى او كان فيمن استثنىٰ الله

Muslim had reported also that:

"Narrated by Anas that a man came to the Prophet (Slm) and addressed him to be the best of the creations. But the holy prophet (Slm) asserted that it was prophet Ibrahim (As)."

عن انس قال جاء الرجل الى النبى صلى الله عليه وآله وسـلـم فقـال يـا خير البريه فقال رسول الله صلى الله عليه وآله وسلم ذاك ابراهيم .

The excellence of the holy Prophet is his sublime characters which is proved from the text of the holy Qur'an and no other prophet had been prophesied like him.The second attribute is that his Satan had become muslim which has been proved by traditions of "Sihah". Still it is a fact that all prophets are equal by virtue of their being "Saheb-e-Biyyana, Imam and innocent".

It was already proved that the subline excellence of the holy Prophet (Slm) also was inherited by Imamana (As), since he comes from the Ahl-e-Baith(Rz), is the Kahlifatullah, Saheb-e-Biyyana and his Satan too had become muslim like that of the holy Prophet (Slm).

Peculiarity of Qur'anic verses:

Imamana (As)had, under the directions of Allah, particularized some verses of the Holy Qur'an for himself to which the author of Hadia had objected in Hadia's chapter 3, argument No.11. Therefore their sanctity is being verified. Allah ordains that:

"It is He who sent amongst the unlettered ones an apostle from among themseleves to rehearse to them His verses and to purify them and to teach them the Book (Quran) and teach wisdom; although they were surely in manifest error before that. And He will send the one more Imam (Imam Mahdi As) also to others (who would come later) who have not joined them (the previous ones). He is exalted in might and wisdom. Such is the bounty of Allah which he bestows on whom He wills and Allah is the Lord of the higest bounty," (62:2-4)

هوالذى بعث فى الامين رسولا منهم يتلوا عليهم آياته ويزكيهم ويعلمهم الكتاب والحكمة وان كانو من قبل لفى ضلال مبين وآخرين منهم لما يلحقوا بهم وهوا العزيز الحكيم ذلك فضل الله يوتيه من يشآء والله ذو الفضل العظيم

From this verse it is clear that there existed long period in between Ummiein and Akhereen who would not meet each other any time in future. When it is not proved that Ummien would meet with the last ones, then how could it be proved that the holy Prophet (Slm) would meet the last ones?(It is just imagination and nothing else.)

Now remains the discussion about the Akhereen, the last ones.

Whenever and wherever the advent of any prophet took place, it is necessary for the people of that nation to be in the company of that prophet. When the people who came later (Aakhireen) did not get the period of Ummiyeen (the people of Rasoolullah's period), how would they get the chance of being in the company of Rasoolullah (Slm).

Kalamullah proves that the recitation of verses of the Scriptures, purifying, teaching the Book and wisdom are the attributes of the prophets.It is a fact that the holy Prophet (Slm) had rehearsed the scriptures, purified their souls, instructed them about the Book and taught wisdom to the Ummiyeens but he could not do any thing like that for the people who would come later in future for the reason that they (Aakhireen) would not get the chance even to see Rasoolullah (Slm) except his sermons, traditions and teachings are the source for the last comers to get benefit out of them.

As regards ranks of both groups are concerned their ranks are equal with each other. In this regard Imam Fakhr-e-Razi (Rz) narrates from Haz. Ibn-e-Abbas about "Zabika Fazlullah:

"Narrated Ibn Abbas (Rz) that Allah is all Powerful Who compares the non-Arabs with the Qureysh, it means that when non-Arabs accepted the faith, they too have got the excellence of those who had witnessed (had seen) Rasoolullah (Slm). Thus they (non-Arabs) are associated with them (Quresh)."

قال ابن عباس عزيز حيث الحق العجم و ابناء هم بقريش يعنى اذا آمنو الحقوا فى درجة الفضل بمن شاهد الرسول عليه السلام وشاركهم فى ذلك .

From this narration two issues emerge: First: About the people to come in the later period are those who are Non Arabs. Second: Both the Ummien and the Akhereen have equal excellence. Now it is necessary that some one should be commissioned in the Akhereen like that of the holy Prophet (Slm), otherwise their ranks cannot match with the ranks of the companions of the holy Prophet (Slm).Therefore, as per the Qur'anic prophecy some one should emerge among the Akhereen (and he is "Mahdi-e-Akhiruz Zaman").

From the above tradition it is proved that the Akhereen are from the Non Arabs who are called the Ajamis. Author of "Durrul Manshoor" commented on this verse that:

"Sayeed Bin Mansur, Abd Bin Hameed, Ibn Jareer, Ibn Manzar and Ibn Hatim all narrated that "Ummien" are Arabs and "Akhereen" are Ajamis. They all base their statement as reported by Abu Huraira (Rz) that when the Soorai-e-Jum'aa (62) was revealed we were with the holy Prophet (Slm). The holy Prophet (Slm) recited it and when he reached at "Akherrena Minhum", a person asked the Prophet (Slm) as to who were those people who have not met us? Holy Prophet (Slm) then put his hand on Salman Farsi's head and asserted: "I swear to Allah in Whose hand is my life, if Faith were even at an exalted place like Surrayya, some of these people would reach to it."

اخرج سعيد بن منصور وعبدبن حميد وابن جريروابن المنذر وابن ابى حاتم عن مجاهد فى قوله هوالذى بعث فى الامين رسولاً منهم قال العرب وآخرين منهم لما يلحقوا بهم قال العجم واخرج سعيد بن منصور البخارى ومسلم والترمذى والنسائى وابن جرير وابن المنذر وابن مردويه وابونعيم والبيهقى معاً فى الدلائل عن ابى هريره قال كنا جلو ساعند النبى صلى الله عليه وسلم حين انزلت سورة الجمعة فتلاها فلما بلغ و آخرين منهم لما يلحقوا بهم قال له رجل يا رسول الله من هؤلاء الذين لم يلحقوا بنا فوضع يده على راس سلمان الفارسى وقال والذى نفسى بيده لو كان الايمان بالثريا لناله رجال من هؤلاء

From this it becomes clear that Akhereen are Non-Arab people among whom Indians are also included. Much emphasis has been given to their Faith. These are the same Ajamis whose period will neither be connected to the period of the holy prophet (Slm) nor the people of this period would have the honour of having in the holy company of the prophet (Slm).

As regards the prominence of the Akhereen, other verses of the Qur'an testify that:

"1. Multitude of those will be from the foremost period (awwaleen).

2. And a few of those will be from the later period. (56: 39,40)

(١) ثلة من الاولين وقليل من الآخرين .

(٢) ثلةمن الاولين وثلة من الآخرين

In this verse "Sullathun Minal Awwaleen"; and "Sullathun Minal Akhereen" denote to two groups, both of them belong to the Ummah of the holy Prophet (Slm). Author of "Mu'allam-e-Tanzeel" had commented on this verse that :

"It is clear from "Sullatain" that both groups belong to the same Ummah. Abul Alia, Mujahed, Ibn Rabah and Zahhak tell that Awwaleen means previous people and "Khaleelum Minal Akhereen" means some men of this ummah who would come in the last period."

وذهب جماعة الى ان الثلتين جميعا من هذه الامة وهو قول ابى العاليه هو مجاهدو من الاولين سابقى هذه لا مة وقليل من الآخرين من هذه الامة فى آخر الزمان و عطا ابن رباح والضحاك قالوا

"Narrated Ibn Abbas (Rz) that both groups "Sullatun Minal Awwaleen and Sullatun Minal Akhereen" as asserted by the holy Prophet (Slm), both belong to my Ummah."

عن ابن عباس فى هذه الآية ثلة من الاولين وثلة من الآخرين قال رسول الله صلى الله عليه وسلم همـاجميعا من امتى

Thus it is certain that "Sallatum Minal Awwaleen" means Ummieen, among whom the holy Prophet (Slm) was commissioned. And "Sallatum Minal Akhereen" means those people who are from Non Arab countries, including India, and who would come at a later period. Their prominence also will be like that of the Ummieens who had the privilege to have the company of the holy Prophet (Slm). Now if we say that holy prophet's religion had reached to the Akhereen through the learned people, then it could be said that the prophecy had completed, as had been asserted by author of "Kasshaff" that:

"When the teaching reached step by step upto the Akhereen of the end period it may be said that it had the authority from the inception to inculcate the same teaching. Thus it can be said that the holy Prophet (Slm) himself was the admistrator for imparting such teachings which reached from the beginners to the last ones."

لان التعليم اذا تناسق الى آخر الزمان كان كله مستند الى اوله فكانه هوالذى وتولى كل ماوجد منه

Thus, as per Qur'nic prophecy there woud be a single personality in the Akhereen and not a group, as maintained wrongly by Moudodi. And he would be known as Mahdi-e-Akhiruz Zaman, and none else from the Akhereen..

That personality about whom Rasoolullah (Saw) has prophesised will be the Caliph of Allah, who would establish Deen as has been established by the Prophet (Saw), would become the saviour of Ummah, would exactly be similar to the Prophet in characters and as prophesied by the Holy Prophet(Slm) Deen would be concluded on him by Allah Subhan Wa Taallah.

Apart from this Prophet Ibrahim (As) prayed for:

"And grant me an honourable position in the later generation (Aakhireen)" (26:84)

اجعل لى لسان صدق فى لآخرين

Tafseer-e-Baizavi narates that:

"Send one truthful person from my progeny who would revive principles of my religion and invite people, as I used to invite, and that personality is none but of the holy Prophet (Slm)."

صادقا من ذريتى يجد واصل دينى ويدعو الناس الى ماكنت ادعوهم اليه وهومحمد صلى الله عليه وسلم.

When Kalamullah mentions the prominence of the Akhereen particularly, then the prayer of prophet Ibrahim (As) should be for "Sullatum Minal Akhereen" also. Because from the formers the holy Prophet (Slm) had already been commissioned, who was surely not from the Akhereen. Thus the following prayer of Prophet Ibrhim (As) was for the holy Prophet (Slm) only:

"Our Lord: Send amongst them an apostle of their own, who shall rehearse thy Versess to them and instruct them in Scriptures and teach wisdom and sanctify them, Thou art the exalted in Might and the Wise." (2:129)

ربا وابعث فيهم رسولاً منهم يتلوا عليهم ايتک ويعلمهم الكتاب والحكمة ويزكيهم انک انت العزيز الحكيم

In this Verse the particulars about the prophet to be born from the Formers are the same what have been described in the verse "Ba'sa Fil Ummien". It does not say about the Akhereen.

Apart from this there are two groups. One begins from prophet Adam (As) and ends at the holy Prophet (Slm). The second group begins from the holy Prophet (Slm) and ends at the Doomsday. Author of "Mualamut Tanzeel" states that:

"Thus the holy Prophet (Slm) asserted that one group is from Prophet Adam (As) upto me and the other group is from me upto Doomsday."

فقال رسول الله صلى الله عليه وسلم من آدم الیناثلة ومنى الى يوم القيامة ثلة

Thus, according to the Prophecy, the one who would be commissioned should be born from the Akhereen, and he is none but Imam Mahdi (As).

Jesus Christ (AS) not from Akhereen

It is clear that the person to be born from the Akhereen could not be Jesus Christ(As) , because he was already born even before the holy Prophet (Slm) of the Ummiien.

It may be clarified that Imamana (AS) after the proclamation of his Mahdiat, lived for just five years and out of those five years he lived in Farrah for two years five months he was busy in instructing the Non Arabs/Ajmis in Khurasan.

Now we like to discuss about the Verse"Summa Inna Alaina Biyanahu" (thus its interpretation is our responsibility), which does not mention who would interpret it? But Allah himself has taken its responsibility to interpret through a person of his choice at a proper time.

As regards narration of Qur'an, Allah ordains the holy Prophet (Slm) that:

(ا)وما انزلنا عليک الکتاب الاتبين لهم الذى اختلفو فيه

"And we have not sent down the Book (the Quran) to you (O Mohammed Saw), except that you may explain clearly unto them those things in which they differ." (16:64/part)

"And We have sent down clear signs and Revealed Qur'an unto you to explain to men what is sent down to them." (16:44/Part)

These verses affirm that explaination of the holy Qur'an is the domain of the holy Prophet (Slm). In another verse "Allah takes the responsibility to interpret the Qur'an. But through whom? Naturally by the one who is going to be commissioned among the Akhereen. About which Jesus Christ (As) had stated that "at the last period Farqaleet would come to interpret (Taveel), (Since prophets brought Tanzeel)_:

نحن ناتيکم بالتنزيل واما التاويل فياتى به الفار قليط فى آخر الزمان

"We (All prophets) have brought Revelations, and for interpretation (Taveel) Farqaleet would come at the end."

From this saying it is clear that it covers all prophets on whom Scriptures have been revealed. This saying of Haz. Isa (As) is just like the the saying of Rasoolullah (Saw): "Nahnu Muashirul Anbiah, La nuriso, Wala Nawaris". The prophets are neither the heirs of anyone, nor anyone is their heir.

The holy Prophet (Slm) is one on whom the Qur'an was Revealed and on that Revelation only he had fought against the infedels.. The holy Prophet (Slm) had asserted:

قاتلت المشركين على تنزيله.

"I fought with the infidels after the Revelation of Qur'an."

As regard Farqaleet, he is the one who would interpret the Qur'an (As prophesied by Jesus Christ (As). Thus these two personalities are different entities and there is no Sharai reason to accept them as one.

Author of Hadia had made a point that as per Ibn Abbas (Rz) "Summa Inna Alaina" refers to the holy Prophet (Slm) by telling that: it is our responsibility, to get it explained through their tongue." but it does not suit what Ibn Abbas (Rz) had claimed and such assertion becomes null and void in view of the holy Prophet's asseretion that Imam Mahdi (As) is the Khalifatullah, through whom Allah would ("Yakhtamaallha Bihid Deen") conclude the Deen. Thus from this it is clear that holy Prophet (Slm) confirmed that interpretation of Qur'an rests with Imam Mahdi (As) alone.

The difference is that the emphasis was made on Iman and Islam for the Ummiyeen (former group) where as the emphasis was made on Ihsaan with the revival of Iman and Islam for the Aakhireen (the people of later period). The word "Bayan" is exclusively meant for the explanation of the meaning of Quran in Daira-e-Mahdavia.

The impact of the Qur'anic prophecy is that Imamana (AS) became the authority on Qur'an by telling that "in the Qur'an there is no abrogation or extra alphabets and declared its continuity and consistency as was prevailing at the time of the holy Prophet (Slm)". The details have been discussed in Chapter 6 of Part 2.

The fault finder requires particularity of the verses (regarding Imamana (AS). The answer for it is that the prophecies mentioned in the Scriptures of the prophets regarding the holy Prophet (Slm) are not as clear as those prophecies mentioned about Imamana (AS). (Vide Part One, Chapter 3 for Prophecies mentioned in the Scriptures).

Eighteen Verses Pertain to Imamana (AS):

Imamana (AS) had asserted eighteen verses of the holy Qur'an pertain to him and his Qoum.

A. Bandagi Miyan Abdul Malik Sujawandi (Rh) has written answer to third question of Miyan Shaik Mubarak (Rh):

"Thus be it known that Imamana (As) has claimed many verses of Qur'an which are related to him and his Qowm."

ثم اعلم يا اخى ان المهدى ادعىٰ فى حقه و حق قومه آيات كثيره .

B. Regarding question No.11 of Miyan Shaik Mubrak (Rh), Miyan Abdul Malik Sujawandi (Rh) has answered thus:

"As we have explained before, Imamana (AS) has claimed some verses of Qur'an to be in his favour."

ادعىٰ فى حق نفسه آيات كما ذكرنا قبل.

C. Those verses of Qur'an which provide proof of Imamana's Mahdiat are mentioned in the oldest source "Aqeeda-e-Shariefa" which was compiled by Bandagi Miyan Syed Khundmir (Rz) and was authenticated by consensus of all companions of Imamana (AS). The same is mentioned below:

"For the proof of his Mahdiat, Haz Mahdi (As) gave the evidence from the Book of Allah and the practice of Rasoolullah (Saw), as the verse of Quran is: "Is he who is on a clear proof from Allah..." There are many other verses like this."

بر ثبوت مهدیت حجت از خدا واز کلام خداد به موافقت رسول بیاورد کقوله تعالیٰ افمن کان علی بینة من ربه .... ومثل این آیت دیگر آیت با بسیار مشهور اند ـ

Before this it has been stated that Imamana (AS) has argued his Mahdiat from Kalamulla. Then the verse "Afa Mun Kana" was presented as a concrete proof and then presented many verses relating to his Mahdiat along with the verse "Wa Akhereena Minhum".

D. Bandagi Miyan Abdul Ghafoor Sujawandi (Rh) belongs to the descendants who had stated that:

"Certainly I decided to describe the Sayings of Imamana (AS) which are relating to Qur'an, and they are about eighteen. Among them some relate to Imamana (AS) and some relate to his Qowm."

انی اردت ان اوضح نقول صاحب الزمان خلیفة الرحمن وهوالمهدی الموعودعلیه الرضوان ماورد فی القرآن بنقل مشهور هو ثمانی عشرة آیة بعضها مختصة لذات المهدی الموعود وبعضها متعینة لقومه

E. Author of "Majmual Aayaat" has referred to a poem of Malik Ji Mehri (Rz) who had written that:

"Imamana had pointed out about some verses relating to him and some relating to his Qowm. Therefore Malik Ji Mehri (Rz) had stated that "Afa Mun Kana" is the categorical Qur'anic injunction about Imamana (AS), and there are eighteen verses for both Imamana and his Qowm."

فرمود هاند که این آیت درحق من است و این آیت در حق قوم من است چنانچه بندگی ملک جی رضی الله عنه فرموده اند چون نص افمن کان علی بینه اصدق هژده دگر اشها دوی وقوم دی از حق ـ

F. Author of "Anwarul Oyun" has stated that:

"Be it known that Imamana (As) has pointed out eighteen verses relating to him and his Qowm."

بدان که هشده آیات قرآنی بامر الله تعالیٰ قراة کرده انند

G.Particularly those eighteen verses pointed out by Imamana (As) on the commands from Allah alone have been mentioned by Shah Burhan (Rh) in "Shawahedul Vilayet", chapter 17 under the caption" Empahsized Proclamation at Badhli".

(Note: For the benefit of the readers, those 18 verses have been translated and properly interpreted and have been provided in Addendum to this Book. Translator)

H.Shah Burhan (Rh) stated in his "Hadiqatul Haqaeq" that:

"Advent of Imamana (As) has been mentioned in the holy Qur'an in eighteen verses which are famous in favor of Imamana (AS)."

خبر مجى موعود در كتاب آسمانى خصوصاً در هژده عدد آيات قرآنى كه اشهر المشهود و درحق آنحضرت مسطور شده است

Opponents of Mahdavis contend that the verse "Wa Akhereena Minhum" relates to the holy Prophet (Slm) which is wrong as we have discussed it in detail above. As against the contention of the opponents, Bandagi Miyan Syed Khundmir (Rz) asserted in his "Maktoob-e-Multani", which was written as a "Propagation Maktoob" to the scholars of Multan, emphasizing that the Verse "Wa Akhereena Minhum" relates to Imamana (As) and not to the holy Prophet (Slm), since the Holy Prophet (Slm) belongs to the Awwaleen and not to the Akhereen. And we assert that it is our firm Faith and belief as such.

Angels Inspire Imamana (AS):

It may be pointed out that Bandagi Miyan Syed Khundmir (Rz) has mentioned in "Maktoob-e-Multani" about Shaikh Akber's statement just to emphasize his argument:

"Thus Mahdi would order as inspired by Angel sent by Allah to keep him on the straight path."

لا يحكم المهدى الابمايلقى اليه الملك من الله الذى بعثه ليسد ده

Opponents could not argue against Imamana (AS) by presenting the said statement of Shaikh Akber that the Angels used to inspire Imamana (As), because Bandagi Miyan Syed Khundmir (Rz) has categorically mentioned in "Aqeedai-e-Shariefa" that Imamana (As) used to get instructions directly from Allah Jall-e-Subhanahu without the medium of any angel as confirmed by Imamana (AS) himself:

" Imamana (AS) informed that "I get inspiration and teachings from ALLAH directly without any medium each day."

قال الامام المهدى صلى الله عليه وسلم علمت من الله بلا واسطة جديد اليوم .

"Yaghbita Hum ul Anbiah"- A TRADITION:

In the "Maktoob-e-Multani" just to emphasize the prominence of the companions of Imamana (As) the tradition "Yaghbita Hum ul Anbiah" (the prophets would envy them) has been mentioned. Author of "Zubdatul Haqaeq" had mentioned that tradition:

"You are (holy Prophet (Slm) the last of the prophets, and there would be no Nabi after you."

انت خاتم النبين ولانبى بعدك

A. Author of "Zubdatul Haqaeq" has mentioned another tradition :

"Did you not hear that tradition in which the holy Prophet (Slm) stated that verily I recognize that group of people who have the ranks like me before Allah. They are not the prophets or martyrs, yet prophets and martyrs would envy them because they had an exalted position before Alllah;. They love each other with the grace of Allah."

اقواما هم به منزلتى عندالله ماهم انبياء لاشهداء يغبطهم الانبياء والشهداء بمكانهم عندالله هم المتحابون بروح الله

In this tradition although "Yughbita hum ul Anbiah" is mentioned, emphatically.

This tradition is available in "Sihah"; thus Hzt.Omer's narration reported in "Abu Dawood":

"Narrated by Omer (Rz) who heard the holy Prophet (SDlm) telling that among Allah's creation there are certain pious people who are neither Nabi nor martyrs, but on the Doomsday by seeing their exalted position before Allah, Anbiah and martyrs would envy them."

عن عمر رضى الله عنه قال قال رسول الله صلى الله عليه واله و سلم ان من عبادالله لانا ساماهم ليسوا با نبياء ولا شهداء يغبطهم الانبياء والشهداء يوم القيامة بمكانهم من الله

C. In these traditions also it is mentioned that Anbiah and martyrs are said to become envious. But in this connection Seuyuoti had mentioned some six narrations in his "Addural Manshoor." In three of them the words "Yaghbat Humul Anbiah wush Shuahda" has been mentioned and in other three, the words "Yaghbutul Nabiyyuna wush Shauda" had come. D.Bandagi Miyan Abdul Malik Sujawandi (Rh) had narrated about "Yaghbatul Anbiah and Shuhada" with reference to Omer Ibnal Khattab (Rz), Abu Huraira (Rz) and Abi Malik alAsh'ari (Rz), as mentioned in "Sirajul Absar".

E. Ibn Abi Sheeba had commented on "Yaghbata Humal Anbiah wush Shahda", but here also these words are missing.

F. Author of "Insaf Nama" although had mentioned the words "Yuabathumal Anbiah", but other words are missing.

Argument Against Real Purpose is Wrong:

In such a situation, when a part of the narration is missing, no blame could be inflicted on Mahdavis. By furnishing the said narration in the "Maktoob-e-Multanai", author's intention was just to emphasize the prominence of the conmpanions of Imamana (AS). It is not a commentary on the verse "Khatimun Nabbien."Unnecessary discussion in this regard is against the principle of argumentation.

Kabatullah and 360 Idols:

Before the victory of Makkah (7 Hijri), there were 360 idols in and around the House of

Allah; hence, could any one argue that muslims who were offering prayers by facing the Makkah were also prostrating before those idols? *(Requires thorough research)*

Whatever the author of "Maktoob-e-Multani" has written, he has before him those words which were used by Shaik-e-Akber (Rz) in respect of the companions of Imamana (As), and the contents of the discussion. Bandagi Miyan Shah Abdul Ghafoor (Rh), the descendant, also has written that:

"As reported by Imamana (As)" Allah had ordained me that the verse" Wa Akhereena Minhum" is meant to my Qowm only and the one who is commissioned among the Aakireen is none but you. You are the same person to appear at the last.

روى عـن الـمهـدى الموعود انه قال ان الله تعالى امر لى ان المراد من قوله آخرين منهم قومك فقط ومن الرسول منهم ذاتک .

Author of "Anwarul Oyuoon" had written that:

4. "Immana (As) stated that Allah has informed me that the word "Akhereen" denotes to your Qowm alone and the promised one among them is your personality."

قـال الـمهـدى ان الـله امرلى ان المرادو آخرين منهم قومک ومن الرسول منهم ذاتک

5. Thus Imamana (As) has particularised the Verse" Wa Akhereen Minhum"for his Qowm as ordained by Allah. This fact has also been reported by Imamana's descendant, Bandagi Miyan Abdul Malik Sujawandi (Rh):

"Thus be known, Brother; Imamana (As) has referred many verses of the holy Qur'an for himself and for his Qowm, including what Allah has asserted" I Sent those among the "Akhereen" who did not meet the "Ummiyeen."

اعـلـم يا اخى المهدى ادعى فى حقه و حق قومه آيات كثيرة ....منها قوله تعالى و آخرين منهم لمايلحقو ابهم .

"Sirjul Absar" and "Akhereena Minhum" is as under:

6."Allah has informed about Qowm-e-Mahdi (AS) in His Book many a time which also includes His commands". And sent (Mahdi As)" among the Akhereen whose period was not adjacent to the period of Ummiyeen."

قـد اخبر الله عن هذا القوم فى مواضع جمة من كتابه منها قوله تعالى و آخرين منهم لمايلحقو ابهم .

7. The disciple of Imamana (As), Bandagi Miyan Syed Khundmir (Rz) stated that Imamana (As) gave the evidence for himself (his Mahdiat) from the verse "Wa Aakhereena Minhum"

واز آیات دیگر هـم حجـت فـرمـوده اسـت کمـا قال سبـحانـه وتـعالیٰ هوالذی بعث فی الامیین رسولاً منهم .... وآخـریـن منهم لما یلحقوا بهم (مکتوب ملتانی مطبوعه)

8. Miyan Abdul Ghafoor Sujawandi (Rh) commented on that verse:

"I say that the truth is what Huzoor Mahdi-e-Mawood (As) has said, as the meaning of the verse is apparently clear. The words of Allah "Wa Aakhireena Minhum" is conjoined with ummiyeen by means of a conjunction. Hence the Rasool sent by Allah in Ummiyeen is Huzoor Mohammad Rasoolullah (Slm) and (the Ptromised one) sent by Allah in Aakhireen is Huzoor Mahdi-e-Mawood (As).

اقـول الـحـق ماقال لان هذالمعنی ظاهر فی بیان الایة لان قوله و آخرین منهم معطوف علی الامین والمعنی هـوالـذی بعـث فی الامیین رسولاً وهو محمد وفی الآخرین رسولاً وهوالمهدی الموعود ..

9. Author of "Maahiat-e-Taqleed" wrote:

"Allah's word "Akhireen" joined together with "Ummiyeen" by means of and Allah sent the promised one, in the "Akhereren" and he is Mahdi Alaihis Salaam."

وقولـه آخـرین مـعـطـوف علی الامیین ای بعث الله رسولا فی الآخرین المهدی صلی الله علیه وسلم

10. Author of the pamphlet "Ummal Aouliah" also mentioned a person as the "Mahdi-e-Akheruz Zaman (As)."

"In Ummiyeen the Rasool is Mohammed (Slm)and in the Aakhireen is the Promised Mahdi (As)."

فی الامیین رسولاً وهـو مـحمد صعلم وفی الآخرین المهدی صلعم .

"Shawahedul Vilayat and Ma'asheral Ambiyah":

It was already discussed what Shah Burhan (Rh) stated about the advent of Mahdi (As) in the Scriptures and Qur'an in which eighteen verses point out about Imamana (As). Among these eighteen verses the words "Akhereena Minhum" also exist. Accordingly, Shah Burhan (Rh) asserts that the verse"Akereen Minhum" denotes to Imamana (As) and not to the Holy Prophet (Slm).

Thus Shah Burhan (Rh) accepts "Mahdi-e-Akheruz Zaman (As)" is none but the personality alone of Imamana (As).

Shah Burhan (Rh) has made the following heading in the chapter 28: "The demise of Imam

(As) in the city Farah".

"Mohammed (Slm) is none but a Messenger of Allah, and indeed (many) messengers have passed away before him."

"Shawahed-ul-Vilayat and Moulood" of Abdul Rahman:

It may be pointed out that writings of the predecessors can not be negated by the successors. For example the most oldest biography of Imamana (AS) is "Moulood" of Shah Abdul Rahman (Rz). While Shah Burhan (Rh) referred both "Janatul Vilayet" and "Matleul Vilayet", but omitted to refer "Moulood" of Shah Abdul Rahman (Rz); although "Moulood" was already existing as the oldest source.

Shah Burhan (Rh) maintained that "Rasool-e-Ummyeen" means the holy Prophet (Slm), while "Akhereena Minhum" points out both "Qoum-e-Mahdi (As)" as well as Mahdi-e-Maood (As)" himself, hence there is no ground for the opponents to argue against Imamana (As), since any non-innocent could not negate the Sayings of Imamana (AS), particularly when it is based on the consensus.

The succession (tawatur) of the claim of Imam (As) Based on the verses of Quran:

Bandagi Miyan Abdul Malik Sujawandi (Rhg) was the descendant who replied to the third question of Shaik Mubarak Nagori (Rh) with reference to "Wa Akhereena Minhum" and "Summa Inna Alaina Biyana":

"The explanation of the verses of the Holy Quran by Haz. Mahdi (As), which are about himself has reached the succession (tawatur)."

وهذه الآيات بلغت روايتها عن المهدى حد التواتر .

Haz. Abdul Malik Sujawandi has written about the verse which had been specified by Haz. Mahdi (As) for himself thus:

" When it is proved that Imamana (As) has specified some verses of the Holy Qur'an relating to him and to his Ummah, then it becomes an obligation for us to accept them without any reservation. And further that we should avoid any objection about them."

فــاذاتـحقـق ان الـمـهدى ادّعـىٰ حق نفسـه آيـات وكذلك فى حق قومه وجب علينا قبول قوله وترك المعارضة لقول .

What Imamana (As) has stated about certain verses of the holy Qur'an, every Mahdavi is bound to accept them as an obligation.

When it is proved as stated by Imamana (AS), that "Akhereena Minhum" means Imamana's ummah and himself, it becomes an obligation and to accept whoever objects or does not believe, he is accountable before Allah on Doomsday.

As after believing the claim of Rasoolullah (Slm) it becomes mandatory for us to believe without any proof what ever he (Slm) has said for example: the existence of Allah, the revelation of Quran by Jibrael (As), Miraj, Split of Moon etc. No Muslim can deny them, otherwise he will be called Kafir (infidel).

"And those who have faith in Allah and His prophets, they are trustworthy and martyrs before Allah."

والذين آمنوا بالله ورسله اولٰٓئک هم الصديقون والشهدآء عند ربهم

C. Allah states that:

"Those who are obedient to Allah and His prophets, they would be raised (on the Day of Judgment) along with those to whom Allah has rewarded, i.e. prophets, siddiqeens, truthworthy, martyrs and pious; and these are good friendly people"

ومن يطع الله والرسول فاولٰٓئک مع الذين انعم الله عليهم من النبيين وصديقين والشهداء والصالحين وحسن اولٰٓئک رفيقا .

According to the traditions it is stated that whoever loves any of the degnified person, he would be with him on the Day of Judgment. According to Ibn Masood it is said in "Sahih Bukhari" and "Muslim" that:

Ibn Masood narrated that a person came to the holy Prophet (Slm) and enquired what was his opinion about a person who hold dear a group, but has not met them? Holy Prophet (Slm) said that he would be raised with them whom he holds dear."

قال جاء رجل الى النبى صلى الله عليه وآله وسلم فقال يارسول الله كيف تقول فى رجل احب قوما ولم يلحق بهم فقال المرء مع من احب .

In "Seheheen" also it is reported that:

"Narrated Anas that a person asked the holy Prophet (Slm) when the Dooms Day would come? The holy Prophet (Slm) felt pity on him and asked "what preparation has he made for that Day?" He told that he did not keep any thing for that Day, but he holds dear Allah and His Prophet (Slm). The Holy Prophet (slm) answered that he would be raised along with him whom he holds dear."

عن انس ان رجلا قال يا رسول الله متى الساعة قال ويلك وما اعددت لها قال وما اعددت لها الا انى احب الله

Author of "Madarijul Nabuwwat" has written that:

"Thus you would be resurrected with the Holy Prophet (Slm), because the Holy Prophet (Slm) has said that every one will be with him whom he loves."

رسوله قال انت مع من احبت

940

Here the words "Along with" have been used in the traditions, which proves that those who are obedient to the prophets, would be raised with Anbiahs.

D. Allah has also informed that:

And the Earth would be brightened and the records would be placed opened and Anbiah and the witnesses would be brought forward and verdict would be granted before them with truth."

واشرقت الارض بنور ربها وضع الكتاب وجاىء بالنبين والشهدآء وقضى بينهم الحق (الزمر. ع٤)

Allah ordains that:

"And when Allah took covenant from Anbiah".

واذا خذالله ميثاق النبين

E. Allah mentions about Ashabul Jannah and their affirmation as below:

"Those are the people of paradise who will reside there forever and if any ill feeling they had, We shall eradicate. Under them will be flowing canals and they would exclaime; "all praise is to Allah who has guided us otherwise we would have lost the right path, had Allah not directed us towards the right path? Verily prophets came from Allah with the truth."

اولئك اصحاب الجنة هم فيها خالدون ونزعنا مافيصدور هم من غلتجرى من تحتهم الانهار وقال الحمدلله الذى هذانا لهذا اوماكنا لنهتدى لولا ان اهدينا الله لقد جآءت رسل ربا بالحق.

F. Allah further informs about paradise that:

"Rush towards Allah's generosity and towards the paradise whose breadth is equal to the breadth of the Earth and skies which has been prepared for those who had faith in Allah and His prophets."

سابقوآالى مغفرة من ربكم وجنة عرضها كعرض السمآءِ والارض اعدت للذين آمنو بالله و رسله.

H. Allah also states that:

"And We never punish until We send any Rasool."

وماكنا معذبين حتى بنعث رسولا.

J. Allah further asserts about the Holy Prophet that:

"Verily (The Holy Prophet) came with the truth and certified the previous prophets."

بل جآء بالحق وصدق المرسلين

It is a fact that the holy Prophet has certified not only the prophets but also the Messengers.

K. Allah also tells that:

"Mohammed (Saw) is none but a Messenger and indeed (many) messengers have passed before him."

وما محمد الا رسول قد خلت من قبله الرسل

L. Allah ordains that:

1."Then if there comes to you guidance from me."

۱. فاما ياتينكم منى هدى

2."Oh Bani Adam (As) if there come to you prophets from among you."

۲. يا بنى آدم اما ياتينكم ورسل منكم

These two verses address the children of the prophet Adam (As). Thus it is clear that in order to guide the people prophets are sent by Allah. Mahdi (As) is the Khalifatullah who has brought guidance from Allah, therefore Imamana (AS) is sent from among the Akhereen as Mahdi-e-Akheruz Zaman (As).

Opponents of Imamana claim that Rasool brings a new Book and the Nabi brings a new Shariat which is nullified in the light of Qur'anic doctrine. Thus those who are commissioned by Allah, but did not bring any new Book or new Shariat, still they are in the category of the Commissioned ones.

N.The Holy Prophet (Slm) had been named "Khatimun Nabiyeen" in Kalamullah. And Bandagi Miyan Ilahdad (Rz), the companion of Imamana (As) had said in 911 H.that:

"Mohammed Awwal Muhar Umoor-e-kul Rusl."

محمد اول مهرا مور كل رسل

Here Mohammed Awwal means, the holy Prophet (Slm) has been mentioned as the Seal of all prophets.

S. Allah ordains that:

"Tell Oh Mohammed, verily, Allah has guided me towards the straight path."

قل اننى هدانى ربى الىٰ صراط مستقيم

By the words "Hadaani Rabbi" Allah has guided the holy Prophet (Slm).Like Imam Mahdi (As) also is the one who is guided by Allah, hence he is mentioned as "Khalifatullhil Mahdi"in the tradition of "Sihah".

Hzt. Umroo Bin Jamooh, companion of the holy Prophet (Slm) has addressed "Al Mahdi" to the holy Prophet (Slm), which explains how the holy Prophet (Slm) was guided by the words "Hadani Rabbi" (Guided me my Lord).

Thus Mahdi Alihis Salaam declared himself to be the "Promised Mahdi (As)" by the command of Allah.

"Verily We Revealed Torah which contained guidance light. Anbiah used to issue orders accordingly."

انا انزلنا التورٰة فيها هديو نوريحكم بها النبيون

Those who were giving orders according to Torah were also called "Al Rusl":

"Verily We gave Torah to Moosa (As) and after him We sent Prophets one after another." لقد آتينا موسى الكتاب وقفينا من بعد بالرسل

After Moosa (SAs), prophets Yushe, Iliyas, Shamuel, David, Sulaiman (As) were sent one after another who used to give orders according to Torah. It may also be clear that since in the verse "Ba'asa Fil Ummieen" the name of the holy Prophet (Slm) is not mentioned and in the same manner, the verse "Akhereena Minhum" doesnot mention the name of Mahdi-e-Maood (As). Hence Akhereena Minhum" means Imamana Alaihis Salaam and none else.

"WAMA ALAINA ILLAL BALAGH".

*******THE END*******

BOOKS REFERRED IN WRITING:

THE MUQADDAM-E-SIRAJUL ABSAR ALONG WITH THE SUPPLEMENT:

Serial	Book's name	Author's name
1	Kashfuz Zuinoon	Mustafa Ibn Abdullah
2	Muqaddama-e-Ibn Salah	Taqiuddin known as Ibn Salah (D.643 H.)
3	Sahieh Muslim	Abul Husain Muslim Bin Hajjaj (D.261 H.)
4.	Al Muallim-e-sani (Translation of Muslim)	Waheeduz Zaman
5	Minhaj Sharh-e-Sahieh Muslim	Yahiya Ibn Ashraf Novi (D.672 H.)
6	Sanan-e- Abu Dawood	Abu Dawood Sulaiman Ibn Asshas (275 H
7	Kitabul Fakhri Fil Adaabus- Salateenat-e- Dawalul Islami	Mohammed Bin Ali Tabataba, alias Baban Al Taqtaqi (D.702 H.)
8.	Tareekh-e- Aadabul Fatha ul Arabia	Jurji Zaidan (D 1233 H.)
9	Muqaddam-e- Ibn Khaldoon	AbdulRahmanBin Mohd.Bin Khaldoon(808
10	Muqaddam-e- Fathul Bari	Ibn Hajr Asqalani (852 H)
11	Muqaddam-e-Shahnama (1245 H)	Turner Maccan
12	Muqaddam-e-Ja ameul Hikayat	Mohammed Nizamuddin
13	Muqaddam-e- Hidaya	Abdul Hai, Farangi Mahli (1204H)
14	Ma Yambagi In Yataqaddimul Falsafa	Muallim-e- Sani Abu Nasar Farabi (339 H)
15	Jazbul Quloob Ila Dayarul Mahboob	Abdul Haq Muhaddis-e-Dehlavi (1052 H)
16	Muqaddamus Surathul Hindia	Abul Shaddad Khan Shirwani
17	Andracoles and the Lion	Bernard Shah
18	Juanpur Nama (W.1216 H)	Khairuddin Mohammed Ilahbadi
19	Education in Muslim India	S.M. Jafer
20	Akhbarul Akhiyar	Abdul Haq Muhaqiq-e-Dehlavi (1052 H)
21	Tuhfatul Kiram (W.1181 H)	Ali Sher Khaney
22	Tareekh-e-Sindh	Syed Mohammed Bhakker (1019 H)
23	Farhang-e-Asafia	Syed Ahmed Dehalvi
24	Mazahebul Islam	Najmul Ghani Khan Rampuri
25	Kanzul Ansaab	Translated by Syed Murtuza Ilmul Huda
26	Reehanatul Adaab Fi Tarajim Al Maroofeen Bil Kuniata wal Qalb	Mohammed Ali Tabrezi (1373 H.,(P.Iran)
27	Umadatul Talib Fi Ansaab Ahl-e-Abi Talib	Kamaluddin (828 H)
28	Madarijul Nabuwwat	Abdul Haq Muhaddis-e- Dehlavi
29	Rouzatul Ahbaab	Jamaluddin Shirazi (917 H)
30	Al Muahebul Ludnia	Shaik Ahmed Bin Mohammed Bin Abi Baker Al Qistalani (923H)
31	Al Uqdul Fareed	Shahabuddin Ahmed Alias Ibn Abdia 328 H)
32	Jameul Tawareekh	Qazi Faqeer Mohammed (1260 H)
33	Kanzul Ansaab	Syed Ata Husain
34	Tafseer-e-Fakhr-e-Razi(Tafseer-e-Kabeer)	Fakhruddin Razi (606 H)
35	Al Burhan Fil Alamat-e- Mahdi-e-Akhiruzaman	Shaikh Ali Bin Hissamuddin (975 H)
36	Kanzul Ammal	Shakh Ali Bin Hissamuddin
37	Khazeenatul Asfia (w.1281)	Ghulam Serwer
38	Tabqat-e-Akberi	Nizamuddibn Ahmed Bakhshi (1003 H)
39	Tareekh-e-Farishta (W.1015 H)	Mohammed Qasim Farishta
40	Tareekh-e-Khiqi (Zikrul Mulook)	Abdul Haq Muhaddis-e-Dehlavi
41	Mua'sirul Ikram	Mir Ghulam Ali Azad (1299 H)

42	Mira'tul Aalam	Bakhtawer Khan
43	Hatyat-e-Wali (Shah Waliullah)	Mohammed Raheem Baksh
44	Tazkeratul Khitaaba	Mohammed Osman Imadi
45	Imperial Gazeteer of India	English Government
46	Promotion of Learning in india during Mohammedan Rule	by Narender Nath
47	Indian Education in Ancient and Later Times	by F.A.Keay
48	Hayat-e-Shibli	Syed Sulaiman Nadvi
49	Usool-e- Ibrahim Shahi	Shahabuddin Dowlatabadi (849 H)
50	Muqaddama-e-Tafseer (Nizamul Qur'an)	Hamneeduddin (Rtrd. Principal Darul Uloom
51	Riyazus Salaateen (W.1202 H)	Ghulam Husain Zaidpuri
52	Masnad-e- Ahmed Ibn Hunbal	Ahmed Ibn Hunbal Shaibani (221 H)
53	Ash'atul Lam'aat	Abdul Haq Muhaddis-e-Dehalvi
54	Sharh-e-Safarus Saadaat	-------- do --------
55	Al Isharaat	Bu Ali Seena (427 H)
56	Sharh-e-Al Isharaat	Fakhruddin Razi (606 H)
57	Sharhul Isharaat	Naseeruddin Tusi (672 H)
58	Zubdatul Haqa'eq	Ainul Quzzat Hamdani (533 H)
59	Al Yuaqeetul Jawaher	Abdul Wahab Sherani (973 H)
60	Kitabul Fitan	Nayeem Bin Hammad
61	Tareekh-e-salateen Gujrat o Malwa	Hasan Bin Hasan Gujrati
62	Hindustan Ki Qadeem Islami Darsgahain	Abul Hasnath Nadvi
63	Oriental College Magazine 1940	Abul Hasnath Nadvui
64	Uqdud Durer Fi Alaamat-e-Al Mahdi- Al Muntazir (W.958 H)	Yousuf Ibn Ahmed
65	Lisanul Arab	Jamaluddin Bin Manzur, Afriqui (711 H)
66	Zadul Muttaqeen (W1003 H)	Abdul Haq Muhadis-e-DehAlvi
67	Najatur Rasheed	Abdul Qader Badayuni (1004 H)
68	Muaheb-e- Elaih (P.in Kanpur)	Husain Ibn Ali Waez Kashefi (910 H)
69	Maghzanul Karamat(Translation of Maadan-e- Jawaher)	Kareemuddin
70	Muntakhabatut Tawareekh	Abdul Qader Badayuni
71	Aaieen-e-Akberi	Abul Fazal (1101 H)
72	Miratul Sikandari(W.1020)	Sikander Bin Miohammed Bin Manjhu
73	Maadanul Jawaher	Abdul Qader Bin Shaik Ahmed Bin Multani
74	Mir'at-e-Ahmedi (W.1172 H)	Mirza Mohammed Hasan
75	Zaferul Wala Ba Muzafer wala	Abdullah Mohammed Bin Omer Makki
76	Tuhfa-e-Asna-e-Ashria	Shah Abdul Aziz Dehlavi (1239 H)
77	Nazhatul Khawatir	Abdul Haasi Bin Fakhruddinal Husaini
78	Al KItabul Muqaddus (Arabic),	---------- do------
79	Kitabul Muqaddus (Urdu)	-------------do----
81	Holy Bible	Abdul Hai Bin Fakhruddinal Husaini
82	Sanan-e-Ibn Majaa	Mohammed Bin Yazid Bin Majaa (273 H)
83	Tabqat-e-Ibnn Sa'ad	Mohammed Bin Sa'ad, Katibul Waqedi(230
84	Tafseer-e-Zahedi (W.519 H)	Imam Zahed Abu Nasar Ahmed Binal Hasan
85	Tajul Uroos	Syed Murtuza Zubaidi (1205 H)
86	Usl-e-musfa	Mirza Khuda Baksh
87	Jaama-e-Tirmizi	Abu Moosa Mohammed Bin Moosa Tirmizi

88	Uqrabul Mua'arid	Sayeedul Khoori Al Shartuni
89	Muntahi'ul Arab	Abdul Raheem Safipuri
90	Muheetul Heet	Batrusul Bustani (1305 H)
91	Nujoomul Mishkat	Siddiq bin Mohammed bin Zafer Makki
92	Izalatul Haqain Un Khilafatul Khulafa	Shah Waliullah Muhaddis-e-Dehklavi (1176
93	An Nihaya Fi Ghareebul Hadees wal asr	Ibnul Aseer Al Jazri(606 H)
94	Tafseer-e-Madarik	Hafiz Abdullah Bin Ahmed Bin Mhmood 710
95	Al Khasaes-e-Kubra	Jalaluddin Seoti (411 H)
96	AlWarful Wardi Fil Akhbarel Mahdi	-------- do ------
97	Mua'jjimul Baldan	Yaqoot Hamvi (626 H)
98	The Land of the Eastern Caliphate	G.L.Strange
99	Geography of Eastern Caliphate	Jameelur Rahman
100	Lam'at-e-Sharh-e-Mishkot	Abdul Haq Muhaddis-e-Dehalvi
101	Minhajul Sunnatul Nabuwat	Ahmed Bin Abdul Haleem Ibn Tamima (726
102	Shawahedul Nabuwat	Abdul Rahman Jami (898 H)
103	Shamaail-e-Tirmizi	Abu Eisa Tirmizi (279 H)
104	Al Fawedul Jaleela Alash Shamael	Mohammed Bin Qasim Haboos
105	Tareekh-e- Aouliaye-Gujrat (Translation of Mir'atul Ahmadi-886 H)	Syed Abu Zafer Nadvi
106	Al Rahmatul Mahdatul Ma'aroof	Nasrullah Bin Khaleelullah Bin Hibatullah
107	Al Kashif Sharh-e-Mishkot	Taibi (Husain Bin Mohd. Bin Abdullah (732 H
108	Umdatul Qari Sharh-e-Bukhari	Badruddinal Aini (885 H)
109	Fatawai Hadeesia	Ibn Hajral Haitami (973 H)
110	Al Dureral Muntashira Fil Ihadees-e-mashura	Jalaluddin Sioti
111	Kasshful Istelahatul Funoon(1158 H)	Mohammed Aala Ibn Ali Thanavi
112	Tazkera	Abul Kalam Azad
113	Mashaheer-e-Islam	Khaja Ibadullah Akhtar
114	Kimia-e-Sa'adat	Mohammed Ghizali (505 H)
115	Ash shifa	Qazi Aiyaz (544 H)
116	Sanan-e-Nisaai	Abu Abdula Rahman Nisaai (303 H)
117	Mirqatul Mufateh (Sharh-e-Mishkot)	Mulla Ali Qari (1016 H)
118	Sahieh Bukhaeri	Abu Abdullah Mohd. Bin Ismail (256 H)
119	Tareekh-e-Hundustan	Mohammed Zaakaullah
120	Al Faslil Milal	Ibn Hazam (456 H)
121	Aijazul Qur'an	Qazi Abu Baker Baqilani (404 H)
122	Darbar-e-Akbari	Mohammed Husain Azad
123	Tanqeed-e- Shairul Ajam	Mahmood Shirani
124	Muntakhabul Bab (1142 H)	Mir Mohammed Hashim Khafi Khan
125	Tareekh-e-Tabri	Mohammed Ibn Jareer Tabri (310 H)
126	Dastan-e-Ghum (1251 H)	Badrud Dowla
127	Aqaaed-e-Islam	Abdul Haq, Author of Haqqani
128	Mu'asirul Umara	Shah Nawaz Khan, Shamsamud Dowla (1171 H)
129	Hindustan Main Musalmanoun ka Nizam-e-Taleem wa Tarbiat	Manazir Ahsan Gilani
130	Tozak-e-Baberi (persian)	Mirza Abdul Raheem Khan Khanan (1036 H)
131	Tozak-e-Baberi (Turkish)	Baber Badshah (937 H)
132	Rouzatus Sifa	Mir Khu'wand (903 H)

133	Muasir-e-Raheemi	Abdul Baqi Nihavandi (1042 H)
134	Ansaabul Ashraaf	Abu Jafer Ahmed Ibn Mohd.Bin Jaber (279 H)
135	Qoul-e-Haq (Jubili No. 11 & 12/1946	Akber Shah Khan Najeebabadi
136	Jamia Jubili No. of Nov. and Dec/1946	------------do--------
137	Maghzan-e-Afghani(W.1020 H)	Khaja N aimatullah Bin Habeebulla Hervi
138	Say Dafter	Abul Fazal (1011 H)
139	Shairul Ajam	Shibli Numani
140	Tahzeebul Akhlaq	Sir Syed Ahmed Khan
141	Devan-e- Faizi	Abul Faiz Faizi (1004 H.)
142	Annorul Safer Akhbar Al Qurnan Ashir	Abdul Qader al Edroos (1038 H)
143	Padmawat	Malik Mohammed Jaisi
144	Malik Mohammed Jaisi,	Syed Kalab-e- Mustafa
145	--- Do---Nigar 12/1961	--------do-----
146	---- Do---Urdu Risala of July 1943	-------DO----
147	Bahr-e-Zakkhar	Wajihuddin Ashraf
148	Tareekh-e-Mahdavian	----—do----
149	Zikr-e-Wahdat	Peer Baksh Qamber Shahdad Zai
150	Tarjumai Tareekh-e-Sir John Melcom	Mirza Hairat
151	Khazana-e-Rasool Khani	Mohd. Faizullah Munshi wa Fazl-e-Ali Khan
152	Tareekh-e-Rasheeduddin Khani	Ghulam Imam Khan
153	George Nama	Mulla Feroz Bin Kaaus (1242 H)
154	Mir'atul Akhbaar	Mohammed Faizullah Munshi
155	Alamgir Nama	Mohd. Kazim Bin Mohd.Ameen Quzveni
156	Basateenuas Salateen (W 1240 H)	Mirza Ibrahim Zubairi
157	Nishan-e- Hyderi (1217 H)	Mir Husain Ali bin Syed Abdul QaderKirmani
158	Karnam-e-Hyderi (W.1263 H)	Abdul Raheem
159	Hamlaat-e-Hyderi (Trns. Of Karnam-e-Hydri	Shaik Ahmed Ali Gopamvi
160	Yadgaar-e-Makkhan Lal	Makkhan Lal
161	Gulzar-e-Aasafia (W 1260 H)	Hakeem Ghulam Husain Khan
162	Mahboobus Salateen	Mohammed Husain
163	Saulat-e-Afghani (W 1289 H)	Haji Zar Dar Khan of Karoli
164	Tareekh-e-Asaf Jahi	Mohammed Qader Khan Munshi
165	Khazanaa-e-Gowher-e-Shawar -	----------=-do-------
166	Waqaey Chanchaklguda	------------do------
167	Tareekh-e-Khurshid Jahi -	---------do------
168	History of India	Elliot
169	Hayat-e-Masih	Muzaffeer Husain Khan Sulaimani, Shah Abadi
170	Sihah Sitta Ki Pesheen Goyian	Khaja Hasan Nizami
171	Oriental College Magazine 2/ 1941	----------do-------
172	On Mahdis and Mahdiism	D.S.Margoulioth
173	Seerat-e-Ibn Hissham	Abu Mohd. AbdulMalik Bin Hissham (218H)
174	Devan-e-Hissan	Hazrat Hissan Bin Sabit (40 H)
175	Devan- Mansoob Ba Hazrat Ali Rz.	Hazrat Ali Rz. (Martyred 60 H)
176	Murawijul Zahab	Abul Hasan Ali Husain Bin Ali al Masoodi
177	Tareekh-e-Yaqoobi	Ahmed Bin Abi Yaqoob (240 H)
178	Sharh-e-Moota	Mohammed Bin Abdul Baqi Zarqani (1112 H
179	Musfa Sharh-e-Moota	Shah Waliuallah Muhaddis-e-Dehlavi

180	Aarizatal Ahwazi	Abu Baker Mohd. Ibnal Arabi al Maliki (542
181	Sharh-e-Tirmizi	---------------------do----------
182	Shurootul Aimmatul Khamsa	Hafiz Abu Baker Mohd. Bin Moosa Al Hazimi (584 H
183	Nazhatul Nazar Fi Touzih Najatul Fiker	Ibn Hajer Asaqalani (852 H)
184	Al Mustadrak	Hafiz Abu Abdulla Mohd. Bin Abdulla (405)
185	Abrazul Wahamul Maknoon	Ahmed Bin Mohammed Siddiq
186	Tahzeebut Tahzeeb	Ibn Hajer Asqalani
187	Risalatul Mahdi	Mulla Ali Qari (1016 H)
188	Meezanul Aitadal	Hafiz ShamsuddinMohd. Bin Ahmeduz Zahbi
189	Tafseer-e-Kasshaff	Abul Qasim Jarulla Mohd. Bin Omer Zamha
190	Tafseer-e-Baizavi	Qazi Nasiruddin Abu Sayeed Abdulla(685h)
191	Tafseer-e-Tabseerur Rahman	Ali Bin Ahmed al Mahaemi (835 H)
192	Tafseerul Jameul Bayan	Mohammed Ibn Jareer Tabri
193	Ahkaamul Qur'an	Imam Jassas (370 H)
194	Mualimul Tanzeel	Mohammadul Husain Bin Masoodul Bughvi
195	Talkhees	Zahbi
196	Tafseer-e-Roohul Muani	Aaloosi (1270 H)
197	Noorul Anwaar	Mulla Jeevan (1130 H)
198	Qamrul Aqmar Hashia Noorul Anwar	Mohammed Abdul Haleem
199	Sharh-e-Maqasid	Saaduddin Taftazani
200	Akhlaq-e-Nasiri	Naseeruddin Toossi
201	Minhajus Sunnatul Nabvia	Hafiz Ibn Tamima (728 H)
202	Manasib-e- Ghousia	Mohammed Sadeq Shahabi
203	Seeratun Nabi	Shibli Numani
204	Ad Dural Manshoor	Jalaluddibn Seoti
205	Tafseer-e-Safi	Mulla Mohsin Kashani (1091 H)
206	Ahsanal Wadia Fi Tarajim Ulemai Shia	Syed Mohammed Mahdi Khwansari
207	Kulliyat-e-Talib	Talib Amili (1035 H)
208	Al Istaiaab Fi Marifatal Ashaab	Ibn Abdul Bar Undlisi (230 H)
209	Bahrul Muaani	Syed Mohammed Ibn Jaferul Maliki
210	Hujjatul Baaligha	Shah Waliullah Muhaddis-e-Dehalvi
211	Hashia-e-Sharh-e- Mulla Jami	Mulla Hisamuddin (943 H)
212	Mukhtasirul Muaani	Sa'dudiin Taftazani
213	Asadul Ghaba Fl Marifata Ashaba	Ibn Aseer Jazri (238H)
214	Al Kaamil	----------do---------
215	Jazbul Quloob Ila Dayar-e-Mahboob	Abdul Haq Muhaddis-e-DEhlvi
216	Devan-e-Jareer	Abu Hazra Jareer Ibn Atita (111H)
217	Tazkiratul Mouzu aath	Mohammed Bin Therul Fitni
218	Hasibat Minul Sunnta Fi Ayyamul Sunnat	Abdul Haq Muhaddis-e-Dehlavi
219	Al Jawaherul Muazzam Fi Ziaratul Qabrul Mukkarram	Ibn HajrulHaitami (973 H)
220.	Hadeqwul Balagha	Shamsuddin (1183 H)
221	Farhang-e-Nizam	Syed Mohammed Ali, Preacher of Islam
222	Bahar-e-Ajam (W.1154 H)	Tek Chand Bahar
223	Sheereen Khusraow	Nizazmi Gaunjvi
224	Awariful Muarif	Shaik Shahabuddin Suharwardi (632 H)
225	Nathatul Uns	Mulla Abdul Rahman Jami

226	Zawarif-e-Sharh-e-Awarif	Shaik Ali Bin Ahmedul Muhaimi
227	Maktubat-e-Imam Rabbani	Shaik Ahmed Sar-e-Hindi (1032 H)
228	Masnad-e-Abu Dawood	Abu Dawood Tiyalsi
229	Sawaeqw-e-Muhrriqa	Ibn Hajr Haitami (973 H)
230	Tareekhul Khulafa	Jalaluddin Seoti
231	Dalael-e-Nabuwwat	Abu Nayeem Asfahani (444H)
232	Muntakhabul Lughat	Abdul Rasheed Tatvi
233	Hujjatul Balegha	Shah Waliullah Muhaddis-e-Dehlavi
234	Sikander Nama	Nizam Gunjvi
235	Kitab Ibn Seeayreen	Mohammed Ibn Seeayreen (!10 H)
236	Kitabul Isharaat	Khaleel Ibn Shaheen (872 H)
237	Al Itqan Fi Uloomul Furqan	Jalaluddin Seoti
238	Mu Habt-e-Uzma	Sirajuddin Ali Khan Arzoo
239	Nahjul Adub	Najmul Ghani Khan Rampuri
240	Hashi-e-Sharh-e-Jami	Abdul Rahman Asfaraini
241	Al Bahrul Muheet	Asseruddin Mohd. Abu Hayan Gharnati (745
242	Al Nadva Vol.2 No. 10	Published by Nadvah
243	Al Fouzul Kabeer Fi Usoolul Tafseer	Shah Waliullah Muhaddis-e-Dehlavi
244	Tareekh-e-Khurshi Jahi	-------------
245	Mughniul Labaib Un Kutubul Ahareeb	Jamaluddin Ibn Hussham (763 H)
246	Sharh-e-Mulla Jami	Mulla Abdul Rahman Jami
247	Qamoos	Mujadduddin Mohd. Bin Yaqoob (817 H)
248	Mukarer Rat-e-Qur'an	Shamsuddin Mohd. Kirmani (786 H)
249	Ahya al M aita Ba fazael-e- Ahlal Bait	Jalaluddin Seoti
250	Masalikul Hanfa	Jalaluddin Seoti
251	Bushra	Inayet Rasool Chiryakoti
252	Al Futoohatil Makkia	Mohiuddin Ibn Arabi (638 H)
253	Majmaul Bahaar	Mohammed Bin Taher Patni
254	Sharh-e-Najbatul Fikr	M ulla Ali Qari
255	Fatawa-e-Alamgiri	Mulla Nizam and other
256	Talbees-e-Iblees	Ibn Jozi
257	Takmeelul Ieman and Taqviat-e-Ieman	Abdul Haq Muhaddis-e-Dehlavi
258	Fathul Bari	Ibn Hajr Asqalani (852 H)
260	Tafseer Tavielat-e-Qur'an	Abdul Razzaq Bin Jamal, Kashi Samarqandi
261	Al Kabriatul Ahmar	Abdul Wahab Shirani(973 H)
262	Takmila-e-Izalatul Ghain Un Basaratul Ain	Hyder Ali Faizabadi (12299 H)
263	Al Isha'a Fil Isharatul Sha'a	Mohd. Abdul Rasool Barazanji (1103 H)
264	Hajjul Kirama Fe Aasaril Qiama	Nawab Siddiq Hasan Khan
265	Al Istasqala Khabarad Wa lil Maghrib al Aqsaa	By Shaik Ahmed Bin Khalidun Nasiri
266	Sarwe Azad	Mir Ghulam Ali Azad
267	Dafiatul A'yan	Ibn Khalkan(681c H)
268	Al Talveeh alal Touzeah	Sa'aduddin Taftazani
269	Tahzeebul Kalaam	Yaqoob Abu Yousuf Al Baniani
270	Dastan-e-Jehan	Abu Rija Mohd. Zaman Khan
271	Safernama-e-Misro Roomo Shaam	Shibli Numaani
272	Tareekh-e-Ibn Khaldoon	IIbn Khaldoon
273	Sahi Muslim Mai Sharh-e-Akmaal	Ibn Khaldoon (808 H)

274	Shmamatul Anber Fi Maward Fil Hind Minal Asr	Mir Ghulam Ali Azxad
275	Ittehaful Nabla	Nawab Siddiq Hasan Khan (1307 H)
276	Kitabul Islam	Nazeerul Haq
277	Fawaedul Fikr Fil Imamul Mhdi Al Muntazir	Ibn Yousuf Almuqdasi Al Hanbali
278	Sharas Sunnat	Husain Bin Masood ul Bughv (516 H)
279	Shazratuil Zahab Fil Akhbar Min Zahab	Abul Falah Abdul Hai Al Hunbali (1089 H)
280	Siraj-e-Muneer Sharh	Shaik Mustafa Ibn Ahmerdul Azizi(1045 H)
281	Kitabul Tayassir Ba Sharh Jameus Saghir	Shaik Abdul Raoof Al Munadi (1039 H)
282	Koukab-e-Muneer Sharh-e-Jama-e-Saghir	Mohd. Bin Abdul Rahman AlQami
283	Hasti Ila A'male-Tawareekhun Nabi w All	Shaik Abbas Qumi
284	Seerath-e-Ibn Hishshaam	Abu Mohd.Abdul Malik B in Hishshaam
285	uslul Jamal	Abu Mohammed Abdul Malik Bin Hishsham
286	Akhbarul Hamqi Wal Mughalafeen	Ibn Jozi (597 H)
287	Tabqat-e-Kubra	Abdul Wahab Sharani (73 H)
288	Mirqatul Masood	Jalaluddin Seoti
289	Ta'nur Rimah	Syed Mohammwed Bin Syed Dildar Ali
290	Tashiadul Mutaeen	Syded Mohammed Quli Kanturi (1260 H)
291	Hidayetur Rashhed	Khaleel Ahmed Saharanpuri
292	Risala-e-Jamal	----------------
293	Kutubkhana-e-Iskandaria	Shibli Numani
294	Ash'ar Mushir-e-Islam	Rafeeq Bukul Azam
295	Subhatul Mirjan	Mir Ghulam Ali Azad Bilgrami
296	Juamaul Kalam	Khaja Gaisoo Daraz (835 H)
297	Burhanul Muasir (W1004 H)	Syed Ali Tabataba
298	Khataerus Quds	Khaja Gaisoo Daraz
299	Al Kashf Fil Mujaweza Hazal Ummat anil Alif	By Jalaluddinn Seoti
300	Tafseer-e- Siddiqi	Abdul Qadeer Hasrat Siddiqi
301	Farogh-e-Kafi	Abu Jafer Mohd. Bin Yaqoob Klini (329 H)
302	Bajarul Anwar	Mulla Baqar Majlisi (329 H)
303	Tazkera-e-Qartabi	Shamsudduin Mohd. Al Qartabi (678 H)
304	Tarjumanul Qur'an	Abul Aalaa Moudodi
305	Tafseer-e- Bahr-e- Muwaj	Shahabuddin Doulatabadi
306	Gharaeb-e-Qur'an wa Ragha-e-Qur'an	Nizamuddibn Hasan Naishapuri
307	Qasisul Anbiah	Ghulam Ali Bin Inayetullah
308	Al Taseer FIl Tafseer	Abul Qasim Abdul Karim Qasheeri (465 H)
309	Al Fatavial Azizia	Shah Abdul Aziz Dehlavi
310	Majmuatul Risaelus Khams	Abdul Hai Faringi Mahli
311	Rajarun Nass Alal Inkar Hadees UIBn Abbas	-------d0 -------
312	Dafeul Waswas un Ibn Abbas	---------DO--------
313	Imtenaun Nazeer	Fazl-e-Haq Khairabadi (1278 H)
314	Tahqeequl Fatwa Fi Abtalul Taghvi	--------do-----
315	Akhbar-e-Sanadeed (Rampur)	Najmul Ghani Khan Rampuri
316	Nuqoosh-e-Makateeb Number	---------------
317	Irshadus Sari, BA Sharh-e-Bukhari	Shahbuddin Qastalani (D 923 H.)
318	Shahab-e-Muarriqa	Asad Makki (1164 H.)
319	Risala-e-Nigar ,Vol 74, No. 4	Niyuaz Fateh Puri
320	Muqaddam-e-Tarekh-e-Tabri	M.J.De Goete

321 Qateebul Ikhwan — Mohammed Idrees Bilgirami

322 Majmual Nafaes (About Persian Poetys) — Sirajuddin Ali Khan Arzoo

323 District Gazateer of Unitred Provinces Vol.28 — ----------------

324 Lisanul Muslameen Fi Ruddal Masihata Wal Kalimi (Printed Asfahan 1349 H. — Shaik Abdul Husain Najfi

325 Farhang-e-Nizam Vol.3 — Islamic Preacher Aqaa Mohammed Ali

326 Masnad-e-Juz-e-Salis(Hadees-e-Gharbi) — Abu Ya'li Moosli (307 H)

327 Injeel-e-Mati — -------------

328 Urdu Tarjuma-e-Qur'an (Printed Lahore) — Mohammed Ali Lahori

329 The Times Gazateer of the World — G.G.Chisholum

330 Iqbal Nama Qalmi, Persian. — -------------

331 Amal-e-Saleh (Shah Jehan Nama) — Published by Asiatic Society of Bengal

332 Islamic Studies — ----------

333 Tareekh-e-Adil Shah — Noorullah

334 Waqiat-e-Abdul Karim (1289 H) — -----------------

335 Tareekh-e-Dawoodi, published by Aligadh University — Abdullah

336 Muqaddam-e-Anwarul Bari — Syed Ahmad Raza Bijnouri

337 Ijala nafia Arabic (QWalmi) — Shah Abdul Aziz Dahalvi

338 Ifadatul Ifham — Mohammed Anwarullah

339 TayassirulAQari, Sharh-e-Bukhari — ------------

340 Nizhatul Abrar Fil Asami wa Manasib-e-Akhbar-------------

341 Addinul Yasir — Published by Saqafat-e-Islamia, Lahore

342 Al Kaashif (Arabic, Qalmi)min Haqaeq — Taibi (739 H)

343 Masnavi –e-Moulana Rome — --------------

344 Haft Tamasha-e- Qateel — Mirza Mohammed Hasan Qateel

345 Journal of the Central Institute iof Islamic Research Karachi

346 Al Tauzih Maet Talveeh — Published in Egypt

347 Al Jama-e-Saghir FI Ahadees-e-Basheerun Nazeer (Arabic, Qalmi)

348 Maqdoom Zadagan-e- Fatahpur — -------------

349 Mu'aarif of July 1963 AD — --------------

350 Maktubat-e-Shaik Ahmad Sar-e-Hindi (Pwersian, Qalmi)

351 Urdu Translation of Mujaddad-e-Alif-e-Sani — Printed at Lahore

352 Tazkera-e- Ulema-e- Hind (Nowal kishore) — Rahman Ali

353 Tarjuma—e- Ulema-e-Hind (Karachi) — Mohammed Ayyub Qadri

354 Shaik Abdul Quddoos Gangohi and his Teachings,(Published at Karachi)

355 Risala-e-Ek Rozi (publkished by Matba- e-Farooqi) — Mohammed Ismail Dahalvi

356 Faravi Bur Aqaed-e-Wahabia, Dev Band — Shah Ahmed HusainKanpuri

357 Anwar-e-Satiah, Matba-e-Nayeemi, Muaradabad — Abdus Sami Kanpuri

358 Hisamul Harmain (Printed in Lahore) — Khaleel Ahmed Ambaitwi

359 Baraheen-e-Qatia (Taba Hilali , Ilahbad — ---------- do ---------

360 Aqrabul Muiwarid, Printed at Bairoot ---- — -----------

361 Tajul Urooas printed at Egypt — -------------

362 Albustan Printed in Bairoot — Abdullah Albustani

363 Taqviatul Ieman printedat Kamal Printing Press — Mohd. Ismail Dehlavi

364 Siratul Mustaqeem (Printed at Matba Hidayetullah) — -----do--------

365 Al Kaukabutul Ash Habia — Printed at Kalimi Press

366 Atbul Bayan Radd-e-Taqviatul Ieman — Mohd. Nayeemuddin Muradabadi

367	Minhajul Sunnathun Nabuwwat	Printed in Egypt
368	Mubahasa-e-Shahjahanpur	Mohammed Qasim Nanuthvi
369	Seeratun Nbi and Mustashriqain	abdul Haleem Ahaerari
370	Talmeezul Nass	Mohammed Qasim Nanuthvi
371	Safarus Saadaat	Abdul HAaq Muhaddiss-e-Dehlavi
372	Hajjul Akrama Fi Asaar-e-Qiamat	Shahjehani , Bhopal
373	Ruhul Muaani	Printed Emarate Bilani
374	Kitabul Fitan	Nayeem Bin Hammad
375	------------Do-------Printed In Arabic	Ibn Abi Sheeba
376	Asbabul Nuzool-e-Qur'an	------------
377	Tareekh-e-Habeeb Ilah	printed inMajeedi mKanpuri
378	Hujjatul Islam	Printed in Easim Press
379	Monthly Tajjalli, Sep. & Oct. 1965	Aamir Osman i
380	Mazaher-e-Haq	Printed at Nowal Kishore
381	Usaoolush Shashi	Nizmuddibn Shashi
382	Tazkeratul Mouzooaat	Idaratut Tabal Munira Egypt
383	Rouzatul Ahbab	------------
384	Translatrion of Tareekh-e-Sir John Melcam	----------------
385	Sharh-e-Qseeda Banth Saa'ad	Allama Abu Mohammed Jamal
386	Jamassaghir, Arbic, Qalmi	Jalaluddin Seoti
387	Tareekh-e-Shiraz-e-Hind, Juanpur	-----------
388	Encyclopedia of Religion and Ethics	James Hastuings
389	Waqae-e-Shoorish-e-Afghanan	Lala Brijnath Dehalvi
390	Ujala-e-Nafi'aa	Shah Abdul Aziz Dehlavi
391	Tuzak-e-Jehangiri, Qalmi	----------
392	Iqbala Nama	---------
393	Mah-e-Naw	Karachi
394	Amal-e-Saleh	Mohammed Saleh Kumbooh
395	Tareekh-e-Ali Adil Shah	Nurullah
396	Mhnam—e- Qoumi Zaban Karachi	-----------
397	Aswa-e-Sahaba	Abdu Salaam Nadvi
398	Ifadatul Ifhaam	Mohammed Anwarulla
399	Tareekh-e-Dawoodi	Abdullah
400	Tajdeed-e- Ih'a-e-Deen	Abul Aalaa Moududi
401	Kitab—e-Ahkamul Qur'an	Qazi Abu Baker Mohd. Bin Abdullah, Baban
402	Ajjam-e-Saguir Min Hdeesul Basheerun Nazeer	Jalaluddin Seoti
403	Lughat-e-Alamgiri	Mohammded Fazil Khan
404	Sanan-e-Dar-e-Qatni Mat-ta'leequl Mughni	Abul Hasan Bin Ali bun Omarul Darelqatni
405	Al-Frooq	Shibli Nu'mani
406	Ghiyasul Lughat	Ghiyasuddin Rampuri
407	Noorul Lughat	Noorul Kakori
408	Risala-e-Mu'arif	Volume of July 1964
409	Mahnama Tajalli	Volume 1964 & 1965
410	Tareekh-e-Farishta Sceond Volume	Mohammed Qasim Farishta
411	Journal of the Central Institute of Islamic Research, Karachi(Pakistan).	

Siraj-ul-Absar

Bismillahir Rahmaanir Rahiim

Siraj-ul-Absar

Preamble

All praise is for Allah Most High Who held the appointment of the *Imam-e-'Adil* as goodness for this *ummat* [The Muslim Community], raised his mention to unprecedented heights and chose him for the governance of this community. Hence, he has been raised to heights both in this world and in the Hereafter. I praise Him in the morning and evening. And I send salutations to Hazrat Prophet Muhammad[SLM] who is the leader of all the Firsts and the Lasts. He is the selected among the most selected [and distinguished] people and is among the loftiest descendants of Marrah, son of Ka'ab, son of Lui, son of Ghalib, and the pure and genuine Arab race. And (I send salutations) on his descendants and on his wives who are the women of rank, honour and dignity, and who have been mentioned in the book of Allah Most High, the Quran. And in whose favour the following Quranic Verse has been revealed: *"...And Allah only wishes to remove all abomination from you, ye members of the Family and to make you pure and spotless."*[8] And salutations on the Companions[RZ] of Prophet[SLM] who are embellished with the Virtuous Manners of the Prophet[SLM] and adorned with his cherished characteristics [and salutations] most particularly on the Perfect *Imam* whose superiority has been established in the galaxies of this universe and whose strands of equity have been drawn across the stars of the sky. No praises are worthy of consideration unless their adornment is centered on the blessed *zath* [nature, essence] of the Imam[AS]. And no dignity can be discussed unless its superiority is centered on the sacred zath [nature, essence] of the Imam[AS]. And no trait of character can be mentioned unless its elucidation and beauty is centered on the praised *zath* [nature, essence] of the Imam[AS]. And no illuminated condition is considered to be worthy of grandeur unless the manifestation of its arguments reverts to his *zath* [nature, essence]. This is the Mahdi[AS] who had been promised to be sent during the Last Era.

After the praises (for Allah Most High) and salutations (to Hazrat Prophet Muhammad[SLM] and Hazrat Imam Mahdi Al-Mau'ood[AS]), be it known that when I saw the tract which has come from Makkah-e-Muazzamah, and is associated with the Sheikh who is known as Sheikh Ali Muttaqi. The title of this tract is *Ar-Rad.*[9] Allah Most High may have it rejected as its name is manifest. I have decided that I would write the refutation or rebuttal of this tract, because I have seen at various places his deviation from the Truth. He has written things without any certainty and his sayings are without *iman* [Faith]. And I have given my tract the title of *Siraj al-*

---

[8] Quran, S.33: 33 AYA.
[9] *Ar-Rad* means rejected; turned down.

Absar li-raf'al-zulm 'an- ahl-al-Inkar [Lamp of the Sighted to remove the Veils of Darkness from the Eyes of the People of Denial.]

[The initial writing of the tract, *Ar-Rad* is as follows:]

In the name of Allah, Most gracious, Most Merciful.

He [Muttaqi] says:

All praises are for Allah Most High Who is the Lord of both the worlds and salutations for our leader Hazrat Prophet Muhammad[SLM] and his descendants and his Companions[RZ]. And after praises for Allah and encomiums for Hazrat Prophet[SLM], this tract which I have titled as *Ar-Rad* is in refutation of those people who ordain and decree that Hazrat Mahdi Al-Mau'ood[AS] has come and gone. Allah Most High may bless you. There is no doubt that the existence of the Mahdi Al-Mau'ood[AS] is proved by the Traditions of Hazrat Prophet Muhammad[SLM] and by the *aasar* [the sayings of the Companions[RZ]]. These Traditions are more than three hundred. And then there is a sect in the cities and towns of India that has the belief regarding a person who passed away about fifty years ago that he is the Promised Mahdi.

We say: The critic has taken unnecessary liberties in quoting the Arabic passage. In other words, he has written يعتقدون فى شخص مات (...believe that a person who died...). There is no need for the word فى . It should have been written like this: يعتقدون شخصا مات

He says: And the obvious Traditions contradict it.

We say: This saying of the critic is because of his flawed view of conditions, ranks and meanings of the Traditions: whether they are correct or infirm and faulty; strong or weak; in factual or metaphorical language. It is also because the critic has not taken care to consider the beliefs of the *mutaqaddimin* [people of the first few centuries of Islam] regarding clinging to Traditions [*tamassuk-bil-hadees*]. They have held that a person who does not have the status of a *Mujtahid* is not permitted to cling to the Traditions [*tamassuk-bil-hadees*]. Therefore it has been stated in the books of principles that for an ordinary person clinging to Traditions is not permitted. And the status of the person who presents proof but has not reached the rank of the *mujtahid* is that of an *'ami* [common man]. In the margins [*Hashia*] of the book *Husami*, it is mentioned under the discussion of *ijma'* [consensus] that a person who is not a *sahib-e-rai* [man of opinion] and *Sahib-e-ijtihad* [person entitled to interpretat Islamic Law] is decreed to be an ordinary man. This goes to show that the person, who draws conclusions from the Prophetical Traditions in spite of not reaching the rank of a *mujtahid*, is, like the Sheikh [Muttaqi], ignorant about the religion of the pious predecessors (*Salaf-us-Saliheen*).

I have myself seen eleven Prophetical Traditions in which it is said that Mahdi[AS] and Esa[AS] would appear together. Some of these Traditions say that Esa[AS] would lead the prayers and some of them talk of Mahdi[AS] leading the prayers. Despite the presence of these Traditions, Allamah Tuftazani^{RA} has clearly stated in the book, *Sharah-e-Maqasid*, that they will not appear together and that neither would follow the other in ritual prayers.

> It is stated that Esa^{AS} would follow the Mahdi or *vice versa*. But this is something that has no basis or authority. Hence, one should not trust such sayings.

Hence, O Just Man! Know that the experts in the knowledge of Traditions are perplexed in pinpointing and ascertaining the Mahdi on a definite and certain issue in such a way that there remains no possibility of contradiction. They have come to this conclusion after a consensus that he [the Mahdi] is among the descendants of Bibi Fatima^{RZ} [the daughter of Prophet Muhammad^{SLM}] and that he would be sent to help the religion. Hence, Imam Bayhaqi has written in his book, *Shu'b-ul-Iman*, that:

> People have differed in the matter of Mahdi^{AS}. Hence, one group has refrained and assigned its knowledge to its Knower [that is, God]. This group holds the faith that he [Mahdi] will be among the descendants of Fatima^{RZ}, the daughter of the Messenger of Allah^{SLM}, that Allah Most High would send him into the world when He wills and that He will commission him to help His religion.

O Just Man! Look at the saying of Bayhaqi that 'one group has refrained'. This refrainment becomes manifest when arguments clash and where there is no preference for one argument over the other. Sheikh Ali Muttaqi, who has authored this tract, *Ar-Rad*, had himself written in a long tract earlier, quoting the *Imams* of *Hadis* [experts in the science of Prophetical Traditions], that:

> Qurtubi has stated in his *Tazkira*, in respect of a long story, that the statement that Mahdi will emerge from the *Masjid-e-Aqsa* has no basis.

Hence, see O Just Man! Despite his being expert and most proficient in the science of Traditions, Imam Qurtubi has written in respect of the attribute of Mahdi^{AS} and his emergence that this has no basis. This shows that the critics of the science of Traditions are puzzled in identifying the Mahdi.

It is narrated by Ibn Manada that Ka'ab Ahbar has said that there would be twelve Mahdis and after that Esa Roohullah^{AS} would descend and kill Dajjal [Anti-Christ]. This is quoted from the book, *Sharah-Ghayat-ul-Ahkam*. And then, Sheikh Najibuddin Abu Muhammad Waiz Dahlavi has written in his book, *Madar-ul-Fuzala*, that the co-existence of Mahdi^{AS} and Esa^{AS} is an issue of the Shia *Mazhab* [religion or school of thought]. If somebody has any doubt in accepting our assertion, he may refer to the said book.

Further, in the same book Sheikh Najibuddin writes that Tuftazani had written in the book, *Sharah-e-Aqaid*, that Esa^{AS} would lead the people in ritual prayers and Mahdi^{AS} will follow Esa^{AS}. However, he retracted that saying and has written in the book, *Sharah-e-Maqasid*, that:

It is said that Esa^AS would follow the Mahdi^AS in ritual prayers or that the Mahdi^AS will follow Esa^AS in ritual prayers. This is something that has no *sanad* [authority]. And it should not be relied upon.

Hence, in describing these differences [of opinion], our objective is to let the Just Man know that the identification of the Mahdi^AS is not possible based on any one thing, because we find no substance in this subject that leads to finality and certainty. Then, how can anybody say that the obvious Traditions oppose our Imam Hazrat Syed Muhammad^AS of Jaunpur?

O brother! Know that even if the *mujtahidin* [jurist entitled to independent opinion or judgment] had explained [regarding the Mahdi], their explanation would have only been their presumption. And if the things they mentioned were found in Mahdi^AS, then their *ijtihad* [legal reasoning] would have been accepted as correct. Otherwise, their error would have come to light. However, when they have not given any explanation on the subject [of Mahdi^AS], how can it be permissible for a *muqallid* [imitator/follower of a *mujtahid*] to draw conclusions from the Prophetical Traditions? If one were to ask, when in a given period of time there is no *mujtahid*, what are we expected to do? The reply to this would be that we would go to the person who is superior to all of us and act according to his opinion. Hence, it is said that when a new issue arises and we need to solve it, and no saying of any *mujtahid* is available, we will accept the saying of the person who is superior to others at the given time.

And there is no doubt whatsoever that during the period of the Mahdi^AS and his companions they were the most superior of all people of the period and no one else. Now, there remain the arguments that prove the *Mahdaviat-e-maujooda* [the present *mahdaviat*] in favour of the *zath* [essence or nature] of the person whose *tasdiq* [affirmation and confirmation] we have performed. We will deal with them shortly, Allah the Most High willing!

Doubts regarding *Tavil*

He [Muttaqi] says: Most often these people explain the Prophetical Traditions on the basis of their opinions, as they do in respect of the Quranic Verses in order to prove their objective.

We say: We do not explain the Traditions and the Quranic Verses in accordance with our opinions. On the contrary, when our opponents consider themselves to be *mujtahidin* and confront us with their arguments on the basis [of their opinions] of the Traditions, we too assume their (*mujtihidin's*) status and give a fitting, rational and traditionally reported reply. And if they accuse us of any prohibited matter, we counter their argument by explaining them in the same way. Allah willing, we will deal with this matter shortly.

He [Muttaqi] says: The *ulama* know that *tavil* [interpretation] is acceptable only when the text is of a person who is free from error [*kalam-e-ma'soom*] and it is not possible to accept the manifest meaning because of its impossibility.

We say: The critic has written these words :

ان التاويل لا يسوغ الا اذا كان الكلام المعصوم لم يمكن حمل العبارة علىٰ ظاهرها للزوم المحال منه

However, the correct text, free of presumption and interpretation, is like this الا اذا كان الكلام المعصوم لم يمكن حمل العبارته علىٰ ظاهرها [except when the speech of a person who is free from error is such that its text cannot be interpreted in its manifest form]. It means that the innocent speech should not be such that it is interpreted as its manifest meaning. Adding the condition of *Ismat* [being free from error] to the speech is also not correct. Instead, he should have said it like this الا اذا كان الكلام المقتضى للتوجيه لم يمكن حمل العبارته [(*tavil* can be done) when the text requires additional instruction and its manifest meaning cannot be taken] so that it includes the speeches of the saints [of Allah] also. This point is evident from what the Sheikh himself has written at the end of his tract that, "if the person concerned is abstinent and strictly follows the *Shari'at* and if his speech can be interpreted to be in accordance with the *Shari'at*, that too can be interpreted [as *tavil*]."

Further, his saying لم يمكن [...it is not possible to accept the manifest meaning ...] too is not correct. This is so because, the *ulama*, at some places, in reverence to the *mazhab* [religion] of the *Mutaqaddimin*, have allowed *tavil* to be done without any necessity. If this had not been their *mazhab* [religion], they would not have interpreted the hadees الخلافة من بعدى ثلثون سنة [after me *Khilafat* (Caliphate) is for thirty years] as the perfect *Khilafat* wherein there was no dissidence and there was no disobedience of the Messenger[SLM]. This kind of *Khilafat* would subsist for thirty years. After this, it would exist at times and would not exist at other times. This interpretation became necessary simply because the *mutaqaddimin* [ancients] had applied the term '*Khulafa*' [Caliphs] on some of the Abbasid Imams and Marwani rulers, like Umar bin Abd-ul Aziz[RA], even though there was no need for deviating from the concerned Tradition. But according to the saying of the Sheikh [Muttaqi] these people should have been called the lords, nobles and kings.

And the Prophet[SLM] told Ammar bin Yasir[RZ], 'Soon a rebel group will kill you.' This *hadis* has been interpreted by some *ulama* in a very farfetched manner. Thus it is written in the book, *Sharah-e-Tajreed:*

> The presumption would be that the rebel group would purport to mean the people who demanded the revenge for the blood of Usman[RZ]; and this was the *tavil* despite the fact that Ali[RZ] had accused Muawiyah[RZ] and his followers as the rebel group. He had said, 'Our brothers had rebelled against us.' He then issued orders that were commensurate with the crime of rebellion, because rebels are those people who extricate themselves from the obedience of the *Imam-e-Haq* [the incontrovertible leader]. What was the need for them to

resort to this deviant interpretation? And they resorted to it to avoid the use of the word 'rebel' against the Companions[RZ]. The word 'rebellion' is such that if applied to the Companions[RZ], it would deprive them of their attribute of *adl* [justice]. Some *ulama* have said that the word 'rebel' cannot be applied to those companions[RZ] who have erred in their *ijtihad* [exercise of judgment]. Whereas Prophet Muhammad[SLM] has clearly defined the rebels. [Prophet Muhammad[SLM] had told Ammar bin Yasir that 'Soon a rebel group would kill you'].

Hence, when our opponents present Traditions against us, we too interpret them in the best manner we can so that it is favorable before the men of justice in such a way that mistakes and errors are not attributed to the person who has the capability to be the Mahdi[AS]. We will deal with the arguments shortly, Allah willing. And our *tavil* is not beyond reason and possibility.

It is reported in the *Musnad* of Ahmad ibn Hanbal by Abdullah ibn Haris, that:

> When returning from Suffain, I was walking along with Muawiyah and 'Amr bin 'Aas. Abdullah ibn 'Amr told his father, "O my dear father! Did you not hear the Prophet[SLM] telling 'Ammar, 'Alas! O ibn Samiah! A rebel group will kill you.'" 'Amr told Muawiyah, "Are you not listening to what he is saying?" Then Muawiyah said, "We always blame each other and you people say that we have killed him. He was killed by those people who had brought him with them." [Upto the end of the narration].

O Just Man! See the interpretation of the Companions[RZ]! We do not resort to such interpretation!

Mahdi[AS] will fill the earth with equity and justice

He [Muttaqi] says: The interpretation of these people [the Mahdavis] is like this: In this *hadis*, it has come that Mahdi will fill the earth with justice from east to west. [They say that] if even one person accepts the obedience of the Mahdi, the objective will be achieved, because *insan* [human being] is *Alam-e-Kabir* [macrocosm]. Hence, see their open disavowal! Which prohibited matter had the text of the hadis demanded that they needed this interpretation?

We say: I have not heard this interpretation from my contemporaries. Nor have we heard it from our non-contemporaries. No such narrative has reached us from them. I do not know wherefrom did the Sheikh [Muttaqi] get wind of it. Why do we need this kind of an interpretation? Instead, to counter the allegation of our opponent [the Sheikh], there is so much ample material in the *hadis* that it is not easy to remember and list them. [That is, we have a large number of proofs. Why do we need this *tavil* (interpretation)?] Perhaps this argument has reached the Sheikh from those people who are neither the followers of the Mahdavis, nor are they reliable. Hence, accusing the community on the basis of the word of a person who is neither well-known as a just man nor as a man of piety, is not justified.

Be it known that the objective of the Sheikh [Muttaqi] in bringing this *hadis* ان المهدى يملاء الارض كلها قسطا و عدلا كما ملئت جورا و ظلما [verily the Mahdi will fill the earth with justice as it is filled with oppression and tyranny] here is to show that oppression and tyranny will be completely eradicated from the earth; and since this did not happen during the lifetime of that person who claimed that he was the Mahdi^{AS}; hence, they say, he is not the Mahdi^{AS}.

I say that if the meaning of the *hadis* is taken to be this way, then it is contrary to the Quran and the *sahih hadis* [correct Traditions]. From among them, is the saying of Prophet^{SLM} that is narrated by Sawban^{RZ}:

> The Messenger of Allah^{SLM} said, 'When the sword is placed in my *ummat* [community], it will not be lifted from them till the Day of Judgement.'

Hence, which period would it be when the entire earth will be filled purely by justice and equity? This is so because the fight with the sword will be between the people of the justice and the people of oppression and tyranny. It will be between the people of the Truth and the people of the non-Truth. Hence, it becomes known that oppression and tyranny will never be completely eliminated from the earth.

Further, the saying of Prophet^{SLM} is that 'a group from my *ummat* will always fight for the Truth and will be dominant till the Day of Judgement.' This Tradition is in *Muslim* as narrated by Jabir Ibn Abdullah^{RZ}.

Hence, know that the fighting by the group of the Truth gives proof that the other group would be that of *batil* [Falsehood], oppression and tyranny. Is there a greater oppression and tyranny than fighting with the people of the Truth? And according to the wording of the Tradition, this killing will continue till the Day of Judgement. Hence, it is evident that the filling of the earth with justice and equity completely eradicating oppression and tryranny is an impossibility. The person who adheres to the meaning of the hadis [that the Sheikh holds] is certainly ignorant.

From these contentions is that which Imam Zahid says under the command of Allah: "...O Jesus! I will take thee and raise thee to Myself..."¹⁰ :

> The Prophet^{SLM} has informed that Esa^{AS} will come down from the Heaven, even as Dajjal [Anti-Christ] will emerge and roam over the whole world. Then there will be famine. Work will become very difficult. [That is, the condition will deteriorate extremely]. And the *muminin* will assemble in Makkah and Madina. And Dajjal the accursed will reach the whole world, except Makkah and Madina. When he intends to enter Makkah, Esa^{AS} will come down from heaven in Makkah. He will perform the morning [pre-dawn] ritual prayers with a few *muminin* [faithful] in congregation. Then he will leave along with

10 Quran, S.3:55 AYA.

the few *muminin* to fight Dajjal. [Here the speech of Imam Zahid comes to an end.]

See, O Just Man! If at the time of the emergence of the *Dajjal*, had Mahdi^AS been the king of the whole world, the *Dajjal* will not be the master of the horizons. And if the *Dajjal* were to become the master of the whole world and were to spread oppression and injustice all over the world during the lifetime of the Mahdi^AS, then how can the earth be filled with justice and equity after eradicating the oppression and injustice? And which oppression would be greater than that of the *Dajjal*?

Prophet Muhammad^SLM has said about the *Dajjal* that:

> He would spread tumult and disturbance on the right side and on the left side [of the face of earth]! O the servants of Allah! Be steadfast on your religion!

Hence, do justice! Allah May bless you with His Mercy! In the face of so many contentions, how can the meaning of the [said] *hadis* be as you have understood?

And besides these contentions, there is the command of Allah Most High:

> "...And We have put enmity and spite among themselves till the Day of Resurrection..."[11]

Know that the existence of enmity and spite among themselves till the Day of Resurrection proves that they are the oppressors and perpetrators of injustice. Then know that the oppression with respect to its meaning of "usage of a thing inappropriately" is included in *zulm-'alal-ghair* [oppression against others] like the killing or the usurpation of things over which one does not have a right, beating, swearing and abusing, causing injury or hurting. It also includes *zulm-'alan-nafs* [oppression of the self] and that is infidelity and all kind of sinfulness. Hence, how can the eradication of the very root of all kinds of *zulm* [oppression] from the face of the earth be possible? And the *hadis* does not give any evidence as to which kind of *zulm* from among the various kinds of *zulm* is meant here.

Under the same Quranic Verse, it is mentioned in *Madarik*:

> All of them would be in disagreement with one another forever and their hearts will be diverse. There would be no conformity among them, nor would they help each other.

And then there is the Command of Allah:

> "Had thy Lord pleased, He would have pressed all mankind to form but one community [ummah]. But the differences will continue among them even then, (because of the freedom of action vouchsafed to man). Only those deserving the Mercy of thy Lord will not deviate (from the straightway)—to follow which man hath been created..."[12]

---

[11] Quran, S. 5:64 SAL.
[12] Quran, S. 11:118 and 119 SAL.

Hence, the Quranic Verse bears witness that Allah Most High did not intend to make the whole mankind as one community [*ummah*], and, therefore, He did not make it one community. And the saying of Allah Most High that differences would prevail among them explains that no period of time will be free of differences between the people of the Truth and the people of Falsehood. How, then, can it be imagined that oppression will vanish from the face of the earth in all its kinds, denominations, shades and manifestations? Hence, whoever specifies a particular kind of *zulm* [oppression] without any reason for it being specific, it should be understood that this is his whim (or personal opinion) [and not the truth].

Then again, know, O Just Man that the filling the earth with justice and equity is stated as a simile that has been given to compare with oppression and injustice. This simile can be of two kinds: either it is *Tashbih-fil-kaifiy'yat* [simile in its state or condition] or it is *Tashbih-fil-kamiy'yat* [simile in its quantity]. If it is *tashbih-fil-kaifiy'yat*, it is *musallam* [accepted]. In other words, as there is oppression and injustice among the people of the earth, the Mahdi[AS] will be capable of establishing justice and equity in that part of the earth. And the *hadis* does not give any indication that he would establish justice and equity in the whole or a large part of the earth.

However, if it is the *Tashbih-fil-kamiy'yat* [simile in quantity] and if it purports to mean those people who are filled with oppression and injustice, then it is unacceptable because of the contentions that we have already mentioned earlier. And this is a *hasan*[13] [good] Tradition. A command about the correctness of such a *hadis* is issued when its content is found in the person for whom it has been specified. The exegesis of the meaning of this *hadis* will not be done in such a manner that it contradicts the Quran or the *Ahadis-e-Sahiha* [Sound Traditions].

Thus the correct meaning and interpretation [of this *hadis*] can only be that Mahdi[AS] will fill some inhabitants of the earth with justice and equity. And the word *ba'z* (some) is absolute with respect to abundance or deficiency. If among the parts of the earth, even one part is filled with justice and equity, it would be deemed correct to say that the earth is filled with justice and equity. This is so because there is *mulabisat* [close relationship] between various parts of the earth, as they are adjacent to each other. And this interpretation is supported by what has been written in the book, *Madarik*. The command of Allah is:

"And hath placed therein the moon as a light, and hath placed the sun as a lamp."[14]

Under this Quranic Verse, the author of the book, *Madarik*, writes as under:

> In other words, [Allah] made the moon a *nur* [light] in the skies, even though it is in the sky of the earth, because there is *mulabisat* [close relationship] among the skies in the sense that they are parts. Hence, it is allowed to say as such, even though it [moon] is not the *nur* [light] for all the skies. Further, it is

---

13   *Hasan* – It is a rank of *hadis*. It is below the various ranks of *Sahih* (sound), but above the *zaeef* (weak).
14   Quran, S. 71:16 SAL.

said that such-and-such a thing has happened in so and so city, even though what has happened is in a part of the city [and not in the whole city]. [The speech of the author of *Madarik* ends here.]

And the following passage in praise of the attributes of Prophet^SLM, from the book, *Sharah-e-Aqaid*, supports the writing of the author of the *Madarik*. It is as under:

[Prophet Muhammad^SLM] made perfect a number of people in the excellences of knowledge and deeds and he illuminated the world with the Faith [*iman*] and righteous deeds.

Hence, see! O Just Man! The *Sharah-e-Aqaid* author's words 'illuminated the world' are like the saying '*yamla-al-arz*' [fill the earth]. This does not mean that the whole of the world or a large part of the world will be illuminated. It means a part of the earth will be illuminated.

If one were to count the number of the Muslims during the period of Prophet^SLM, one would find that the number of Muslims was not even one-tenth of a million of the whole population of the earth, because at the time of the death of Prophet Muhammad^SLM the number of the Muslims was one lakh twenty four thousand [124000], according to one narrative. Now, see how small in number Muslims were when compared to the entire population of the world. In this kind of speech, the reality [or the exact number] is not taken into consideration. But its purport is *majaz-e-muta'araf* [outward appearance as is known].

And the *majaz-e-muta'araf*, in this case, is that the thing that was not manifest becomes manifest; the thing that was not to be found becomes available.

This interpretation is supported by what Kirmani has said in respect of the saying of Prophet^SLM, 'Allah will eradicate *kufr* [infidelity] on account of me.' 'Eradication of infidelity' means that it will be eradicated from the towns and cities of Arabia or that the proof is dominant and the evidence is manifest.

The example of this is that it is said that the market is full of wheat. It means that wheat is available in the market, it is visible and it is not hidden. The purport is not that wheat is available in abundance in every nook and corner. And similarly, it is not understood that wheat is available in a large quantity as compared to other food grains. Similarly, here too the term '*yamla-al-arz*' [world filled with] has come. And it is difficult to comprehend the real meaning of the term because of the contentions that we have presented earlier. And the *majaz* is both *musta'mal* and *muta'araf* [the outward appearance is both known and in use]. Hence, we have to revert to the *majaz* [outward appearance] and it is that justice and equity being found and being manifest is in a part of the world.

All the arguments I have advanced in respect of this *hadis* are only one-tenth of the arguments that I can advance in this respect. Hence, see the negligence of this Sheikh [Muttaqi], who is the tormentor of the Saints of Allah and who has come out in the field to wage a war against Allah. How negligent is he of the said meanings? And because of his ignorance, he is taunting a community that is earnest in reviving the religion of Allah like the Companions^{RZ} of the Messenger^{SLM} did. For us, in respect of the Sheikh [Muttaqi], the command of Allah Most High is sufficient: '*And leave Me (alone to deal with) those in possession of the good things of life, who (yet) deny the Truth; and bear with them for a little while.*'[15]

Kings of the Earth

He [Muttaqi] says: There has come in *hadis* a thing that rejects the interpretation of the Mahdavis. And it is this: The kings of the earth are four; two of them are believers [*mumin*]. They are *Zul-Qarnain* and Prophet Suleiman^{AS}. The other two are infidels [*kafirs*] Namrood [Nimrod] and Ba<u>kh</u>t Nasr. Then, the fifth would be from among my descendants and would be the ruler of the world.

We say: I am astonished at how the Sheikh [Muttaqi], who is ignorant of the science of knowledge, has made allegations against us on the basis of this *hadis* when this *hadis* does not have the capacity to become proof, because none of the *imams* of *hadis* [experts in the science of Traditions] have held this *hadis* to be *sahih* [sound]. Even if these *imams* had certified its health, it would not have been of any use so far as the beliefs are concerned, because this issue of Mahdi^{AS} is not a issue related to deeds that could depend on the presumptions, because presumption is enough in respect of deeds. Rather, this is an issue of beliefs, and it requires positiveness and certainty. Then how did the Sheikh [Muttaqi] say that a thing had come in the *hadis* that rejects the interpretation of the Mahdavis? If we, in accordance with the overweening pride of the Sheikh [Muttaqi], were to accept the interpretation of the said *hadis*, then we would say: Do you not see that there are two Traditions about the number of the Prophets that have been narrated. One of them says that there were 220,000 prophets, while the other *hadis* gives their number as 120,000 prophets. Since, this does not give the benefit of exactitude and certainty, the *ulama* have hesitated in fixing the exact figure of the prophets, and said, 'We will not confine ourselves on the number of the prophets.'

Different Types of *Ahadis*

Then, know that the <u>kh</u>abar [report or *hadis*] could be in three conditions: It could be a report the acceptance of which is obligatory. This is the report, on which the *imams* [experts] have quoted *nass* [categorical Quranic injunction]. Or it is the *hadis* the denial of which is obligatory and the categorical Quranic injunction has been produced to prove its falsehood or its weakness [*za'if*]. Or it could be the *hadis* about which the *ulama* hesitate to categorize it. Hence, the *hadis* that is to be known as correct is not a proof in the matters of beliefs. It only gives the benefit of a dominant presumption. Then, comes the *hadis* about which the *ulama* have hesitated. Such a

---

[15] Quran, S. 73:11 AYA.

hadis does not give the benefit of its being correct by itself. Then, how can it be of benefit to the belief in other matters?

Then, know that the text of the *hadis* does not enter the domain of credence, except in rare cases. On the other hand, the attribute of weakness or strength or a state between the two extremes is envisaged with reference to the attributes of the narrators, that is, their sense of justice and equity, *zab't* [control and discipline], memory, etc. Or [it is judged] in respect of its credentials, like *ittisal* [being adjacent], *inqita'* [separation or amputation], *irsal* [dispatch] and *iztirab* [impatience].

And the *sahih hadis* is the one, whose chain of authority is unbroken and is narrated by a person who is disciplined as a Just Man and he narrates it from a person who has similar qualities and it has remained free of irregularities and defects. It is of seven kinds: (1) the best and the highest is that *hadis* which has the consensus of *Muslim* and *Bukhari*; (2) Then comes the *hadis*, which has been narrated only by *Bukhari*; (3) Then comes the *hadis* that has been reported only by *Muslim*; (4) Then comes the *hadis* that satisfies all the conditions of both *Bukhari* and *Muslim*, even if both have not described it with authorities; (5) Then comes the *hadis* that satisfies the conditions of *Bukhari*; (6) Then comes the *hadis* that satisfies the conditions of *Muslim*; and finally (7) comes the *hadis*, which has been treated as correct by *imams* of *hadis*, other than *Bukhari* and *Muslim*. Hence, the *hadis* that has been narrated with grammatical patterns, like 'said so-and-so' or the verb or the command or [prefixed by] 'narrated by' in the *ma'roof* [active] tense also is treated as sound. And the *hadis* that has been narrated in a *majhool* [passive] tense is not considered to be sound. It has been described in books of principles like the *Husami* and others that:

> If the reporter of the *hadis* is well known in *Fiqh* and *ijtihad* [in the exercise of judgment] – like the *Khulafa-e-Rashidin* [the first four orthodox Caliphs of Islam] or the *Ibadilah-e-Salasa* [the three Abdullahs][16] and Zaid ibn Sabit, Mu'az ibn Jabal, Abu Musa Ash'ari and Ayesha[RZ] and others who are well-known in *Fiqh* and judgement –, the *hadis* reported by these personalities is treated as *hujjat* [incontrovertible proof] and *qiyas* [analogy] is abandoned.

Hence, the Sheikh [Muttaqi] who is inclined towards devious ways and who has deviated from justice and equity should establish the soundness of the *hadis* and then make allegations against us.

Whereas the fact is that this *hadis* is not from the *Sihah*[17] and a *hadis* similar to it has been narrated by Kalbi that: The kingship of the whole world will be given to none but three virtuous men – Suleiman, Zul-Qarnain and Abu Karb; and three infidels – Namrood [Nimrod], Ba<u>kh</u>t Nasr and Zahaak. This *hadis* is taken from the book, *Sharah-e-Shifa*. Hence, this *hadis* requires that the masters of the world should be six,

---

[16] The three Abdullahs are: Abdullah ibn Masud, Abdullah ibn 'Abbas and Abdullah ibn Umar[RZ].

[17] *Sihah-e-Sittah* are the six famous Sunni collections of the sayings of the Holy Prophet[SLM], made by Bukhari, Muslim, Tirmizhi, Abu Dawood, Nasai, and Ibn Majah.

excluding the Mahdi^AS. The people who argue on the basis of such Traditions and sayings are those who are devoid of knowledge and learning.

He [Muttaqi] says: And all their other interpretations will be analogous to these interpretations.

We say: O scandal-monger Sheikh! May Allah accept your repentance! You have scandalized us in respect of these interpretations as you had done in respect of other interpretations earlier.

On the charge that Mahdavis are misled because their beliefs are against the Traditions

He [Muttaqi] says: From this belief these people [the Mahdavis] have become *bid'ati* [innovators] and *gumrah* [misled], because they have beliefs which are against the clear and open meanings of the Traditions.

We say: We do not accept this contention that our beliefs are against the clear and open meanings of the Traditions. On the contrary our belief is as per the ranks of the Traditions and we do not do *tamassuk* [clinging] to the Traditions, because the *salaf* [first few generations after the Prophet^SLM] have decreed that the *'aami* [common man] is not allowed to do *tamassuk* [clinging] to the Traditions [that is, the common men are not allowed to draw conclusions or commands on issues directly from the Traditions]. But this prejudiced Sheikh [Muttaqi] has done *tamassuk* from the Traditions [that is, he has drawn conclusions and commands directly from the Traditions] in violation of the beliefs of the *salaf* and has thus become a *bid'ati* [innovator] and *gumrah* [astray] himself, because he placed every tradition that has come in favour of the Mahdi^AS on par with the *mutawatir ahadis* [the Traditions with continuity or constancy] by giving them the benefit of firmness and certainty. He did not distinguish between the ranks of the Traditions nor on the ranks of their narrators. He has himself said in the last part of his tract as follows:

> In short, the Mahdi^AS will not be proved to be true unless he manifests all those Traditions that have come in his favour, because, if the Mahdi is ascertained after some Traditions are found in him, then there would be no use mentioning the other Traditions. [Here ends the passage of the Sheikh (Muttaqi).]

O Just Man! See the ignorance and ineptitude of the Sheikh [Muttaqi], how he has jumbled up the *sahih* [sound], *hasan* [good] *and za'if* [weak] Traditions, which are conflicting and clashing with each other, and has tried to give the benefit of firmness and certainty to them like the Traditions with constancy. This is sheer *bid'at* [innovation] and *gumrahi* [depravity]. The charge he is making against us is reverting back to him. He has fallen into the very thing he was running away from.

The meaning of *Bid'at*

He [Muttaqi] says: When the matter pertaining to the *bid'at* [innovation] of these people is under discussion, I felt it appropriate to explain the meaning and kinds of *bid'at*, so that it becomes known what kind of *bid'at* these people [the Mahdavis] indulge in. In *shari'at*, all those things which were not present during the period of the Messenger of Allah[SLM] and were introduced later are termed as *bid'at*. They are of two kinds: *hasana* [good] and *qabiha* [bad]. Hence, Sheikh Imam, whose *imamate* is universally accepted and whose title is *Sultan-al-Ulama* Abu Muhammad Abdul Aziz bin Abdus Salam has written at the end of his book, *Qavaid-al-Aqaid*, that the kinds of *bid'at* are: *Wajibat* [obligation], *muharramat* [forbidden], *mandubat* [recommended] and *makroohat* [disapproved things though not unlawful] and *mubahat* [permissible].

And he has given the procedure for segregating as follows: The *bid'at* should be juxtaposed with *Shari'at* laws; if it falls under the rules of *wajoob* [obligation], it is *wajibah* [obligatory]. If it falls under the rules of *tahrim* [forbidden], it is *muhramah* [forbidden]. If it comes under the rules of *mandubat* [recommended], it is *mandoobah* [recommended]. If it comes under the rules of *makroohah*, it is *makroohah* [disapproved but not unlawful]. And finally, if it comes under the rules of *mubah* [permissible], it is *mubahah* [permissible].

There are many examples of the *bid'at-e-wajibah* [obligatory]. One among them is the learning of the science of *nah'v* [syntax]. This is obligatory because the protection of *Shari'at* is obligatory; and this protects *Shari'at*. And the thing that helps complete the obligation, it is obligatory. And among them are the *ghara'ib* [rarities] of the Quran and the *Sunnat*. It also includes the compilation of the principles of *Fiqh;* criticism and cross-checking and the issues of the correct performance of various actions in ritual prayers; the discussion of the *sahih* [correct] and *saqim* [faulty]. Further, the rules of the *Shari'at* prove that the protections in matters that exceed the fixed things in *Shari'at* are a *farz-e-kifayah*.[18]

There are many examples of the *bid'at-e-muhramah* [forbidden]. Among them are the religions or the schools of thought of the *Qadriyah, Jabriyah, Marjiyah and Mujassimah* sects. To contradict the religions of these sects is *bid'at-e-wajibah* [obligatory].

There are many examples of the *bid'at-e-mandoobah* [recommended], like the construction of the caravan, serai and schools. In the earlier times these things were not seen as being constructed. And among the many *bid'aat-e-mandoobah* are the performance of the *taravih* [special night prayers in the month of Ramazan] and discussing the minute details of the *tasawwuf* [mysticism] and talking about the *jadal* [contentions and fighting], etc. Among them are also the issues of convening the *Majalis-e-Mujadilah* [congregations for arguing various issues], provided the objective of these congregations is to invoke the pleasure of Allah Most High.

The examples of *Bid'at-e-Makroohah* are the decoration of the mosques, beautification of the Holy Quran, and others.

Some of the examples of the *bid'at-e-Mubahah* are the shaking of hands by the *musallis* [performers of daily ritual prayers] after the pre-dawn and *Asr* prayers, eating of tasty meals, drinking of beverages, wearing of good dresses and residences, wrapping shawls and *chadors* and garments with loose sleeves, etc. Some of the *ulama* have disapproved some of these things that they are the *bidaat-e-makroohah*. Some others hold that these are the *Sunnats* that

---

[18]   *Farz-e-Kifayah* is a general obligation, whose performance by an adequate number absolves all; adequate obligation.

were in practice during the era of Prophet[SLM] and later too. [Here, the speech of the Sheikh (Muttaqi) comes to an end.]

We say: Let it not be hidden that *bid'at* is an *amr-e-ghamiz* [ambiguous matter]. All the *bid'aat* have not been affirmed by the *ulama*. They have differed [in their opinions] on whether they are the *Sunnat* [the practice of the Prophet[SLM]] or the *bid'aat* [innovations].

Different kinds of *Bid'at*

He [Muttaqi] says: Imam Shafei[RA] has said that there are two kinds of the newly created things [*Bid'at*]. One of them is the *bid'at* that violates the Book of Allah Most High [Quran], or it violates the *Sunnat* [the practice of the Prophet[SLM]] or the *aasar* [the sayings or deeds of the Companions[RZ]] or the *ijma'* [consensus]. This is the *bid'at-e-zalalat* [deviation from the right path].

The other *bid'at* [innovation] is the *bid'at-e-khair* [good innovation]. This *bid'at* is free from the violation of all the four sources of the *Shari'at* that is, the Quran, the *Sunnat, the Aasar* and the *Ijma'*. This innovation is not blame-worthy. And it is said in the book, *Nihayah*, that anything that is new is *bid'at*. The purport is to say that anything that violates the principles of *Shari'at* and is not in consonance with the *Sunnat* is a *bid'at*. The word 'bid'at' is usually used for disapproving something. Hence, know, may Allah may make you fortunate that the *bid'at* of the Mahdavis is certainly the most unlawful evil.

We say: Whatever the Sheikh [Muttaqi] has said, he has said out of sheer prejudice and hostility. The person who does justice and considers the issues [in their proper perspective], Allah Most High will shower mercy on him. See how he [the Sheikh Muttaqi] has accused us of the most severe *bid'at-e-muharramah* [unlawful innovation]! This allegation is proved against only those people who abandon the *sunnat-e-sahiha* [the correct practice of the Prophet[SLM]], in which, there is no scope of interpretation or use of *majaz* [metaphorical language] and no other *Sunnat* [Prophet[SLM]'s practice] is violated. The Traditions that have come on this subject are *ahad* [Traditions transmitted by only one narrator in each link of the chain]. They do not give the benefit of finality and certainty. Besides, some of the Traditions contradict some other Traditions. And there is scope in them for interpretation and use of metaphorical language. Therefore, in this subject the constancy alone is worthy of inclusion and the only conclusion from such Traditions is the existence of the Mahdi[AS]. It is for this reason that Bayhaqi[19] has said that the people have differed in the matter of Mahdi[AS] and one group of people have hesitated and have left the knowledge about him to its knower [Allah]. They hold the belief that he [Mahdi[AS]] is among the descendants of Fatima[RZ], the daughter of Prophet Muhammad[SLM]. And none has finally and with certainty identified the Mahdi[AS] since in this matter there is no particular clue that can definitely identify him, except this *Sheikh-e-palid* [the

---

[19] His full name is Ahmad Ibn Husayn al-Baihaqi. His famous book is *Kitab as-Sunan al-Kubra*.

defiled Sheikh (Muttaqi)], who has said that the Mahdi^{AS} cannot be proved unless he possesses all those attributes that have been described in all the Traditions.

He [Muttaqi] says: Because, the command of the *Shari'at* are of two kinds; one is the principles or the *etiqadiyat* [beliefs] and, two, the *furoo* [the manifest deeds]. The *bid'at* of the beliefs is more serious than the *bid'at* of the deeds. Only the person who is an expert in the Prophetical Traditions, particularly those that are in respect of Mahdi^{AS}, can identify the *bid'at* of the beliefs.

We say: I am astonished at the words of this disoriented Sheikh [Muttaqi], because at times he talks as a sane and wise man and says that *bid'at-fil-eitqad* is known only by a person who is an expert in the Prophetical Traditions. And at times, he talks like a lunatic and says that the person should be an expert especially in the Traditions that have come with respect to the Mahdi^{AS}, because, according to him, the *bid'at-fil-usul* purports to mean the beliefs. Then, which are the vitiated beliefs which we learn from the Traditions that have come in respect of the emergence of the Mahdi^{AS}? All the sects of Islam argue on the basis of the Book of Allah [Quran] and the *Sunnat*, and call each other as *bid'ati* [innovators] and *gumrah* [misled]. Now [the question is] among these sects which *bid'at* is evident in order to charge them on the basis of those Traditions which have appeared in favour of the Mahdi^{AS}? If you look at the afore-quoted passages, the *baladat* [stupidity] of the Sheikh [Muttaqi] will become obvious.

He [Muttaqi] says: It is for this reason [it is said] that fighting against a *bid'ati* [innovator] is superior to fighting against a *kafir* [infidel], because a *kafir* is identified by his bodily appearance and dress that he is a *kafir*. Hence, the Muslim does not go near him, nor does he accept his opinions and contentions. As for the *bid'ati:* He remains in the garb of the Muslims and the righteous. Hence, he is recognized only by the person who has a profound knowledge of *Kitab* [Quran] and *Sunnat*.

We say: The saying of the critic is like the *illat* [illness] of his saying, 'The *bid'at* of the beliefs is more serious than the *bid'at* of the deeds'. His objective is to say that the *bid'at* of the Mahdavis is the *bid'at* of the beliefs. Hence, waging a *jihad* against Mahdavis is superior to waging a *jihad* against *kafirs*, because these Mahdavis hold the belief that a person who is not the Mahdi is Mahdi^{AS}. I am astonished at the Sheikh [Muttaqi] that he has, without any rhyme or reason, just on the basis of his own enmity and injustice [towards us], and for the simple reason of our belief, he holds that our killing is permissible and justified. Even if it is accepted that there is flaw in our belief, on the basis of the vast differences of opinion among the predecessors and others, and on the basis of uncertainity in interpretation and metaphorical language, and because there is no *mujtahid* to whom we could revert [for guidance], even then in ambiguous matters we do not consider that any Muslim who has erred in his judgment is liable to be killed, because this supposed error is like the mistake of a person who cannot find the direction of *Qibla* [Makkah] on an intensely cloudy day and on the basis of the testimony of his heart selects a direction and performs his ritual prayers in the selected direction.

If one were to argue as to how this supposed error could be like the error of the person who has erred in finding the direction of the *Qibla* because his error is the result of the absence of a person who could have guided him in finding the correct direction of the *Qibla*. Now in the matter we are discussing, there are many Traditions which describe the attributes of Mahdi[AS]. Then, how can this mistake be like the error in finding the direction of the *Qibla*?

I say that this has been repeated many times that of these Traditions, some are very weak and some Traditions contradict some other Traditions, because they are equal in their weakness and strength; some Traditions are such that the attributes described in them are found in the *zath* [person] in whom we have reposed Faith. And in this subject [of Mahdi[AS]], there is not even one Tradition which gives the benefit of finality and certainty, because the Traditions are decreed as *ahad* [Traditions transmitted by only one narrator in each link of the chain]. This is so because, even if *ahad* Traditions are *sahih*, such Traditions can only strengthen the *zan* [presumption], and a presumption does not give the benefit of belief, as has been stated in the books of *usul* [principles]. Hence, this is doubtful,[20] because the necessary information is not available from the Traditions. Therefore it is like the error in identifying the direction of the *Qibla*. The purpose of the Sheikh [Muttaqi] would be that it is permissible, rather excellent, to kill the disavower of the real Mahdi[AS], because he [the Sheikh] has associated him with going astray and of leading the community astray, or has treated the killing as justifiable. Read the record of your deeds, O Sheikh! Your 'self' is enough in giving evidence against you.

Manifest deeds of Mahdavis

He [Muttaqi] says: And it is for this reason that you see that the ignorant and the common people have reposed faith in this innovative group, because they see the manifest deeds of the people of this group, like the daily ritual prayers, fasting and seclusion from the common people.

We say: Allah may bless him who has said that even a liar tells the truth once in a while. The Sheikh [Muttaqi] has told a truth [for a change] in praise of our predecessors that they possessed laudable morality and graceful character, which was the fruit of the *tasdiq* [affirmation and confirmation] of Mahdi Al-Mau'ood[AS]. The attribute of the *tasdiq* of the Prophets[AS] [of the yore] too is the same. Hence, it is written in the book, *Sharah-e-Aqaid*, that Prophet Muhammad[SLM] had perfected the nobility of character to its pinnacle. He also made many people perfect in matters of beliefs and deeds. He had illuminated the world with faith and virtuous deeds. Hence, Raghib has said that there are two signs for every Prophet[AS]: One of them is

---

[20] This means the identification of the Mahdi[AS].

of wisdom which is recognized by the people of *baseerat* [insight], for instance, they display *anwar-e-raiqa* [glow of pure radiance] and *Akhlaq-e-Karimah* [bountiful disposition]. They possess the manifest knowledge in such a manner that their speech becomes authentic and *sahib-e-hujjat* [worthy of being treated as proof]. Their explanations bring satisfaction to their listeners. These circumstances are such that in their presence, no man of insight would demand a miracle, except those who are prejudiced. Since most people suffer from spiritual ailments, hence when we see someone who can cure the spiritual ailments and make people perfect, then we know that he is a skillful and expert physician and a true prophet. The other sign is the miracle. The demand for it is essential for one who cannot comprehend the difference between the divine word and the word of man.

And you know that all these attributes were achieved by our people after performing the *tasdiq* of Mahdi Al-Mau'ood[AS]. And which ailment is bigger or more serious than the love for the world and its people? And which *sifat-e-karimah* [generous attribute] is greater and more preferable than giving up and rejecting the world and its people? This lone attribute of giving up the world and its people is equal to all the good attributes. And our people have achieved the noble attribute of rejecting the world and its people through the *tasdiq* [affirmation] of Mahdi Al-Mau'ood[AS]. The Sheikh [Muttaqi] himself has given evidence about this. However, a blind person cannot see! The Sheikh has associated the people who have reposed faith in Hazrat Imam Mahdi Al-Mau'ood[AS] with ignorance. This is similar to the opponents of Islam associating the companions of Prophet[SLM] with ignorance and saying, '*They say: "Shall we believe as the fools believe?"*'[21] And Allah may bless the poet who had said:

> I find the goodness in a noble person to be praiseworthy
> The same goodness becomes a sin among the mean
> The person whose mouth is bitter, is an ailing person
> Because of it, even the sweet water tastes bitter [to him],
> As the rain water is like a pearl in the oyster shell
> And it is the poison in the mouth of a snake.

He [Muttaqi] says: The ignorant and the common people do not know that the manifest deeds [of these Mahdavis] are related to their immanent deeds which are the beliefs and principles. When the beliefs are correct, their manifest deeds too will be correct. When the beliefs get mixed up with *bid'aat* [innovations] the manifest deeds too will become null and void. Hence, it is said in Traditions that Allah Most High will not accept the ritual prayers [Namaz] or the fasting of a *bid'ati* [innovator] or his *sadaqa* [charity], or *Haj* or *umrah* [off-seasonal pilgrimage to Makkah], *jihad*, repentance, justice, *fidyah* [ransom]; and he is pulled out of Islam as the hair comes out of the kneaded flour. This tradition has been narrated by Huzayfah[RZ] in the book, *Ibn Majah* that Allah Most High would not accept the deed of a person who is a *bid'ati* unless he gives up his *bid'at* [innovation]. This Tradition has been narrated in *Ibn Majah* with correct authorities. And Ibn 'Asim[RZ] too has narrated it in his book, *Sunan*, on the authority of Ibn 'Abbas[RZ]. Further, Allah Most High has barred the

---

[21] Quran, S.2:13 AYA

repentance of every *bid'ati*. This Tradition has been narrated by Ibn Fil and Tabarani in his book, *Ausat*, and Bayhaqi. Further, there are those Traditions that have been narrated in this matter, as narrated by Anas bin Malik[RZ].

We say: The purport of the Sheikh [Muttaqi] in quoting these Traditions is to show that because of their innovation of accepting a person who is not Mahdi[AS] as Mahdi[AS,] their deeds are abrogated. And as stated earlier, it is impossible to prove that we are practicing *bid'at* in a matter which is ambiguous. Then how can *bid'at* be proved against us, when Mahdi himself is the adjudicator to distinguish between *sunnat* and *bid'at*, when there are differences of opinion concerning them, because this is from the particularities of Mahdi[AS]. We will further deal with this matter in our discourse about the proofs of Mahdi[AS] on the occasion of the Sheikh's [Muttaqi] example of the mosquito.

Then again, let it be known that the Traditions pertaining to the harshness and severity on the people of *bid'at* sound the death knell for the deeds of *munkirin* [disavowers], because when Mahdi[AS] has been proved and affirmed, how can the deeds of the disavowers of Mahdi[AS] not be decreed as void and wasted, as these people have reached a high station of *gumrahi* [going astray] because they accuse the Mahdi[AS] and his Companions of going astray and leading people astray. May Allah have Mercy on some of our brothers who hesitate in declaring the disavowers of Mahdi[AS] as infidels!

On the charge that only the ignorant are joining the Mahdavis

He [Muttaqi] says: Our saying "that the manifest deeds [of these Mahdavis] which are *furoo* (branches) are related to their immanent deeds which are the beliefs and principles" is not understood by commoners and the ignorant. But if the same meaning is explained along with an example that is perceptible to him, he can easily understand and will accept it. The example is this:

The science of construction is of two kinds: *usool* [principles] and *furoo* [branches]. The knowledge of the principles is known to the expert engineers. That is, determining the foundation to be straight, or its being tilted; and there are some nuances which are known only to the engineers. And the knowledge of the *furoo* [brances] is known to the construction labourer. He knows how to place one stone on another stone. He also knows that his daily wages are just a few dirhams. The wages or the remuneration of the engineers is based on their depth of knowledge of the rules of construction. They are appointed to a post by the kings and wealthy people. The reason for this is that the knowledge of construction is a manifest deed and this deed is related to the immanent knowledge with respect to the soundness or faultiness of the building, which is possessed only by the engineers. The ordinary and ignorant people are not aware of these issues. And they are deceived by the manifest deeds of these people [the Mahdavis] and are ensnared by them.

We say: I am astonished at the deception of the Sheikh [Muttaqi] that he has tried to sow doubts in the minds of people who are unaware about this group that all the people of this group [the Mahdavis] are ordinary and ignorant. The reality, however, is not as he says. Rather, some of the Mahdavi *ulama* are like the prophets of the Bani Israel [Children of Israel]. They have themselves rejected and given up the world and they invite the ordinary people to reject and give up the world. They trust in Allah Most High in all conditions and in all frightening situations, they assign all their work to Allah Most High. Their manifest knowledge is profound and they excel in the immanent knowledge and receive *kashf* [divine unveiling]. Many among them are unlettered and common people too, as the companions of Prophets^AS have been in every era. Hence, it has come in verses of the Holy Quran:

> "He it is Who hath sent among the unlettered ones a messenger of their own to recite unto them His revelations and to make them grow, and to teach them the Scripture and Wisdom, though heretofore they were indeed in error manifest."[22]

> "But the Chiefs of the Unbelievers among his People said: 'We see (in) thee nothing but a man like ourselves: nor do we see that any follow thee but the meanest among us, in judgment immature: nor do we see in you (all) any merit above us: in fact we think you are liars.'"[23]

> "They said: 'Shall we believe in thee when it is the meanest that follow thee?'"[24]

The saying of Heraclius when he was answering Abu Sufyan supports this. He says, 'I asked you whether the nobles amongst the people had followed Prophet^SLM or the weakest among them; you said that the weakest among them had followed Hazrat Muhammad^SLM. In fact such people are the only ones who follow the prophets.'

Further, the saying of Ibn Mas'ood^RZ also supports this contention. He said,

> 'In our day, the people who recite Quran are few and people who understand Quran [or people who act in accordance with Quran] are many. The letters of Quran are neglected [that is, they do not properly pronounce the letters from their *makharij* [proper outlets of sounds], but its limits are protected. They protect the limits of Quran and they neglect the letters of Quran. The beggars are few and the people who give [charity] are many. They perform long ritual prayers and shorten the *khutbah* [sermon]. People begin their deeds before their desires. However, a time will come when the people who recite the Quran will be more, and those who understand it [and act accordingly] will be few. The letters of the Quran will be protected and its limits will be broken. Beggars will be more and those who give [charity] will be few. They will give long sermons and hurry in saying their ritual prayers. They will act according to the desires of their baser self before their deeds.

This is how it is stated in *Sharah-us-Sunnah* in the chapter "Transformation of the people and departure of the pious".

---

[22] Quran, S. 62:2 MMP.
[23] Quran, S. 11:27 AYA.
[24] Quran, S. 26:111 AYA.

Further, Ali Karamallahu Wajhu[RZ] in response to Huzayfah[RZ] or Ibn Mas'ood[RZ] had given a *fatwa* [opinion] on an issue based on his independent judgement [*ijtihad*] after deliberating for two months. An Arab tendered evidence on this *fatwa*, saying, 'I have heard the Messenger of Allah[SLM] saying exactly like this.' Huzayfah[RZ] or Ibn Mas'ood[RZ] expressed their pleasure on hearing the evidence of the Arab. Then Ali[RZ] told Huzayfah[RZ] or Ibn Mas'ood[RZ], 'Why are you pleased with the saying of a person who urinates at his heels?' This is stated in the book *At-Tahqeeq*, which is the *sharah* of *Husami*.

Hence, it is known[25] that the followers of the Prophets[AS] were unlettered and common people. Therefore opponents like the Sheikh [Muttaqi] have maligned them. Therefore, Mahdi[AS] and his community are followers of the Prophets[AS]. (As opponents had maligned the Prophets[AS] and their Companions[RZ], so have opponents maligned Mahdi[AS] and his Companions[RZ].) Hence, we do not take notice of the allegations made by the disavowers against Mahdi[AS] and his Companions[RZ].

Further, know that the objective of the Sheikh is to frighten the people away from socialising with the community of the Imam[AS] and to get them to shun the community. And he ought to do this very thing, in accordance with the command of Allah Most High:

> "Their intention is to extinguish Allah's Light (by blowing) with their mouths but Allah will complete (the revelation of) His Light, even though the unbelievers may detest (it)."[26]

It has been stated in the book, *Futuhat-e-Makkiah*, in favour of Mahdi[AS] that:

> When the Mahdi[AS] emerges, there would be no enemies of his other than the *fuqaha* [Muslim jurists], because their leadership would not remain. When the Mahdi[AS] would issue commands against their *mazhab* [religious thought] they would think that he is misled, because their belief would be that the era of *ijtihad* had expired and that after their *mujtahid imams* none would reach the rank of a *mujtahid*. (Further, their belief would be that the person who emerges with the claim of the *ma'rifat-e-Ilahi* (intimate knowledge of Allah Most High) and *ilham-e-Rabbani* (divine inspiration) would, in their opinion, be a lunatic and a *fasid-al-khayal* (man of vitiated thinking). Hence, they would

---

25   Hence, it is known that the followers of the Prophets[AS] were unlettered and common people. They were not people who read and write. Hence, the Companions[RZ] of Prophet[SLM] like Huzayfah[RZ] or Ibn Mas'ood[RZ] became happy at the narration of an unlettered Companion[RZ]. An adage in Arab is that if there is one who does not know reading and writing, they repeat the saying of Hazrat Ali[RZ]. The intention is not to ridicule anybody. It is just a joke. And the joke that is in accordance with facts is permitted. Hence, it is narrated in the book, *Bustan al-Fiqh*, that one day Hazrat Prophet[SLM] arrived at the house of Hazrat Bibi 'Aishah[RZ]. There was an old woman sitting in front of 'Aishah[RZ]. Hazrat Prophet[SLM] said, "O 'Aishah! Old woman will not enter Paradise." Hearing this, the old woman started lamenting. Then the Prophet[SLM] said, "The men of paradise will be young men (without beards). Among them, there would be no old woman." The old woman became happy. The Prophet[SLM] and 'A'ishah[RZ] both started smiling. This kind of a joke is permitted.— Quoted from the book, *Sharah-e-Siraj al-Absar*, compiled by Muhammad Qasim[RA].

26   Quran, S. 61:8 AYA.

not pay any attention to him.) If he did not have the sword [of miracles] in his hand, the *fuqaha* would have issued the *fatwa* of killing him. If he were a wealthy man and had great power in his hands, they would have become his obedient people in their greed of his wealth.

Further, Sheikh Izzuddin Abdur Razzaq Kashani has written in his book, *Tafsir-e-Taveelat*, under the Divine Command:

> *"Those who disbelieve among the People of Scripture and the idolaters could not have left off (erring) till the clear proof came unto them, A messenger from Allah, reading purified pages, containing correct scriptures. Nor were the People of the Scripture divided until after the clear proof came unto them."*[27]

that, "they are veiled from the path that led to the religion and the truth like the People of the Book, or they are veiled from the truth itself like the *mushrikin* [idolators]. And the *mushrikin* were not those who would break away from their polytheism, until there came a *bayyina* [clear proof; one with indisputable evidence], who guided them to reach the *matloob* [the object of one's love—God]. This is so because various groups of the Jews, the Christians and the polytheists, who had, under the influence of their carnal desires, gone astray and who were hostile to each other; and every group claimed that it was on the true path and invited others to join its path and denounced the faith of the others as false. Despite all this, they used to remain united on the point that they would not give up their faith, until the prophet who was promised in the Torah and Bible appeared. Hence, they said, they would follow the promised prophet, and remaining on the one *Kalimah* [creed], would reach a consensus on the *tareeq-e-Haq* [the right path]."

"In exactly the same way, different people of the religion [the people of the seventy-two sects of Muslims] are behaving like the above-mentioned intolerant people. They are waiting for the emergence of the Mahdi[AS] in the *Aakhir Zamana* [the Last Era]. They promise that they would follow the Mahdi[AS] on the consensus of one *kalimah* [creed]. I do not think that the condition of these people of the seventy-two sects [of the Muslims] is any different from the groups of the Jews, the Christians and the polytheists described in the previous paragraph. They presumed that they would follow the Mahdi[AS] when he emerged and Allah Most High might save them from the mischief of opposing the Mahdi[AS]. Hence, Allah Most High mentioned their utterances and explained that the hostility and severe discord and arrogance of these people was exposed after the emergence of Mahdi-e-Mau'ood who came with the *bayyina* [indisputable evidence] [that is, the *Vilayat* (Sainthood)]. This is so because not just each sect but every person thinks that the Mahdi would be according to his desire and would uphold his opinion to be true. His pretense is because he has camouflaged his false faith

---

[27] Quran, S. 98:1-4 MMP.

and belief as the true religion, and so he is veiled himself from the true religion of Allah. So, when the Mahdi^{AS} appears in a condition that is not in accordance with his presumed thoughts, his infidelity and hostility would grow; his malice and enmity will aggravate." [The statement of Sheikh Izzuddin Abdur Razzaq Kashani comes to an end here.]

And Abu Abdullah Husain ibn Ali^{RZ} narrates that he said:

"If Mahdi^{AS} were to establish himself, people would essentially oppose him, because Mahdi^{AS} would revert to them in a condition that he would be a young man while these people would be thinking that he would be an old man."

This is what is written in the book, *Iqd-ud-Durar*. Further, in the book *Mazhar*, the *Sharah* of *Masabih*, it is written that:

"Mahdi^{AS} would be a *Mard-e-Aziz* [Mighty Man]; only *'arifin* [people with intimate mystic knowledge of God] will recognize him."

The purpose of quoting these sayings is to show that the opposition of the people is proof in itself of the *tasdiq* [affirmation] of Mahdi^{AS}.

Further, the saying of Waraqah bin Nowfal, that has been narrated in the Book of Traditions, *Bukhari*, too supports us. When the Prophet^{SLM} asked, 'Would these people expel me?' Waraqah said, 'Yes. Whenever someone staked a claim like the one you did then he earned the enmity of others.' This narrative proves that the people's enmity against the Prophets^{AS} is a *Sunnat-e-Jariah* [continuing practice]. Since the Mahdi^{AS} is the follower of the Prophet^{SLM} in establishing the religion, as the Prophet^{SLM} has himself said that 'He [the Mahdi^{AS}] will re-establish the religion in the *Aakhri Zamana* [Last Era] as I had established in the beginning period.' Hence, Mahdi^{AS} gave the call towards the same religion that all the Prophets^{AS} had brought. He invited the people unto the religion and made the call of being the Mahdi^{AS}, who was sent by Allah similar to how the Prophets^{AS} invited people to the religion and their call of being sent by Allah Most High as Prophets^{AS}. However, if one were to say that the Mahdi^{AS} did not bring a new religion from Allah Most High but he invited the people unto the religion of the Prophet^{SLM}, I would in reply say that most of the Prophets^{AS} were like that. Even they did not bring any new religion, but their call was for the establishment of the *Deen-e-Qadim* [the old religion of Allah Most High], like the Prophets^{AS} among the Children of Israel had invited people to follow the teaching of the Torah. Hence, the enmity of the people is the result of establishing the religion and inviting the people towards it, as Allah Most High has said:

"...Is it ever so, that, when cometh unto you a messenger (from Allah) with that which ye yourself desire not, ye grew arrogant, and some ye disbelieve and some ye slay?"[28]

On the charge that Mahdavis forbid their people from acquiring knowledge

He [Muttaqi] says: These people [the Mahdavis] forbid their companions from learning *ilm* [knowledge] and think this ignorance to be an excellence. They argue on the basis of their *hamaqat* [ineptitude] that Hazrat Prophet Muhammad[SLM] was *ummi* [unlettered]. See their ignorance! They compare their ignorance with the *ilm* [knowledge] that was bestowed by Allah Most High as the *Ilm-e-Ladunni* [divinely inspired knowledge.] Allah Most High may ruin them and terminate their relics.

We say: O Just Man! See the enmity and hostility of the Sheikh [Muttaqi]; how he has camouflaged the virtues [*tawakkul* (Trust in Allah), indifference towards the people] of our companions who were like the *As'hab-e-Suffah* [People of the Bench] as their evil. With respect to people like the Sheikh [Muttaqi], Allah Most High has said:

"...And a crier in between them crieth: The Curse of Allah is on the evil-doers. Who debar (men) from the path of Allah and have it crooked, and who are disbelievers in the Last Day."[29]

Further, Allah Most High says:

"Those who work against God and His Apostle—it is they who shall be of the most humiliated."[30]

Further, know that our Companions[RZ] do not prevent or prohibit anybody to learn. On the contrary among them are scholars who are expert in the manifest sciences, who have acquired their *ilm* [knowledge] from reputed and accomplished teachers and their immanent *ilm* from their [spiritual] exercises, perpetual remembrance of Allah Most High, seclusion from the people and by their constant companionship with their *murshidin-sadiqin* [truthful preceptors]. All this they have achieved in accordance with the saying of Hazrat Prophet[SLM] who has said:

"Whoever sincerely and genuinely worships Allah for forty days, the fountains of wisdom will flow from his heart and his tongue will wax eloquent."

However, the Mahdavi *ulama* [scholars] instruct the people to develop the desire for Allah Most High and to give up the desire of things other than Allah Most High. They also command that people should disassociate their *batin* [immanence] from

28 Quran, S. 2:87 MMP.
29 Quran, S.7:44 and 45 MMP.
30 Quran, S. 58:20 SAL.

both the worlds—the Here and the Hereafter. Where Allah Most High intends to grant good for any person, that person gives up the world and remains in the company of the *murshidin-sadiqin* [the truthful preceptors]. His preoccupation is to remain in the activities described above. Then, within a very few days he acquires all those things that others cannot achieve in years. This is the result of the *tasdiq* [affirmation and confirmation] of Mahdi^{AS} and the sincerity of the immanence [of the seekers of Allah].

Hence, these people [the Mahdavis] do not need to achieve the sciences that are achieved by formal lessons and teachings in schools, because among them [the performers of perpetual remembrance of Allah Most High] are such people who have, by their efforts, achieved the manifest sciences. If they need any information about the issues concerning the *Fiqh* [Islamic Law], they ask their companions who are experts in those manifest sciences. This has been the practice of those people who are engaged in the deeds of the heart, like *zikr* [remembrance of Allah Most High], *fikr* [thinking], *muraqabah* [meditation], and *tavajjoh il-Allah* [attention directed towards Allah Most High]. They did all they could do in immanent matters. They adopted an easy-going attitude in the manifest matters. They achieved perfection in the matters of principles of religion [did research in the commands relating to daily ritual prayers—*namaz*, *rozah* (fasting), *halal* [legitimate] and *haram* [unlawful; forbidden]. All these are indispensable. Then there is the saying of *Sheikh-ash-Shuyookh* Shihabuddin^{RA}, which is narrated in the book, *Awarif*, supporting this. It is this:

> It is narrated in *hadis* [Tradition] (that Prophet^{SLM} said), 'The excellence of the *'alim* [scholar] over the *'abid* [worshipper] is like my excellence over my *ummat* [Muslim community].' Here, it is not the knowledge about the sale, purchase, marriage, divorce, and *'itaq* [manumission or freeing of slaves] that is being referred to. What is referred to here is the knowledge conferred by Allah Most High and strengthening of the certainty of that inspired knowledge. Sometimes a slave of Allah becomes an *'alim bi-Allah* [a learned man on whom Allah Most High confers the divinely inspired knowledge], but he does not know what is *farz-e-kifayah* [a general obligation whose performance by an adequate number absolves all; adequate obligation]. The Companions^{RZ} of the Messenger of Allah^{SLM} knew more about the realities and the intimate knowledge of Allah Most High than the *ulama* [scholars] of the *taba'een* [followers of the Companions^{RZ}]. And among the scholars of *taba'een* [the followers of the Companions^{RZ}], there were people who were stronger than their compatriots. They were pious and had the competence to issue *fatwas* [religious edicts] and command over the manifest knowledge. May Allah Most High be pleased with them all!'

Further, it is also written in the book, *Awarif*, that:

The minds of these *ulama-e-zahiri* [scholars of the manifest knowledge of the religion] had been filled with the minor points. They were engaged fully in them. And due to this engagement with minor points they were separated from the comprehensive knowledge.

And the minds of the *ulama-e-zahidin* [the scholars among the mystic hermits] acquired the knowledge of the minor points to the extent of the principles of religion and the basics from the *Shari'at* and then turned their attention towards Allah Most High and became fully absorbed in His *talab* [desire].

On the charge that Mahdavis consider the killing of scholars as permitted

He [Muttaqi] says: It is for this reason that these people [the Mahdavis] consider the killing of the *ulama* [religious scholars] as *jaiz* [allowed or permitted]. And they prefer their killing to the killing of the *kafirs* [infidels]. May Allah kill them!

We say: Allah's curse is on the Sheikh [Muttaqi] who has scandalized the sincere servants of Allah Most High! We do not consider the killing of the *ulama* as absolutely allowed or permissible as the Sheikh [Muttaqi] has said. On the contrary, what we say is: If on the basis of our belief, someone like the Sheikh [Muttaqi], concludes that our killing is allowed or permitted, then the killing of such a person becomes allowed or permitted. Otherwise, not! And the opinion that lends justification to this is the saying of the Sheikh [Muttaqi] himself that: 'The *jihad* against the *bid'atis* [innovators] is superior to the *jihad* against the *kafirs* [infidels].' But then the condition of the *munkir* [disavower] is worse than a *bid'ati* [innovator], particularly those who consider the killing of our brothers as permitted.

He [Muttaqi] says: Their [the Mahdavis'] treating as allowed or permissible the killing of our *ulama* [that is, the non-Mahdavi scholars] is the proof of their *jahl* [ignorance] and *zalalat* [going astray]. This is also sufficient to prove that they are incapable of proving their false faith.

We say: We have proved our claim in the same manner as the *ulama* have proved the Unity [Oneness] of Allah Most High and the Prophethood of the Prophets[AS]. In other words, we have proved our claim by rational arguments and through our [superior] character and behaviour. Hence, we will advance the necessary arguments when we deal with the Sheikh's example of the mosquito. However, the person who has covered his eyes with veils of enmity and hostility will not be able to see. Allah Most High says:

"Say—For Allah's is the final argument—Had He willed He could indeed have guided all of you."[31]

"This is the Book; in it is guidance, sure, without doubt, to those who fear Allah."[32]

---

[31] Quran, S. 6:149 MMP.

That is, in reality, [guidance is] for the people of equity and for those who repose Faith, and not for those who disavow and are hostile.

Tafsir on the basis of opinion

He [Muttaqi] says: Then among their evils is the writing of commentaries [exegesis] of Qur'an on the basis of their opinion. Hence, it has been reported that a person, who writes the commentaries in this manner, has committed a blunder, even if his commentary or exegesis is correct.

We say: The speech of the Sheikh [Muttaqi] is mixed with the voice of the animals. It is not even comparable to the speech of the ordinary people. The question of it being akin to the speech of the eloquent people does not arise. Look at the فاء . What relation does this فاء of فورد have with its preceeding phrase? The right phrase would have been تفسيرهم القرآن بالراى و ذالك غير جائز لانه قد ورد . We have ignored other such sentences previously.

The Sheikh [Muttaqi] has made the allegation that we comment on the Quran on the basis of our opinion. This is one of his slanders against us, because our reliable brethren read the various *tafasir* [exegeses] and they explain them in accordance with the Arabic grammar. If any of their sayings is not found in one *tafsir* [exegesis] it will certainly be found in another *tafsir*. I have not heard any of their sayings, which is against the categorically proven beliefs.

The conditions that the Sheikh [Muttaqi] has subsequently mentioned are not essential. The reasons for this will be dealt shortly, Allah willing. And which prohibited matter can be blamed on the person who is an *'alim* [scholar] of lexicography, and knows the background of the revelation of a Quranic Verse; even if he does not know some of the things that the Sheikh [Muttaqi] has mentioned in his later passages.

From the point of view of eloquence, the Verse that holds the highest rank in Quran is as follows:

وَقِيلَ يَا أَرْضُ ابْلَعِى مَاءكِ وَيَا سَمَاء أَقْلِعِى وَغِيضَ الْمَاء وَقُضِىَ الْأَمْرُ

وَاسْتَوَتْ عَلَى الْجُودِيِّ وَقِيلَ بُعْداً لِّلْقَوْمِ الظَّالِمِينَ

33

And this is so because this verse has such fine points which the experts in the science of *fasahat* [eloquence] and *balaghat* [rhetoric] have failed [to explain], so much so, that even the disavowers have asserted that this is not the speech of a human being, but it

---

[32] Quran, S. 2:2 AYA.

[33] Quran, S. 11:44 MMP. The meaning of verse is: *"And it was said: O earth! Swallow thy water and O sky! Be cleared of the clouds! And the water was made to subside. And the commandment was fulfilled. And it (the ship) came to rest upon (the mount) Al-Judi and it was said: A far removal of the wrong doing folk!"* - AYA

is the *kalam* [speech] of Allah Most High. Most of the commentators [of Quran] have explained this verse without going into the details of the relevant points. Hence, if somebody explains the Quranic Verses in the following manner – *'yaaa-arzub-la-'ii maaa-'aki'* ['O earth! Swallow up thy water]; *'wa yaa-samaaa-'u 'aqli-ii* [O sky! Cease pouring']; that is hold back your water and stop raining; *'wa giizal-maa-'u* [and the flood abated]; *wa quzi-yal-'amru* [and the destruction of the community of Nuh^AS was completed]; *wasta-wat 'alal Juu-diyyi* [and the ark settled down on the Judi] – then, which prohibited matter can he be accused of?'[34]

Then I will explain the difference between the *tavil-e-masmu'* [the permissible interpretation] and the *tafsir-e-mamnu'* [the prohibited exegesis], *Insha-Allah.*"

Five kinds of *Tafsir-bir-Rai*

He [Muttaqi] says: This *Hadis* has been narrated with credits and authority by Abu Daud, Tirmizi and Nasai[35]. There is another *Hadis* on this matter which says that 'The person who explains the Quran without the [necessary] knowledge should search for his place in the Hell.' This *Hadis* has been reported in Abu Daud as narrated by Ibn 'Abbas. And Sheikh Jalaluddin Suyuti^RH has said in *'Al-Itqan fi Uloom-il-Quran'*, copying from the writing of Ibn-e-Naqib that there are five sayings about *Tafsir-bir-Rai* [exegesis on the basis of one's opinion]: (1) writing the *tafsir* without the knowledge of those *uloom* [fields or branches of knowledge] which should be known for writing the *tafsir* [exegesis].[36] (2) The writing of *Tafsir* of the *mutashabihat* [allegorical Quranic Verses] the meaning of which is known only to Allah Most High. (3) The writing of the *tafsir* that proves the *fasid mazhab* [corrupt religion] to be correct in a manner that places the depraved religion as the core and subjugates the *tafsir* to it; and making the *tafsir* to conform to such perverted religion in whichever way possible, even if such a way is weak. (4) To say, without a valid argument, that certainly the purport of Allah is this. (5) To write the *tafsir* with lenient interpretation and under the influence of one's carnal desires. All these kinds [of *tafsir*] are found in this group [of Mahdavis].

We say: The Sheikh's saying that all these kinds of *tafsir* are found in this group [of Mahdavis] is a slander against us [Mahdavis], because none of these five kinds of *tafsir* is found among us. And we will refute the allegations about every kind of the above mentioned *tafsirs*. We have already answered the allegation about the first kind under the saying of the Sheikh "Then among their evils is their writing the commentaries [exegesis] on the basis of their opinions."[37] We would not repeat it.

Tafsir of Allegorical Quranic Verses

The answer to the second kind [about the allegorical Quranic Verses] is as follows: We do not do the *tafsir* of the allegorical Quranic Verses. Neither do we do the *tafsir*

---

34   Judi is the name of the mountain on which the ark finally settled.
35   Abu Daud as-Sijistani, Muhammad ibn Isa at-Tirmizi and Ahmad bin Shu'ayb an-Nasai are the three of the eight Imams of Prophetical Traditions of the ninth Century AD.
36   Writing of *Tafsir* without the knowledge of these branches of knowledge is not allowed or permitted.
37   Refer Page 30

of *yad* [hand] as the 'organs [of the body].' Nor do we prove in the *tafsir of wajh* [face], the face which includes the eyes, nose, ears, tongue and lips. Similarly, we do not do the *tafsir* of *istava* [to sit firmly on] as *istiqrar* [residing] (as sitting on the *arsh* [Empyrean]). Rather, with regards to *Mutashabihat* [allegorical verses] our creed is the same as that of the *salaf*[38]. That is, we repose faith in *mutashabihat* [allegorical Quranic Verses] and we do not engage in the details of their conditions. Allah Most High may void the deeds of the Sheikh for he has slandered us by alleging that we do the *tafsir* of the *mutashabihat* [the allegorical Quranic Verses]. In fact, the *ulama-e-khalaf*[39] have done the *tafsir* [in the past] of the *mutashabihat* [allegorical Quranic Verses] by interpreting various words. They have done the *tafsir* of *yad* [hand] as the divine omnipotence; they have interpreted *wajh* [face] as the *zath* [essence, nature] and *istava* as *istila* [hegemony, intention]. Hence, this is what we found in the various *tafsirs* [exegeses]. Therfore the charge of interpreting on the basis of one's own opinion, the ambiguous Quranic Verses, the meanings of which nobody other than Allah Most High knows, is a charge on the *ulama-e-khalaf* of the *Ahl-e-Sunnat-o-Jama'at*.

Tafsir that Proves the Depraved Religion

The answer to the third kind of exegesis — according to the Sheikh [Muttaqi], "the writing of the *tafsir* that proves the *fasid mazhab* [depraved religion] to be correct in a manner that places the depraved religion as the core entity and subjugates the tafsir to it; and making the *tafsir* to conform to such perverted religion in whichever way possible, even if such a way is weak" — is that this too is a slander against the Mahdavi group, because our religion does not depend on our opinion, so that we could make the religion as we like it and then make the *tafsir* conform to it in a manner we like. On the other hand, Mahdi[AS] has asserted that the Quran is the real basis of the religion. Hence, the commands [and interdictions] from among the various schools of thought of the religion that are in conformity with the Quran, are correct and good; and what is not in conformity with the Quran is not correct, according to the commands of Mahdi[AS]. This is the *mansab* [position] of Mahdi[AS], as there is a *Hadis*, wherein the Prophet[SLM] has said, 'Mahdi[AS] will establish the religion in the Last Era, as I have established it in the First Era.'

And it is narrated by Jaafar[RZ] that the Prophet[SLM] was asked, 'When Mahdi appears, what would be his *sirat* [biography]?' The Prophet[SLM] said that he would be on the same *sirat* as that of the Prophet[SLM]. He would demolish the innovations of those times as the Prophet[SLM] had demolished the untruths [of his time]. We will, Allah willing, deal with this issue in detail presently.

---

[38] See next footnote for meaning of *Salaf*.
[39] *Khalaf* means one who comes after or successor. *Salaf-as-Salihin* purports to mean the Companions[RZ] of the Prophet[SLM], their successors and the followers of the successors. And those who followed them are the *Khalaf*.

Deciding the Purport of Allah without Corroborating Argument

And the answer to the Sheikh's fourth kind of exegesis—saying that "the purport of Allah Most High is like this, without any corroborating argument"—is that we do not issue any command in this manner. On the other hand, the *zath-e-muqaddas* [the holy person] whom we accept as the Mahdi Al-Mau'ood[AS] has said that certain Quranic Verses are in his favour or in favour of his group [that is, Mahdavis]. This is among his distinctive features because, as his knowledge about he being the Mahdi Al-Mau'ood[AS] is categorical and absolute, so also his knowledge that some of the Quranic Verses are in his favour or in favour of his group too is categorical and absolute. When we have performed the *tasdiq* [affirmation and confirmation] that he is Mahdi Al-Mau'ood[AS] on the basis of the very proofs, which makes the *tasdiq* of the Prophets[AS], compulsory [and we will go into the details, Allah willing, of this presently], then what proof is more authentic and reliable than the word of Mahdi[AS]?

Interpreting with Leniency and as per One's Desires

However, the reply to fifth kind of exegesis, according to the Sheikh [Muttaqi]—that is, "doing the *tafsir* on the basis of the matters interpreted with leniency and one's carnal desires"—is that we do not do any *tafsir* in this manner. On the other hand, this issue is one of the issues that have already been dealt. It is not correct to enumerate here as another issue.

O my brother! I have stayed in the company of the Companions[RZ] of Mahdi[AS] and have heard their *bayan* [explanation of Quran]. Hence, I have seen many of the listeners crying and weeping on hearing the *bayan*.[40] Many of them were lamenting with their heads bowed down in humility and fear of God! There were many whose faces were changing colour! And many who had fallen unconscious! And many who were shivering! And many who were so impressed by the *bayan* that their body hair used to stand up while the birds of their thought flew in the gardens of the meanings and secrets of the Holy Quran! They found the gardens full of their cherished fruits. No tree in these gardens was cut. There was no let or hindrance. Whenever the horses of their thought were let loose in the fields of the treasures of the meaning of the Holy Quran, they found the fields free, open and unconcealed. O my brother! After having seen this open and obvious matter, who would demand oratorical eloquence from them?

---

40 The author has described the glory of the *bayan* of Quran by the Companions[RZ] of Hazrat Imam Mahdi Al-Mau'ood[AS]. This shows the exaltation of the *bayan*, full of the intimate knowledge of God, of the *noorani zath* [the luminous essence] of the Companions[RZ] of Hazrat Imam Mahdi Al-Mau'ood[AS]. They were so close to God. Their nearness to God and the depth of their *bayan* are the result of their *tasdiq* of Hazrat Imam Mahdi Al-Mau'ood[AS]. It appears that the author [Hazrat Bandagi Abdul Malik Sujawandi[RA], 'Alim Billah] has seen this rare incident with great solemnity. Hence, he has addressed the critic as *Ya Akhi* [O Brother!].

Specifying Verses of Quran with Mahdi^AS and his Companions^RZ

He [Muttaqi] says: These people especially reserve the divine command of Allah for Mahdi and his companions:

> *"Say: This is my way; I call (men) to God resting my stand on firm conviction—I and he who follows me. And glory to God! I am not of those who set up peers for God,"*[41]

We say: The Sheikh has written this incorrectly. There is no mention of 'and his Companions'. Here the Arabic word '*man*' (he) [in the above verse] purports to mean the *zath* of Mahdi^AS, and not the companions of Mahdi^AS. This is a narrative that is proved with constancy [*tawatur*].

He [Muttaqi] says: About the divine saying:

> *"...soon will Allah produce a people whom He will love as they will love Him..."*[42]

They say that its purport is Imam Mahdi Al-Mau'ood^AS and his Companions.

We say: I do not know whether this horrible passage is really that of the Sheikh [Muttaqi] or it is the *tas'heef* [mistake of the copier or the calligrapher], because the correction of the passage is not possible in any manner. [The Sheikh says] و فى قوله تعالىٰ فسوف ياتى الله بقوم يحبهم و يحبونه هم المهدى الموعود و اصحابه . The correct phrase should have been وقولَه تعالىٰ , with *nasab* (*zabar* on the letter lam) so that this *qual* becomes *ma'toof* (dependant) upon the first *qual* which is the *maf'ool* (object) of و يخصون ذلك القول و هذا القول (these people specify). That is يخصون (The people specify that saying and this saying). Or it can be stated this way, و يقولون فى قوله تعالىٰ فسوف ياتى الله الخ هم المهدى و اصحابه .

And the mention of the Mahdi in the *tafsir* of this community is not done by our [Mahdavi] Companions^RZ of their own accord. But it is narrated with constancy from Mahdi^AS that the purport of 'this community', whose arrival is promised, is the community of the Mahdi^AS, and no one else.

And this is among the peculiarities of Mahdi^AS, after the Prophet^SLM. We will deal with it presently, Allah willing.

Difference between *Tafsir* and *Tavil*

Hence, now I begin to discuss the difference between the *tavil-e-mubah* [permissible or lawful interpretation] and *tafsir-e-muharram* [forbidden exegesis]. I say that from amongst the common meanings of the '*Mawwal*'[43], is that meaning which has

---

[41] Quran, S. 12:108 SAL and AYA.
[42] Quran, S. 5:54 AYA.
[43] The object of *tavil* [interpretation] i.e., the thing which is interpreted.

preference with a predominant opinion. *Mawwal* is derived from *aal* or *yaul*. And *aal* is used for the person who returns. When you return something and turn it around, you say *awlatahu*. It means: I have returned and turned it around. Thus when you reflect upon the usage of a word, and you turn it towards a certain meaning, then truly you are doing *tavil* towards that meaning of the word. And this opinion, in the end, is the possible result. Allah has said:

> *"Do they wait to see the [tavil] results (of evil activity) on the day when the [tavil] results of what they were warned against will manifest themselves?"*[44]

In other words, they see only its *tavil* or its consequences.

And the meaning of *mufassar* [made clear] is that the purport of the statement that has come from the *mutakallim* [person who makes the statement] is so clear from the words themselves, that there is no scope for *tavil* [interpretation] or *takhsis* [specialization]. That is why it is called *mufassar* [made clear] because it is open, without a doubt and visible. And this word is derived from the Arabic expression *asfar-us-subh* [unveiling of the morning]. When the morning becomes bright and there is no element of doubt in it, then the Arabs call it *asfar-us-subh*. And this is a derivative from *asfarat al-maratu 'an wajhiha*. This is said when a woman removes the veil from her face. Hence, this word is a transposition of the word *tafsir* [exegesis]. And this is the meaning of the saying of the Prophet[SLM] that, 'the person who does the *tafsir* on the basis of his own opinion should search his place in hell.' In other words, if a person does *ijtihad* [legal reasoning] and on the basis of his own opinion and interpretation issues the command that this is the real purport of Allah Most High, then the above threat is held open for him.

Hence, the difference between *tafsir* and *tavil*, which we have mentioned earlier, is discussed in the books of *Usul* [principles], like *Manar* and others. Our brothers [that is, the Mahdavis] do not do the *tafsir* in this manner. Hence we do not fall under the injunction that 'he who did the *tafsir* of the Quran on the basis of his own opinion should search his place in the hell'.

Bayan of Mahdi[AS]

Now turning to Mahdi Al-Mau'ood[AS]'s *bayan*: it is not as per his opinion and interpretation for it to have the likelihood of being right or wrong, because the rank of *Mahdiat* [the station of being the Mahdi[AS]] is above *ijtihad*. This is by virtue of the saying of the Prophet[SLM] in favour of Mahdi[AS], that 'he [Mahdi[AS]] would follow in my footsteps and will not err'. And further, on the basis of the saying of the Prophet[SLM] that he [Mahdi[AS]] will establish the religion in the Last Era as he [the Prophet[SLM]] had established it in the First Era. We will present all the remaining arguments shortly.

It is impossible for a person to establish the religion in the Last Era in the same way as the Prophet[SLM] had established it in the First Era without posessing the *mushahida-*

---

[44] Quran, S. 7:53 SAL.

e-ruhani [spiritual vision of divinity] to inquire from Allah and His Prophet^SLM. This is because the person who is subservient to such conjectural differences which result from the *tavil* [interpretation] of the Quranic Verses and the Prophetical Traditions, and selecting some of them while rejecting some others, it cannot be said about him that he had established the religion in the same way as the Prophet^SLM had established it in the First Era. The reason for this is that the Prophet^SLM is subject to certainty while the other person would be subject to his conjecture, and consequently he would not be free from error. The difference between certainty and conjecture is like the difference between the heaven and the earth. Allah Most High says:

> *"Most of them follow naught but conjecture. Assuredly conjecture can by no means take the place of truth. Lo! Allah is Aware of what they do."*[45]

And the *bayan* [explanation of Quran] of Mahdi^AS comes from the command of Allah [*amrullah*] and His teachings. Hence, if it is asked on this occasion as to what is the meaning of the command of Allah, because the command of Allah is specific to the Prophets^AS and Mahdi^AS is not a Prophet, because the door of the Prophethood has already been closed and a curtain has been hanged to cover it [Prophethood].

The reply to this is that we do not accept that the command of Allah does not come to anybody other than the Prophets^AS. Do you not see that when Khizr^AS took leave of Musa^AS, he replied to all the matters on which Musa^AS was not patient and said, *"...I did it not on my own accord..."*[46] It is obvious that the meaning is that 'I did not do this on my own but on the command of Allah Most High.' And some of the narratives prove that Khizr^AS is a *vali* [saint] among the Saints of Allah. Hence, the expression '*amrullah*' [command of Allah] is being applied to a saint by the Holy Quran. Then, how could it not apply to Mahdi^AS? It has been stated in some of the Prophetic Traditions that Jibrail^AS [Gabriel] will be in front of Mahdi^AS and Mikail^AS [Michael] would be behind him.

Obligatory to accept the word of Mahdi^AS and reject the word of *Mujtahidin*

In short, after it is determined that he is the Mahdi^AS, whatever is confirmed to have been said by Mahdi^AS is essentially a *hujjat* [incontrovertible proof] and it is obligatory on everyone to accept it. It is also obligatory to eschew all the sayings of the *mujtahidin* that go against the sayings of the Mahdi^AS, because if we assume the co-existence of the Mahdi^AS and the four *mujtahid Imams*^RH, the situation will present two alternatives: either he will be subservient to the *mujtahidin* or the *mujtahidin* will be subservient to him. The Mahdi^AS becoming subservient to the *mujtahidin* is inconceivable, because Mahdi^AS is protected from erring because he is the Vice-

---

[45] Quran, S. 10:37 MMP.
[46] Quran, S. 18:82 AYA.

Regent of Allah, he is the *khalifa* of the Messenger of Allah[SLM], his mission is to invite the people unto Allah and obedience to him is obligatory for every person. The *mujtahid* is not like this. Hence, his [the Mahdi[AS]] being a *matbu'* [one to whom others are subservient] is proved. When the Mahdi[AS] is proved on the basis of those arguments with which the Prophets[AS] are proved, then his sayings are in themselves evidence for us, irrespective of whether the sayings of scholars match his sayings or not, because that [the saying] in itself is *hujjat* [incontrovertible proof]. No argument is required to support the *hujjat* nor is it in need of any further proof. Hence, Abu Shukoor Salimi[RH] has discussed in his book, *Tamheed*:

> Because they [Prophets[AS]] are the *hujjat* [incontrovertible proof] of Allah Most High for the people. And no further proof is produced to prove something that is already proven. Nor is it in need of any further proof. [Here ends the statement of Abu Shukoor Salami].

Specification of Verses of Quran by Mahdi[AS] is not excluded from principles of Arabic

Then, know O Just Man! That the Mahdi[AS] making the two Quranic Verses specific to himself and his community [It is on these that the critic (Sheikh Muttaqi) has raised his objection] is not excluded from the principles of Arabic grammar because the common is sometimes taken as special. It is stated in the book, *Bazdooi*, that:

> The Arabic word *'man'* (who; the one who; those who; whoever) possesses the probability of both the common and the special [meaning]. And in the *Sharah-e-Mutavassit* of *Kafiah*, which is known in our cities as *Vafiah*, it is written that *'man'* (who) and *'ma'* (what) are used for singular, doublet [*tasniyah*], plural, and male and female genders. [Here ends the statement of *Bazdooi*].

In summary, there is need for a system for *takhsis* [specificity], which proves the specificity like the command of Allah Most High: *"'Afa-many-yakhluqu ka-mallaa yakhluq..."*[47], the purport of *'many-yakhluqu'* (the one who creates) is *Haq-Vahda-hoo* [God Alone], because creation by anyone other than Him is impossible. Hence, in the command of Allah, *''ana wa man ittaba'anii'* ('...I and the one who follows me...'[48]), the arrangement of the words indicate that the *'man'* (the one who) is specific because it forms a conjunction with the personal pronoun which is present in *'aduu'* [I invite]. Then the meaning of this Verse is this: 'I invite unto Allah on *baseerat* [vision] and the one who follows me will also invite people unto Allah on *baseerat* [vision].' This *'atf* [conjunction] demands that the *d'avat* [invitation] of the *tabe'* [follower] and the *matboo'* [one who is followed] should be one and the same. Otherwise, there will be

---

[47] Quran, S. 16:17. The meaning of the quoted words is: *'Shall He then who createth and he who cannot create anything be given the same regard?"*

[48] Quran S. 12:108. The meaning of the complete verse is: *Say: "This is my way: I invite unto Allah, upon vision — I and the one who follows me. Glory to Allah! And never will I join gods with Allah!"*

discord between the two calls or invitations.[49] The harmony in a conjunction is among the virtues of a joined sentence.

Further, it is known that inviting [the people unto Allah] was obligatory for the Prophet[SLM]. Similarly, it should be an obligation on his follower. Hence, the *tabe'* [follower] on whom the inviting of the people of the *ummat* towards Allah is obligatory cannot be anybody other than the *zath* of the Mahdi Al-Mau'ood[AS], because the Mahdi[AS] is sent only with this mission. Hence, the saying of the Prophet[SLM] is: 'How can my *ummat* be annihilated when I am at its beginning, Esa[AS] is at its end and Mahdi[AS] from among my descendants is in the middle.' Hence, as the Prophet[SLM] and Esa[AS] are inviters towards Allah Most High, so also the Mahdi[AS] is the inviter towards Allah. And It is so particularly because the command of Allah *'man ittaba'anii'* [the one who follows me] is absolute. And in perfect emulation one would turn towards the *fard-e-kamil* [the Perfect individual]. In this particular situation, the perfect individual is the Mahdi[AS] only, because the Mahdi[AS] is the Seal of the *Vilayat* [Sainthood] of our Prophet[SLM]. And what I have mentioned is possible, probable and likely. But the irrefutable argument in this matter is the saying of Mahdi[AS], the acceptance of which is obligatory on us by the same evidence on which it becomes obligatory to accept the saying of the Prophets[AS] and that [the evidence] is his character. Besides, Allah Most High is the One [God] who inspires the good [deeds].

Further, in the Word of Allah Most High; '...fa-sawfa ya'-tillaahu bi-qawminy-yu-hibbhum wa yuhib'-buunahuu...'[50] Mahdi Al-Mau'ood[AS] has specified the word *qawm* for his community. This is not improbable on the basis of *'aql-o-naql* [rationality or narration]. Hence, we will deal with it.

Imam Baghawi[51] has written in his book of *Tafsir, Ma'alim-at-Tanzil,* under the divine saying: *'O ye who believe! Look to your own selves.'*[52] That:

---

[49] It is proved by the Holy Quran that the *Tabe'* and the *Matbu'* are one. Hazrat Bandagi Miyan Shah Burhan[RA], author of Shawahid Al-Vilayat, writes that:
"Hence, Know O Musaddiq! The positions of *Vilayat* [Sainthood] and *Nubuvvat* [Prophethood] are the attributes of Hazrat Prophet Muhammad[SLM]. *Vilayat* is his immanent attribute and *Nubuvvat* is his exoteric attribute, as Hazrat Bandagi Miyan Syed Khundmir[RZ] has said that Prophethood is the manifestation of the Prophet[SLM] while Vilayat is his immanence. Hence, know O Musaddiq! That Allah Most High has terminated Prophethood with the Seal of Prophethood. And He terminates *Vilayat* with the Seal of Sainthood. And Muhammad[SLM] and Mahdi[AS] are equal [to each other] by the irrefutable arguments in *Shari'at, Tariqat* and *Haqiqat.* It is for this reason that the Mahdi[AS] is called the Seal of Sainthood, *nazir* [equal] of the Prophet and his perfect follower. Hazrat Bandagi Miyan Syed Khundmir[RZ] has said in his book, *Ba'az al-'Aayaat,* quoting Hazrat Prophet Muhammad[SLM] who has said that 'In every *ummat* there is one like its prophet and the *misl* [equal] can be only he who is like the prophet of that *ummat* in the view Allah Most High. Hence, when the follower gets the rank of the prophet, it is necessary that he becomes a *Khalifatullah* [Vice-Regent of Allah]. And in the *ummat* of the Seal of Prophethood too there would be his equal, and that equal is the Mahdi Al-Mau'ood[AS]. [Here ends of statement of Hazrat Shah Burhan[RA].]— From *Shawahid Al-Vilayat.*
[50] Quran, S. 5:54 SAL. Transliteration. It means; "Allah will bring a people whom He loveth and who love Him..." [Translation by MMP.]
[51] His full name is Husayn bin Mahmud al-Farra' al-Baghawi.
[52] Quran, S. 5:105 SAL.

Some of the [Quranic] Verses are such that their interpretation has occurred even before they were revealed. The interpretation of some other Verses has occurred during the period of Prophet Muhammad^{SLM}. The interpretation of some other Verses has occurred sometime after the Prophet^{SLM}. And some Verses are such that their interpretation will occur in the *Aakhir Zamana* [Last Era] (Here ends the statement of the *Ma'alim-at-Tanzil*).

Now I say that the interpretation of this Verse has occurred at the time of the emergence of Mahdi^{AS}. Hence, if it is said that the *mufassirin* [commentators of Quran] have explained that the purport of the *qawm* [community] is the community of *Ansar* [helpers of Madina] or Abu Bakr^{RZ} [Siddiq] and his community, or Salman Farsi^{RZ} and his community. Its reply is that this is not so, because Allah Most High says '*fa-sawfa ya'-tillaahu bi-qawm*' [*Allah will bring a people whom He loveth and who love Him…*]. However, the *Ansar*, Abu Bakr^{RZ} and his community and Salman Farsi^{RZ} and his community, were already present during the period of the Prophet^{SLM}. And the Arabic word '*sawf*' indicates that the advent of the *qawm* [community] will be in the distant future. Then how is it possible for that *qawm* to be present during the period of the Prophet^{SLM}?

The statement of Hasan Basari supports the meaning we have expressed. He has said that Allah Most High knew that a *qawm* will renege on its commitment to Islam after the demise of the Prophet^{SLM}. Hence, He has announced that He will bring a *qawm*. That *qawm* will be friends with Allah and Allah Most High will be the friend of that *qawm*. Same is what the *Ma'alim-at-Tanzil* too has said under this Quranic Verse. This shows that the emergence of the expected *qawm* will occur after the demise of the Prophet^{SLM}. And the purport of this *qawm* is not the *Ansar*, or Abu Bakr^{RZ} and his community or Salman Farsi^{RZ} and his *qawm*, as has been mentioned earlier by some commentators.

This is also supported by the saying of Qazi Shihabuddin who has said in his *tafsir*, *Bahr-e-Mawwaj*, that:

> It is narrated that after the *irtidad* [the revolt of apostates], two thousand people of the Nakh'ee Tribe and three thousand people of the Kundi Tribe, and three thousand from various [miscellaneous] other tribes came into the Religion of Islam and became sincere *muminin* [believers]. '*Fa-sawfa ya'-tillaahu bi-qawm*' [*Allah will bring a people whom He loveth and who love Him…*]' purports this group and this revelation has come in reference to them.

> Some say that that the Prophet^{SLM} was asked who these people were. The Prophet^{SLM} said that they were the *Ansar* [Helpers]. Some others say that the Prophet^{SLM} gestured towards Salman Farsi^{RZ} and bestowed this glory to his *Qawm*. Then, he [the Prophet^{SLM}] said, 'Even if *Iman* [Faith] were hung on the *surayya* [Pleiades], some men of *Faris* [Iran, Persia] will achieve it.' Yet some others have said that this Verse is in the *shan* [glory] of Abu Bakr^{RZ}, who fought and killed *murtidin* [apostates—people who had rebelled and refused

to pay *zakat*—poor-due] with a large army.[53] He made such an arrangement for the killing and did not stop and was not bothered by the blame of the blamers. He did not compromise with them, and said, "By God! Even if they [people who opposed the killing] shackle me to prevent me from fighting, I will continue the killing [the rebels]." Then he hurried to fight the *jihad* [holy war] with them. And by Allah's help and will, he was successful. Some among the rebels were killed while others converted to Muslims.

However, the above-mentioned Quranic Verse, wherein the promise to bring a *qawm* [community] is stated to happen in the future, is difficult to relate to Abu Bakr[RZ], the Ansar [Helpers] or Salman Farsi[RZ], who were present at the time of the revelation of the Verse. However, by the Verse: '*Fa-sawfa ya'-tillaahu bi-qawm*' [*Allah will bring a people whom He loveth and who love Him…*]' purports to bring the new community in the future. If the purport is not to bring or create the community in the future, it will create ambiguity, difficulty and complications. [Here ends the statement of the book, *Bahr-e-Mawwaj*].

Mahdi[AS] and his community are mentioned in the Quran

In the book, *Tafsir-e-Naishapuri*, it has been [clearly] stated that:

"Probably the purport is the community of Mahdi[AS]."

Then, know, O Wise man! The correct meaning of this Quranic Verse is the one that has been stated by Mahdi[AS]. And Allah Most High has given the news of the community of Mahdi[AS] at many places in His Book [Quran]. Among the many Quranic Verses [that have given the news] is the following one:

---

[53] The Muslims residing in the outskirts of the city of Madina refused to pay *zakat* [poor-due] and *ushr* [tithe] after hearing the news of the demise of Hazrat Prophet Muhammad[SLM]. They also revolted against most of the commands of *Shari'at*. Hazrat Prophet Muhammad[SLM] had, while on his death bed, sent a contingent of the army under the leadership of Osama bin Zaid to the frontiers of Syria. The contingent had gone about ten leagues from Madina and had stopped there because the health of Hazrat Prophet[SLM] was deteriorating. When the death of Hazrat Prophet[SLM] occurred, the people of the villages around Madina had refused to pay the poor-due. Hazrat Abu Bakr[RZ], the first Caliph of Islam, ordered that the rebels be attacked. Hazrat Umar[RZ] and all the Companions[RZ] of Hazrat Prophet[SLM] opposed the orders of Hazrat Abu Bakr[RZ]. Their argument was that the rebels were Muslims and had only refused to pay the poor-due and how could they be killed for not paying the poor-due? Hazrat Abu Bakr[RZ] said, "If you do not cooperate with me [in fighting the rebels], I will fight alone against them till my last breath. Even if you tie my hands and feet, I will not stop [fighting them]." Hazrat Umar[RZ] asked, "What is your argument in continuing to fight against them [those who had refused to pay the poor-due], despite the saying of the Prophet[SLM] that I have been commanded to fight the people until they accept that God is one and that I am His Messenger. If one did this, he would save his life and property from me, except by a right." Hence, Hazrat Abu Bakr[RZ] said, "By God! I will fight with that person who differentiates between *namaz* [ritual daily prayers] and *zakat* [poor-due], because *zakat* is the right of the *maal* [property]. And the Prophet[SLM] has said that by suppressing [or misappropriating] somebody's right, their *maal* [property] and *khoon* [blood] would not be safe." Hazrat Umar[RZ] says, "By God! I had seen that Allah Most High had guided [Hazrat] Abu Bakr[RZ] to fight. And this matter is certainly *haq* [Truth]." Up to the end.—[Excerpted from the book, *Mojez-Numa Mutavassit Quran-e-Sharif*, printed at Latifi Press, Delhi.]

"As well as (to confer all these benefits upon) others of them, who have not already joined them..."[54]

In this Verse, the purport of the word *'Aakhariina'* [others of them] is the community of Mahdi[AS].

Along with this is the command of Allah Most High:

"A number of them will be from among the earliest believers, And a smaller numbers will be from among the later believers..."[55]

This command also supports the same meaning. The saying of Imam Baghawi in his book, *Ma'alim-at-Tanzil*, under this Quranic Verse, which is as follows:

"One group of ulama, that is, Abu'l Aa'liah Mujahid 'Ata' bin Abi Riyah and Zahhak, are of the opinion that both the groups mentioned in this Quranic Verse are from the ummat [community] [of Prophet[SLM]] and 'Sullatum-minal-'awwaliin' [a number of them...] are the early people of this ummat [community], and the purport of 'qaliilum-minal-'aa-khiriin' [a small number...] are those people who will be born in the aakhri zamana [Last Era]. (They are the group of Mahdi[AS]).

In the *tafsir* [exegesis] of the Quranic Verse, *'A number of them will be from the earliest believers, And a smaller number will be from among the later believers'*, it is narrated by Ibn 'Abbas that Prophet Muhammad[SLM] had said, 'Both these groups are from my *ummat*.' Hence, the group that has been promised to be brought is the group of Mahdi[AS].

If it is asked wherefrom is this matter understood that the promised *qawm*, which is mentioned in the two Quranic Verses[56] is the community of the Mahdi[AS]? It is probable that there could be any other community from the *Ummah* of the Prophet[AS] whose emergence is awaited. What is the reason for specifying this community to be that of Mahdi[AS]?

The reply to this question is this: Allah Most High may grant you *barkat* [blessings in abundance]. Do justice! Do not resort to crookedness! When we have proved that a *qawm* would emerge after the Prophet[SLM], then it should be seen that besides the *qawm* of Mahdi[AS], is there any other *qawm* whose coming is mentioned in the Quran, when the Mahdi[AS] and his group possess certain specific qualities which are not found in others? And it is these specific qualities which increase the preference for choosing them. Then, what reason do we have to reject this *qawm*, that performs *karamaat* [wonderworks], and look for others?

---

[54] Quran, S. 62:3 AYA.

[55] Quran, S. 56:13-14 SAL.

[56] Quran, S. 5:54 and S. 56: 13 and 14. *"Fa-sawfa ya'-tillaahu bi-qawminy-yu-hi-bbuhum wa yuhib-buunahuu..."* and *"Sallatum-minal-'awwaliin, Wa qaliilum-minal-'aakhiriin."* Meaning *"Nay! God will raise up others, loved of God and loving Him..."* and *"A number of them will be from among the earliest believers, And a smaller number will be from among the later believers..."* —English transliteration and translation from *Al-Qur'an* rendered into English by Syed Abdul Latif.

If it is said that it is possible that the said *qawm* could be purported community of Esa^AS [Jesus Christ], then what is the reason to reject the *qawm* of Esa^AS and to prefer the *qawm* of Imam Mahdi^AS? The reply to this question is that your argument could of course be correct with respect to *aql* [rationality]. But the *naql* [narratives or traditions] rejects it. This is so, because the Prophet^SLM has informed [us] that the *qawm* of Mahdi^AS would come before that of Esa^AS. He has said that Masih [Messiah—Jesus Christ] would meet the various *aqwam* [communities] of the [Muslim] *ummat* that could be like you or better than you in strengthening the religion. This has been mentioned by Ibn Jarjan^RA in his book, *Irshad*, with relevant authorities, as narrated by Ali Sayeed ibn Marzooq Kindi upto RasoolAllah^SLM. Similarly, Imam Qurtubi has narrated it in *Tazkirah*. Further, it is narrated in *Hadis* in *Sihah.*[57] Anas bin Sam'an narrates in the story of Dajjal [Antichrist], 'Then a community whom Allah will protect from the *fitnah* [mischief] of Dajjal will come to Esa^AS. He will wipe his hand over their faces and will talk to them in accordance with their ranks and grades. (Up to the end of the Tradition).

Hence, if it is asked, how is it understood that the *qawm*, which will come to Esa^AS, whom he would caress their faces with his hands and would talk to them in accordance with their ranks and grades and that Esa^AS will find them to be emulating the Companions^RZ of the Prophet^SLM, is the *qawm* of Mahdi^AS. Rather, it is possible that it could be some other *qawm* too.

The answer to this question is that, the matter is not how the questioner has assumed, because the Prophet^SLM has said:

> 'How can the *ummat* [community] be destroyed, when I am at its initial part, and Esa^AS is in its final [or last] part, and Mahdi^AS from my descendants is in the middle part?'

And Razin^RA has added the following words in the *Hadis* [Tradition]: 'And there would be a long period between Mahdi^AS and Esa^AS and during this intervening period there would be a crooked group.[58] Neither this group is from me nor am I from it.'

Hence, the *Hadis* with its connotation proves that the advent of the Mahdi^AS would be before that of Esa^AS. Now the situation presents two alternatives with respect to the people who will be protected from the mischief of the Dajjal. They will either be from the people who have performed the *tasdiq* [affirmation] of Mahdi^AS or they would be from the ones who have rejected the Mahdi^AS. The second alternative is *batil* [void]. Hence, the first alternative will prevail.

If it is said that [in the Quran] at one place, the word *qawm* [community] has been used, while in another place, the word *aqwam* [communities] has been used. How

---

57 *Sihah* are the six famous Sunni collections of Holy Prophet's Traditions made by Bukhari, Muslim, Tirmizi, Abu Daud, Nasai and Ibn Majah.
58 Terha تیڑھا crooked.

can there be any conformity and consonance between the two? The reply to this is: In reality, the *qawm* is one single unit. However, since there are many places and many tribes, the word *aqwam* is used due to their number.

Investigation about Mahdi^{AS} being mentioned clearly or symbolically in the Quran?

He (Muttaqi) says: Despite this, nobody has said that there is a clear or symbolic mention of the Mahdi in the Holy Quran.

We say: If the purport of the Sheikh [Muttaqi] is that the *ulama* of the past have not given the proof of existence of the Mahdi^{AS} from the Holy Quran, because none has quoted Prophet Muhammad^{SLM} as saying that a particular Quranic Verse is in favour of Mahdi^{AS}, then it is correct.

However, the possibility of explanation remains. It does not disappear because it has not been explained in the previous eras. This is because, despite not obtaining any narration from the Prophet^{SLM} regarding some Quranic Verses, the *ulama* [scholars] have extracted commands from these Verses. And they have proved [the validity of] those commands through those verses. Hence, it is mentioned in the books of principles of *Fiqh* [Islamic Code of Law] that the Messenger of Allah^{SLM} departed from this world without clearly explaining the details of the *riba* [usury]. Therefore, for the matters, which he has not clearly explained, the possibility of explanation still persists. It will not fade away only because the *ulama* [scholars] of the past have not explained them. The delay in explaining an issue is allowed until the need for explanation arises. This has been clarified by Imam Nawawi in his book, *Sharah-e-Muslim*, in respect of Osama killing a person who on being pursued had recited: *La ilaha illa Llah* [There is no god but Allah]. That clarification is as follows:

> The Prophet^{SLM} did not make it obligatory upon Osama *qisas* [capital punishment], *kaffarah* [expiation] or *diyat*. Hence, the argument for the annulment of these three alternatives is made. However, the *kaffarah* [expiation] is obligatory on the person [who kills by mistake] and *qisas* [capital punishment] is annulled on the basis of doubt. This is so because the killer [Osama] had presumed the killed person to be a *kafir* [infidel] or he had assumed that the recitation of the *Kalimah* [the Islamic Creed—*La Ilaha illa Llah*] in the given circumstances did not make him a Muslim. On the obligation of *diyat* [blood money], there are two sayings of Imam Shafei^{RA} and the *ulama* have accepted either one of these sayings. The answer to the lack of mention of the *kaffarah* is, that *kaffarah* [expiation] is not immediate; it can be given after a delay. And to delay the explanation of a matter until the need arises is permissible as per the scholars of the fundamental principles of Islamic Jurisprudence. [The saying of Imam Nawawi ends here.]

And what has been stated in the book, *Tawale'*, [59] too supports this view.

> The Jews say: Either there would be an explanation in the *shariat* of Musa[AS] which would make it clear that Musa[AS]'s *shari'at* would be annulled in the future or there would be no mention of it. If it was explained, it would have been well-known with constancy in that *shari'at*, like the real religion of Musa[AS] is well-known and is *mutawatir* [constant]. Hence, if there is mention about its perpetuity in the *shari'at* of Musa[AS], then its annulment would be impossible. If the point that proves the perpetuity of the *shari'at* is not there, then his *shari'at* would not be repeated (the *shari'at* of Musa[AS] would not have been constantly applicable to the Prophets[AS] of the Bani Israel). Hence, the commands of this *shari'at* would not have been obligatory more than once.

> We [the author of *Tawale'*] would answer this point by saying that there exists in the *shari'at* of Musa[AS] the proof which points towards it annulment. However, it was not repeatedly narrated because the need for narrating it did not occur many times, as the need for narrating the original religion had occured. Or, on the face of it, it supports the contention that it would persist forever, but this is not absolute, because its annulment is not *mumtana'* [prohibited or impossible].

Hence, see, O Just Man! The saying of *Tawale'* لم يتوافر الدواعى الىٰ نقله [the need for narrating it did not occur many times] indicates that the lack of narration of it is possible, because the reasons for it were not needed often. The matter we are now discussing is similar.

And this is supported by the saying of Sheikh Abu Shukoor Salami in his book, *Tamhid*, under the discussion about vision of angels. He says:

> Some of the *fuqaha* [Muslim Jurists] have hesitated because there is no *nass* [categorical statement] in the matter of the angels. And prohibition is also not allowed when there is no proof. Hence, there should be hesitation on the matter.

Hence, see, O Just Man! See the saying of Salami that, 'prohibition is also not allowed when there is no proof'. Therefore prohibiting without the proof of prohibition is itself prohibited.

If the purport of the Sheikh [Muttaqi] is that lack of proof about the existence of Mahdi[AS] in the Quran is irrefutable, then we do not accept it, because the finality is achieved by a clear statement [*nass*] from the Book of Allah [Quran] or the *Khabar-e-Mutawatir* [Tradition with constancy] of the Prophet[SLM] or the *ijma'* [consensus] of the *ummat* [Muslim community]. And from among these things, none is present. Hence, how can finality be achieved in future regarding the lack of proof about existence of Mahdi[AS] in the Quran? On the other hand, there is not even a *Khabar-e-Wahid*

---

[59] Its Arabic spelling is طوالع.

[solitary Tradition of Prophet Muhammad^SLM] or a narrative from the Companions^RZ [of Prophet^SLM] that there is no Verse in favour of Mahdi^AS. Similarly, there is no narrative in this respect even from the *mujtahidin* [Muslim Jurists entitled to independent judgment].

Hence, if one were to say that how a thing that has not been proved in the past can be proved in our times, the reply to this question is that it will be proved by the *bayan* [speech] of Mahdi^AS after his *zath* [the person] is proved as the Mahdi al-Mau'ood^AS, because he is the *'alim-e-Rabbani* [scholar on whom the divine knowledge is bestowed]. The secrets of the Book of Allah that have not been revealed to anybody after the Prophet^SLM have been revealed to him [Mahdi^AS]. We will shortly submit the [relevant] arguments in this respect.

The same is the case with Esa^AS. Thus, with respect to the Book of Allah, the explanation and certainty of Esa^AS and Mahdi^AS is final and binding, there is no doubt about this. This is because the final command that they would issue could either be based on their presumption or *ijtihad* [interpretation of the Islamic Law] or opinion. Or it could be based on the basis of the command of Allah Most High or by *kashf-e-yaqini* [convincing divine unveiling] or the *ilham-e-Rabbani* [divine inspiration].

If you accept the first proposition, you would be deemed to attribute certain things to both these eminent personalities that should lawfully not be attributed to them. This is so for the simple reason that calling a matter that is *zanni* [presumed] as *qata'i* [categorically imperative] is *kufr* [infidelity], because it is tantamount to giving evidence against Allah Most High. A presumption gives the benefit only of a presumption.

If you accept the second proposition, the objective is achieved. Then, if you say that the divinely inspired commands cannot give the benefit of being imperative because the *ulama* [scholars] have already proved that *ilham* [divine inspiration] is not a *hujjat-e-qaviah* [strong argument or proof] (because the comparison of *ilham* is possibile only with other similar type of *ilham*).

The reply to this is that the *ilham* [divine inspiration] and *kashf* [divine unveiling] of one who is not Mahdi^AS or Esa^AS does not give the benefit of absolute finality because such a person is not definitely *ma'soom* [sinless or free from error] or *mahfuz* [protected from error]. However, the *ilham* and *kashf* of Esa^AS and Mahdi^AS is absolute and imperative, because both of them have been commissioned to invite people unto Allah Most High. Hence, it is necessary that they should have the correct knowledge of the beliefs and deeds from Allah Most High. But Esa^AS issuing commands on the basis of *ilham* and *kashf* is obvious and manifest, because when Esa^AS descends he will not be a person who receives *wahi* [divine revelation]. Jibrail^AS [Gabriel] too will not be sent to him. Esa^AS will issue his commands on the controversial issues of the Muslim *ummat* [community] on the basis of his *ilham* and *kashf* [divine inspiration and unveiling]. He will not be subservient to the *mazahib* [schools of religious thought] of the four Imams. On the contrary, he would abolish them, because this matter is among his specialties. Similar is the case of Mahdi[AS] who is protected from committing errors [or sinless] on the basis of the arguments and proofs that we have already mentioned.

In short, the proof of the existence of Mahdi[AS] from the Book of Allah is liable to be awaited till it is explained, in case it has not been explained by anybody. Hence, all the sayings of Mahdi[AS] that are proved to have been issued by him are the final and absolute arguments or proofs. They cannot be compared with the presumptive arguments on the basis of the *dalil* [argument or proof] which we have already mentioned in the discussion about Mahdi[AS] joining the *mujtahidin* [Muslim Jurists entitled to independent judgment]. The specialties that have come in favour of Mahdi[AS] also guide us in this matter.

Specialities of Mahdi[AS]

Besides these is the narrative in which the Mahdi[AS] was mentioned before Husain[RZ], son of Ali[RZ]. Husain[RZ] is quoted as saying, 'If I were to get Mahdi[AS], I would have served him all my life.' The Sheikh [Muttaqi] has quoted this narrative in his *risala* [tract]. Similarly, it is mentioned in the book, *Iqd-ud-Durar* also. Apart from these specialties, there is the saying of Prophet[SLM], which is narrated by Ali[RZ]. He said, 'I asked, O Messenger of Allah! Is Mahdi from us or from other than us?' Prophet[SLM] said, 'He is from us. Allah Most High will conclude the religion with him as He had initiated it from us.' [up to the end of the Tradition]. A group of *huffaz* [people who have memorized the Quran or Traditions] have narrated this *hadis* [Tradition] in their books with *sanad* [authorities]. Besides these, Abul Qasim Tabarani, Abu Na'im Asfahani, Abdur Rahim bin Hatim, Abu Abdullah Na'im bin Hammad and others have also narrated this Tradition.

See, O Just Man! The person whose *Zath* is the concluder of the religion, how can such a person not ascertain [issues and commands] with Allah Most High and His Messenger? Hence, it is known from this Tradition that everything that Mahdi[AS] says or does or the thing he decrees as lawful or *haram* [unlawful or prohibited] is the true religion of Muhammad[SLM]. The whole mankind is bound to repose *iman* [Faith] in his sayings.

And among the specialties is what is narrated by Ka'ab Ahbar. He said, 'Without doubt, I find Mahdi[AS] written in the books of the Prophets[AS] of the yore. There is no oppression or defect in his commands.' This Tradition has been narrated with authorities by Imam Abu Amr Muqri in his book *Sunan* and this Tradition has been narrated with authorities by Hafiz Abdullah Na'im bin Hammad. Hence, see, O Just Man! When Mahdi[AS] is mentioned in the books of the previous Prophets[AS], on the basis of rational argument, there is all the more reason that he must also have been mentioned in our Book (Quran), as Mahdi[AS] has explained. Among the specialties is what Salim Amsal[60] has said. He said, 'I have heard Abu Ja'far Muhammad bin Ali[RZ] as saying that Musa[AS] has seen in the *Sifr-e-Awwal* [the first book of Torah], the rank and grade that were given to the *Qayam-Aal-e-Muhammad* (Mahdi[AS]).' He told Allah Most High, 'O Allah! You make me the *Qayam-Aal-e-Muhammad*.' Then he was told, 'He would be from the descendants of Ahmad[AS] [that is, Prophet Muhammad[SLM]].' Hence, he saw in the *Sifr-e-Sani* [second book]. There too he found a similar thing. Then he said the same [as he had said before]. Then he was given the same reply. Then he saw in the *Sifr-e-Salis* [third book]. It was the same here too. Then he said the same. Then he was given the same reply. This has been narrated in the third chapter of the book, *Iqd-ud-Durar*.

Hence, see, O Just Man! How could the explanation of a person who has been mentioned in the three books in the Torah essentially not be final and absolute? It has been mentioned in the book, *Awarif*, as narrated by Ibn Mas'ood[RZ], 'For every Verse [in the Quran] there is a *qaum* [people] that will know its meaning shortly.' The author of the book, *Zawarif*, which is the *Sharah* of *Awarif*, Maulana Ali Peero has said that it is understood by the saying of Ibn Mas'ood[RZ] that some of the meanings of the Holy Quran that did not occur in the minds of the Companions[RZ] of the Prophet[SLM], will occur in the minds of the *Mashayakhin* [saintly guides], particularly the Companions[RZ] of Mahdi[AS].

Hence, see, O Just Man! And ponder over the saying of Ibn Mas'ood[RZ]. In the past there was no explanation about the mention of the Mahdi[AS] in the Quran. Can this be taken as an argument that there would be no such explanation in the future also, especially when the people giving the explanation are Mahdi[AS] and his Companions[RZ]? From the quotation of the *Zawarif*, it is understood that the explanation of the Companions[RZ] of Imam[AS] would be such that it would not be found in the past. Then, how could the explanation about Mahdi[AS] be found in the past? (When the rank and grade of the explanation of the Companions[RZ] of Mahdi[AS] is manifest from the saying of Ibn Mas'ood[RZ],) Their explanation cannot be treated as the *tafsir bir-Rai* (exegesis of the Quran on the basis of the commentator's opinion). Hence, the one who reproaches has become the reproached, the one who curses has become the accursed, the one who drives has become driven…!

And Sheikh Abdur Razzaq Kashi too in his *tafsir*, *Tavilat-e-Quran*, mentioned that the explanation of Quran will be done only by Mahdi[AS] as it should be done and none other can do it. Hence, he has specified that '*Alif-Laaam-Miiim*' as a *qasam* [oath] and its reply is *mahzoof* [dropped]. The dropped reply is this: 'Verily, I will explain this Book [the Quran that was revealed to Muhammad[SLM]] which was promised through the tongues of the Prophets[AS] of the past in their books. And in their books, it is written that the Quran will be with Mahdi[AS] in the Last Era. And no one, other than Mahdi[AS], will know the real explanation of the Quran as it should [be known and

---

[60] The Arabic spelling is سالمامثل

understood]. Esa^AS has stated that, 'We bring to you the words, and *Farqalit* [Paraclete] will bring you the meaning thereof in the Last Era.'

Sheikh Abdur Razzaq has understood the term *Farqalit* used by Esa^AS to be the *zath* of Muhammad Mahdi^AS, although others have understood it as purporting to mean Prophet Muhammad^SLM. However, the truth is what Sheikh Abdur Razzaq has said, because the saying of Esa^AS is, 'We bring to you the *tanzil* [revelation or words].' This purports to mean all the Prophets^AS to whom the divine books were revealed, as Prophet^SLM has stated, 'We are the group of the Prophets^AS. We are neither the heirs of anybody nor anybody could be our heir.'

Hence, see, O Just Man! Without proof, how can it be said with certainty that the existence of Mahdi^AS is not present in the Quran when the absence of an explanation in the past does not preclude the possibility of its explanation in the future? On the other hand, the explanation will be awaited till it comes from Mahdi^AS whose mention is found in the books of the Prophets^AS, as has been revealed in the sayings of Ka'ab Ahbar, Ja'far Sadiq and Sheikh Abdur Razzaq.

This is supported by the saying of Kirmani which he has made under this saying of Ali^RZ, which Ali^RZ had said in reply to a question by Abu Juhaifa. The question is this: 'Do you have anything that the Quran does not have?' Another time he said, 'That which is not with the people.' Then Ali^RZ said, 'Oath on the *zath* Who split the grain and created the soul in it. There is nothing with us that is not in the Quran [We have only what is in the Quran], except for the comprehension of His Book which is bestowed by Allah and that which is in this *sahifa* [tract]. [That *sahifa* was handed over by the Prophet^SLM to Ali^RZ and there were some commands.] Abu Juhaifa says, 'I asked, what is there in the *sahifa*?' Then he said, 'It has information about blood money and the freeing of a prisoner; and that a Muslim should not be killed in place of a *kafir* [infidel].' Kirmani says: Hence, it can be said that, it is mentioned in the chapter on '*Haram* [sanctuary] of Madina' that it is stated in the *sahifa* that, 'for Madina also [like Makkah Mukarramah] the *haram* is upto so-and-so place so if a person perpetrates an incident or shelters the perpetrator, Allah's curse will be upon him.' [Here ends the statement of the *Sahifa*.] Despite this being present in the *sahifa*, Ali^RZ was content to describe only three issues and did not explain the fourth issue that was in the *sahifa*. This necessitates a contradiction. In reply to this complication, Kirmani says that not mentioning the presence of a thing does not mean that it does not exist. Hence, there is no contradiction [Here ends the statement of Kirmani].

The saying of Ali^RZ is to be found in the 28th part of the thirty parts of Bukhari, in the Chapter *Aaqila*.

Hence, see, O Just Man! Look at Kirmani's saying that, not making an explanation of the thing that is there in the *Sahifa* does not mean that it does not exist, for the simple reason that the explanation was not made [either way]. And this is supported by the statement made in the *Tamhid* of Abu Shakoor in favour of the vision of angels. Abu Shakoor has said that some *fuqaha* [Muslim Jurists entitled to independent judgment] have hesitated in this matter, because there is no categorical command about the vision of the angels. And denying it too is not allowed, because there is no proof of even that. Hence, one is bound to hesitate in this matter. Hence, if it is said that the explanation of Quran is not permitted in any way other than *sama'at* [listening][of traditions], because the commentator may not be protected from the misfortune of doing the exegesis on the basis of one's own opinion; the reply to this is that we do not accept this contention that it is not permitted even if the explanation of the commentator is in accordance with the principles of *tafseer* and the words of the Quran support it; rather, till the Day of Judgment, the deducing of the meaning of the Quran will remain entrusted to the commentators who have the rank of extracting commands from the Quran. We will give all the detailed arguments about this shortly.

In addition to all these arguments, is the narrative in the Bukhari Sharif, as narrated by Abu Juhaifa, who has said, 'I had asked Ali^RZ, is there any book with you?' He replied, 'I have no book other than the Book of Allah and the comprehension that is given to a Muslim man.' Kirmani has explained this *Hadis* by saying that there is a guidance in this saying of Ali^RZ that a person of understanding is permitted to extract certain things from the text of Quran, in accordance with his comprehension, that have not been extracted by the earlier commentators. However, this permission is subject to the condition that such extractions should be in accordance with the principles of *Shari'at*. This has been narrated from the *Bukhari Sharif*, Chapter *Kitab-ul-Ilm*.

Besides all these arguments, is the saying of the Prophet^SLM that the person, who was present in the company of the Prophet^SLM and heard it, should convey this *Hadis* [Tradition] to those who are absent because those who are absent may comprehend it better than those who were present. Kirmani has mentioned in the first part in the chapter of 'Some people to whom knowledge is conveyed comprehend it better than those who hear it', that it is obligatory on an *'alim* [scholar] to convey the *ilm* [knowledge] to the people to whom it has not reached and to explain it to the people who have not understood it. And it is a promise that Allah Most High has extracted from the *ulama* that they would "...*make it known and clear to mankind, and not to hide it...*"[61]. And in it is also the matter that verily there will come in the Last Era, those people who will be given the knowledge and understanding that was not bestowed to the people before them. But this will be among a very few people because the term *rubba* [some] was coined for *taqlil* [minimizing].

And besides all these arguments is the one that the author of *Ta'aliq*, has said in the introduction of his book:

> 'Since all knowledge is the bestowal of Allah Most High and, in particular, special gifts, it is not impossible that people from later periods of time are given more than what is given to earlier people'.

---

[61] Quran, S. 3:187 AYA

And among all the arguments is the one that Imam Hujjat-ul-Islam Abu Hamid Muhammad Ghazali[RA] has said in his book, *Ihya ul-Uloom*, that decreeing a speech as *haram* [prohibited] without hearing about it is taboo. The reason for this [prohibition] is because we have not heard anything from Prophet Muhammad[SLM] on some of the Quranic Verses and there is so much disagreement amongst the Companions[RZ] and the people of the later periods that a consensus is impossible and hearing from the Prophet[SLM] on all matters too is impossible. And the *akhbar-o-aasar* [Prophet's Traditions] argue in favour of their expanse in meaning. The Prophet[SLM] said in favour of Ibn Abbas[RZ], 'O Allah! Make him a *faqeeh* [Muslim Jurist] in religion and confer on him the knowledge of *tavil* [interpretation of Quranic Verses].' If *tavil* was based on hearing [that is, it was not permitted beyond stating what was listened], then there was no reason for specifying [of Ibn Abbas[RZ] by the Prophet[SLM]]. Allah Most High says, "...*those among them who are able to think out the matter would have known it...*" [62] And said Abu Darda[RZ], 'A person does not become a *faqih* [Muslim Jurist] unless he is able to explain many perspectives of the Quran.' And Ali[RZ] has said, 'If I wanted I would have written the exegesis of the Surat *Fatiha* which would be enough to load seventy camels.' Ibn Mas'ood[RZ] has said, 'When a person intends the knowledge of the Firsts and the Lasts, he should choose the Quran.' Some of the *ulama* have said that every Quranic Verse has sixty meanings. And what remains without being understood is in addition [to the sixty meanings]. They have also said that the last part of the Quran is comprised of 77,200 sciences, because every *kalma* [word] has a manifest and an immanent meaning and a beginning and end. And there are signs and indications about all sciences. And for a person who thinks, every matter that appears to be difficult to him, there are hints in the Holy Quran about it.

From among all these is the one that has been mentioned in *Zawarif* in the explanation of the saying of Ibn Mas'ood[RZ], 'There is no [Quranic] Verse, except for it there is a community, which will learn the meaning of the Verse.' This statement of Ibn Mas'ood[RZ] incites every seeker who is a man of courage that his courage should not cease on the matters that are listened to, but clear the place in his heart for the matters that are heard so that he understands the nuances of the meaning thereof, the meaning that even the Companions[RZ] too had not comprehended. In fear of improper length [of this discourse], I have abridged some of the arguments and for the wise Just Man only one word is enough to understand.

Exegesis of Quran by the Sufis

He [Muttaqi] says: It is said in *Itqan* that the *tafsir* [exegesis] of the Quran by Sufia is not *tafsir* at all. And Ibn Salah has said in his *Fatawa*, 'I have obtained this point from Imam Hasan Wahidi who is a commentator of Quran. He told me that Abu Abdur Rahman Salami has written "*Haqaiq-ut-Tafsir*" [the realities of the exegesis]. If his belief is that the realities he wrote is a *tafsir* [exegesis], then he has become a *kafir* [infidel].'

[62] Quran, S. 4:83 MMP.

We say: This saying of Imam Wahidi [that he had called Abu Abdur Rahman as *kafir* [infidel] for his belief that his *tafsir* was the realities] is not correct, because the realities that Abu Abdur Rahman has written can be called a *tafsir*. There is no objection to calling it a *tafsir*, because it is clear that there are exoteric and esoteric meanings of Quran. And there are nine esoteric meanings of the immanence of Quran. Hence, the term *tafsir* is applicable to each one of the nine esoteric meanings. Then what happened to Wahidi that he treated Abu Abdur Rahman like this? Abu Abdur Rahman has used the sayings of great saints like Abu Yazid Bistami, Junaid Baghdadi and Sheikh Shibli in his *tafsir*. These sayings have illuminated the *ummat* [community] of Muhammad[SLM] in its desire for Allah as a dark night is illuminated by the stars. One is astonished how Sheikh Wahidi, despite his knowledge that Abu Abdur Rahman is among the [eminent] Saints of Allah Most High, could use the term *kaj*[63] for him. This is despite the fact that Abu Abdur Rahman has written very few things of his own accord. If an ambiguity arises from such exegesis, the same ambiguity would be true for the exegeses of other commentators also because at some places [in the Quran] most of the exegists have given commentary just like Abu Abdur Rahman. Under the Quranic Verse, '*Yet of mankind are some who take unto themselves (objects of worship which they set as) rivals to Allah, loving them with a love like (that which is the due) of Allah (only) - those who believe are stauncher in their love for Allah...*,'[64] Qazi Baizavi has written that *andad* [objects of worship which they set up as rivals to Allah] are the idols and also said that they are the *sardars* [chiefs] of the infidels and the infidels were obedient to their chiefs as Allah has said: '*(On the day) when those who were followed disown those who followed (them)...*'[65] And perhaps the purport of *andad* could be something other than the above mentioned two meanings and that is the thing which keeps them away from the remembrance of Allah Most High. And this meaning of Baizavi is similar to the meaning of Abu Abdur Rahman. That which is written in *Tafsir-e-Madarik* under the Quranic Verse: '*...Give them such a deed if ye know any good in them,*'[66] is so similar to the statement of Abu Abdur Rahman that it is almost exactly the same. See the *Tafsir-e-Madarik* if you have any doubt.

He [Muttaqi] says: And it is for this meaning [that the explanation of the Sufia does not have the rank of *Tafsir*], that some of the *ulama* [scholars] have criticized it. The statement of the Sufia is as follows: Under Allah's saying, '*And remember thy Lord when thou forgettest,*[67] the Sufia explain the meaning of *nasiita* ['forgettest'] as [*nasiita nafsika*] 'you forget your *zath* [essence, nature].' And before the said Verse, is the Verse which says, '*Never say in any matter, I will surely do it tomorrow,*'[68] On the other hand say, 'I will do it

---

63   Here the author has used the word 'mu'wajj' [crooked] or 'kaj' (in Urdu) كج *instead of 'kufr'*. This shows that the seekers of Allah know the eminence of the seekers of Allah. How can the seekers of the world know the eminence of the seekers of Allah? Here, Sheikh Muftari has slandered Hazrat Seal of Saints[AS] [or Imam Mahdi[AS]] and his Companions[RZ].
64   Quran, S. 2: 165 MMP.
65   Quran, S. 2: 166 AYA.
66   Quran, S. 24: 33 AYA.
67   Quran, S. 18: 24 MMP.
68   Quran, S. 18: 23 SAL.

God willing. [Then remember your Lord's will or pleasure].' Apart from this, there are many places in Quran where the *ulama* have taken objection. And the commentator of the Quran needs to master fifteen *uloom* [sciences].

We say: The Sheikh's Arabic quotation is much below the standard of correct language and idiom and it does not give the fullest meaning that he intended to convey, because it is devoid of the relative pronoun. On the other hand, the passage written eloquently is و ما يحتاج اليه المفسر من العلوم خمسة عشر علما .

Sciences a *Mufassir* should master

He [Muttaqi] says: The fifteen sciences are as follows: 1. Lexicon; 2. Grammer; 3. Morphology; 4. Derivation; 5, 6 and 7. Meaning, Explanation and Science of rhetoric; 8. Recitation of Quran; 9. Principles of Religion; 10. Principles of Fiqh [Islamic Law] or commands, interdictions, story [Tradition], abridged, clear or manifest, common and special, absolute or confined, strong, ambiguous, manifest, *mawwul*, reality, outward appearance, obvious and allusion or metaphorical; 11. Reasons for the revelation of Quran; 12. Annulling and Annulled; 13. Fiqh [Islamic Law]; 14. The Traditions that explain the abridged and ambiguous matters [or verses].

We say: A commentator of Quran need not know all the sciences that the Sheikh [Muttaqi] has mentioned. The commentator needs to know some of these sciences and the *mujtahid* [Muslim Jurist] needs to know some others of them, because the *mujtahid* has to extract the commands and explain the *Shari'at*. However, the *mufassir* [commentator] does not have the responsibility of extracting the commands from the verses of the Quran. Hence, he does not need to know all those sciences. The commentator needs to know [or master] some of these sciences, like grammer, morphology, lexicon, explanation and the *shan-e-nuzool* [circumstances of the revelation of a Quranic verse]. Hence, these sciences are found necessary for commentary. Most of the commentators, while writing the commentary, have not explained these sciences, which the Sheikh [Muttaqi] has presented as a condition for writing the commentaries of Quran. The argument for not needing all the sciences that he has enumerated, is that Faqih Abul Lais Samarqandi has written in his book, *Bustan,* that the Quran was revealed for the people as a *hujjat* [clear proof]. Hence, if the commentary of Quran was not permissible, then the Quran would not have been a *hujjat* for the people. When such is the case, it is permissible for any person who knew the lexicon and the circumstances of the revelation to write the *tafsir* of the Quran. But for the person who has not mastered the circumstances of the revelation of the verses of the Quran and the lexicon, it is not permitted to write the commentaries. However, he can say or write what he has heard, as a story and not as a *tafsir*. In these circumstances, there is no fear for him. If such a commentator knows that his *tafsir* is confined to what he has listened, and he wants to extract a command or commands from a verse of the Quran, for him also there is no fear.

Hence, know, O Just Man! Our brothers [who have given up the world and become the seekers of Allah Most High] do not comment on the Quran on the basis of their thinking. Rather, they study the exegeses [written by others] and they take only those points from these exegeses that are excellent, in accordance with the command of Prophet Muhammad[SLM], who said, 'The Quran is the treasure of many facets, take only the best from among them.' Since our brothers have turned their faces away from the world and turned them towards Allah Most High, sometimes a point is revealed in their pure hearts that is not found in the exegeses. From among their explanation is the command of Allah Most High, '*O Messenger! Proclaim the (message) which hath been sent to thee from thy Lord. If thou didst not, thou wouldst not have fulfilled and proclaimed His mission...*'[69]. Its meaning is understood as 'The thing you have conveyed would be deemed that you had not publicized it if you did not practice it yourself.' The reason for this meaning is that the preaching of a message is of two kinds: one is oral, that the preacher simply says through his tongue, and the other is expounded by action or deed of his limbs. The point [to be noted here] is that it is obligatory on the *muballigh* [preacher] to practice the message he conveys, so that the oral preaching of the preacher should have definite effect on the people preached. Hence, it is said that the *zaban-e-hal* [practical conveyance of message] is more effective than the *zaban-e-maqal* [oral word]. If the *muballigh* [preacher] does not practice what he preaches, he becomes disgraced in the eyes of the people he preaches. They dislike him. Hence, the preacher by word of mouth is ineffective. Hence, he is not fit to be called a preacher.

Apart from this is the explanation of the command of Allah Most High, '*Say: Short is the enjoyment of this world: the Hereafter is the best for those who do right...*' [70] Its meaning has been given as 'for the person who keeps his *zath* [essence, nature] away from the little wealth of the world.' Hence, it is obligatory on the seeker of the Hereafter that he abstains from his desires, which pollute the purity and cleanliness of the heart. Allah Most High says, '*As for that Abode of the Hereafter we assign it unto those who seek not oppression in the earth, nor yet corruption. The sequel is for those who ward off (evil).*'[71] The meaning of this Quranic Verse is given as 'wickedness and rising [in revolt] are both mentioned in the Quranic Verse; the abode of the Hereafter is given to those who abstain from both these [evils].' Apart from their explanation, is the command of Allah Most High, '*Every soul shall have a taste of death: and We test you by evil and by good by way of trial. To Us must ye return.*' [72] *Fitna* [trial] is testing. *Shar* [evil] is the world. And *khair* [virtue] is the Hereafter. As the world and its *ne'maten* [good things of life; divine blessings] are a trial for the people from Allah Most High and *sadiq* [true or sincere] is the person whose heart is not involved in the love of the world. So much so that he saves his heart from the love of the world and comes out of it; similarly, the *ne'maten* of the Hereafter are the testing (examination) for the *sadiqin*

---

[69] Quran, S. 5: 67 AYA.
[70] Quran, S, 4: 77 AYA.
[71] Quran, S. 28: 83 MMP.
[72] Quran, S. 21: 35 AYA.

[true, sincere people]. Hence the *sadiqin* too, should not show respect or inclination towards them, because this respect or inclination will be a veil for the *visal* [meeting, union with God] of *matlub-e-haqiqi* [real objective] as has been said about the *matlub-e-majazi* [worldly objective]:
[Couplet]

I have left to the people, their religion and their world
For being engaged in Your remembrance, O my religion, O my world!

Hence, see, O Just Man! Which prohibited matter have our brothers adopted and which unlawful matter have they accepted? Can it be called the exegesis on the basis of one's opinion, even if this explanation is not found in the exegeses of the past, despite the fact that the commentators are the Companions[RZ] of Mahdi[AS] and the *tabayeen* [followers of Companions]? They are of lofty ranks and grades that the predecessors of the past did not excel them. Nor did the Saints of Allah of the later period have reached such ranks of excellence. Hence, Pure is the *Zath* that has kept the Companions[RZ] of Mahdi[AS] and the *tabayeen* away from the excessive useless conversations [and He guided them to remain in His remembrance]. He also gave them the ease and comfort of *mo'ainah* [inspection or seeing] and *mushahada* [observation of divinity] and thus made them carefree and indifferent to the anguish of excessive argument.

Divinely Bestowed Knowledge for Exegesis

He [Muttaqi] says: The fifteenth science that is among the science for the exegesis is the divinely bestowed Knowledge. It is a kind of knowledge that Allah Most High bestows on him who works in accordance with his knowledge. Hence, it is stated in the *hadis* that the person who acts in accordance with his knowledge is made the heir to a knowledge that he does not know.

We say: The lone *fazilat* [mastery] of this divinely bestowed knowledge is enough to support the things that the Sheikh [Muttaqi] has enumerated earlier for the lawfulness of the exegesis, because the person who is among the ones who are endowed with the bestowed knowledge will not do a thing that angers Allah Most High. And the matter that angers Allah Most High is the exegesis on the basis of one's own opinion. Even if a person has done the exegesis despite his ignorance of the sciences that the Sheikh [Muttaqi] has enumerated, it is because Allah Most High protects such people from falling into error and he inspires them on the path of correctness. Hence, Allah Most High may keep some of our brothers unharmed and steadfast on the truth in this world and in the Hereafter, because they knew some things and practised what they knew, their practice made them the inheritors of the unknown sciences. The evidence of our explanation is given by their obvious condition.

He [Muttaqi] says: If a person has learned these sciences and practiced according to them, then Allah Most High bestows on him the *ilm-e-ladunni* [divinely inspired knowledge or the bestowed knowledge].

We say: It is astonishing that Sheikh [Muttaqi] has exaggerated in his apostasy, and said that, 'the person who has learned these sciences...' [up to the end]. The astonishment is because the Sheikh has mentioned some of the sciences for the purity and cleanliness of the immanence. Nobody else has laid down the condition of learning these sciences. The cleanliness that makes Allah Most High bestow the *ilm-e-ladunni* is granted to the special people of Allah Most High. Hence, Sheik-ash-Shuyookh Sheikh Shihabuddin[RA] has written in his book, *Awarif*, and I have mentioned this before. It is that sometimes, the servant of Allah becomes *'Alim Billah* and becomes the Man of Certainty but he does not have the knowledge of the *Farz-e-Kifaya*. Hence, what is the use of the *ilm-ul-ishtiqaq* [etymology], syntax, lexicon, *badi'* [science of rhetorical devices], *qira'at* [recitation of Quran] etc. for a seeker of the Truth. He needs the knowledge that enables him to correctly perform *namaz* and *roza*. A seeker of Truth who is a *faqir* [one who has performed the obligation of giving up the world—*Tark-e-Dunya*] need not know the knowledge of *zakat* [poor-due] and *haj* [pilgrimage to Makkah]. Similarly he need not know the detailed knowledge of marriage, divorce, *ila*, *Khula'* and *zihar* [various kinds of divorce], if he is unmarried and without a wife. On the contrary, learning these sciences, which the Sheikh [Muttaqi] has mentioned precludes the achieving of the *ilm-e-ladunni*.

Hence, Imam Ghazali has said about the science of *Fiqh*, in his book *Ihya ul-Uloom* that the science of *Fiqh* is of course the science of religion, but it hardens the heart if one is engaged in reading it all the time. It also removes the fear of God from one's heart. Hence, this characteristic is seen in the people who have become the people of *Fiqh*.

Hence, ponder, O Just Man! Always engaging oneself in reading the science of *Fiqh*, which is a science of religion, renders hardness to the heart then what do you think about being engrossed in sciences other than *Fiqh*? Whatever I have mentioned are the sayings of the saints of Allah, who had received the *Ilm-e-Ladunni* [the knowledge bestowed by Allah Most High to His Friends (*Awliya*)]. According to a saying of the Prophet[SLM], if a person engages himself continuously for forty days in pure remembrance of Allah then fountains of wisdom overflow from his heart and tongue. The books of the *Awliya-Allah* are full of their sayings.

Among the sayings is the one mentioned in the book, *Awarif*, in the matter of the person who reads or recites the Holy Quran. Such a reader of the Quran should not confine his comprehension to the emulation of the *mazhab* that he follows. Then the reader gets the *barkat* [bounty] of the Book of Allah with the manifestation of its secrets. And that *barkat* [bounty or abundance] is proved for the sacred *zawath* [personlities] of the people of wisdom. And that *barkat* is achieved by these *nufoos* [souls] through remembrance [of Allah]. (Here ends the statement of the Sheikh-ash-Shuyookh^{RA}).

He [Muttaqi] says: And he, who has done the *tafsir* [exegesis] of the Quran without the above-mentioned sciences, is deemed to have done it on the basis of his own opinion.

We say: The answer to the issue of the exegesis on the basis of one's own opinions has already been given many times and we do not repeat it.

Question about the knowledge of the Companions^{RZ} and its response

He [Muttaqi] says: The language of the Companions^{RZ} of the Prophet^{SLM} and their followers was Arabic and for this reason they had by nature achieved the sciences of the Arabic Language, not by the benefit of their teachers, and also not by the usual processes of learning. And the *uloom-e-ukhravi* [the sciences of the Hereafter] was known to them from the Prophet^{SLM}. This has been mentioned in the book, *Itqan*. The author of *Itqan* has copied from *Allamah* Tuftazani^{RA}, who has written in his *Sharah* that the *mulhid* [heretics] have been named as *Batiniah* [Carmathian sect of the Shi'ites] on the basis of their claim that the clear commands of the Quran and Traditions [of the Prophet^{SLM}] are not based on their manifest meaning but they have an immanent meaning, which is known only to the person who has been bestowed the inspired knowledge, by Allah Most High. The purpose of this claim of the heretics is the total negation of the *Shari'at*. However, the *mazhab* [belief] of some *muhaqqiqin* [research philosophers] is that there are clear manifest meanings for *nusoos* [categorical Quranic commands], despite the fact that there are hidden hints about the immanent nuances, which are revealed to the *arbab-e-suluk* [people of the mystic initiation]. The consonance between the immanent nuances of the clear Quranic commands and their manifest meanings are possible. Hence, that revelation of the minute points is because of the *Iman* [Faith] and pure *Irfan* [intimate knowledge of God and highest form of mystical experiences].

We say: That the Sheikh [Muttaqi] has referred to the *Itqan* for this narrative is proof that he is unaware of the *Sharah-e-Aqaid*, because this narrative is as evident as sunlight in the book, *Sharah-e-Aqaid*. Had he read this book, he would never have referred to the book, *Itqan*. Hence, the Sheikh's mentioning of this narrative from the book, *Itqan*, is proof of his *Adm-e-Itqan* [total absence of perfection], in the knowledge of those books that are current among the *ulama* as the Quran is current among the children.

Then again, know, O Just Man! *Allamah* Tuftazani^{RA} has clarified that the nuances are revealed to the people of the mystic initiation and said that these revelations are because of their perfect *Iman* [Faith] and pure *Irfan* [intimate knowledge of God]. And you, O Sheikh! You know, because you have lived [for some time] with our brothers, that our brothers are those who seek the proximity and nearness of Allah Most High; they fight their *nafs* [self, concupiscence], they perform religious and spiritual exercises, they assign their own work to the will of Allah Most High and they are happy with the pleasure of Allah, making themselves devoid of the love of the world and keeping themselves aloof and away from their own and other people. They also live in loneliness and seclusion for the remembrance of Allah and lay down their lives in the path of Allah and they help and benefit others. Hence, all these virtues of our brothers are manifest and are well known to the people. And nobody knows their hidden conditions and what has been kept concealed for them: that is, the vision of God in this world, [which is] the eternal coolness of the eyes [that is, the cherished desire of the heart]. That is the reward for their good deeds. They are the leaders of those who follow them [in time]; they judge the opinions of those who have gone before them. They explain the Quran and their commentary of it is the best.

The author of the *tafsir* entitled *Tabsir-ar-Rahman*, Maulana Ali Peero has, in the *Sharah* of his book *Awarif,* known as *Zawarif,* quoted the saying of Ibn Mas'ood[RZ] that 'There is no verse, but there is a community for a verse, and the community would shortly know the meaning of that verse.' Under this saying, he said:

> The saying of Ibn Masood[RZ] incites every man of courage, so that his courage is not confined to what he has listened to. And that he should clear the place in his heart where the saying reaches, so that he understands what he has heard, that is, the nuances of the meanings that were not understood even by the Companions[RZ], despite their extreme purity and their hearts being free of things other than Allah Most High and their being the source and fountainhead of the asceticism and continence. May Allah Most High be pleased with them all!

> The Sufi that has both the attributes, that is, his heart being free of the things other than Allah Most High and giving up the world, gets the information about the meaning of every Quranic Verse that is opposed to the thinking and comprehension of common man. On the other hand, he achieves a new meaning from the Quran every time he reads it. This is for the simple reason that whenever he is given the comprehension of the new thing, a new good deed is born and this new deed becomes the cause of the purity of his comprehension. And this is because the *nur* [divine light] reaches from the manifestation to his immanence. Then, he acts in accordance with his second comprehension, with the result that this second purity begets a new comprehension. And this chain of events continues. These deeds that are born one after another are not the deeds of the *qalib* [mould], because there is a fixed limit by the manifest *Shara'* [divine law]. On the other hand, these are the deeds of the heart, which are as good as known. They are as comprehensible as the others. Thus it happens like this: the reasons for the comprehension are not dependent and the deeds of the heart are known, because they are a clean anecdote as they are the deeds or motives or intentions; in other words they are the intentions or the beliefs. They are also the flattery or the lamenting of the soul in the presence of the Almighty. It

also learns the etiquette of the heart in the presence of the soul, which is latent, and then becomes *munawwar* [illuminated]. And from these matters, every matter becomes the cause of a new inspiration. Hence, for that Sufi a large number of sciences get accumulated and it is also expected that the knowledge of one person is different from that of the other. Hence, under these circumstances, how can the reasons be limited? [Here ends Maulana Ali Peero's saying].

Under the command of Allah Most High, '*And such of your slaves as seek a writing (of emancipation), write it for them if ye are aware of aught of good in them, and bestow upon them of the wealth of Allah which He hath bestowed upon you,*'[73] it is stated in *Madarik* that if the other servant of Allah Most High is the *khudawand-e-ishrat* [Lord of pleasure]; then he is the 'confidant' of the court of the Almighty. He meets the people to test them. He sees them admonishingly and commands them to rekindle their sense of honour. He is the successor of the Prophet[SLM]. He commands like the command of Allah Most High. He takes [things] for the sake of Allah Most High and he spends in the path of Allah Most High. He understands from Allah Most High and he speaks to Allah Most High.

Oath in the name of Allah Most High! The Companions[RZ] of Mahdi[AS] were endowed with the attributes, which have been mentioned in the *Madarik*. Allah Most High has sealed the heart of the Sheikh [Muttaqi]. He has made him deaf. He [God] has blinded his [the Sheikh's] eyes. He [the Sheikh] lived in the company of the Companions[RZ] of Mahdi[AS] at one time. However, he [the Sheikh] did not achieve the thing that the other Companions[RZ] were divinely bestowed upon. He did not come to know that their *bayan* [explanation of Quran] was perfect *Iman* [Faith] and pure *Irfan* [intimate knowledge of God], as has been stated by *Allamah* Tuftazani[RA].

Narration from Baizavi and its response

He [Muttaqi] says: And its [the saying of *Allamah* Tuftazani[RA] و اماما يذهب اليه بعض المحققين الخ] *nazir* [precedent] is the command of Allah Most High, '*The recompense for an injury [evil] is an injury [evil] equal thereto (in degree): but if a person forgives and makes reconciliation, his reward is due from Allah: for (Allah) loveth not those who do wrong.*'[74] Baizavi has said that the second *sayya'ah* [evil deed] is named as *sayya'ah* because there is alliteration between the first *sayya'ah* and the second *sayya'ah* or it could be because the second *sayya'ah* takes revenge on one who behaves in an evil manner. And the Sufis[RZ] have acquiesced to the manifest meaning of the Verse and then taken the hint. They have said that the path of *tariqat* [mystic way of life] is that the sinner is rewarded with *jaza* [blessings] along with an evil, which is appropriate to his sin. So, the *salik* [seeker] should forgive the evil-doer. He should not compensate with an evil deed. Ponder over these things so that the difference between the *Batiniah* sect and the Sufis becomes obvious.

---

[73] Quran, S. 24: 33 MMP.
[74] Quran, S. 42: 40 AYA.

We say: May Allah Most High give right guidance to the Sheikh [Muttaqi] for he has produced arguments from the conditions of the Sufis so that the conditions of our brothers could be compared with the conditions of the Sufis, because our deduction or drawing conclusion is similar to the Sufis. Then again know, O Just Man! The *ulama-e-zahir* [the scholars of the manifest knowledge] have tried to decree that the Sufis are the misguided people and they have spared no effort to brand them as ignorant, even after the scholars of the manifest knowledge had realized the difference between the *Batiniah* sect and the Sufis. Like the saying of Wahidi regarding Abu Abdur Rahman even though he has quoted only the most eminent Sufis in his *tafseer*. Hence Sheikh [Muttaqi] accusing our brothers of infidelity and innovation is like the scholars of the manifest knowledge accusing the Sufis of *gumrahi* [being misguided] and *bidat* [innovation], etc.

Under the command of Allah Most High, *'They take their priests and their anchorites to be their lords in derogation of Allah, and (they take as their Lord) Christ the son of Mary; yet they were commanded to worship but One Allah: there is no god but He.'*[75] the *Tafsir-e-'Arais* says that Junaid Baghdadi[RA] has said that when Allah Most High intends to do *neki* [goodness, virtue] with the *Murid-e-Aakhirat* [the disciple of the Hereafter], He gives right guidance to him to remain in the company of the Sufis, and protects him from the company of the *qaris* [readers or reciters, who do not act upon what they preach]. If the *be-'amal ulama* [scholars who do not perform deeds according to their knowledge] are engaged in their work and in accumulating the goods and chattels of the world, in vexing and provoking the friends of Allah Most High, in trying to disgrace them, even then their misfortune was enough to disgrace them, more particularly when they taunt the truthful people and the *'arifin* [those who have the intimate knowledge of God]. [Here ends the quotation from Junaid Baghdadi[RA] in the book, *Tafsir-e-'Arais*.]

Calling the Disavower of the Mahdi[AS] as *Kafir*

He [Muttaqi] says: And one of the evils of these Mahdavis is that every Mahdavi has the belief that the person who disavowed the 'dead person' [Imam Mahdi Mau'ood[AS]] became a *kafir* [infidel]; and on the basis of this belief of theirs, they call the Muslims as *kafirs*. Since they unreasonably call the Muslims as *kafirs*, they themselves become *kafirs* [infidels]. This is so because none has said that the disavower of the Mahdi[AS] is a *kafir*.

We say: It is not known whether the last horrid passage of the Sheikh [Muttaqi] is written by him or it is the distortion of the calligrapher. Rather, the passage that completes the objective is this: لان انكار المهدى لم يقل احد بسببه الكفر [This is so because not even one has said that the disavowal of Mahdi[AS] is the cause of infidelity.] Or it could have been said, لان منكر المهدى لم يقل احد بكفره [This is so because nobody acquiesces that the disavower of the Mahdi[AS] becomes an infidel.]

---

[75] Quran, S. 9: 31 AYA.

Then, one is astonished why the Sheikh [Muttaqi] overlooked the *fatwa* of the *muftis* of Makkah, which he himself has quoted as an argument in his previous long tract. In this *fatwa* he has happily and contentedly accepted the contention that the disavower of Mahdi^AS is a *kafir* [infidel]. And the infidelity charge against the disavower is the *fatwa* of the *muftis* of Makkah. Hence, the *Muftis* of Makkah have written that:

> But this group of Mahdavis is calling a person from among the Muslims as *kafir* who has opposed their wrong belief, that is: 'One who accepts is *mumin* and the one who disavows is *kafir*.' If, by this, the purport of the Mahdavis is that, in accordance with their belief, the Muslims are on *na-haq* [unjust or untruth], and that they are expelled from Islam, then the Mahdavis have become *murtid* [apostate]. Allah Most High may protect them. However, the decree about the person who disavowed the Mahdi^AS: Verily, the Prophet^SLM has given the news of infidelity for the person who has disavowed Mahdi^AS. [Here the *fatwa* ends. The person who has given the *fatwa* is Yahya bin Muhammad Hanbali].

The thing which is even more astonishing is what the Sheikh says a few lines later in this tract while calling us as *kafirs* because of our disavowal of that Mahdi (who according to him will emerge later) in whom, as per his opinion, will be found all the signs. In his opinion, our acceptance of this Mahdi is a testament of the rejection of their (Sheik's and his brothers') Mahdi, who they think will manifest all the supposed signs. Hence, it is clear that the allegations he is making against us are reverting to him. He has fallen into the thing which he had run away from! The point to be noted in this is that Allah Most High has brought the truth on the tongue of the Sheikh and has placed the accussation back on him from his own saying. Had it not been this, it is does not behove the glory of a wise man that his first word was nullified by the last part of his saying without a considerable distance between them! It is like the Arab woman who spun the thread for half a day and later in the day she destroyed the spun thread with all her strength!

Is the issue of Mahdi^AS part of beliefs?

He [Muttaqi] says: But the issue of Mahdi^AS has not been discussed in the books of beliefs, despite the mention of those things whose disavowal renders a person *kafir*, like the chastisement in the grave, the affirmation of the *pulsirat* [straight bridge][76] and others.

We say: This statement of the Sheikh [Muttaqi] is like his reference of *Itqan* for issue of *Sharah-e-Aqaid*. It bears witness to his lack of study of the well known books. Had he studied the books, he would never have said what he said, because the issue of Mahdi^AS is mentioned in lengthy and detailed books, like *Sharah-e-Maqasid* and

---

[76] *Pul-sirat* is the extremely narrow bridge over which the righteous pass into Paradise, according to the Muslim beliefs. This bridge is the only pathway to the Paradise.—Urdu English Dictionaries.

others. "However, the emergence of Mahdi^AS is narrated by Abdullah Ibn Mas'ood^RZ." And this statement is mentioned in the book, *Sharah-e-Maqasid*, along with a detailed description. Similarly, it is mentioned in the book, *Sharah-e-Aqaid* also, under the topic of Esa^AS in dealing with the conditions and signs of the Doomsday. Allah Most High may destroy those people who repose faith and beliefs in such a Sheikh who is devoid of the manifest religious sciences and immanent inspirations.

Is the *Munkir* (disavower) of Mahdi^AS a *Kafir*?

He [Muttaqi] says: Hence, if it is said that the *hadis* [Prophetical Tradition] says 'He who disavows the Mahdi^AS is a *kafir*' then it is evident that the *munkir* [disavower] of Mahdi^AS is *kafir* [infidel]…

We say: Jabir bin Ibn Abdullah has narrated this *hadis* [Tradition] and Imam Abu Bakr Al-Askaf has reported in the book, *Fawaid-al-Akhbar*, in these words: 'He who disavows the emergence of Mahdi^AS, verily, he has committed *kufr* [infidelity] on what had been revealed on the Prophet^SLM.'

Know, O Just Man! The meaning of the words of the Tradition is suggesting that the emergence of the Mahdi^AS is included in those things that were revealed to the Prophet^SLM, that is, in Quran. And Imam Abul Qasim Suhaili has copied this hadis in his book, *Sharah-e-Siyar*. Similarly, it is also narrated in the book, *Fasl-ul-Khitab*.

Reason for *Takfir* of a Disavower of Mahdi^AS

He [Muttaqi] says: … the reply to this is that the Tradition about the disavowal is a weak *ahad*[77] Tradition and gives only the benefit of presumption. Hence, its disavower's *kufr* [infidelity] is not certain under this Tradition.

We say: This issue can be unveiled only by Mahdi^AS whose disavowing this hadis mentions. If the Mahdi^AS decrees *kufr* on his disavower, that would be the [correct] belief. And if he does not decree, then that would be the [correct] belief. When we research the issue of the disavower's *kufr*, we find that there are many arguments that support the infidelity of the disavower. The reason is that the Mahdi^AS is the *khalifa* of the Messenger of Allah; he is the one who revives the religion of the Messenger of Allah, according to the proven consensus of the Muslim *Ummah* [community] from the day of the Prophet^SLM to our day.

It is said in the book, *Nawadir*, that the person who has not accepted, one who invites people to follow the *Shara'*, on the basis of contempt, becomes a *kafir*. Here, the person who invites people to follow the *Shara'* is the *Qazi* [judge] or the *Muhtasib* [censor]. When the disavowal of the judge or the censor on the basis of contempt is *kufr*, the disavowal of the Mahdi^AS is *kufr* for a better reason. [One may ask the

---

[77] *Ahad* are the Traditions transmitted by only one narrator in each link of the chain, though its core text is not disputed.

disavowal of the judge or the censor was on the basis of contempt: is the basis, here contempt too?] Yes. Here too, it is contempt on account of not performing the *tasdiq* [affirmation and confirmation] of the Mahdi^AS and attributing falsehood and wrong claim to the Mahdi^AS is tantamount to insulting him.

Hadis-e-Ahad and *Hadis-e-Mutawatir*

Then, know, O Just Man! The disavowing of a thing that is proved by the *ahad* Traditions is tantamount to not being certain that the *hadis* [Tradition] has emanated from the Prophet^SLM. This is so because even if the *ahad* Tradition is *sahih* [sound], it gives only the benefit of presumption. And the person who denies a thing that is proved by a *hadis-e-mutawatir* [the tradition with repeated continuity] his being a *kafir* is proved by a Prophetical Tradition and it is certain and there is no doubt about it. Because of the large number of the narrators, certainity is achieved and the doubt is erased. Hence a thing which is proved by *ahad-e-zanni* [solitary traditions which give the benefit of presumptions] becomes certain without a doubt after the fact predicted by the Tradition comes into existence. Hence, the rise of the sun from the west is proved by a *hadis-e-ahad* [Tradition narrated by only one narrator]. In the exegesis of the command of Allah Most High, '*In the day when one of the portents from thy Lord cometh*,'[78] it is stated that when the sun rises from the west and the people see it, the presumption will vanish and certainty will be achieved. At that time, the disavowal or the doubt about this *ahad* Tradition of the Prophet^SLM will not persist in the heart [or mind] of the *mumin* [believer]. Similar is the case of the *hadis-e-ahad* in the matter of Mahdi^AS. [The doubt about the *hadis-e-ahad* will persist till the emergence of Mahdi^AS. After his advent, the doubt will vanish and the matter becomes certain.]

And what has Imam Ghazali^RA said in the fourth chapter of his book, *Ihya-ul-Uloom*, about the dangers of *Munazarah* [dialectical speech or controversy], supports this view about the *hadis-e-ahad* becoming correct after the manifestation of the predicted event. The Prophet^SLM has said that when the people learn the sciences and give up deeds, express love with their speech and nurture hatred and enmity in their hearts, and terminate relations with their near and dear ones, Allah Most High will curse them, make them deaf and blind. This Tradition is narrated by Hasan bin Ali^RZ and verily, this Tradition is proved to be *sahih* by *mushahidah* [observation]. (Here ends the statement of Imam Ghazali^RA).

Hence, see, O Just Man! The saying of Imam Ghazali^RA that, "this Tradition is proved to be *sahih* by *mushahidah* [observation]", means that the *hadis* of the Prophet^SLM became *sahih* [sound] among the *ulama* by the manifestation of the predicted event. And what Kirmani has said in the *Sharah-e-Bukhari*, under what Umar^RZ had told his son Abdullah^RZ, is close to the matter mentioned above. (Umar^RZ had told his son Abdullah^RZ that) 'If Sa'ad bin Abi Waqas^RZ narrates any *hadis* from the Prophet^SLM, do

---

[78] Quran, S. 6:158 MMP.

not ask any questions of him.' Kirmani has said that sometimes the *hadis-e-ahad* is systematically surrounded by circumstances, and such *hadis* gives the benefit of certainty. Under those conditions, there remains no need for raising questions. And this saying of Umar^RZ is in the first part of the thirty parts of *Bukhari*, about the chapter on *mas'h* [wiping] of the *mauzah* [socks or footwear].

And among the arguments of *takfir* [decreeing *kufr*] is the saying of the Sheikh [Muttaqi] at the end of his tract and that is: 'In short, the Mahdi^AS cannot be proved unless all those Traditions, which are narrated about him [Mahdi^AS] are found in him.' And the Tradition, 'He, who denies the Mahdi^AS, verily became a *kafir*,' is also among those Traditions that have been narrated about the Mahdi^AS. And if the Mahdi^AS does not decree the command of *takfir* against his disavower, then as per the condition put by the Sheikh [Muttaqi], the Mahdi^AS's *Mahdiat* does not stand proved, because the command of the Mahdi^AS will not be in conformity with the *hadis*. Thus it is astonishing at the Sheikh's lunacy and lack of adequate knowledge of the science of *Hadis* and *Usul* [principles] for he has issued his command only on this *hadis* ['He who denies the Mahdi^AS, verily became a *kafir*,'] that it is weak and does not give the benefit of finality and correctness, despite the fact that most of the *ahadis* about Mahdi^AS are *ahad* and do not give the benefit of their being final and certain. Yes! (It is the answer to the question of its *taqdir*. The question is whether anything has been narrated with constancy in the subject of Mahdi^AS?) The *ahadis-e-ahad* about the existence[79] of Mahdi^AS, despite not having proof of finality, have achieved *tawatur* [constancy], because the narrators themselves have reached the limit of *tawatur*. Because the narrators of the *ahadis-e-ahad* are in a large number, their number makes it impossible that all of them are saying things that are false. Their large number is perpetual to this day. Hence, the beginning of this *khabar* [Tradition] is like its end and its end is like its beginning. All the Traditions that have been reported about the emergence of the Mahdi^AS are unanimous and consistent, except in the matter of signs and attributes. This is so because a large group of people from each of the Islamic sects has narrated it.

He [Muttaqi] says: Certainly the Tradition ('He, who falsifies the Mahdi^AS, verily became a *kafir*') argues in favour of the belief in a Mahdi; it does not argue in favour of the belief in a specific Mahdi.

We say: It would have been better if he had said لان الحديث with *lam jar'ah* so that it could be the reason for his saying فلا يجزم بكفر جاحده or he could have said مع ان الحديث.

I say that the Sheikh's statement لا المهدى المعين [and not a specific Mahdi] is meaningless. The reason is that the obligation of belief in a Mahdi commands that one should believe in the Mahdi al-Mau'ood^AS, who has actually been proved. And it

---

79 The Sheikh [Muttaqi] has written after praises of God and Prophet^SLM, 'There is no doubt that the existence of the Mahdi^AS is proved by the *ahadis*, that are more than three hundred in number.—See Sheikh's first saying.

does not mean that one says that 'one who disavows the Mahdi[AS] is a *kafir* [infidel]' and then say, 'Whoever is Mahdi, I will believe in him; but I do not believe in this Mahdi because of the doubts that occur to me.' If this belief is enough for him, then he is like the person, who says that: 'I believe that the Seal of the Messengers[SLM] will come during the Last Era. But I do not hold the belief that Muhammad is the Seal of the Messengers[SLM].'

Hadis of Sufiani is *Ahad* and not *Mutawatir*

He [Muttaqi] says: If it is accepted that the disavower of the Mahdi is a *kafir*, then the Mahdi, whose disavower is an infidel and whose acceptance is obligatory should conform to the Ahadis and signs that have been narrated for him. However, this person [who has staked the claim] does not possess most of the authentic signs which are particularly related to the Mahdi and are stated in well known Traditions. For example The Sufiani will be present during the era of the Mahdi and the Mahdi will come with Esa[AS] on the soil of Palestine to kill Dajjal, and there are other signs.

We say: The scholars of science of Traditions in their authentic books have not ascertained the soundness [*sahih*] of the Sufiani Tradition. Since they have not clarified whether this Tradition is *sahih* or *mawdu* [sound or fabricated] therefore it cannot be determined whether it is *sahih* or *mawdu* [sound or fabricated]. Rather one would hesitate because of the silence of the scholars of the science of Traditions. This point has been stated in the principles of Traditions. Hence, the Tradition, which one is obliged to accept as sound, is not considered as a *hujjat* [final proof] in respect of dogmatic beliefs. This is so because such a Tradition does not give the benefit of finality and certainty, as the Sheikh [Muttaqi] has mentioned earlier in his saying in answer to some other point, that the *Khabar Ahaad*[80] gives only the benefit of presumption, despite its being *sound*. In our reply, we say the same thing as the saying of the Sheikh [Muttaqi]. The Tradition whose soundness the Imams have hesitated on, does not give the benefit of its own correctness, then, how can it give the benefit of the correctness of the belief for others? [If the confirmation of a given Tradition is lacking, it cannot give the benefit of finality and certainty, and it cannot be taken as a proof in the matters of beliefs]. Then, how can the Tradition about which the authorities have remained silent be taken as reliable? Because the Tradition, which does not give benefit of its own correctness, how can it give the benefit of the correctness of the belief of others? Hence, I have already mentioned this point clearly.

Hence, the Traditions of this kind, about which the authorities have hesitated, will not be decreed as correct, until they actually occur. Thus, if later when the fact predicted in such a Tradition[81] comes to happen and is manifested, it would be understood that the Tradition was pronounced by the Prophet[SLM]. Otherwise, when

---

80 *Khabar Ahad* is the Tradition transmitted by only one narrator in each link of the chain.
81 In other words, the matters mentioned in the Tradition are treated as correct after these matters have come to happen and are manifested.

these matters do not come to happen and are not manifested, the Tradition concerned would be treated as fabricated. Hence, how can such Traditions be presented against the person concerned whose claim is proved by those things with which the claim of Prophets^AS is proved? That is, their character and behavior. I will deal with these matters shortly, Allah willing, when discussing the Sheik's [Muttaqi] example of the mosquito. We have already dealt with the issue of Mahdi^AS appearing along with Esa^AS and we do not reiterate it here.

The Sheikh's saying about the matter of the *Bab-e-Lud* [Gate of Lud], on the soil of Palestine, is just a hint about the Tradition, which is narrated in Qurtubi. This is a very weak Tradition. Hence, Imam Bayhaqi[82] has said in the book, *Shu'b-al-Iman* that the consensus of the *ulama* is on the unambiguous belief. Then again, know that bringing the Sufiani Tradition among the Traditions issued by the Prophet^SLM is proof of the ignorance of the Sheikh [Muttaqi], because this Tradition is not among the Traditions issued by the Prophet^SLM. And the argument is on the point that the Traditions about the attributes of Mahdi^AS do not specify any particular attribute of the Imam^AS. Some of the *ulama* have hesitated about these Traditions, as Bayhaqi has mentioned in his book, *Shu'b-al-Iman*. I have already dealt with this matter earlier.

If the Traditions had been issued in specifying the attributes of the Mahdi^AS, there was no need for the *ulama* to hesitate. However, the ignorance about the Traditions and the suspicion about such ignorance is not justified against the authorities who examine the quality of the Traditions.

Charge of *Kufr* on Mahdavis because they do not believe in the supposedly real Mahdi who is yet to come

He [Muttaqi] says: Hence, his disavowal becomes necessary, because it is necessary to believe in that person who will possess all the signs. Under these circumstances, their *kufr* [infidelity] is the result of their belief in the *Mahdiat* of a person, which makes it necessary for them to disavow the *Mahdiat* of the Mahdi who would possess all those signs.

We say: Verily, it has been mentioned earlier that this saying of the Sheikh [Muttaqi] contradicts his earlier saying in his discussion about the disavower of the Mahdi^AS not becoming a *kafir*. That saying of the Sheikh is this: '...they themselves become *kafirs* [infidels]. This is so because none has said that the disavower of the Mahdi^AS is a *kafir*.' And the Sheikh [Muttaqi] has become a *kafir* under his own saying because he has made the charge of *kufr* against us, just on the basis of our *tasdiq* [affirmation and confirmation] of our Mahdi^AS. His contention is that our *tasdiq* of our Mahdi^AS is tantamount to the denial of his supposed Mahdi that he expects in the future. [This is so because his charge of *kufr* against us is without a justification of the *Shari'at*.]

---

82   His full name is Ahmad ibn al-Husayn al-Bayhaqi^RH.

Hence, you [the reader] think over it, so that contradiction between the two sayings of the Sheikh becomes obvious to you.

He [Muttaqi] says: And among the follies of the Mahdavis is that they mention some of the Traditions that have no reality [significance] in the opinion of the *Sarrafan-e-Hadis* [experts of Traditions] and in their imagination they compare these Traditions with the correct Traditions that have come through various manners. And it is not a hidden fact that the comparison is done only between those Traditions that are equal in the matter of their strength and weakness. The comparison does not take place between the Traditions that are *mashur* [well-known], *mutawatir* [repeatedly constant], and *mustafiz* [favoured] Traditions, which have been proved in various manners and some of those Traditions are *mat'oon* [blame-worthy] Traditions that are not considered to be Prophetical Traditions.

We say: I have found that in the saying of the Sheikh [Muttaqi], المطعون فيها the feminine pronoun ها turns to the *alif* and *lam* of المطعون and this is not correct. On the other hand, the pronoun should be masculine. I do not know whether it is the mistake of the calligrapher or of the Sheikh. It could well be the mistake of the Sheikh, because the last [part of the] saying proves the point that I have mentioned with reference to the Arabic syntax. And the saying is الذى لا ثبوت له اصلا . Then know that this is the folly of the Sheikh [Muttaqi] that he has accused us of folly. Hence, there has been no discussion between us and the *Sarrafan-e-Hadis* [Hadis experts] at any time. If there had been a discussion, we would have advanced our contentions about those Traditions, which do not exist in the view of the *Sarrafan-e-Hadis*. This is another one of the malicious accusations of the Sheikh against us [the Mahdavis]. One can understand from the sayings of the Sheikh that the Sheikh claims to be a *Sarraf-e-Hadis* [Hadis expert]. However, the Sheikh's folly and his lack of proficiency in the science of the Prophetical Traditions are obvious and are being witnessed, where he has said, 'In short, the Mahdi^AS will not be proved unless all those attributes that have come in the Traditions are not found in him.' We will shortly deal with this matter.

I swear by Allah! Even a person, who has an iota of understanding of the Traditions, will not pass an order the like of which the Sheikh has passed. The question of an expert in the science of the Traditions passing an order like that of the Sheikh does not arise at all.

Folly of the Shaikh [Muttaqi]

The Sheikh [Muttaqi] has accused us of *himaqat* [folly]. It is like a Gujarati parable, which is uttered as a proverb. It is like this: A Dakhani [south Indian] was talking with a Gujarati. The Dakhani told the Gujarati, "How strange is the language you speak in your everyday life [of Gujarati language] where you utter a word, and then dropping the first letter of the word you add an 'em' [or *mim*] in its place and utter it again? Instead of saying '*roti*', you say '*roti moti*'; for '*pani*' you say '*pani mani*'; and for '*talwar*' you say '*talwar marwar*'." The Gujarati in order to free himself of this defect replied that 'Such utterances are used by people who are *bazaari mazaari* [or traders]'. Hence, by saying *'bazaari mazaari'*, the Gujarati confessed his defect in his effort to deny his defect.

Similarly, the Sheikh [Muttaqi] has associated us with *himaqat* and arrogated himself to the title of *Sarraf-e-Hadis*. Despite this, he talks like a *havan'naq*[83] [fool, simpleton]. Hence, the Sheikh's sayings are not hidden from the people of wisdom.

He [Muttaqi] says: Despite verification and contentions, it becomes necessary that the obligation of belief is discarded by both sides. Then, how can the claim of the Mahdavis about the belief of *Mahdiat* be accepted as obligatory? This is nothing but their ignorance.

We say: Even if, according to the rule laid down by the Sheikh [Muttaqi], inconsistency is accepted, the acceptance of claim of the claimant becomes obligatory on the basis of the *akhlaq* [morality or ethics] of the claimant. This is so because the *akhlaq* prove the miracles of the Prophets[AS] and the evidence of their *Nubuvvat* [Prophethood] is provided by the witnesses. Had there been no *akhlaq*, the miracles and the evidence of the witnesses would not have been proved. This is so, because if we compare the Prophet who performs miracles with a sorcerer who creates extraordinary imagery, and each of them claims to be a prophet, how can we differentiate between the two and accept one as the Prophet and disavow the other as a sorcerer? Ordinarily, it is not possible to differentiate between the two, except by their *akhlaq*. Hence, if the *akhlaq* of the person are like the *akhlaq* of the Prophets of the past, then it becomes obligatory to accept him as a Prophet. Otherwise, he would not be accepted as a Prophet. Hence, the correctness of the miracle depends on the *akhlaq* of the claimant. Similarly, the evidence of the witness is rejected, unless the witness is just and a person of good and likeable *akhlaq*, in which case, he is accepted [as a good and reliable witness]. Hence, the factor that decides the acceptance of the evidence too, is the *akhlaq* of the witness. A detailed discussion about the matter will follow while dealing with the Sheikh's example of the mosquito.

He [Muttaqi] says: Among the matters besides their ignorance, is the breaking of the *ijma'* [consensus].

We say: Allah Most High may increase lunacy in the treasure of the Sheikh! How he spends his lunacy without any fear of its being spent! Allah Most High says: *'On account of their arrogance in the land and their plotting of Evil, but the plotting of Evil will hem in only the authors thereof.'*[84]

---

[83] *Havan'naq* is a person who talks like a lunatic at times and like a wise person at other times.
[84] Quran, S. 35: 43 AYA.

Belief of Mahdi^AS being Free of Error

He [Muttaqi] says: Their 'breaking the *ijma*'' is that they hold the belief of the '*ismat* [being free from sin] in favour of a *vali*. Hence, they [the Mahdavis] do not allow any mistake or *zillat* [ignominy] for a *Vali*.

We say: The Sheikh [Muttaqi] is aware that we [Mahdavis] believe that, except the Mahdi^AS, a *mutlaq vali* [ordinary saint] does commit mistakes. However, the Sheikh has tried to confine the Mahdi^AS as an ordinary saint. This manifests his enmity and hostility. However, we do not think it to be lawful for the Mahdi^AS to commit mistakes in his *ma'loomat* [information] which is achieved from Allah Most High, because the position and rank of being the Mahdi^AS keeps him free from error. This is so, because if we make it lawful for the Mahdi^AS to err in his *ma'loomat*, it becomes lawful for the Mahdi^AS to commit mistakes in his knowing that he is the Mahdi^AS. In those circumstances, it would not become obligatory for the people to repose *iman* [Faith] in him as Mahdi^AS. The benefit of his being commissioned [by God] to invite the people unto Allah Most High will perish. Then the Imam^AS becomes a person who bears a burden that he is not obliged to bear. And this is not allowed for the Mahdi^AS [because the Mahdi^AS is the *Khalifatullah* (Vice-Regent of Allah) and *Hujjatullah* (proof of Allah Most High)]. Whatever I have so far written are the rational arguments. However, I will submit the traditional arguments on the matter shortly, Allah willing.

He [Muttaqi] says: It is not like what the Mahdavis believe. On the other hand, the *vali* [saint, friend of Allah] is *mahfooz* [protected from sin]. In other words, it is possible that a *vali* may commit an error. However, a *vali* will not insist on [committing] the error. And despite this, there will be no change [for the worse] in his ranks. Hence, it is said that a *vali* is a *vali*, even if he becomes subject to a *sharyi had* [penalty for transgressing the limits of *Shari'at*] and is punished for it. [This will not expel him from his *vilayat* (the rank of a saint)] unless he transgresses the limits of *fisq* [sinfulness] by insisting on and repeating [the sin perpetually]. This cancels the manifest rank of the *vilayat*.

We say: Our brothers hold this kind of belief in favour of the non-Mahdi [*vali* or saint].

Response to the point that Mahdi^AS should possess characteristics mentioned in all *ahadis*

He [Muttaqi] says: In short, the Mahdi will not be proved, unless he possesses all those attributes that have come in the Traditions about him.

We say: I have already mentioned the mischief of this statement of the Sheikh [Muttaqi] many times. Hence, I will not repeat it. Allah Most High may have mercy on him who did justice and observed the waywardness of the Sheikh who has disobeyed the *mazhab* [creed] of the authorities of the Principles and the *muhaddisin* [experts in the science of the Prophet's Traditions] and has applied the condition that all Traditions must be found in the Mahdi, despite the fact that the Traditions differ from one another like day and night.

Hence, see, O Just Man! This is the condition of the person who has claimed to be among the *sarrafan-e-hadis* [experts of Hadis]. What would be the condition of the people who are not among the claimants of *sarrafan-e-hadis*, and yet argue on the basis of the Traditions to prove their disavowal? Woe to the Sheikh [Muttaqi] and his brothers!

He [Muttaqi] says: [This is so] because if the Mahdi is proved by some of the Traditions, there would be no use of the mention of other Traditions.

We say: The contention of the Sheikh indicates that he does not know the principles, arguments and interpretations of Traditions by the *mujtahidin* [Islamic jurists entitled to independent judgment]. Further, he does not even know that the Traditions, the *mujtahidin* hold to be strong, are classified as *asl fil-bab* [fundamental in this subject] and they ignore the Traditions that they consider to be *za'if* [weak] and contradict the strong Traditions.

If the Sheikh were to see the *ahadis-e-Sihah* that deal with raising the hands [during the ritual prayers] with justice and equity, he will find more than ten Traditions. In spite of this, these Traditions are abandoned by the Hanafis. Similarly, if he sees the Quranic Verses and the Prophetical Traditions, which deal with the *iman* [Faith] increasing and decreasing, he would find that they are innumerable. In spite of this, they are subjected to *tavil* [interpretation] by the Hanafis. In the same manner, those Traditions that deal with scarcity of water for cleanliness [for ablutions] are abandoned by the Hanafis. In the matter of estimating the amount of water for cleanliness using the ten by ten [10x10] [yards] method there is no authority near all the *muhaddisin* [experts in the science of Prophetical Traditions] that could be relied upon. Hence, *Faqa'iy Sharah-e-Masabih* and other books mention it. Despite this, that is the *mazhab* [creed] of the Hanafis. It is astonishing that the Sheikh and those of his ilk, know that in all the matters of religion like divorce, poor-due, *le'an* [mutual cursing (by a couple in a court of law in a case of adultery)], *Khula'* [divorce obtained by the wife], *su'lam* [advance payment in a sale agreement], *hi'bah* [gift], *riza'* [foster relationship], *atuqa* [freeing the slave], *taharat* [cleanliness], *najasat* [impurity], *ightisal* [washing, bathing], and other matters, there are Traditions pertaining to them. However, the *mujtahidin* [jurists entitled to independent judgment] have not been able to draw conclusions because there are controversial issues in them. Hence, they have drawn conclusions where they thought that a given Tradition was preferable in the matter of its correctness. Thus they have decreed only such Ahadith as sound and correct. Besides these Traditions, they either abandoned the other Traditions, or they interpreted them. And in the matters of the religion, there is no subject in which they arrived at a consensus and did not disagree.

If the *mujtahidin* had pondered in fixing the signs of the Mahdi^AS, they would have certainly differed from one another because of the contradictions in the Traditions, as they have disputed in all the other matters of the religion. Hence, how can a wise person imagine that all the Traditions that have come in respect of Mahdi will be found in him? This is a thing that the intellect refuses to accept. Please think over it because it is obvious.

He [Muttaqi] says: Verily, Tirmizi has mentioned in his book, *Shama'il*, that the Prophet Muhammad^SLM used to protect his *zuban* [tongue] [that is, he did not speak without an objective]. He used to speak only when there was an objective.

We say: The purpose of the Sheikh [Muttaqi] in bringing the saying of Tirmizi is to support his contention, "if the Mahdi is proved by some of the Traditions, there would be no use of the mention of other Traditions". In other words, the Prophet^SLM did not say anything without an objective. Hence, if [some of the attributes mentioned in the] Traditions are not found in the Mahdi^AS then he is not the Mahdi. And if inspite of some [of the attributes mentioned in the] Traditions being found and some other Traditions are not found; if in these circumstances, the Mahdi^AS is accepted, then it becomes imperative that the Prophet^SLM said something without an objective and as such, it becomes unlawful. In this respect, I say that the reply to this contention has already been given. We do not reiterate it. How can the nation prosper, whose [imaginary] grinding hand-mill is running on the strength of people like the Sheikh [Muttaqi]?

Real *Shari'at* is what Mahdi^AS explains

He [Muttaqi] says: If somebody stakes a claim of being the Mahdi^AS his claim should be juxtaposed with the *ahadis* and the *Shari'at* and examined. If it is in consonance with them [Traditions and *Shari'at*], the claim should be accepted and its *tasdiq* [affirmation and confirmation] should be performed; otherwise, it should not be affirmed and confirmed. If the claimant is pious, a strict follower of the *Shari'at* and his sayings are capable of being interpreted and can be set right in accordance with the *Shari'at*, his sayings will be interpreted and it will be set right in accordance with the *Shari'at*, in good faith in favour of the *muminin* [believers].

We say: Verily, we found the claim of our *matbu'* [leader—Imam Mahdi al-Mau'ood^AS] to be perfectly in consonance with the *Shari'at* of Prophet Muhammad^SLM; moreover, we found him to be one who issues commands as the commander of *Shari'at-e-Ijtihadi* [Interpretative Islamic Code of Law] and one who also explains it, because this point is among the conditions that validate him as the Mahdi^AS. This is so, because Mahdi^AS and Esa^AS will repeal some of the commands of the interpretative Islamic Code of Law. If they do not do this [repeal some of the commands of interpretative Islamic Code of Law], and follow the commands of the *mujtahidin*, the claims of both the celebrities will become suspicious. Hence, both of them will not be the *muqallid* [conformists, followers, and disciples] of the *mujtahidin*.

He [Muttaqi] says: If the claimant does not accept the interpretation of the *Shari'at*, then rejecting the claimant and disavowing his claim and following the *Shari'at* will become obligatory. But interpreting the *Shari'at* on any issue violating the *ijma'* [consensus], and turning it in accordance with one's own claim, affirming it as the reality, and making the *Shari'at* subservient to one's own opinion is sheer apostasy. Allah Most High may protect us from this heresy.

We say: What the Sheikh [Muttaqi] has said is correct in respect of all the *awliya* [saints]. [Every word and deed of the saints of Allah Most High must be seen in accordance with the *Shari'at*.] However, with respect to Imam Mahdi al-Mau'ood^AS, when his being the Mahdi^AS is proved, it is not lawful for anybody to juxtapose any proven saying of the Imam^AS with the *Shara'-Ijtihadi* [interpretative Islamic Code of Law] and accepting it if in consonance, otherwise, rejecting it. On the contrary, the real *Shari'at* is what the Imam^AS explained. The good *tavil* [interpretation] is that which the Mahdi^AS has decreed as good and the bad *tavil* [interpretation] is that which the Imam^AS decrees to be bad. This is so, because the controversies that exist among the *mujtahidin* cannot be brought to consensus. Hence, it is necessary that the Mahdi^AS issues commands regarding some controversial matters as correct and some other controversial matters as incorrect.

The example of this controversy is this: In the view of Imam Abu Hanifa^RA intending the manifest and reality from one and the same word is not correct. But it is correct in the view of Imam Shafei^RA. Similarly giving preference to the confined over the absolute is not correct, except under certain conditions, in the view of Imam Abu Hanifa^RA, whereas it is correct without any condition in the view of Imam Shafei^RA. Similarly, the generality of the manifest is correct in the view of Imam Abu Hanifa^RA and it is not correct in the view of Imam Shafei^RA. Using this analogy for all the differences among the *A'imma-e-Mujtahideen*, is it permissible for every follower of each of the four *mazahib* to examine and compare the saying of Mahdi^AS and accept it if it is in consonance with the thing of his own *mazhab* [creed], otherwise, reject it? [It is not like this.] Rather it is obligatory on all the followers of all the *mazahibs* [creeds] to accept the sayings of Mahdi^AS and reject the sayings of all the imams of the four *mazahibs*. This is so because Mahdi^AS is the final argument [*hujjat*] of Allah Most High, like the Prophets, on all the people. And no other argument is valid over the final argument of Allah Most High.

And our explanation is supported by the thing that Abu Shukoor Salami has mentioned in his book, *Tamhid*, in the matter about crossing the *pul-sirat*.[85]

> This affair [of crossing the *pul-sirat*] will be for the believers and infidels, and not for the Prophets^AS and Messengers^AS. This is so, because entering the hell and crossing the *pul-sirat* is necessary for common *muminin* and is related to [divine] rewards, accountability, weight and the record of deeds. They are necessary for all the *muminin* [believers]. They are not necessary for the

---

[85] *Pul-sirat* is the extremely narrow bridge providing the only approach to Paradise; or Paradise Pathway.

Prophets^AS and the Messengers^AS of Allah Most High. The reason is that all these things that have been mentioned are for the manifestation of good and evil and for giving the reward for the good or punishment for the evil [deeds]. And the Prophets^AS are born free and undefiled of these evils because they are the proof of Allah Most High for the people. And no *hujjat* [argument or proof] is advanced over the *hujjat* [argument or proof] of Allah Most High. Nor is it in need of any argument or proof! [Here ends his (Abu Shukoor Salami's) statement].

Answer to the charge that many Mahdis will be emerge if only some Traditions are required for proof of Mahdiat

He [Muttaqi] says: If the Mahdi is proved by only some of the Traditions, then the *Mahdiat* of every person will be proved for one in whom some of the Traditions will be found. Hence, many *Mahdis* would be found in one and the same period and, similarly, many Esa^AS and Dajjal too will be found.

We say: One is astonished at the short-sightedness of the Sheikh [Muttaqi]. If some of the signs [described in the Traditions] are found, how does it become necessary for many *Mahdis* to be gathered together [at the same time]? This is so because, along with the proof of *Mahdiat*, the Mahdi has to necessarily invite the people unto Allah Most High with the divine teachings, his good *akhlaq* [virtues and morality], and he should remain constantly and consciously insistent on his claim to being the Mahdi until his death. And Allah Most High does not want to give a wrong-doer and a liar the position of a virtuous and likeable person, and leave him in that exalted position till his death. Further, He will not leave the signs of such an imposter alive after his death.

Hence, the Prophet^SLM said when he was close to his demise, 'Verily I had intended to send word to Abu Bakr^RZ and his son and make a declaration that the aspirants are desirous, or the gossipers are gossiping. Hence, I said that Allah Most High would never permit and the believers will not allow that, in the presence of Abu Bakr^RZ, some other person becomes the *Khalifa* [Caliph].' Similar is the case in the matter of the discussion about *Mahdiat*.

If in any person, some of the signs of the Mahdi^AS are found, and in reality he is not the Mahdi^AS, Allah Most High does not want to fulfill his desire and He does not allow his claim to continue.

Example of the Mosquito

He [Muttaqi] says: I did not find any example for this group of Mahdavis other than this one. A person caught hold of a mosquito and tied a thin thread on one of its legs. Then, holding the mosquito in his hand, went to another person, and said, 'Is there someone who will buy an elephant from me.' The other man said, 'How much does it cost?' He named the price. The other person said, 'Bring the elephant so that I can buy it.' He opened his palm and said, 'This is the elephant.' Hence, the other person [the intending buyer] was astonished at the folly of this person who had offered the elephant for sale, and said, 'How do you call a mosquito an elephant?' Then he said, 'Did you not see its trunk?'

Hence, the example of the group of the Mahdavis is like the man of the mosquito. Simply on the basis of their knowledge that he [Syed Muhammad^{AS}] is among the descendants of the Messenger of Allah Most High and his name is Muhammad, they became the believers that he is the Mahdi^{AS}. Allah may protect us from their ignorance.

We say: The Sheikh [Muttaqi] has told the truth! He could not find another example because of his blindness! His truth is like the truth of a blind person, who said that he had never seen the sun and its light! This is so because he has exposed his own condition through his own words. Similar is the case of the person, on whose heart, ears and eyes Allah Most High has placed the veil of blindness. His thinking becomes confused like that of the blind she-camel in a dark night. Hence, Allah Most High has told the story of people such as the Sheikh [Muttaqi]: He says: '*And when they saw them they said: Lo! These have gone astray.*'[86] In other words, the infidels and the hypocrites say about the *muminin* [believers] that they have been misled. But when the believers go into the Paradise, the infidels and the hypocrites will say wistfully and repentantly [in the Hereafter], '*...What has happened to us that we see not men whom we used to number among the bad ones? "Did we treat them (as such) in ridicule, or have (our) eyes failed to perceive them?*'[87] The infidels had called the believers as having gone astray. However, the believers were the perfect ones.

However, the saying of the Sheikh [Muttaqi] that – 'simply on the basis of their knowledge that he [Syed Muhammad^{AS}] is among the descendants of the Messenger of Allah Most High and his name is Muhammad, they became the believers that he is the Mahdi^{AS}. Allah may protect us from their ignorance,' – is the negligence of the Sheikh because the thing which makes the reposing of Faith in Mahdi al-Mau'ood^{AS} as obligatory is the same thing that made the reposing of Faith in the Prophets as obligatory. And this thing is their *akhlaq* [virtues and morality], because *akhlaq* alone are the foundation of reposing Faith in the Prophets^{AS}. Hence, we too repose our Faith on the basis of the *akhlaq* of Mahdi^{AS} as the people of insight and discernment had reposed their Faith in the Prophethood of Prophet Muhammad^{SLM}. This is so, because we have found some Traditions that are proved in the *zath* [personality] of Mahdi^{AS}. We also found some Traditions that did not have the rank of being the [correct] beliefs and proper arguments in the matter of Mahdi^{AS}. Further, we found some of the sayings of the *ulama* [scholars] contradicting each other, so much so that some of the *ulama* have remained silent on the conditions of identifying the Mahdi^{AS}.

---

[86] Quran, S. 83: 32 MMP.
[87] Quran, S. 38: 62-63 AYA

Morality of Mahdi^{AS}

Now I will present the arguments about the *akhlaq* [morality] of the claimant [Imam Mahdi^{AS}] which are worthy of being presented. From among the various arguments is the one, which has been mentioned in the book, *Sharah-e-Aqaid*, in respect of the argument about *nubuvvat* [Prophethood].

And the people of vision have argued on two counts about the Prophethood. First, the condition and the situation just before the *dawat* [call, invitation], during the period of the call and then after the completion of the call is taken into account. And then the great *akhlaq* [morality] of Prophet Muhammad^{SLM} and his sage-like commands, his proceeding towards a place where great wrestlers were poised for a confrontation with him, his Trust in Allah Most High in every adverse situation, and his straightforwardness was such that even his bitterest enemies who tried their best in their efforts to be hostile and taunt him, could not find enough room to find fault with him. Hence, verily the intellect can be certain that all these matters will not come together in the ordinary people who are not the Prophets. Further, the intellect does not accept that Allah Most High accumulates all the excellences and perfections mentioned above, in a person about whom Allah Most High is aware that he slanders Him and then He gives him a respite period of twenty-three years, and makes his religion overpower all other religions and defeat all his enemies, and keep his Signs alive even after his death till the Day of Resurrection.

Secondly, the Prophet^{SLM} staked claim to a great matter, that is, the Prophethood among the people of a community, which had neither a Book nor *hikmat* [wisdom]. He manifested upon the community a Book and wisdom. He taught them the religious commands and illuminated paths and perfected them with grand *akhlaq*. He also filled most people with the excellence of knowledge and deeds. And he illuminated the world with *iman* [Faith] and righteous deeds. Then Allah Most High made his religion predominate over all other religions as He had promised. And Prophethood and Messengership have no meaning other than these matters. [Here ends the statement of *Sharah-e-Aqaid*].

Hence, see, O Just Man! When the people of insight and discernment have argued on the basis of *akhlaq-e-hamidah* [praised morality] and *ausaf-e-mahmoodah* [praise-worthy attributes] for the proof of Prophethood, then which *hadis-e-zanni* [conjectural Tradition] prevents you from accepting a person who is perfectly endowed with these moralities and attributes as the Mahdi al-Mau'ood^{AS}? The reason is that the *akhlaq* [morality] are the final arguments for the acceptance and cannot be compared with *Ahad-e-zanni* [conjectural Traditions][88].

This matter has been established beyond doubt that the attributes and moralities of Imam Mahdi[AS] have been illuminated in the world like the light of the sun. The effectiveness of his speech is well-known all over the world. And verily, by remaining in the company of the Imam[AS], cowards have become courageous, the most ignorant have become great scholars, the great sinners have become the most obedient worshippers, and the great misers have become most generous. The real meaning of eradicating the oppression and injustice from the hearts [and minds] of the people of the earth and filling them with justice and equity is that the oppression is the opposite of the things that have already been mentioned. *The doom will be doubled for him on the Day of Resurrection, and he will abide therein disdained forever; Save him who repenteth and believeth and doth righteous work; as for such, Allah will change their evil deeds to good deeds. Allah is ever Forgiving, Merciful.*[89] According to this, this community of Mahdavis in reality is the *ahl-e-arz* [People of the earth]. Apart from them, the other people are like their donkeys.

From among the other arguments is the one, which is mentioned in the book, *Tawale*, that:

> His [the Prophet[SLM]'s] great *akhlaq* [virtues and morality] are the witnesses to his truth: for instance, his adherence to the Truth and his remaining abstinent from the world throughout his life [or *tark-e-dunya*: rejecting the world], his great generosity that he did not preserve more than one day's food; his bravery was so great that he did not run away even if he had to confront the great pomp and power like that of the battlefield of Uhud [about five miles from Madina]; his eloquence was so great that great orators among the Arabs became dumb before him [the Prophet[SLM]]. Despite great difficulties and hard work, he was insistent on his claim to be the prophet; he was disdainful of the wealthy people, he was courteous to the *faqirs* [indigent people]: all these *akhlaq* [virtues and morality] are not to be found in people other than Prophets[AS]. The attributes that were his are not found in the other people. The manifestation of all these attributes in his *zath* is a great miracle, and it was a strong argument in favour of his *nubuvvat* [Prophethood]." (The statement of *Tawale* ends here).

High Morals are Adequate Proof of Mahdiat

Hence, ponder over it, O Just Man! When it is found that a person stakes his claim to a possible matter [that of being the Mahdi[AS]], which is close to the matter of

---

[88] *Ahad-e-zanni* are the Prophetical Traditions, which are transmitted by only one narrator in each link of the chain. [*Zanni* means conjectural]. Then the meaning of the Arabic expression is Conjectural Traditions of the Prophet[SLM].

[89] Quran, S. 25: 69 and 70 MMP.

Prophethood; and he is bestowed with the attributes which would have made it obligatory, during the period of the Prophethood, to accept the claim of Prophethood; would these attributes not make obligatory, the affirmation of this possible matter [the *Mahdiat*] of the claimant of being the Mahdi[AS], and the rejection of the relevant Traditions based on conjectures?

And among the arguments, is the one, which was adduced by Imam Raghib that:

> There were two signs for every Prophet: one of them is based on wisdom, which is recognized by the people of insight, and that is the manifestation of *anwar-e-ra'iqa* [pure radiance] and the existence of *akhlaq-e-karima* [bountiful virtues] and their being experts in manifest sciences in such a way that their sayings become the *sahib-e-hujjat* [master of arguments] and their explanations gives contentment to their listeners. These matters are such that in their presence no man of insight will demand miracles. Only those who are obsessed with hostility will demand the miracles.

> The second sign is the miracle, the demand for which is necessary for the person who is incapable of differentiating between the sayings of man from that of God! Some of the research philosophers have said that the person who is deficient in wisdom demands proof through miracles over and above the true beliefs and virtuous deeds of the claimant. And the person who is perfect in his wisdom considers the perfection of the true beliefs and virtuous deeds as the proof of the truthfulness of the claim of the claimant and of the obligation of his emulation, because the spiritual diseases are dominant on most of the people because their beliefs and deeds are defective. When we have seen that a person cures spiritual diseases and makes them perfect, then we have understood that he is an expert physician and a truthful prophet. His statement ends here.

This narrative has been written under the Quranic Verse, *'The way of those on whom Thou hast bestowed Thy Grace'*[90], in the book, *Tafsir-e-Rahmani*.

Hence, see, O Just Man! That when an expert physician, who cures spiritual diseases [like the troubled beliefs, defect in deeds, hardness of heart, negligence and the spiritual love for those other than Allah Most High], and who has cured thousands of people from their spiritual afflictions, is the Mahdi[AS], why should we not accept him as such and repose faith in him as the Mahdi[AS]? And how can he be rejected on the basis of conjectural Traditions?

['*Alim Billah*[91]—Bandagi Miyan Abdul Malik Sujawandi[RA], the Author of this book] says: Decidedly and verily, I have found my companions [*ta'bayeen* (next generation of) of Mahdi[AS]], as those who lament at the separation from their beloved [that is, God Almighty]; who remained standing throughout the night in the remembrance of

---

90 Quran, S. 1: 7 AYA.
91 *Alim Billah* means the scholar bestowed with the divine knowledge by Allah Most High.

Allah, their legs swollen of the stress and strain of standing, their eyes swollen with profuse flow of tears and being awake in prayers during the night, and among them are people whose eyes remain open all the time, and most of them remained crying, and many of them remained standing all the time grieving and sighing, many more wailing and weeping, lying on their back and crying loudly — these are the followers of the Companions[RZ] of Mahdi[AS]. Whereas the Companions[RZ] of Mahdi[AS] were the perfect physicians who cured the people suffering from spiritual illness. What are your evil thoughts, O slanderer, about the *zath-e-pak* [pure and unblemished personality] of Mahdi[AS]? Allah Most High is the One Who guides to the right path and inspires rectitude and correctness [in His pious servants].

Ambiguity of Imam Razi regarding Prophethood

And among the arguments is the one, which the author of the book, *Tafsir-e-Naisapuri* gave in reply to the ambiguities of Imam Fakhruddin Razi. And the ambiguity of Imam Razi is his saying:

> I do not know that Iblis [the Devil] was not truthful, his uttering falsehoods and his not being protected from deception other than through the heard arguments [that is, from the Quran and Traditions]. And the truth of the heard arguments depends on the truthfulness of Muhammad[SLM]; and the truthfulness of Muhammad[SLM] depends on the fact that the Holy Quran is a miracle from Allah Most High, and not from *Shaitan-e-khabis* [the wretched devil]. And the achieving of this knowledge [that the Quran is a miracle from Allah Most High and that it is not from Shaitan] depends on achieving the knowledge that Jibrail[AS] is truthful and free from the evil deeds and deceit of the devils. And it necessitates rotation [*daur lazim aata hai*].[92] And this is a hard position. [Here ends the statement of Imam Fakhruddin Razi's ambiguous statement; and the reply of Naisapuri[RA] follows.]

> He says, 'I have often said that the difference between the miracle and necromancy is that he who performs the miracle invites people unto goodness, while the sorcerer invites people towards evil. And the difference between an angel and devil is that the angel gives the inspiration of good while the devil inspires evil. When this is the situation, how can the miracle become like the necromancy and Jibrail[AS] become like the devil? And how can the *daur* [rotation] become necessary? End of Naisapuri[RA]'s statement, under the command of Allah Most High: '*Man is made of haste. I shall show you My portents, but ask Me not to hasten.*'[93]

Hence, see, O Just Man! That the ambiguity of Imam Razi[RA] has been safely overcome from a narrow and difficult position by *khair* [good]. This is the

---

[92] In other words, achieving the knowledge of the truthfulness of Jibrail[AS] depends on the truthfulness of heard arguments, and the truthfulness of the heard arguments depends on the truthfulness of Hazrat Jibrail[AS].
[93] Quran, S. 21: 37. MMP.

comprehensive name of all the praised ethics and morality. And that which is achieved from the *shar* [evil] is the blame-worthy morality. When it has been proved that the person concerned and his community are endowed with the nobility of character of the Prophets[AS], then no fair-minded person will have any doubt about the truthfulness of that person.

And among the arguments is what Imam Muhammad Nasrabadi says in his book, *Tafsir-e-Kashif al-Ma'ani*, under the command of Allah Most High, '*Behold! Allah took the covenant of the prophets, saying: "I give you a Book and Wisdom; then comes to you a messenger, confirming what is with you; do ye believe in him and render him help." Allah said: "Do ye agree, and take this my Covenant as binding on you?" They said: "We agree." He said: "Then bear witness, and I am with you among the witnesses."'*[94] Under this Quranic Verse, Imam Muhammad Nasrabadi has said that:

> The purport of the saying, 'The Messenger, confirming what is with you' is that the Messenger will follow the commands of the Book, in his speech, deeds and condition.

> Although this Verse in the Quran is specifically for the affirmation and confirmation of our Prophet[SLM], the command also applied to the Prophets[AS] preceding Muhammad[SLM]. Hence Abu Mansur Maturidi[RZ] has said that the *tafsir* of the phrase is that the Messenger[AS] would be the one who affirms and confirms all the Prophets[AS] and Messengers[AS]. Hence, any Prophet[AS] or any *ummat* [community of the prophet] was not commissioned except for acting according to what He had made obligatory and what He had desired. And when a righteous person with true sayings, deeds and conditions, which are in consonance with the conditions of the Prophets[AS] of the past and the present, stakes his claim to be a Prophet[AS], then it becomes obligatory on them to accept him as the Prophet[AS]. And then the person from the *ummat* who remains doubtful and suspicious, demands a miracle. However, the person who reposes Faith in the claimant before seeing the miracle becomes the one whose *iman* [Faith] is the strongest, like the *iman* of Abu Bakr Siddiq[RZ]. The reason is that the most important thing in accepting the Prophethood is the morality and ethics of the claimant of the Prophethood. However, the miracle conflicts with necromancy. Both are similar in that they surpass reason and experience. But they are not similar in reality. However, the person who does not accept the *akhlaq* [morality and ethics] as the basis and associates miracle with necromancy, will never repose *iman* in the claimant.

However, in the *ummat* of Prophet Muhammad[SLM], when a person possessesing the attributes of the Prophets in perfect Sainthood comes [upon his claim of khilafat and Mahdiat] with the commands of Allah Most High and the Prophet[SLM] [and says that 'Allah has commanded me,' or that 'the Messenger[AS] of Allah has ordered me'] and he gives the details of his own

---

[94] Quran, S. 3: 81 AYA.

condition under the divine command, under circumstances which are possible and in a manner which the Shari'at does not disapprove, then it becomes obligatory upon the people to accept him [and his claim]. His disavowal is not lawful, because, prior to his staking the claim, he has not uttered anything that violates the Shari'at and his [divine] trance is blended with his consciousness, but his consciousness dominates his trance; it will not be only trance [that is, he will not be devoid of his senses during divine ecstasy.] Hence, his denial will be deemed to be the denial of the Prophets^AS, because his rejection becomes a charge of infidelity against him. And charging infidelity against a *mumin-e-saleh* [virtuous believer] is infidelity in itself. This is an obvious matter.

And his giving the information from Allah Most High through the soul of the Prophet^SLM becomes a final proof. When final proof comes in conflict with conjectural argument, the latter becomes annulled, because the person, who reaches that position, does not utter slander and falsehood against Allah Most High. Hence, his *tasdiq* [affirmation and confirmation] becomes obligatory, because the *tasdiq* of the Prophets^AS did not become obligatory but for the reason of their *akhlaq* [morality and ethics] that were like those of the Prophets^AS of the past era. Hence, praised character would become the cause of the obligation of the affirmation and conformation. And that praised character is present in this Saint [that is the claimant to the Mahdiat]. Hence, the command of the obligation of the *tasdiq* [affirmation and confirmation of the Imam^AS] will continue to persist. [That is, the *tasdiq* of the claimant of the Mahdiat becomes obligatory.] And this matter that has been mentioned is among the principles of the Fiqh Hanafiah. Up to this point is the statement of Imam Abu Muhammad Nasrabadi^RA.

Hence, ponder over it, O Just Man! that, after this satisfactory statement, how can a Just Man argue on the basis of *ahadis-e-ahad* [Traditions transmitted by only one narrator in each link of a chain] and reject the claim of a person whose claim has been proved by a thing that proves the claim of the Prophets, that is, [it is proved] by good character and conduct and likeable morals and ethics.

Among the arguments is the one that has been mentioned in the Bukhari [Book of *Hadis*—Traditions], the saying of Bibi Khadija^RZ who told the Prophet^SLM after he asked her to cover him with a blanket, 'I am afraid of my *zath*!' In reply to this Bibi Khadija^RZ said, 'By Allah! Allah will never disgrace you! You treat your [uterine] relatives with kindness. You do hard work. And you achieve such things that others do not achieve. You treat your guests hospitably. In times of trouble, you support and help the people who are on truth.'

Hence, see O Just Man! How Bibi Khadija^RZ has commended the character and conduct of the Prophet and said the Satan will never be able to give trouble to the Prophet because of the latter's good character and conduct.

Kirmani, the commentator of *Bukhari*, has said under the saying of Bibi Khadija[RZ] that good conduct becomes the cause of avoiding evil deeds. And the noble character becomes the source of eradicating the evil deeds.

And among the arguments is the saying of Imam Abu Hamid Muhammad Ghazali[RA] in his book, *Ihya-ul-Uloom*, in the matter of Prophethood of Prophet Muhammad[SLM]. After enumerating the virtues in the Prophet[SLM]'s character and conduct, he says:

> Verily all those traits that are mentioned, cannot be expected or imagined in any imposter. Those character and conduct cannot even be concealed. On the other hand, the Prophet[SLM]'s praised qualities and the likeable conditions are the witnesses to his truthfulness. So much so, that an ignorant person saw the Prophet[SLM] and spontaneously cried out, 'By Allah! This is not the face of a liar!' And had there been no immanent matters in the Prophet, the manifest matters themselves were enough for his *tasdiq* [affirmation and confirmation]. Here ends the statement of Imam Ghazali[RA].

Hence, O Just Man! See the arguments that make the *tasdiq* of the Prophets obligatory!

And among the arguments is the one, which Imam Ghazali[RA] has said in his book, *Ghayat-al-Uloom*:

> If you have a doubt about a particular person being a prophet or not being one, you cannot achieve certainty about him, except with the knowledge of his conditions and circumstances; or after seeing his conditions and circumstances with your own eyes; or by repeatedly listening to the narratives about him by narrators. Hence, verily when you come to know about the science of the medicine or the science of *Fiqh* [Islamic Code of Law], it will be possible for you to know the physician and the jurists by seeing their conditions and listening to their sayings. Hence, if you do not see the conditions of the physicians and the jurists with your own eyes, you will not be able to know that Imam Shafei[RA] was a jurist and Jalinos [Jalon] was a physician. This is so because you recognize them from your knowledge and not because of the emulation of others. On the other hand, when you learn the two sciences, that is, the science of medicine and Islamic Code of Law and read their books and writings, you acquire the necessary knowledge about their characteristics that one is a jurist and the other is a physician.
>
> Similarly, when you come to know the meaning of Prophethood and ponder over the meaning of the Prophetical Traditions, you will come to know that the Prophet[SLM] had a high ranking, and then you strengthen this knowledge with the experience of those things: the worship and its effectiveness and the purity of the heart. About them, the Prophet[SLM] has said a very good thing! When a person works according to his knowledge, Allah Most High bestows on him a knowledge, which he does not know. This is the *ilm-e-batin*

[immanent knowledge]. Further what a good thing the Prophet^SLM has said. He said, if a person helps an oppressor, Allah Most High appoints that oppressor over him.

Further, the Prophet^SLM has said another good thing that if a person rises in the morning and his objective was only one: that of achieving the Vision of Allah Most High, then Allah Most High frees him from the intentions and thoughts of this world and the Hereafter. Hence, when you have experienced the saying of the Prophet^SLM among thousands of people, you have achieved the necessary knowledge. You should not have any more misgivings about that knowledge.

Hence, do not achieve the certainty about the proof of Prophethood from the miracles such as the staff of Musa^AS or the splitting of the moon into two. Because if you were just to see the staff become a serpent and not consider the innumerable facts which are not included with it, then under these circumstances then there is high possibility that you would suspect it to be necromancy. And that this is just your thought. And it is due to being misled by Allah Most High, because Allah Most High misleads whom he will. And all that has been mentioned earlier was the condition of the *ilmi iman-e-qavi* [strong Faith based on knowledge]. However, the *zauq* [fervour] that is, seeing with one's own eyes or holding with one's own hands can only be achieved by the practices of the *Sufis*. Hence, whatever proof I have mentioned is enough to support the proof of the Prophethood for that objective which I had intended. Up to here is the statement of Imam Ghazali^RA.

Conditions of the Community of Mahdi^AS

Hence, know O Just Man! The mystic knowledge of Mahdi^AS is proved by his condition, words and their effectiveness. Hence, many of the powerful and arrogant people, who used to exploit and drink the blood of [other] people, gave up all their evils after being in the august company of Mahdi^AS for a day or two. And then they distributed their wealth in the way of Allah Most High. They took to indigence, hunger and contentment. Many of the thieves and highway robbers and burglars quit their evil deeds after remaining in the company of Mahdi^AS. They then took to the remembrance of Allah Most High and meditation and then immersed themselves in their obedience to Allah Most High. All their spiritual maladies were cured and they started sporting the condition of the *Sufis* [mystics]. In other words, they distanced themselves from the people [and became closer to Allah Almighty]. They spent their time in seclusion; remained in indigence and hunger; spent their nights in the worship of Allah Most High. They also remained content with little, were patient in difficulties, remained aloof from others for the remembrance of Allah Most High. They used to remain ashamed of their misdeeds and indulged in the remembrance and meditation of Allah Most High. All these virtues were manifest among the followers of Mahdi^AS and the followers' followers. I have examined the effectiveness of the companionship of Mahdi^AS among thousands of people.

Hence, O Just Man! If you do not achieve certainty about the *tasdiq* [affirmation and confirmation] of the Imam^AS from his praise-worthy character and conduct, how did the wise people of the time of Prophet Muhammad^SLM achieve the certainty about the affirmation and confirmation of his Prophethood? The condition of the call of Mahdi^AS towards Allah, which was always in chaste and eloquent language, was such that people would come to him out of their own desire and yearning. Never was his condition separated from being engrossed with *tajalliyat* [divine manifestations] and *mushahidaat* [observations], immersed in the ocean of *mukalamaat* [dialogues] and *mua'inaat* [inspections]; perishing in the *zath* of Allah Most High and remaining with Him under all conditions. Every word he uttered was from the divine command. His every saying was a verse from among the verses of the Holy Quran. So much so, that had his *zath*, which possesed the characteristics of a Prophet, come during the periods of the proclamation of the claims of the Prophets, reposing faith in his Prophethood would have been obligatory on the basis of those arguments which I have already mentioned. Then, how can his claim to be the Mahdi^AS be disavowed? How can he be opposed on the basis of the *Ahad-e-Zanniah* [the conjectural Traditions transmitted by only one narrator in each link of the chain]? His *tasdiq* is made obligatory by the thing that makes the *tasdiq* of the Prophets obligatory, in other words, his exemplary *Akhlaq* [character and conduct].

Tradition of Emperor Heraclius

And among the arguments is the one that has been mentioned in the *Hadis-e-Harqil* [Tradition of Byzantine Emperor Heraclius] of *Bukhari*. This Tradition is narrated by Abul Yaman Hakim Bin Nafe'. He said that he was informed by Shu'yeb and he narrates from Abdullah bin Utabah ibn Mas'ood quoting Abdullah ibn 'Abbas who quoted Abu Sufyan bin Harb that Harqil sent a man to him [Abu Sufyan] when he was sitting among some mounted Quraysh nobles—they had gone to Shaam [Syria] as traders. This incident happened at the time when the Prophet^SLM had concluded a limited treaty [of peace] with Abu Sufyan and other infidels of Quraysh.

In short, all the Quraysh came to Emperor Heraclius. These people were in Ailia. Then Heraclius summoned them to his court. At the time, he was surrounded by the nobles of Rome. He then called an interpreter. Heraclius told the interpreter: 'Ask these people who among them has a very close family relationship to him [Muhammad^SLM] who calls himself a prophet.'

Abu Sufyan says, 'I said I am genealogically closest to him.'

On hearing this, Heraclius said, 'Bring him [Abu Sufyan] closer to me. And bring his companions too near me.' This meant that these other people should be made to stand at the back of Abu Sufyan.

Then Heraclius told the interpreter, 'Tell these people that I will ask Abu Sufyan about the person who calls himself a Prophet. If he [Abu Sufyan] lies to me, they should immediately contradict him.' Abu Sufyan says, 'By Allah, Had I no sense of honour that these people would allege that I was lying, I would certainly have told lies about him [Muhammad[SLM]].'

In short, Abu Sufyan says, Heraclius first asked me, 'How is his lineage among you people?'

I told him, 'He [Muhammad[SLM]] is of [great] lineage among us.'

Then Heraclius asked me, 'Had anybody among you made a similar claim [to be a Prophet] earlier?'

Abu Sufyan says, 'I said, No.'

Heraclius asked me, 'Had there been a king among his ancestors?'

Abu Sufyan says, 'I said, No.'

Heraclius asked, 'Have the wealthy people supported and followed him or the weak people?'

Abu Sufyan says, 'I said, Only weak people [have supported and followed him].'

Heraclius asked, 'Are his followers increasing or decreasing [in number]?'

Abu Sufyan says, 'I said, They were increasing.'

Heraclius asked, 'Does anybody after entering his religion abandons it being displeased with it?'

Abu Sufyan says, 'I said, No.'

Heraclius asked, 'Were you accusing him of lying before he staked his claim?'

Abu Sufyan says, I said, No.'

Heraclius asked, 'Did he ever go back on his promise?'

Abu Sufyan says, 'I said, No. Now we are in a period of truce with him. We do not know what he will do. [Whether he will keep his word or not, we do not know.]'

Abu Sufyan says that he did not get any chance to add anything other than the facts about the truce.

Heraclius asked, 'Have you ever fought a war with him?'

Abu Sufyan says, 'I said, Yes.'

Heraclius asked, 'How was your war with him?'

Abu Sufyan says, 'I said, it was like a contest. Sometimes we won and sometimes they won.'

Heraclius asked, 'What does he command you to do?'

Abu Sufyan says, 'I said, He commands us to worship only Allah. Do not assign partners to Him. Give up all that your forefathers used to do. [Besides this], he commands us to say our ritual prayers, pay poor-due, tell the truth, be pious, be kind to your relatives.'

After this, Heraclius told the interpreter, 'Tell Abu Sufyan this: I asked you about his lineage and you told me that he was of a high pedigree. All Prophets are of high pedigree among their communities. Then I asked you if anybody among you had staked the claim to be a Prophet and you said no. Then I thought if you had said yes [to this question] I would say that he was emulating the earlier claimant. Then I asked you whether there was a king among his ancestors. You said, no. If there was a king among his ancestors, I would say that he was such a person who wanted to regain the country of his forefathers. Then I asked if you had accused him of lying before he staked his claim to be a Prophet. You said, no. I am certain that a person who does not like to lie about people in general, how could he lie about Allah specifically? Then I asked whether wealthy people were following him or weak people, you said weak people were following him. Indeed, only such people who were weak have followed the Prophets. When I asked if his followers were increasing or decreasing, you said they were increasing. In reality, this is the way *iman* [faith] flourishes till it finally reaches perfection. Then I asked if his followers ditch him after being displeased upon entering his religion, you replied in the negative. *Iman* [Faith] is like that. Once its cheerfulness enters the hearts, it stays there. Then I asked if he went back on his promises, you said, no. All prophets keep their promises. Then I asked what commands did he issue to you, you said he commanded you to worship Allah and not to assign partners to Him. He commanded you not to worship idols. He commanded you to perform the *namaz* [daily ritual prayers] to Allah. He also commanded you to be pious and being truthful. […upto the end of the *hadis*]

Hence, Know O Man of Wisdom! The *zath* [essence, nature] of the person whom we have accepted as Imam Mahdi al-Mau'ood[AS], his glory and that of his Companions[RZ] is the same as has been described in the *Hadis-e-Harqil* [the Tradition of Heraclius]. His morals and ethics and those of his Companions[RZ] are exactly like the morals and ethics of the Prophets[AS]. Hence, how can one whose attributes are like those of the Prophets[AS] be disavowed?

Hence, O Man of Wisdom! It is necessary for you to think in the matter of the *zath* of Mahdi[AS] in the same way as the people of wisdom had pondered over the *zath* of Prophet Muhammad[SLM]. Hence, see O Just Man! Most of the Companions[RZ] [of the Prophet[SLM]] saw the cherished morals and exalted ethics of the Prophet[SLM] and performed his *tasdiq* [affirmation and confirmation]. This has come to be known because of the reason of their *tasdiq*. For instance, Abu Bakr Siddiq[RZ], Ali[RZ], Abu Zar Ghifari[RZ] and Zamad Tayyab[RZ] joined Islam and their story of joining Islam has been described in the book, *Bukhari*. Similar is the case of Buraidah[RZ] and sixty mounted

Companions[RZ] converting to Islam. This story is mentioned in the book, *Rozat-ul-Ulama*. Similar is the case of other people reposing Faith in the Prophet[SLM]. If you want to count all those instances, you will not be able to count them. Similarly, the Arabs too reposed Faith in the Prophet[SLM] after the conquest of Makkah. They joined Islam in droves. Hence, this is learnt from the *Bukhari*, the book of Prophetical Traditions, from the reply of Abu Jamila. The Arabs used to censure those who joined Islam before the conquest of Makkah and used to say, 'Ignore him and his community! If Muhammad[SLM] overpowers the people of Makkah, he is a True Prophet.' Hence, when Makkah was conquered, every community hastened in joining Islam. 'And my community overtook me in joining Islam.' Hence, when Abu Jamila came from the Prophet[SLM] to his community, he said, 'I have come to you from the Prophet[SLM] who is True!'

Hence, see O Just Man! Abu Jamila's saying, 'Every community has hastened in joining Islam.' What miracle had they seen in the conquest of Makkah? And in which book had he read that the conquest of Makkah was the truthfulness of the Prophethood of Prophet Muhammad[SLM]? All this, despite the fact that they had seen and heard about the miracles of the Prophet[SLM], but had refrained from reposing Faith in him. Hence, it is known that Faith is the sheer generosity and bounty of Allah Most High. The story of Abu Jamila is mentioned in the seventeenth of the thirty parts of *Bukhari*, in the chapter about the station of the Prophet[SLM] at the time of the conquest of Makkah. Similarly, the Bedouins of Arab reposed their Faith in the Prophet[SLM] after hearing that the people of Makkah had joined Islam. As has been mentioned in *Kirmani*, the Bedouins of Arabia were waiting for the people of Makkah to repose faith in the Prophet[SLM]. Hence, when the people of Makkah became Muslims, all the wild Arabs too became Muslims. All Praise is for Allah Most High at their joining the religion of Islam. And this narrative is mentioned in the *Kirmani* in chapter ten of *Bukhari* about the treaty with the idolaters.

Hence, see O Just Man! The wild Arabs reposed Faith in Islam just in emulation of the people of Makkah. They were neither impressed by the miracles nor were they persuaded by the *akhlaq* [morals and ethics of Prophet[SLM]] like the people of insight and vision. They joined Islam simply by the Guidance of Allah Most High. Allah guides whom He will!

Similarly, Abdullah bin Salam [a Jew scholar residing in Madina] asked three questions and then reposed Faith in the Prophet[SLM]. It is mentioned in *Bukhari*. *Bukhari* says that the Tradition was narrated by Hameed as quoted by Anas. He said that Abdullah bin Salam heard that the Prophet[SLM] had arrived in Madina. At that time he was collecting dates from the ground. He came to the Prophet[SLM] and said, 'I ask you three questions, which none other than the Prophet[SLM] knows. 1. What is the first condition among the conditions of the Day of Resurrection? 2. What is the first thing that the people of Paradise will eat? And 3. What is the thing that causes the likeness of the mother or father in a child?' The Prophet[SLM] said, 'Just now, Jibrail[AS] has informed me about the answers.' Abdullah asked, 'Has Jibrail informed you?' Then the Prophet[SLM] said, 'Yes.' Abdullah said, 'Jibrail is the enemy of the Jews among the angels.' The Prophet[SLM] recited this Quranic Verse: '*Say (O Muhammad, to mankind): Who is an enemy to Gabriel! For he it is who hath revealed (this Scripture) to thy heart by Allah's leave, confirming that which was (revealed) before it, and a guidance and glad tidings to believers.*'[95] Then the Prophet[SLM] said, 'The first condition of the Day of Resurrection is the Fire. It will herd the people from the East to the West. The first thing the people of Paradise will eat is the liver of the fish. When the water of the mother is dominant, the child assumes the likeness of the mother and when the water of the father is dominant over that of the mother, the child assumes the likeness of the father.' Abdullah spontaneously cried, 'I testify that there is no god but Allah, and that you are the Messenger of Allah.'

Information given by the Prophet[SLM] does not give certainty about his Prophethood

Hence, know O Just Man! Giving mere information about the three things does not give the certainty about Muhammad[SLM] being the Messenger of Allah Most High, for the apprehension that he [Muhammad[SLM]] might have heard these things from the Jews who used to visit Makkah for trade and commerce or he might have heard it from the idolaters who went to the Jewish cities for trade. On the basis of this apprehension the eternal disavower would not be certain that Muhammad[SLM] is the Prophet. And this narrative is to be found in the 18th of the 30 parts of *Bukhari* about the hostility towards Jibrail[AS].

Further, according to a *Bukhari* narrative, the cause of the conversion to Islam of Abdullah bin Salam is his listening to the Quranic Verse: '*O ye unto whom the Scripture hath been given! Believe in what We have revealed confirming that which ye possess, before We destroy countenances so as to confound them, or curse them as We cursed the Sabbath-breakers (of old time). The commandment of Allah is always executed.*'[96] It is narrated that when Abdullah bin Salam returned after his journey to Syria, he heard this Quranic Verse. He joined Islam, came to the Prophet[SLM] and said, 'I was not certain that I would return to the members of my family before my face got distorted.' It is narrated this way in *Tafsir-e-Madarik*.

Hence, think over it O Just Man! What miracle had Abdullah bin Salam seen [that he joined Islam]. Hence, if it is said that he had seen a great miracle that would stay put till the Day of Resurrection, and that miracle was the *kalam* of Allah [that is, Quran]. The reply to this is that, this would have been a strong argument if Abdullah had presented this Verse before the experts of Arabic eloquence and demanded from them a verse of this nature and excellence, and when the experts failed to create a

---

[95] Quran, S. 2:97 MMP.
[96] Quran, S. 4:47 MMP.

verse of this excellence then Abdullah would have been certain that this speech was the speech of Allah and no human being was able to create such an eloquent Verse.

What a beautiful thing is written in some of the books, that the basis for the *tasdiq* of the Prophets is the immanent harmony between them and their followers. And then, the correct Tradition of *Bukhari* speaks a lot about this immanent harmony, that a legion of human souls were created and the soul that recognizes the Prophet loves him and the one that does not recognise the Prophet, differs from him.

And similarly, Abdullah ibn Salul and his followers joined Islam after the battle of Badr. Hence, it is narrated in the *Bukhari*, Chapter 18 ولتسمعن من الذين اوتوا الكتاب. Thus when the Prophet[SLM] fought the Battle of Badr and killed the heads of the Quraysh then Ibn Salul and his companions, that is, the idolaters said, 'This virtuous man has come.' therefore they took the oath of allegiance on the hand of the Prophet[SLM] and became Muslims.

Hence, see O Just Man! The reason for Abdullah and his companions joining Islam was not the victory of the Prophet[SLM] over the idolaters of Badr but it was the guidance of Allah to his servants. Otherwise, how could the overpowering of the idolaters be a proof of the veracity of Prophethood, because the Prophets and non-prophets become victorious sometimes and vanquished at the other times. Hence, this cannot be the correct argument for the veracity of Prophethood. Hence, it becomes obvious that Allah Most High provides guidance to whomsoever he wishes with whatever thing He wishes! The miracle was the proof of the truthfulness of the Prophethood for the people of the past.

Similarly, when the Jewish boy who used to serve the Prophet[SLM] became ill, and the Prophet[SLM] went to enquire about his health and asked him to become a Muslim, he instantly became a Muslim. Hence, see O Just Man! The Jewish boy who used to serve the Prophet[SLM] became a Muslim at the time of his death at the mere saying of the Prophet[SLM]. Whereas the miracles and the good manners of the Prophet[SLM] had no effect on him. Allah Most High says: '*It is not for any soul to believe save by the permission of Allah. He hath set uncleanness upon those who have no sense.*'[97] It is obvious from this Quranic Verse that *Iman* depends on the command of Allah Most High and not on the miracle, although the miracle puts blame upon the enemy. The story of the Jewish boy is in the thirteenth part of the *Bukhari*, under the matter of visiting the sick idolater to enquire about the health.

Similarly, Negus, the king of Abyssinia, his companions, monks and intellectuals reposed faith in the Prophet[SLM] immediately after listening to the Quran without any investigation or analysis, despite the fact that experts in Arabic eloquence were present and there was a possibility of confrontation with them. The Quran is eloquent about the immediate reposing of faith. Allah Most High says: '*When they listen to that which hath been revealed unto the messengers, thou seest their eyes overflow*

---

[97] Quran, S. 10:100 MMP.

with tears because of their recognition of the Truth. They say: Our Lord, we believe. Inscribe us as among the witnesses.[98]

Similarly, the Jinns [or *Jinnat*] too became Muslims immediately after listening to the Quran. *'… and they said: Lo! we have heard a marvellous Qur'an, which guideth unto righteousness, so we believe in it…'* [99] Some among them are such who reposed Faith after demanding miracles, because the correctness of the miracle too is dependent on *Akhlaq.* Hence, the person, who does not repose Faith on the basis of *Akhlaq,* associates the miracle with sorcery.

Morals are the only thing to recognize the Prophet[SLM]

Our foregoing submissions are the proof that in the matter of *tasdiq* [affirmation and confirmation], the real thing is the *akhlaq.* Allah Most High says: *'Or do they not recognise their Messenger that they deny him?'*[100] In other words, they did not recognise him by his honesty, truth, perfect wisdom achieved without being taught by somebody, perfect knowledge and good character and conduct. In other words, they recognised that he possessed the above listed attributes. All the commentators of Quran have developed a consensus on this meaning of the above Quranic Verse. None of them has differed on the matter of this meaning of the Verse, because this Verse is in favour of the polytheists. And the polytheists recognised the Prophet only by those attributes. If this Verse had addressed the *Ahl-e-Kitab* [people of the Book], the exegesis of this Verse would possibly have been that they recognised the Prophet[SLM] by what their Book had said [about him]. Therefore, their disavowal of the Prophet was the result of their hostility and malice. Similar is the exegesis in the *Tafsir-e-Madarik.* And in *Tafsir-e-Kawashi* [under the foregoing Quranic Verse] it is said that, enquiry is done merely for the purpose of reprimand and disavowal. In other words, they recognised the Prophet[SLM] from those attributes, but even then they disavowed him. Hence, it becomes known from this Verse that the reason for *tasdiq* [affirmation] of the Prophet was their knowledge that the Prophet was endowed with those attributes. Had this not been the cause of the *tasdiq,* what would have been the cause of the reprimand? Hence, it becomes evident that, after acquiring the knowledge, their disavowal is the result of their malice and hostility. *(It will be said to him:) "Read thine (own) record: Sufficient is thy soul this day to make out an account against thee."* [101]

[98] Quran, S. 5:83 MMP.
[99] Quran, S. 71:1-2 MMP.
[100] Quran, S. 23:69 AYA.
[101] Quran, S. 17: 14, AYA.

Companions^{RZ} of Mahdi^{AS} are like the Companions^{RZ} of the Prophets^{AS}

The reason that I have quoted these arguments and narratives is that our opponents, who have resorted to exaggeration in our disavowal, have concluded that the community of Mahdavis is ignorant and it does not know anything. Then, what would be the condition of these people who charge a community of having been misled despite their [the Mahdavis'] arguments about the *tasdiq* of the Mahdi^{AS} being similar to that which the companions of the Prophets have advanced during all periods of time regarding their *tasdiq* of the Prophets and the attributes of the companions of Mahdi^{AS} are just like the attributes of the Companions^{RZ} of the Prophets?

O brother! If you ponder over the Quranic Verse about the *Ibad-ur-Rahman* [servants of the Merciful God[102]], you will find that the group of Mahdavis are the true servants of Allah Most High. When you read the Verse: [Allah says:] *'Lo! men who surrender unto Allah, and women who surrender, and men who believe and women who believe, and men who obey and women who obey, and men who speak the truth and women who speak the truth, and men who persevere (in righteousness) and women who persevere, and men who are humble and women who are humble, and men who give alms and women who give alms, and men who fast and women who fast, and men who guard their modesty and women who guard (their modesty), and men who remember Allah much and women who remember - Allah hath prepared for them forgiveness and a vast reward.'*[103], you will recognise that they alone are the true Muslim men and Muslim women. When you read the verse, *'Successful indeed are the believers.'*[104] you will come to know that the successful believers are these Mahdavis. And if you desire the verse: *'Not so those devoted to Prayer; Those who remain steadfast to their prayer.*[105], you will always find them steadfast in their prayers. And if you ponder over the Quranic Verse: *'Whenever the Signs of (Allah) Most Gracious were rehearsed to them, they would fall down in prostrate adoration and in tears.'*[106], you will be certain that these are the same people who prostrate and who weep in prostration. The community of Mahdi^{AS} has obtained all these qualities by virtue of reposing faith in the Mahdi^{AS}. Hence, these people were like the dead and became alive after performing the *tasdiq*. Who is more generous than Mahdi^{AS} in distributing the *Faiz* [Bounty] of *Vilayat*? Who is more veracious than Mahdi^{AS} in his speech? And who is more effective than Mahdi^{AS} in curing the spiritual maladies? Allah Most High says: *'And who is better in speech than him who prayeth unto his Lord and doeth right, and saith: Lo! I am of those who are Muslims (surrender unto Him).'*[107]

---

[102] Quran, S. 25:63
[103] Quran, S.33:35 MMP.
[104] Quran, S. 23:1 MMP
[105] Quran, S. 70:22-23 AYA.
[106] Quran, S. 19:50 AYA.
[107] Quran, S. 41:33 MMP.

Proof for veracity of Mahdi^AS is the same proof which is given for the veracity of the Prophets^AS

And I have given lengthy arguments here so that the just man comes to know that when Mahdi^AS being Mahdi^AS is proved by that thing which proved the Prophethood of the Prophets^AS, then that thing which plagues the mind [of the just man] on the basis of *Ahad-e-Zanniah* [conjectural Traditions transmitted by only one narrator in each link of the chain] creating doubts and misgivings will not prevent the just man from performing the *tasdiq* of Mahdi^AS. This will make it obligatory on the just man to emulate the sayings of Mahdi^AS without any more arguments.

Traditions in Favour of Mahdi^AS

Now, I will produce those Prophetical Traditions and the sayings of the predecessors that are found in favour of Mahdi^AS and his community. Among the Traditions is the one about which Abu Is'haq has quoted Ali^RZ as saying after seeing his son, Hasan^RZ, 'Truly, this son of mine is a Syed, as the Prophet^SLM has named him. Soon Allah Most High will bring forth from him a man whose name will be like the name of the Prophet^SLM and who will resemble the Prophet^SLM. He will fill the people of the earth with justice.' Abu Daud has narrated this Tradition with proper authorities in his book, *Sunan*. Besides him, Imam Abu Esa Tirmizi has quoted it in his *Jami'* and Imam Abdur Rahman Naisapuri in his *Sunan* also.

I say that Mahdi^AS has the *akhlaq* [morals] resembling those of the Prophet^SLM. What remains to be addressed is the discussion about the filling of the earth with justice in the saying of Ali^RZ. This matter has been elaborately dealt with earlier.

Among the other things is the saying of Ali^RZ that 'I asked the Prophet^SLM whether Mahdi^AS will be from among us or from among others?' The Prophet^SLM said, 'He will not be from others. On the other hand, he will be from among us. Allah Most High will conclude the religion with him.' In other words, Allah Most High will perfectly manifest the religion in his era and he will deliver his companions to the ranks of the *muqarriboon* and *siddiqoon* [closest trusted favourites of Allah; and the Truthful]. They will be the people of the *mushahadah* [divine observation or contemplation], *mo'a'enah* [seeing with eyes] and *mukalama* [dialogue]. However, no one will recognise them except Allah Most High and His saints, as Allah Most High has said, 'My *awliya* [saints, friends] are under my tunic. One who is stranger to me will not recognise them.' This Tradition has been narrated by a group of people, who have memorised the Prophetical Traditions, and quoted them in their books. This group includes Abul Qasim Tabarani, Abu Na'im Asfahani, Abdur Rahman bin Hatim, Abu Abdullah Na'im bin Hammad and others.

And among many others is the Tradition narrated by Ka'ab Ahbar^RZ that Mahdi^AS is one who performs *muraqabah* [meditation] especially for Allah Most High like the *gidh* [vulture] hiding its head in its feathers. This Tradition is narrated by Imam Abu

Muhammad Husain in his book *Masabih* and it has been explained with authorities by Imam Abu Abdullah Na'im bin Hammad.

And among them is the one narrated by Abu Sayeed Maula Ibn Abbas. He said he had heard it from Ibn-e-Abbas that he used to say, 'Without doubt, I hope that the days and nights will not come to an end unless Allah Most High will send from among us, the *Ahl-e-Bait*[108], a boy who would be in the prime of his life and young and the shenanigans of the time will not encounter him, and neither will he encounter the shenanigans of the time. He will restore the rule of this *ummat* [the Muslim Community], as it was established through us in the beginning.' This has been narrated by Hafiz Abu Bakr Bayhaqi with relevant authorities, in the discussion about the *ba'sa* and *nushoor* [Emergence (of the Mahdi^AS) and Resurrection].

Verily , this attribute was found in Mahdi^AS that he did establish the rule of the *ummat* [the Muslim Community] as it was during the period of Prophet Muhammad^SLM. The purport of the *ummat* [Muslim Community] here is the community that is obedient to Mahdi^AS and which has accepted him as Imam Mahdi al-Mau'ood^AS. It does not mean all the people who were invited. As for the disavowers (who are from among the people who were invited), the Prophets^AS too did not establish the rule of the disavowers.

And among the narratives is the one that has been narrated by Jabir bin Abdullah^RZ. He said that a person came to Abu Ja'far Muhammad bin Ali^RZ and told him, 'Take this five hundred *dirham* from me. They are the *zakat*[109].' Abu Ja'far replied, 'You take it yourself and spend it on your poor Muslim neighbours, the poor and brothers. Then, when our Mahdi from our *Ahl-e-Bait* arrives, he will distribute with equality and justice among the people. He, who obeys him, obeys Allah Most High. He who disobeys him, disobeys Allah Most High.' This has been narrated with relevant authorities by Imam Abu Abdullah Na'im Bin Hammad in the *Kitab-al-Fitan*.

I say, Verily, I found in Mahdi^AS this distribution (among the free people, the slaves, the children and the elders) and I found the Mahdi^AS's justice among those who obeyed the Mahdi^AS. And he, who disobeyed the Mahdi^AS, he disobeyed Allah Most High. Hence, the disobedient does not accept the justice of the Mahdi^AS.

And among them is the narrative narrated by Ka'ab Ahbar^RZ that, 'Verily, I find Mahdi^AS written in the Books of the earlier Prophets^AS that there would not be any *zulm* [oppression] and *Aib* [defect] in his commands.' This has been narrated with relevant authorities by Imam Abu Abdullah Na'im Bin Hammad.

I say that verily, this narrative of Ka'ab Ahbar^RZ is proved by Mahdi^AS. He has said that he is mentioned in the Book of Allah Most High and the Books of the

---

[108] *Ahl-e-Bait* are the members of the Holy Prophet^SLM's family comprising Hazrat Fatima^RZ, Hazrat Ali^RZ, and their children, Imam Hasan^AS and Imam Husayn^AS [according to the Shi'ites].

[109] *Zakat* is Religious tax as a basic in-function in Islam.

Prophets^AS. And there was no *zulm* and no *'aib* [no oppression and no defect] in his commands as is well-known.

Further, from among the others is the narrative, narrated by Abu Ja'afar bin Ali^RZ. Abu Ja'afar says that Amir al-Muminin Ali^RZ bin Abi Talib was asked about the attributes of Imam Mahdi^AS. Ali^RZ said, 'Mahdi^AS would be young, of medium height and face. The hair of his head would spread on his shoulders. The *nur* of his face would dominate the hair of his head and beard. I say that the attribute of Mahdi^AS, whose *tasdiq* [affirmation and confirmation] we have performed, was all like this.

And among them is the narrative that is narrated by Haris bin Mughaira Basari, 'I asked Abu Abdullah Husayn bin Ali^RZ as to what would be the sign by which Mahdi^AS will be recognised?' He said, 'By his *sukoon* [peace] and *vaqar* [prestige and dignity].' And I asked, 'And by what other thing?' He said, 'by his knowledge of *halal* and *haram* [by his knowledge of the things allowed and prohibited]. And by his not being *muhtaj* [needy]. Other people will be needy of him and he will not be needy of others.' I say that Haris had spoken the truth. Mahdi^AS was like that.

And apart from those is the narrative that has been narrated by Abu Abdullah Husayn bin Ali^RZ. He said, 'If Mahdi^AS is established, people will disavow him, because he would go to those people when he would be young and they would think that he is very old.' Hence, O Just Man! See the saying of Husayn ibn Ali^RZ that when Mahdi^AS is established, people would disavow him. This means that the disavowal of Mahdi^AS by people is among the *mo'ay'yidat* [supporting factors] of Mahdi^AS.

And among other things is the narrative that has been narrated by Ali bin Huzail and he quotes his father to say, 'I reached Prophet Muhammad^SLM and he was in a condition in which his blessed soul was being seized. What I see is that Fatima^RZ was near the head of the Prophet^SLM.' The Tradition is long. At the end of it, Prophet Muhammad^SLM is quoted as saying: 'O Fatima! By Him WhoWho has sent me with the Truth! The Mahdi^AS of this *ummat* [Muslim Community] is from these two: Hasan and Husayn. When the world plunges into turmoil and trials will emerge, paths will be cut off and one will plunder the other; the elder will not show pity on the younger and the younger will not show respect to the elderly; in those circumstances Allah Most High will send a person from these two. That person will conquer the forts of misguidance and closed hearts. He will establish the religion in the Last Era as I had established in the Beginning; he will fill the world with justice as it would have been filled with oppression and injustice.' This narrative has been narrated with relevant authorities by Hafiz Abu Na'im Isfahani in the matter of the attributes of Mahdi^AS.

Hence, see, O Just Man! *Quluban ghulfa* [closed hearts]. This saying of the Prophet^SLM is *atf-e-tafsir* [conjunction] with his saying *husun-az-zalalah* [forts of misguidance]. Hence, it has become known that Mahdi^AS will open the closed hearts by his *faiz* [beneficence] and he will fill the hearts with his justice. And this is the meaning of the expression: 'He will fill the earth with justice as it would have been filled with oppression and injustice.'

Hence, Imam Ahmad Ibn Hanbal has mentioned in his *Musnad* that 'Allah Most High will fill the hearts of the *ummat* of Prophet Muhammad^{SLM} with contentment and it will include *adl* [justice].'

And among the others is the narrative, which has been narrated from Amir-ul-Mumineen Ali^{RZ} bin Abi Talib. He quoted Prophet Muhammad^{SLM} as saying that Mahdi^{AS} will be from among us, the *Ahl-e-Bait*,[110] and Allah Most High will create the needed ability and capacity in one night. That is, in a part of the night. This story has not been recorded because of its length. By Allah! The narrator has spoken the truth narrating from Amir-ul-Mumineen Ali^{RZ}.

And among the others is the Tradition, narrated by Taus^{RA} that the sign of the Mahdi^{AS} would be that he would be hard in dealing with the rulers and he would be merciful while dealing with the poor and meek [*masakin*]. I say that Mahdi^{AS} was hard on the worldly people and it was impossible for them to befriend him because they were afraid of him. However, the *fuqara* [the people of religion] had friendship with Mahdi^{AS} as a brother has friendship with his brother and a father has friendship with the son. Abu Abdullah Na'im bin Hammad has narrated this Tradition with relevant authorities.

Among the other things is the Tradition narrated by Abdullah bin Ata who said, 'I asked Abu Ja'far Muhammad Bin Ali^{RZ}, 'when Mahdi^{AS} appears, what would be his *seerat* [biography or character].' He replied, 'he will demolish the things that existed before him as did Prophet Muhammad^{SLM} and he will revive Islam.' This is stated in the book, *Iqd-ud-Durar*. In other words, he would demolish the innovations. And he would also demolish all those mistakes in the matters of deeds and beliefs that the *mujtahidin* might have committed in the course of their work. This is among the peculiarities of the Mahdi^{AS}. Hence, we have mentioned this earlier. The saying of the Prophet^{SLM} that, 'he [Mahdi^{AS}] would establish the religion in the *Aakhir Zamana* [Last Era] as I had done in the *awwal zamana* [First Era]' guides the statement of Abu Ja'far, because if the Mahdi^{AS} does not command that the mistake of the *mujtahidin* is a mistake, the establishing of the religion in the Last Era as the Prophet^{SLM} did will not be established. Hence, this shows that the Mahdi^{AS} is the ruler over the four *mazahib*.[111]

And among them is the Tradition, which is narrated by Ali^{RZ} Bin Abi Talib who has said in the matter of Mahdi^{AS} that, 'he will not leave any *bid'at* [innovation] without demolishing it, and he will not leave any *sunnat* [Prophet^{SLM}'s Tradition or practice] without re-establishing it.' This is stated in the book, *Iqd-ud-Durar*. The meaning of

---

110   *Ahl-e-Bait* are he Holy Prophet^{SLM}'s family comprising Hazrat Fatima^{RZ}, Hazrat Ali^{RZ} and their children, Imam Hasan^{AS} and Imam Husayn^{AS} and their descendants [according to the Shi'ites].

111   The four *mazahib* are the Hanafi, Shafei, Hanbali and Maliki named after the great Imams of these Islamic sects.

this saying is that Mahdi^{AS} will act on his deeds and command others to follow him in those deeds. And the Persian couplet of Sheikh Sa'adi supports it. Sa'adi said, 'he is the orphan who, before reading or writing the Quran, has washed some of the books of the religion.' In other words, he issued the edict that they were cancelled. And the believers thought that the edict was correct, because the heavenly books are not washed with water; they were washed away from the hearts of the believers who had reposed Faith in the Prophet^{SLM}. In other words, the deeds [as per those books] were given up. All these narratives are taken from the book, *Iqd-ud-Durar*, although some of them are weak. However, when they were found in the *zath* of the person who claimed to be Mahdi^{AS}, it became obvious that they were correct, even if they had not reached the stage of correctness.

And among them is the one, which is narrated by Tabari in his history that Mahdi^{AS} will appear in the year 905 Hijri, and the emergence of the Mahdi^{AS} occurred in that year. [The *da'wa-e-Mu'ak'kad* (claim with emphasis) came in that year. The claim was, 'He who accepts me is a *mumin* (believer) and he who disavows me is a *kafir* (infidel)'].

And among them is that which is said in the commentary of Tradition narrated by Abu Huraira^{RZ}. He said, "Amongst the things that I learnt from the Prophet^{SLM} is that he said, 'Allah will send in this *Ummat* at the beginning of each century a person who will revive the religion and the reviver of the religion in the tenth century is the Mahdi.'" This Tradition is present in the book *Tambeeh-ut-Taharruz*, etc. and it has been mentioned by Nawawi. Similarly, the true Vali, Syed Muhammad Gesudaraz has mentioned it in his *Malfuz* [utterances].

He [Muttaqi] says: Thus we learn that the departed Syed [Mahdi^{AS}] is not the Mahdi^{AS} because he did not have those qualities in him which have come in favour of the Mahdi^{AS}. In summary, those qualities are that Mahdi^{AS} will be the Imam [he will be a king having worldly splendour].

We say: The truth is that the Sheikh [Muttaqi] should have said ﹷ instead of ﹪ because the pronoun is for the ﹶ which is masculine.

Mahdi^{AS}'s Imamat is proven even if people oppose him because Allah has made him an Imam

He [Muttaqi] says: And the Mahdi is not an Imam because Imamat is ordinary leadership and it is established by one of the three ways. One among them is when those in power from among the scholars and wealthy people pay fealty without any condition of numbers. It is not necessary for the entire city to pay fealty, but only those who can assemble easily. Rather, even if one person agrees to follow it is enough for the fealty of Imamat. The second way is that the king makes him his vice-regent and takes fealty from the people. The third way is that the Imam vanquishes and triumphs. This is written in *Sharah Maqasid* and none of these three ways was found in him [the Mahdi^{AS}]. The last two ways not being found in him is evident. As for the first way, he did not obtain fealty from those in power from amongst the scholars and the wealthy people. Thus the saying of the person who proved his [Mahdi^AS] *imamat* is null and void.

We say: The Mahdi^AS is Imam by verification although the opposing disbelievers in their ignorance have rubbed dust on their noses (i.e. they oppose paying fealty to him). This is because Mahdi^AS has been made an Imam by Allah Most High and hence his Imamat is proven. This is similar to prophets, that they are prophets because Allah Most High made them prophets and not because the people accept and follow them.

Its example is this: A king appoints someone as a Qazi (judge) of the city and commands the inhabitants of the city to obey the Qazi. Then with the command of the King he becomes a Qazi irrespective of whether the people obey him or not. Thus if they obey him they will get prosperity. If they don't obey him and do not heed to his call, then if the Qazi has the means, he will subjugate and punish them. But if he does not have the means to subjugate and punish them, he will not lose his position of Qazi because the proof of he being the Qazi is his appointment by the King and not the obedience of the people.

And I produce arguments in favour of my statement. Among them is the one that Abu Shukoor Salami has stated in his book, *Tamheed.* He says: Some people have said that when the Imam is not obeyed, he would not be the Imam. We [Abu Shukoor Salami] say that it is not like that, because the obedience of the Imam is obligatory on the people. If they do not obey, the fault is with the people who do not obey and their fault does not adversely affect the *imamat.*

Have you not seen that Prophet Muhammad^SLM was not obeyed in the beginning of Islam, and due to his nature neither could he be severe on his enemies. The infidels had rebelled against helping him and his religion. However their rebellion was not detrimental to the Prophet^SLM nor did it deprive him of his Prophethood. Similarly Imam Mahdi Mau'ood^AS definitely is at the same station as Rasoolullah^SLM. Similarly, Ali^RZ bin Abi Talib was not obeyed by all the Muslims. Despite this, Ali^RZ was not deprived of his position as the Vice-Regent of Prophet^SLM. Hence, our contention has become correct. Even if the people abandon Islam, the Imam will not be deprived of his position as the Vice-Regent. Similarly, people indulging in sins will not deprive the Imam of his Imamate. Further, if the Imam loses his dominance, it is the result of the rebellion of the people and their rebellion does not deprive the Imam of his Imamate. Hence, O Just Man! See the saying of Abu Shukoor Salami with deliberate consideration.

Among the other things is the saying of Hujjat-al-Islam, Imam Muhammad Ghazali^RH, has said in his book, *Mukhtasar al-Ahya*:

> And know that whoever has an inclination of the desire of the world and turned his face away from the Hereafter, such a person is the Dajjal of the religion and the one who establishes the religion of the Satan. He is not an

Imam of the religion because an Imam is one who is followed because he induces people to turn their faces away from the world and become attentive to God Almighty, like the Prophets[AS], their Companions and the religious scholars among the ancestors. (Up to here is his statement.)

Hence, see, O Just Man! The statement of Imam Ghazali[RH], that he did not impose the condition of fury and dominance for the correctness of Imamate.

And among other things, is that which has been mentioned in *Hameedi*, the *Sharah* of *Hedaya*, that:

The person who is suitable for Imamate is one who has all the attributes of Imamate in himself. In other words, he should have in himself the attributes like Islam, freedom, *bulugh* [maturity], *aql* [intelligence], and justice. Further, one becomes an Imam when a group of Muslims takes an oath of fealty to him and that group is pleased with his Imamate. Further, that Imam should raise the *kalmah* of Islam and have the intention to strengthen the Muslims. And the blood, property, chastity, of the Muslims should be safe in his hands. He should behave like a loving brother and merciful father to his group of people.

And one who does not posses these attributes is not a suitable person and is not suitable to become an Imam. Supporting him and helping him is not obligatory on the people. On the other hand, it is obligatory on them to attack and wage war against such a person till he is corrected or he is killed. And these are the meanings that open up and remove the doubts. [Here ends his statement.]

Hence, see, O Just Man! The commentator has not imposed the condition of the fealty of the people of the authorities, as some others have imposed such a condition. On the contrary, he has mentioned only the absolute fealty of a group of Muslims.

By Allah! Verily, that person, whose Imamate we proved [that is, Imam Mahdi[AS]] has all the attributes that are mentioned in *Hameedi*. Verily, the perfect group of Muslims who turned their faces away from the seekers of the world, who gave up the life of the world to remain in the quest for Allah, performed *bayat* [paid fealty] of Imam Mahdi[AS] through divine inspiration, unveiling and mystical experiences of the divine omnipresence. Many years before Imam Mahdi[AS] manifested his claim to be Mahdi[AS], Allah Most High had revealed to the members of this group that this *zath* is to be the Imam Mahdi[AS]. Hence, they came in the presence of the Imam[AS] and told him about their inspirations, the Imam[AS] told them Allah Most High would soon manifest the claim.

Hence, the saying of the Sheikh [Muttaqi] that 'those in power did not pay fealty to the Imam[AS], hence, the saying of the person who proved the Imamat became null and void' is the convincing proof of the ignorance of the Sheikh [Muttaqi] about the attributes of the people who paid fealty to the Imam[AS]. What rank do the people in power have when compared to the people who paid fealty to the Imam^{AS}? They are a group of people who are surrounded by the angels. They have achieved the peace of Allah Most High. Allah Most High has counted them among his *musahiban* [Companions]. He who sits with them is fortunate.

Hence, the *hadis* [Tradition] too is saying the same thing that, 'Allah has raised their stations. Although they are not from the Prophets and Martyrs, but the Prophets and Martyrs will desire for their status.' [When a community which has received such a status from Allah pays fealty to Imam Mahdi^{AS}] the saying of the person who did not accept the Mahdiat and Imamat of the Mahdi^{AS} is nullified and the saying of the person who accepted the Mahdiat and Imamat of the Mahdi^{AS} is proved.

Qualities of the Community of Mahdi^{AS}

I have previously described the qualities of the community of Mahdi^{AS}. Now I will describe some of those qualities of the community of Mahdi^{AS} which are in conformity with those things that are stated in the hadees that mention the qualities of the *Awliya* [Saints].

Allah Most High says, '*Lo! Verily the friends of Allah are (those) on whom fear (cometh) not, nor do they grieve.*'[112]

Omar bin Khattab^{RZ} narrated that the Prophet^{SLM} said, 'Among the servants of Allah, there are some people who are not Prophets^{AS} and Martyrs, but the Prophets^{AS} and the Martyrs would desire their station and ranks which Allah Most High would confer on them on the day of Resurrection.' The Companions^{RZ} said, 'O the Messenger of Allah! Give us the news of these people, as to who they are.' The Prophet^{SLM} said, 'They are a group of people who love one another for the pleasure of Allah Most High, despite the fact that they have no close relationship among themselves, and despite the fact that they have not given any riches to any one of them. By Allah! Their faces will be lit with the *nur* [divine light] and they will be sitting on the pulpits of divine light. They will not be afraid while others will be afraid. The will not be scared while others will be scared. They will not grieve while other people greive.' Then Prophet Muhammad^{SLM} recited the Quranic Verse: '*Lo! Verily the friends of Allah are (those) on whom fear (cometh) not, nor do they grieve?*[113] Listen! Those are the people who are the Friends of Allah, they are not afraid of anybody and they will not grieve. Abu Dawud has explained with relevant authorities in his *Sunan*. And this *rivayat* [Tradition] is treated as *agreed* by the *Sahihain* [Sahih Bukhari and Sahih Muslim].

It has been narrated by Abu Hurayrah^{RZ} that on the day of resurrection, Allah Most High will ask the Prophet^{SLM}, 'Where are those people who had friendship with each other. By My *Jalal* [Majesty]! Today I will give refuge to them under My shade.

---

[112] Quran, S. 10:62, MMP
[113] Quran, S. 10:62 MMP.

Today there is no shade other than My shade.' Muslim has narrated this with authority [*sanad*]. It has been narrated by Ma'az bin Jabal that 'I heard Rasoolullah[SLM] say that Allah will say, 'Where are those people who had friendship with each other. By My *jalal* [Majesty]! There are the pulpits of *Nur* for them. The Prophets and the martyrs will desire for those pulpits and positions.' Tirmizhi has narrated this.

Baghawi has narrated with authority that Abu Malik Ash'ary said, 'I was near the Prophet[SLM] who said, 'Truly there are servants of Allah. They are not the Prophets and Martyrs on the day of Judgement but Prophets[AS] and Martyrs will desire their positions because of their positions' proximity to Allah Most High'. Abu Malik Ash'ary said that at that time an Arab was sitting amongst a group of the community. Hearing this he sat on his haunches and stroked both his hands on his thighs and said, 'O Rasoolullah[SLM], inform us about them as to who those people are.' Then Abu Malik said that he had seen the holy face of the Prophet[SLM] that it was very happy. Then, the Prophet[SLM] said, 'These are the servants of Allah Most High from various cities and various tribes. They will not have close relationship with each other so that there could be love and affection between and among them. They will also have no money because of which they could be in close love and affection between or among them. Their relationship and love will be simply because of their seeking the pleasure of Allah Most High. Allah Most High will make their faces *noorani* [illuminated] on the Day of Resurrection. He will also make tall pulpits of pearls and gems for them. Because of the dread of the Day [of Resurrection], people will be scared but these people will not be afraid.'

It has been narrated from the Prophet[SLM] that he had said quoting Allah Most High as saying, 'From among My servants, My friends are those who remember Me and I remember them.' Similarly Baghawi too has narrated without authorities quoting Abu Huraira[RZ], who said quoting Prophet[SLM] that from among the servants of Allah Most High, there are His servants whose station and positions the Prophets and Martyrs will desire. The Companions[RZ] asked the Prophet[SLM] as to who these people were so that they could also love and respect them. The Prophet[SLM] said they are a group of people who love each other and one another among themselves because of their love of Allah Most High. Their faces would be illuminated and they would be sitting on the pulpits of *nur* [Light]. They will not be afraid while others will be afraid. They will not grieve while others will be in grief.

Hence, see O Just Man! That the above mentioned attributes that are the attributes of the Saints of the *ummat-e-Muhammadiah* [Friends of Allah among the community of Prophet Muhammad[SLM]] are to be found among the members of the community of the Imam Mahdi[AS] (the Mahdavis). Thus how can their pledge of allegiance not be taken as proof of his (the Mahdi[AS]'s) Imamat? And how can their conclusion be not taken as the argument for others? And Allah says the truth and shows the path of truth.

Claimants of Mahdiat

He [Muttaqi] says: Then know that Allah Most High have Mercy on you. From the beginning of Islam to the present, many people have claimed to be Imam Mahdi^{AS} from among the wealthy people and the *mashayakheen*. From among them, there is a Sheikh whose name was Syed Muhammad Nur Bakhsh and among them was a Sheikh who lived in Rum.

We say: I found in the Sheikh's original saying كان the *kana* is placed before the word Sheikh and this is not correct. He should have said و منهم شيخ كان فى الروم .

He [Muttaqi] says: The name of the Sheikh who lived in Rum is Owais. He was a contemporary of Bayazid and he had eighty vice-regents. When the issue of the Mahdiat came before him, he called his vice-regents, and told them that, 'the issue of Mahdiat is presented before me in this manner, so you turn your faces towards Allah.'

We say: The eloquent phrase would have been فتوجهوا الى الله انتم .

He [Muttaqi] says: [The Shaikh further said to his vice-regents] 'And tell me the thing that is revealed to you.' His friends became busy with the issue of Mahdiat for a few days and then came to him and said, 'It has been revealed to us that you are on the truth. [and the issue of Mahdiat is proven in your *zath*].' When the issue of Mahdiat was told to the Sultan of that time, since the Sultan was from amongst the Awliya-Allah, he said, "Mercy be upon you. Come out with the call of Mahdiat, we are with you and will help you." After a few days Owais no longer had the thought of the call of Mahdiat.

We say: Even in this saying of the Shaikh [Muttaqi], there is an proof for the soundness of our contention about Mahdiat which is that Allah Most High does not leave a *Vali* [Saint or Friend of Allah] on the wrong path — a mistake that creates a defect in his religion. Allah Most High will make the *Vali* aware of the mistake so that the *Vali* then corrects his mistake. On the other hand when Allah leaves the *Vali* on his call of Mahdiat till his death, then it is known that either the *vali* was true in his claim. Or alternatively he is not a *vali* at all because remaining on the wrong path is impossible for a *Vali* which the Sheikh himself has mentioned it earlier.[114]

He [Muttaqi] says: Then there is a person who is virtuous and is a Syed in a western country. He is now alive. And he is an elderly respected person and is the leader of an army. He has won victories in the western countries for as long a distance as could be traveled in four months. He is now prospering and claims that he is the Mahdi.

We say: We have come to know of this information from the traders who have come from Makkah that this virtuous person has been killed. He was a *kimiagar* [alchemist]. His intention was to conquer the cities of the Muslims. His invitation was not the *tark-e-dunya* [renunciation of the world] and *ishtgihal ma'Allah*

---

[114] The Sheikh's saying is that it is not like that. On the other hand, the *vali* is protected from a mistake, it means that it is possible for a *vali* to commit a mistake but he does no insist on continuing to repeatedly commit the mistake.

[engagement with Allah]. All the Prophets were sent to the people to propogate the *tark-e-dunya* and *ishtgihal ma'Allah.* Allah Most High says that, '...*We have made some of you as a trial for others...*'[115] It is said in *Tafsir-e-Kashshaf that* 'O Muhammad! We have made you a test for the others. This is so because if you had owned wealth and gardens, they [the people] would have flocked to you in the lust of wealth and desire of other acquisitions. We have made you a *faqir* [indigent], so that the people who follow you would do so exclusively with the desire to achieve Us. Hence joining your group for the sake of world, even if it is in thousands, is not considered to be for the sake of the religion. Allah Most High says, '*Say: Not equal are things that are bad and things that are good, even though the abundance of the bad may dazzle thee.*'[116]

Conclusion

He [Muttaqi] says: Allah Most High be Merciful to you! Know that the *aakhirat* [the next world or the life after death] is the home of the reward and blessings while the world is the House of Testing. Allah Most High has tested His servants in various ways. Hence, some of the servants of Allah Most High are those who were tested by the hardships of penury and starvation, some others are those who were tested by disease and many other calamities and difficulties in succession one after the other, still others are those who were tested by health and well-being [this was the calamity of good (*hasanah*)], yet others are those who were tested by a large number of enemies, and they were tested by the great number of infidels, innovators and the famous seventy—one sects [of Muslim *ummmat* or community] and the innovative sect, the Mahdavis, in our day. We seek refuge in Allah from them.

We say: In being inimical to our Companions [the Mahdavis] the Sheikh [Muttaqi] has gone to such an extent that he has troubled himself by travelling from Makkah to Gujarat [India] to oppose them. He intends to extinguish the *Nur* of Allah Most High by blowing his breath. However, his deceit has dissolved as salt dissolves in water. He did not achieve his objective. Then he returned to Makkah. And after a long time he wrote a letter to the Sultan of Gujarat urging him to kill our brothers in Gujarat. The Sultan accepted the advice of the Sheikh [Muttaqi] and murdered eleven of our Mahdavi brothers, who were sincere in believing in the religion of Imam Mahdi[AS] and acted according to the Mahdavi religion thinking it to be the source of divine rewards. But Allah Most High took revenge against him within four months. One of the servants of the Sultan killed the Sultan and his ministers. Hence, the sword is in use since that time up until now [the time of writing this passage by Hazrat Sujawandi[RA]. The period since then is in turmoil and there is no peace. Allah Most High says, '*Ah woe, that Day, to the Rejecters of Truth!*'[117]. Hence the Shaikh [Muttaqi] saw their Tasdiq in Mahdi[AS] to be upright and firm which was similar to the way that Abu Sufyan replied to the question of King Heraclius 'Is anyone leaving Muhammad's religion after joining it because of the hardships he is facing?' that 'No [they aren't leaving his religion].'; thus the Shaikh [Muttaqi], disheartened by the

---

[115] Quran, S. 25:20 AYA
[116] Quran, S. 5:100 AYA
[117] Quran, S. 77:15 AYA. Allah has repeated this verse ten times in this Surah (*al-Mursalaat*).

rejection and refutation of the Mahdavis, said, that 'Allah has tested us through this innovative sect'. If you see the writing of the Shaikh [Muttaqi] with justice you will find that it is similar to the saying of the idolators when they said, 'Verily this talk benefits [Muhammad^SLM]. We haven't heard of this in the previous religions so it is a fabrication.' Thus, what a joy it is for the believers of Mahdi^AS and what a devastation it is for the deniers of Mahdi^AS.

He [Muttaqi] says: May Allah have mercy on you! Know that it is the habit of Allah pertaining to his servants that sometimes a person is a *vali* by nature, he adheres to the Book [the Holy Quran] and the Sunnah. After the death of this *vali* a group which transgresses the limits of religion is born. In the cities of Persia is a person by the name of Syed Nematullah *vali*. The Rafzis are his believers but they have no connection to this *vali*. Then there is a person whose name is Shahbaz Qalandar. We have heard that he was a pious man and the Qalandariya group found today is related to him, although this group has moved away from the path of Shahbaz Qalandar. Then another person Shah Qasim Anwar was from the Awliya Allah. Most of his companions were apostates and proud. Then in the cities of India was a person by name of Badi'uddin Shah Madar who was from the *Ahlullah* [people of Allah]. His companions are called Madaris but they are far away from him [from his path]. There are many others apart from these people. The purpose of mentioning these Awliya-Allah is that after the demise of these Awliya-Allah their sects went out of their religion. Similarly, because of the innovations of the believers of this deceased Syed [Imam Mahdi^AS] it is not necessary that the deceased Syed [Imam Mahdi^AS] was also an innovator, because one cannot have such a suspicion about him.

We say: The saying of the Sheikh [Muttaqi] that after the demise of the Awliya their communities turned away from their path would have been true if they did not have the correct traditions of their leader through constancy. But when they have written those things upon which their beliefs and actions are based from those narrators who were liked and considered truthful by their leader, then how can one suspect that they have started a thing which was not sanctioned by their leader or they have made a mistake in noting the narration of their leader. In summary, the intellect does not accept this and the narrations refute it. If this is made permissible, the entire religion will be cast in doubt and hadith of constancy [*mutawatir*] and singular hadith [*ahad*] will become equal and will not give the benefit of certainty.

Thus see, O Just Man! Allah has protected the Mahdi^AS from the slander of an opposing person like the Shaikh [Muttaqi] and has firmly established the high morals of the Mahdi^AS upon the Shaikh [Muttaqi] to such an extent that the Shaikh himself had said that one cannot suspect innovation in the *zath* of the Mahdi^AS despite his knowing that some of the verses in Qur'an have been specified in favour of Mahdi^AS. by the Mahdi^AS himself, and not by the companions. Otherwise, who has the power to make specification in the Book of Allah and believe in it unless such a thing has been narrated through constancy from the Mahdi^AS himself? And how can one suspect that the Mahdi^AS has fabricated lies against Allah or has committed a mistake because the reason for accepting the Mahdi^AS are those morals that keep his denial far away. Thus with respect to these very meanings the Shaikh [Muttaqi] has said that 'one cannot have such a suspicion about him.'

He [Muttaqi] says: And for Allah is the Authority of Eloquence. He casts astray whom He wills and guides whom He wills. He knows best who they are that receive His guidance.

We say: It is He who has astounded the *wasileen* [newcomers] and has made the perfect people to reflect upon the fruit of their actions. *"He cannot be questioned for His acts, but they will be questioned (for theirs)."*[118] The Shaikh's [Muttaqi] tract along with its answers has been completed. All praise is for Allah and all virtues are completed by His blessings.

---

[118] Quran, S. 21:23 AYA

SUPPLEMENT

I then decided that apart from all these discussions (which are present in Siraj-ul-Absar) I should write a short discussion in Persian language. Hence I say: [text follows]

Question: If someone asks what proof do you have for the affirmation of Meeran Syed Muhammad Mahdi Mau'ood Alaihis Salam, then my answer is [as follows].

When we pondered regarding the time of the advent of Mahdi Alaihis Salam we found without doubt that his advent would be at a time which would be bereft of the *Mujtahidin* [jurists entitled to independent opinion or judgment] as per the consensus between us and the scholars. And we saw that our position did not surpass *taqleed* [adherence]. Thus it is not appropriate for us to cling [*tamassuk*] to the hadees for the proof and rejection of any matter because this is the speciality of the *Mujtahidin*. Even if we suppose that *tamassuk-bil-hadees* [clinging to a hadees] is permissible, the rectification of *ahadees*, its adaptation, harmonizing and conveying the phrase either factually or metaphorically is not within our possibility. This is because, the people who were unique pearls in this field made mistakes in specifying the rank of the hadees as per its attributes.

Therefore, Ibn Salah, who was an Imam of ahadees, taunts a leader of the science of Hadees like Ibn Juzi saying, 'Ibn Juzi has composed books on the *Mauzuaat* [Fabricated Traditions]. However there is no proof that these are *Mauzu* [fabricated]. The truth is that they are counted among the *za'if* [weak traditions].' This narration is present in *Arjuzah* which is about the principles of Hadees.

Similarly there is consensus amongst the exegesists that Satan threw (some suggestions) into the recitation of the Prophet[SLM] whereupon he said, 'These are the lofty idols and their intercession is hoped for'. This is explained for the verse, '*And We have sent before thee no apostle or prophet but when he read the Satan cast forth suggestions in respect of his reading;...*'[119] and no exegesis fails to mention this narration, except those which Allah wills. The traditionists have consensus on *alqa* (throwing of suggestions) being *Mauzu* [fabricated] to the extent that they say that whoever believes in the narration of *alqa* is feared to have fallen into infidelity.

Similarly, the *usuliyan* [principle-ists] of hadees narrate that the Prophet[SLM] said that, 'Soon after me, you will have many *ahadees* with you. Present them upon the Book of Allah. If they conform [to the Book of Allah] then accept them, else reject them.' The *Muhaddisin* [traditionists] are of the opinion that this tradition is *Mauzu* [fabricated] and has been introduced by disbelievers. Similarly, in the explanation of the hadees — if there is conflict between two traditions and neither of them are invalid then the Mujtahid [independent jurist] can act upon any one of the two as per the testimony of his heart. The *usuliyan* [principle-ists] present the hadees 'fear the vision of the

---

[119] Quran, S. 22 :52

believer because he sees with the light [*nur*] of Allah.' But the Muhaddisin have mentioned this hadees amongst the fabricated.

Further, it is popular amongst the commoners and the elite that after the Quran, Bukhari and Muslim are the more correct books. Despite this Ibn Salah says that Bukhari and Muslim contain weak traditions. This statement of Ibn Salah is present in *Arjuzah*. With regards to accepting the traditions of the people with differences, the correct religion is that his tradition is acceptable if he does not keep the belief of the fabrication of hadees like the Khitabiyah [rhetorics]. And he says in *Arjuzah* that Bukhari and Muslim is full of traditions of the Shia.

And further some of the ahadees which are mentioned in *Hedaya*, have also been criticised as fabricated. Similarly some traditions of Ihya-ul-Uloom have been criticised. The purpose of this lengthy discourse is that one should see with justice that inspite of such differences and their likelihood, how can we reject the claim of such a person (the claim of Imam Mahdi Mau'ood Khalifathullah[AS]) who has been bestowed with the qualities of the Prophets[AS]? Therefore, following the scholars becomes necessary for us.

And the Prophet[SLM] has described two ranks for the scholars. He[SLM] said, 'The scholars are the successors of the prophets[AS]. They are those who do not desire the world. And if they desire the world, stay away from them' And similarly, the Prophet[SLM] said, 'Scholars[120] are the trustees of Allah as long as they do not mix together with the kings. So when the scholars start associating with the kings, avoid them. Verily they are the thieves of religion! They are the thieves of religion! They are the thieves of religion! And robbers too!' Thus it becomes imperative for us to investigate both kinds of scholars and follow those scholars who are the trustees of the Prophets[AS].

And we see that the scholars who are deniers of Mahdi Alaihis Salam are inclined towards the world and associate with the kings. Thus when we see the condition of those scholars who accepted the Mahdi Alaihis Salam, we find that they renounce the world and its constituents, possess the desire for Allah, have trust on Allah, lead a shar'ee [Islamic code of conduct] life and shun the world for the sake of Allah so much so that they attain the status of being the 'trustees' of the Prophets[AS.] Then why should we not follow them? Thus, you understand this matter and do justice. May Allah have mercy on one who does justice.

Translated by:

Ahqar Dilawer alias Gorey Miyan Mahdavi [Hazrat Moulana Syed Dilawer[RH] Saheb of Begum Bazar, Hyderabad]

---

[120] The scholars are the trustees of the Prophet[SLM] as long as they do not mix together with kings and do not desire the world. When the scholars mix together with the kings and desire the world, they have committed treachery with the Messenger[SLM], so you avoid them (Refer: Jame-ut-Tafseer, Jild Duwam, Pages 57-58 by Imam Jalaluddin Suyuti[RH], published in Egypt)

1056

English Translation by:

Hazrat Syed Ziaullah Yadullahi Saheb. Completed in December 2010.

The above English translation of Sirajul Absar has been published in this book with kind permission and courtesy from the Team of "Khalifatullah Mehdi.Info" for the benefit of the readers to have access to the original Sirsajul, Absar in one book.

BISMILLA—HIR-REHMAN-NIR-RAHEEM

ADDENDUM

Comprising various important topic which provide "food for thought"

INTRODUCTION:

At the completion of the book, I ventured into some such topics which have strength and useability for the readers who could ponder over them to qualify their usefulness.

They teach Islam, Ieman and Ihsan, in detail subsequently they take the reader towards Vision of Allah. They teach the basics of Good Governanace. they inculcate learning how to face the decliners of our Faith and convince them to join the main stream of Mahdaviat.

You will love to read about Zikris, belonging to our FAith who live mostly in Baluchistan of Pakistan and of Iran. Then you will read about the only Mahdavia Kalhora Dynasty which ruled Sindh and brought a new system of governance through Dairahs; where Collective Farming brought Green Revolution through massive Canal System out of Indus River. Imamana(AS) stayed in Sindh for more than 18 months and give a new philosophy to the tillers that the lnds belongs to Allah and the cultivators are temporary guardins of that land on behalf of Allah and the produce of that land belongs to the cultivator. Thus his such philosophy brought Green Revolution in Sindh.

As far economic welfarte of a society, Imamana(As) emphasised the continuous rotation of the wealth among the inhabitants of a country. He declared Momins do not hoard wealth eitherr in kind or currency. Produce of the land and the earnings of a man through his labour and skills have an equal status, hence as per Allah's dictate, both are charged with Ushr, which is ten percent of either of the produce of a land or ernings of a man plus Zakat. Thus the Diarah's economy was based on it, where every one was equal without any distinction.

This Addendum provides two major Dialectic discussions between Mahdavi preachers and non-mahdavi scholars, one of which took place in the Royal court of Akber the Great, who himelf presided the discussion, the other was conducted by a judge of Auranga Zeb Alamgir. These dicussions provide ample khowledge about our Faith. The beauty of those discussions is that our preachers became successful by defeating the decliners.

Thus, the above important essays are furnished for information of the readers who may appreciate my desire to bring forward such topics which are not only important but provide wide range of academic value. These essays provide you basic knowledge about Islam, Mahdavit, and their preachers who taught and guided about the basics of the Religion of Allah, as presented by prophets and Aoulia Allah.

Faqeer Syed Shrief Khundmiri

TOPICS:

Principles of good governance as determined by Ameerul Momineen Hazrat Ali ibn Abi Talib(Rz)

- Imamana's letter to the kings
- Imamana's Mission—Vision of Allah
- Aqeeda-e-Shariefa by Hazrat Bandagi Miyan Syed Khundmir(Rz)
- Risala-e-Haszda Aayaat by Bandagi Abdul Ghafoor Sujawandi(Rh)
- Five Sessions of Discussion by Hazrat Shaik Mustafa Gujrati in the court of Akber the Great
- Mubahisa-e-Alamgiri with Mahdavi Preachers of Chichind, Ahmadnager.
- Zikri Mahdavi of Balochistan
- Mahdavia Kalhora Dynasty of Sindh, Pakistan
- Excerpts from the Essay written by Mr. Namdar Khan on Kalhora Dynasty
- Golden Period of Kalhora Dynasty by an eminent Kalhora living Descendant
- Excerpts from the Internationl Conference on Kalhora Dynasty held in 1995 in Pakistan
- Shah Inayet Shaheed, Mahdavi of Pakistan
- Who was Zul Qarnsain?

khundmiri

1. ISLAMIC PRINCIPLES OF GOOD GOVERNANCE
ADOPTED by IMAM ALI IBN ABI TALEB(Karamallhu Wajhu)

- The 4th. Caliph of Islam, Hzt. Imam Ali(Rz) wrote a letter to Maalikal-Ashter, the governor of Egypt in 678 Ad/ 58 H. This letter is available in a famous religious book "Nahjul Balagha.

- **I order you to use your head, heart, hands and tongue** to help the creatures of Allah, because the Almighty Allah holds Himself responsible to help those who sincerely try their best to help Him . . . . Let. it be known to you, Maalik, that I am sending you as a governor to a country which has seen many regimes before this.

Some of them were benign, sympathetic and good. While others were tyrannical, oppressive and cruel. People will judge your regime as critically as you have studied the activities of other regimes and they will criticize you in the same way as you have censured or approved other rulers.

- **KINDNESS, COMPASSION AND LOVE**: Maalik you must create in your mind kindness, compassion and love for your subjects. Do not behave towards them as if you are a voracious and ravenous beast and as if your success lies in devouring them.

- **TWO KINDS OF PEOPLE**: Remember Maalik, that amongst your subjects there are two kinds of people: those who have the same religion as you have, they are brothers to you, and those who have religion other than that of yours, they are human beings like you. Men of either category suffer from the same weaknesses and disabilities that human beings are inclined to, they commit sins, indulge in vices either intentionally or foolishly and unintentionally without realizing the enormity of their deeds. Let your mercy and compassion come to their rescue and help in the same way and to the same extent that you expect Allah to show mercy and forgiveness to you.

- **FORGET AND FORGIVE:** Do not feel ashamed to forgive and forget. Do not hurry over punishments and do not be pleased and do not be proud of your power to punish. Do not get angry and lose your temper quickly over the mistakes and failures of those over whom you rule. On the contrary, be patient and sympathetic with them. Anger and desire of vengeance are not going to be of much help to you in your administration.

- **AVOID ARROGANCE**: Take care never to bringing yourself as par with Allah, never to matching your power with Him contesting His Glory and ever to pretend that you possess might and power like Him because the Mighty Lord will always humble pitiless tyrants and will degrade all pretenders of His Power and Might. Every tyrant and oppressor is an enemy of Allah unless he repents and gives up oppression.

- **POLICY BASED ON EQUITY**: You must always appreciate and adopt a policy which is neither too severe nor too lenient, a policy which is based upon equity will be largely appreciated. Remember that the displeasure of common man, the have-nots and the depressed persons more overbalances than the approval of important persons, while the displeasure of a few big people will be excused by the Lord if the general public and the masses of your subjects are happy with you.

- **DEMANDS OF THE RICH:** Remember, Maalik! That usually these big personages are mentally the scum of the human society. They are the people who will be the worst drag upon you during your moments of peace and happiness, and the least useful to you during your hours of need and adversity, they hate justice the most, they will keep on demanding more out of the State resources and will seldom be satisfied with what they receive and will never be obliged for the favor shown to them if their demands are justifiably refused, they will never accept any reasonable excuse or any rational argument and when the time changes you will never find them staunch, faithful and loyal.

- **DO NOT CREATE DIVISIONS:** Do not give cause to the people to envy each other (man against man, tribe against tribe or one section of the society against the other). Try to alleviate and root out mutual distrust and enmity from amongst your subjects.

- **BE FAIR AND kEEP YOUR DIGNITY:** Be fair, impartial and just in your dealings with all, individually and collectively and be careful not to make your person, position and favors act as source of malice. Do not let any such thing or such person come near to you who does not deserve your nearness and your favor. Never lower your dignity and prestige.

- **CREATE GOODWILL:** Try carefully to realize that a ruler can create goodwill in the minds of his subjects and can make them faithful and sincere to him only when he is kind and considerate to them, when he reduces their troubles, when he does not oppress them and when he never asks for things which are beyond their power.

- **DEALING WITH DIFFERENT GROUPS OF THE SOCIETY**: You must know that the people over whom you rule are divided into classes and grades and the prosperity and welfare of each class of the society individually and collectively are so interdependent upon the well-being of the other classes that the whole set-up represents a closely woven net and reciprocal aspect. One class cannot exist peacefully, cannot live happily and cannot work without the support and good wishes of the other.

- **TAKE CARE OF ALL SEGMENTS OF THE SOCIETY:** The army and the common man (common citizens who pay taxes or tributes) are two important classes, but in a welfare state their wellbeing cannot be guaranteed without proper functioning and preservation of the other classes, the judges and the magistrates, the secretaries of the State and the officers of various departments who collect various revenues, maintain Law and order as well as preserve peace and amity among the diverse classes of the society. They also guard the rights and privileges of the citizens and look to the performances of various duties by individuals and classes. And the prosperity of this whole set-up depends upon the traders and industrialists. They act as medium between the consumers and the suppliers. They collect the requirements of the society. Then comes the class of the poor and disabled persons. It is absolutely necessary that they should be looked after, helped and well-provided for. The Merciful Allah has explained the ways and means of maintaining and providing for each of these classes. And every one of this class has the right upon the ruler of the State that at least minimum necessities for its wellbeing and contended living are provided.

- **TYPE OF ADVICE TO ACCEPT**: Remember that back-bitters and scandal-mongers belong to a mean and cunning group, though they pretend to be sincere advisers. Do not accept the advice of misers, they will try their best to keep you away from acts of kindness and from doing good to others. They will make you frightened of poverty. Your worst minister will be the one who had been minster to the despotic rulers before you and who had been a party of atrocities committed by them. Select honest, truthful and pious people as your companions. Train them not to flatter you and not to seek your favor by false praises because flattery and false praises create vanity and conceit and they make a man lose sight of his real self and ignore his duties.

- **HONEST JUDICIARY:** So far as dispensing of justice is concerned, you have to be very careful in selecting officers for the same. You must select people of excellent character and high caliber having meritorious records. They must possess the following qualifications: Abundance of litigations and complexity of cases should not make them lose their temper. They should not develop vanity and conceit when complements and praises are showered upon them. They should not be misled by flattery and cajolery. Pay them handsomely so that their needs are fully satisfied and they are not required to beg or borrow or resort to corruption. Give them such a prestige and position in your State that none of your courtiers or officers can overlook them. Let judiciary be above of every kind of executive pressure or influence, above fear and favor, intrigue or corruption. Take every particular care of this aspect because before your appointment this State was under the sway of corrupt, time serving and wealth grasping opportunists who were lewd and greedy and vicious and who wanted nothing out of State but a sinful consent of amassing wealth and pleasures for themselves.

- **OFFICERS OF THE STATE**: Then come the officers of the State. You must supervise their work. They must be appointed after careful scrutiny of their capabilities and characters. These appointments must be made originally on probation without any kind of favoritism being shown or influence being accepted otherwise tyranny, corruption and misrule will reign in your State. Keep them also well-paid so that they may not be tempted to lower their standard of morality and may not misappropriate the cash of the State which they hold in their trust and if after being paid handsomely they prove dishonest, then you will be right to punish them. Therefore keep a careful watch over their system of work and rule.

- **REVENUE AND TAX COLLECTION:** So far as collection of land revenues and taxes are concerned, you must keep in view the welfare of the taxpayers which is of primary importance than the taxes themselves because these taxes and the taxpayers are the original sources on which the welfare of your State and its subjects depend. If the taxpayers complain to you of the heavy incidence to taxation, of any accidental calamity, of the vagaries of monsoon, of the recession of the means of irrigations, of floods or destruction of their crops on account of excessive rainfall and if their complaints are true, then reduce their taxes. This reduction should be such that it provides them opportunities to improve their conditions and eases them of their troubles.

- **POVERTY CAUSES RUINATION OF A COUNTRY**: Remember Maalik! If a country is prosperous and its people are well to do, then it will happily and willingly bear any burden. The poverty of the people is the actual cause of the devastation and ruination of a country and the main cause of the poverty of the people is the desire of its ruler and officers to amass wealth and possessions whether by fair or foul means. They are afraid of losing their posts or positions and sway or rule and want make the most during the shortest time at their disposal. They never learn any lesson from the history of the nations and never pay any attention to the Commands of Allah.

- **TREAT BUSINESS PEOPLE WELL:** I want to advise you about your business men and industrialists. Treat them well, and order your officers to follow the same policy. There may local businessmen carrying on their trade in certain places or those who send their merchandise from one place to another place. There may even be those who import or export of goods. Similarly, there may be industrialists and manufacturers as well as industrial labor or men engaged in the handicrafts. They all deserve sympathy, protection and good treatment. One more thing about these traders and industrialists: While treating them most sympathetically you must keep an eye over their activities as well.

- **TAKE CARE OF THE POOR:** Then I want to caution you about the poor. Fear Allah about their condition and your attitude towards them. They have no support or resources and no opportunities. They are poor, they are destitute and many of them are crippled and unfit to work. Some of them may be begging and some (who maintain self respect) do not beg, but their conditions speak of their distress, poverty, destitution and wants. You must fix a share for them from Baitul Maal (Government treasury). Beside this reservation in cash, you must also reserve a share in kind of crops etc. from government granaries in cities where food grains are stored as are cultivated on State-owned lands, because in these storage, the share of those living far away from any particular city is equal to the share of those who are living nearby. Let me remind you once again that you are made responsible for guarding the rights of the poor people and for looking after their welfare.

- Therefore be very careful of the welfare of the poor people. Though every one of these poor persons deserves your sympathy and you will have to do justice for Allah's cause to achieve His favors, yet you should pay more attention to the young orphans and the old cripples. They neither have any support, nor they can conveniently come out for begging. They cannot reach you, therefore you should reach them.

- **LISTEN TO PEOPLES' GRIEVANCES:** Out of your hours of work, fix a time for the complaints and for those who want to approach you with their grievances. During this time you should do no other work but hear them and pay attention to their complaints and grievances. For this purpose you must arrange public audience for them during this audience, for the sake of Allah, treat them with kindness, courtesy and respect. Do not let your army and police be in the audience hall at such time so that those who have grievances against your regime may speak to you freely, unreservedly and without fear.

- **STAY IN TOUCHJ WITH PEOPLE:** You must take care not to cut yourself off from the public. Do not place a curtain of false prestige between you and those over whom you rule. Such pretensions and show of pomp and pride are in reality manifestations of inferiority complex and vanity. The result of such an attitude is that you remain ignorant of the conditions of your subjects and of the actual cases of the events occurring in the State.

- **NEVER AWARD LANDS TO YOUR FRIENDS AND RELATIVES**: You must never give lands in permanent lease with all proprietary and ownership rights to your friends and relatives. You must never allow them to take possession of the source of water-supply or lands which have special utility for the communes. If they get possession of such holdings they will oppress others to derive undue benefits. And thus gather all the fruits for themselves leaving for you a bad reputation in this world and punishment in the hereafter.

- **BE FAIR IN DISPENSING JUSTICE**: Be fair in dispensing justice. Punish those who deserve punishment, even though he may be your near relative or a close friend and even if such an action may give you pangs of sorrow and grief. Bear such a sorrow patiently and hope for Divine Rewards. I assure you this will bear you good results.

- **PEACE BRINGS PROSPERITY:** If your enemy invites you for a peace treaty that will be agreeable to Allah, then never refuse to accept such an offer because peace will bring rest and comfort to your armies, will relieve you of anxieties and worries, and will bring prosperity and affluence to your people. But even after such treaties be very careful of the enemies and do not place too much confidence in their promises, because they often resort to peace treaty to deceive and delude you and take advantage of your negligence, carelessness and trust. At the same time be very careful, never break your promise with your enemy, never forsake the protection or support that you have offered to him, never go back upon your words and never violate the terms of the treaty. You must even risk your life to fulfill the promises given and the terms settled because of all the obligations laid by Almighty Allah upon man (in respect of other men) there is none so important as to keep one's promises when made.

- **DO NOT SHED BLOOD:** Beware of the sin of shedding blood without religious justification and sanction, because there is nothing quicker to bring down the wrath of Allah to take away His Blessings, to make you more deserving of His wrath and to reduce the span of your life than to shed innocent blood. On the day of judgment, Allah will first attend to the sins of bloodshed carried out by man against man. Therefore never try to strengthen your power, position and prestige by shedding innocent blood. Such murders instead of making your position strong, will not only considerably weaken it but may also transfer your power totally, taking it away from you and entrusting it to somebody else.

- **AVOID SELF-ADMIRATION**: Beware and do not develop the trait of self-admiration. Do not get conceited of the good points that you find in your good character or good deeds that you have done. Do not get flattery and cajolery make you vain and egoist. Remember that of all the cunning ruses of the devil to undo your good deeds and of the pious people and to affect their piety, flattery and false praises are the ones on which it relies the most. The practice of boasting over the favors done, undo the good done and the habit of breaking one's promises is disliked by both Allah and by men.

- **DO NOT TAKE DECISIONS IN HASTE**: Do not be hasty and do not precipitate your decisions and actions, when time comes for an action to be done, or a decision to be taken, then do not be lazy and do not waste time and do not show weakness. When you do not find a true way to do things on hand, then do not persist on the wrong way and when you find a correct solution, then do not be lethargic on adopting it. In short do everything at a proper way and keep everything in its proper place.

- I beseech Allah that by His Limitless Mercy and by His Supreme Might He may Grant our prayers, that He may lead both of us to the Divine Guidance of achieving His Pleasure of successfully pleading our cases before Him, justifying our deeds before men, of gaining good repute, of leaving good results of our benign and just rule with ever expanding prosperity and ever increasing welfare of the State and of our meeting our ends as martyrs and pious persons as our return is towards Him only.

- May the peace of Allah be upon the Holy Prophet (Saws) and His chosen descendants.

* * *

- It is a Manul of Goods Governance for any Govrenment particularly to Islamic States, also generally to other states of of the World. Peace and Trnquility comes through these guide-lines for any Goverrtnment.

I have ventured to transmit this venerable piece of guidance to persons engaged in administration in the newly created democratic governments in Pakistan. May Allah help them to read, understand and administer accordingly, if they really want to bring Pakistan on the ideals of Qaed-e-Azam, Mohammded Ali Jinah. Amen

Wama Alaina Illul Balaagh.   **Faqeer Syed Shrief Khundmiri**

—

2. IMAMANA'S LETTER TO THE KINGS.

"OH. Mankind: Understand that I am Mohammed (As), son of Abdullah and the namesake of Prophet Mohammed(Slm), the Messenger of Allah. Allah has made me the seal of Vilayet-e-Mohammadia (the sainthood of Prophet Mohammed(Slm), and the Caliph of the Prophet's august followers (Ummah).I am he who was promised to be sent during the Last Era. I am he about whom the Prophet had given advance information. I Am he who has been mentioned in the sacred books of the earlier prophets(As). I am he who invites the people (created by Allah) to come to Allah at the bidding of His Prophet(Slm).

And further, I am not intoxicated at the time of making the claim. I am in my senses. I have been provided with pure and clean food from Allah. I am in need of none other than Allah, the Eternal. I do not desire a throne or crown. I am not hankering after a dominion ore authority. I consider them as absurd and filthy. I am your liberator from worldliness.

The reason for this invitation is that I have been enjoined upon to invite you. I convey my invitation to jinn and mankind, in the sense that I am the seal of the Vilayet-e-Mohammedi (Slm) and Caliph of Allah. Obedience to me is obedience to Allah, and disobedience to me is the disobedience to Allah. Accept my creed so that you are liberated, and obey me.

If you refute me, Allah will seize you. Save yourself from the punishment of the Day(Doomsday) when mountains will be blown to smithereens.

Do not go from this world when you face(spiritual) ruin (in the Hereafter). Choose the reward of the Hereafter. Do not sell it for counterfeit coins. I am telling you all this because you are intelligent. If you consider that I am concocting and maligning Allah, you are bound to inquire into my work (As the Caliph of Allah). Start the work fast.

If you are inattentive to my work, it would mean that you are trying to refute me. You are capable of finding out the truth. IF you allow me to continue (what you consider to be) false claim, you will be liable to Divine Punishment. On oath in the name of Allah, I say that Allah Is enough as a witness to my claim that I am sent to prevent the annihilation of Mohmmed's Ummah and cleanse it of its deviation. Never get deceived. Compare my words, deeds and facts with holy Qur'an. and think over them. If they are in accordance with holy Qur'an, obey me. Otherwise, kill me. This is the best course for your salvation. otherwise your so called ulemas would say that I am left unhindered to preach, as they interpret my mission as an innovation. Therefore, fear Allah and turn to him with humble heart. He is merciful to his servants. This advice is for those, who try to listen with understanding.

* * *

3. IMAMANA'S MAIN MISSION "VISION OF ALLAH IS POSSIBLE".

These are certain verses of the holy Qur'an which Imamana Alaihia Salaam had referred regarding sighting the "Vision of Allah" through our eyes. The Ulema-e-Herat put a question to Imamana (As):

"It is heard that you challenge to cause Vision of Allah in this mortal World?

Imamana politely presented these Verses in this connection: The following verses and some excerpts are reported from "Muqaddama-e-Sirajuil Absar". And some from my Essay" Khuda ho so Khuda Ko Dekhey"

1. "Thus whoever wishes to meet Allah must practice virtuous deeds".(Here meet means, it does not mean that when you meet, you shall shut your eyes. Naturally when you meet Allah, you will see and speak)
2. "The man who is blind here, would be blind in the hereafter".
3. "Beware: Those who are doubtful about their meeting with Allah. Beware that Allah surrounds everything".
4. "Tell Oh Mohammed: This is my path on which I call upon you towards the vision of Allah. Not only I, but my follower also".(Here follower is meant for Imamana(As).)
5. "Oh the Faithful who have faith (after seeing Allah) clinch to your faith firmly".
6. "Do you not see in yourself? Keep in mind that Allah is present in you".

That is thetranslation of these verses, which point out that Allah's Vision is possible during this mortal World.

Request of prophet Musa was: Can I see you? Prophet cannot claim anything which is not possible; hence Musa(As) requested: Could I see you?

Allah's answer was: You cannot see me (in an incarnate form). That is to say Allah is "Noorun Ala Noor" a glimpse of a brilliant light which is not possible to be apprehended., but can be visualized and imagined in your dream while sleeping or in the day time if you have gained that much spirituality through perpetual exerting righteousness and have the sublime firm desire for the vision of Allah. Thus You must have the desire to see Him with your heart, mind and eyes. The above first verse informs that you can see him only when you are on a righteous path. The third Verse directs that you should not doubt His vision, that surrounds you from all corners. The fourth one clearly informs that the Mission of the Holy prophet(Slm) and his follower (Imam Mahdi (As) was to direct you towards vision of Allah. The sixth Verse is explicit in itself.

"It derives from the central belief that Allah is unknowable. To know about Allah, one must study his 'signs' (isharat), i.e., the natural world, the Cosmos. Perception of nature is regarded as a necessary prelude to the awareness of God. Thus, the pursuit of knowledge is equated with faith and a religious duty." A Quote from "Al Qur'an, Science and Renaissance."(My Book under print)

Allah declared before the Angels that He is going to create Adam by molding with His own hands on best of His own Form and image and had blown His spirit unto Adam and says He is near to your jugular vein and surrounds you from all corners. If you do not look into your heart and take the guidance, it is your fault.

My Essay on "Khuda ho so Khda ko Dekhey" published in April 2004, in Noor-e-Vilayet" you may have an idea what that proverb means. Further my Book "Qur'an And Science", chapter 8, examines how emotions and intellectual egoism are shattered by altruism and generate ideas of universality and a spiritual realization transcends ordinary intellectual to a peculiar state of exaltation of "Self"; where the realm of duality melts down merging into the ultimate Unity; the all powerful Unity of natural forces in whom the existence of universal spiritual Essence is manifested." This paragraph tells you to crush your Self by merging into the ultimate Unity that is Allah's and nothing but Allah.

When you put a drop in the ocean, the drop becomes the part of the ocean or say it has become the ocean itself. The same is the situation of a Seeker, when he immerses his self unto the Divine Self, he becomes part and parcel of that Divine Self, hence we may say that the Seeker had merged unto the Divine and became DivineSelf. That is what the Holy Prophet(Slm) directed by saying "Mootu, Qabla Anta Mootu". That is to say, unless you annihillsate your self and your "ANAA" you cannot imagine to have His Vision.

Now we go to securitize the Ihadees-e-Nabavi:

First of all Go through the "Hadees-e-Gabrial" With respect to IHSAN which expilicitly directs:

"Offer prayers as if you are seeing Allah, otherwise think that Allah is seeing you, or think that Allah is witnessing your prayers".

Had it not been possible to see, then the Holy Prophet(Slm) would not have instructed Ummah in these clear and understandable words to at least have imagination that Allah is witnessing your prayers. On that Imamana said: "At least have a firm desire to witness His Vision in the dream while sleeping". Thus if any person submerges his Self and his own attributes unto the sublime attributes of the holy prophet(Slm), I am sure, with Holy Prophet's benevolence, you may have Vision of Allah.

Ibn Abbas(Rz) stated that the Holy Prophet became very joyous one morning and exclaimed that: "Rayatha Rabbi" I had seen my Lord". On this Hadis, Imam Ibn Haunbal commented that the prophet(Slm) might have seen Allah in his dream, since the prophets' dreams are true.

The holy prophet(Slm) had further described the features of Allah by saying "I saw my Lord in the form of a curly haired and a beardless young man wearing a green robe and wearing golden shoes and drops of gold water on His face. "At another time the holy Prophet(Slm) also informed his companions that" Allah came to me in His best Form while I was sleeping. And asked me about the "Dispute of the Sublime Council". When I told that I do not know, He put his palm between my shoulders which caused me coolness in my inner most, and "I got the knowledge of all creations between the Earth and the Skies". And Allah informed me that He made known to Ibrahim(AS) the secrets of the heaven and the Earth like that."

Ibn Sadaqa and Abu Zarr accepted these Hadies as true and when they asked "Verily you did see Allah? The holy Prophet(Slm) said: "I just sighted a brilliant light, then how could I see Him?." The same was the situation with Prophet Musa(SAs) who asked Allah: "Can I see you"? Allah told him "You cannot see me" Then further Allah directed him "You can see me if the mountain (Before you) stands at its place and directed him to see towards the mountain. With the power of His brilliant light the mountain was reduced to ashes and Prophet Musa(As) fell down unconscious and when came to his senses he exclaimed "You are great and most powerful". Do you think that without seeing Allah, Musa(As) had addressed to Allah: "You are great and most powerful?" The difference in witnessing Allah's Vision by the holy Prophet(Slm) and by Prophet Musa(As) is that Musa(As) fell down unconscious, and the holy Prophet(Slm) withstood that brilliant light and said that" how could I see Him in a brilliant light?" Surely that brilliant light was the Vision of Allah alone and nothing else what Musa(As) had seen and fainted.

Shaikhul Islam Imam Taimiyya had commented Ibn Abbas' Hadis that "The Holy Prophet (Slm) saw Allah does not contradict the claim (of seeing Allah) nor his statement that "I saw my Lord with the eyes of my heart, and also during my sleep". Prophet's assertion that "I saw Allah in the most beautiful Form should be taken in positive sense ; since the Holy Prophet(Slm) (speaks truth and nothing but truth. The same is the opinion of Ibn Khateer and Ibn Qayyum, the most prominent Muhaddis and commentators.

Verse 53:2, of Al Najam: certifies that "Neither the holy prophet had deviated from the right path nor he had trodden on a wrong path."

Another verse 53:11 testifies that the prophet "never did tell a lie what he witnessed." Further verses: 53:13 emphatically states that "Indeed he did see the spectacle again near Sidrathul Muntha". Second time near the Lot tree at the last boundary (53:13)"

"Closed to which is the everlasting paradise".(53:15). "The sight did not shift nor did it cross the limit (53:17). Lastly Allah informs "Indeed he saw the supreme signs of His Lord." (53:18) Now I ask you: Do you have still any doubt whether the holy prophet(Slm) did not witness the Vision of Allah during the M'airaj?

And what do you say, when the Holy Prophet(Slm), on the advice of Prophet Musa(As), visited several times to get reduced the 50 prayers to 5 prayers daily? Do you think that he, without seeing Allah "One to One", he got his suggestion granted by Allah and the prayers got reduced to 5 for the Ummah? This dialectic discussion was very important and should have been consummated by looking "Eye to Eye" to each other!!!

The same is asserted by Mu'dah Ibn Jalal, Abdul Rahman Ibn A'ish and Behaqi, all prominent Muhaddisseen, (Tirmizi 237) when Ibn Abbas very emphatically told that the holy prophet had sighted the Vision of Allah two times with the eyes of his heart. (Tirmizi 335) Imam Ahmad Hunbal took it seriously by telling that the prophet never says lies. He confirmed that Prophet(Slm) might have seen Allah in his dream and the prophet's dreams are always true in all respects. When Abu Zarr inquired the prophet (Slm) "Whether did you see Allah?" Prophet(Slm) told him that "There was a brilliant light how can I see?" (Tirmizi, Book one Item 342) Thus, the same brilliant light is the vision of Allah.

Do not ever think that when Hazrat Musa requested Allah that "I want to see you" And Allah forthwith informed him that "You cannot see me". Here Hz. Musa wanted to see Allah in a personification, which was not possible. Because Allah is "Noorus Samawati wal Arz." Still more than that "Noorun Alaa Noor. "Qur'an also informs that perception is not possible but sighting is possible. There is much difference in between Perception and Sighting.

What you see isn't necessarily what you get' is a good way of summing up the difference between seeing and perception. The eye sees because it responds to varying light inputs. However, what we perceive is a combination of the sensory input into the eye and what we already know or expect. (Wickipedia) Further it may accurately be described as "Allah is beyond to be grasped either physically or mentally.

Perception is really connected to the five senses viz; smell, taste, hearing, touch, which, in our view, is not possible but as far as sighting or seeing is concerned, it is possible to look or behold with our own eyes. To further elborate this difference, I like to go back to refer the dialogue between the Prophet(Slm) and Abu Zarr(Rz):

"There was a brilliant light how can I see?" (Tirmizi, Book one Item 342) Thus, the same brilliant light is the vision of Allah, to my understanding, it is possible to which Imamana (As) said "Every person sees Allah, but is unablde to differenciate for want of real knowledge or guidance." Further he said "HER KE KHUDA-E-RAA MUQQIED BEENAD, WO MUSHRIK ASTH." Means, whoever personifies Allah, he is a mushrik infidel.

Yet in another "Saying" of Imamna (As) he emphatically stated that "Her Ke Tasawwour-e-Khuda, bairoon-e-Zat-e-Kheesh mikunad, woo mushrik asth." Measns: who ever imagines Allah being away from one's own person, he is a mushrik. Immana(As) by saying this he proved Allah's assertion "He surrounds every body and that He is in your own self."

Thus Imamana(As) asseted that "whenever you inhale, the breath represents "Huwwal Bathin" by uttering "Illalah toun hai" whenever you exhale tell" La Ilahun Nahien". This outgoing breath represents "Huwaz Zahir". Both are Allah's attributes. "HUWAL BATHIN AND HUWWAZ ZAHIR".

You are supposed to reckon these breaths, which is called "Paas-e-Anfas". Here you are supposed to imagine that, you are viewing your Heart and the sound you get from the breath is "Hoo" which represnts "Allah". If you concentrate profusely, then you are sub-merging your self unto the "Divine Unity" and you become "Haq from top to toe". That is the stage in which you have annihillated your "Self" and merged unto the Divinity, there is nothing but AllAH AND NONE ELSE EVERY WHERE, BUT ALLAHi Allah. That is how Allah surrounds you and He is in your Self. The power which runs your body represents Entity of Allah, and the body becomes your entity. Thus Allah and you are "Hands in Glove' with each other". Imagine your "ROOH" is Allah and your body is your entity. I request you to give deep thought: who is he that tells "I"? Is it you or Some One in You!!!

That is the stage when you ponder on to your "Inner Self", which is called 'Zikr-e-Khafi' in which you imagine yourself as "HAQ", in which your 'Self' and all of your attributes are totally anihillated by merging unto the Divinity, thus what remains, nothing but Allah every where. That is why Mansur asserted "Anal Haq". what is wrong in it? Still we are bound to the advice given by Imamana(As) "Knowing is Ieman, and uttering it, is Kufr".

Hence to know we must imagine by having firm faith that my life, my humble prayers, my death and everything belongs to Allah alone, who is Omnipotent, Omniscient and Omni presence, who is alone to be worshipped and none has the power to provide sustenance in this world of multifarious creations, in and upon the Earth, and in the oceans and in between the Earth and the Skies. That is how you are surrendering to the will of Allah which will lead you to understand Him through your Self and when you visualize Him, by submerging your own Self unto His Self then only you may have the possibility to have a glimpse of his vision.

To further elaborate the above contention, Remembrance of Allah, is the first stage. When you indulge yourself in remembering Allah, you are supposed to forget yourself by continuously utterring:

"Illalah Toan Hai; La Ilaha Houn Nahin". That means to say "Toan hai, Mien Nahin", meaning only Allah is present and nothing else not even me. That is why the holy Prophet (Slm) had said:

"MOOTU QABLA ANTHA MOOTU." On that score only the Holy Prophet(Slm) became jubillient and said "RAYETHA RABBI". This brings you near to Allah. With utmost concentration and humility you are immersing yourself unto His Divine Entity. Every breath of yours declaring "thou art; not me" with intensity and have the faith that there is "Nothing But Allah". This is called "Unity of Divine Manifestation."

GHALIB-E-MURHOOM' SAYS IN HIS POEM THAT:

"NA THA KUCH THO KHUDA THA, KUCH NA HOTA THO KHUDA HOTHA"

"DUBOYA MUJHKO HONEY NE, NA HOTHA MIEN THO KEYAH HOTHA"

Meanings: There is nothing but Allah, and Allah alone. I HAVE IMMERSED UNTO THE DIVINE UNITY OF ALLAH, AND BECAME ALLAH."

On the othder hand Mir Taqi Mir complaints submissively:

"SUB KUCH KARO HAI AAP HI HUM KO ABUS BADNAAM KIYA."

Like-wise, Imamana's companion, Hazrat Miyan Bheek, exclaimed: "Allah is all". However, this concept is not exclusive to Mahdavis. Even before Mahdi (as) a man named Mansur, in Baghdad, uttered "Anal Huq", meaning "I am the truth. I am Allah". However, he was executed by the ruler for such a bold statement which was against Sharia. Of course there is no other diety but Allah. Hence his statement was perceived as a very bold statement and was taken at face value, while Mansur meant Truth and nothing but Truth. That is why, when Mansur was executed, his every drop of blood asserted loudly "Anal HUQ".!!!

Later on, after Mahdi Maood (as) came and gone, Hzrt. Khalifa-e-Groh explained what Mansur meant. After having Deedar-e-khuda only Munsoor dared to asseret "Unal Haq" Further Hzrt Khalifa-e-Groh said, "My body became Huq, my heart became Huq, my soul became Huq. Huq hi Huq hai, and nothing but Huq." The same was told by Hzt. Miyan Bheek that" All is Allah" Then Imamana asked him: "What are you witnessing". Miyan Bheek replied: "Allah is in everything". Then, Imamana reprimonded him "Knowing Allah is Ieman; uttering is infedility. (Kufr)". It means, "Do not utter so opdenly, otherwise you will face the same verdict what Mansoor got by openly utterring". then Immana read the Couplet of Moulana Rom:

"Bezaar Manaum Kuhna Khuday ke thoo dari" "Hur Lahza mara Tazaa Khuday deegarey Hust."

It means thus:

"I am tired of your old vision of Allah, because in every moment of time, I witness His fresh Glory and a new Splendor."

Thus Imamana asserted "Do not tell what you had witnessed openly, because common people who do not understand the inner meanings of the Divine Knowledge, they may indulge in wrong beliefs of "Hama Oost" meaning they will get the wrong impression that "All is God" it might be taken to the extremity. To tell openly about the glimpse of the Divine splendor is against Shariat. Therefore Mansur being immersed in the Unity of Allah had uttered openly "Anul Haq" (I am Huq), He was right by telling that "I am Huq" since Allah ordained that I have surrounded everything of this Universe. But to tell openly was against Shariat, according to Imamana. Hence Mansoor was martyred because he went against the Shariat and that act of execution of Mansur also was correct since the Rulers had the authority to uphold the dictates of the Shariat. But they failed to destroy Mansur's drops of blood which were pronouncing "Anal Huq".

Further Imamana(As) had also clarified that: To view Allah from the view point of common knowledge which is implanted on your heart, is an old impression of Allah. Such sticking to the old notion, is boring, since every moment of time His splendor is new and afresh. This can be proven with the Qur'anic Verse: "Kulla Yumin Huwa Fish Shun" (55:29) that "Every new day or new moment of time brings a fresh splendor and a fresh Glory of Allah".

This is one aspect of the Divine Knowledge. Another aspect is as mentioned by Allah Himself in hadith al-Qudsi that:

"When my servant offers his servitude by remembering Me continuously with concentration and from the depth of his heart and soul, he nears to Me. If he tries to reach Me one inch, I go towards him one yard till I become his hand through which he holds anything; I become his leg through which he treads; I become his eyes through which he sees." (Bukhari—8-131-6502)

When Allah becomes Eyes of the Seeker, what will the Seeker see? Is it not Allah's Glory what the seeker wished to see? Therefore the holy prophet asserted "Raitha Rabbi" I had seen My Allah through the Eyes of My Lord. Then the prophet said "If you want to see Allah; See me." That is what Imamana also said" If you want to see Allah; See me" And really Haz. Bandagi Miyan, at the very first glimpse of Imamana uttered "My eyesight may be shatterd, Had I seen Mahdi; I saw in you the Glory of Allah." On that utterance of Bandage Miyan, Imamana told "Yes, Khuda ho so Khuda Ko Dekhey". Meaning: Only if you have reached that sublime stage of seeing Allah, then you can see Him, because you have immersed spiritually and not physically at that point unto the Entity of Allah.

Furthermore, the holy prophet (Slm) has said that every action of the real lover of Allah impresses Allah so much that in the result: Allah becomes the Lover's hand, leg and eye. When, Allah becomes the eye of the lover, what will the lover see? Will he not see his Beloved, Allah? That is the meanings of: Khuda ho so Khuda Ko Dekhey".!!!

Thus to arrive at this sublime stage the seeker had to pray to Allah as if he is Seeing Allah, if not, then he must keep in mind that Allah is witnessing him. From that sort of worship the seeker gets His Vision, only when he becomes pious by adopting righteous way of living. That means to Follow the dictates of Shariat first and obey Allah according to His dictates. When the Seeker is perfect in Shariat, then he has to proceed on the path of the Tareeqat which had been taught by Imamana. Therefore Imamana ordained "Shariat, Baad uz Fanaey Bashriat."

It means to say the Seeker had to annihilate his Self and get immersed in the Divine Unity of the "Zat-e-Bariey Ta'alah."

It is stated that during a Sermon, one Mullah pointed out to Imamana (As) that:" The Vision of Allah is possible only after death." Imamana replied: When did I say that it was possible in one's life time? Then he read a tradition: Mootu Qabla unta Mooto" and explained that: Unless you die before your death, Allah's vision is not possible." This is what annihilation of the Self and immersing unto the Divine Unity means, which is Allah and nothing but Allah. The following couplet is clear about this situation:

"Bey Irada Murney Waley, Bil Irada Markey Dekh—Woh Tamasha Karchuka, tho tamasha karkey Dekh." This couplet tells the Seeker to annihilate and get out of his Self if he wants to witness the Vision of Allah during his lifetime.

Zat-e-Khuda is absolute, Allah (swt) is not bound to time and place and He can not be perceived. However, Allah (swt) can be visualized in dreams during sleep or even in the day time while one is submerged in sincere and deep meditation (zikr) with perfect concentration and with the depth of his mind and heart. In fact, Imamana (As) said:

"To have atleast the desire to witness the Glory of Allah, is an obligation". He also said that, without that desire, one is not a Momin. Hence remember Allah (swt) while sitting, standing or lying, as Allah mentions in Quran. This will lead one to annihilate the Self/Nafs and once it is annihilated and immersed into the Divine Unity of the Almighty, the seeker becomes part and parcel of that Divine Entity. When the Seeker attains that position he becomes "Fana Fillah" and when he merges unto His Divine Unity, he becomes Baqi Billah." Then what is left: "Thoo hi Thoo and Kuch Nahien". Meaning, as the companions of Mahdi (as) Miyan Bheek and Khalifa-e-Guruh(Rz) said, "Allah is everywhere inside and outside, in you and around you. "This is the result of Zikr-e-Dawam, the teaching of Mahdi Maood, which makes the Seeker annihilate his self and witnesses the Sublime Glory of Allah. This stage is called by Imamana: Fana-e-Bushariat" which enables a person to clinch to the Shariat-e-Mustafavi.

Let me remind you the Verse" Mun Kana Yarju Liqa-e-Rabbi" (18:110) which tells that: whoever has the desire to witness Allah, must adopt the righteous way of life. This righteous life is called "Amal-e-Saleh."

What is Amal-e-Saleh? To adopt a rightuous and virtuous life. To adopt "Amr Bil Muaroof" and Nahi unil munkir". "to remember continuously "La ilaha Ilal lah". Then only you are able to have the Vision.

Let me further elaborte: When we view an object, we require the light of our eyesight, first. Then, the object also needs to be surrounded by light for it to be viewed. Likewise, if we want to have Deedar-e-Khuda, we require two lights: one is that of the Shariat (the teachings of Prophet Muhammad (Slm) and the other is that of the Tareeqat, which is the light of the Vilayet-e-Mustafavi (the teachings of Mahdi Maood). What does Tareeqat involve?

1. Tark-e-Dunia: To renounce worldly connections to concentrate our mind and heart towards Allah.
2. Tark-e Alaeq: To retire from the huzel and buzel of the worldly life for remembrance of Allah.
3. Suhbat-e-Sadeqan: Cultivate friendship with those who will guide you towards the right path.

4. Zikr-e-Dawam: Perpetual Remembrance of Allah with concentration.
5. Tawkkul: Reliance on Allah for each and every need of yours.
6. Talab-e-Deedar-e-Khuda: Perpetual Desire to witness the Vision of Allah. One who does not desire to witness, he cannot witness. Thus Desire is a Must.

These are the tenets of Tareeqat which teach you "Amal-e-Saleh, pre-requisite for" Liqa-e-Rabbi", the Vision of Allah.

Thus These are the two Lights. 1. Shariat and 2. Tareeqat ; through which we may have our desire accomplished and Zikr is the key to achieve the vision of Allah.

Importance of Zikr in seeking the vision of Allah:

Imamana asserted that he had brought a very straight path on which if any one treads he is sure to get his desire accomplished. He further elaborated that:

"We have been given authority. You relinquish that authority by fulfilling the dictates of Allah. Actually when You relinquish your authority, and when you follow Shariat and Tareeqat; both of which will bring you to the nearest way to the stright path to achieve Beneficence of Allah".

To adopt obedience and humility is to relinquish that authority. To disregard honor and wealth, to suppress passion and desire for worldly life and to die before your physical death (Mootu Qabla unta Mootu) is called relinquishment of that authority.

This is what Amal-e-Saleh is through which we can accomplish our desire to witness the vision of Allah. This is what Imamana had taught elaborately to us. He asserted:

"Be with Allah, where ever you are."

Once Hzrat Bandagi Miyan had a conversation with a Hindu Raja who asked Bandagi MIyan:

"How can an Aakaar (man) see Nirakaar (Allah, that which cannot be seen)".

Bandagi Miyan replied "One has to annihilate one's Self into the Divine Self of Allah by perpetually negating his Self." Only then one can visualize the glimpse of "Nirakaar."

The Raja then asserted:" there was a curtain, which is now burnt up and there is nothing but Allah everywhere." It is told that after just three days of this incident the Raja passed away. Upon which, Bandagi Miyan commented that the Raja had that much capacity only to bear and passed away being annihilated into the Ultimate Divine Unity.

The Holy Prophet (slm) has informed us that: what you inhale, it runs through your heart and infuses whole of your body. Therefore if you take the name of Allah with every breath, then

Zat-e-Khuda, that is "Entity of Allah" penetrates into your body and helps Ieman to flourish in yourself. Hence Perpetual Remembrance of Allah is a must according to Imamana(As). This is called "Pass-e-Anfas" to Reckon each breath. Thus Imamana (As) taught us in view of the holy Prophet's instructions that when you inhale Say: "Illalah Toun Hai" and when you exhale say "La Ilahoun Nahien." Not just by the words of mouth but actually understanding the meanings and the purpose of negation of self and assertion of existence of Allah everywhere. This is the key through which you open the door of Enlightenment to attain Allah's Beneficence: "leading you towards accomplishment of your desire to have the Vision of Allah".

For this Imamana(As) instructed to exercise at least twice a day, in the morning after Fajr prayer, before the Sun Rise and in the evening after Asr prayer before the Sun Set, Namaz-e-Maghrib.

This is the perfect time to annihilate your Self and immerse yourself unto the Divine Self through which the Divine vision is possible and there is a big list of those venerable personalities who had the Vision of Allah through their eyes of the heart and also from the eyes of their head, they had the vision of Allah. In this regard Khaja Gaisoo Draz, a saint from Gulberga (Karnataka) who lived prior to Mahdi Maood (as), states that:

"I, Mohammedul Husaini speak about such pious personalities who had witnessed the vision of Allah. Among them are Hazrat Imam Razi, Imam Ghizali, Ibn Arabi and many more who had certified that Vision of Allah is possible in this mortal world."

Lastly, I conclude with a quotation regarding Allah Subhana Wat Tallah, from Futuhat-e-Makkiah written by Mohiuddin Ibn Arabi, a mystic, philosopher and a reputed sage, one of the greatest spiritual teachers of Islam who had prophesied about the Advent of Mahdi in the Tenth Century which came true:

"It is He who is revealed in every face, sought in every sign, gazed upon by every eye, worshipped in every object of worship, and pursued in the unseen and the visible. Not a single one of His creature can fail to find Him in its primordial and original nature."

How beatifully an imminnt poet Ghalib had stated the above utterances of IBn Arabi in a poetic exaltation:

JAB KEY TUJH BIN NAHIN KOIE MOUJOOD PHIR YE HANGAMA AI KHUDA KEYA HAI

*WHEN YOU(ALLAH) SAY, except Me, nothing is EXISTING THEN why and WHAT IS THIS FANFARE IN THE WORLD?

That is the beauty of His manifestation, if still not visualized, I have only to refer the Qur'anic Verse:" "Whoever is blind here, he is also a blind in the hereafter."(17:72) God Forbid.

Let me tell a statement of a pious man who told about his dream: "I saw a dream, in which I witnessed some fourrteen eminent personaliteis, includiug prophets, Imamana and Bandagi Miyan, who passed befofre me, on which I became very astonished to see them all at a time, and humbly enquired the Almighty, that "Although all such exalted personalities passed before me one by one, but none had told about You" Then a voice was heard telling "Aaiena Dekh, Khudi ko Bhool Ja". "look up on the mirror, and forget about your entity". He told further that the figure of Prophet Moosa and the words of the voice: "look the mirror and forget your self" are clinging in my mind to get the clue".

In order to find out the clue, I pray Allah, the Almighty, from deepest of my heart and soul to guide me further and direct me to that straight path brought by Imamana (As) by treading on which I may be able to have the Sublime glimpse of Thy Vision to request Allah alone to decode the sacred wordings of the voice: "Aaieena Deykh" by this you witness your own figure, if you can annihillte yourself, then surely you wil witness the Almighty. that is the nearest path brought by Imamana(As) Wama Alaina Illul Balaagh!!!

—

4. AQEEDA-E-SHARIEFA

Hzazrat Bandagi Miyan Syed Khundmir, Siddiq-e-Vilayet(Rz) had written four important booklets regarding Mahdavia Faith: They Are:

1. **Aqeeda-e-Shariefa,**
2. **Maktoob-e-Multani,**
3. **Maqsad-e-Sani,**
4. **Risala-e-Khatim-e-Vilayet.**

Among them all, "Aqeeda-e-Shariefa" became most important because it provides the Basic Beliefs of our Faith, which was consented and authenticated by all companions of Imamana(As), word by word and belief by belief and was attested by all jointly and signed as the Basic Tenets of our Mahdavia Faith. It is also known as "Ummal Aqaayed"(Mother of beliefs).

It was written when Haz. Bandagi Miyan(Rz) while in Gujrat, became serious to hear wrong versions of our Faith from various sources. In order to eradicate any false notion which might have emerged about the Faith, he took trouble to compile this valuable booklet, in order to familiarize and adopted by Mahdavis the fundamentals of the basic tenets of the Faith which were asserted by Imamana(As).

It is a fact that human memory fades away by the course of time and as regards basic tenets of the Faith, they are prune to be misrepresented as time passes on. In view of this critical situation, Bandagi Miyan (Rz) was very vigilant and felt his utmost responsibility to compile these Basic Tenets which were asserted by Imamana(As) during his long residence in FARAH.

When Bndagi Miyan (Rz) compiled this book and became satisfied, he called an IJMA in which all companions and prominent elite were present, then the contents of the "Aqeeda-e-Shriefa" ware read, one by one, and clause by clause, and got it approved and attested as the most corrected version of our Faith and signed jointly and kept as the First ever Mahzara, a Public Record, and also published and circulated to various Dairahas and places where Mahdvis were living in order to inculcate them these Basic Tenets of our Faith.

(The URDU—Ageeda-e-Shariefa, with elucidations by Hzt. Khoob Miyan Saheb Palanpuri, duly translated in English, Just the Aqeeda itself.—Khundmiri)

TEXT OF "AQEEDA-E-SHARIEFA:

In the name of Allah, the most benevolent and most merciful

I, Syed Khundmir, son of Syed Moosa, known as Chajoo, do hereby subscribe what I had heard the following injunctions from the mouth of Imamana(As):

Imam Mahdi said: "I am directly taught by Allah daily to declare that I am the servant of Allah and the follower of Mohammed Rasoolullah(Slm), the Last Messenger of Allah. I, Mohammed Mahdi(As) of Juanpur, is the Imam Mahdi of the last period, and the heir of Mohammed, Allah's Messenger. I am authority on the meanings and substance of Qur'an and Faith (Iemaan). I am the Interpreter of the Reality in its inner and outer Manifestations. (Since Allah declared "Summa Inna Alaina Bayana"—It is Our responsibility to interpret. hence that task is resting with me to interprtet.)

Imam Mahdi(As) declared that he was Mahdi(As) as commanded by Allah. To prove his claim he cited Allah's Kalaam, the holy Qur'an, and by toeing to the footsteps of the holy Prophet(Slm) and practicing the Prophet Mohammed's Shariat without any error.

Allah said: Is he to be counted equal with them who rely on a clear proof from his Lord, and a witness (Qur'an) from which he recites, and before it, the Book of Mosses, an example was a mercy to all? Such is his belief, if any one disbelieves, his abode is Hell. Hence, do not be in doubt concerning it. Since it is the truth from thy Lord; but mostly of mankind believe not (11:17). (There are many verses in Qur'an on this subject.)

Imam Mahdi(As) maintained by ordaining: The refusal to "believe me as Mahdi(As) tantamount to as if to refuse to Allah, His Book Qur'an and His Messenger, (the Holy Prophet (slm)

Imam, Mahdi(As) said: I am assigned the responsibility of propagating the word of Allah among the masses.

Imam used to say, if any tradition of the Prophet (Slm) is recited by any one to argue his opinion, it is possible that any contradiction may arise, since there are various traditions like that one, hence it is difficult to correct them. Imam (As) said, in such situations, the criterian is that, if any tradition has conformity with Qur'an and according to the circumstances of such Revelations, should be taken as correct. As a proof, Imam Mahdi(As) presented the Saying of the Prophet(Slm), "there would be many traditions spread by the followers after my demise, hence those traditions only to be accepted which have conformity with Qur'an, otherwise should be rejected."

With regard to a tradition in which it is asserted that Mahdi(As) would fill the earth with justice, as it would have been filled with injustice, oppression and violence. This tradition, as it is understood, means that all the people on earth would accept me as Mahdi(As) and obey me, thus all believers had believed me and accepted me as Mahdi(As).

Imam Mahdi(As) cited a verse of the Qur'an which he claimed it be regarding his devotees: "So those who fled and were driven away from their houses and suffered troubles for Allah's cause, and then fought and were slain.(3:195). Imam Mahdi(As) asserted about this verse that the attributes described in this verse are the attributes of his devotees (Mahdavis). Among those attributes all have happened except war, which would occur when Allah determines and it would manifest itself at his Will and Pleasure. Imam Pointed out the person who possessed this attribute in the verse would be among the Mahdavis.

Imam Mahdi(As) decreed as hypocrite a man who after accepting Mahdi, did not migrate along with him; and thus he had avoided the company of the Imam(As). This decree is in conformity with the Qur'an which states that, those of the believers who avoided to go to jihad and sit idle in their houses, having no reason, are not equal to those who actually took part in the jihad along with their wealth and life. Allah had granted the jihadists high rank comparing to the sedentary ones. Allah Is always merciful and forgives(4: 95,96).

As regards repentance, Allah says: Those who repent, amend and hold fast and make religion pure for Allah, they are among the believers, to whom Allah grants high rewards.(4:146).

Imam Mahdi(As) asserted that the process of Verification is a fact. To whom he accepted, Allah too accepted him, and those to whom Imam Mahdi(As) rejected, Allah too rejected them.

Imam Mahdi(As) sternly decreed his devotees not to offer prayers behind a non believer, if by mistake any one prayed, he must repeat his prayer.

Imam Mahdi(As) asserted that all commentaries and explanation of the Holy Qur'an, if they are against his own interpretations, they should not be taken as his interpretation, since his assertions and commands are completely in conformity with that of the holy Prophet's deeds and commandments.

Imam Mahdi(As) declared emphatically that he is not bound to adopt any one of the four Schools of Doctrine in relation to Fiqha. Hence if one desires to examine the truthfulness, he should verify their adherence to the Holy Qur'an and compliance with the precepts and practice of the holy Prophet (Slm) in their manner of conducting, keeping in view Allah's assertion: "Inform thou; This is my way, I do invite towards Allah, on evidence which is clear, as if seeing with one's eyes. I and who (Mahdi) follows me. Glory to All. I and my follower will never associate idols with Allah." (12:108)

Imamana(As) categorically said: Allah had sent me particularly to explain His Commands in connection with "Vilayet-e-Mahmmadi" and Allah had ordained "Say more it is for Us to explain (and make it clear) (75:19) and this explanation is to be furnished by me and none else.

Imamana(As) asserted that Allah has to be seen in this world with one's own eyes. Imamana(As) had given the testimony of the "Vision of Allah" as mentioned in the Holy Qur'an and as pointed out by the Holy Prophet(Slm).

In this connection, Imamana(As) further asserted that the desire to witness Allah is an obligation on every individual, man or woman. Further declared: one may not be a true Momin, until he or she had seen the Almighty through the physical eyes, or spiritual eyes, or even in his or her dream. He further explained that a true seeker is he or she who has relinquished worldly desire, and who has devoted himself or herself towards Allah with heart, mind and soul and should be completely absorbed in remembrance(Zikr) of Allah and kept himself or herself in seclusion and who have ability to come out of himself or herself; they are alone who are the blessed one having complete Faith (Ieman) on Allah.

Imamana(As) declared the Zaath—e—Khuda,(Divinity) of Allah is Faith, and real Faith is Vision of Allah.

Imamana's explanations about some of the verses of the Holy Qur'an, basically differ from the elucidations given by the earlier commentators who are known as Mujtahids.

According to the Holy Qur'an, the true believers are those who, when Allah is mentioned, feel a tremor in their hearts, and when they hear His Revelations and Signs rehearsed, find their Faith strengthened, and put all their trust in their Lord; those who establish prayers, and spend freely out of the gifts We have given for their sustenance. Such in truth are the believers; they have gardens of dignity with their Lord, and forgiveness, and generous sustenance.(8:2,3,4). According to Imamana(As) the seekers of Allah whose attributes are enumerated in those verses, maintained and adhere to the limits of Faith.

Imamana(As) ordained about those who are condemned that their destiny is eternal in the hell as per the Qur'anic dictate "Nay, those who seek gain in evil, and are strapped round their skins, they are verily the companions of the Hell, therein they shall abide forever".(2:81)

Imamana(AS) pointed out the verse of the Holy Qur'an "If a man kills a believer intentionally, his recompense is Hell, to abide therein forever and the wrath and the curse of Allah are upon him, and a dreadful penalty is prepared for him"(4:93) and reprimoneded to avoid such unholy things.

According to the Imam(As), the following verse declares Hell for the seekers of the worldly desires: "If anyone does wish for the temporary things of the present life, We readily grant them those things, as We will grant to such persons as We will; in the end We have provided Hell for them; they will be burned therein, disgraced and rejected."(17:128)

And who relinquishes the worldly life, for them the Imam(As) declared as per the verse: "Whoever works righteousness, man or woman, and has Faith, verily, We will give new life, which is good and pure and We will bestow on them our reward according to the best of their actions". (16:97)

As regards forsaking things, other than Allah, Imamana(As) pointed towards the Verse:" Oh. Ye, the believer, Fear Allah alone. And let every soul look to what provisions he had sent for the Hereafter? Ye, Fear Allah Alone, for He is well acquainted with all that you do.(59:18)

Imamana(As) referred the verse of the Holy Qur'an regarding Perpetual Remembrance (Zikr-e-Dawam): "When Ye pass the congregational prayers, celebrate Allah's praise, standing, sitting, or lying down on your side, but when Ye are free from danger, set up regular prayers, which prayers are obligatory on Believers at particular times."(*4:103)

Thus I call upon the Seekers of Truth, who are the Devotees of Imam Mahdi(As) you should know that the Injunctions mentioned above by this servant, syed Khundmir(Rz), who was constantly in the company of Imam Syed Mohammed Mahdi(As) from his first meeting to the last breath of the Imam(As), and he found no deviation in observance of the above said Injunctions at any time. We should all believe and have Faith in them. Any explanation, elucidation or interpretation for these Injunctions would be against the teachings of Imam Mahdi(As).

Faqeer Syed Sharief Khundmiri

* * *

5. EIGHTEEN (HASZDA) AYAAT

5. 18 VERSES OF THE HOLY QUR'AN, ABOUT WHOM IMAMANA(As) HAD PARTICULARIZED BY SAYING THAT SOME OF THEM PERTAIN TO HIS PERSONALITY AND SOME TO HIS FOLOWERS(QOUM)

Accordingly Bandagi Abdul Ghafoor Sujawandi(Rh) brother of Bandgi Abdul Malik Sujawandi(Rh) author of "Sirajul Absar", had compiled in a Riasala by name "Risala-e-Hazsda Ayaat" (A Risala on the Eighteen Verses). The same verses also had been already recorded by Bandagi Miyan Syed Khundmir(Rz) in his "Aqeeda-e-Shariefa" which had been authenticated and consented by all the companions of Imamana (As). The gist is hereunder:

The proof of Mahdiat, from the word of Allah, Kalamullah and the prophecies which confirmed by the Holy Prophet(Slm), Imamana(As) had substantiated his claim as the Definite Evidence(Hujjat) based on these Eighteen Verses of the Holy Qur'an.

It is a fact that Imamana(As)had argued his Mahdiat from Kalamullah by presenting the verse "Afaa Mun Kana" as a concrete proof and then presented many verses relating to his Mahdiat along with the verse "Wa Akhereena Minhum" as the fulfillment of the intent of the Holy Qur'an.

Bandagi Abdul Ghafoor Sujawandi(Rh) belongs to the Descendants who had stated that:

Certainly I decided to describe the Sayings of Imamana(As), as mentioned in the Holy Qur'an, they are about Eighteen. Out of them some relate to Imamana(As) and some to his Qoum.

Particularly these eighteen verses pointed out by Imamana(As) on the Commands of Allah, having been mentioned by Shah Burhan(Rh) in his "Shawahedul Vilayet". Apart from it, Shah Burhan(Rh)had also recorded them in his "Hadiqatul Haqaeq", by mentioning: "Advent of MAHDI(As) as had been mentioned in the Holy Qur'an in eighteen verses which are famous in favour of Imamana(As).

These verses also had been presented in a poem written by Malek Ji Mehri(Rz) also.

In the following paragraphs we shall try to elucidate each Verse, first with its meanings then shall elaborate it how it pertains to Imamana(As) or to his Qoum:

(Note: The numbering of the Soora and the Verse and translation in English is given from Yousuf Ali's Qur'an. Further Verses 1,2,5,7,8,10,13 and 17 pertain to Imamana(As), and verses 3,4,6,11,12,14,15,16, and 18, pertain to Groh-e-Mahdavia. Further, there are some sort of repetition in interpretation of those verses, but there is consensus among the Groh, therefore, we are bound to accept them As they are. If there is difference in calculation and interpretation of each verse, the same may be pointed out to rectify if agreeable.)

• "Wa IZABTALA IBRAHIMA(As) RABBAHU BE KALAMTE FATEHUNNA INNI JAELUKA LIL NAS IMAMA, WA QAALA MIN ZURRAITINI" (2:!24);

"And remember that Ibrahim(As) was tried by His Lord with certain Commands, which he fulfilled. Then Allah asserted: I will make thee an Imam of the Nations. (On that) Ibrahim (AS) pleaded "Also make an Imam from my progeny". Allah answered: But my promise is not with in the reach of the evil doers."

Through this verse Allah Has revealed that when Ibrahim (AS) fulfilled successfully the Command of Allah, Ibrahim (As) invoked three Blessings from Allah, they are:

• To create a Muslim Ummah who would maintain peace and harmony among themselves and adhere to the dictates of the holy Qur'an;

To commission an apostle from among the Ummah of their own who shall rehearse the signs and verses of the Holy Qur'an and teach them wisdom and sanctify them and to cleanse them from the evils; Thou art exalted in might and wisdom.

• To create another Imam from his progeny who would lead the Ummah on the right path by interpreting the intricacies of the Divine Knowledge revealed on the holy Prophet as recorded correctly in the Holy Qur'an.

Imamana(As) asserted that Allah had pointed out that the third request of Ibrahim (AS) "for creating an Imam, was for you and for none".

Imamana (AS) asserted further that the Holy Prophet(Slm) had claimed himself to be the Result of his Father's plea, I too claim that I am also the result of my Forefather Ibrahim's (As) plea to create an Imam from his progeny.

Now we have to study what were the Commands of Allah which Hzt. Ibrahim (AS) had successfully fulfilled and whether they have bearing on us too:

• After bathing clean your hair of the head and make a line in between the hair;
• Cleanse the nostrils by inhaling water in the nose;
• Gargle properly with water in order to clean the mouth and teeth;
• Prune your mustache;
• Clean the teeth with Miswak;
• Trim hair of the armpit;
• Trim the nails;
• Trim hair of your private parts;
• Circumscribe your kids;
• Clean all waste to keep the house clean.

According to traditions they are thirty commands: Ten in Soora-e-Momin, Ten in Soora-e-Ahzab and ten in Soora-e-Mu'arif. These all are the dictates of Allah which are binding on all human beings.

Thus Imamana(As) asserted emphatically that this verse pertains to me alone asper the Command of Allah that he is the Imam as per the Plea of Hzt. Ibrahim (As) and if any one has any doubt he must investigate my character, then only he must accept me as the Imam Mahdi(As)

2. "FA INNA HAJJOOKA . . . . (3:20)"

> "So if they dispute with thee, Tell: I have surrendered completely to Allah and the one who follows me."1mamana (As) had asserted that this verse Also pertains to him in which the holy Prophet had categorically informed the infidels that on some matters if you dispute, I surrender to Allah to decide and so also my follower shall surrender. That follower, according to Imamana(As) was he who was the Taba-e-Taam, toeing the footprints of the holy Prophet(Slm) step by step.

Imamana (As) further told that the word "Mun" in the verse points to him alone as per the Command of Allah. Thus this verse also pertains to Imamana(As)

3. INNA FIL KHALQIS SAMAWAT-E-WAL ARZ . . . . (5:57)

> "Behold! In the creation of the heaven and the earth, and in the alternation of night and day there are indeed signs for men of understanding."

Imamana(As) asserted that Allah informs me that the people mentioned in the verse as "Olaika" are his followers. They are the one who are firm in their faith and they remember continuously Allah whether standing, or sitting or even lying on their sides. They are perfect in their faith and will never turn back, since they contemplate and ponder on the signs of Allah and firmly confirm that these signs are not created for vain or as a play.

Thus Imamana(As) informed that this verse is for his followers, Qoum.

4. "MUN YURTID MINKUM . . . . (3:190,191)

> ""You who believe! If any one among you turns back from his faith, soon will Allah bring people whom He loves them and they too love Allah intensely."

Imamana(As) asserted that Allah had informed him that the people who love with intensity with Allah, mentioned in the verse, are your followers.

In this verse Allah reprimands those who were present during the period of the holy Prophet that if someone among them turns back from the faith after accepting it, it is certain that Allah would bring a people to whom Allah loves them and they too would love Allah intensely.

The Word "SOUFA" in the verse points out for a period which would come in remote future. And that period would be of Imam Mahdi (As); since the holy Prophet(Slm) had prophesied "KAIFA TAHLAKA MY UMMAH, IN WHOSE INCEPTION I AM, IN THE LAST JESUS CHRISAT(As) WOULD BE THERE AND IN BETWEEN US MAHDI(As) WOULD BE THERE."

According to a tradition the holy Prophet desired to see those people who would love Allah intensely, about whom the prophet(Slm) pointed out that they are such exalted people, neither they would be from the prophets nor martyrs, still the prophets and martyrs would envy of their ranks granted by Allah. About those people, author of "Addurul Manshoor commented that:

"Reported by Ibn Huraira(Rz) that when the "Soor-e-Jumaa" was revealed, we were sitting along with the Holy Prophet(slm). When the holy Prophet(Slm) recited it and when he reached at "Akhereena Minhum", on that a companion asked to the Prophet(Slm)as to who were those people? Holy Prophet then put his hand on the head of Salman Farsi(Rz) and asserted" I swear to Allah in Whose Hand is my life, if Faith is even at Suriyya, like exalted place, some of these people would reach it".

From the above it becomes clear that by putting his hand on the head of Hzt. Salman Farsi(RZ) an Ajmi, coming from from Persia, the Holy Prophet(Slm) pointed out clearly that those people are from Ajam(Non Arab country) and in which India also is included. Thus those people about whom Allah had ordained to bring are Ajmis, certainly they are Indians about wehom Imamana(AS) pointed out.

Imamana's assertion has also been sanctified by Imam Fakhr-e-Razi who had commented that:

"Narrated Ibn Abbas that Allah is all powerful who had assembled the Non Arabs with the Qureysh, since when non Arabs accepted Faith, then they too became prominent, because they have joined to them who had witnessed the Holy Prophet(Slm).

Thus this verse pertains correctly to the followers of Imamana(As) that is his Qoum.

5. "WA OOHI ILA HAZAL QUR'AN . . . . (PART 6:19)

> "This Qur'an had been revealed to me by inspiration, that I may warn you, and he will also warn you who will reach to my place."

Allah had informed Imamana(As) that the word "Mun" points out to you alone. Further the words "ILA MIN BALAGH" clarify that the Qur'an which was revealed to the Holy Prophet (Slm) also had been revealed to Imamana(As) by inspiration directly without any medium. Thus the interpretation of the Qur'an is the domain of Imamana(As) who will also warn the people as the holy Prophet(Slm) had warned to the Qureysh. Thus the Mission of the Prophet(Slm) was also the Mission of Imamana(As), by asserting "Summa Inna Alaina Biyana". Thus Allah intended to reveal the interpretation of the Qur'an by inspiration to Imamana(AS) who is to complete the Deen as had been prophesied by the Prophet(Slm), because Mahdi is the authority to warn the people to act without reservation as per the dictates of the holy Qur'an and to strictly follow on "AMR BIL MA'ROOF-E-WA TANHUNA UNIL MUNKER" MEANING:" ENJOIN WHAT IS RIGHT AND ABHOR WHAT IS WRONG."

Thus this verse also pertains to Imama

6. FA IN YAKFIR BEHA . . . . (PAFRT 6:89)

> "If these(infidels) reject (what is mentioned in the Qur'an): Behold! We shall entrust the charge to a new people who would never reject like them, (but rather they would cling to the Qur'anic dictates as their guide)."

According to Imamana(As) Allah had informed him that the "New People" mentioned in this verse are your followers only, and none else, who will never deny the dictates what had clearly been mentioned in the Qur'an. Their mission would be to propagate Islam to its entirety and thus they shall inculcate the true intent of the Qur'an and teach them all three elements of Deen-e-Haqqa: Being: Islam, Ieman and Ihsan. Most particularly they shall insist on Ihsan, since it directs to understand the secrets of the Divine Knowledge, which is nothing but the "Vision of Allah", and thus to annihilate oneself unto the Entity of Allah and become FANI FILLAH.

Thus it is the great Blessings of Allah to whom he likes bestows and never to those who are transgressors. His Blessings upon them are un-measurable by appointing Imamana(As) as the Promised Mahdi who is the Khaliftullah, Khatim-e-Vilayet-e-Mustafavi(Slm) and also as had been prophesied by the holy Prophet that, Mahdi(As) is from the Ahl-e-Bait(Rz) and the Saviour and the annihilator of innovations and Bid'aths from the Ummah. Thus the followers mentioned in the verse are well taught by Imamana(As) on the strict principles of Deen-e-Islam of the period of the Holy Prophet. Thus this verse is meant for Imamana's followers only upon whom Allah had decided to entrust the charge.

7. "YA IUUOHUN NABI HASBIKA . . . . (8:64)

> "Oh. Apostle: Sufficient unto thee is Allah and also to him who follows thee among the believers."

Through this Verse Allah had consoled the Holy Prophet who had suffered much trouble and misery on the hands of the infidels by emphasizing that Allah is with you and also with him who followed you in word and spirit, that is Mahdi(As).

It is a fact that during the period, when the Holy Prophet started propagation about monotheism as mentioned in the Revelations, the Qureysh became hostile to him and started troubling and created troubles for him for which he suffered much. That situation became very troublesome for the Prophet. Hence Allah tried to console him not to be afraid and become perturbed since Allah was with him who would help him in his thick and thin.

With regard to Imamana(As), situation was different. Here the worldly scholars were hostile to Imamana(As) since Imamana's Mission was against their worldly life. Imamana(As) was teaching austerity and asceticism and denouncing the innovations, rituals and bidats being practiced by the worldly scholars who were busy in amassing the wealth by fraudulent and unethical ways. Thus the teachings of Imamana(As) were deadly against them and their illegal practices, hence they had become hostile to Imamana(As) by instigating the authorities for issuing Imamana's expulsion orders so that in the absence of Imamana(As) these so called scholars could amass the wealth unhindered.

Therefore as Allah had consoled the holy Prophet(Slm) not to be disheartened from the miseries being inflicted against the person of the holy Prophet(Slm)by stating that Allah is Sufficient for him, as well as, for the Holy Prophet's perfect Follower, Imam Mahdi(As), since Mahdi(As) also was suffering from the hostile attitude of the worldly scholars.

Imamana(AS) informed that Allah had pointed out towards the Word "MUN" used in this verse. Thus Allah mentioned that it is used for you and for none else. Hence this verse is meant for Imamana(As), alone and for none else.

8. "SUMMA FAZALTO . . . . (11:1)

"Further explained in detail by the one who is wise and well acquainted with all things."

Through this verse Allah asserts that whatever knowledge had been revealed to the holy Prophet(Slm)in the Qur'an, the same shall be inspired to the one who is wise and who is perfect in understanding them all, and that person is Mahdi who would propagate them according to the commands of Allah who directly taught Imamana(As) and instructed him about those secrets for whose clarification Allah, had taken the responsibility by asserting "SUMMA INNA ALAINA BIYANA", through the mouth of that wise man who is called the Promised Mahdi who would interpret the Divine Secrets of "Ihsaan" so as to envision the Divine Entity of the Creator of this gigantic Universe.

In this verse the word "MUN" points out to Imamana(As) as determined by Allah, hence this verse also pertains to Imamana(As).

9. "AFA MUN KANA ALAA BIYYANA" . . . . (11:17)

"Can they be like those who accept a clear sign from their Lord and to whom
a witness was also there, which they accepted without reservations; and those
who denied all above."

Imamana(As) asserted that Allah had informed him that the Word "Mun" in the verse pertains
to me alone. Imamana(AS) further pointed out that he is also the result of Hzt. Ibrahim (As)
who pleaded before Allah to create an Imam also from his progeny. And also that the holy
Prophet had prophesied about him that Mahdi comes from the Ahl-e-Bait(Rz) and Mahdi
shall follow toeing my footsteps and never will err, as well as Mahdi is the Khalifatullh, who
will complete the Deen as the holy Prophet(Slm) had established it during his life time. Holy
Prophet further asserted through a tradition: "Kaifa Tahlaka". Thus through this tradition Mahdi
is the Saviour of the Ummah, like the holy Propht(slm) and Jesus Christ(As). On account of all
these attributes, can anyone who does not possess such attributes compare to Imamana(As)?

Apart from the prophecies of the holy Prophet(Slm), Jesus Christ (AS) had also prophesied
that: We the prophets of Allah had brought Revelations from Allah, and "Farqaleet"
would come to interpret these Revelations." This reference is made in the Bible and Torah
also. These Scriptures clearly prophecy that Allah shall commission Farqaleet(Mahdi)
for interpretation of Qur'an. Thus Qur'an becomes a witness for Imam Mahdi, and other
Scriptures also witnessed. Apart from the scriptures, the holy Prophet(Slm) had foretold
in his many continuous (Mutawatir) traditions that Mahdi(As) shall carry my characters,
"Khulqahu Khulqi", whose appearance is must to complete the Deen, before establishment of
the Day of Judgment.

The words "Olaika Umenoon" point to the followers of the Imam who have firm faith on
Imamana(As) as the "Khatim-e-Vilayet-e-Mohammed Mustafa(Slm) who will complete the
Deen. Deen means: Islam, Ieman and Ihsan according to the Gabreil's Trdition. Thus this
verse is for both, Imamana(As) and for his followers (Groh-e-Mahdi(As).

10. QUL HAZA FI SABILI . . . . (12:108)

Allah addresses the holy Prophet(Slm): "Say: This is my way. on which I
Invite you towards Allah on the clear evidence as you witness with your own
eyes. And he also would invite accordingly who is my perfect follower. Glory
be to Allah. I, and aslo my follower, will never join any god with Allah."

Through this verse Allah declares that He had deputed the holy Prophet(Slm) to inform
the people of the Qureysh that I am on the right path, which leads me towards the Vision
of Allah. Therefore, for your own betterment, I invite you to follow that right path, so that
you also may get the Vision of Allah. And this sort of invitation would be given also by my
perfect follower, Imam Mahdi(As). What is the Right Path? Right Path is that which would
take you to the audience of the Almighty.

For that Allah had directed that if anyone is desirous for the Vision of Allah, he must do virtuous deeds and should not make anyone Allah's partner. Allah further informs that "WAMA KHALAQTAL JINNA WA INSA, ILLAH LIABUDOON"(I did not create Jinn and Ins, except for my worship"). And how the worship, to be performed: the holy Prophet(Slm) had advised: if you want to worship: "IN TA'ABADULLHI KA'ANAKA TARA" (Worship Allah keeping in mind that you are witnessing Allah, if not, at least think that Allah is seeing you) it mean to say that while worshipping, concentrate on the wordings of the verses of the holy Qur'an, which you are reciting during the prayers. If such is the intent of your worship, then it is possible that your worship is accepted by Allah, Subhnawat Ta'aallah. And your regular worship in that way shall bring you to the audience of Allah.

It may be kept in mind that with regard to Imamana(As), he, as a proof of his Mahdiat, had substantiated his claim, on the word of Allah, Kalamullah and the prophecies by the Holy Prophet and as mentioned in the Scriptures, and then presented the verse "Afa Mun Kana ala Biayyana Min Rabbihi" as a concrete Proof of his person as Imam Mahdi(As), and then presented many verses relating to his Mahdiat.

Another point for consideration is that the words "Manit Tab'eni" are abstract ones, denoting to a single person who should be the "Ta'bae'Ta'am" toeing the footsteps of the Holy Prophdet(Slm) and he should be from the Ahl-e-Bait, and should possess Holy Prophet's characters and should not ERR. These all qualities, as per authentic historical record and biography are found in that single person who is named Khalifatullah by the holy Prophet(Slm). Thus this verse pertains to him alone and none elso.

11. "SUMMA AOURASNAL KITAB . . . . (35:32)

> "Then We have given the Book for inheritance to such of our servants to whom We have chosen. But there are among them who wrong themselves."

According to Imamana(As), Allah had informed him that the words" for inheritance to such of our servants to whom We have chosen" are the persons who accepted you as the Promised Mahdi(As).(As). Thus the peculiarity of these persons had been mentioned in another verse that they are busy in remembrance of Allah, sitting, standing, and lying on their sides, and ponder and contemplate on our Signs regularly and exclaim in praise of Allah that these Signs are not created for sport purpose but to guide humanity and to get the beneficence out of them.

We would like to present another verse which generate the reasons for inheritance, which is as under:

"INNAL LAZEENA YATLOON KITABA . . . . (22:

"Those who recite Qur'an and establish Prayers and spend from that amount which We had provided them, either openly or secretly, and they pretend that they had established such a business which would never vanish and which would bring to them higher profits with the

Grace of Allah. Thus according to the above verse, these persons are the true inheritors of the Kalamullah, as mentioned in the first verse, which clearly relate to the followers of Imamana(As), that is "Groh-e-Mahdi(As) alone.

Hzt. Abdul Ghafoor Sujawndi(Rh) had further elaborated about these persons who are of three categories:

- "Zalimun Nafs" who have relinquished the worldly fanfare and "Mata-e-Hayat-e-Duniya" and enhanced their position from worldly life to the spiritual life. Still they come across worldly fanfare which drag them towards the charms of their passion, but with their will power they subdue their evils and kill their passions which are influenced by satanic temptations.

- Those who are inclined to do justice for everyone and with Grace of Almighty, they have overpowered their temptations and human passions and thus they had embarked towards a higher stage which is called "Lahoot", the place of Divine Entity, and after accomplishing that stage the Seeker immerses himself unto that Divine Entity and becomes "Fani Fillah" the most exalted position, which is not easily acquired by everyone unless Allah Himself Grants that position.

- These are those who are immersed always unto the Divine Entity and busy in glorification of the Creator of this gigantic Universe by offering worship day in and day out, sitting, standing or even lying on their sides. They are those who always are found lamenting and groaning and making their eyes red and their legs swollen on account of continuous worship whole nights and annihilate their baser self in order to obtain self-satisfaction by the Grace of Allah.

These are the persons to whom Allah had made them the inheritors of the Book and infused unto them the capability to interpret the holy Qur'an. Thus this verse pertains to Imamana(As) and his qoum.

12. "WA IN TATAWALLO . . . . (47:38)

"And it is they that are needy. If you turn back(from the path), Allah will substitute in your stead such people who would not be like you."

Imamana(As) had stated about the information given by Allah that the reference regarding some such persons had been given in this verse, are your followers only whose attribute is that they would not be like the people who would turn back from the right path.

It is a fact that Allah had ordained to His Apostle(Slm) to advise the faithful to obey the Holy Prophet(Slm) so as they get higher reward. Allah never demands much of your wealth, but a very little portion, even lesser than one fourth of your Ushr (if you spend for the betterment of the Ummah) and for that meager amount also if you show miserliness in not spending, then Allah is not dependent on you. Thus on the basis of your miserliness, Allah is all powerful to bring such people who would not be like those about whom the verse points out, surely they are the followers of Imam Mahdi(As), who are better than the above in religious matters and they would place their belongings under the control of Allah. These are the facts of those people about whom reference hsas been made in many traditions and also in the commentaries(Tafaseer). They would never become afraid or feel sad. Thus this verse also pertains to the Groh-e-Imamana(As).

13. "KHALAQAL INSANA WA ALLAMAHUL BIYAN . . . . (55:3,4)

> "He had created Man, taught him the faculty of speech (and intelligence to interpret Qur'an)"

Allah informed Imamana(As) that the reference of the "Man" in the verse is for you and none else. It is a fact that Allah had Revealed Qur'an on to the holy Prophet(Slm) to recite it intermittently, word by word, and had taken the responsibility not only to safeguard it permanently, but also to interpret it later on through someone whenever He felt necessary. And for the purpose of interpretation, Allah commissioned Imam Mahdi(As) by infusing in him the capacity to interpret the intent and purpose of the Revelations directly without any medium. Thus this verse pertains to Imamana(As).

14. "SULLATA MINAL AWWALEEN WA QALEELA MINALAKHEREEN". "One group pertains to the former people and some belong to the Akhereen."(56:39)

15. "SULLATA MINAL AWWALEEN WA SULLATA MINAL AKHEREEN."(56:40) "One group pertains to the Akhereen". (Both verses carry almost same meanings)

Sullata Minal Awwaleen and Sullata Minal Akhereen, denote to two groups which belong to the Ummah. It is clear from Sullatain that Awwaleen means previous people, and Khaleelum minal Akhereen means some men who would appear in the last period.

It is certain that Awwaleen means "Ummieen" among whom the holy Prophet(Slm) was born and was commissioned by Allah as the Last of the Apostles. And Minal Akhereen means those who are Non Arabs and who would come at the last period whose prominence would be like that of the Ummieen, since both belong to the same Ummah of the holy Prophet(Slm), with a difference that the Awwaleen had the privilege to enjoy the company of the holy Prophet and those who came at the end, missed the venerable company of the holy Prophet(Slm), nor they heard the recitation by him and not even had the opportunity to hear his instructions from the holy Qur'an regarding wisdom. However the teachings and instructions given by the holy Prophet(Slm)reached to the Akhereen also through the learned people of the Ummah. Thus it can be ascertained that the prophecy had completed. Because learning reached step by steps until the end of the period. Then surely it may rightly be claimed that the Holy Prophet himself had been the administrator for imparting the learning which reached from the inception to the last ones.

Apart from this there are two groups of peoples. One started from Hzt. Adam(Ass) to the Holy Prophet(slm). The other started from the Holy Prophet(Slm) to the Day of Judgment.

First group includes Prophet Ibrahim(As) whose one of the pleas was to create a truthful man from the Akhereen. It means to say that who would emerge after the holy Prophet(Slm) about whom information was given in both Kalamullah and Torah that "Farquleet" would come to interpret them on direct commands by Allah, and who would come from the progeny of the holy Prophet(Slm).

Some scholars still presume that the holy Prophet(Slm) may again emerge as the commissioned one at the last stage, which is wrong. Since the holy Prophet(Slm) himself had informed that the one to be commissioned one from the Akhereen is the Khaliftullah, coming from the Ahl-e-Bait(Rz) carrying Holy Prophet's characters and shall follow his footprints and will never Err. Thus that is the personality of Imam Mahdi(As) who would complete the Deen, as was started by the holy Prophet(Slm). And also that Imam Mahdi(As) is the Savior of Ummah and Khatim-e-Vilayet-e-Mustafavi(Slm).

Thus both verses belong to Immana(As) and his Followers;

16. "WA AKHEREENA MINHUM LAMA YALHAQU BIHIM . . . . (62:3)

> "As well as (to confer all these benefits upon) others of them, who had not already joined them, and He is Exalted in Might and Wise."

"Allah ordained that: "It is He who had sent amongst the unlettered ones an apostle from among themselves to rehearse to them His signs and to sanctify them and to instruct them the Scriptures and teach wisdom; although they were surely in manifest error before that. And he would commission also from the Akhereen from among the Ummah and who had no chance to meet the Ummiyeen that is the Awwaleen, and such is the bounty of Allah. From this it is clear there occured long period in between Awwaleen (Ummiyeen) and the Akhereen who would never meet each other any time in the remote future. When it is proved that Ummiyeen would not meet with the last ones, then how could it be possible that the holy Prophet(Slm) would meet the Last ones?

It is the practice—Sunnat—of Allah Jalle Shanahu, that whenever an apostle is commissioned in a nation even with a small number of people who witness that apostle and that apostle, according to Kalamullah, rehearses the meanings of the Scriptures, sanctifies their passions, instructs his followers about the Book and teaches wisdom to them. Thus all was done correctly by the holy Prophet(Slm) as pleaded by prophet Ibrahim(As) about him. But it was not possible for the holy Prophet(Slm) to act liked that to the people who wuld come in the last. But it was Allah alone who arranged that action as mentioned by Ibn Abbas(Rz):

"Narrated Ibn Abbas(Rz) that Allah is all powerful who had assembled the Non-Arabs with the Qureysh, thus the non Arabs accepted the Faith and became prominence, because they joined to them who had witnessed the holy Prophet(Slm)".

From the above narratiopn it is proved that the last ones are the Non Arabs, including Indians. These are the same Ajmis whose period was out of reach of the holy Prophet(Slm)— Lum Yalhaqu—will never meet therefore these Ajmis would never get the company of the holy Prophet(Slm).

17. "SUMMA INNA ALAINA BIYANA" . . . . (75:19)

   "Nay, More. It is for Us to explain it, and make it clear."

The meanings of this verse had already been discussed along with the explanation of the verse 13, however since it is an important verse we have to go through it minutely.

According to Bandagi Abdul Ghafoor Sujawandi(Rh), Allah ordains Imamana(As)that We have given the responsibility to you to interpret the secrets of the Holy Qur'an and for that We inspire you regularly. It means that Allah shall teach Imamana(As) how to explain and what to explain.

As regards Revelations, Gabreil(As) had brought the verses of the Qur'an during twenty three year long period, piece by piece and advised the Holy Prophet to first listen them carefully and recite them intermittently, slowly, since the responsibility to safeguard the Holy Qur'an, Allah had taken for Himself. Accordingly, the holy Prophet, although he was an unlettered man, used to recite them whenever those Revelations came to him. Now see the beauty of the Prophet's memory that sooner the Revelation started pouring onto the conscious mind of the Prophet (Slm), he started reciting them spontaneously in a well toned form, in a well attributed masterly worded sermons, that even the well versed scholars of that period around him astonished to hear from the mouth of that Mohammed(Slm) who was publicly known as an unlettered man. The force of the properly worded sermons was so impressive and challenging that no renowned poet of that period dared to compose a single verse like that, since Qur'an was the word of the Almighty, therefore no body could create like that. In order to sanctify it to be the Word of Allah, the Holy Prophet reminded the audience: "I had been with you for the last forty long years, did you hear such beautifully worded sermons before? "I am now reciting as being directed by my Sustainer."

Now the situation for ImamanaAs) was unique, since he was chosen by Allah for the interpretation of the Qur, an was the responsibility to explain and interpret the intent of the holy Qur'an was taken by Allah Himself by telling "Summa Inna Alaina Biyana". For that purpose imamana(As) was being nourished from the very childhood under the stewardship of a learned mystic Hzt. Shaik Daniyal, under whom he became well versed with all the worldly and religious branches of education and was acclaimed as "Syedul Ulema", was it not a miracle that a boy of just 12 years was decorated with a title "Syedul Ulema" by the scholars of Juanpur? Further, he was acclaimed as "Syedul Aouliya" at his age 21 years. It was Almighty alone who made him to attain the capability and proficiency in order to unfold the secrets of the ambiguities of the holy Qur'an and interpret its intent and objects in a sweet, elegant and well toned style which attracted not only the commoners, but also the scholars. The force of his selfless interpretations was so impressive and touchy, whoever heard became spell bound and mesmerized and tears popped out from the eyes of some listeners spontaneously. Is it not a miracle that at that period there were no loudspeakers and the audience was so immense that at the time of the sermons, people used to gather in thousands, if there was no place in the premises, they used to climb on the walls, on the trees and in the balconies of their houses and hear and understand equally by all whether they are near or far off. And another beauty of his sermons was that he travelled thousands of miles from the East to the West, and wherever he went he gave his sermons in the colloquial language of that place which was easily understood by one and all. Thus Imamana(As) became the embodiment of "Summa Inna Alaina Biyana" who gave a new meaning to the Shariat-e-Mustafavi(Slm) of the early period of Islam. The attributes of his sermons were unmatchable, fluent and elegant that could not be recorded easily, since at that remote period of time there were no appropriate implements to record them as we possess now a days.

Thus as prophesied by Jesus Christ(As) that all prophets had brought Revelations and for their interpretation "Frqaleet" would come to interpret. And that Farqaleet is Imamana(As) alone. Thus this verse pertains to Imamana(As) and none else.

18. "WA MAA NAFIR RAQIL LAZEENA." . . . . (98:4)

> "Or did the people of the Book make Schism, until after, there came to them
> clear evidence."

The last eighteenth Verse is about those who had even after receiving clear evidence and advice through revelations they had transgressed and became enemy of the Promised Mahdi(As). Imamana(As) informed that, according to the dictates of Allah, those who were given the Books are the Scholars of the period of Imamana)As) and the "Biyyana" denotes to Imamanal(As) alone. Those worldly scholars transgressed against the verdict of Qur'an and tried to change the meanings according to their wishes, as the Jews and Christians did during the period of the holy Prophet(Slm). Thus such mentality of the worldly scholars still prevailed during the period of Imamana(As). Thus they became enemy since the teachings of Imamana(As) were against their wishes. Imamana's teachings were becoming hurdle against those scholars, since Imamana(As) was propagating the tenets of Islam as taught by the holy Prophet(Slm) asking the people to adhere to the dictates of Qur'an which call upon Muslims towards: "Amr Bil Maroofe Wa Tanhuna unil Munkir" (Enjoin Virtue and abhor evil), and towards 'Vision of Allah'.

Imamana's Teachings were based on Ihsan. He openly taught the meanings of Ihsan, leading towards the Vision of Allah, the most cherished goal should be of every God-Fearing Muslim for which Allah had already declared that He had created Jinn and Ins for his worship only which accomplishes Vision of Allah, if worship is performed as advised by the Holy Peophet(Slm) "Ka'anka Tarah" as if you see Allah.

Faqeer SYED sharief khundmiri

* * *

—

6. Majalis-e-Khamsa

Majalis-e-Khamsa is the account of five debates between scholars of Mughal Emperor Akbar's court and **Hazrat Shaikh Mustafa Gujarati***. These debates took place in the presence of Akbar himself. The debates have been translated into English by Faqir Syed Ziaullah Yedullahi Sahab. Given below is an extract from the book which is the introduction of Hazrat Shaikh Mustafa Gujarati.*

In the name of Allah, Most Gracious, Most Merciful.

HAZRAT SHAIKH MUSTAFA GUJARATI

Mian Shaikh Mustafa Gujarati, the author of this book, was born in Naharwala (now the city of Patan) in Gujarat in 932 AH (1527 AD). He was the scion of a Bohra family and the son of Mian Shaikh Abdur Rashid, an eminent scholar and the author of Naqliat Mian Abdur Rashid, an authentic record on the traditions of Imam Syed Muhammad Mahdi al-Mau'ood of Jaunpur (Uttar Pradesh in India). He received his early education at the feet of his illustrious father. When he reached the age of discretion, he took the vows of discipleship at the hands of Bandagi Mian Pir Muhammad, a murshid (guide) of great spiritual achievements. Then he took the oath of fealty in the service of Hazrat Shihabul Haq and Bandagi Mian Syed Mahmood Syedanji Khatim-ul-Murshideen. Hazrat Syedanji saw signs of great spiritual accomplishments in Shaikh Mustafa and permitted him to set up his own Daira and start preaching. Hazrat Shaikh set up his Dairas at many places. Innumerable people received the blessings of Allah as his disciples.

Hazrat Shaikh was called to the court of Mughal Emperor Akbar and was incarcerated for two years. During this period, a debate on the Mahdavi faith and beliefs went on for eighteen months. He made a record of the debates as the process went on. Due to the passage of time, these records have perished. Of them, the record of only five sittings have been retrieved. The original is in Persian. It had been translated into Urdu by Hazrat Syed Dilawar alias Goray Mian of Begum Bazar, Hyderabad Deccan. This Urdu translation is being repeatedly published for over half a century.

Malik Sulaiman author of Tarikh-e-Sulaimani writes: Pleased by the speeches and arguments of Mian Shaikh Mustafa Gujarati in the court during the debates on Mahdavi beliefs, Emperor Akbar wanted to grant some jagirs to him. But the Shaikh used to reply that the celebrated personalities of the Mahdavi sect refused to accept worldly wealth from kings. He said that they considered such grants, fixed periodical and other sources of income as haram (prohibited). When the Ulema of the court saw that they were unable to defeat the Shaikh in debate, they conspired to find an excuse which would cause his continued imprisonment.

They insisted on the Emperor not to release him unless he accepted a jgir, which he had termed as haram (prohibited). The Ulema did their worst to torment the Shaikh. Finding no other way, they again conspired to ask the Shaikh what he thought of the Emperor who had not accepted Syed Muhammad of Jaunpur as Imam Mahdi al-Mau'ood. When they repeatedly insisted on an answer Shaikh Mustafa finally said: "I call a person, who accepts Syed Muhammad as Mahdi al-Mau'ood as a momin (faithful). I call a person, who refutes Mahdi, as a kafir (infidel). I call Akbar akfar (worse infidel), if he refutes Mahdi." On hearing this, the Ulema were angry, but could not say or do anything without the permission of the Emperor.

Continuing the narrative, Tarikh-e-Sulaimani says that the Emperor called the Shaikh for a private audience late one night and asked for an explanation for the disrespect. The Shaikh replied that Prophet Muhammad and Imam Mahdi, standing on his right and left, asked him to reply boldly that one who refuted Mahdi was akfar. "I got the courage to tell the truth after this," he added. The emperor believed him and permitted him to go where he pleased. "But, please, accept the jagir," he pleaded. Finally, the jagir was granted in the name of the Shaikh's son, Shaikh Abdullah.

After his release from captivity, the Shaikh came to Bayana (in Rajasthan) and set up his Daira there. He died the same year, 984 AH (1578 AD) at the age of 52.

A collection of his letters to his contemporaries had been compiled by him and was recently published with its Urdu translation. The letters reveal his profound devotion to Allah and ways and means to do penance to reach spiritual heights and finally realise the Ultimate Truth. (From Muntakhab-ut-Tawarikh and prefaces to the translation of two books, Majalis-e-Khamsa by Hazrat Syed Dilawar, and, Makateeb by Hazrat Syed Khuda Bakhsh Rushdi, respectively.)

SESSION I

I was taken in shackles to the court where the Mughal Emperor Akbar, Emirs and some Ulema (religious scholars) were already seated.

I said: Assalaam Alaikum They suitably replied. They sat in a circle and made me sit in the middle. First, the **Emperor asked my name**. **I said**: Mustafa. The Emir of Surat Fort (in

Gujarat), who was present in the court said he had never seen so unclean a Mustafa in the world.

The Emperor was irratated at this and said: Shame on you. He is an elderly person and one should talk to him respectfully.

Turning to me, the Emperor said: We know you are a respected elderly person and a guide. Veiled women, emirs and the king of Gujarat wait at your door-step. Your benediction and paskhurda (what remains after eating and drinking) is respectfully taken to Agra, Gaur (in Bengal) and Surat (in Gujarat). Reference to you is very often made in our court. At the instance of the Ulema and as the need arised, you have been brought here in shackles. What do you think of us?

In reply, **I said**: Somebody asked a murshid (spiritual guide) to define faqiri (the life-style of a faqir). The murshid said it was like sifted and moistened dust; it did neither soil the back of the foot, nor caue pain to the sole. I belong to the religion of of ahl-e-batin (saintly heart) and my heart is untainted and pure. I am happy about everyone.

The Emperor then said: The Ulema and mashayakh (religious guides) are very hostile to you. They have petitioned to us many times that great trouble had occurred in Gujarat. The son of a Shaikh had adopted the religion of innovators (bid'atis) and invites all people to his cult. Poladis, Afghans and many others, including some Ulema, had also joined it. Hence, it is the duty of the Emperor to suppress this trouble. It is because of the efforts of the Ulema that you have fallen into this predicament. How far is your heart afflicted by this?

In reply, I recited a Persian couplet which means that I am not afflicted by what others do, because, whatever is done to me, is done by my Friend (Allah).

After this the discussion veered round to Mahdait. The Emperor asked: What do you say? Mahdi al-Mau'ood is yet to come? Or that he has come and gone?

I said: Mahdi al-Mau'ood has come and gone.

Pandemonium broke out among the courtiers. They started abusing and making acrimonious remarks. Some of them menacingly came towards me.

They said: Killing this man will bring great rewards (from Allah).

Kalan Khan, one of the courtiers, said: I will kill him with my own hands. If the Emperor becomes angry, he will be angry at us. We will respond. We will tell him that this man deserved to be killed, according to Shariat. And, therefore, we killed him.

The Emperor said: Silence. We ask him for his arguments. Let us see what he has to say. We should enquire into his beliefs. After the enquiry, we will take suitable action.

Silence prevailed at this point.

Turning to me, the Emperor said: Describe in detail how you accepted and reposed faith (iman) in Imam Mahdi and how did you know that Syed Muhammed, who migrated from Jaunpur, claimed to be Mahdi al-Mau'ood in Gujarat and was laid to rest in Farah (in Afghanistan) was in fact Mahdi al-Mau'ood? How did you find out that the place of birth of Mahdi al-Mau'ood was Jaunpur, the place of the announcement of his claim to be Mahdi al-Mau'ood was in Gujarat and his place of burial was Farah? There is a Hadith (Prophet Muhammad about the places of birth, claim and death of Mahdi. Ulema from Arab and Ajam (non-Arab lands) and the imams of Makkah and Madina are all convinced of the mischief and falsehood of the claim. You are learned, wise, and a spiritual guide. In spite of all this, how did you accept the claim and now invite the people of these beliefs. You should tell us all about your acceptance, the whole of your story.

I said: My ancestors belonged to the Sufi order and were mashayakheen (religious patriarchs) of tariqat (religious observances). It is generally accepted that in the religion of mystics, the refusal to accept the word of a vali (saint) is prohibited; it is worse than a killer poison. Many from among the *ahl-e-zahir* (worldly people) did not accept the word of the saints and lost their iman (faith) and divine knowledge. They went astray in the wilderness of spiritual destructions. All this is clearly written in the books of Khwaja Junaid Baghdadi, Imam Muhammad al-Ghazali and Shaikh Shihabuddin Suhrawardi. Be that as it may, we knew for sure by tawatur (continuity of the narrations) that Hazrat Syed Muhammad had claimed in congregations of Ulema and mashayakheen that he was Mahdi, he stood by his claim to his last breath and the signs of his sainthood (vilayat) manifested themselves all overthe world. The manifestations of his grace became well known every where. So much so, that illiterates became fully acquainted with the nuances of Shariat (Islamic Code of Law) and recognition of Allah through his (Imam Mahdi's) companionship to a degree that their knowledge and competence are beyond description. Their commendable attributes and illustrious actions. Like tawakkul (trust in Allah), truth, obeisance, gentleness, politeness and other virtues reached excellence. This again is beyond description. Each one among his followers became a spiritual guide in his own right. Thousands of followers flocked around such spiritual guides. They renounced worldliness and became the seekers of Allah within the limits of tariqat and Shariat and realised the Ultimate Reality. On the basis of the religion of Sufis, we accepted the Imam as Mahdi al-Mau'ood and knelt at his door-step. We abstained from wordy duels and discussions which is the usual practice among the Ulema-e-zahir (experts in worldly knowledge). Mashyakheen of tariqat have written in their books: "O the traveler of the path of the (Ultimate) Truth: Be careful ; keep yourself away from rejecting the aulia Allah (saints) so that you do not destroy the fruit of your Faith (Iman). And, look at the word of Allah that Prophet Moses who was endowed with the glory of Prophethood told Prophet Khizr, in view of the compulsions of the Laws of Torah, that 'Truly, a strange thing hast thou done' (18:71), and then how in utter humility and modesty Prophet Moses said: 'Rebuke me not for forgetting, nor grieve me by raising difficulties in my case.' (18:73). But the light of the Prophethood of Moses is required so that we could identify the nur (light) of the sainthood, that is Imam Mahdi al-Mau'ood. What do the ignorant and worldly pirs know?

In short, the beliefs of Mashayakheen of Tariqat are manifest. But let not the Ulema of your court think that the proof of the Mahdiat of Syed Muhammad of Jaunpur is confirmed to what I have just said. No. We know that what we have just said is not the final argument for the Ulema of Shariat. But, since you had asked me to describe from the beginning to the end, my story in detail, I said all that I have just said. We now come to the scientific argument that when Imam Mahdi al-Mau'ood was accepted on the basis of what has been described above, that is, the beliefs of the Mashaykheen of Tarqat, the Ulema-e-zahir disputed our acceptance of the Imam and started a debate on the subject. They asserted that our beliefs were wrong and that we were faithless. They went to the extent of issuing fatwas (religious edicts) ordering us to be externed or killed. They got some Mahadavis killed just for saying that Mahdi had come and gone. We were astonished. We were intrigued whether our beliefs were wrong under the Quran and Hadith-e-mutawatir (continuity in narration of Hadiths) and the consensus of the Ummah (followers of Islam), and if so, it was our duty to repent and return to the truth. But if our beliefs are correct according to the Quran, the Hadith and consensus of the Ummah, we need not bother about the opposition, reproach and torture by the opponents of Imam Mahdi. For Allah says: "Whoso works righteousness benefits his own soul; whoever works evil, it is against his own soul:" (41:46). Hence, it is not necessary for us to repudiate Hazrat Syed Muhammad Mahdi al-Mau'ood on the basis of what the *Ulema-e-Zahir* say. (To take two instances:)

The sayings of the *Jamaat Asaba* (the group of paternal relations) about their younger brother (Joseph): "They said: 'Truly Joseph and his brother are loved more by our father than we; but we are a goodly body! Really our father is obviously wandering (in his mind)! Slay ye Joseph . . . .'" (12:8). And the sayings of the group of angels about Adam: ". . . They said: 'Wilt thou place therein one who will make mischief therein and shed blood . . . .' (2:30). We do not give credence to the words of the brothers of Joseph and the group of angels. The Ulema-e-zahir of our times do not command more dignity or excellence than them. How can we reject the claim of Imam Mahdi on the basis of the blind following of these Ulema? To find out the truth we studied the books of our predecessors. We found references to Imam Mahdi in the books of Hadith (traditions of Prophet Muhammad). We found that no Hadith-e-mutawatir (a number of traditions giving continuity to prove an event) had been reported in respect of Imam Mahdi as Mutawatir-ul-ma'ani (continuity in meaning). However, no mujtahid (religious director) or mufassir (commentator of Quran) has said anything definite about the signs of Imam Mahdi, because

the ahadith (traditions) are obviously ahaad (single traditions without corroboration); such traditions give only the benefit of assumption and assumptions cannot be relied upon in matters of beliefs. Besides, there are obvious contradictions. Some traditions say that Mahdi and Jesus will come at the same time, while others say that they will come at different times. Similarly, some traditions say that Dajjal (Anti-Christ) will come during the time of Imam Mahdi while others say that he would come after the appearance of the Imam. Again, there is contradiction in various traditions about the places of birth, claim and death, and dates of appearance of Imam Mahdi. Hence, the Ulema of the past hesitated and deliberated about the matter because of their immense intellectual honesty. They finally left it to Allah.

They agreed on the point that Imam Mahdi wHistory of Sindh is as rich as its culture, its traditions, its language, its moral value, its social diversity and its civilization. With such obvious attractions it was destined to offer temptation not only to immediate neighbors but to far flung invaders like the Portuguese and the English. **Excerpts from "Kalhora Dynasty's Governance" an overview by Janab Mohmmed** Such political and cultural pressures resulted in local intellectual as Aadil (just and righteous). He will be among the descendants of Fatima, daughter of Prophet Muhammad. He will appear when Allah wished to help His religion. In short, contradictory statements in the traditions give rise to doubts. Ulema in the Emperors court and of Naharwala town tried their best to disprove the possibility and create doubts about Imam Mahdi but they failed. They came to the conclusion that the appearance of Syed Muhammad as Imam Mahdi was possible and that those who reposed trust in him were not liable to be derided. They said that the Mahdavis should not invite others to their religion and beliefs on the basis of the possibility because the possibility alone was not a final argument. In short, a study of the books of traditions showed that it did not become necessary to find fault with and deride a follower of Imam Mahdi. It was not just, they said, to attribute kufr (infidelity), zalalat (deviation from the right path) and bid'at (innovation) to the followers of Imam Mahdi. To issue a fatwa (religious edict) to behead them was unjust tyranny. May Allah bless him who does justice.

The Court Ulema argued that it appeared from the speech of Shaikh Mustafa that, according to the Ulema of the past, it was proved that Mahdi called Mahdi al-Mau'ood was not proved to be Imam Mahdi. Hence, the Shaikh deserved to be blamed (as wrong) by his own confession.

I replied: It is necessary that Mahdi's imamat (leadership) was bound to be similar to the imamat of the Prophets and not that of the worldly kings because all Prophets were imams and their leadership was not dependent and contingent upon their having possessions of kingdoms and wealth. In respect of Prophets, Allah says: "And We appointed, from among them, leaders, giving guidance under Our command, so long as they persevered with patience . . . ." (32:24). A few hundred prophets suffered certain poverty and were martyred by their detractors. Where did they have a country in possession, a large army and immense riches? On the basis of this meaning, it is proved that Syed Muhammad was Mahdi and under the Quranic injunction, "giving guidance under Our command," invited the people to Allah. In short, it is proved from a study of the books of Hadith that Syed Muhammad was an imam (leader).

The Ulema quoted the Hadith in which Prophet Muhammad had said that Mahdi would fill the earth (al-arz) with justice and fair-play, as it was filled with oppression and tyranny. They asked me whether I considered it to be correct or contrived (mauzu). **I said**: We consider it to be correct.

The Emperor asked: How does it reconcile with your stand? **I replied**: Allah had said in respect of Shu'aib (identified with Juthro, According to Pickthal): "Do no mischief on the earth, after it had been set in order . . . ." (7:56). In this Verse, the word al-arz (the earth) means the land of Madyan because Shu'aib appeared on the land of Madyan as Allah says: "To the Madyan people we sent Shu'aib, one of their own brethren:" (7:85). The consensus of the commentators of Quran is that there were in all 400,000 mounted soldiers in Madyan but none other than the two daughters of Shu'aib accepted him as Prophet and obeyed him. In spite of this, Allah says "Do no mischief on the earth of Madyan, O followers of Shu'aib after it had been set in order." The point to be considered here, is that nobody in Madyan had reposed faith in Shu'aib and abstained from mischief:

yet, Allah says: "After it had been set right" What does it mean? Hence, it is obvious that here "setting right" means Shu'aib's call to the people to set right or invitation towards good. Whether somebody obeys him or not is immaterial. In accordance with the commandment of Allah. it can be said that Shu'aib invited the people of the land of Madyan to set it in order. Some of the commentators have said that Shu'aib did good deeds and invited others to do good deeds. In this sense of Shu'aib inviting the people of the earth (al-arz) to set it in order, Imam Mahdi also invited the people of the earth (al-arz) to justice. Many people reposed faith in Imam Mahdi, obeyed him and sacrificed their life and property for him and made themselves the target of reproach.

At this point, the Ulema said: Your argument on this count is not correct because all your trouble is confined to the town to Patan (in Gujarat). It is not known in any other town or country. Hence, your argument that Mahdi had filled the whole world with justice as had been done by Shu'aib in the town of Madyan is wrong. By your own admission, you have made yourself blameworthy.

I replied: There is contradiction in your contentions. Just now you were saying that during the reign of Salim Shah, when Shaikh Ala'i was produced for beheading, he refused to retract from his faith in Imam Mahdi, while some of his followers had reneged, that somebody asked why he did not renege while his followers did, he had said that as the leader, he had to act according to the highest principles while the followers could adopt easygoing ways. In short, you know that nobody was known to be as strict in piety, discipline and devotion as Shaikh Ala'i. He had made the doorstep of Imam Mahdi his object of veneration and sacrificed his life at that doorstep. This news spread all over the world that a devout aalim (scholar), strict follower of the Shariat and a leader of tariqat had given the information that Imam Mahdi had come and gone, and that he had fought kings, emirs, Ulema and mashayakhs with convincing arguments. There is hardly a person in Arabia or elsewhere who can say that he had not heard of this news. Besides, you were just now saying that the Ulema of this city had sent their complaints to the Ulema of Makkah and that they (the Ulema of Makkah) had issued a fatwa to kill the group of Mahdavis. It is thirty years since this fatwa reached Gujarat. The Ulema of Arabia know that a large group of Mahdavis exists on this earth and this had astounded the Ulema of the non-Arab lands (Ajm). A large number of people follow the group of Mahdavis, that is, it believes that Imam Mahdi has come and gone. The news had spread both to Makkah and Madina; may Allah protect these cities. But then again you say you had heard that somebody had claimed to be Mahdi in Patan town and that you had not heard anything more than that. In another breath, you say that the misfortune of your waywardness had reached Gaur (in Bengal) and East, where there are thousand of people who follow our claim that Imam Mahdi had come and gone and fallen into this waywardness (gumrahi). You also say that our waywardness had reached Badakhshan where our friends killed a Badakhshani. People of Shiraz had fallen into perversity in following our ways. Mullah Alauddin has come from Shiraz and joined our company. There is a group of Mahdavis in Hirat, Farah and Qandhar. Furthermore, Shaikh Abdunnabi, who is the president of (the Ulema of) the Emperor's court, and Qazi Yaqub, who is the Malik-ul-Quzat (chief justice), have both said in this very court before the Ulema that Emperor Akbar had come all the way to Gujarat to put down the Mahdavi menace; otherwise, an ordinary servant of his was enough to conquer Gujarat because the Gujarat army was not strong enough to warrant the invasion by the Emperor, while I am as insignificant as a straw among the group of Mahdavis. But to put me down, the mighty Emperor Akbar had to come himself to Gujarat. In spite of all this evidence how can you in fairness say that the news of Imam Mahdi's claim was confined to a town like Patan and that you had not heard about it from anywhere else. In fact, the whole world is agog with the news that a big group of Mahdavis had spread and invites the people to give up innovations, strictly follow Prophet Muhammad and Quran, observe the commands ofShariat and abstain from what had been prohibited therein; that in prayers and supplications, it adopts the highest standards. Piety, truth, renunciation, honesty, secludedness, acceptance of the life of poverty with resignation and philanthropy are the cornerstones of the Mahdavi faith and practice. Day and night the group sings the paeans that Imam Mahdi had come and gone. Therefore, the Ulema should not falsely say that the news of Imam Mahdi was confined to the town of Patan only.

At this stage, the Emperor said: There is no way other than to say: 'Unto you your religion, and unto me my religion.' (109:6). Because, it is impossible to defeat you in argument. But why is it that the commentators of Quran have decreed this Verse as repealed?

I said: Some of the commentators have treated the Verse as not repealed. **The Emperor asked**: Which of the Commentators? **I replied**: Qazi Baizavi, for instance.

The Ulema of the court told the Emperor: There is no need to discuss this matter. Shaikh Mahdavi's word does not deserve to be taken into consideration. He is the mischief-monger of our era. We are the people of learning who sit with the king. When we listen to the Shaikh with attention, we sometimes feel that the Shaikh is probably right. His word casts influence on our minds. Such a mischief-monger should not be allowed to go free. The fatwa of the Ulema of Makkah is enough as the final argument for us, because they are the best in the world and their fatwa would not be wrong. Under their fatwa, the Shaikh should be beheaded.

The Emperor asked me: Had you been to Makkah? **I said**: No. **The Emperor asked**: Had the Ulema of Makkah come to Gujarat? Again **I said**: No. **The Emperor said**: What kind of a people are they! Without coming to Gujarat and without enquiring or issuing a warning, they have issued a fatwa to behead the Mahdavis on the issue of Imam Mahdi's appearance and death, on the basis of what their (the Mahdavis') enemies had to say. This is not the work of Allah-fearing Ulema.

The Ulema of the court said: O Emperor, compared to the Ulema of Makkah, we are illiterate. It does not lie in our mouth to criticise or contradict their word. We have to follow their word and act accordingly.

Addressing one of the Ulema, the son of a mullah, the Emperor said: Tell us about the story of your father who had lived in Makkah for a long time and was famous as a teacher and a leader. But then the Ulema of Makkah issued a fatwa charging your father of being a rafzi (heretic), an enemy of religion and, therefore, liable to be beheaded. What do you say now? Was the fatwa of the Ulema of Makkah correct and was your father liable to be beheaded? Or, was it that the Ulema of Makkah were jealous of the good name of your father and falsely issued the fatwa against you father? **The son of the mullah said**: If the Emperor himself shames the Ulema in front of the Mahdavi innovators, who will come to the help of the Ulema of the religion?

The Emperor said: Yours in an unreasonable argument in a learned discussion. Your reply should be based on scientific argument and knowledge of religion. Now, you follow your father and believe that your father was among the Ahl-e-Sunnat-o-Jamaat. You do not consider your father to be a rafzi (heretic). In this sense, the Ulema of Makkah could bejealous of your father. When the Ulema of Makkah could be jealous of your father, what argument do you have to believe that they are not jealous of the group of Mahdavis. You answer my question. The son of the mullah kept quiet.

Feeling defeated, the **Ulema** changed their tactics. They quoted Prophet Muhammad as saying that Truth (Haq) always surmounted falsehood (batil), and **argued**: The group of Mahdavis, wherever it was, lived in poverty and disgrace. We always dominate them. Had they been on the right path, why should their condition be so bad? Please ask this question of the Shaikh. **The Emperor said**: It is not necessary to ask this question of the Shaikh. I can tell you the answer that is in the Shaikh's mind. **The Ulema asked**: What is it?

The Emperor said: The truth triumphs over falsehood as the Shaikh triumphs over us. See, We are fifty or sixty people here trying to corner the Shaikh by our questions. The Shaikh, despite his poverty, shackles, being away from his father or brother and relatives and friends, sits in our court as if he is our master. He is answering each and every one of our questions with dignity, aplomb and steadfastness. This is the triumph of the Truth over falsehood. **The Ulema said**: This argument is beside the point. Triumph, as it manifests itself from outside, is needed.

The Emperor said: Your argument is unreasonable because when two hundred mounted Mughal soldiers seen ten Firangi (European) soldiers, they run like sheep which see a wolf. According to your arguments, the Firangis were on the right path. You should not indulge in unreasonable arguments. Then turning to me the Emperor said: From the contents of Hadith, you have proved the possibility and probability. In other words, it is possible and probable that your claim of Imam Mahdi having come and gone may be correct. This shows that because of this belief, you are not liable to be beheaded or externed. Had you been steadfast in this belief and not invited other people to accept you belief, it would not have landed you in trouble. The arguments of possibility and probability should not have been used to raise a hue and cry and deceive people that Imam Mahdi would no more come, that all the Ulema were misled. All this is sheer waywardness. You have fallen into this predicament by your pride and ignorance. You should now repent and say that your pir (spiritual guide) was a perfect saint of the highest order (vali-e-kamil). He had claimed on his own to be Mahdi. According to Hadith, it is possible and probable that his claim could be true and you are in his (spiritual) order. It is not justifiable for you to reject the word of your pir, which is possible and probable in Shariat. If, by chance, a Mahdi were to come as is being claimed by experts in Hadith, you will accept him and you will think that you pir had erred in interpreting the revelation or intuition. If, on the contrary, no Mahdi were to come in future, it will be obvious that the real Mahdi al-Mau'ood is the person, who has come and gone. Either you say this, or you give a final argument (to prove that Syed Muhammad of Jaunpur is the real Mahdi).

I replied: Since you had asked me to tell the whole story of my acceptance of Syed Muhammad as the Mahdi al-Mau'ood from the beginning to the end, I presented the arguments of the Sufi saints and experts in Hadith. Otherwise, I know that the Ahadith-e-Ahad (Solitary uncorroborated traditions of Prophet Muhammad) cancel each other under the principle that when two ahadith contradict each other, they cannot be relied upon in arguments. But these arguments in this sitting have proved that even if we (the Mahdavis) have intentionally committed a mistake, we are not liable to be beheaded or externed. Howcan we beconsidered liable to be beheaded and externed when it is obvious that we are on the right path.

Therefore, whoever says that Mahdavis are liable to be beheaded and externed and considers that this order is correct and permitted (jayaz), is himself liable to be inflicted with the same punishment. Now, I present the final argument, by the grace of Allah, the one. **The emperor said**: Go ahead.

I said: Ulema of the past have laid down in the books of beliefs some conditions of character and conduct to prove the prophethood of a human being. These conditions have been described in detail. They have arrived at a conclusion by consensus that a person who possess certain qualities, attributes and character, will never be a false pretender. All these qualities can be seen in Sharah-e-Aqaid, Tawale', Sharah-e-Muaqif, Tafseer-e-Madarik, Ahya-ul-Uloom and other books of beliefs. The characteristics and attributes, which have been laid down as a condition for a prophet, we found in Syed Mohammed of Jaunpur who claimed to be Mahdi. Hence, according to the standards, laid down by the Ulema of the past and jurists of the subsequent era, we came to know that truly and certainly Syed Muhammad was the Mahdi al-Mau'ood and there as no doubt about it. Prophet Muhammad has said with reference to Mahdi that he would follow in my footsteps and would not err. This saying of the Prophet has come true in respect of Syed Muhammad of Jaunpur. In other words, the character, conduct and behaviour of Prophet Muhammad was flawlessly followed by Syed Muhammad of Jaunpur. Hence it was realistically known that he alone, and none else, was

Mahdi al-Mau'ood. And the probability shown by Hadith finally became a certainty. For, all that was laid down by the Ulema of the past was in conformity with the character and conduct of Imam Mahdi.

The emperor said: You have not seen Syed Muhammad: how did you come to know that the character, conduct and behaviour, laid down by the Ulema of the past, were present in him ? **I Said**: We investigated the character of Imam Syed Muhammad as the Ulema of the past had investigated through their research in the books of beliefs the character of Prophet Muhammad and came to the conclusion that this person alone was Mahdi al-Mou'ood.

The Emperor said: From your arguments it appears that the person who bears this character is to be accepted. Suppose in future, some person is born, has all the qualities in him and claims to be Imam Mahdi, what will you say about him?

I Said: No such person will be born and will never claim to be Mahdi al-Mou'ood. **The emperor said**: To suppose that the impossible will occur is not impossible. Hence, suppose that somebody is born and makes the claim, what will you say about him? **I replied**: Suppose somebody with the character of prophet Muhammad is born and claims that he is the Prophet, what will be your and our reaction? Whatever can be said in that event, will also be said in respect of Imam Mahdi. But such an event will never come to happen. The seal of the Prophets has come and gone and the Seal of the Sainthood (vilayat) too has come and gone.

At this point, the trend of the discussion changed and questions not related to the discussion of Mahdavi beliefs began to be asked. Some of them were: Can an underage (unadult) person be called a companion of the Prophet? What is your opinion about a person who says Hazrat Ali (the fourth Caliph of Islam) was superior (afzal) and more respected than Hazrat Au Bakr (the first Caliph of Islam)? What is your belief in respect of the quarrel between Hazrat Ali ad Hazrat Mua'wiah? What do you say about cursing Yazid? What are the conditions for a Mujtahid (religious director), according to you? These and similar other questions were asked and replied according to my light. The emperor and the Ulema did not controvert my replies. They appeared to be happy about them. Since these questions and their replies were not related to the subject under discussion and to be brief, they have been omitted. This sitting had started at dusk and went on till midnight. When the sitting was over, I was handed over to the jailor in-charge.

SESSION II

I was again taken in shackles to the Emperor's court where, besides the Emperor and Ulema, some emirs, who were not present in the earlier sitting, were already occupying their seats. I was made to sit in the centre and all others sat around me in a circle. **To the Ulema, the Emperor said**: This is Shaikh Mustafa Mahdavi. You may ask him whatever you want.

The Ulema told me: You are an elderly person and a leader. You possess abilities that people like us can benefit from. On the basis of which argument, do you call Syed Muhammad of Jaunpur as Mahdi al-Mau'ood? Why do you subscribe to beliefs which are against the ahadith (traditions of Prophet Muhammed)? There are signs for Mahdi in the ahadith.

I Replied: There is great contradiction in ahadith describing the signs of Imam Mahdi. It is impossible to identify him on the basis of ahadith. All that can be said on the basis of the ahadith is that Imam Mahdi has come and gone or will come.

The Ulema said: Alas ! It does not lie in your mouth to say such unreasonable things because there cannot be any contradiction among the ahadith of Prophet Muhammad. **To the Emperor, I said**: Please listen to me attentively. We say that contradiction does occur among the ahadith, while these Ulema say that there is no contradiction among them. We will concede that we are wrong in our claim about Mahdi, if these Ulema prove, according to the rules of the science of ahadith, that there can be no contradiction among them.

The Emperor told the Ulema: At the beginning of the discussion itself, you are saying a very unreasonable thing. I would be a rafzi (heretic) if there is no contradiction among the ahadith. Today itself, I was reading a book of ahadith. I came across two ahadith about the appearance of Dajjal (Anti-Christ). They contradicted each other. It is obvious that the ahadith about Imam Mahdi too would not be without contradiction.

The Ulema did not reply. Instead, they asked me another question.

The Ulema said: According to a tradition, Prophet Muhammad said in respect of Mahdi that those living on earth and in heavens, would be friendly to Mahdi. In another tradition, it is said that those living on earth and in heavens will be contented, satisfied and happy with Imam Mahdi. How is it that the people of the city are hostile to your Imam and his followers, and keep them at a distance ?

I replied: Look at what Allah has to say. Allah had commanded that people should be benevolent to those who troubled and tormented Prophet Muhammad. Allah says "Nor can goodness and evil be equal (Evil) what is better: then will he between whom and thee was hatred becomes as it were thy friend and intimate". (41:34). In other words O Muhammad Mustafa, have a good word to those who are hostile to you, treat them with a better morality and remove their evil with your good; for instance, be patient against their anger, be forbearing against their ignorance. Pardon their evils, be benevolent against their miserliness and so on. In consequence, your enemy will become your friend as if he is your close relative. If you follow this regime, your difficulties will come to an end. Now, think it over. Prophet Muhammad followed the commandment with utmost devotion. But did all those, who were hostile to him, become his friends? Did they eschew their hostility? It is obvious that the hostility of the opponents had reached its zenith. Hence, the Verse should be understood to mean the negligence, ignorance, hostility, malice and belligerence of the kafirs (infidels), so that the meaning of the Verse reflects the situation in favour of Prophet

Muhammad because the malicious people are prominent here. With respect to these hostile elements, Allah says: "Even if they see all the signs, they will not believe in them". (7:146). Similarly, except the *Ulema-e-Zahir* (worldly Ulema) and their followers, ask anybody. They will all say that they had not seen anybody except the group of Mahdavis who had pleasantness, elegance, courage, uprightness, affection, honesty, brotherhood, bravery, generosity, trust in Allah, surrender to the will of Allah and such good character and conduct. As the Quranic Verse came true in case of Prophet Muhammad, the Hadith has come true in respect of Imam Mahdi and his followers. Further, Prophet Muhammad has said: "verily when Allah makes one of His servants His friend, He calls Gabriel and tells him that He makes so and so His friend. He asks Gabriel to be friendly to him. Gabriel becomes friendly to him and then announces in Heavens that Allah has made so and so His friend and all others should make him their friend. Hence, all in Heavens make him their friend. He also becomes popular among the people on earth. From this, Hadith, it becomes obvious that all prophets and saints, whether they are from the *sabiqoon* (eminent virtuous people of the past) or *as-hab al-yameen* (people of paradise), are popular among the inhabitants of the earth and the Heavens. All this inspite of Allah's saying. ". . . And, in defiance of right, slay the Prophets, and slay those who teach just dealing with mankind, . . . ?" (3:21), and the Hadith, "Verily the prophets and saints were subjected to most difficult trials and tribulations. "Both the Quaranic Verse and the Hadith manifest that trials and tribulations were inflicted on Prophets and saints. It should, therefore, be noted how the saints were subjected to difficulties and how people slandered them. And then Allah tells Prophet Muhammad: "Patiently persevere, as did all apostles of inflexible purpose; . . ." (46:35). Besides, Prophet Muhammad is quoted as saying that his (grandsons) Imam Hasan and Imam Hussain are the leaders of the young men of paradise. But they were subjected to trials and tribulations at Karbala (now in Iraq), so soon after the demise of Prophet Muhammad, by the descendants of his companions. Now you should know that the Hadith, "he becomes popular among the inhabitants of the earth", applies to all prophets and saints. Similarly, the Hadith, "all the inhabitants of the earth and the Heavens make him their friend", applies to Imam Mahadi and his followers.

The Ulema then said: The Hadith should not be interpreted (taveel). The world of Hadith should be believed as it was. One should abstain from violating this rule.

I replied: The religion of Imam Abu Hanifa is based on taveel (interpretation), so much so, that the Ulema of Shafei school of Fiqh call them *as-hab-ur-rai* (opinionated Ulema) and their own Ulema as the *as-hab-al-hadith* (Ulema of Hadith). Prophet Muhammad has said that the actions are related to the intentions. Besides, Prophet Muhammad has also said everyone gets what he intends to achieve. Further, he said wazu (ablution) will not be valid unless there is nee'at (intention) for it. Imam Shafei bases his beliefs on the word of the Hadith, while Imam Abu Hanifa on taveel (interpretation). This is no secret to those who know the differences of opinion among the *mujtahids* (religious directors).

The Ulema said: We accept all that you have said. But if you go in for taveel, the taveel should satisfy us.

I replied: It is not necessary for me to satisfy you. We have satisfied ourselves and our followers by the rules of the religious commandments and Islamic theology. For, a perfect man like Imam Abu Hanifa, despite his immense capabilities and the goodness and superiority in faith, could not satisfy Imam Shafei and the differences between the two imams persisted. I am not superior to Imam Abu Hanifa and you are not superior to Imam Shafei in comprehension and justice. How can the difference of opinion between us be removed? Allah says: "Already has our word been passed before (this to Our servants sent (by us). That they would certainly be assisted, and that our forces, they surely must conquer. (37:171, 172, 713). Allah further says: "Allah has decreed; it is I and my apostles who must prevail': for Allah is one, full of strength, able to enforce his will". (58:21). Allah further says "Ye Must gain mastery if ye are true in Faith". (3:139). Allah says: ". . . and it was due from us to aid those who believed" (30:47). There are many other similar verses in Quran. Now will you argue on the basis of the manifest wording of the verses or would you explain them in a manner applicable to the condition of the prophets and the faithful? The prophets did not attain outward or manifest dominance over the people hostile to them. They were actually beheaded by their opponents. What do you say about the sorcerers of Fir'aun (Pharaoh) and *As-hab-e-akhood* and such others; whether they were dominant or not? If you rely on the outward meaning of the words, you are bound to come to the conclusion that they were not dominant. To infer this meaning is tantamount to blaming the momineen (believers). But the reality of these momins is proved by convincing arguments. Therefore, we are bound to interpret the Quranic Verses and hadith in a way conducive to the realities of the prophets and their followers so that we are not thrown out of our religion. Allah knows better.

SESSION III

I was brought to the Emperor's court in shackles. **Abdunnabi Danishmand** who was the head of the Ulema of the durbar **told the Emperor**: O Emperor, please do justice. These Mahdavis are few. How can one accept their argument? The majority of the people say that Mahdi al-Mau'ood will come while these few Mahdavis say that Mahdi al-Mau'ood has come and gone. Then, O Emperor, please ask what Shaikh Mustafa has to say.

I asked: Has the Emperor heard the conversion of Prophet Joseph and his brothers or not? **Abdunnabi said**: I have heard it many times **The emperor said**: Please say. I have not heard it from you.

I said: O Emperor, Ten brothers were the children of one mother. Joseph and Bin yamin were from the other mother. Joseph's brothers, out of jealousy, said that Joseph should be killed, thrown at a place where there was no human being or thrown into a dry well. However, they told their father they would take Joseph out to play with. They took him and threw him into the well of Kin'an. They came a second time and sold him to a trader. Joseph's brothers were many but Joseph was alone. But who was a liar among them?

The Emperor said: All brothers of Joseph were sinners and Liars. **I said**: Joseph's brothers were many. How could they be sinners and liars? **The Emperor said**: You are turning it on us.

I said: I related the story of Joseph to you because number of mullahs and shaikhs is great and they say that Imam Mahdi will come. I am alone and my brothers are few and we say that Imam Mahdi has come and gone. Who are the liars? O Emperor, please do justice. Again the Emperor conceded that Joseph was right.

I said: If that is so, we Mahdavis, who say that Imam Mahdi has come and gone, are on the right path, because we are few. Allah says: ". . . Among them are some who have faith and most of them are perverted transgressors". (3:110). At every point of time, every prophet has been opposed by a majority and only a few people reposed faith in them. Similarly, at the time of Imam Mahdi also, many people opposed and refused to accept him and only a few people accepted him. Hence, it is proved by convincing argument that Imam Mahdi had come and gone. Besides, O Emperor, before creating Adam, Allah told all the angels, 'Behold, thy Lord said to the angels: I will create a vicegerent on earth.' They said: 'Wilt Thou place therein one who will make mischief therein and shed blood?'—whilst we do celebrate Thy praises and glorify Thy Holy (name)?' He said: I know what ye know not.' And he taught Adam the nature of all things; then placed them before the Angels and said: "Tell me the nature of these if ye are right". They said:'Glory to Thee: of Knowledge we have none, save what Thou has taught us: In truth it is Thou who are perfect in knowledge and wisdom". (2:30-32). Two thousand years before the birth of Adam, Allah had told the angels that he intended to create Adam, who would be his vice regent on earth. The angels said O Allah, will you create a person on earth who will shed blood and cause destruction while we sing praises of your purity? Allah said: What We know, you do not know. And when Adam was created, He was instructed in the nature of all things. He informed him of their names and explained all creation. Then, all the things were set before the angels. He asked them to tell the names of all things that were created, if they (the angels) were truthful. The angels were momins (faithful). They repented and said they knew what He had taught them. They said: Verily, He knew everything and He alone issued commandments to the Creation. The point to be noted here is that the angels were all in the Heavens, they had been created out of light (noor). Inspite of this, they were jealous of Adam. Why should not the people who are sinful and are madly wedded to worldly desires, not be jealous of Imam Mahdi, his followers and the seekers of Allah? When the angels repented and reposed Faith in the commandments of Allah, in humility, they were accepted by Allah. Similarly, those people, who refute Imam Mahdi, listen to the arguments in proof of Imam Mahdi. Those who are blessed with iman (Faith), repent with modesty and humility and accept Imam Mahdi. They thus become the loved of Allah. Satan has sinned. He refused to prostrate before Adam and said: 'I am better than Adam'. He does not repent now. Similarly, the person, who is not blessed with iman (Faith), does not repent. He too is proud. He does not accept Imam Mahdi. He is therefore, kafir (infidel). Allah said: "If they do fail to judge by (the light of) what Allah hath revealed, they are (no better than) Unbelievers". (5:47). Prophet Muhammad has said "Whoever disbelieved Mahdi, verily, he is Kafir (infidel)". This Hadith has been reported in *Tabaqat Al-Fuqaha*. O Emperor, please do justice. Allah Says: "O David ; we did indeed make thee a vice regent on earth ; so judge thou between men in truth (and justice) . . ." (38:26). And Prophet Muhammad said: May Allah bless him who does justice and curse of Allah be on him who does not do justice".

After listening to this, **the Emperor said**: O Shaikh Mustafa, May Allah bless you and may He shower his bounties on you.

Turning to the Ulema, the Emperor said: You also present some arguments in reply to the Shaikh's arguments.

However, none said anything **(Shaikh Mustafa writes)**: Allah says: 'Truth has (now) arrived, and Falsehood perished ; for Falsehood is (by its nature) bound to perish. (17:81). Prophet Muhammad has said ; Truth will dominate; it will never be dominated. Hence, it is proved that Imam Mahdi has come and gone. A few hundred Ulema and Shaikhs had gathered in the Emperor's court for the debate in which by the grace of Allah they were defeated.

The Ulema asked: How many years have passed since Imam Mahdi came and went away? **I replied**: Imam Mahdi came in 905 AH after the migration of Prophet Muhammad from Makkah to Madina and claimed to be Mahdi al-Mau'ood in the tenth century AH. Thus he supported the religion of Prophet Muhammad. We (Mahdavis) followed him. Historians have by consensus quoted the Hadith that, according to Abu Huraira, Prophet Muhammad had said that Allah would send at the head of every century a person who will revive the religion for this ummah. Historians have also arrived at the consensus that at the head of the tenth century AH, none other than Imam Mahdi will appear. After this, I recited a Persian couplet, which means: Sun has arisen in the skies, what is the use if a blind eye does not see it? The sun is on the head and my shield is in my hand. If the ant does not pick up the grains of sugar, tell it not to pick; and if a blind person does not see, tell him not to see.

After this I told the Emperor: Allah says in Quran: . . . . And get two witnesses, out of your own men . . . ." (2:282). In other words, Allah has asked to call two men from among our men as witnesses. Allah has not asked for the evidence of eunuchs. Prophet Muhammad has said that the seeker of worldliness is a eunuch, the seeker of life in the hereafter is a woman and the seeker of Allah is the man. Further, Prophet Muhammad has also said: Fasting is obligatory for the person who has seen the crescent moon (of Ramzan) and if others accept his evidence, fasting is obligatory on them also. Similarly, we have seen the arguments of Quran and Hadith and listened to the evidence of Allah and his prophet, and therefore, it is obligatory on us to accept Imam Mahdi. It is for this reason that we have accepted and say that Imam Mahdi has come and gone. And on my saying so, many people have accepted the Imam. And if somebody does not accept, divine vengeance for refusal falls on his head. In other words, his abode will be in Hell. O Emperor, I have presented evidence from Quran, Prophet Muhammad and reliable books. Please now ask your Ulema also to present evidence from Quran, Hadith and reliable books and put forth their arguments to show, when Imam Mahdi, according to them, has to come.

The Emperor told the Ulema: Shaikh Mustafa has argued his case and you have listened to him. Now, you can go ahead with your arguments.

Nobody said anything. **I told the Emperor**: You may listen to one more argument. In Quran, Allah says about people who read Quran but do not act according to it: "The similitude of those who were charged with the (obligation of the) Mosaic Law (Torah), but who subsequently failed in those (obligations) is that of a donkey which carries huge tomes (but understand them not). (62:5). In other words, people, who read Quran but do not act according to it, are like the donkey which is loaded with stones or wood on its back. Prophet Muhammad has said: The scholar, who does not act according to his knowledge, is like a donkey".

(Here Shaikh Mustafa quotes a Hindi doha, which, in translation, reads) O half wit, you are loaded with the burden of a donkey. You are led by your ear and you are asked to walk silently.

(Again, he quotes a Persian couplet, which in translation, reads) That you see around and (believe that) they are men. They, in fact, are donkeys and bullocks without tails. (Shaikh Mustafa quotes Shaikh Mohiuddin ibn Arabi as saying) All praise be to Allah who had created donkeys in the shape of men. (Then Shaikh Mustafa quotes a stanza of Persian Poetry which, in translation, reads) O ignorant scholar, how much would you learn, I know the knowledge of inner (Truth) and you do not, The hair of your head have greyed in learning the grammar and syntax. But you have not acquired a single letter of the divine knowledge. (Another couplet, he quoted, reads in translation) you have put a number of books on the back of a donkey. But you cannot say that it is the scholar of the inner divine knowledge. (After quoting these lines of poetry, Shaikh Mustafa continues his address and says) Allah says: "They are like cattle—nay more misguided; . . ." (7:179). So they do what Allah has created them for. They praise Allah. But some people do not remember Allah and worship Him. They would, therefore, always burn in Hell. Dogs, pigs, donkeys and other quadrupeds will not be tormented in Hell. But people, who oppose Allah and his Prophet and die in a state of opposition will always burn in Hell. Therefore they are worse than the animals. Allah says: "Ye people of the book! Why do ye cloth truth with falsehood, and conceal the Truth, while ye have knowledge?" (3:71). That is, the knowledge of Prophet Muhammad being the true apostle of Allah. Similarly, Imam Mahdi's attributes are obvious. Why do they conceal it?. But what can one, who is blind, see?

Prophet Muhammad has said that the fly which sits on filth is better than the Ulema and fuqaha (Islamic jurists) who go to the doorsteps of kings, or in other words, who go to kings seeking (pleasures of) worldliness. Hence, how can the people, who possess such attributes, accept Imam Mahdi? But people, who seek the Truth and who are just and who have forsaken the profane world, will surely accept Imam Mahdi and have actually accepted him. Allah says: "Those who reject (Truth), among the people of the Book and among the polytheists, were not going to depart (from their ways) until there should come to them Clear Evidence. (98:1) In other words, they believed that Prophet Muhammad would come but when he actually came with Clear Evidence, (they refuted him). Allah says: "Nor did the people of the book make schisms, until after there came to them clear evidence. (98:4) Similarly, the Ulema and shaikhs have arrived at a consensus that Imam Mahdi will come in 905 AH. When Imam Mahdi Actually came, the Ulema and shaikhs made schisms except for a few who were just and seekers of Allah. They accepted Imam Mahdi and the rest refuted him. They said: This is not the Mahdi that was promised (Mau'ood). This extract is from the book, Tafseer-e-Taveel by Abdur Razaq Kashi.

Finally I said: O Emperor, I say that I will write a letter to you, and please ask your Ulema and shaikhs to write a similar letter that the person or persons, who argue without the support of Quran and Hadith, should be made to blacken their faces, ride a donkey and go round the bazaars of the town, while people should be allowed to stone them.

I wrote the letter and handed it over, to the Emperor, while he Ulema and shaikhs did not. The Emperor asked the Ulema and shaikhs to explain their reluctance to write the letter. One of the Ulema, who was an elderly person, said: We are not as well versed in Quran and Hadith as Shaikh Mustafa is. He studies the Quran and Hadith day in and day out. **The Emperor said**: You have studied so much but you cannot argue on the basis of Quran and Hadith. Quran and Hadith are the basic things. Why did you not become well versed in Quran and Hadith?

The Emperor was angry with Abdunnabi Danishmand and said: Bring donkeys. Blacken the faces of these Ulema and shaikhs, make them ride the donkeys. Then take them round the town. All the courtiers rose and started begging off the emperor to forgive them. When the emperor ordered blackening of their faces and making them ride the donkeys, it was as good as their being disgraced. At this point the scholar who was arguing was expelled from the court. The meeting ended thus.

SESSION IV

The Ulema asked the Emperor to tell Shaikh Mustafa that Prophet Muhammad had **said**: "The world is like a stinking and decaying cadaver and its seekers are curs. Stinking cadavers have a smell. Then worldliness too must have a smell. How does it smell? **The Emperor told me**: What is this? What is your answer?

I said: People who could smell the stink of worldliness and the seekers of Allah have renounced the world because to them the smell of the world is dirtier than that of a stinking cadaver. Insensate people do not understand because when dogs go to eat stinking cadavers, their sense of smell becomes blunted, and therefore, they relish eating decaying cadavers. Similar is the case of the seekers of worldliness. They do not smell the stink of worldliness; they seek the world and they enjoy eating with an open heart and are happy. It is narrated that Prophet Muhammad was going with his companions and saw the decaying and stinking parts of the body of a rat. The stink was strong enough to make all of them cover their noses with cloth. To his companions, Prophet Muhammad said: Friends, Is there anybody among you who could buy this? The companions said: Nobody will accept it. The Prophet asked: Will anybody take it free of cost? The companions said: It is of no use. What can we do with it? The Prophet then said: There are worms in this decaying body of the rat. They eat rot and become fat. He dies when he is taken out of this worldliness. He is like the worm which is accustomed to the stink of the cadaver. Similarly, the person who lives and loves the worldliness, does not feel the smell of the rot, because his mind is accustomed to that smell and has become fat. When he is retrieved from worldliness, he dies. In other words, such people relish and enjoy the wealth and love of worldliness. And what wealth (*mata*)? It is worse than used sanitary towels. The world is worse than them but it appears to be good to its seekers. So saying one's prayers daily, listening to the explanations of Quran and acting according to the Holy book *tark-e-dunya* (renunciation), piety, trust in Allah and to accept Syed Muhammad, who is the seal of the Muhammadan Sainthood (*Vilayat-e-Muhammadi*), as Mahdi al-Mau'ood do not appeal them till their last breath. Another incident is narrated that a scavenger chanced to come into the locality of perfumers. The smell of the perfumes went to his head. It appeared to him as intolerably bad. He lost consciousness and fell to the ground. The people of the locality wondered what had happened to him. Incidentally, Shaikh Fariduddin Attar happened to pass that way. He asked what kind of a person was he. They said he was a scavenger. Shaikh Attar asked somebody to bring some fresh excrement. It was brought, The Shaikh asked him to place some of it near the nose of the scavenger. An hour later, the scavenger regained consciousness. He rose and cleaned his face and nose with a cloth. He was happy. Reaching home, he related the incident to his wife and other members of his family. He promised that he would never again go to the locality of the perfumers. Similar is the case of the person who seeks the world. The seeker of the world does not like saying his daily prayers, listening to the commentary of Quran, piety, trust in Allah, renunciation, love for Allah, spending his wealth and sacrificing his life for Allah do not appeal to him because all these things are like perfume. Allah says: "And whose word can be truer than Allah's ? (4:87) To the others (seekers of worldliness) this word will not appeal. In fact, this makes them lose consciousness and, like the scavenger, they regain their consciousness when they smell the stink of worldliness. Prophet Muhammad has said that the world was the place for the descendants of Adam to defecate. The smell of the worldliness was worse than the stink of the decaying cadaver. To the seekers of the (Ultimate) Truth, the smell of worldliness is a stink. Therefore, they renounced it. They sought Allah. They won the divine robe of honour as Men. Allah says: "By men whom neither traffic nor merchandise can divert from the remembrance of Allah . . . ." (24:37). In other words, they are men or the seekers of Allah and trade does not make them neglect the remembrance of Allah. The minds of the seekers of worldliness are accustomed to the stink. If one of them goes to his house and tells his family members about renunciation or explanation of Quran, the members of the house become angry and scold him like the members of the scavenger's family on his going to the locality of the perfumers. They say they earn worldly wealth. All this talk of renunciation and other things does not please them.

SESSION V

One day, I was brought to the court of Emperor Akbar and the Ulema started the debate on Mahdism. All the Ulema said their zuhr (afternoon) prayers in congregation but I said my prayers separately and did not join their assembly. The prayers over, all came to the court.

Abdunnabi told the Emperor:

please ask Shaikh Mustafa why he calls Muslims as kafirs (infidels). **I said**: O Emperor, please ask Abdunnabi whom have I called kafir, or am calling kafir. Also, please ask Abdunnabi to produce some evidence to prove his allegations. **The Mullah Said**: If you do not call us kafirs, why did you not say your prayers in our leadership (imamat).

I asked the Emperor: Which religious order do you belong to and who is your murshid (spiritual guide)? With great respect, both his hands touching his ear lobes and a bowed head, the Emperor said: I am the disciple of Hazrat Khwaja Moinuddin Chishti (of Ajmer).

I said: Suppose somebody were to say that Hazrat Khwaja Moinuddin Chishti had deviated from the religion or that he had gone astray and had misled other people, what would be your reaction? What would you say?

The Emperor said: I would call such a person a kafir and will kill him with my own hands. **I said**: My murshid is Imam Syed Muhammad Mahdi al-Mau'ood. When somebody were to say that Imam Mahdi and his followers are apostates and are misleading the people, how can I say my prayers under the leadership of such a person? Besides, I do not call anybody kafir. But I recite the Hadith, in which Prophet Muhammad has said: "Whoever refused to accept Imam Mahdi, verily he is a kafir." This Hadith is reported in the book, *Tabqat al-Fuqaha*. I only recite this hadith. I do not call anybody kafir on my own.

Then I told the Emperor: Please ask the mullahs: What is the punishment under the Shariat for falsely slandering anybody? The mullahs did not reply.

I said: Allah says in Quran that people who falsely slander, should be punished with eighty stripes. The Mullahs have become liable to this punishment. Allah says: "And those who launch a charge against chaste women, and produce not four witnesses (to support their allegations), flog them with eighty stripes; and reject their evidence ever after: For such men are wicked transgressors . . . . (24:4). **The Emperor said**: O mullahs and shaikhs, you have falsely slandered Shaikh Mustafa and, therefore, you are liable to Quranic hadd (punishment).

I said: O Emperor, prophet Muhammad has said: May Allah bless him who has done justice and curse him who does injustice.

The Emperor then asked me: O Shaikh Mustafa, these mullahs and shaikhs are devout persons and guide the people in religious affairs. But you did not say your prayers under their leadership. Why? **I said**: Prophet Muhammad has said that the seeker of the world is impotent, the seeker of the Hereafter is a woman and the seeker of Allah alone is a man. Allah says: "By men whom neither traffic nor merchandise can divert from the Remembrance of Allah, nor form regular Prayers . . . ." (24:37). In other words, these people had renounced the world and kept themselves busy in nothing other than regular prayers and remembrance of Allah. They listen to the explanation of Quran and they act according to it. These are the men. All others are impotent. O Emperor, please do justice. Ask Abdunnabi and all other Ulema to produce one commandment from the books of Hadith and Fiqh asking a man to say his prayers under the leadership of impotents. Many books are eloquent about the prohibition of an impotent person from leading a group of men in prayers. Therefore, I did not say my prayers in the congregation led by an impotent.

The Emperor laughed and said: O Shaikh Mustafa, you have spoken the truth. **To the Ulema, he said**: Shaikh Mustafa did not say his prayers under your leadership because you are impotents and to say one's prayers under the leadership of a eunuch is not allowed. Now, come, answer him. And produce an argument based on Quran and Hadith and reliable books to prove that saying one's prayers under the leadership of eunuchs is permissible. Nobody gave a reply and appeared to be defeated.

The Emperor Said: O Shaikh Mustafa, you have given a fitting reply. May Allah bless you. **Then, I told the Emperor**: I have recalled another narration. I will tell you if you feel like listening. There was a eunuch sitting among a group of God-fearing devout men. These men of God were talking about Allah, Prophet Muhammad and Makkah. One of them said he had been to Makkah. Great rewards from Allah await those who go to Makkah. He had been the wonders of the oceans and forests. This created a desire in the mind of the eunuch to go to Makkah. He went to his house, took some food for the journey and started his sojourn to Makkah. He had hardly gone a couple of leagues when his legs and loins began to ache. He saw a tree on the way and tried to reach it. He found reaching it very difficulty. With a great effort, he somehow reached the tree and started lamenting like a woman and fell down. He saw an approaching man at a distance. When he came near, the eunuch asked him how far Makkah was. The newcomer asked how long he had been travelling. The eunuch said he had started from his house the same day and intended to go to Makkah. His house was about a couple of leagues from the place. The traveller said: O Eunuch, return home because when you see the ocean you would die of fear." The traveller went away. The eunuch felt scared of what the traveller had said. He returned home. His relatives scolded him for undertaking the journey. They said going to Makkah was the task for men.

After narrating the story, I told the Emperor: As Prophet Muhammad has said the seekers of Allah alone were men and the seekers of the world were eunuchs. Hence, they do not follow the Prophet, they do not renounce the world. They go to the kings and emirs and seek pensions and other worldly possessions. For this they indulge in flattery and sycophancy.

They cannot repose trust in Allah and they cannot become pious. The seekers of the world were like the eunuch who returned from his intended journey to Makkah.

The Emperor was happy to listen to the narration and the arguments. He said: May Allah bless you and may He Shower his bounties on you, O Shaikh Mustafa. Then, he ordered the Ulema to put forth their arguments in reply to me. They did not reply. They did not have the strength to reply.

With courtesy from "Khalifatullahilmehdi.com"

* * *

—

7. Mubahisa-i-Alamgiri:

The Debate on Mahdaviat between Hazrat Miyan Shaykh Ibrahim[RH] and Qadi Abu Sa'id ordered by the Emperor Aurangzeb Alamgir at Ahmadnagar Compiled in Persian by: **Hazrat Miyan Abu al-Qasim** Translated into English by: **Scott A. Kugle** Research Scholar Graduate Programme in Religious Duke University, Durham, USA. Published by: **MARKAZI ANJUMAN-E-MAHDAVIA** Chanchalguda, Hyderabad—500 024.

In the name of Allah, the most Beneficent, the most Merciful

Introduction

"The Aurangzeb Debate" is the second major text to record the disputations which raged between Mahdawi and Sunni scholars during the Mughal period. These debate texts are very important sources that reveal how Mahdawi scholars of a particular age understood their faith, and how they expressed it in the potentially threatening context of inquisitions instigated by the scholars of the Mughal court. It could be argued that the tradition of disputations and debates started with Sayyid Muhammad Jaunpuri himself. It is recorded that he encountered his first systematic opposition after he announced his mission as the Mahdi at the town of Barhli Gujarat in the year 905H/1499 AD. Sayyid Muhammad wrote a letter to the Sultan in his own defence and to further explain his mission and delayed his departure from Barhli in order to receive a reply, while waiting, he received a contingent of scholars from Ahmadabad and Patan who came to pry him with questions. This may be said to be the first Mahdawi debate and it is recorded in the classic Mahdawi records of *Sirat Imam Mahdi Maw'ud* and *Shawahid al-Wilayat*. A second major debate took place when Sayyid Muhammad arrived in Farah (Afghanistan). The chief scholar of the court of Herat (which ruled Farah at that time) deputed some scholars for the purpose of questioning the Sayyid, with the implicit threat that failure to pass the inquisition would result in imprisonment and perhaps punishment. The contents of this debate were recorded in *Sirat*, as well as in the non-Mahdawi source, *Nijat al-Rashid* by Abd al-Qadir al-Badauni.

However, the formation of debate literature as a distinct genre came only after the death of Sayyid Muhammad himself and the growth of the Mahdawi community under his first generation of followers. The first of these texts, and by far the most substantial of them, is *Majalis-i-Khamsah*, "Five Debates in the Court of the Emperor Akbar" by Shaykh Mustafa Gujarati. This text set the precedent for all subsequent records in the genre of Mahdawi debates. Shaykh Mustafa displayed his brilliance as an orator and his keenness as a politician, as he answered the questions of the Sunni scholars and turned the Emperor himself against them. The arguments and examples put forth by Mustafa Gujarati in the records of these debates were repeated again and again by later scholars in later disputes. He argued that the followers of the Mahdi are like Sufis but qualitatively different from them and superior to them. He also argued that the followers of the Mahdi were the true moral leaders of the *Ahl-i-Sunnat o Jama'at* community. Each argument he presented was designed to prove that the Mahdawi community was not liable to punishment under the terms of the *shari'at*, and further that other Sufis and scholars who had not joined the Mahdawi community were hypocritical, corrupt or mislead by their pride. In his argument, the true followers of any Prophet are always a minority, and their unwavering insistence on the truth always leads them to be persecuted and oppressed by others.

The debate of Shaykh Ibrahim that is recorded in this text, *Mubahisa-yi-Alamgiri*, is both concise and tranquil when compared with the debate that was recorded about one century earlier. Shaykh Mustafa's debates were in many sessions spread over the course of his eighteen month imprisonment at Akbar's court. In contrast, Shaykh Ibrahim's debate lasted only one day. While Shaykh Mustafa was physically threatened with summary punishment on the spot, Shaykh Ibrahim was treated respectfully and came to the debate on his own power. While Shaykh Mustafa had to deal with over one-hundred antagonistic scholars and courtiers as well as the vacillating Emperor Akbar himself: Shaykh Ibrahim had only to face the judge, Qazi Abu Sa'id, who had been deputed by Aurangzeb to question the Mahdawi scholars and ascertain what their beliefs might be. But let this contrast not place Shaykh Ibrahim in a bad light! He well knew that in being called to a debate, his community's future in Ahmadnagar was in jeopardy and that if he did not impress the judge with his interpretation of Qur'an and Hadith sources, his community might become vulnerable to execution, imprisonment or exile. The background of each of these Mahdawi debates is the potential use of state violence against them, no matter how calm and tranquil the debater may appear. Furthermore, this contrast between the long series of debates which raged in Akbar's court and the single debate ordered by Aurangzeb should not be understood as a judgment on the capabilities of the two protagonists, Mustafa Gujarati and Shaykh Ibrahim. Rather, the contrast show the marked change in the social position and aspirations of the Mahdawi community in the hundred years which had lapsed between these two debates.

In the first instance, resistance to the Mahdawi movement was fierce. Although the movement's arch-opponent, Shaykh Ali Muttaqi had died (in 975 Hijri /1568 CE), one of his primary students was alive and actively opposing the Mahdawi community's growth in Gujarat. He is Miyan Muhammad ibn Tahir of Patan (also known as Nahranwala) who was a hadith specialist. He continued his teacher's opposition to the Mahdawi community by contending that they disrespected the Prophet by disregarding or misinterpreting the Prophet's sayings about the coming of the Mahdi. So vociferously did he make this claim that he demanded a personal interview with the Emperor Akbar when he invaded Gujarat, and tried to steer the invading Emperor toward a full state persecution of the Mahdawi community. Miyan Muhammad ibn Tahir must have come into acute conflict with Shaykh Mustafa Gujarati himself, for both were resident at Patan; in addition the hadith scholar was from the Bohra community, and is known to have focused his efforts on trying to keep the Bohra community from joining the Mahdawi circles, while Shaykh Mustafa's own father had come from the Bohra community and joined the Mahdawi community[1]. In addition to resistance by a network of hadith scholars and Sufis in Gujarat, the Mahdawi community faced persecution by the chief scholar of the court in Delhi, Abdullah Sultanpuri, who was just as active in the Mughal court as he had been in the Suri court. He seemed to engage in inquisitions and persecutions in order to reinforce his own power at court, and attacked not only Mahdawi leaders but Sufi shaykhs as well. All these factors meant that the Emperor Akbar was

1 In *Majalis-i Khamsa*, the court scholars were noted to have said, "The trouble that you Mahdawis have caused is confined to the town of Patan in Gujarat." This is a reference to the work of Muhammad ibn Tahir and his pressuring the Mughal governor, Mirza Aziz Khokha, to suppress Mahdawis by breaking up their da'irahs. In a military attack on one such da'irah, in 890. Hijri / 573 CE, Shaykh Mustafa Gujarati was imprisoned and his father was killed. He ridiculed the court scholars and questioned not only their morality, but even their masculinity.

The Mahdawis bear witness to oneness of Allah who sent the Prophet on a mission. They cherish the memory of all four of the Prophet's close companions, and believe that all four legal methods are validly based on the truth. They are certainly members of our Sunni community. They say that 'Mahdi of the end of time (Mehdi Akhir-u-zaman) is their leader who has come and gone . . . . They are not liable to any Qur'anic punishment, nor to summary execution, nor to imprisonment or exile. I have found no cause for punishing them in any way.

This shows that by the time of this second debate, tensions had abated between the two formerly rival groups. The Sunnis on the one hand, though suspicious of Mahdawi doctrines, did not openly accuse them of infidelity, ignorance and rebellion as they had before. The Mahdawis on the other hand had learned to check their claims to absolute moral leadership of the whole Muslim *ummah*, in the interest of building up viable and vibrant regional communities in which to practice their religious convictions.

After noting the content of the debates and the social background which called them into being, one must look carefully at the genre of debate literature itself. These texts are not simply the records of a debate that happened; rather, recording them is a strategy for the community to protect itself in further debates in the future. Arguments and illustrations from early debate texts are reused in later debates and are refined for new audiences. By writing and reading these debate texts, scholars in the Mahdawi community prepared themselves to defend their community against subsequent accusations or potential persecution. In *Mubahisah-yi-Alamgiri,* the judge complained to Shaykh Ibrahim that the Shaykh always had the upper hand in debating, for he had studied the controversial points and had already memorized useful quotes, traditions and examples. Shaykh Ibrahim replied that debating was his job, and that he naturally studied in advance all the possible accusations and their appropriate rebuttals, as well as combing earlier scholarly works for points to support his argument. These debate texts are not only evidence of this scholarly preparation for community defense, but are also a primary tool to achieve such preparation. The fact that Mahdawis have been constantly challenged to debate and dispute, usually under the implicit or explicit threat of persecution, explains why this genre of debate literature features so prominently in the body of extant Mahdawi literature.

It is said that history is always written by the winner. Debate texts as a genre are even more complicated than historical texts. Debate texts are always written by those who portray themselves as the winner, whereas in any actual debate it may be very hard to decide who had actually won. It should not be surprising, then, that in both of these debate records, the Mahdawi scholar appear to score a clear victory. In the case of Shaykh Mustafa, he shames the court scholars into an awkward silence, while in the case of Shaykh Ibrahim, he wins from the inquisition judge the admission that Mahd'awis are stalwart members of the *Ahl-i Sunat o Jama'at* community.

Debate texts as a genre are also always written in the form of a dialogue,/each side giving its question, answer and counter-question in the form of an argument. In a debate, answers have to not only be right, but they have to be quick and sharp as well. This gives the debate text an immediacy and drama which a scholarly tract lacks. To highlight this feature, *Mubahisah-yi Alamgiri* has been translated with all the grammatical framework of a dialogue, including quotation marks which the original Persian does not feature. However, this style of writing the debate in the form of a dialogue should not mislead the reader into assuming that the debate text records the dialogue as it actually happened, word for word. Rather, the dialogue was most likely reconstructed by the writer from memory, after the actual event had already passed. In the case of *Majalis-i Khamsah*, Mustafa Gujarati was a prisoner in chains during the course of the debates, and was most likely physically unable to write the content of his debates during or immediately after the event. He most likely composed the debate records after his release from the court, while preparing to travel back to Gujarat. Yet at least in the case of *Majalis-i Khamsah*, the writer of the debate text was also the primary debater, and this accounts for the vividness of his account and the dramatic tone of his record.

The case of composition of *Mubahisah-yi Alamgiri* is even more complicated. The writer of the text, Abu al-Qasim, is not one of the primary debaters. Furthermore, the writer may not have been directly present during the debates as a witness to what was actually said. Abu al-Qasim notes that he accompanied Shaykh Ibrahim along with other Mahdawi leaders to the official court building in the town of Ahmadnagar; however, he then says that only Shaykh Ibrahim and Shaykh A'zam entered into the judge's private chamber where the debate ensued. It may be possible that the other Mahdawi leaders (including the writer) could have overheard the debate inside, but most likely they learned of the content of the debate after the actual event as Shaykh Ibrahim recreated the dialogue verbally for his companions who had not been present[4]. This should not cause the reader to dismiss this debate text as inauthentic, for all debate texts depict only one side of the argument in an idealized manner. Rather the reader should simply bear in mind that the distance between the writer and the events that he "records" accounts for lack of vivid conflict in the record itself Shakh Ibrahim is portrayed as giving long lectures in place of an answer for each question. Whereas in reality he was most likely interrupted and challenged more frequently. These elements of dialogue have been erased from the form of the debate which was finally recorded and passed down within the Mahdawi community.

This hypothesis is substantiated by the fact that the writer, Abu al-Qasim reports the discussion of the judge with the Emperor Aurangzeb as a verbal dialogue, whereas he could not have possibly overheard this dialogue that happened in the Emperor's court after the Mahdawi leaders had been released to return to their lodging.

The translator has tried to render the text of this debate in clear, modern English from the Persian text of the original that had been published by the Markazi Anjuman-e-Mahdavia in Chanchalguda, Hyderabad in 1994. The Persian text had been published face to face with an Urdu translation; however, this English translation makes no reference to the Urdu and derives directly from the Persian. (WITH COURTESY FROM kHALIFATULLAH.COM)

With courtesy from "KHALIFATULLAHILMEHDI.COM"

*　*　*

—

8. ZIKRI MAHDAVI OF PAKISTAN:

Before partition a few knew the word Ziikri Mahdavi who are living mostly in Makran, Baluchistan and Karachi., it was Hazrat Mashaeq Moulana Syed Murtuza Saheb of Gujrat, known as Hyderabdi, since he settled down at Hyderabad, after leaving Channapatna as a Reformer, he then established "Masjid-e-Shamsia" at Khalla of Chanchalguda, Hyderabad, India, some where in 1930s. When the air was thick about the creation of Pakistan in 1940s, he pragmatically planned to migrate to Sindh in 1945 or so and settled down at Hyderabad(Sindh) and established a Dairah at Shadadpur, where he constructed a Masjid and started preaching Mahdaviath. Meanwhile he had the opportunity to read some literature on

Mahdaviat, and luckily he came to know about these Zikri Mahdvis who are predominantly residing in Makran, Qallat, Kharan, Las Bela and many hilly villages of Baluchistan, and their educated elites live in Karachi also. With much curiosity Moulana found out some such learned ones of the Zikri Mahdvis from them he tried to understand their beliefs about Imamana (As) and the basic facts about being called Zikri.

In this venture, Moulana's younger son Syed Shahabuddin Yadullahi, took utmost interest and not only he discussed these issues with the Zikri scholars, and gone through their literature, but he personally visited their places and lived among them for months and learned their way of practicing Mahdavi basics and their social, cultural and economic way of living. He happened to come to Hyderabad(India). Since I came to know about the Zikri Mahdavis who are living in Pakistan I visited him at his residence for the purpose of getting first hand information about them. Very kindly he gave me some literature about the Zikris and narrated to me his experience while living with them at their remote places.

In order to introduce and familiarize with them, I am jetting down some facts about them for information of the readers.

A majority of the adherents of the Zikri sect live in Makran, Qallat, Kharan,. Las bela. But they are also found in Mashkai, Jhalan and Karachi. In the last decade of the 19th. Century, they extended their influence in to Lasbela, where a good many of the Converts are to be found chiefly along the Baluchistan's ocean side, particularly in the vicinity of Gawader Seaport. This religious minority, mostly comprising Baluchis, consisting of Sajadis, Barohi, Baladi, Hasani, zardaris and Bazanji clans who, are little known people in a setting of Islamic Orthodoxy living in the regions of Baluchistan, along the Iranian border and in the cosmopolitan Karachi and its adjoining localities.

It is a general belief that they are the Followers of Hazrat Syed Mohmmed Juanpuri(As), "Mahdi-e-Aakhiruzzaman" whom they believe that for a considerable long time he stayed at a hillock, known as "Koh-e-Murad", and prolaimed and propagated his Doctrine. it was a common belief that a mere look at Hzt. Syed Mohmmed(As) was enough to convert one to the Mahdavi Fold. Thus a majority of them, mass converted to Mahdavi Faith.

(Vide, Stephen and Pastner's "Aspects of Religion in Southern Baluchistan Anthropoloca 1972").

His techings and his way of life became a constant danger to the worldly Ulemas, and being unable to defeat him in theologicl discussions, they sought to have recourse to persecution. They tried to evict him from their jurisdiction by poisoning the ears of the authorities, and made him to leave to Khurasan. Then Imamana(As) went to Afghanistan after crossing the hilly ranges of Baluchistan and reached Qandhar and from there he went to Farah in the Helmond Valley of Afghanistan, situated about a distance of 180 miles from Qandhar, and just 20 miles from Iranian Border on the West, where he passed away after staying there for 29 months on 19th. Zeeqaieda,910 H/1505 Ad, was burried at Farah. His Mausoleum is regarded as a venerable place where people visit with devotion and offer their homage.

Makran is an arid track of a desert and mountainous region, comprising about 23000 Sq.miles with a Zikri population of about more than ten lakhs, a distinct minority, bounded on the south by the Arabian Sea, on the East by the rugged peaks of the Jhalwan Region. (Vide Baluchistan Gazetteer Series, Bombay 1970).

Makrani Zikris believe that Hzt. Syed Mohammed(As) whom they call "Muradullah" after visiting Makkah and Madinah, came to Laristan from Iran to Keech (now Makran) and settled down on a mountain top, known as "Koh-e-Murad" for some years, where he preached his Doctrine of Mahdaviat and converted the whole population of that region.

It is a well known fact, and also certified by the contemporary Historians that Hzt. Syed Mohammed(As) was the first person after centuries to launch a Puritan Movement in India, and particularly in Makran which had no political nuances behind it. The movement for moral and social reforms was the first expression of religious thought as an active and assertive social and predominently a religious force in the Indian Muslim Society. It was launched with a single aim of presenting the Faith in its original form, as practiced by the Holy Prophet(Slm) to the masses in all its purity.

(Vide Mushtaq A. Kayani's Essay, published in the Pakistan Times, Rawalpindi, May 26, 1968)

According to another legend it is said that the missionary work in that area was done by one or two Indian Mahdavi Preachers; and in all probability it was Miyan Abdullah Khan Niyazi(Rh), after Imamana(As), who after converting as Mahdavi, resided at that place for a long time, which resulted in mass conversion of the Baluch Tribes to the Mahdavi Faith. It is said that after leaving Biyana, the Khan went on traveling to many places then arrived Afghanistan somewhere about 1549, then arrived Makran and started preaching the Mahdavia Faith and mass conversion took place on his hands. Then he settled down in Sar-e-Hind (Vide Baluchistan Gazetteer Series Vol:vii, page 116.)

Yet another legend speaks that Bu Said, founder of the Buledai Rule in Makran, helped the spread of Zikri Faith with full enthusiasm. According to the local traditions, the Zikri Faith came up simultaneously with the Buledais. The founder of the Buledais Dynasty came from Germsel of the valley of Hilmond, which is close to Farah. He was contemporary of Hzt. Syed Mohammned Juanpuri(As) of Farah, with whom Bu Said came into contact with the Syed (As) and converted to the Mahdavia Belief on Hzt. Syed Mohammed's hands. Then Bu Said migrated to Makran and established his rule in the first quarter of 15th. Century. Thus the Buledais are the first Zikri Rulers of Makran who dominated most parts of Baluchistan where the Zikri Faith struck roots and flourished and prospered.

(Vide Henry Field's "An Anthropolical Reconnaissance in West Pakistan, Cambridge, USA, in 1959).

According to the Zikri Faith, Imamana(As) raised the system of "Perpetual Zikr" to the status of an obligation and made it one of the foremost duties upon the followers to repeat the name of Allah with devotion and complete absorption. He was against any worldly act during the Zikr performance. Anything likely to interfere with Zikr was prohibited. As reported earlier, Shaik Abdullah Khan Niyazi(Rh) brought the light of the Faith to Baluchistan. Afterwards his followers laid excessive stress on Zikr. They abandoned other tenets preached by Imamana(As) and exaggerated by sticking to Zikr only. On that score they came to be called Zikris.

Apart from Moulana Syed Murtuza and his son and followers, Mahdavis living in Pakistan have direct contact with these Zikris and they are slowly, but steadily, trying to mingle with them by regularly preaching among them the real tenets of Mahdavi Faith, in which Perpetual Zikr has its own dominating position. They have established "Pakistan Zikri (Mahdavi) Anjuman, and through this Forum they have close contact in order to bring the Zikris into the mainstream of Mahdavis and also in order to safeguarding the rights of the long neglected Zikris of Makran. This Organization is busy in publishing literature and using other means to acquaint these people with the social, economic and political conditions of the Zikris. They have been trying through mass media to enlighten them about the different aspects of Mahdavi Faith.

In 1995, this organization arranged for a "two day Seminar" on "Kalhouda Dynasty" of Sindh, under the chairmanship of Mr. Yaqoob Ali Zardari. Many important leaders like the then President Farooq Ali Khan Laghari, Begum Be Nazeer Bhatto, Prime Minister, Mir Asif Ali Zardari,(Present President of Pakistan) and many more ministers and elites sent their well wishes for conducting the "Sminar" on the Kalhouda Rulers of Sindh" (The Mahdavi Rulers, who ruled Sindh about a century and propagated "Mianwali Movement" as prescribed by Imamana(As) for the "Green Revolution in Sindh" prescribing agriculture reforms). A town by name "Mianwali" is located in southerrn Punjab whose MNA is Mr. Imran Khan the fomous creckiteer—turned politician of Pakistan.

Religious practices of the zikris:

From the literature available, particularly the Biography "Safer Nama-e-Mahdi(As)", their religious practices consists 1. **Zikr, and 2. Kishti**.

Zikr consists of daily prayers at six fixed intervals. Zikr consists, Zikr-e-Jali and Zikr-e-Khafi. Each zikr consists of 10 to 12 lines. Zikris do not have their mosques, but the place where they practice Zikr is known as Zkikrkhana where they perform both Rukoo and Sajda. Zikris form two rows facing each other and repeat the following: When first Row states, the second Row answers:

First Row	Second Row
La Ilaha Illallah (There is no god)	Illallah (But Allah)
Hasbi Rabbi (Allah is enough to help me)	Jallalah (Allah is Great)

Ma Fil Qalbi (I renounce every thing)   Ghair Allah (Except Allah)

Hadi (who is my Leader)   Mahdi (the leader is Mahdi)

This zikr is repeated six times at intervals:

1. **Zikr—La ilaha Illulllah (Zikr-e-Khafi)** is repeated 13 times before dawn.
2. **Zikr-e-Jali** at early dawn spoken loudly. The words are: "Subhan Allah Yarju" while going in Sajda. Then repeat above Zikr, after sun rises, another sajda is performed
3. **Mid Day Zikr-e-Jali** with the words mentioned above, without prostration.
4. **Zikr, a little before the sun set**. It is Zikr-e-Khafi as mentioned in Item 2 above, with prostration.
5. **After sun set, Zikr-e-Jali**, as mentioned in item 1 above loudly.
6. **Mid Night Zikr-e-Khafi**, repeated by individuals 1000 times, and at each 100, they go in prostration.

They read Qur'an. They have firm belief on the Holy Prophet (Slm) as the Last of the Prophets. but have some differences in other tenets. As regards, Kalema, they urge:

"La ilaha Illullahu noor-e-pak, noor-e-Mohammed, Mahdi Muradullah".

They have the faith that the Holy Prophet was "Saheb-e-Qur'an". His Mission was to preach and spread the Doctrine of Qur'an, literally only, while Mahdi(As) was the "Saheb-e-Taveel-e-Qur'an". Therefore Mahdi's interpretation and elucidation of Qur'an is final and binding on all.

They avoid performing five times Prayers, instead they practice Zikr-e-Jali and Zikr-e-Khafi as mentioned above six times a day.

They do not pay Zakat, but they honestly pay Ushr, 10% of their income as ordained by Imamana(As).

They believe in "Renunciation" of the Worldly life and Hijrat as an obligation.

2. Kishti: This is another form of Worship, performed at special occasions, like: Birthday, Marriage, Circumcision and other religious or social functions. Particularly on all Friday nights and every 14th. of the month(Since Imamana was born on 14th. Jamadiul Awwal), as well as ten nights of the month of Zilhajja, every year. It is performed at Zikrkhana building. Fire is lit in the middle surrounded by both men and women in a circle. No drums or musical instruments are used. A sweat throated lady stands in the middle and sings the praises for Mahdi(As), while others repeat in chorus. The singer often changes from song to song accompanied by men. When the singer states the word "Hadiya", the men answer "Gul Mahdia". The whole gathering starts dancing till ecstasy enveloped upon them.

3. CHAUGAN

This is also a social gathering, particularly at wedding ceremonies which continues for many nights. Those verses recited at **Kishti**, the same are recited in front of Zikrkhana Building. This is a folk dance of the Baluchis in which both men and women take part as a recreation under the moonlight. They sing songs praising Allah and Mahdi(As).

KOH-E-MURAD

It is located some two miles away from Turbat., the capital city of Makran. It is called "The House of Mahdi(As)". It is just like a place of worship as Mecca to them. Therefore they perform pilgrimage to Koh-e-Murad, once as year. Baluchis all over Makran and other places come at the end of Ramazan to perform 27th. night of the "Lailatul Qadr" in congregation.

The primary holy area consists of a large plateau about one and half mile on one side. The entire area is surrounded by a low wall of loose stones. Zikris remove their shoes before they enter this environ. The central hillock is 60 to 70 feet high, whose upper part is cup-shaped, with a deep hollow in the center. It is said that Imamana(As) while going to Afghanistan, stayed on this hill top for some time and preached his Mission here. Apart from Imamana(As), in the later period his descendant preachers stayed at that hill and preached the Mahdavi Doctrine for a longer time. Thus they believe that Prophet Moosa emerged from the Mountain of Sina, prophet Eisa came from the mountain Sayeer, while the Holy Prophet came from mountain of Faaraan (Jabal-e-Noor) our Mahdi(As) came from Koh-e-Murad of Makran. Therefore they regard Koh-e-Murad as a place for pilgrimage like Makkah. Thus they come from far off places, by travelling long journeys, and even by bare footed, they visit as a holy place. They respect their leader like a holy Man, to whom they offer devotion and accept his verdicts as a Farman.

They are also known as "Dair-e-Waley", because, for performing Lailatul Qadr, they erect a circle of stones (Dairah), within which they perform their rituals of the Lailatul Qadr whole night, praising Allah and Mahdi(As) in chorus and perform folk dance.

But on account of spread of education among the Zikris, some differences have emerged among the educated generation. The new generation does not give much respect to Koh-e-Murad as Makkah. However they devotedly join the prayers of Shab-e-Mairaj, Shab-e-Barat, Lailatul Qadr and two Id Prayers regularly.

In view of their differences regarding religious rituals, they were subjected to persecution by the Sunni Muslims. Particularly the Nawab of Qallat and his courtiers have many a time persecuted and harassed them. It happened, particularly on Lailatul Qadr. The army of Qallat attacked and killed many Zikris. They are segregated as non muslims and are being treated even as Kafir by the Sunnis.

(Vide: 1.R. Hughes Buller's thesis published in Baluchistan Gazetteer, Vol. VII, 1937 AD
2.G.P. Tsate's Memoir on the country and family of Nawab of Qallat.'
3. Pir Bakhsh Qamber Shah-dad-zai's "Zikr-e-Wahdat wa Ibadaat of Shuh'dai Jakigore (Karachi 1937)

FAQEER SsYED sHARIEF kHUNDMIRI

*   *   *

—

9. MAHDAVI KALHOURA DYNASTY OF SINDH

'*Kalhora*' Claims to be the First Pir (Spiritual Leader) of Sindh.

Masjid Khudabad Kalhoro, Interior Sight

After the death of Ibrahim Khan, Kalhora family distinguished for centuries, none of his descendants rose to be of importance, except Amir Adam Shah Kalhoro, who was 7th of his descendant. Who rose to occupy the holy seat vacated by the celebrated saint (Amir Chenai Khan Abbasi) of the time, Amir Adam Shah Kalhoro started his career from small village with the support of the Abro who remained a powerful force behind him. Sardar Khabar Abro was the first person to embrace Mahdaviat, who enrolled Amir Adam Shah as his follower, who was a pious and staunch Mahdavi. Miyan Adam Shah, after the demise of Imamana(As) settled down in a small village which became the centre for learning for the Mehdvis.

Masjid Khudabad Kalhoro, Interior Sight

At that time Nawáb Khán Khánán having come to pay respects to Amir Ádam Sháh and to ask his blessings, at the request of Wadera Kabar abro, granted to him the zamindarí of Chándúkah,. After some time Ádam Sháh went over to Multán, to pay a visit to Lál l'san the celebrated living saint of the time, and a descendent of Shekh Baháuddín Multání. A large number of disciples joined him here and he was obliged to occupy a spacious tract of country. This excited the jealousy of the landowners of the place, at whose instigation the ruler of Multán had him killed and thus he became a martyr.

Later on, his descendant visited many area of Sindh, many people joined them gradually. Thus Kalhoras arose and flourished in Sindh for over many centuries as Mahdavi Religious and Political leaders. Many Communities of Sindh Enrolled as their followers Abro, Bhatti, Jokhiyo, Junejo, Sial, Sahta, Rajputs, Kalwar, Jatoi, Khosa, Chandio, Leghari, Talpurs, and many others.

In History, it is reported that in the battle of Halani Majority of Balouchs stood against their Murshid, the Two Followers never go astray to them and remained Loyal till their Death, those were Jatoi And Khosa Tribesmen who Fight at their last gasp in the Battle of Halani.

The Mehrabpur City in Khairpur District is stil on the name of Abbasi Army's Soldier Mehrab Khan Jatoi, who fought for the dignity of his Spiritual Mahdavi Leaders and thus became martyr.

After the end of Abbasi Dynasty in Sindh, Abbasi's take their loyal Army with themselves and settled in Khanpur and Shikarpur. So even uptil now the Chief Sardar of Abbasi Tribe and Jatoi Tribe live together and enjoy great relationship with each other.

The Kalhora Dynasty succumbed to King Nader Shah who invaded India in 1739 AD. One of the most famous Nawab Kalhora was Mian Ghulam Shah Kalhoro. He is known to have assisted Ahmad Shah Durrani against the Hindu Marathas during the Third Battle of Panipat in order to restore Mughal prestige. Ghulam Shah commanded a large army and fought against the Rao of Kuchh, an ally of the Maratha and an adversary of Sindh in the Thar Desert in the year 1762.

The kalhora Dynasty declined later when Mian Abdul Nabi lost control of Sindh in 1783 and was defeated by his own disciples Talpur Amirs in the Battle of Halani. Mian Abdul Nabi Kalhoro was the last Kalhoro Nawab.

The Kalhoro period is most important for the development of Sindhi literature, arts, crafts and irrigation. During Kalhora rule several wah (canals) were dug in every part of Sindh to irrigate the uncultivated land.

Main Adam Shah Kalhoro	
Sultan And Saint of Sindh and the other Parts of Todays Pakistan	
Reign	Kalhora Dynasty
House	Royal House of Abbasid

Mian Ilyas Muhammad Kalhoro brought new agricultural lands in his custody and increased disciple's number. He died in 1620 in a small village of Mujawar in taluka Dokri District Larkana. After the death of Mian Ilyas Muhammad Kalhoro all disciples made Mian Shahal Muhammad Kalhoro as their new spiritual guide and who became governor of the area.

Mian Shahul Muhammad Kalhoro took over the lands of Abro and Sangi tribes and in retaliation he was killed in the uprising initiated by Nawab Sheikh Ahmed Bakhri in 1657.

Mian Nasir Muhammad Kalhoro (1657-1692)

After the martyrdom of Mian Shahal Muhammad Kalhoro by Mughals, Mian Nasir Muhammad Kalhoro succeeded the governorship in 1657 A.D. He acquired more celebrity for piety and virtue than any of his predecessors, and therefore was envied by most of the people of his time. Accordingly the natives of the place came and incited the Mughals of Bakhar Sarkar (Northern Sindh) to harass and trouble him. Mian Nasir Muhammad Kalhoro was therefore obliged to leave the place and go to a sandy desert near Shahdadkot.

Mian Noor Muhammed Kalhoro With Mian Muradyad Kalhoro

Mian Nasir Muhammad Kalhoro lived much time in Punjab in this way. After some days of hardship and want, he left Larkana and settled in the plains of Kachho where he established his capital. Seeing this Mír Panhwar, the chief of the Panhwars, taking an army from the Governor of Bakhar, commanded among other leaders by Mirza Khan Pini, the Governor of Siwi came and fought with Mian Nasir Muhammad Kalhoro, but soon a truce was made and Mian Nasir Muhammad Kalhoro was sent to the Emperor Aurangzeb, who kept him in confinement at Gawaliyar for some time. During this period, fighting went on with the Mian's followers, until Mian Nasir Muhammad Kalhoro managed to escape and returned to his native place with the help of Amir Muhammad Bahadur Khan Daudpota of Shikarpur who did his arrangements in Chanduka Parguna.

Mian Nasir Muhammad Kalhoro spearheaded the Mianwali Movement from 1657 to 1692 A.D, leaving behind a legacy in the form of the shrines of his disciples. The leaders of Mianwali Movement struggled against the foreign rule of the Mughals and eventually succeeded in overpowering them. After a successful reign of 35 years in 1692 A.D Mian Nasir Muhammad Kalhoro died and was buried in Gaarhi near Kakar taluka Khairpur Nathan Shah, District Dadu Sindh.

Mian Din Muhammad Kalhoro(1692-1699)

Mian Nasir Muhammad Kalhoro was succeeded by Mian Din Muhammad Kalhoro in 1692. He rose to become the leader of Mianwali Faqirs and subsequently, led the movement wisely. The Kalhoras had already become strong under the leadership of Mian Nasir Muhammad Kalhoro and brought many areas under their rule. Mian Din Muhammad Kalhoro continued the mission of his father and gained great popularity, which constantly irritated the Mughal Governor of Bakhar. They had become politically strong and captured more areas where they then established their rule. The rising power of the Kalhoras was not acceptable to the Mughals and their loyalists. The Mughals and their supporters were scared of the rising power of Mian Din Muhammad Kalhoro and his movement in Chandukaka Parguna of Bakhar sarkar (Northern Sindh).

A fierce battle was fought on 1699 A.D in which a number of soldiers from both sides lost their lives. The Kalhoras completely routed the Mughals in that battle emerging as a formidable force. Amir Sheikh Jehan lost his life and Allah Yar Khan fled from battlefield. When the Mughal Prince Muizuddin heard the news of the defeat of his governor Allah Yar Khan, and the death of his military officer, Sheikh Jehan by the Kalhora army he marched from Lahore to Sindh to retaliate. Mian Din Muhammad Kalhoro deemed it wise to send his brother Mir Muhammad Kalhoro, and two advisors Qasim and Khaman to prince Muizuddin at Bakhar to submit. They appeared before the prince and convinced him with their intellect. After the submission of the Kalhoras, he returned to Lahore. The prince was on his way to Lahore when the news of looting and ransacking of villages by Mianwali Faqirs reached him. He set out for Sindh again in a flash and ordered his army to attack on Sindhi villages. Mian Din Muhammad Kalhoro kept mum over the plundering of villages by the prince. A fierce battle was fought on the banks of Nai Gaj in <u>Dadu District</u>. However he asked for clemency and presented himself before the prince who took him to Multan, where, subsequently he was murdered. The dead body of Mian Din Muhammad Kalhoro was buried in Sindh. After this incident Mian Yar Muhammad Kalhoro, along with his followers went to <u>Kalat</u> for a refuge. On his entry there he was resisted by the <u>Brohis</u>. During this exile he was compelled to live on Khirthar Range on Mian Gun Peak, which was later named after him. After passing a year Mian <u>Yar Muhammad Kalhoro</u> returned back to Sindh in 1701.

Muhammad Muradyab Khan Kalhoro (Nawab Sarbuland Khan) (<u>urdu</u>) (محمدمرادياب خان كلهورو والعمروف باون سربلندخان), was the <u>Subedar</u> of <u>Sindh</u> appointed by <u>Mughal Emperor Muhammad Shah</u>, and was given the imperial title *Sarbuland Khan*.

On receiving the news of Mián Núr Muhammad's death, the king, who had again been influenced by the slanders of some malicious people of his court, named Ismáíl Khán Piní to be his agent in Sind, and the latter had already proceeded as far as Muhammadábád, and had sent off a few men under Sayyed Sháh Muhammad to Tattá, and others towards the sandy desert, where they pillaged the villages of Thár and Hingórjah. Soon after the arrival of lsmáíl Khán's men, one Sálih Khán came to Tattá on behalf of the late administrator Gul Muhammad Khán Khurásání to collect the revenue demands. But just before that the king's ambassador Muhammad Beg Shámalí had come to Tattá and appointed Áká Muhammad Sálih as the agent in charge of Tattá and taking some nobles of the place had started for the royal camp. Sálih Khán's men would not allow Áká Muhammad Sálih to carry on the State duties. When Muhammad Beg Shámlú, who on receiving orders to that effect had sent back the nobles, arrived at the camp, he was blamed for not making a good selection for the collection of revenue at Tattá. A fresh order was therefore issued appointing Kází Muhammad Mahfúz to the post. Again the nobles were required to pay respects to the king at his camp.

Muhammad Murádyáb Khán appointed to be the ruler with the title of Nawáb Sarbuland Khan.

While the Kázi's eldest son was quarrelling with Sálih Khán as to who should collect the revenue and other Government dues, information was received that the king had appointed Muhammad Murádyáb Khán to be the ruler of Sind with the title of "Nawáb Sarbuland Khán." It would appear that all this time the late Mián's envoy Díwán Gidúmal had been at work in the court of the king and had now succeeded in securing the king's good will, as the chiefs and nobles had paid allegiance to the king and Muhammad Atur Khán had been given up as a hostage. So the nobles went direct to Umarkót to meet their new ruler, who on receiving the honour now marched to his capital. Shekh Zafarulláh was appointed to be the administrator of Tattá and once more there was peace and order at that place.

Muhammad Murád dethroned and Mián Ghulám Sháh elected.

Mustering strong among themselves on the night preceding 13th Zí-Hajj, 1170 A.H. (1757 A. D.) the Sirái nobles besieged the Mián's residence and took him and his favourite chiefs prisoners. The next morning his brother Mián Ghulám Sháh was placed on the throne. He tried his best to please the nobility as well as the common people, who had been much oppressed by Muhammad Murád.*

The town of Alahábád founded, and the revolt of Muhammad Murád's brother Ahmadyár Khán.

Soon after the Áshúrah (the 10th of Muharram) of the new year, that accursed town was surrounded by the floods of the river, so that Mián Ghulám Sháh deserted it and built another city near his father's Muhammadábád and called it Alahábád. All the chiefs and nobles recognized him as their ruler and paid homage to him, except Ahmadyár Khán, brother by the same mother to Muhammad Murádyáb, who was then at Khudábád, and Maksúdah Fakír, son of Bahár Sháh, who at first left his father's side with the intention of adhering to Mián Ghulám Sháh's cause, and subsequently came and entered the Mián's service, apparently to avoid unpleasant results.

The Mián's other brother Atur Khán appointed as ruler by the royal decree.

Meanwhile Atur Khán, who was a hostage with the king, represented his case in person very strongly and succeeded in having the order of rulership passed in his own name. Hearing this, Ahmadyár Khán began to collect forces. The Siraí chiefs now repented of what they had done and knowing that Atur Khán had been duly appointed as a ruler by royal decree, thought it prudent to submit to him. Mián Ghulám Sháh therefore had no other alternative but to move with his whole army to the sandy desert on 25th of Saffar of the same year. After he had travelled a few stages, Maksúdah Fakír having received letters from Atur Khán to that effect, set Muhammad Murádyáb at liberty, and deserting Miáu Ghulám Sháh's cause, and taking some Siraí chiefs with him started to meet the newly appointed ruler, while Mián Ghulám Sháh with Rájah Líkhí, a few other friendly chiefs and a selected band of soldiers hastened away to a distance.

Ghulam Shah Kalhoro	
Shah Wardi Khan	

ميان غلام شاه كلهوڙو

Reign	1757-1772
Birthplace	Kalhora Dynasty
Died	1772
Place of death	Hyderabad, Sindh, Pakistan
Buried	Hyderabad
Predecessor	Noor Mohammad Kalhoro
Dynasty	Kalhora Dynasty
Father	Noor Mohammad Kalhoro
Mother	Mai Gullan

Dr. Lakho's comments on Mian Naseer Muhammad are correct, when he considers him as first Kalhora ruler starting from 1681 AD. His views cannot be questioned as the last half of seventeenth century was the climax of worst drought from 1550-1850 AD. And Mughals had only one fifth land revenues in 1665 compared to 1600 AD. At that time there were anti government rebellions all over India. Mian Naseer's, strategy was to take over land of loyalist tribes, who paid taxes to Mughals, and occupied present Larkana district, Mehar and Khairpur Nathan Shah Talukas as author has detailed. It was a clever strategy, as contours of the area are such that it can easily be irrigated, even when river level was low. No other area of Sindh had this advantage, before opening of barrages from 1932 to 1962. In support of the weakening of Mughal power and native rebellions, Dr. Lakho has correctly quoted the case of civil resistance of Khattak and Yousif Zai tribes of Kabul, Hassan Abdal and Peshawar, of Marathas in South India, of Hindus all of India and of Sikhs in the Punjab. Aurangzeb in his own letters as governor of Multan to his father Shah Jehan, described rebellions in terms of Sindh's affairs. Dr. Lakho mentions about execution of Guru Tegh Bahadur at the orders of Aurangzeb, unsuccessful invasion of Shia Kingdom of Bijapur, shivajis coronating himself as Shahanshah and on his death Sambhoji's becoming king of kings, and finally the rebellion of Aurangzeb's son Akbar-II against his father. Interesting story is that Aurangzeb's famous daughter, a poet in her own right, Zaibun Nisa, was the informant of her brother Akber-II, and Aurangzeb had sent her to Gawaliar fort vitrually as a prisoner for the rest of her life. All such setbacks compelled Aurangzeb to release Mian Naseer Muhammad conditionally from jail, some five years (1675-1680/81) after his arrest. He is right in his arguments that Mian Naseer Muhammad did not escape the prison, but was released conditionally.

Author has quoted a rare collection of letter and materials by Riazul Islam "A Calendar of documents on Indo-Persian Relations" which gives conditions of acceptance of Yar Muhammad Kalhoro as ruler of Sindh, showing Mughal's weakness against safavids of Iran and Kalhoras help to watch the borders, as well as Iranian activities, hitherto not properly projected by historian of Sindh. The same documents also show that Nadir Shah wanted to liquidate Noor Muhammad Kalhoro by suggesting to Mughal emperor Muhammad Shah fort his murder.

Author has successfully described a series of capitals of Kalhoras from 1681 to 1722 AD. Abandoning of Khudabad is actually connected with change of the course of the branch of the river passing west of the Khudabad near Phaka around 1749 AD. It is known that in that century, 1740 AD, was the hottest year and 1760 AD., the coldest. These frequent cold years intercepted by warm years, causing changes in discharge of water in the river Indus. From 1754-1760 AD, due to these fluctuations, the river Indus started hydrological changes in its course. Even when it started flowing along the present alignment of it between Hyderabad and Kotri to Keti Bander and Shah Bander, it changed its courses every year in different lengths to stabilize and to fix final coruse, which process can take one or two decades. It is because of this that construction of new canal had to wait for 12-15 years and the first major canal was Sarfraz Wah constructed between 1772-1775 AD. The river took long to stabilize, and almost year after year changes in its course made Kalhoras to change sites of their capitals. Thus these were not true capitals but camp sites. The issue is controversial, but the author has successfully enumerated them chronologically. On the other hand he claimed that Hyderabad fort was constructed in 2 months in 1768 AD., is clarified by the author, that it look much longer and was occupied only in the last years of Ghulam shah Kalhoro. This investigation of the author breaks this myth. There is another myth that Rani Kot fort was constructed by Mir Sher Muhammad or Nawab Wali Muhammad Leghari, almost overnight and Saiful Maluk had changed course of the river Indus in the darkness of one night or a first barrage across the Indus was constructed by Barmaki the governor of Sindh at Sukkur or the Persian wheel existed during Mohenjo Daro times, whereas History says it was invented 2000 years later by the Greek.

He also throws new light on Muradyab's intention to abdicate and settle in Musqat as he had married a daughter of Imam of Masqat. The author has detailed wars of succession of Kalhoras after death of Noor Muhammad Kalhoro and Jagirdars playing role of king makers, creating chaotic situation for five years, but these five years also saw hydrological changes in the old course of the river from north of Hala to Kadhan and Lowari and Jagirdars' lands were being deserted and they had to get new lands and thus sided with those who could deliver them the best advantages of new settlements. The divided loyalties of Jagirdars are fully described and looking to these incidents of 1754-1759 AD. One can judge what could become the shape of things from 1754-1759 AD, one can judge the emerging shape of things from 1775-1783 AD, which too he has detailed.

The author has also described Ghulam Shah's putting a Bund across eastern Puran to deprive Lakhpat in Kutch of irrigation water, based on report of Dr. James Burnes. The statement is correct, but reason for doing so was not vengeance as stated by Burnes, against Kutchis. The fact is that with change of course of river Indus and eastern Nara or Hakra not getting spill water from the river Indus and Sutlej during a few weeks of inundation in seventeenth and eighteenth centuries, there was limited water in western Puran fed by Phulleli canal after 1758 AD, and Ghulam Shah had to stop whatever little water was flowing in the Puran to irrigate land of Sindh. Thus it was no vengeance. Almost every author including Dr. Lakho seems to have accepted Hyderabad as old Nerunkot, but with establishment of Hyderabad and its expansion since early British days, no pottery or artifacts or ruins of any kind have been located. This needs future research.

Author has detailed about the fall of Kalhoras, and also settled the borders, administrative st up and divisions for the purpose of administration. An interesting part is that for nearly a century 1657-1750 AD, concentration of Kalhora cities and settlements is in upper Dadu and Larkana districts and after 1750 AD. On the left bank but in Central Sindh. Author describes this in the capitals of Kalhora. He has also listed 60 administrative units. They also correspond nearly though not exactly with the present Talukas of Sindh and it seems Kalhora administrative divisions were inherited by the British in 1843 AD, and there is very little change in them. The administrative hierarchy is detailed. It seems, it was the copy of Mughal system with similar advantages and disadvantages, though Kalhoras made many changes in the system. An interesting observation is that the total financial system was in the hands of nationals, the Sindhi Hindu accountants and tax collectors, this monopoly continued upto early British rule. Author mentions that Hindus occupied special position since Mian Adam Shah's days. It is to be realized that syllabus used in the Madersahs included Persian and Arabic literary texts, while syllabus of Hindu schools included many subjects separately for Brahmans (priests), Khatris (princes and army), Vaishas (businessmen) and Sudras (working class). Vaishas had to learn mathematics, due to this Sindhi accountants were well known for their work under Abbasids Caliphate. Taxation system is also detailed. Foreign relations with Kalat, Bahawalpur, Multan, Jodhpur, Jaisalmir, Kutch, Delhi, Afghanistan, Muscat, East India Company and Dutch are discussed in details.

The economic conditions depended on primary industry like agriculture, animal husbandry and fisheries. Minor industries also existed specially textiles, cotton goods, indigo, salt petre etc. Agriculture was supported by irrigation. Kalhoras created Jagirdars, who ultimately developed estranged relation with those, who thus allotted them the land. This state of things has been repeated in history every where and Sindh Jagirdars were no exception. Author has listed field crops as well as horticultural crops. The industrial centres too are listed. Trade articles, trade routes, sea and inland ports are mentioned along with articles of import and export. In terms of coins and currency, author mentions that during the period under study, coins were minted in Hyderabad, Thatta, Bakhar and Shikarpur.

Author lists tribes, castes, indigenous Sindhi and Balouchi tribes and Hindus and mentions that Sindhi tribes did not get special concessions from Kalhoras. This argument is valid because Kalhoras tried and succeeded in taking over lands of some Sindhi tribes of Dadu and Larkana districts, and distributed them to their disciples from Dera Ghazi Khan, Dera Ismail Khan, Sibi, Kachhi and the southern Punjab. The Sindhi tribes opposed it as they were regular tax payers and their complaints brought periodic Mughal expeditions. Dr. Lakho correctly divides immigrant tribes into groups are Jatts of southern Punjab. This is an important classificati8on that all immigrants were not Balouchis of Sibi, Kachhi and others of Kalat etc. do not consider those from D.G. Khan etc as real Balouchs. Recently Nawab Akbar Bugti stated that they are not Balouchs, but Barochs. .

Language literature and education system has been discussed in details along with syllabus. The author has shown that Sindhi language was also taught along with Persian and Arabic. This disproves the claim that Sindhi was introduced in the primary schools by the British, though credit of standardization of alphabet goes to Bartley frere in 1853 AD. He gives names of prominent Madrasahs and well known teachers of Sindhi, Persian and Arabic and some of it is an addition to our knowledge. He also gives list of books written then in Sindhi and Persian and names of authors, and finally details of Sindhi literature.

A chapter describes architecture and archaeology, an important ingredient of any history indeed. Certain sites belonging to sixteenth, seventeenth and eighteenth centuries, now in ruins, can be excavated. I have listed 729 canals, as they existed in 1843 AD, and belong to Kalhora-Talpur period. They now are merged in new barrages. A field study can tell new tales.

The Mian receives the title of Shahnawaz Khan and his sons return from Persia

In 1161 AH (1748 A.D.) Ahmad Sháh Dúrání, who settled the boundaries of Nádir Sháh's share of the country with the Emperor of Dehlí, and secured it for himself, confirmed Mián Núr Muhammad as the ruler of Sind, giving him the new title of "Sháhna wáz Khán." In the next year, the Mián's sons Ghulám Sháh and Atur Khán, who had been taken away as hostages, returned from Persia. In 1163 AH. (1750, AD) Gul Muhammad Khurásání became Miáns agent at Tattá. In the same year news was received of the Miáns third son Murádyáb Khán's arrival at Muscat and the death of Shekh Ghulám Muhammad, who had been in his company. Accordingly Shukrulláh Khán was ordered to proceed immediately to bring the young nobleman home.

In 1164 AH (1751 AD) ships left for the port of Muscat, but Shekh Shukrulláh died soon after. In due course of time Muhammad Murádyáb Khán arrived and was received with great affection by his father, who entrusted him with the entire management of the financial business of the state, and appointed Khudábád to be his head quarters. Sháhnawáz Khán, who used to be at Khudábád, came to reside at the new built town of Muhammadábád. Khudádád Khán, who during the absence of his elder brother, had put on the turban of an heir-apparent, had now to resign that honourable position to the rightful owner Murádváb Khán. Being much chagrined and mortified at this, he left his native land and went to Hindustán. But Muhammad Murádyáb Khán soon proved a failure as a financial manager and so that office was taken back from him.

The king comes to Sind and Diwan Gidumal is sent as an envoy to him

In the beginning of 1166 AH (1753 AD) it was rumoured that Sardár Jahán Khán was coming to Sind. And about the close of the year a different rumour was circulated to the effect that the king himself was coming in order to pass on to Hindustán. On the 4th of Muharram 1168 AH (1755 AD) information was received that the king had moved from Muhammadàbád to the sand-hills. Diwán Gidúmal was therefore sent in a hurry as an envoy to meet him at his camp and assure him of the Mián's loyalty and faithfulness, and if possible to induce him to turn back without marching further by the route. The Diwán met the king's camp at the bridge of Sakhar. As the king was angry and out of humour, the Diwán could not get an audience for 3 days. At last the king encamped at Naoshahrah. Here Diwán Gidúmal was fortunate enough to secure the king's audience and to conciliate him.

Death of Mian Noor Muhammad and the election of his son Muradyab Khan

It was about this time, on the 12th of Saffar of the same year 1168 AH (1755 AD) that the ruler of Sind Mián Núr Muhammad died of quinsy or the inflammation of the throat in the vicinity of Jesalmer.

The nobles of the state lost no time in electing the late ruler's eldest son Muhammad Murádyáb Khán to the throne. That young nobleman, fearing lest he might be again given away as a hostage, had left his father on the way and betaken himself in a different direction, from which he had to be brought to fill the vacant throne. This ceremony of enthronement took place on 16th, i.e. 4 days after the late Mián's death.

Mian Nasir Muhammad Kalhoro (urdu) ميان نصير محمد كلهوره:was the famous king of the Kalhora Dynasty that ruled Sindh from 1108 AH (1696 AD).

On his death, Mián Sháhal Muhammad was succeeded by his son Mián Nasír Muhammad, in the year 1108 AH (1696 AD) This Mián acquired more celebrity for piety and virtue than any of his predecessors, and therefore was envied by most of the people of his time. Accordingly the natives of the place came and incited the Mughuls of Bakhar to harass and trouble him. Mián Nasír Muhammad was therefore obliged to leave the place and go to a sandy desert. After some days of hardship, he returned and fixed his residence in the land of the Panwhárs. Mír Panwhár, the chief of the Panwhárs, taking an army from the governor of Bakhar, commanded among other leaders by Mírzá Khán Piní, the governor of Siwí, came and fought with Miàn Nasír Muhammad, but soon a truce was made and Mián Nasír Muhammad was sent to the Emperor Álamgír, who kept him in confinement for some time. During this period, fighting went on with the Mián's followers, until Mián Nasír Muhammad managed to escape and returned to his native place. He once more settled his affairs satisfactorily and began to lead a comfortable and secure life among his followers. He laid the foundation of a new town on the land of the Panwhárs, bounded on one side by the hills of Róh and on another by a stream of cool water. He called the town by the name of Khárí and himself took up his residence in it. The village of Hatrí he gave to Faojah Fakír, one of his followers, and the land of Káchhah to another of his Fakírs by name Ináyet Sháh. His followers, who so long had deserted their villages and strongholds, returned and settled permanently and occupied themselves in extending their landed property and territorial possessions. On one occasion they had to fight in an open field with Mír Yakúb Khán, the governor of Bakhar * and were victorious Similarly they fought several times with the governors of different neighbouring places and on all these occasions they bcame successful. The parganah of Lákhát was taken from the Mughuls of Síwistán on a farming contract. Makan Mórah was secured through the exertions of Faríd Bhágat, and the parganah of Sáhtí was brought into possession through Feróz Wírar, who built a town there calling it Naoshahrah. After this, the Siráís were firmly established in different parts of the country. After a successful reign of 35 or 36 years Mián Nasír Muhammad died and was buried on a red sand-hill in the village of Khárí.

Mian Shahul Mouhammed Kalhoro: (urdu) ميان شاهل محمد خان كلهوڙو : was the famous king of the Kalhora Dynasty that ruled Sindh from 1701 to 1783.

On his death, Mián Iliás was succeeded by his brother Sháh Alí better known as Sháhal Muhammad. In this pious mahdavi's time the number of his disciples increased largely and they occupied themselves in cultivating land. The canal of Ládkánah was dug by them. He secured land on both the banks of the canal from the tribes of Sángí and Abrah and divided it among his children and brothers, and himself selected his residence in the village of Habíbání. This rise of Mián Sháhal Muhammad excited jealousy in the hearts of some of the Abrah chiefs killed him under the orders of the governor of Bakhar. He was buried at the village of Marandhah in the out-skirts of Chándúkah in the parganah of Khárí.

Mian Sarfraz Kalhoro (Khudayar Khan) (urdu) ميان سرفـراز محمد خان كلهوڈو وابن المعروف خدايارخـان): was the famous king of the Kalhora Dynasty that ruled Sindh from 1701 to 1783. He was given the title *Khudayar Khan* by the Mughal Emperor Shah Alam II ans is known to have assisted Timur Shah Durrani prior to the Third Battle of Panipat.

The Rule of Mián Muhammad Sarafráz Khán

Muhammad Sarafráz Khán confirmed by the new king with the title of "Khudáyár Khán." The next day after Mián Ghulám Sháh's death his son Mián Muhammad Sarafráz Khán was placed on the throne of Sind with the unanimous consent of the nobility of the Fakírs, or followers of the late Mián. Timur Shah Durrani the viceroy, hastened to send a robe of honour with his sanad confirming the new ruler with the title of "Khudáyár Khán" in addition to his father's title. The Derahs were also attached to him. Mián Muhammad Sarafráz Khan therefore prepared to go in that direction and started about the close of Zulhajj of the same year 1186 A.H. (1772 A.D.) He had to spend some months in settling the affairs of the Derhas, and on the 12th of Rabíussání, 1187 A.H. (1773 A.D.) he returned to Hyderabad.

(With courtesy from Khalifatullahmehdi.info)

Khundmiri

*　*　*

——

Excerpts from "Kalhora Dynasty's Governance" an overview by Janab Mohmmed Namdar Khan Bozai

History of Sindh is as rich as its culture, its traditions, its language, its moral value, its social diversity and its civilization. With such obvious attractions it was destined to offer temptation not only to immediate neighbors but to far flung invaders like the Portuguese and the English. Such political and cultural pressures resulted in local intellectual resistance which slowly and gradually attained its full strength by the advent of Islam in this part of the world. This began a new era in the history of Sindh. From then onwards awareness of "Human Rights" in general were publicized and practiced unreservedly. A growing sense for the establishment of a "Just Society" which can offer:

—1. Equal opportunity to masses. 2. Respectable living to every citizen. 3. Protection against all kinds of 'Exploitation of Man by Man'. 4. Freedom of thought and speech. 5. Freedom to earn their living. 6. Protection against 'Forced Slavery' 7. Right of 'Self Determination' of their social religious and political status. 8. Protection against 'Imperialistic Forces' existing at that time etc. was but a natural and well justified thinking. Sindh was therefore looking for a radical change in social and political life structure. It had tasted the Hindu Imperialism, the Arab Dominance, the Turkish Monarchy, the Afghan Rule, Hegemony of Mughal India so on so forth.

The Kalhora dynasty was perhaps the first to represent the locals' aspirations. The most probable reason which made them 'Revolutionary' and become Torch Bearers of 'Self Determination' in Sind was against the oppression and injustice they faced from the Mughal imperialism and the un-magnanimous attitude of 'Ulmas' of the time. Kalhoras had no political ambitions. They were basically 'Darwaish Sifat' Religious sect and followers of Syed Mohammad(As) of Jaunpur who believed him to be the 'Mehdi-e-Maud' whose grandfather Syed Osman Sherazi, an Aalim of high stature, came to Delhi along with King Taimoor in 801 A.D. After the departure of Taimoor, Syed Osman Sherazi stayed in Delhi and then shifted to Jaunpur which was the centre of Ilm-o-Adab and was commonly known as SHIRAZ of HIND. Unfortunately, contemporary historians intentionally avoid to mention his name and give due credit to him or his followers who have been part and parcel of histories of Sindh, Baluchistan, Makran, Afghanistan, Masqat, Kirman, Southern Khurasan and Central Punjab the whole of 'Seraiki' speaking area Gujarat, Mando, Palanpur, Ahmed Nagar, Jodhpur, Jaipur, Jalore, Nagore, Bijapur, Burhanpur, Bayana, Berar, Marwar, Deccan, Madras, Mysore etc. etc.

The fact is that millions of Imamana's followers have contributed to the progress, welfare and prosperity of the places wherever they lived. Their contribution is in every walk of national lives. How can we forget Qazi Qaden RZ, Shah Inyat Sofi, Shah Abdul Latif Bhitai, Sachhal Sarmast, Mir Shahdad Khan Talpur, Mir Chakar Khan Laghari, and Nawab Bahadur Yar Jung?

Kalhoras religious belief was an integral part of their glorious history. Any attempt to isolate them from their strong religious character which was the main source of their strength. People gathered around them in the time of their "poverty" and "Faqiree". They had a very large community of followers and Peerbhais comprising of multitude of nationalities. With regard to their Peerbhais religious character Maulana Azad writes on page # 41 of "TAZKARA" (Urdu Published by Javaid Brothers, Lahore): "These people had strange habits and living, peculiar enough to remind the living habits of Sahaba-e-Ikram". On page 54 he writes and admires by saying: "Much information is available in Tazkarat-ul-Wasileen in the chapter related to Shaikh Dawood and by reading these a strange and mind wondering feeling is experienced and one desires to leave everything aside and just keep on talking about those truthful and clean people"! He continues: "Centuries have passed by and yet if their reference is made even today it leaves us wondering and questioning what could have been the impact on our hearts if we were in their company?" These people used to live outside the city in their own colonies, which they used to call 'Daira'. This word under the influence of local linguistic affects appears as 'Dero' or 'Dera' etc but some of them still exist in their original from like, 'Daire Langar Khan' in Lahore, 'Daire Deen Punnah' near Kot Addu in the Punjab, 'Daira Drazo' originally 'DARAZ' where Hazrat Sachal Sarmast Shrine stands in Sindh, or 'Diara Gurgi Balgator' in Turbat Baluchistan. Others are 'Nao

Dero' near Larkana which is 'Naya Daira', 'Rajo Dero' near western border of Khanpur with Baluchistan, 'Daira Basti' outside Multan. Dera Ghazi Khan and Dera Ismail Khan are also 'DAIRAS' because these towns are famous for Mehdavia Population and these two Mehdavi Generals were sent by King Aurangzeb from Gujarat to Punjab. Expulsion and persecution of Mehdavis had been a very popular 'Sport' of many worldly Ulmas/Mullahs and at times even the Kings and provincial Governors were involved in this 'Cruel game'. Mian Adam Shah Kalhora, a very pious and saintly follower of Syed Mohammad Mehdi A.S. did not escape the wrath and crucifixion by Multan's Governor who imprisoned him and eventually martyred him for no reason.

He did not belong to 'Qabza Group' and occupied lands of others by force. History admits and recognizes him as a holy religious leader. He believed in Quranic inference: AL-ARZO LILLAH! He also believed in "APNA OGAO APNA KHAO". The teachings of the Masluk certainly have stronger inclination towards 'Amar Bil Maroof wa Nahi Anil Munkir' and even greater emphases on 'Honesty", "Equality of Human Rights", "Social Justice", recognition of "Hoqooq Allah and Hoqooq-ul-Ibad" etc.

In those days Muslims had drifted from the real teachings of Islam and Shari'a was manipulated to cater individual needs. Practicing judiciary had double standards and Fatwas to suit the needs of people were available at a price, details can be read in 'TAZKARA' by Maulana Abul Kalam Azad who said "There was a need to revive the true spirit of Islam".

Followers of the Masluk including Mian Adam Shah and his followers had undertaken revival of the spirit of Shari'a which involved re-introduction of the practice of:—I. Total submission to Allah and his Messenger (PBUH). II. Amar Bil Maroof (Practicing of Rightful actions and stopping of wrong acts). Sawieth (equality of Human rights and equal distribution of resources). Ijma (Democratic approach on matter of collective importance). Usher (10 percent tax on income). Tawakkal (Reliance on Allah). Hijrat (Migration for Tableegh). Sohbat-e-Sadiqeen (company of Truthfuls) Tarak-e-Hubbe-Dunnya (discarding the love of worldly charms).

Zikr Allah (Remembrance of Allah). Uzlat (loneness for meditation and Tuzzakia). Talab-e-Deedar-e-Ilahi (Urge to see and meet Allah Subhanah-wa-Taala in order to achieve real Ma'arefat).

The economic structure of the society was looked after by imposing 10% Tax on the income or productivity of the "Kasib"—a person who works outside the 'Daira'. This tax called 'USHER' along with the Zakat was collected from 'Sahib-e-Nisab'. Another approach was that country's resources are created for all the human beings and a "just and fair distribution" based on the individual contribution and efforts, is the responsibility of the 'Ool-ul-amar'. On the other hand accumulation of wealth, hoarding of commodities or for that matter anything in excess of one's need was regarded as violation of tenants of the Masluk, which proved to be a stumbling block for those who believe other than these principles. In-fact their practical system of Usher and distribution of community resource itself is a separate subject of research.

Mian Adam Shah Kalhora while practicing the above tenants happened to annoy lot of his neighboring feudal and land lords because the Haries (actual kashtkars) were now getting equal share from the income of their cultivated crop in addition to humanly treatment, like brothers of one family and at the same time getting groomed as good practicing Muslims. Truth and social justice prevailed attracting the masses. The friction between the powerful Feudal supported by the Government and helpless locals increased resulting in the growth of an "Opposition" which gained strength day by day. Leadership of the sect was imprisoned not only in Sindh but throughout India, some were tortured to death. Hundreds and thousands of families were driven out and forced to migrate from their placers to other places. Armies were used to extinguish the sect and their 'Dairas' in Gujarat and Bayana. Judiciary and clergy were used and mobilized to justify state's action.

Dr. Ishtiaq Hussain Qureshi in his Book "BARRE SAGHIR PAK-O-HIND KI MILLAT-E-ISLAMIA" writes on page no. 173:—"Religious beliefs are never suppressed in this manner. MAKHDUM-UL-MULK (ABDULLAH SULTANPURI) had to run a campaign in order to overcome the Mehdavis which eventually destroyed them but the doctrine of 'Correct Believes' suffered an irreparable damage. At that time the only disagreement between Muslims and Mehdavis was that the latter had accepted Syed Mohammad as Mahdi-e-Mauood(As) and were strict observers of the Islamic statutes (FRAIZ-E-ISLAM). In reality, a strange situation had emerged whereby those who were the leaders and fore-runners in adhering and following the Shari'a were being doubted as deviators from the Shari'a". Thus, state and its cultivated religious machinery provided complementary services to each other. Their tyranny was unchecked as there was no "Human Rights Organization" or "International Courts of Justice" to reprimand the governments of that time. As a result a lot of its followers went underground. Shaikh Mubarak Sindhi, father of Allama Faizi and Alma Abdul Fazal was forced to go into hiding. He lived a fugitive life for years together. Detail account is given by Mohammad Hussain Azad in his famous Darbar-e-Akbari. Mian Mir Balapir of Lahore a maternal grandson of Hazrat Qazi Qadan(Rh) had to take refuge in Lahore and live an anonymous life for almost forty years. He has been labeled as "Qadri' by his well-wishers and followers who did not like to expose him as Mahdavi to the state authorities or 'Ulmas'. So also Mian Mir's Murshid Hazrat Sayed Kizr who lived an anonymous life in Sevestan. The history does not know who he was! His real identity is—he was Syed Mohammad's great grandson! It goes like this—Syed Kizr bin Syed Ashraf bin Syed Yaqoob bin Syed Mehmood bin Syed Mohammad Mahdi A.S. Such is the sad history of early Pirs and Pirbhais of Kalhoras of Sindh.

According to Tuhfatul Ikram in 995 A.H. on the expedition of conquest of Sindh, Abdul Rahim Khan-e-Khanan approached Mian Adam Shah Kalhora for his blessing and with a request to pray for his success in his mission. Khan-e-Khanan gifted some land at Chanduka as his "offering" for Fuqra's Mudad-e-Muash. Mian Adam Shah's prayers were answered and Khan-e-Khanan conquered Sindh. A similar case in history is about Sardar Khan who was blessed by Mian Naseer Mohammad to become ZARDAR KHAN whose progeny runs up to present Zardaries. After the hanging of Hazrat Adam Shah Kalhora R.A., time passed by wounds was healing but the Ulmas and the land lords did not forget them. They again framed fictitious charges against his third Gaddi Nasheen. Mian Shah Mohammad who was killed in prison in 1657 A.D. by the authorities. He was succeeded by another very pious young man Mian Naseer Mohammad. He also was arrested in 1675 A.D. and handed over to King Aurangzeb. Here again, after few years of imprisonment the 'HAQ' prevailed. The King was pressurized by Ulmas and so he organized a Manazira between the Ulma-e-Waqat and the Mehdavi Ulmas to determine the truth about the faith and also to pass a decree for Mian's persecution. This Manazira is known as 'Mubahisa-e Alamgiri' and took place in the year 1095 A.H. (1678 A.D.) in Ahmed Nagar. Once again neither the Ulma nor the King could find anything seriously objectionable to enable them pronounce a decree of 'Kufr'. It is believed that Mian Naseer Mohammad was released as a consequence of the MUNAZIRA. In 1738 A.D. Nadir Shah invaded Sindh and Hind, completely destroying and wrecking the economy of both earlier mentioned parties. He looted their wealth and divided Mian's Dominion into three parts and only one third was left with them. He also, either destroyed the books and libraries or taken away most valuable scripts of Holy Quran and many other important manuscripts. This was not the end of his loot! Mian Noor Mohammad Kalhora had to pay One Crore Rupees, and a yearly ransom of Rs. 20 lakhs. He took away Mian's two sons Muradyab Khan and Ghulam Shah as 'security' to ensure timely payments by Mian Noor Mohammad.

These two sons being of young age Hazrat Belawal Zardari was entrusted to accompany them and look after them in Iran while in Nadir Shah's custody. This important assignment signifies the diplomatic caliber, the royal dependency, the closeness and trust worthiness of Hazrat Belawal Zardari (1705—1754 A.D.) with Mian Noor Mohammad Kalhora. It appears that younger generation of Kalhoras drifted away from the original teachings and desired the pomp and glory in this world and it was fulfilled by Allah Subhana-wa-Taala. In 1715 A.D. Mian Yar Mohammad was officially appointed by Delhi as official 'Ruler' of the province. So, from hence forth with royal decree in their hands the young Kalhoras started collecting the land revenue, money started pouring in, reins of power was in their hands. Regular army was employed. Slowly and gradually a system of governing and running of the country was shaping up, demanding more time, more attention of the leadership who were basically of religious discipline and who preferred to opt for devotion to Allah, sit in isolation purifying their souls, Qalab and Nafas by Zikerwo-Fiker and establishing Salat. From the point of view of the Historians and the worldly people "Golden Period of the Dynasty" started. Their achievements in the introduction and development of:—1. Human relations. 2. Provincial administration and economic structure. 3. Land management, Agriculture and Irrigation system of the country. 4. Education in masses. 5. Military training in Mosques along with religious education. 6. Literature and Poetry. 7. New architecture. 8. Maritime Logistics. Including building of new Towns etc. etc. are an unforgettable chapters of Sind's history.

Each topic itself had been a subject of research on their own. Later on, his descendant visited many area of Sindh, many people joined them gradually. Thus Kalhoras arose and flourished in

Sindh for over many centuries as Mahdavi Religious and Political leaders. Many Communities of Sindh Enrolled as their followers Abro, Bhatti, Jokhiyo, Junejo, Sial, Sahta, Rajputs, Kalwar, Jatoi, Khosa, Chandio, Leghari, Talpurs, Zardaris and many others. The Mehrabpur City in Khairpur District is stil on the name of Abbasi Army's Soldier Mehrab Khan Jatoi, who fought for the dignity of his Spiritual Mahdavi Leaders and thus became martyred.

After the end of Abbasi Dynasty in Sindh, Abbasi's take their loyal Army with themselves and settled in Khanpur and Shikarpur. So even uptil now the Chief Sardar of Abbasi Tribe and Jatoi Tribe live together and enjoy great relationship with each other.

The Kalhora Dynasty succumbed to King Nader Shah who invaded India in 1739 AD. One of the most famous Nawab Kalhora was Mian Ghulam Shah Kalhoro. He is known to have assisted Ahmad Shah Durrani against the Hindu Marathas during the Third Battle of Panipat in order to restore Mughal prestige. Ghulam Shah commanded a large army and fought against the Rao of Kuchh, an ally of the Maratha and an adversary of Sindh in the Thar Desert in the year 1762.

The kalhora Dynasty declined later when Mian Abdul Nabi lost control of Sindh in 1783 and was defeated by his own disciples Talpur Amirs in the Battle of Halani. Mian Abdul Nabi Kalhoro was the last Kalhoro Nawab.

The Kalhoro period is most important for the development of Sindhi literature, arts, crafts and irrigation. During Kalhora rule several wah (canals) were dug in every part of Sindh to irrigate the uncultivated land.

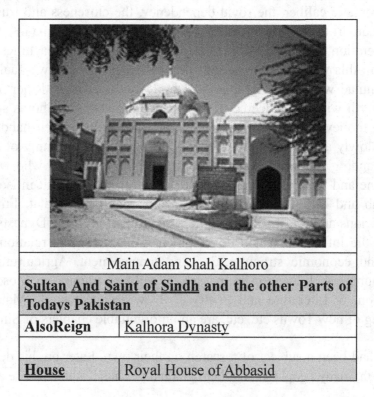

Main Adam Shah Kalhoro	
Sultan And Saint of Sindh and the other Parts of Todays Pakistan	
AlsoReign	Kalhora Dynasty
House	Royal House of Abbasid

With Courttesy from Mr. Reehan Fareed who
PROVIDED me Books on Sindh History.
And from Wickipedia. Compilded by Faqeer Syed Sharief Khundmiri

* * *

—

10. Shah Inayet Shaheed(Rh) OF SINDH

TRANSLATION OF THE EXCCERPTS FROM URDU WITINGS OF HZT. MIYAN ABDUL GHANI BHEEK (RH) of Channapatna, migrated to Pakistan in 1947.

10. Shah Inayet Shaheed: Author of Tuhfatul Ikram had mentioned with great respect about Shah Inayet that he was a pious, God fearing, murshid of murshids, vali-e-kamil, who went to Gujrat and benefitted himself from the company of Hzt. Abdul Malik Sujawandi (Rh).

Under the influence of the Sawwiyat Doctrine of Imamana(As) he had experimented Equality of Action, and Collective Farming in Sindh, which is the pioneering bright period written in the annals of history on Kalhora Kingdom of Sindh. This Islamic experiment of Collective Farming was unique and new to the prevailing environment which was alien and was vehemently rejected by the feudals and landlords. Not only Government, but the jagirdars, wordly priests and the so called mashaeqeen, under the influence of their old habits, never tolerated the new way of life under the Collective Farming. But Shah Inayet proved its benefits and utility.

The Northern Sindh was under Multan's administration, whose headquarter was Bakkhar. When Alamgir was unsuccessful in his expeditions, he granted the upper Sindh to Miyan Yar Mohmmed Kalhora. While the Southern Sindh was under Jahan Mirza Jani Baig Tarkhan, whose Headquarter was Thatta. During the period of Jehangir both portions of Sindh were made a separate province of Sindh, in 1614 AD. In 1732 AD Sindh was granted as the Jagir of Nawab Amir Khan, who granted the Southern Sindh to Miyan Yar Mohammed Kalhora. Thus entire Sindh province came under Kalhora Dynasty. After some time, Delhi Government granted the title of "Khuda Yar Khan" to Miyan Noor Mohammed Kalhora.

Under Islamic conviction, land belongs to Allah. And those who are actual cultivators of a certain portion of land, become temporary owners of that portion of land. Later on, these temporary owners were made permanent jagirdars who used to employ Hawaris (cultivators) for cultivation against a paltry share in the produce. This Hawari System became intolerable for the cultivators because the jagirdars were exploiting the real cultivators by making them the Bonded Labor."

That was the atmosphere when Shah Inayet started his movement in Miranpur (It is said that Imamana(As) stayed here for some months. Hence this town was named after him as Miranpur) where Shah Inayet propagated his novel scheme of Collective Farming which was a Shot in the Blue for the cultivators who surrounded Shah Inayet. Although Shah Inayet was a pious Vali, still he was against the exploitation of the cultivators, hence he started his own doctrine of collective farming for the cultivators living in his Dairah. In view of the Qur'nic Injunctions, Shah Inayet adopted the principle of Sawiath (sharing equally) in the produce out of their cultivated harvest, as advised by Immana(As).

Shah Inayet had the blessings from Imamana (As) which was basically founded on the principle of Equality. It is a fact that Imamana(As) lived in Thatta for 18 months, during the period of Jam Nanda. Hundreds of people embraced Mahdaviat, among them were many elites and Miyan Adam Shah Kalhora and his follower Shah Inayet also, who was living in the Dairahs where Sawwiat(Equality) was the order of the day. Thus Shah Inayet's scheme of collective farming had a magnetic power towards which the Hawaris (cultivators) left their jagirdars and flocked around Shah Inayet. Hawaris became satisfied that they were being treated as equals as against the inhuman treatment of the jagirdars. This experiment became successful in which all were working as the members of a family, getting equal share not only in the produce, but as brothers of the Dairah, where there was no harassment and tyrannical treatment of the jagirdars under whom they were bonded labor and were being mal-treated. Thus this scheme became very popular and hundreds of Hawaris started collective farming, making the lands barren pertaining to the jagirdars and feuds. These Hawaris left their jagirdars and embraced Mahdaviat. Thus these tyrant jagirdars could not digest it and started enmity against Shah Inayet by influencing authorities to take stern measures against the very Collective farming scheme. They approached Mir Lutf-e-Ali Khan, administrator of Thatta, and requested him to stop Shah Inayet from his scheme of Collective Farming. But, as he was himself a Mahdavi, he did not like to interfere with the scheme which was flourishing day in and day out.

When these elements saw that Mir Lutf-e-Ali Khan, administer of Thatta, was not taking any action, they amassed a sizable force and attacked Miranpur, but their onslaught was repulsed by the Fuqara-cultivators. Still there were some casualties whose relatives filed a petition in Delhi Court against illegal attack by the jagirdars. Orders were issued in favor of the complainants and the lands of the attackers were delivered to the relatives of the victims. This legal success brought a fresh awakening to the Hawaris, who left their jagirdars and joined the collective farming scheme. Shah Inayet became successful and strong and none could dare to confront him.

When the enemies of Shah Inayet approached Delhi's Sultan Farrukh Sier who was against Mahdaviat, he expelled Mir Lutf-e-Ali Khan from Thatta and appointed Nawab Aazam Khan, being an arch rival of Mahdavis, wrote against Shah Inayet wrongly that he was defying the orders of government and claiming himself to be the government. On this utterly false complaint, Farrukh Sier without conducting any Inquiry, ordered to crush them by force.

After getting orders, Aazam Khan started to attack Miranpur, asking jagirdars to join him along with their men to fight against the Fuqaras. When the news of attack reached to Shah Inayet, he lamented by telling "I did bring this scheme to make the cultivators equal by bringing them out from the clutches of tyrannical behavior of the jagirdars and feuds, instead so much rancor, tumult and bloodshed are being arranged. When his aids suggested since they did not have ammunition, they shall attack on them in the night. Shah Inayet did not agree. But, when enemy's army was advancing against Miranpur, Fuqaras started "Night Attacks" on the enemy. Even after four months the army could not overpower the Fuqaras, the enemy planned covertly to offer "Peace Deal". Shah Inyet accepted peace and for the purpose of signing the Treaty, went to Aazam Khan, who ordered to arrest instead of a Peace Treaty".

After arresting Shah Inayet by their covert planning, they started killing the Fuqaras and their thatched roof houses were burnt down and after looting their belongings the dairah's boundary wall was dismantled.

After this destruction Aazam khan came to Thatta and called Shah Inayet to see him. It is said there was a lot of conversation between them, but he was dead against the Shah and on 7th. January 1718, the Shah was martyred. Inna lillahi wo inna alaihi wa rajeoon.

Note: Some more material can be had regarding Shah Inayet Shaheed Rh. from the writings of Janab Namdar Khan Sahebe.

Faqeer Syed Shrief Khundmiri

* * *

—

Zulfiqar Ali Kalharo, Anthropologist, Qaed-e-Azam University, Islmabad, subscribed this article as the representative of the present day kalharo generation living in Karachi.

11. A Glorious Past: (KALHORA RULE)

THE beginning of the 16th century witnessed the rise of the Kaihoras in northern Sindh. Mian Adam Shah Kaihoro, a celebrated religious scholar was greatly influenced by the teachings of Syed Muhammad Jaunpuri alias Mehdi Jaunpuri, and spent all his life in preaching and spreading the Mehdvi thought and ideology. He was a disciple of Mian Abu Baker Jatoi, who accompanied Syed Mohammad Jaunpuri to several places in Sindh and also in India. Once when Syed Mohammad Jaünpuri arrived in the town of Mandu, a large number of people gathered around him. Sultan Ghiyasuddin Khalji (1469—1500), who was imprisoned in the same town, also wanted to meet him, but could not do so because he'd been taken into custody by his son, Nasiruddin. However, he informed Syed Mohammad Jaunpuri about his inability to pay him respects and requested him to send his one or two disciples so that they could benefit from him. Syed Mohammnad Jaunpuri deputed two *of* his disciples, Mian Salmullah and Mian Abu Bakar, on whom Ghyiasuddin showered sliver and gold coins and inquired about Syed Mohammad in detail. The place where the Mehdvis settled was called the Daira.

Mian Adam Shah Kalhorô established his first Daira, a religious settlement in a small village named Haitri which is now known as Haitri Ghulam Shah in Dokri taluka of Larkana. He started his Career from this small village with the support of the Abro tribe who remained a powerful force behind him. A man, Khabar Abro, was the first person to enrol as his follower. This small village became the centre for learning for the Mehdvis. A lot of other people flocked to the village to seek his blessings. Many people believe and argue that Syed Muhammad Jauripuri was the propagator of a new religion. However, he did not claim to have founded or propagated any new religion. He only professed that as a Mehdi he was commissioned by the Almighty to restore Islam to its pristine purity. He did not confine himself to the interpretations of the four orthodox schools of the Sunnis, but claimed to have followed the religion of Muhammad and beliefs and practices as enjoined by the Holy Quran, who claimed God, His Prophet and His book were his sole guides. According to him, not all the members of the Daira were equally righteous. He said that there were three types of people in his Daira: believers, hypocrites and the Kafirs. The latter two he credulously asserted, were not destined to die in the Daira—they would generally leave it before their death. After each week, the Mehdsavis of the Daira would assemble and individually make an open confession of the sins they had committed during the week. Anyone guilty of some serious offence would offer himself before the leader of the Daira voluntarily to receive punishment in accordance with the laws of the Shariat. With the passage of time, the Daira of Mian Adam Shah Kalhoro received a number of disciples who popularized the teachings of Syed Mohammad Jaunpuri. Due to his teachings, the Mehdavi thought and ideology, and the name of Mian Adam spread to far-flung areas. Even Abdul Raheem Khan Khanna, the soldier of Akbar the great who had captured Bukhar, on hearing his name, visited him. When he met him, he was hugely influenced by him, and granted him the Chandka Parguna, which now comprises the Larkana district. As time passed by, the circle of his disciples kept on increasing which annoyed the local jagirdars, zamindars and Mughal officials who became against him and influenced the the Mughal governor in Multan. His growing popularity as a religious and spiritual leader, not to mention his emergence as a political figure, eventually led the Mughals to attack him.

Ultimately, he was taken captive and was brought to Multan where he was martyred. Afterwards, his body was brought to Sukkur where he was buried in a hillock, which was then named after him as Adam Shah Ji Takkri. After his martyrdom, his successors continued his mission remaining in their Dairas and gained popularity, which consistently irritated the Mughal governor of Bukhar. Even after such brutal attrocities, they became strong and captured some areas where they established their Dairas and began to rule. As a result, troops of both the Kalhoras and the Mughals met in a battlefield near Gerello. In that battle, Feroz Verar, (founder of Nausharo Feroz) a disciple of Mian Nasir Mohammad Kalhoro and a general of Mian Deen Mohammad's army, spearheaded the Kalhora army, while Mughal

Governor of Bukhar Shaikh Amir Jahan led his forces. The battle was fought in 1699 in which a number of soldiers from both sides lost their lives. The Kalhoras achieved victory in that battle.

Among these two men who lost their lives, Mir Mondar Khan Chandio and Hajji Khan Marri, were known for their bravery and fighting skills. Mondar Khan Chandio, the valiant fighter of the Kalhora army, was a disciple of Mian Shahal Mohammad Kalhoro and belonged to the Husnani section of the Chandio tribe, Sono faqir Janwari Chandio, a folk storyteller, has narrated in his Writings about the chivalry, valor and intrepidness of Mondar Khan and his other tribesmen. The heroic stories of Mondar Khan Chandio are still preserved in the folklore of the countryside. Some locals believe that it was he who killed Mughal Governor Sheikh Amir Jahan. Descendants of Mondar Khan Chandio, known as Mondarni Chandia, still have that sword with which he killed Sheikh Amir Jahan in the battle of Gerello. His body was taken to his native place in Jagir for burial. The grave yard contains several graves of those who died along with him in the battle of Gerello, prominent among those were Paliyo Janwari Chandio, Nando Khan Janwari Chandio, and Dinar Khan Janwari Chandio. Haji Khan Marri, like Mondar Khan, died fighting bravely against Mughal troops. He was the father-in-law of Mir Suelman alias Kaku Than who was the ancestor of the Talpurs of Sindh and settled down in the Kachho area of Dadu.

There he heard the name of a pious man named Mian Nasir Mohammad Kalhoro, he went to meet him, and later on became his disciple. His descendants, who are known as the Hajizai, subsequently moved out of Kachho to the present districts of Hyderabad and Khairpur. Gerello, a small town in the Dokri taluka of Larkana district, served as the Daira for the Kalhoras over a century. He founded a village here in the 16th century that assumed the name which indicated their place of origin. It was once a very important trading center. The Hindus controlled the business of the town. The buildings of that period include a three-domed mosque, which is lavishly decorated with glazed tiles, and the tomb of one of the members of the Kalhora family. The mosque here is believed to have been built by Noor Mohammad Kalhoro.

* * *

12. EXCERPTS FROM SEMINAR ON KALHORA DYNASTY, 1995

Report on an Internationl Seminar on Kalhora Rule in Sindh, published by the Seminar Orgnising Committee, Karachi:

A Two Day Seminar was held in Commemoration of the Mahdavi Kalhora Rule in Sindh held in September 1996 under the chairmanship of Yaqoob Ali Zardari. The following are a few Excerpts of the opinions from out of 30 Dignitaries of the Seminar on the Kalhora Rule in Sindh, Pakistan.

1. Farooq Ahmed Khan Laghari (The then President of Pakistan): Kalhora Rule which is considered to be the Golden period in the History of Sindh, was characterized by political stability, Economic Prosperity, Religious Harmony and Social Justice. Our History is rich with personalities who have contributed to shape our present history. Mian Adam Shah, the First Kalhora ruler was a very pious and religious man.

2. Muhtarima Benazir Bhutto, (the then Prime Minister of Pakistan): The 18th. Century was the period of enlightenment and learning under the Kalhora Rule. I appreciate the efforts of the organizing committee for organizing this Seminar.

3. Hakim Ali Khan Zardari (Finance Committee Chairman, father of Asif Ali Zrdari, present President of Pakistan): Kalhora belonged to Upper Sindh, known as "Dera Jaat". Being religious leaders they attracted a large number of Serikai speaking section of the people, particularly the Baluchis. My ancestors were also part of kalhora army, migrated along with them from Dera Jaat to Nawabshah, where my great grand farther Bilawal Faqir Zardari (a pious Mahdavi) was buried in their graveyard at Bilawal-Ja-Koba.

4. Asif Ali Khan Zardari, president of Pakistan: Kalhora Rulers provided the people of Sindh an opportunity by laying of wide ranging irrigation Canal Network throughout the country. Poetry and literature also received special attention. As a result eminent scholars like Ali sher Qanai. Makhdoom Moin Thattvi, Mohsin, Artard, Shah Abdul Latif Bhitai and Baba Bhullhay Shah, Sofi Sarmust and many more belong to the Kalhora period.

5. Pir Mazharul Haq (the then minister for Parliamentary Affairs): Kalhora's was a Golden Period of the HIstory of Sindh. In fact they never posed themselves to be the Rulers, but due to their humble posture and Faqeeri background of Mahdavi culture, they served the people of Sindh with great zeal and untiring efforts in the fields of agriculture, irrigation, literature, art and Mysticism. They promoted the feelings of Brotherhood among the various sections belonging to different religions, sects, caste and creed which created atmosphere of peace and tranquility in Sindh.

6. Abdul Hameed Akhund, (Secretary Culture and Tourism, Sindh): Many Kalhora chieftans, Mian Adam Shsah, Mian Shuhal Shah, Mian Deen Mohammed laid down their lives for their motherland. Miyan Shah Inayet (Shaheed) Rizvi appears on the horizon of Sindh, during that period arose great stalwarts like Sufi Master and Shah Abdul latif Bhitai as great Sufi Poets. The foundation of rich cultural and literary traditions were laid down during the Kalhora Rule.

7. Yaqoob Ali Zardari, President, Seminar Committee: The foundations of Kalhora Rule were laid by Mian Adam Shah by initiating his "Mianwali Movement" formed by him on the patron of Mahdavi Movement of Syed Mohammed Juanpuri(Known as Mahdi-e-Akhiruz zaman). He came to Thatta in 906 H and stayed for 18 months. He gave a new Slogan to the cultivators by decalaring "Grower is the owner of the land." With this Slogan, he wanted to bring them under the flag of Mahdavi Movement. Mian Adam shah was born in 1520, just 13 years after the extradition of Syed Mohammed Juanpuri from Sindh. He embraced Mahdavi Movement and formed his own party with the same program and Slogan and gave it the name "Mianwali Movement". He was of a Faqeeri behavior, without any pomp and glory. People liked

his simple way of living on Mahdavi tradition by forming Dairahs, where every one was equal. Kalhora period brought about radical changes in the socio-Economic conditions of the country. A Green Revolution was brought about by laying a comprehensive Canal System through out the country. Urbanization took place during their rule. Consequently, Hyderabad, Naushro Peroze, Mohammedabad, Khuda Abad, one & two, and Allahabad, Hyderabad were built by Kalharos. Eminent scholars and saints like Mian Noor Mohammed, Mian Sarfraz, Shah Abdul Latif Bhitai, Baba Bhooly Shah propagated the message of love and harmony among the people of Indus valley during their period. The triumph of Kalhora was indeed the triumph of the trodden masses of Sindh. An era of ascendency came on the horizan when the Kalhoras gained power and suzerainty over Sindh,.

GOVERNMENT OF SINDH RECENTLY ANNOUNCED 2ND. OCTOBER, A PUBLIC HOLIDAY EVERY YEAR, CELEBRATING THE BIRTHDAY OF GHULAM SHAH KHAN KALHORA, FOUNDER OF HYDERABAD IN SINDH.

Report provided by my nephew, Syed Javeed Nizam.

Syed sharief Khundmiri

13. "WHO WAS ZUL QARNAIN ?"

BISMILLA HIR RAHMAN NIR RA HEEM

This presentation is submitted to determine who was Zul Qarnbain? the very word "Qarn" means Horn, Century, but here it is horns as per the Dream mentioned below.

There are authentic four sources to determine who was he.

1. We have to refer to the dream of the Prophet Danial as mentioned in the Holy Torah.
2. Prophecies of Prophet Eshuwah came to be known 160 years before the Conquest of Babul By Khorus, known as Zul Qarnain.
3. 16 Verses of the Holy Qur'an in Soora-e-Kuhaf (18: 834 to 18:98) about him.
4. Result of the Research of 1838AD clearly determines who was this person.

First we shall discuss about Prophet Danial's Dream:

1. He informed that he saw that a Ram was standing at the bank of a river, having two long horns one behind the other. That Ram was going towards West, East and North. Thus that ram treaded all over the lands of West, East and North. Then Gabriel emerged and interpreted the Dream that the two horn Ram represents the two territories of Media and Paras of the old Persia.

According to the old legends, Persia's northern part was known as Media and the southern portion was known as Paras. And Zul Qarnain would conquer both parts and establish a great Empire. This dream had prophesied that Bani Israiel who were so far in Diaspora and living a nomadic life at the hands of Babul Kingdom who destroyed their Haikal-e-Sulaimani. According to the dream, the same Zul Qarnain would conquer Babul and help Bani Israiel to construct their Haikal and establish them in Palestine.

According to the Dream, Zul Qarnain's advent had been on the same principles ordained by Allah for the Prophets. He was acclaimed to have been the pious and the chosen one by Allah. And who became the savior of the down trodden nations of the East, West and the North. He would construct the barrier to safeguard from the atrocities of the troublesome nation who did not know any language.

Second: Prophet Ushuwah's prophecy: He had informed the destruction of Palestine first, which occurred 160 years before the Fall of Babul. Then he mentioned the rise of Palestine and then he explained about Zul Qarnain by saying the savior of the nations would emerge and would populate Palestine afresh. Further many cities and towns would be established for Bani Israiel. Finally Jeroshelam would be founded on a grand scale. Then he was telling all about Zul Qarnain who was a shepherd and fulfilled the commands of Allah. Allah had grasped his right hand to make him overpower over the nations and punish the tyrant kings.

Third.: 16 verses of the Holy Qur'an regarding Zul Qarnain.

The Mushrik's of Makkah went to the Jewish Rubbies to enquire, according to their Torah, whether the Holy Prophet (Slm) who was posing himself to be the Messenger of Allah, was he correct and was there any prophecy about him in Torah? Jerwish Rubbies suggested three questions and told to the Mushriks to enquire from him. If the Prophet(Slm) furnished correct answers, as mentioned in the Holy Torah, then he should be considered as the Real Messenger of Allah, otherwise disregard him.

Accordingly they came to the Holy Prophet and put to him 3 questioins;1. About the Men of the cave. 2. About Zul Qarnain and 3. About Prophet Khizr. We are concerned here about the second Question of Zul Qarnain. On that the Holy Prophet(Slm) got the Revelation and these 16 verses were revealed, on which they became convinced.

If we minutely go through these verses we come to conclusion as under:

1. The name of Zul Qarnain was proposed by the Jews themselves and which was recorded in the holy Qur'an.
2. Allah had bestowed upon him the sovereignty over a vast Empire. First he conquered the West upto Asia-e-Minor, where he witnessed the sun was setting in the mud; then the East upto Sindh, where he witnessed the sun was rising from the waters; then the North upto Sistan and Balakh and reached at such a place from where the tyrant Gog

Magog used to create trouble every now and then for the peoples of the adjoining areas. Where he, on the request of the people, constructed a strong barrier to stop the tyrants to invade other countries.

3. He ruled his vast empire with justice and given them peace and tranquility, which was never given by the other tyrant rulers of his period.

4. He gave amnesty to his captured populations and declared peace to all as our Holy Prophet(Slm) declared amensty to all the Qureysh of Makkah on It's conquest.

5. He decreed peace and reprimanded not to disturb peace. He particularly announced whoever did good deeds he will be rewarded and those who create troubles would be dealt with iron hands.

6. He was a Monotheist and was God-Fearing. And he had firm faith on the Hereafter. He was not greedy and was selfless as against other kings of his period.

Accordingly, the Commentators decided that such personality was of CYRUS only and none else

Fourth:. From the Research conducted in 1838 it came to notice about an Epitaph found in an expedition on which the name of Cyrus has been inscribed and on his head two horns were clearly displayed and his period had been mentioned from 554 BC to 542 BC, that is 12 years which is recorded as his governing period of a vast empire from east to west and north.

Now we shall find out why and how Cyrus the Great should be designated as Zul Qarnain mentioned in the Holy Scriptures.

On that Epitaph the features of a person had been inscribed having two horns.

In the previous, the present Persia was divided in to two portions, being Media of the North and Paras of the South. According to the prophecies mentioned above the conqueror of these two portions was named as Zul Qarnain since he conquered both portions and founded a vast and strong empire, more than two hundred years before Alexander's conquest of the East upto Sindh.

Thus Media and Paras are denominated as two horns over his head. The epitaph certifies it. Hence he is Cyrus the Great, pronounced as Zul Qarnain by the Jews and adopted by all.

Further it was prophesied that he would become the emancipator of Bani Israiel and help them to build the destroyed Haikal-e-Sulaimani and accommodate them in Palestine.

According to the legends Cyrus built a barrier in between two hillocks to curb the invasion of the Gog and Magog.

According to Qur'an and other Scriptures Cyrus the Great was a pious and God Fearing noble man of charming characters, a Monotheist and have faith in the Hereafter; who established Peace and tranquility in his vast Empire and brought prosperity, and declared amnesty to all and decreed whoever did good deeds he would be rewarded and whoever did mischiefs, he would be dealt with iron hands of law and order. These are the recorded facts about his governance.

On these clear historical facts and evidences, and Prophecies, Cyrus the Great was Zul Qarnain of the Scriptures and none else. This is also the findings of various eminent scholars and Researchers, among them are:

1. Commentator Allama Tehrani, 2. Interpretor of Qur'an, Syed Ahmed Khan; 3. Abul Kalam Azad in his Tarjumajma nul Qur'an; 4. Dr. Bahauddin, Historian Mohammed Ibrahim And many more.

2. They all emphatically declared that the commonly mis-quoted opinion was about Alexader the Great who was wrongly declarted as "Zul Qarnain" on the following findings based on the historical facts:

   A. The carved Stone can still be seen on which the figure of Cyrus the Great had been clearly inscribed as having two horns on his head, while Alexander had no symbol like that.
   B. According to Qur'an Cyrus was the great king who conquered a vast territory during 554 BC to 542 Bc, the 12 year perod mentioned in Qur'an.
   C. As per prophecies and the Holy Scriptures, Cyrus was the Shephard in the beginning, then emerged as a strong Conqueror. Alexander was not a Shephard.
   D. Cyrus was a perfect Monotheist and God fearing. Alexader was a Polytheist and never caring others.
   E. Cyrus after these adventures and expeditions led his life of a pious man of noble chracters and then died in peace, but Alexnder died while battling.
   F. As per Qur'an Cyrus went first towards the West, then to the East and finally to the North. But Alexander just went towards the Esat and died while returning.
   G. Cyrus was the contemporary of Zurtusht and accepted his religion and became Parsi and propagated that religion with firm faith and zeal, while Alexander was the pupil of Aristotle, and never propagated his teacher's philosophy.

Now we have to conclude by determining whether he should be designated as a Prophet?

1. He was a Shehard as other Prophets were Shephards ikn ther beginning.
2. Allah addressed him direrectly "Oh Zul Qarnain" it is the Sunnat-e-Ilahi to addrtess the Perophets directly like that.
3. It must be accepted that Cyrus was also getting directions directly from Allah and some times Revelations also were revealed to him as to other Prophets.
4. Historical recortd certify him as the pious Messenger of Allah.
5. And the older generation of the Prophets claimed him as God-Sent human being, who had obediently accomplished the Mission of Allah, Amer Bil Mruf-e-was N ahi Unil Munkir".

6. He himself declared that Allah had ordered him to construct the Haikal-e-Sulimani and to help the Israelis to settle in Palestine.

Thus I leave the matter to you to ponder deeply on the points above, whether he should be designated as Prophet or not. Wam Alina Illul Balagh.

Faqeer Syed Sharief Khundmiri

*   *   *

THE END

—

THE END